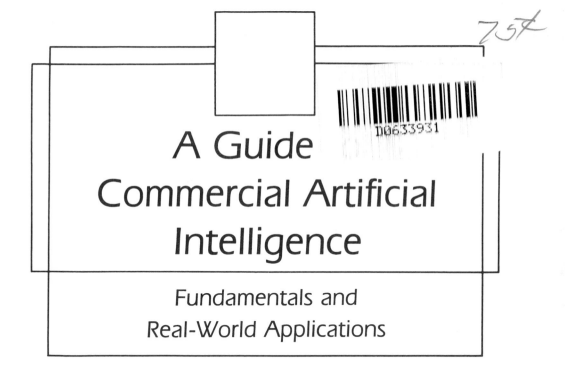

A Guide Commercial Artificial Intelligence

Fundamentals and Real-World Applications

WENDY B. RAUCH-HINDIN

President, Hi-Tech Editorial & Consulting, Inc.

Prentice Hall
Englewood Cliffs, New Jersey 07632

Library of Congress Cataloging-in-Publication Data

Rauch-Hindin, Wendy B.
A guide to commercial artificial intelligence.

Includes index.
1. Artificial intelligence. 2. Expert systems
(Computer science) I. Title.
Q335.R383 1987 006.3 87-19326
ISBN 0-13-368770-8

Editorial/production supervision: Sophie Papanikolaou
Cover design: Lundgren Graphics, Ltd.
Manufacturing buyers: S. Gordon Osbourne and Richard Washburn

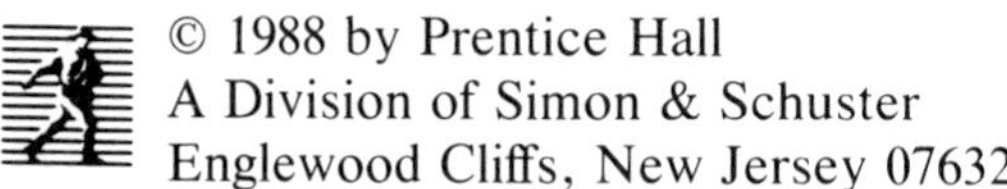

Printed in the United States of America

10 9 8 7 6 5 4 3 2 1

ISBN 0-13-368770-8 025

Prentice-Hall International (UK) Limited, *London*
Prentice-Hall of Australia Pty. Limited, *Sydney*
Prentice-Hall Canada Inc., *Toronto*
Prentice-Hall Hispanoamericana, S.A., *Mexico*
Prentice-Hall of India Private Limited, *New Delhi*
Prentice-Hall of Japan, Inc., *Tokyo*
Simon & Schuster Asia Pte. Ltd., *Singapore*
Editora Prentice-Hall do Brasil, Ltda., *Rio de Janeiro*

To Harvey,
With love and thanks for his help and endurance

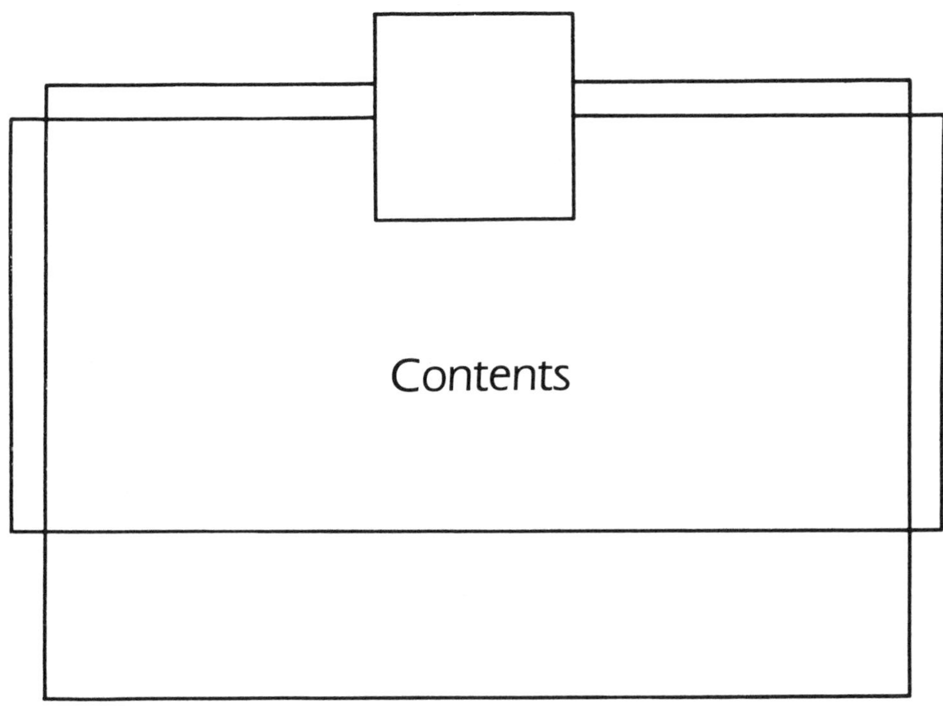

Contents

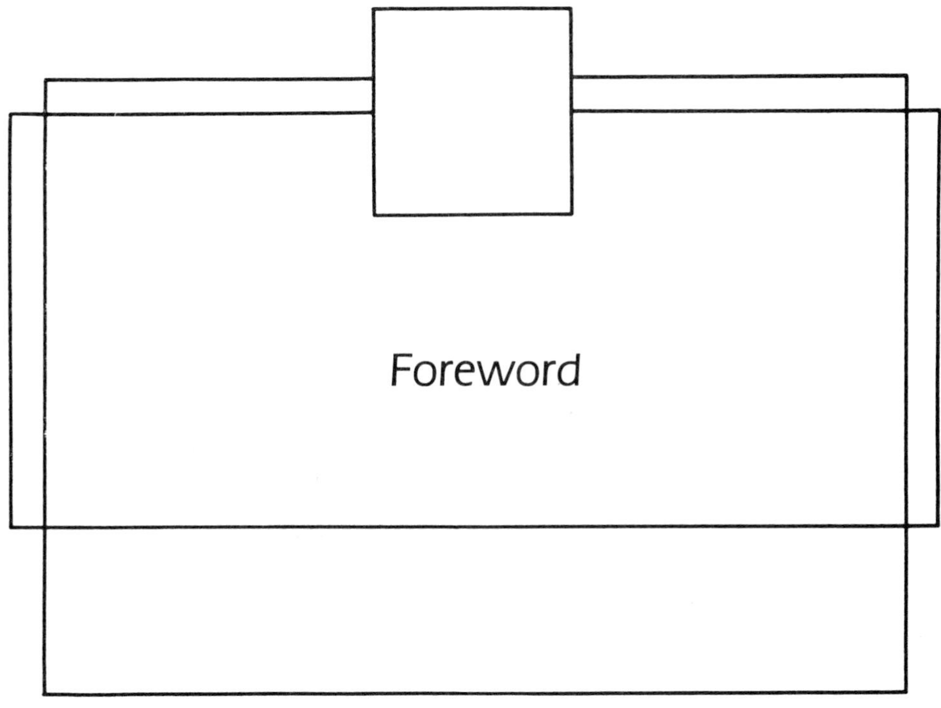

Foreword

A growing concern of mine has been the schizophrenic approach industry has taken to the introduction of AI into its organizations. On one hand, organizations have hailed AI as a new tool which shows promise of solving some difficult problems. On the other hand, many in an organization still do not know much about the technology, often harbouring a certain level of uneasiness. I also find myself uneasy; a lack of understanding of the technology may ultimately lead to unnecessary failure in its application. Why does this ignorance persist? What can be done about it?

I have often compared the study and practice of Artificial Intelligence to that of medieval guild. A guild has a few "masters" whose knowledge and experience place them above the rest, there are "journeymen" who practice the trade, and there are "apprentices" who learn by working with the masters. In the field of AI there are a few well known "masters," who have researched and taught at a small number of universities, and a growing group of journeymen. Because of the lack of educational materials, much of the knowledge was acquired by doing and through an oral tradition. Recently, there has been a proliferation of books, articles, and research papers published on AI, yet few outside of the AI guild have been able to penetrate it.

Wendy Rauch-Hindin provides us with a window into AI by cogently addressing three important issues:

1. WHAT is AI,
2. HOW is AI practiced, and
3. WHERE has AI been successfully applied?

The mist which surrounds and obscures AI is dissipated. I recommend this book highly to both the layman and expert alike.

Mark S. Fox
Carnegie Mellon University

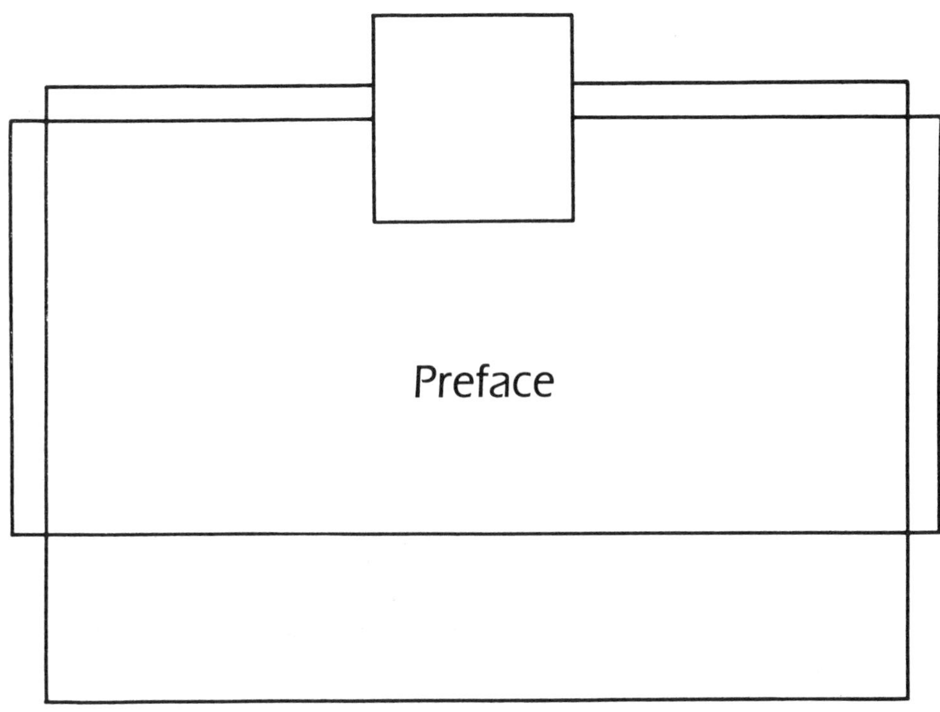

Preface

In the last few years, a number of companies and organizations have become convinced that artificial intelligence can provide leverage for them. They have seen AI tools developed to make AI accessible to corporate and organizational people who are not AI experts. They have watched the prices of AI hardware and software development environments decrease. Most important, they are aware that some companies have demonstrated that they can use AI in production operations to improve their business and save themselves money.

But for most people to commit themselves or their company to using AI in their company's daily operations is a difficult decision because of several technical and nontechnical factors. In particular, potential AI users and company management are concerned with cost, training, risk, tools, programming languages, computer hardware, career decisions, corporate management attitudes, and the ability to evaluate the technology and its applicability to their problems. At the same time, they want to ensure that they are not left behind as new technologies evolve, and that their companies do not lose a competitive edge to another company that is more up-to-date about high-technology advances.

My decision to write a book on commercial artificial intelligence was motivated by the suggestion of many of these users with whom I worked on consulting projects starting in 1984, as well as vendors who had observed the same concerns. The users generally worked for large corporations at which I was helping to evaluate technologies and plan business, marketing, or production strategies. Each company had some business problem to solve that it had heard might better be solved with AI, rather than with an existing technology.

No matter what the problem was to solve, the beginning of every project always turned out the same. What the people in every company needed most was for me to use my combination of experiences as a programmer in industry, and as a writer/analyst about computer technology, to provide them with in-depth AI information. This information had to be presented in a way that was tailored to their problem, but was more generic than what many AI vendors supplied. Once they understood this information, they could evaluate the technology and its applicability to their problems themselves. Only then could real planning begin.

This book is largely based on the explain-by-example techniques (as opposed to teach by lecture) that were successful in my consulting. Users targeted by the text include corporate executives and managerial decision makers; engineering, software, data processing, and industrial middle management; marketing managers; programmers without previous AI training; and students. The book is designed to help these people determine if and how AI is useful for their project, their company, or their personal career, and to help them get started in AI. To provide this help, the book offers enough basic technical and application knowledge about AI so readers can:

- understand the basic concepts of AI
- assess the suitability of AI for their needs
- distinguish between the AI software and hardware claims that are true and those that are naive, misleading, or puffery

With this in mind, I wrote the book to be technically as well as commercially oriented. However, the technical material in the book is geared to the AI nonexpert and assumes no prior knowledge of AI.

Overall, the book provides both a general overview and technical knowledge of AI, its software, hardware, and application-building tools. It also provides extensive application studies showing where and how to use the technology. Besides communicating basic AI knowledge, I had two other goals in writing this book. One was to provide perspective on the AI information presented. Pains are taken to point out the benefits of AI, as well as its problems, what AI can do and what it will not do, the difficulties of getting started in AI, and where in the real world the different AI software, hardware, and techniques fit.

The other goal was to write a book that was readable. Therefore, the general, technical, and application material is presented without jargon, in a straightforward style that is not pedantic, and sometimes folksy. Except for attributions that are woven into the text material, I have intentionally avoided footnotes and references in the text. Instead, an annotated combination of references and bibliographic material is located in the back of the book.

The book is organized into sections and topics. Each section and topic begins with general-interest information and gradually gets into greater technical depth. This organization avoids the need to read the book sequentially. Less technical readers can get a basic understanding of the different AI subfields (expert systems, natural-language, AI hardware) and the applications they need to be aware of, while skipping nitty-gritty details. More technical readers can get an in-depth knowledge of the technical details they need for their work while skipping chapters dealing with certain applications or commercial information.

Chapters 1 and 2 provide a general overview of AI and discuss how it differs from traditional programs, why it is important, its payoffs, limitations, and the strategies and problems involved in bringing AI into an organization.

Chapters 3 through 14 explain how expert systems work and how to build one using AI application development tools. They also explain how natural-language systems work, how to interface one to a database, how to choose a suitable expert system application, how to evaluate the features and capabilities of different AI application development tools, and what to look for and beware of in a natural-language system.

Skipping to chapter 25, chapters 25 through 27 provide basic knowledge about different AI programming languages and the different types of computer hardware that can run AI systems, and describe the key points to take into account when choosing a computer for various types of AI applications.

Chapters 28 and 29 discuss the underlying concepts and potential of state-of-the-art expert systems for automated programming—some of which have entered the commercialization phase—as well as expert programs that learn by experience or analogy.

Since the book is targeted at readers with commercial interests, the heart of the book, Chapters 15 through 24, focuses on what to do with the new technology. These chapters examine, in depth, a large number of real-world AI applications and application areas. The applications examined were chosen because their concepts can be copied and applied to similar problems. The book explains, in depth, what these AI systems do, how they do it, what benefits they provide that cannot be achieved with conventional programs, and why.

The applications selected for examination were generally developed at user companies, often by application experts rather than AI experts. Many are in routine use at the user companies. The AI systems discussed come from the financial, insurance, and investment industries; management consulting firms, companies engaged in all branches of manufacturing; mechanical, electrical, electronic, and civil engineering companies; traditional data processing centers; medical institutions; ships; and scientific laboratories.

The business application areas that these AI systems encompass include portfolio management, insurance underwriting and claims adjustment, accounting, assets and liabilities management and traditional Management of Information Systems (MIS) application development and maintenance. Among the industrial applications are manufacturing planning, scheduling, monitoring, project management, distribution, equipment diagnosis, and real-time monitoring. Scientific and engineering applications include use and maintenance of scientific instruments, interfaces to complex control panels and software systems, statistical analysis, computer algebra, physician's management systems, VLSI design, and circuit-board diagnosis.

However, applications examples are not limited to Chapters 15 through 24. I have woven real-world AI applications into every chapter to illustrate AI techniques and system building. I believe that this approach helps to make the technical information in the book easier to understand, and the general material easier to remember.

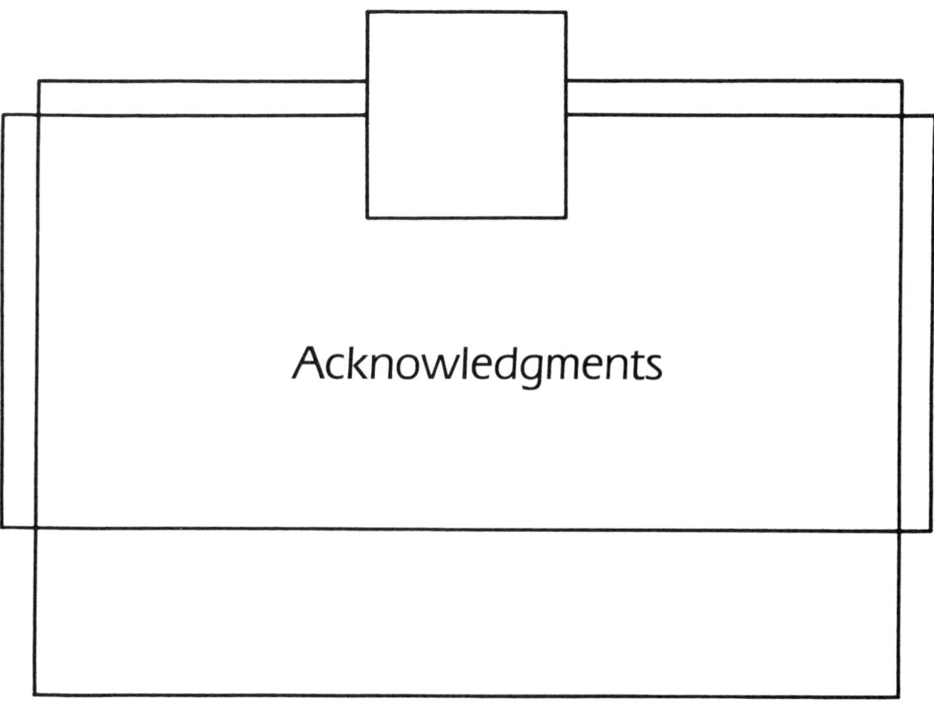

Acknowledgments

It is difficult to provide appropriate acknowledgments to individuals in a book which was written with the cooperation of many people. One person, Mark Fox, stands apart from all others who gave their time and advice, and I am at a loss for words to thank him adequately. An authority in the AI field, he read and criticized every chapter in both volumes of this book. I owe him a great intellectual debt for making many comments and suggestions that improved the book.

I would also like to thank Beau Sheil for critiquing the hardware chapters and Charles Forgy for reviewing the programming language chapter.

Although the book bears the name of a single author, it has been influenced by many people and would not have happened without their help, ideas, and cooperation. It is my pleasure to acknowledge and thank the following people:

James Alexander, Bradley Allan, Howard Austin, Robert Balzer, Ram Banim, Harry Barrow, David Barstow, Roger Bates, Daniel Bobrow, Piero Bonissone, Kenneth Bosomworth, John Seely Brown, Jaime Carbonell, Maria Celocruz, Eugene Charniak, Gregory Clemenson, Mache Creeger, Simon Curry, Stanley Curtis, Jim Dowe, Scott Fahlman, Robert Fallat, Aryeh Finegold, Bernard Finzi, Horace Flatt, Charles Forgy, Mark Fox, Bud Frawley, Roy Freedman, Michael Freiling, Eric Frey, William Gale, Thomas Gannon, Bruce

Gras, Abraham Gutman, Stephen Hardy, Larry Harris, George Heilmeier, Carl Hewitt, Peter Hirsch, Erna Hoover, Alex Jacobson, Peter Jones, Alan Kay, Jerrold Kaplan, Thomas Kehler, Charles Kellogg, Ted Kowalski, Arnold Kraft, Karen Kukich, Fred Luconi, Francis Lynch, John McDermott, Clement McDonald, Marvin Minsky, Jack Munson, John Nairn, Sal Nuzzo, Dennis O'Connor, Marcel Pahlavan, Jeffrey Perrone, Charles Rich, Charles Rieger, Bruce Roberts, Charles Rosen, Roger Schank, Beau Sheil, Herbert Simon, Howard Shrobe, Kenneth Sloan, James Spoerl, Mark Stefik, Albert Stevens, John Strickland, Jay M. Tenenbaum, Christopher Tong, John Vermes, Geoffrey von Limbach, David Walden, Homer Warner, David Warren, Daniel Weinreb, Gio Wiederhold, Karl Wiig, Chuck Williams, Douglas Williams, Michael Williams, Nels Winkless, Patrick H. Winston, and Stephen Wyle.

My apologies to anyone who has been inadvertently left out. Needless to say, any errors of fact, interpretation, or emphasis that may have crept into the book are mine.

I also extend special thanks:

To Eric Hindin for performing the logistics work and preparing the art and manuscript for submission

To David Trowbridge, Susan Metzler, and Gail Jacobs for expediting information transfer

To Eileen Zanni for hours of patient tape transcriptions

To Wordstar

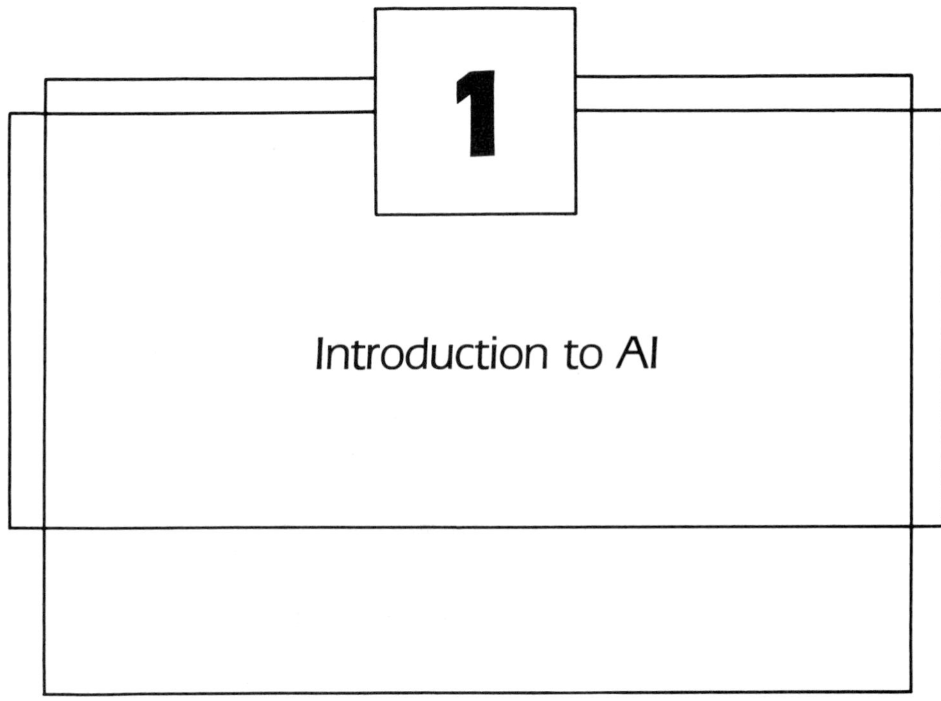

1 Introduction to AI

At 4:00 one morning, the $100,000-a-day drilling operations grind to a halt as an offshore rig automatically shuts down. The foreman holds a brief consultation with the on-site, experienced drilling advisor to explain the manner in which the problem occurred and the characteristics of the rock formations in the drilling area.

The drilling advisor advises that in all likelihood, liquid under high pressure is seeping out of the permeable rock surrounding the drilled hole and forcing the drilling assembly against the side of the hole, thus causing it to stick. The drilling advisor then recommends that the foreman circulate the drilling fluid (mud) at a normal flow rate to homogenize the mud, but at the same time decrease the filtrate and add lubricant products. This procedure frees the stuck drill bit and avoids a half-a-million dollar delay. In addition, the drilling advisor makes some suggestions about how to avoid a recurrence of the same problem.

Later that day, the chief engineer of a large military/industrial complex company is worried about meeting the shipping dates scheduled for several different nonstandard printed-circuit (PC) boards. Technicians to build the boards are plentiful. The engineer's worry exists because the planning of installation procedures that the technicians must follow are time consuming and tedious to do for so many different boards.

The chief engineer confers with the company's industrial engineer. The industrial engineer assigns the PC board planning chores to a skilled assistant. The assistant (a veteran with twelve years' experience) examines the parts list and schematic diagrams output from a computer-aided design program and rapidly draws up complete sets of plans for several technicians to assemble the different

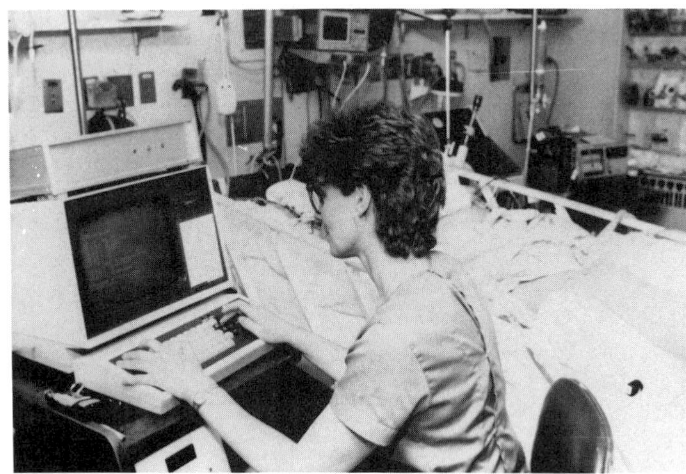

Figure 1-1 At LDS hospital, a computer is wheeled into a patient's room and hooked up to an expert system via a modem. (LDS Hospital)

PC boards. The industrial engineer remains on hand to answer questions about those components the assistant does not yet know. With help from this assistant, the installation procedures are planned in less than a day, the technicians get to work, and the company meets its calendar obligations.

In these examples, the on-site drilling advisor and the industrial engineer's assistant have one thing in common. They are not people. They are real computer programs, at work in commercial environments. The concepts and techniques used in building these programs are part of a field known as artificial intelligence (AI).

AI programs are programs that exhibit behavior normally identified with human intelligence, but until recently, not with computers. In particular, AI programs seem to grasp concepts and ideas. Some understand natural language. Some can see. Others can infer new information.

AI programs do not substitute for people, but they give people leverage. The people leverage occurs because AI systems have the knowledge and reasoning powers to advise and consult with people so that the people perform their jobs more expertly and appear smarter than they would otherwise.

The leverage for people translates to leverage for companies. For example, Schlumberger Ltd. had in mind $200 million a year worth of economic and competitive leverage when, back in 1978, it decided to develop AI capabilities. The AI programs developed help the firm's oil-exploration experts evaluate seismic data to locate oil. The seismic data are measured with proprietary tools. The firm's AI objective was to improve its competitive position and generate an additional $200 million a year in sales-of-service revenues for the use of just one particular tool.

Figure 1-2 GE mechanics can consult with an expert system to help diagnose locomotive faults (General Electric)

As for manufacturing and sales operations, Digital Equipment Corporation, a company that markets its computer systems based on components that customers specify and order a la carte (a time-demanding marketing option), uses AI programs to configure these systems. Digital claims that it saves \$40 million a year by using this program. The firm has now placed similar AI systems in the hands of its sales people who use them to configure orders and quote prices in the customers' offices.

Another group of AI systems provides intellectual leverage. AI-based medical consultation systems at the Pacific Medical Center, Regenstrief Institute for Health Care, and LDS Hospital perform diagnoses and offer treatment recommendations (Figure 1-1). Because these medical systems make sure that routine cases get their due care, they leave physicians freer to spend more time on the difficult, challenging cases.

AI programs have also demonstrated leverage in the equipment diagnosis and financial services fields. For example, General Electric developed an AI system to consult with its trouble shooters about locomotive faults because too many technicians in its repair shops were tying up a million dollars' worth of gear by scheduling locomotives with minor problems for major overhauls (Figure 1-2).

And First Financial Planners uses an AI system to consult with its staff about comprehensive financial planning. The large amount of expertise and time required to produce a comprehensive financial plan for a client can cause a company to reach the point quickly where it cannot handle any more clients. AI significantly compresses the time needed to produce a plan so that a company does not have to turn away clients and shut down its growth.

THREE AI BRANCHES

AI program fall into three basic categories: expert (or knowledge-base) systems (and the tools to build them), natural language (everyday native language) systems, and perception systems for vision, speech, and touch.

Expert systems are programs that contain the knowledge of human experts, encoded so a computer can understand it. A human-like reasoning mechanism uses this knowledge to solve problems in specific domains. With this encoded knowledge and reasoning mechanism, expert systems can tackle problems that are beyond the reach of conventionally programmed computers.

One of the most important types of AI programs associated with expert systems are AI application development tools. These tools help AI novices (experts also) build and maintain their own expert systems. And therein lies their value—because these tools are available to the AI nonexpert, they facilitate the spread of AI technology and AI applications into interested organizations.

The second AI area, called natural language systems, encompasses programs that understand the native language of the user, such as English. The most popular natural language systems are those that act as interfaces to databases. These interfaces allow database users to query databases in fairly unconstrained English instead of formal query languages. This makes database information accessible to noncomputer professionals.

The third type of AI programs are simple perception systems for vision, speech, and touch, Computer vision systems, for example, can interpret visual scenes and decide if objects meet inspection standards and quality control criteria, or move a robot to the proper location to grasp a part for manufacturing.

Currently, computer vision systems have fairly limited capabilities. They can only be used under controlled lighting and simple scene conditions. In addition, most vision system analyses use numeric and pattern recognition techniques, and few have any AI content.

AI TRENDS

The most outstanding, ongoing trend in AI is the gradual elimination of barriers to its commercialization.

For example, cost, training, risk, portability, language, hardware, and integration with traditional hardware and software are major concerns for any project and, in the past, have constituted the major barriers to commercial AI. It is difficult for companies to make a decision to bring in a strange, expensive AI machine that does not match what the data-processing department uses, that most people in the company have never seen, and that runs a nonstandard language that most programmers do not know, to develop applications using new technologies.

However, a number of hardware, software, and economic factors are contributing to the elimination of these barriers and the consequent spread of AI in commercial environments. Advancing semiconductor technologies are decreasing the prices of Lisp machines and increasing the power of general-purpose computers. (Lisp machines are specialized personal computers, designed to execute Lisp—the major AI programming language—fast, and to provide an environment that facilitates AI application development.) As a result, a range of differently priced machines are available that make sense for the job.

There is a standardized version of Lisp, called Common Lisp, appearing on a variety of computers, from Lisp machines and general-purpose minicomputers to PCs. Standardization allows applications to be transported to different computers with minimal program changes. There are also several reasonable tool kits and some packaged AI applications that eliminate the need for programmers to use Lisp at all. Increasing numbers of traditional-application programmers are being turned into good AI programmers. And several companies have demonstrated that they can use AI technology in production operations and save money.

Four basic approaches to using AI have emerged: turnkey applications, semi-custom applications (also known as vertical-market tools), generic application development tools, and fundamental AI languages.

At first glance, it seems that it would be difficult to build turnkey AI applications, particularly expert systems because expert systems contain people's opinions, experiences, and judgments (heuristic knowledge). These differ from person to person and they change over time.

As it turns out, there are some fairly routine judgments and decisions that are made in certain types of applications areas, like assessing a corporation's financial future. If the potential user agrees with the quality of knowledge in such a knowledge system, a turnkey system is possible.

Turnkey systems are less likely to be found in certain domains—for example, manufacturing—because there is no such thing as a generic factory. A compromise—semi-custom applications—is finding favor for these kinds of domains. Such systems are essentially AI application development tools that already contain some generic knowledge applicable to particular application domains. Users can add the remaining knowledge that is specific to a company's problem, usually by picking choices from a menu.

The third approach to building and using AI systems is via knowledge system application development tools. These tools are composed of a template to hold knowledge, a prewritten reasoning mechanism, and an easy-to-use interface for entering knowledge. The tools practically automate the coding of a knowledge system. However, they require general AI knowledge and a good deal of planning, design, and testing work on the part of the developers.

The fourth approach to developing knowledge systems is to develop the system in a low-level AI language like Lisp, Prolog, or a variety of other high-level AI languages. Clearly, this requires more programming and AI knowledge than an application development tool. On the other hand, working in these languages provides the maximum amount of functionality because the developers are not limited to the functionality of a tool.

As can be seen, an infrastructure is emerging that will support AI in commercial environments. Most large companies have already formed AI departments. Most AI systems developed have been expert systems.

The initial commercial AI applications were developed in large, high-technology industries, such as the oil and computer industries. High-technology industries embraced AI first because technology pioneers are most likely to appear first in companies that are constantly closely involved with new technologies.

The next wave of commercial AI applications has been emerging in equipment-fault diagnosis, data interpretation, and a variety of manufacturing applications including scheduling, factory monitoring, and distribution. The Department of Defense requires companies bidding on government contracts to examine the possible productivity and capability gains that may be achieved with AI techniques. The financial and insurance industries have been developing applications that provide advice about investment management, underwriting, credit and loan review, and financial planning. And tools are emerging that support value-added AI capabilities also in small companies.

In short, there are a number of reasons and a good deal of evidence that AI is poised to make its mark in the business, industrial, and scientific worlds. It will not do so overnight. Solving the problems necessary to field a new technology is usually an evolutionary, not revolutionary, process. As in any other field, when a new technology is introduced, it takes years to train people, change attitudes, assimilate ideas, produce products, refine the products, and change the operations of a user company.

However, there seems to be no doubt that AI is commercially feasible, can provide great leverage, and will ultimately become a standard technique that will be viewed as any other data processing technology. When that time comes, managers and professionals will need to understand some AI basics in order to cope with questions and decisions about how AI will affect them personally, their present and future jobs, their departments, and their companies.

WHAT EXACTLY IS AI?

As a subfield of computer science, AI is a software technique that programs use to represent data symbolically, reason with the data symbolically, and, by so doing, solve symbolic, rather than numeric problems. Because they work with symbolic techniques, concepts, and problems, AI programs are often called symbolic processing programs. Symbolic problems are the problems most often encountered in common everyday life. They deal with symbols and symbolic concepts, rather than with numbers.

Symbols can take the form of characters, digits, or words. They may be names of objects or attributes, such as "X", "Y", "7", "3.14159", "hair", "brown", "desk", "typewriter", and "telephone-network". However, symbolic and numeric processing programs both deal with symbols. What's the difference?

FROM OBSCURITY TO POPULARITY

Artificial intelligence has always had an attraction and appeal for people who have dreamed of building machines that think. Toward that goal, in the early nineteenth century, a chess playing machine was presented to the public. It turned out, however, that rather than AI, the intelligence was supplied by a midget inside a large machine-like box.

When the Eniac computer was created during World War II, followed by the Maniac and then other digital computers, several researchers revived the idea of machines that think—without, however, defining what it means for a machine to think. Bypassing this still unanswered question, the British mathematician/scientist Alan Turing devised a test that has come to be known as the Turing test. It is reminiscent of the story of "The Lady or the Tiger."

In this test, a person is required to communicate with a "thing" behind a closed door. The person is unaware of whether the "thing" is a human being or a machine. A typewriter outside the closed door provides the only means of communications. Via the typewriter, the person can ask any questions of the thing, which also responds via the typewriter. The Turing test requires the person to identify, after some period of interrogation, whether the "thing" is a human being or a machine.

As Turing points out in his paper "Can a Machine Think?", which discusses the feasibility of programming a machine to think, any program that deceives a person into believing that a machine is a human being requires more than just knowledge and reasoning capabilities (Turing, 1950). For example, to deceive interrogators, the machine would have to make periodic errors since human beings are not infallible. Also, it would need to know how much time to delay before returning an answer, as well as when to throw up its hands and claim ignorance. The machine would even need to know when to refuse to answer a question by feigning a lack of taste for, say, certain art forms about which the question is predicted. And so on.

In 1956, John McCarthy convened a ten-scientist conference at Dartmouth College to devise the techniques necessary to produce intelligent computer programs, and thus thinking machines. From this meeting, the present field of AI emerged.

In those early days, optimistic AI experts defining the field promised the moon and the stars, and needless to say, could not deliver them. Among the AI goals then was a program that could mimic the full range of human problem-solving abilities—a kind of superman, if you will. One of the earliest and best known AI programs, called the General Problem Solver (GPS), was written by Allen Newell and Herbert Simon of Carnegie-Mellon University and J. Clifford Shaw of the Rand Corp. GPS, the basis of most AI programs today, views problems to be solved in terms of a current situation and a desired goal. Its underlying problem solving strategy, known as "means-end" analysis, was to reach a goal (solution) by defining and selecting steps that would reduce the difference between the current and goal states.

Alas, the dream failed miserably. Except for the simplest cases, the generalized AI programs were overwhelmed by the complexity of the problems and the number of possible paths between the current and goal states.

Another tarnished dream was the AI program that would be able to translate accurately any language into any other. The stories say that when this language program, overwhelmed by language subtleties, translated the statement "THE SPIRIT IS WILLING, BUT THE FLESH IS WEAK," into Russian and back into English, the translated version came out as "THE WINE IS GOOD, BUT THE MEAT IS ROTTEN."

From the heights of hope and optimism, artificial intelligence plunged into an era of disillusionment. Labeled a useless discipline and esoteric science (or art), companies by and large ignored the field. AI progress was left to a few universities and research groups mostly supported by government grants.

Out of these years of obscurity came a number of practical and popular by-products of the quest for intelligent machines. These include time-sharing computer systems, graphic displays, word processing, computer-aided design techniques, and the modern, visually exciting computer interfaces adorned with windows, mice, pop-up menus, and icons. During these dark ages, a great deal was learned and the groundwork was laid to make AI successful. Based on the new knowledge, a number of prototype AI systems were built and tested. To accomplish this system building, the AI community came up with a development environment which is the most productive environment for producing any type of complex software program.

Only in the 1980s did AI tentatively emerge from the depths of obscurity, being very careful this time about what it promised. And the times they have a-changed from the early faddish days.

For the first time in the history of AI, affordable hardware with large enough memories is available to support AI systems. AI developers have learned not to expect perfection. Practical AI systems have been successfully demonstrated. Application development tools are available to ease both AI system development and technology transfer. The time is ripe for that technology transfer because AI is now appearing in the wake of programs such as VisiCalc, which prepared previously computer-naive users for the next wave of technology.

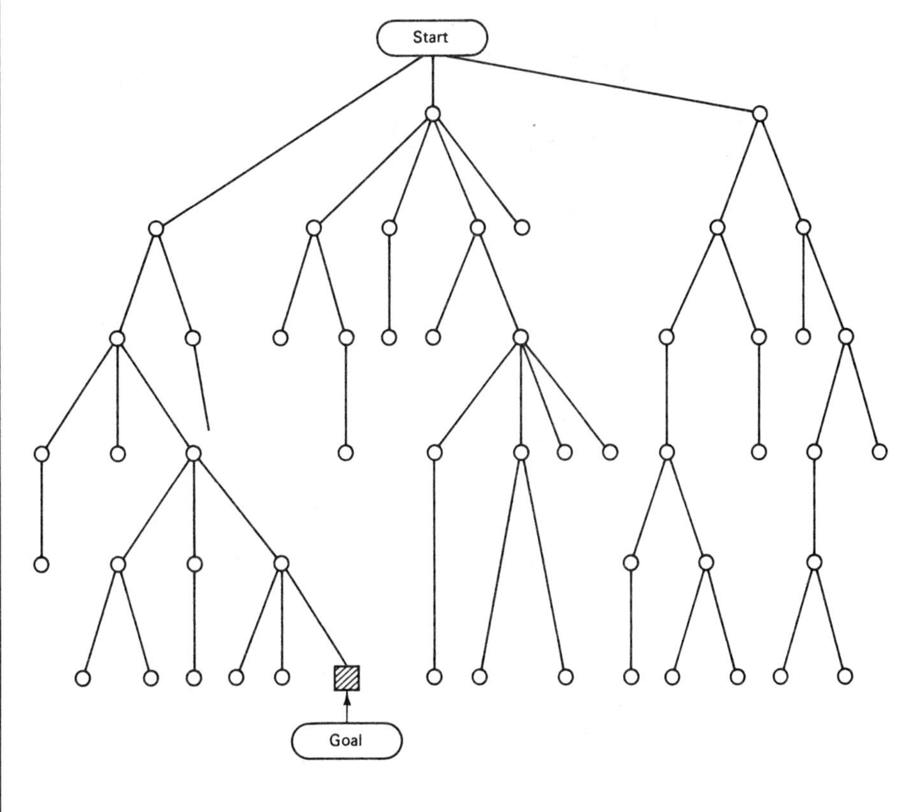

The means-end analysis strategy attempts to reach a goal by defining and selecting steps that will reduce the difference between the current and goal states.

A good way to understand what is meant by AI, or symbolic processing, is to contrast it with more conventional computer programs that perform computational or numeric operations. A numerical program's strong point, for example, is its ability to multiply or add two 10-digit numbers together. It can find the answer to "$X + Y$" if you tell it the values of X and Y. It may perform complex computations very fast, and it may use highly complex algorithms to process that numeric data. A numeric program may also use complex algorithms to sort

Information	=	Collection of separate words or characters
Knowledge	=	· Interconnection of words · Structure present · Relationships indicated

Figure 1-3 The difference between information and knowledge is in the relationships represented between parts in a program.

through information in thousands of database records. The information may be words, numbers, data, or patterns. The program may read the information to determine that 30 *X*-cars, 20 starter motors, and 800 gallons of gasoline were shipped to automobile dealer *Y*. But a numeric program cannot tell you that "$X + X = 2X$," nor can it explain why one of the cars won't start.

AI programs differ from numeric programs in that they understand not just symbols, or information, but the relationships between symbols. In a symbolic program, the information—characters, digits, words, data, patterns, and so on—are interconnected. The information and its interconnections form various structures that are used to represent relationships. These relationships between symbols and information imply what human beings interpret as meaning, or knowledge (Figure 1-3).

For example, an AI program understands the relationship between the symbols "car", "start", and "gas". Since it understands this relationship, it can infer "if a car won't start, it may be out of gas."

Similarly, AI programs seem to understand concepts such as a screwdriver, or ideas such as scheduling, because they are designed to understand the relationships between a screwdriver and a screw, and how scheduling is related to sequences of operations which are related to resources. The ability of AI programs to understand symbols in terms of concepts, ideas, and relationships makes AI programs seem to exhibit, at least to some small degree, common sense.

WHY WORD PROCESSING IS NOT SYMBOLIC

Some people might argue that word-processing programs and databases handle textual as well as numeric information and therefore process symbols. Word-processing programs manipulate words, phrases, sentences, and paragraphs. A database might contain employee or inventory information in textual form. So, why aren't word processing programs, databases, and database management systems that manipulate words and database information, equivalent to the symbolic reasoning capabilities that characterize AI technology?

One answer is that word-processing programs do not see characters that make up words as characters. Instead, they see each character as an equivalent code number (called ASCII code value). For example, upper case "A" equals ASCII code 65 and lowercase "d" equals ASCII 100.

The ASCII codes, representing characters, are strung together to form words. However, word-processing programs do not represent or understand the relationships between words. They do not even represent or understand the relationship of words to a paragraph. As a person types, a word processing program stores the ASCII values of the typed characters into arrays. As such, a word processor sees a document mostly as a bunch of numbers. In addition, typical word processing operations, such as search for certain character and replace it with another, is a clever, but number crunching operation where the program merely matches and substitutes one number for another. Hence, word processing programs are mostly numerically oriented programs.

WHY DATABASE PROCESSING IS NOT SYMBOLIC

Like word processing programs, databases contain textual information. However, the basic types of processing involved in database management operations—manipulation of database data stored as numbers, data storage, and data retrieval—are numerically or computationally oriented.

Database-data manipulation includes operations such as adding payroll information or subtracting items from inventory, which are clearly numeric. The process of storing, locating, and retrieving the database information in computer memory uses a system of addresses whereby each piece of data, such as employee name, has its own address in memory. The addresses are just plain numbers. Therefore, the processing of the information is numeric.

Of course, it is true that all computer programs, AI or otherwise, eventually boil down to numbers in memory. However, unlike with conventional programs, both AI users and programmers are far removed from the need to handle those numbers or addresses. In AI programs, the location of data in memory is handled by the programming language. AI programmers work at a much higher level, with symbolic concepts and interconnected symbols that represent relationships and meaning.

ARE AI AND SYMBOLIC PROCESSING SYNONYMOUS?

AI is a broad field. There is no single, agreed upon definition that holds true for all AI activities. Mostly, however, AI is a set of software techniques for representing data symbolically, and for processing it symbolically. The data is represented symbolically by showing relationships between data that imply meaning and concepts. AI processing of the data is also symbolic because it is performed on symbolic data, and also because it is performed in a way that implies reasoning, inferring, and meaning.

Symbolic processing techniques are not better or worse than techniques used in numeric processing, and may not even be more intelligent. They are merely different. It is possible to achieve the same techniques with ordinary programming languages. However, it is much more difficult, and may prove intractable.

The ability to deal with symbolic information has been associated with knowledge, strength, and power throughout the known history of life on earth. Members of some primitive societies will not tell strangers their names because they believe that to know the names of objects is also to have power and dominance over them. And the Bible tells us that one of Adam's first jobs was to name all the animals, including himself—a task that, according to Biblical commentators, implies recognizing the nature of the animals, separating them by species, and clarifying which are fit to mate with one another. These are symbolic processing activities that require superior intellect and provide much more information and power than simply counting the animals (although the human beings were told to be fruitful and multiply).

Similarly, the ability of programmers and programs to work directly with symbolic concepts, and information structured to show interrelationships, rather than just perform numeric processing, makes a vast difference in the types of programs that can be written and the types of tasks the program can perform.

EMINENT DOMAINS

AI programs, based on symbolic processing, are finding their way into real systems in a variety of problem areas (Figure 1-4). For the manager or engineer, an understanding of these systems is important because their concepts can be copied and applied to similar problems.

Successful AI systems that are transferable to different problem domains fall into several general categories. These include configuration, design, diagnosis, interpretation, analysis, planning, scheduling, intelligent interfaces, database intermediaries, natural language, vision, and automated programming (Figure 1-5).

Computer Configuration programs select and arrange components for computer systems. They were among the first commercial expert systems. In fact,they proved so successful that computer configuration expert systems are currently in use or under development by almost every large computer manufacturer in the United States.

Design Systems perform planning or layout of an object or system to meet specified requirements, in addition to evaluating the consequences of design decisions. Computer configuration systems are actually a simple type of design problem. Electronics firms hope to incorporate artificial intelligence techniques into much more complex design systems to design the next generation of chips. Engineers hope to use similar programs to design systems and structures such as chemical plants, buildings, bridges, dams, and transportation systems and circuits.

Design systems generally perform some system design themselves and check the design performed by engineers for potential problems. This is particularly useful in the design of large systems where it is easy to forget the reasons for some design decisions and difficult to evaluate a change in part of a design.

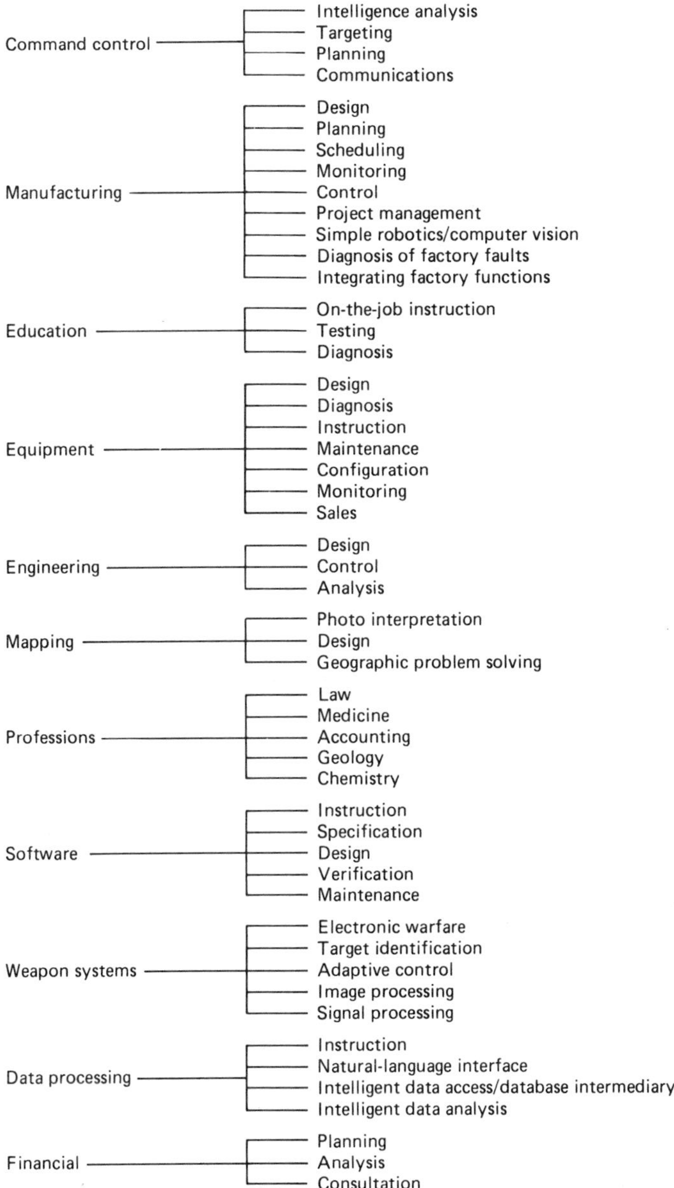

Figure 1-4 Artificial intelligence application areas

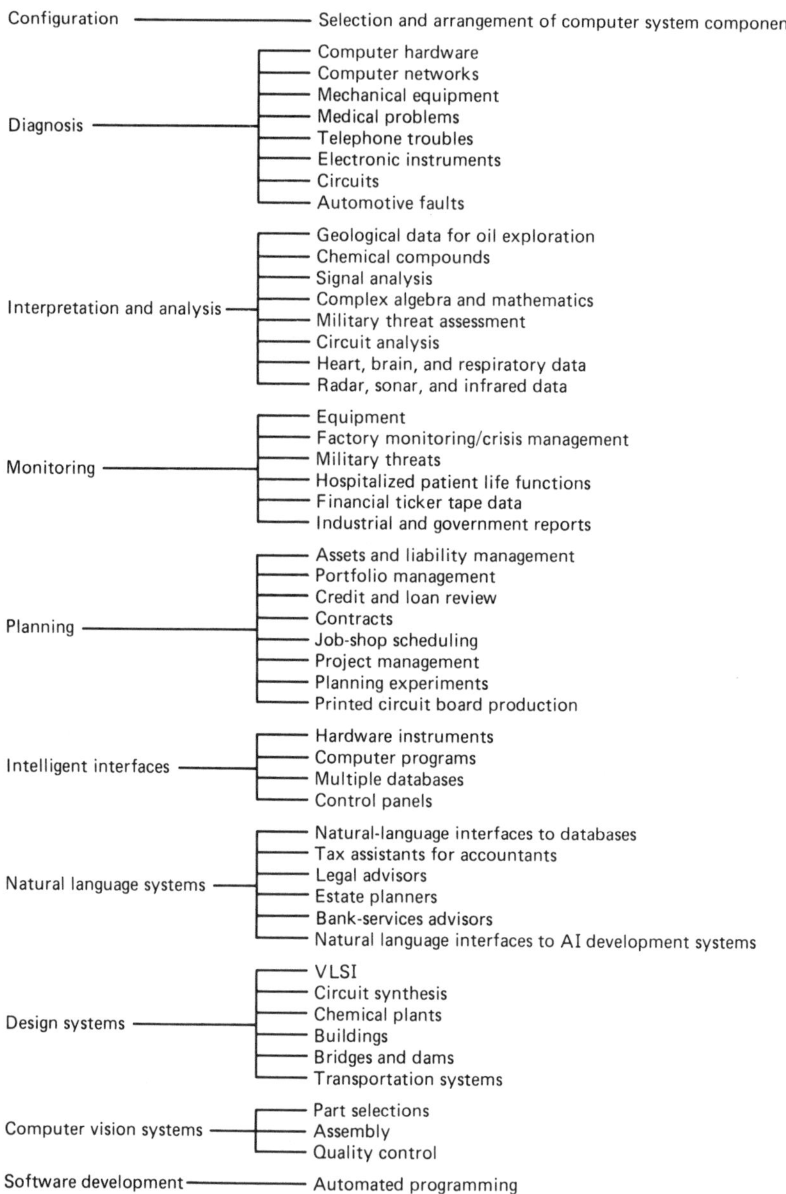

Figure 1-5 Commercial AI applications

Diagnostic Systems that incorporate AI technology apply knowledge and reasoning technic ues to diagnose different types of problems. For example, expert systems in use in the field perform diagnosis of mechanical equipment, computer networks, medical problems, telephone troubles, and factory systems.

Interpretation and *analysis* systems sift through and make sense out of large quantities of data. The data to be interpreted may be received, in the form of graphs that resemble EKG's, as the result of electrical or acoustical signals transmitted, nuclear bombardment, infrared, radar, or sonar scans, or magnetic fields. Interpretative expert systems help experts interpret this data to infer diverse features such as underground geological structure, arrangement of atoms in compounds, cardiovascular dysfunctions, or presence of threatening objects on land, sea, or air.

Analysis systems also evaluate data to help assess earthquake damage for structures, perform military threat assessment and tactical targeting, mathematically manipulate and symbolically solve algebraic problems, and monitor equipment. In addition, monitoring systems frequently must be able to make a critical judgment in a very short time interval in order to avert a potential disaster.

Signal and image processing systems are types of interpretation and analysis systems, and the major challenge for the military. The military tries to figure out, from radar, sonar, or infrared scans and photographs just what is likely to be happening either on land, sea, or in the air.

In one technique used for detecting submarines, pilots try to detect modulations on the ocean's surface waves. The modulations are caused by shock-wave effects created by submarines, as they travel, even a couple of hundred feet below the surface.

These modulations to the ocean waves are imperceptible to the eye. But signal processing and image processing equipment can detect them after going through a complex series of image enhancement steps. The image enhancement steps are dictated, in part, by the image processing system's knowledge about what basic waveforms are involved in the creation of a complex ocean wave pattern and what sort of wave shapes can be changed by objects moving under the water, and in part by what does not look right in terms of the system's understanding of what a wave pattern ought to look like. AI programs use this knowledge to determine if somewhere, built within this pattern, is the characteristic shock wave effect caused by the submarine, and to generate some analysis of what is under the water, how fast is it going, and in what direction.

What an AI program actually does is to go down a bunch of multiple decision paths to arrive at a final answer. Following roadmaps when traveling has this flavor since roads often fork, with only one road being the shortest way to a destination.

Unfortunately, with complex applications such as image analysis, as with complex games such as chess, the number of potential paths through the tree of possible decisions (called the solution search space) is so great that an ordinary algorithmic computer strategy to investigate all the paths would take the fastest computer centuries. The intelligent aspects of many AI programs has a lot to do with picking which paths are more likely than others to be appropriate.

Planning systems are closely related to analysis systems. Expert planning systems are found in the financial, industrial, and scientific arenas. They use knowledge acquired from experts in the field to perform asset liability management, portfolio management, financial planning services, credit and loan review, job shop scheduling, project and organization management, and planning of molecular genetics experiments.

Intelligent interfaces are AI-based computer programs that insulate users from complex, difficult-to-use hardware or software. Unfortunately, most hardware and software systems, especially complex ones, are not blessed with friendly interfaces. As a result, useful systems often become less useful because they require an expert with detailed knowledge of the system to operate it properly.

Experts, in a field, are scarce. Intelligent interfaces to unfriendly systems make them easier to use by the nonexpert. For example, intelligent interfaces make complex laboratory instruments accessible to a broader group of scientists because they perform some of the chores necessary to use or to tune the instruments.

Database intermediaries are expert systems that sit between users and database management systems, and interface to one or more databases. Their job is to intercept database information requests from users or programs. Then, the database intermediaries use their knowledge of the information contained in one or more databases, and the best way to search them, in order to generate intelligent search strategies to retrieve database information that makes sense.

Natural-language interfaces act as front-ends to database management systems. The front-ends accept user's queries in users' natural language, English or otherwise, and translate them into a formal, more difficult-to-learn database query language. Currently, almost every database company in the United States is working on natural-language front-ends to databases.

Computerized vision systems can guide robots to select parts, drill holes, spray paint, or spot weld. Without the vision system, robots must be carefully programmed to perform these jobs in an exactly specified position. Moreover, the robots must be constantly reprogrammed as their parts get out of line. If the robot has even a simple vision system, it becomes an intelligent and adaptive machine because it can identify a piece, locate it, adjust itself for different positions, and then perform manipulations.

Quality control and visual inspection are other important areas for computer vision systems. Some vision inspection systems merely check parts as they pass by on a conveyer belt. When checking, they ensure, for example, that the parts are the correct ones, are not broken, chipped, or bent, and have four holes drilled in exactly the correct place. Currently, most vision systems work algorithmically and have little or no AI content.

Expert programmer systems are under development to create AI programs to automate the creation of other programs. Current automated-programming systems handle only very simple and narrow problem domains such as database retrieval or update. In the future, it will be possible to combine traditional programming with AI techniques such as natural-language and expert-system capabilities to create moderately complex programs that reliably meet specifications.

AI GOOD FOR NON-AI TASKS

AI program architectures, techniques, and tools are designed to allow exploration of programming strategies for ill-understood, ill-specified problems. These methods and tools are applicable to development and rapid prototyping of any computer program, having nothing to do with AI.

An exploratory program construction environment is necessary to build AI programs because AI programs are complex and often not well understood. For example, an AI system might advise about ways to maximize a company's net profit margin or play a game of chess. However, who knows the best way to maximize a company's net profit margin or the best strategy to get an opponent's king in checkmate? And, how should an AI system handle problems that have many correct answers?

In contrast, classical software engineering environments are oriented toward the idea of getting both requirements and design right, and then adhering to those ideas. In software engineering, contractors or end-users decide what they want and communicate their requirements to software engineers. The software engineers design an overall system to meet the contractor's requirements. They partition the system into small, but interdependent, modules that many individuals can work on. Then they check out the system requirements and design with the contractor, freeze those requirements and design, and implement, test, and deliver the system (Figure 1-6).

Clearly, if the contractors don't know what they want, the program design will be incorrect. If the software engineers misunderstand the requirements that the contractors intended, their completed system will be unacceptable. If, after the system is built, the builders and contractors discover important new features that make the system far more suitable, they must tear down the system and rebuild it at great expense. A change in even one part of a program generally necessitates a rebuilding effort, because in conventional programming a change in one place is likely to impact the rest of the program.

In contrast, AI languages and tools have several features that allow developers to explore ideas and to change their minds. First, AI systems are the most modular software systems in existence. The program structures and mechanisms that contain knowledge, infer information, and control the way the program infers information are separate and independent. Even the substructures that hold individual pieces of encoded program knowledge are modular, unsequenced, and largely independent of each other. Separation of these program mechanisms and knowledge structures make it relatively easy to modify one part of an AI system and to add new knowledge incrementally, without affecting other parts of the program.

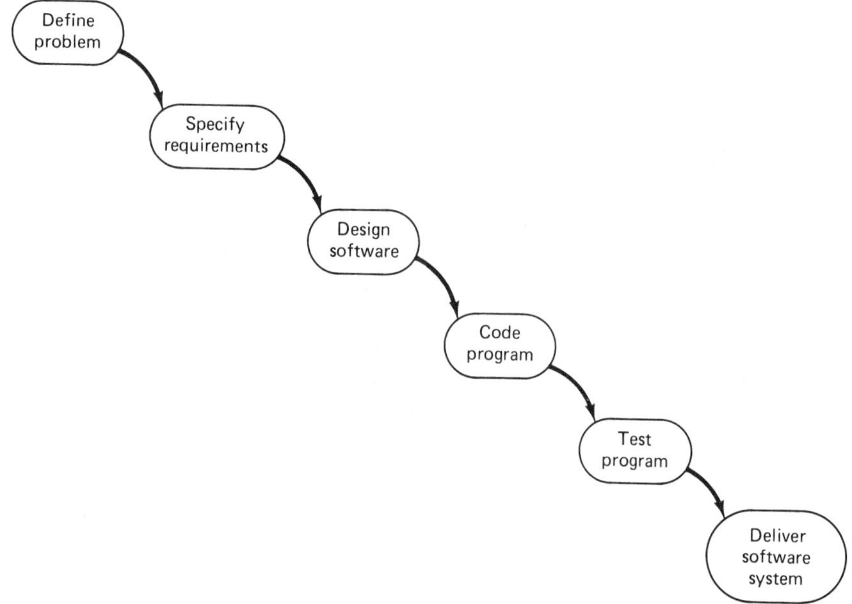

Figure 1-6 Classical software engineering.

AI languages also promote exploratory programming because they are designed to make it easy to build on or use previously designed routines. Other AI language design features allow programs to wait until the last minute, when programs actually are running, to implement many programming decisions. This allows program developers to change the behavior of a module easily and to know that their changes will be implemented properly when the program runs.

The graphical orientation of AI tools and environments helps AI system developers to visualize the framework and structures of the system they are building and the changes they make. The integrated nature of the tools and language allows programmers to develop, compile, debug, modify, and unmodify their programs without hassle.

These tools and techniques invite developers to explore different designs for systems without great grief or the expense of program redesigns. Users or system developers can start with only a few requirements and rapidly build a prototype system. Trying out the prototype system on themselves or on selected users helps them crystallize other ideas, add extra niceties piece by piece, and discover and dump any potential disasters early on.

Before the advent of commercial AI, the idea of rapid prototyping and ability to experiment with programming strategies had been advocated for programming productivity. At that time, however, the idea had insufficient tool, architectural, and environmental support to become widespread in the software industry. There are no current metrics to measure productivity for incremental program development and rapid prototyping capabilities, but few people who have used it want to return to conventional methods.

Examples of rapidly prototyped projects on AI systems include an AI-based process control system built in 4½ months on a Lisp Machine Inc. computer that also runs Unix. A three-month effort on a Tektronix AI workstation produced an expert system prototype that performs simple instrumentation and circuit board diagnosis at Tektronix.

Texas Instruments also chose to prototype Arborist, its PC-based decision tree software, on Lisp machines using AI tools and exploratory programming environments. Decision tree software is not new, but Arborist provides new, and at its design time ill-defined, software capabilities for conventional computers in that it allows users to interact directly with the decision tree instead of with tabular data from which the computer program draws and redraws a decision tree. For the same reasons, IBM sees AI's rapid prototyping capabilities as a future tool to help MIS departments develop applications with end-users.

AI MISCONCEPTIONS CORRECTED

A number of misconceptions surround the field of AI, possibly because commercial AI is young and not personally known to most people. Here is the real story about some of the most common ones.

- Contrary to what many people think, AI is not a black art, nor even revolutionary. Instead, it is a software technique that is very "do-able," provided that it is applied to the appropriate problem.
- Programming is the simplest part of creating most AI applications. The more difficult task is finding some way to represent knowledge in a computer program. If the AI program is an expert system, an equally difficult task is getting the knowledge from an expert in the first place. Acquiring the knowledge to represent in the program, in many respects is not a technical task. It often requires more diplomatic than technical skill, some knowledge of cognitive psychology, and an ability to get along with people, talk to them, and draw them out.
- AI systems do not replace people. They augment them.
- AI systems provide their economic leverage by performing the types of tasks that occupy a high percentage of highly paid people's time, rather than by handling "far-out" tasks that are a figment of science fiction. In fact, AI systems cannot perform tasks or solve problems that human beings do not know how to do.
- AI programs can be written in an conventional programming language. However, most attempts to use conventional languages for AI development

have flopped for practical, not technical, reasons. AI programs tend to be ill-understood and also to have so many possible conditions and solutions at each stage of the program that human beings find it difficult to visualize the program and keep track of the program steps. Since AI-oriented languages and environments are designed to be easy to change and to keep track of complex programs, most AI application developers develop their programs in an AI-oriented language. For practical reasons, the developed AI programs may be translated into a conventional language and run on standard computers in production environments.

- The term *artificial intelligence* is misleading. It turns out that once many of the programming techniques are explained, many people feel they have been duped by the term *artificial intelligence*. This is an unfortunate feeling because, in reality, expert systems can emulate highly paid experts such as doctors, geophysicists, and electronics and mechanical equipment diagnosticians.

The human experts, referred to in the last-mentioned misconception, deserve their compensation because they think, reason, and call on knowledge that they have diligently acquired over time in order to perform their interpretative and diagnostic duties. Are these activities any less intelligent when incorporated into computer programs just because we understand their techniques?

In the minds of many people, the answer to the question is "yes," because of a human foible known as the "witch doctor syndrome." People afflicted with this syndrome tend to view behavior as intelligent if it is mysterious and encompasses things for which they do not have a good explanation. However, once they understand the elegant algorithms underlying this behavior so that the mystery is stripped away, it is questionable whether they still want to call the behavior intelligent or not.

As a consequence, the definition of AI is a moving target. AI ideas are subconsciously defined by many as bizarre, flaky, hairbrained, and questionable ideas at the forefront of technology. But, what is radical AI today is apt to become obvious tomorrow and find its way into computer systems after that. When that happens, the boundary of AI shifts. Yesterday's AI then becomes something else—ordinary computer functionality—but not intelligent.

CAUTIONS

Some words of caution regarding AI are necessary. Although AI systems can give companies a lot of leverage and can solve complex problems that are not solvable with alternative techniques, they still have limited capabilities. They do not, and will not, replace human beings; they augment them.

AI is appropriate only for certain types of applications, and there are surprisingly few of them. Many real-time processing problems (those that have critical time constraints), as well as problems that involve modeling of space and time (such as aircraft flying in radar environments and constantly shifting position coordinates in real time), are particularly difficult. Worse, AI systems must be hand-crafted by both AI, and applications experts. As such, it is not the stuff of economic revolutions. Any AI-induced economic revolution will have to wait until the AI researchers figure out how AI systems themselves can learn some of the expertise they need without requiring so much help from professionals.

There is scarcity of AI talent. AI experts are not the kind of people picked off the streets or found, in most personnel offices, looking for jobs. As such, they are likely to be highly paid. This cost and scarcity is difficult to reconcile with the labor-intensive requirements needed to develop current AI systems.

Resistance to AI exists in many segments of the programming community, and the reasons for the resistance are logical. It is difficult to convince traditional programmers who have been programming in the Fortran, Cobol, or C language for fifteen years that a new technology will increase their productivity. It may increase it, but only after they learn and become experienced with a new programming language, AI concepts, and a variety of new techniques. Under these circumstances, it is easy to understand why many programmers will not see the gain; they will claim that they work pretty productively right now.

The science of knowledge extraction—trying to interview experts to get at their knowledge to encode in an expert system—is another labor-intensive activity. Worse, it is a poorly understood science. No one yet knows how to get someone to tell them everything he or she knows about a subject.

Despite these problems, AI can provide many intellectual and economic benefits. Yet its history has involved passage through several fads where it has been presented to the public with much fanfare and hype. As a result, people have expected a lot from AI which has never been delivered.

Now it can deliver something that people can see, touch, feel, and understand in terms of their personal benefits. A sure-fire way to be disappointed in AI, however, is to expect more of it than it can deliver.

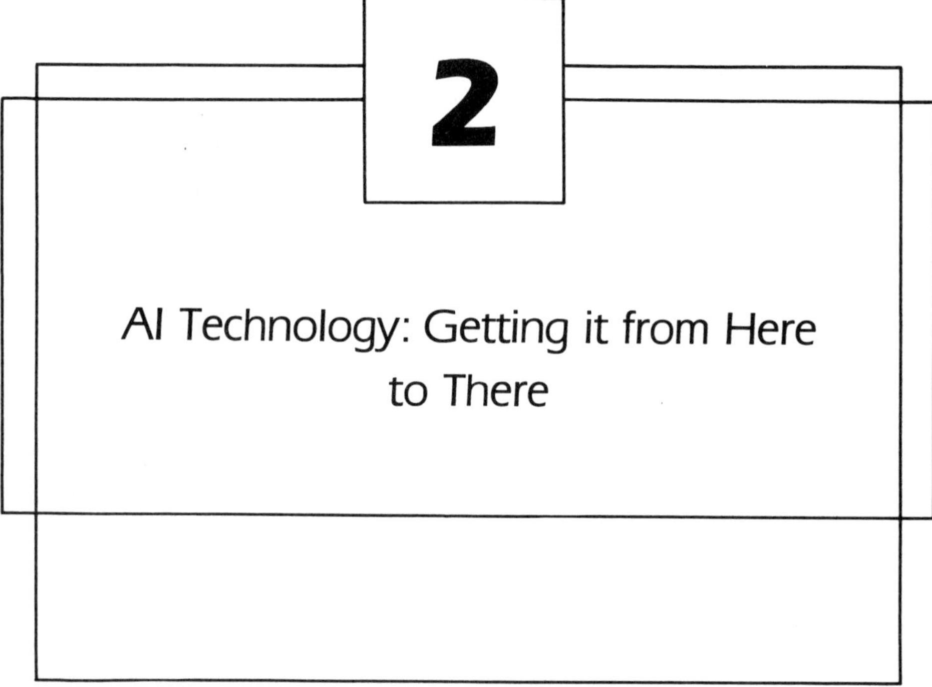

2

AI Technology: Getting it from Here to There

No matter what the benefits are, artificial intelligence cannot reach its full potential if only a select group of people are able to understand it, support it, or use it. For AI to achieve success on a wide scale, interested parties must devise methods to transfer the AI technology between the universities where AI researchers pioneered most early knowledge systems and industrial environments where the bulk of the world resides.

There are two different levels of AI technology transfer. One level involves the sale of turnkey AI-based applications. The other level involves the transfer of the technology necessary to build AI-based applications.

TURNKEY AI SYSTEMS

The idea underlying turnkey AI-based applications is the elimination of the need to transfer any AI technology in order to use the application. Instead, the application developers will use AI technology to hide the complexity of both the problem to be solved and the AI system used to solve it. End users will see only functionality and not even know that the application contains any underlying AI.

IMPORTING AI TECHNOLOGY

Many problems, are not amenable to turnkey AI solutions. They may be specific to an organization, its products, or its techniques, or they may be standard problems for which there just are no off-the-shelf products available.

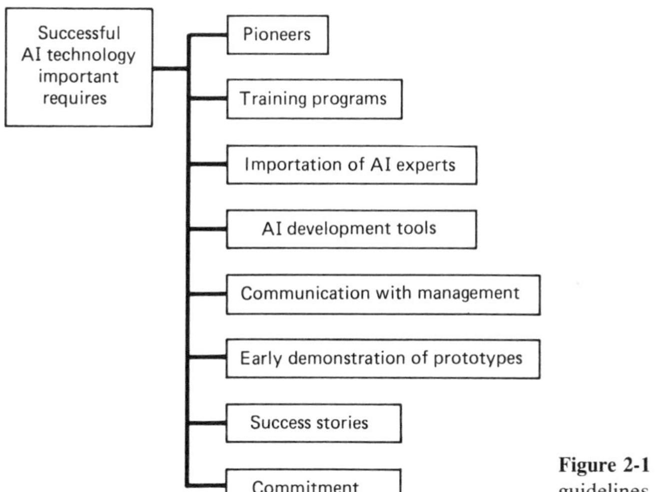

Figure 2-1 AI technology transfer guidelines

Under these conditions, the organization may consider either forming an AI department to develop its own AI applications, or contracting with an AI company to develop the application. Either method involves importation and diffusion of technology—a difficult feat for any technology to accomplish. How much more difficult, then, is a decision to import AI technology and then manage the AI technology transfer simply because the technology is still so new and there are so few precedents to learn from.

Experience in many technologies has shown that the existence of technology, no matter how suitable for solving an organization's problem, does not help to make people aware of the new technology or get them to accept it into the mainstream of their organizational activities. It is, rather, the management of the technology transfer that ultimately determines the success or failure of the new technology and therefore the problem solution within an organization.

Despite the newness of the technology, some observations and guidelines for getting an organization into the AI business and diffusing AI ideas throughout the organization have been noted and established. These observations and guidelines cross technical and non-technical areas, including getting started, personnel, training, money, management involvement, tools, hardware, and attitudes (Figure 2-1).

PIONEERS

In AI, as in any other field that is new, very different, and which requires big steps to adopt, there are people who pioneer and there are other people who copy. The process of adopting AI technology into an organization usually requires a pioneer—a person with some sort of gleam in his or her eye. That pioneer might have heard that AI is a glamorous subject, but is also aware that it might do something for the organization.

AI pioneers generally have read some of the available AI literature. This reading is not enough to inform them how to integrate AI into their everyday workplace. However, it does provide them with enough background knowledge so that what they have heard about how AI might solve their organization's problem makes a modicum of sense to them. Therefore, they are willing to investigate the subject further.

Technology scouts and pioneers often make the initial contacts with AI tool or hardware firms or academic institutions. For importation of AI technology into an organization, that contact must be followed by more comprehensive training and education.

Most AI tool vendors, AI hardware suppliers, and universities offer some sort of educational and training programs in AI. Educational seminars also provide some general AI education, as well as insight into the identification of AI opportunities, roadblocks, and how an organization might get into the AI business. Some educational programs are geared to the use of a particular AI tool. Other programs teach the basic concepts of AI, expert systems, or Lisp programming.

PERCEIVED VERSUS ACTUAL RISK

Because the importation of AI technology is a big and costly step, the impetus and approval for AI projects must come from an organization's top management. The managers who negotiate and approve the entry of an organization into the AI arena must perceive a relative advantage for AI over the organization's present way of operating. Many factors—financial, training, experience—influence whether or not an AI solution to a problem is the best one. Most important, however, the perceived risk associated with adopting an AI solution, in terms of accomplishing a particular task or achieving a specified goal, must lie within acceptable limits.

An AI solution may have a very high perceived advantage. However, the risk perceived may also be very great because the AI field is still relatively uncharted. For this reason, widespread AI acceptance and high-volume AI activity will not take place until there has been a number of success stories.

The tendency to copy-a-success story can already be seen in the computer manufacturing and oil exploration industries. There, venturesome engineers at Digital Equipment Corp. and Schlumberger pioneered XCON and the Dipmeter Advisor (an expert system that interprets oil-well logs and tries to infer the presence of underground oil from them). Once these expert systems demonstrated their feasibility and benefits, almost every other computer manufacturer began development of computer configuration programs, and almost every other oil company began to develop oil exploration programs.

Each of the successor programs is different from its ancestor. But they were developed after company management understood concretely what such a program could do and observed personally that such programs were feasible. Then they were able to translate what they understood and observed into their own situations.

COMMUNICATING ON MANAGEMENT'S TERMS

Once the feasibility of an AI solution to an organization's problem is understood, management needs to be convinced that the new technology will benefit the organization in several ways, but particularly financially. Most organizations' management is generally composed of nontechnical people who are trying to achieve a certain business result. It is up to an organization's pioneers and scouts to create the image and vision of what AI can do for a problem so that management will feel that the benefits are worth the risk.

Upper management generally regards the idea of employing any new technology as any other business investment. Discussions with management reveals that they are pretty matter of fact about what facets of the new technology concern them most. One question is foremost in their minds: "What is my return going to be?" The answer to that question mostly determines why they want to make that investment.

Therefore, the believers—the pioneers, technology scouts, and AI firms—must sell management on why AI technology will net the company a return on its investment. Which of several ways to represent knowledge or infer information, and the elegance and simplicity or sophistication of a solution, are issues for the early research and later implementation stages. However, some understanding of AI concepts is necessary to equip management to evaluate the chances of an AI project's success and the bottom line.

GETTING STARTED IN AI

Once a decision to import AI technology has been made, a host of difficult-to-resolve details must be addressed. For example, AI is a technology that has a very limited number of practitioners. There is a shortage of competent knowledge engineers. They are difficult to locate and to hire.

An organization cannot expect to just plunge into the AI field by hiring a few programmers. Any organization that wants to get into the AI business must be prepared to make a substantial investment in education—in other words, to train technical people.

Because of the substantial investment needed, many companies importing AI technology start with a small system to see if AI is suitable for their needs. Although the first application may not be a company's most meaningful one, most new-to-AI companies use it as a learning experience. During this experience, they develop some expert system building skill and they learn how they can use AI technology on a whole range of company problems waiting in the wings.

Some firms elect to experiment with an AI system before building a department by contracting to have a small expert system built for them. By contracting externally, the firms are able to see how expert systems solve a problem and how applicable expert systems are to the firm's specific problems before they invest in staffing a department and training the staff.

TECHNOLOGY TRANSFER

Most ideas for importing technology are intuitive. They often seem logical, but they do not always work. Regardless of a company's pioneers or entry-level AI applications, eventually it must confront the difficult question of how to train the staff of an organization to employ technologically new AI concepts in products and applications that they build. The problem of "how" is compounded because many programmers in the organization are likely to be resistant to the new technology, and with reason. The exit costs from familiar programming languages, software techniques, and operating systems are very high. It requires a good deal of low-productivity time for experienced, productive Fortran, Cobol, and C programmers to become equally facile with new languages, techniques, and programming environments.

The most successful technology transfer technique (and perhaps the only successful one) used at System Development Corp. (SDC) is to physically transfer the people who already have the technology into the organization so that they can personally transfer the technology to the uninitiated.

"Past software experience shows that technology does not transfer well either from the written word or from discussion about technology theory," claims Jack Munson, a vice president of SDC. Munson explains that cases where a technology is so obviously good that people seek it out are rare. Cases where engineers and software professionals learn the technology almost in a vacuum because the technology is its own reward generally are trivial cases. The notion that a company can import a technology based on a research organization's reports that explain a technology and its benefits just does not work.

In summary, Munson says that a newly formed group will not employ new technology concepts in an application unless they are sure they know how to do it. They will simply go back to techniques they understand. Unless an organization brings in people who already know the new technology and can distribute it throughout the organization, the organization will have a tough time getting its people to seek out, learn, and apply the technology.

A PROBLEM OF CULTURE

Another technology transfer issue to address is how to manage technology transfer between different types of cultures—for example, the different cultures that abound in computer science, manufacturing, engineering, or MIS domains. This issue is of particular importance in AI because AI is such an interdisciplinary subject. More than most subjects, AI involves computer-oriented experts working with and training experts in a variety of application fields.

Each of those fields has its own culture; and one of the biggest problems that impedes the flow of technology between the different cultures stems from cultural resistance. The cultural resistance that occurs is based on how the different cultures understand, preceive, or identify with goals, terminology, and the technology to be transferred. The people in each culture think about the technology in terms of how it affects them. They have different criteria for success. They talk about their functions and processes differently, even when they overlap.

Often, people in the different cultures do not even understand each other's terminology. Software professionals have been criticized for their jargon. But they should not be singled out. As frustrated observers can attest, the aerospace industry sports "leads" and "lags." The communications industry is filled with "acks" and naks." And the financial industry's "puts," "calls," "liquidity risks," and "margins" are enough to cause the "bulls" and the "bears" to hide in their portfolios. Yet these cultures must decide together whether success of a project means a million dollars, a Nobel prize, easier-to-perform jobs, increased efficiency, more jobs able to be run, or fewer jobs that have to be run.

The implications of the various attitudes among heterogeneous cultures is best exemplified by an interesting situation that developed at Daisy Systems. Daisy makes computer-aided engineering workstations that use AI, as well as other technologies, to create intelligent circuit design assistants. The use of AI as one of the underlying technologies gave the Daisy system some modifiability and ease-of-interfacing-to-other-design automation systems benefits that are not common. Yet for the first few years of the firm's existence, Daisy refused to be known as an AI company or even to label its technology as AI. Instead, the firm called itself a "solution" company and called its technology "advanced programming." When pressed for an answer about its use of AI, it described itself only as a firm with an engineering problem to solve and a willingness to apply a multiplicity of solutions—AI or otherwise—to solve it.

Daisy's founder, Aryeh Finegold, blames the difference in research and commercial cultures for his refusal to set up business under an AI aegis. Simply put, researchers emphasize ideas and methodologies. In contrast, commercial organizations are interested in products than can be repetitively manufactured and result in a profit.

Until recently, to label the business AI automatically meant to associate it with advanced research cultures. Unfortunately, according to Finegold, because of the style with which certain circles within this culture operate, AI has traditionally been used as an excuse not to deliver. For many people in these circles, the aura of advanced research frequently legitimized excuses for writing software that was not of production quality. These researchers excused themselves and expected customers not to get angry when software was late or did not do the job because "the problem is complicated," "the problem is too big," "AI is still new technology and it will improve in the future."

The delivery and production quality problems cropped up because instead of concentrating on the problem they needed to solve, some AI people tended to concentrate on the methodologies they were using to solve it. In other words, they concentrated on ideas, not on solutions or products.

Daisy was aware of this "idea" emphasis and did not want to attract these kinds of researchers. Moreover, the firm shied away from being an AI company because it wanted to avoid any hint of the problems associated with the only-ideas-are-important contingent of the AI culture.

It turns out that people who concentrate on solutions find that it may or may not be necessary to use AI to solve a problem. If a problem solution demands AI techniques, then AI techniques should be used as they become available. If the problem can be solved better, faster, or cheaper with traditional techniques, those techniques should be the ones of choice. There is nothing intrinsic about AI as a solution. It is only a means to an end.

INVOLVE MANAGEMENT

It is not sufficient simply to be aware of the training, personnel, cost, and attitudinal obstacles and then let nature take its course. To a large degree, the importation and diffusion of technology throughout an organization, in the face of the obstacles discussed and resistance to change, is dependent on effective planning for change.

For example, an important variable in the process of successful technology transfer and diffusion is who gets the technology to transfer. If the first people who receive the new technology are chosen for their flexibility and rationality, while those who are more dogmatic and rigid are eliminated from the newly forming AI team, the chances are that mental attitudes will be better, resistance to change will be minimized, and as a result, the technology diffusion time will be compressed.

Because AI is so new, technology transfer is facilitated if the senior managers responsible for the new technology are picked because they value and like to nurture innovation. Also, since technology transfer depends on management's commitment, it is most important that both senior and corporate management are involved in the projects they are managing or supporting. It takes dedication on the part of organizations to stick with the new and unfamiliar when, instead of products or services, only potential benefits will be produced for a long time. Under these circumstances, the organization's managers should have something to back up their dedication. They are also entitled to know what they are getting for their money.

To keep managers involved, informal networks between AI experts and management should be developed to communicate the status and progress of the new technology. In addition, AI people must be prepared not only to give presentations on their projects, but also to provide hands-on experience for managers while the project is still under development. Fortunately, in AI, there is nothing farfetched about the idea of operating a partially complete system. It is standard practice to develop AI systems incrementally. Unlike with conventionally developed software, AI developers create simple prototypes relatively quickly. Then they use these prototypes as vehicles to determine what new knowledge needs to be added.

Three classes of people concerned with the expert system development should be able to try out these prototype systems to get a firsthand feeling for the project. One, as discussed, is management, because their support and commitment is absolutely necessary. Application domain experts also need to try out the system because their heuristic knowledge is encoded and they need to evaluate the system's performance as an expert throughout development. Moreover, application domain experts who are being cloned by these expert systems can become attached to them. Finally, end users need to be involved early with expert system development because expert systems are user-driven tools. The final expert system product must satisfy user needs because it is the users whose abilities they amplify and leverage.

The end users also need to be involved because of the fear and insecurity that may otherwise be generated. DEC discovered these fears in its initial trials of XCON, its computer configuration program. Just when the firm thought it had its AI importation program under control and expected its computer configurers to send the XCON-generated configuration outputs to the factory floor with each order, none appeared. After much discussion with the configurers, accompanied by a lot of hemming, hawing, and hedging, DEC management realized that its supposedly convinced configurers were afraid for their jobs. Since then, the firm has involved the end users in expert system development so that they realize early just how it will affect them.

It turns out that DEC's configurers have not been made redundant. They have become XCON supervisors or have gone on to similar challenging jobs. However, part of the reason for no layoffs was DEC's growth; new configurers who might have been hired were not.

In other DEC expert system development efforts, such as XSEL, which helps sales people use XCON to configure orders and quote prices at the point of sale, the sales representatives were involved at the very beginning. From the first, the salespeople were able to weigh the idea of visiting customer sites carrying their computer, telephone link, and keyboard, and also the image of typing while talking, against the potential for getting more orders. Consequently, XSEL has enjoyed a high level of support from its users.

LEARNING AI

Convincing management solves the problem of support for AI projects. But the problem of a shortage of AI practitioners remains. Several solutions to alleviate the shortage are occurring. First, a number of schools, other than those known for their AI departments, have already instituted AI courses in computer science and business departments.

Second, many of the AI companies feel that there are presently enough AI-trained people to seed companies. With these people as the seeds, it is possible to train sufficient people to build systems.

The people that AI companies plan to hire and train are people with some sort of computing background. These people include computer scientists, electrical engineers who have been working with computers, software engineers, and business data-processing professionals. People who understand a particular application domain and who have no computer anxiety and some computer experience are valuable because of the interdisciplinary nature of AI. Data-processing people fall into this category both because they have programming experience and because they know the problems of large database applications and of interfacing to intelligent, but not technically savvy people.

TOOLING UP FOR AI

AI tools improve the ability to transfer the technology and shorten the training time. So, in an effort to make knowledge-based programs and programming more widely accessible, a number of AI companies have simplified knowledge programming methods and designed AI application development tools that incorporate the simplified methods. The power of these tools lies in their ability to be used by people with no AI expertise. Most commonly, the tool user turns out to be a person who is an expert in the application domain in question. He or she works in conjunction with another person with some computer or programming background.

The AI companies' goal, however, is to provide tools so that domain experts can eventually build their own expert systems. In fact, many cases exist where persons ranging from managerial personnel to biology experts and mechanical engineers have done so. Such tool users need not be AI experts, but they must understand at least some of the basic precepts of AI and expert system building.

GRAPHICS FOR AI DEVELOPMENT

Most of the original AI application development systems ran on Lisp-oriented machines with high-resolution, bit-mapped displays and integrated graphics environments. However, many tool vendors are implementing the expert systems developed with the tools, as well as the tools, on standard machines such as IBM mainframes, DEC VAXs, engineering workstations, and high-end micros.

These standard computers already proliferate in users' environments. They may give as good or better run-time performance than that of many Lisp machines. Notwithstanding these benefits, most AI vendors agree that bit-mapped graphics environments are very important for AI development.

These graphics environments have even more significance for AI novices and organizations that are first importing AI technology. The integrated AI and graphics capabilities make it easier for less sophisticated users to grasp quickly the complex ideas and techniques within AI.

There are several reasons for this greater ease of use. For one, a graphics environment provides developers with instant feedback about what their system knows, can do, and why it makes suppositions. In addition, as developers create knowledge-representation structures within an expert system framework, the graphics environment allows the devlopers to move about within that framework and view the structures they have built.

These kinds of capabilities are not generally available on the more common 24- by 80-character screen. Consequently, expert system development on a standard terminal demands a great deal of visual imagery within the minds of developers about what is happening as they build their expert system.

DIGITAL EQUIPMENT CORP. IMPORTS AI

The best way to understand the planning, learning, and support issues in AI technology importation, as well as the need for demonstration and early user involvement, is to examine a case of a company that has imported and established an AI capability, and in so doing has dealt with these issues. The development of XCON at Digital Equipment Corp. is one of the best examples of a successful technology importation and transfer.

XCON, named R1 at Carnegie-Mellon University (CMU) where it was originally developed, configures VAX-11 and some PDP-11 computers. Given a customer's order, XCON determines what, if any, substitutions and additions need to be made to build a complete and functional computer system with the best possible performance. In response to user input, XCON produces printouts showing the components chosen, reasons for adding or deleting others, cable lengths, vector addresses (physical addresses of devices on a computer bus), and a series of diagrams showing the spatial and logical relationships among the devices and modules in a computer system.

Computer configuration at DEC is time consuming and complex because DEC does not offer only a limited number of standard computer systems. Instead, DEC's computer system offerings are based on components that customers specify and order a la carte. The task of configuring a computer system involves examining the components that the customer has selected, and deciding whether the set of components is complete as is or if additional components must be added to make the system functional. In addition, a human configurer must determine the spatial relationships between the components in order to integrate them.

"It used to take an expert configurer about 25 minutes to configure a system manually," says Dennis O'Connor, group manager of DEC's AI Technology Center and an AI pioneer at DEC. When that time is multiplied by 10,000 slightly different VAX orders per year, and adjusted both for the number of customers who change their minds so that the order needs to be reconfigured, as well as for other customers who want to know "what if I added this or did that," the configuration time problem becomes almost intractable.

In his article describing XCON's development and evaluation at DEC, John McDermott, XCON's designer, names three factors that contribute to making the computer configuration task difficult (McDermott, 1981). First, determining completeness is a very tedious task. To determine whether the set of components that has been ordered is complete, it is necessary to descend to a level of detail that is difficult for people to handle. As a result, completeness is not always determined satisfactorily.

Second, equally good configurers tend to configure the same sets of components in different ways. So the DEC system configurations are not consistent.

Third, it is difficult to keep skilled, experienced configurers. Such people tend to be promoted to other jobs. Consequently, configurers are often not as experienced or as knowledgeable as DEC would like.

AI'S RECEPTION AT DEC*

To solve its configuration problem, DEC made several unsuccessful attempts to automate the configuration process by developing a program using traditional software techniques. In 1978, Sam Fuller, who was then a faculty member in the computer science department at CMU, accepted a position at Digital. As he became aware of the problems that Digital was having in automating the configuration task, he proposed and began the negotiations between management at Digital and researchers at CMU.

After half a day of discussions about Digital's computer configuration, the CMU group believed that the configuration problem had characteristics that made it amenable to an expert system solution. So the group proposed that Digital Equipment support an effort at CMU to develop a configuration expert. John McDermott, senior research computer scientist at CMU and inventor of Digital Equipment Corp.'s expert computer configuration program, describes the initial reactions of the people at DEC to the idea of an expert system that configures VAX-11/780 computer systems as ranging from radical skepticism to moderate disbelief.

*This discussion is based on McDermott (1981).

"The only reason we were asked to build the expert system was that the problem was bothering some people enough so that they were willing to try anything," McDermott says. "Yet, despite the seriousness of the problem, no one at Digital was prepared to fund the development of a knowledge-based configurer until after the demonstration version of XCON had been implemented."

After the first version of XCON was demonstrated, some people's skepticism was replaced not with belief but with caution and hope. And after each succeeding developmental stage and demonstration, a few more people became less cautious. Some even committed themselves to making XCON a success. Finally, after about a year, as XCON was able to demonstrate its increasing configuration expertise, staunch believers and supporters began to emerge.

Five factors, according to McDermott, enabled XCON to stay afloat in the sea of caution that surrounded it. First, at each stage in its development, and with each demonstration, XCON convinced a few people who were in a position to assist in its development that it had real promise. Second, the task of developing a computer configuration was of just the right degree of difficulty. As a result, XCON was able to develop at a reasonable enough rate so that anyone who looked could see progress.

Third, only occasionally did XCON do less than was expected of it. Therefore, it never made any enemies. It turns out that not having enemies was just as important as having strong supporters. XCON's place at Digital Equipment was tenuous enough that if a few people had believed that it was a serious mistake, the exploration and development efforts would have stopped.

Fourth, the group of people who were close enough to the program to know about it firsthand was quite small and possessed the characteristics of not being resistant to change or new technologies. They believed that XCON had promise and therefore were willing to accept the times that it stumbled.

The fifth factor entailed maintaining XCON in a proper perspective by not allowing the hyping of any people's expectations for XCON. Keeping the right perspective is particularly important because, after a buildup of expectations, AI has flopped on this score in the past. To prevent such a recurrent experience, "the spokespeople for the project at Digital Equipment Corp. worked hard to manage people's expectations to insure that no one would count on more from XCON than it could deliver," McDermott says.

The initial contact between Digital Equipment Corp, and CMU occurred in 1978. From December 1978 through April 1979, a strategy for attacking Digital's configuration problem was formulated and a minimal expert system to demonstrate the potential of the knowledge-based approach was written and demonstrated. From May through September 1979, a large amount of more computer configuration knowledge was added to the program. From October through November 1979, Digital tested XCON extensively and determined that it was sufficiently expert to be used on a regular basis to configure its VAX-11/780 computer system.

By January 1980, the chief question had become how to integrate the expert configurer into Digital's operational environment without disrupting the existing operations. It took the first half of 1980 to define the type of organization that should support XCON and the functions the group should perform. The second half of that year was spent recruiting people, none of whom had any background in AI, to learn enough AI so that they could continue the development and maintenance of XCON when CMU's involvement was completed.

Since that time, Digital Equipment Corp, has expanded this AI group. Using this initial CMU-trained group as the seed, the computer firm has grown its own internal expertise in AI, and it has grown that expertise without bringing in people who have formal credentials in AI.

However, it is Digital Equipment's usual computer system configurers, rather than this home-grown AI group, who actually operate the expert system. Normally, to operate without an expert system, in each of Digital's final assembly and test plants, people called technical editors configure each system to be built. Then they give their configuration diagrams to technicians, who actually assemble the systems.

Once XCON was ready for routine use, the person who had been the technical editor for VAX-11/780 systems became XCON's supervisor. The supervisor's role was to review XCON's output configuration diagrams for correctness. The output, if correct, was then given to the technicians for use in assembly.

The AI group that Digital formed when XCON was getting ready for routine use was given three principal functions; data collection, process development, and program maintenance and development. The data collection task, performed by engineers, involved extending XCON's database of component descriptions. The process development task was to invent ways to facilitate information flow and XCON's accessibility between the XCON development group and people in other Digital Equipment organizations, such as manufacturing, engineering, and sales. For example, the process development group formalized the reporting of problems with XCON, such as an incorrect configuration performance, and the checking of reported problems, such as "was the configuration produced by XCON indeed incorrect?"

The people responsible for data collection and for process development needed no special training. But the people responsible for program maintenance and development were slated to take over the role that CMU played. They were the people who, in the future, would modify XCON's rules as inadequacies in its knowledge were discovered, and they would extend XCON so that it could configure systems other than VAX-11/780s. To take over this role, they needed to become proficient in OPS5, the specialized programming language used to program the expert system.

On the average, it took each of the new AI group's members about three months of learning and practice to achieve enough OPS5 proficiency to be able to make appropriate modifications and extensions to the program. With this proficiency, however, the group became self-sufficient enough to subsequently extend

XCON's capabilities. First the group extended XCON so that it could also configure VAX-11/750 systems. Later, the group focused on extending XCON to configure PDP-11s. Configuring PDP-11 systems is a more difficult problem than configuring VAX-11s because PDP-11s support a significantly greater number of components.

XCON is now firmly entrenched at Digital. Since its acceptance, the Digital AI group has added other expert systems which it is integrating with XCON. Many of these were developed by or in conjunction with CMU. Some are under development with other academic institutions, and some extensions to the expert systems are the products of Digital's AI technology importation and transfer.

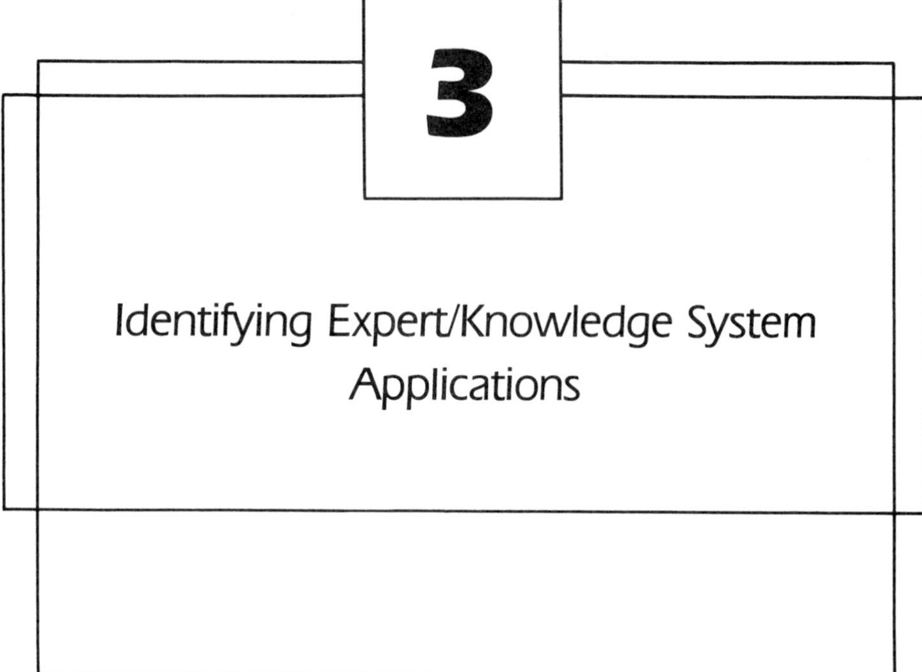

3 Identifying Expert/Knowledge System Applications

It is probable that within the next 30 days yet another company will form an artificial intelligence department or yet another artificial intelligence company will start up. Most likely, both the department and company will investigate, build, use, or market an expert system.

Expert systems are computer programs that capture the expertise of human experts who are knowledgeable in a particular application domain. As such human experts are in very short supply, they are expensive and difficult to get.

Since getting the real human expert has proved to be a problem, the alternative, the expert system scheme, is to represent an expert's knowledge in a form that a computer can use. A computerized model of the expert's reasoning and problem-solving abilities then uses that knowledge to solve problems in humanlike fashion.

The expert's knowledge is contained in what is aptly called a knowledge base. An inference mechanism also does what its name implies. It makes inferences based on its interpretation of the representation of the expert's knowledge (Figure 3-1). These expert systems (or knowledge-based systems), which incorporate these experts' reasoning and problem-solving models, augment the experts' capabilities and are similar to having a consultant on call.

It is important to realize, however, that while expert systems can reason from knowledge in a limited domain and can approach (in some cases, even exceed) human performance, they cannot provide solutions for problems that human beings do not know how to solve. Instead, expert systems contain, in encoded form, the existing knowledge of experts and use that encoded knowledge

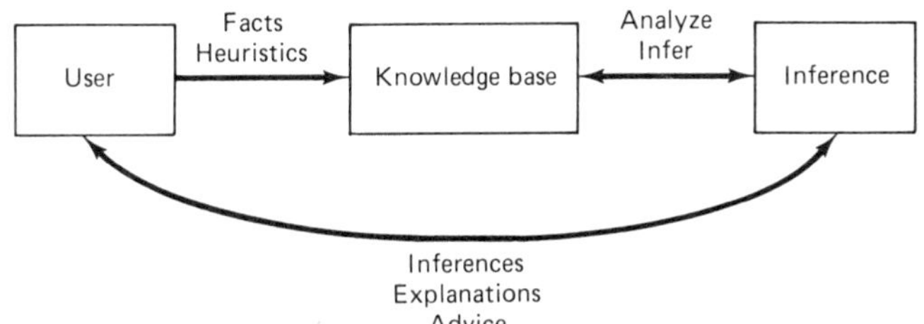

Figure 3-1 Expert systems infer and advise based on interpreting human experts' knowledge.

to reason like a human being. Therein lies the power of expert systems—in that knowledge, not in clever programming.

To reason like a human being, expert systems rely not only on factual knowledge as do conventional programs, but also on uncertain knowledge and observations based on experience and intuition (collectively called heuristics). The facts and heuristics are extracted from experts in a specialized subject area. They are then coupled with methods of analyzing, manipulating, and applying the encoded knowledge so that the program can make inferences and explain its actions.

Expert systems differ from computer programs because their reasoning is not straightforward. Their tasks have no practical algorithmic solutions, and they must often make conclusions based on incomplete, judgmental, speculative, uncertain, or fuzzy information (Figure 3-2). For example, most human beings would interpret the statement, "the boss is never in his office" to mean "the boss is frequently out of his office." "Fire him" would be an unthinkable conclusion to most human beings (and expert systems), who know that bosses are frequently at meetings held elsewhere in the organization.

Typically, to build an expert system, the developer chooses a form to represent the expert's knowledge. The developer and the expert work together to encode some of the expert's basic knowledge and reasoning techniques in that form. Then the developer and the expert together challenge that expert system

Figure 3-2 Expert systems solve problems for which there is no practical algorithmic solution by reasoning with heuristic as well as factual information.

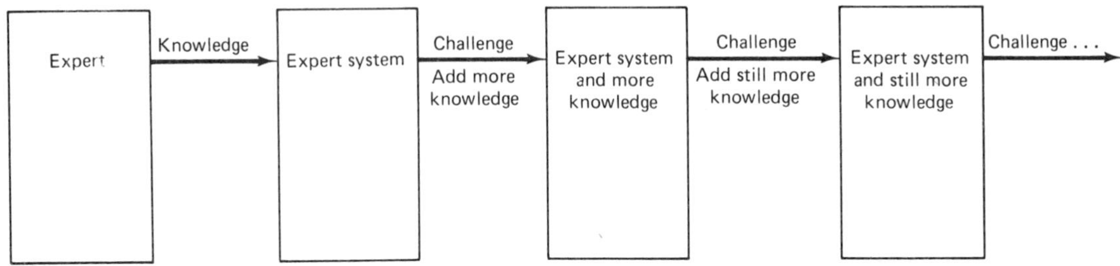

Figure 3-3 Expert system development

with a lot of problems and cases. As the fledgling expert system makes mistakes, its developers add more knowledge and thus try to improve on the model of the expert (Figure 3-3).

EXPERT SYSTEM CHARACTERISTICS

There are several characteristics that expert systems must exhibit to be useful. First, in order to add more knowledge and to improve on the model of the expert developed, expert systems must have the capability to update their knowledge easily. The update capability is necessary not only to correct mistakes that the expert system makes, but to keep pace, for example, with new knowledge that an expert learns or new items that a company decides to handle. Ultimately, expert systems may be able to learn new facts themselves and, in this way, increase their knowledge. For the time being, they are dependent on acquiring their knowledge from human beings, either directly or through data entered into databases by people.

Second, to be able to cope with real-world problems, expert systems must have flexible problem-solving strategies, just as do human experts. This feature is necessary because each problem to be solved, as well as the information available to solve it, may be slightly different each time.

Third, expert systems need to exhibit high performance in terms of their ability to solve their assigned problems correctly. Just as human beings who have difficulty getting the right answer are not considered experts, expert systems that blunder when dealing with the basic problems they were designed to solve are not considered expert systems. Fourth, expert systems need to have the capability to explain what they have done and why, in the same way that human experts explain their actions.

KNOWLEDGE BOTTLENECKS

Not all fields of knowledge are currently suitable for expert system applications. In general, expert system applications are suitable for tasks about which people are more knowledgeable and perform a lot better if they have had years of experience. Usually, the number of such people is relatively small. As a result, their knowledge is scarce, poorly distributed in an organization, often distributed among many people, and unavailable with any degree of reliability. This scarcity, poor distribution, and unavailability results in a knowledge bottleneck for an organization.

The high-payoff expert system applications occur where the knowledge bottlenecks are. Therefore, to identify what is a good expert system application in an organization, it is necessary to analyze the flow of information in the organization and locate the knowledge bottlenecks.

Unfortunately, instead of looking to locate these bottlenecks, there is a tendency among many people when considering potential expert systems to focus on the word "expert." These people frequently overlook excellent candidate expert system applications because they are misled by their perceptions of the word "expert."

Clearly, a geophysicist who interprets geological and oil-well log data is easily recognizable as an expert. The geophysicist is recognized as expert because most people associate geophysicists with such characteristics as university degrees, intellectual sophistication, and the ability to perform tasks that the average person could not conceive of learning—a kind of witch-doctor syndrome if you will. For most people, the combination of the academic associations, together with the ability to perform tasks that are as unintelligible to most people as witch-doctor's methods, adds up to "expert." By this characterization, a physician and a geophysicist are clearly experts.

But knowledge bottlenecks frequently encompass ordinary types of knowledge, such as the planning performed by a travel agent, rather than the more intuitive and academic expertise often associated with expert systems. For example, in the case of expert systems that perform computer configuration, the knowledge bottlenecks comprised some moderately paid, experienced technicians/clerks who were expert at their jobs.

High-payoff expert systems have also been implemented to perform locomotive diagnostic tasks. Migrating to a less technical area of expertise, the loan advice domain has the characteristics of a possibly good expert system application. Knowledge about loans certainly exists in organizations that issue them. However, the information is generally poorly distributed, difficult to use, and difficult for most people to communicate to others. Therefore, loan organizations make a larger number of undesirable loans than they would like. Even something as simple as filling out various forms within an organization may require a fair amount of knowledge to avoid their bouncing back from the accounting department. Making an expert system out of such an application may be a valuable time and money saver. Yet people do not generally view the latter as a "real" expert system application.

KNOWLEDGE SYSTEMS

Since the term *expert system* often suggests misleading notions and features about what these systems can do and what kinds of applications are appropriate, "knowledge system" is the preferred label by many in the AI community. Knowledge systems suggest a greater variety of ordinary knowledge than the intuitive and academic expertise associated with the label "expert."

Knowledge systems that perform more ordinary tasks than, say, oil-exploration systems have several advantages, some of which are particularly relevant to organizations first getting into AI. First, the problems caused by knowledge bottlenecks affect an organization economically. Second, many AI companies claim that compared to systems with intuitive and academic expertise, it is easier to estimate the amount of time, cost, and effort to build ordinary knowledge-based systems. As such, they entail a much lower risk and are more practical.

The ease of estimating development time, cost, and effort are related to the ease with which the non-application expert can understand the subject matter of the application. This ease is important because to build an expert system, the knowledge engineer, who extracts knowledge from an application expert and converts it into a form that a computer understands, must to some degree acquire an understanding of the subject.

Clearly, there is much more to learn for a subject based on academic expertise rather than one based on ordinary knowledge. For example, an intelligent person can sit in a room full of books and figure out to get from here to Tahiti. It may take time, it may not be convenient, and certainly it would be easier to find a route if either a travel agent or a travel information expert system were available. However, sitting in a room filled with geology texts is a different ball game. In contrast to travel agents or other people who possess ordinary knowledge, experienced, expert geologists are more likely to have learned vast amounts of facts and have spent years in training and apprenticeship.

Due to the combination of their vast storehouse of facts and intuitive knowledge, an expert's expertise is difficult for a knowledge engineer to understand at the onset of a project. How, then, can a knowledge engineer estimate how long it will take, how much it will cost and how much effort it will involve to build an expert system that performs the geologist's job? Knowledge engineers can, however, estimate and quantify such parameters for applications that incorporate ordinary knowledge simply because they understand them better.

A third advantage in building ordinary-knowledge systems is the ability to easily find experts who can systematically communicate their knowledge. Systematic communication of knowledge is a much more difficult task when building expert rather than knowledge systems. Expertise tends to be amorphous, unstructured, and intuitive. Like artists, experts, follow a classical pattern of accomplishing their work without thinking, to any extent, how they perform it. These characteristics make it difficult for experts to articulate their knowledge.

In contrast, ordinary knowledge tends to be more structured and systematic. The structure and systematic nature of such knowledge makes it easier for knowledgeable people to state their knowledge explicitly enough to be incorporated into a computer system.

Finally, more people exist who have ordinary knowledge than those who have expertise. This makes it easier to find the experts in a field. Because of the greater abundance of experts in ordinary knowledge, there is no danger that a knowledge system will not be able to be completed because the only articulate, experienced expert at a company has left.

While knowledge systems containing ordinary knowledge are in some ways more practical than academically oriented expert systems, they too have their failings and should not be considered simple to develop or run compared to their more complex counterparts. The problem is that simple systems, such as expert travel planners, may need to contain hundreds of heuristic rules about shortcuts, discounts, and so on. These systems frequently rely on search through a large search space of solutions to find the best solution—a strategy considered a "weak," not necessarily efficient method. In contrast, complex systems are likely to concentrate on representing more knowledge in ways that require less search to arrive at a solution and provide more efficient performance. Thus they classically rely on what is considered to be "strong" methods.

CHOOSING AN APPLICATION

Teknowledge, Inc., suggests eight common situations where a knowledge-based system can be of value.*

- The knowledge required to perform a particular task effectively is available only at a central location. Requests for advice are channeled to a small group of people who are always in demand. For example, a key product design team may be spending an excessive portion of their time on the phone advising repair personnel.
- A written document or flowchart is intended to facilitate the use of a program, procedure, or piece of equipment. However, it is so long and detailed that it is useless in practice. In actuality, the users develop folklore-like methods for accomplishing the task. They rely excessively on previous methods that were determined empirically to work. For example, a flexible and sophisticated computer simulation program goes unused in favor of building expensive models because its user manual fills a shelf of three-ring binders.
- An organization turns away work or loses business to competitors because an overworked human expert is required to make judgments or recommen-

* Evaluating Knowledge Engineering Applications," Knowledge Engineering, Teknowledge, Inc., Palo Alto, Calif., 1983.

dations, even in routine cases. For example, to reduce unnecessary, expensive work, a locomotive repair center requires a supervisor to approve all diagnoses and recommendations before work is undertaken. Although costs are controlled, the average down time increases to a point where it is economical for customers to tow broken equipment to other centers for repair.

- Due to turnover in equipment or personnel, an excessive amount of time is spent training rather than doing. For example, a company updates its line of test equipment each year, and field engineers must spend an average of two months annually attending training sessions.
- A large amount of mainly routine data must be scanned by a highly trained expert on a continuing basis. For example, a high-energy physics laboratory employs a crew of 10 people to look for rare events in bubble chamber images.
- A variety of information from heterogeneous sources must be monitored and integrated to determine the possibility of an important event. For example, a government agency must constantly examine information from multiple sources to determine if a military threat is present.
- A critical judgement must be made in a very short time interval to avoid a potential disaster. For example, a nuclear power plant control center must decide quickly to shut down or cut back a particular unit when a potential problem is detected.
- An optimal solution to a routing, planning, or configuration task is too expensive or time consuming to determine. Instead, a minimally effective process of guesswork has been substituted. For example, a computer company has to configure orders for its equipment, with the proper cables, components, and mounting arrangement, on an individual basis. Errors and delays in this process become a serious problem as orders increase.

KNOWLEDGE SYSTEM PREREQUISITES

To build a knowledge-based system for any problem domain, certain prerequisites concerning the human beings involved and problem characteristics must be met. For example, prerequisite conditions concerning human experts require that there be at least one person who performs the task well enough to be classified as an expert in that task. Experts must be able to articulate their knowledge and explain how to apply that knowledge to a particular task. It is possible to bring the knowledge of several human experts to bear on a problem. Dealing with more than one expert, however, can cause inconsistencies in the knowledge extracted for computer use because different experts often arrive at the same or equivalent answer by what seems to be very different means.

Prerequisite conditions that apply to the problem, rather than the human expert, require that the application area be well bounded. In other words, the problem limits that the knowledge system can handle should be well defined because most knowledge systems today do not deal well with problems at the limits of their knowledge; in fact, many do not even know that problem is beyond their knowledge. In addition, the chunks of knowledge encoded within the program must be relatively well defined so that when solving a problem the knowledge system can select from its various alternative pieces of knowledge. Finally, the problem chosen for a knowledge system application should be solvable by human beings within a period of three minutes to three weeks.

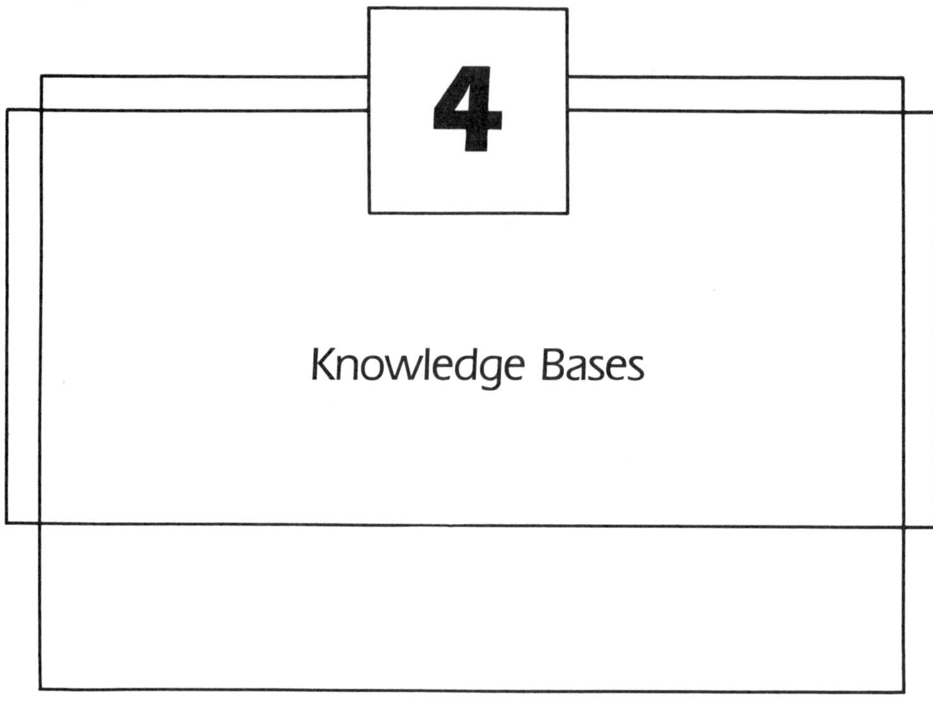

4 Knowledge Bases

Although we can recognize intelligent behavior to some degree when we see it, no one has yet succeeded in defining what intelligence is. The lack of a definition of intelligence makes it difficult to attribute intelligence to computer programs. However, AI researchers have developed a number of ways to represent human knowledge and structure computer programs so that the programs exhibit behavior that we normally associate with intelligence. As mentioned earlier, the computer programs that incorporate these knowledge representations and structuring techniques are our present-day expert or knowledge systems.*

Expert/knowledge systems contain three basic components (Figure 4–1). These components are in addition to the user interface, which varies with the knowledge-based system and insulates the end user from the AI technology. One basic component, called a knowledge base, in some symbolic manner represents knowledge of facts and general information, as well as heuristics such as judgments, intuition, and experience, about a particular narrow problem area. The second component, known as an inference mechanism, interprets the knowledge in the knowledge base and performs logical deduction and certain knowledge base modifications. The third component, the control mechanism, organizes and controls the strategies taken to apply the inference process.

Some components and characteristics are common to knowledge systems and conventional computer programs. For example, conventional computer programs also contain data (facts, as opposed to heuristics) and a means to

*The terms *expert system* and *knowledge system* are synonymous. However, *knowledge system* is considered by many in the AI community to be more descriptive of what these AI systems are and will be used throughout most of the rest of this book.

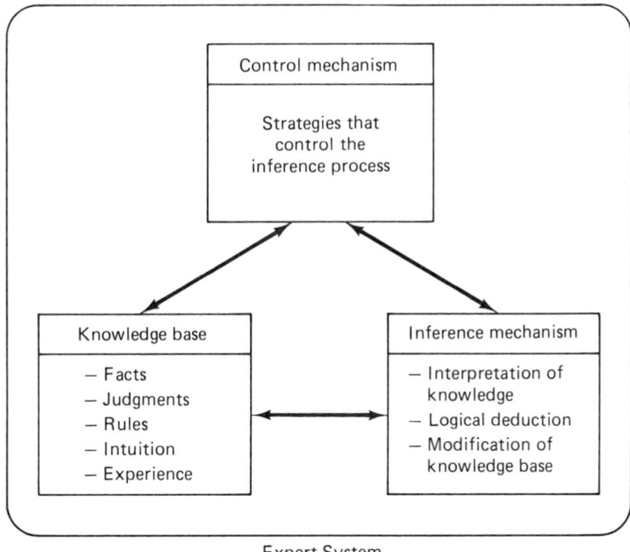

Figure 4-1 Three components of expert systems.

manipulate those data algrorithmically and to control the strategies that the program applies to solve its problem. However, conventional programs differ substantially from knowledge-based systems because in conventional programs, the data, manipulation, and control capabilities are all buried together and distributed throughout the program. In contrast, knowledge systems modularize the knowledge base, inference mechanism, and control mechanism. In other words, these three mechanisms are separate and independent of each other.

This separation of the knowledge base and the inference and control mechanisms contributes to the easy modifiability of knowledge systems and makes it possible to change the system just by modifying the knowledge base. For example, one knowledge-based system for oil exploration was converted to a knowledge system in the area of public accounting by substituting a public accounting knowledge base for the one containing oil exploration knowledge.

Even the chunks of knowledge within the knowledge base are separate from one another. This separation allows new chunks of knowledge to be added fairly easily to knowledge systems. As a result, the knowledge base lives and grows as the expert behind it adds more knowledge to it. In contrast to the knowledge base, the inference and control mechanisms are essentially static. They do not generally change with time.

KNOWLEDGE BASES AND DATABASES

Both knowledge bases and traditional databases are designed to store information. They differ significantly from each other in the types of information they can

DATABASE TABLE FOR EMPLOYEES

EMPNO	ENAME	JOB	HIREDATE	SAL	DEPTNO
5124	ADAM	CLERK	15-DEC-81	800.00	20
5436	PUCCINI	SALESPERSON	28-FEB-82	1,600.00	30
5499	NADER	SALESPERSON	04-MAR-82	1,250.00	30
6012	BING	MANAGER	13-APR-82	2,975.00	20
6078	LYONS	SALESPERSON	23-JUN-82	1,250.00	30
7134	MARTIN	MANAGER	17-OCT-82	4,850.00	30
7488	FLYNN	MANAGER	25-NOV-82	2,450.00	10
7793	FERMAT	ANALYST	09-FEB-83	5,000.00	20
8005	KING	PRESIDENT	12-MAR-83	8,000.00	10
8035	KAREN	SALESPERSON	24-APR-83	1,900.00	30
8456	BACH	SALESPERSON	01-JUL-83	1,500.00	30
8888	ESCHER	CLERK	22-SEP-83	1,100.00	20
8900	EINSTEIN	CLERK	10-OCT-83	950.00	30
9116	GODEL	ANALYST	07-JAN-84	5,000.00	20
9130	JACKSON	CLERK	16-APR-84	1,300.00	10

Figure 4-2 Typical facts stored in databases.

store, the types of interrelationships between data they can handle (that indicate either application-specific or commonsense knowledge), and in what kind of training is needed for the person who updates the stored information.

To illustrate one difference, databases store only facts (Figure 4-2). Moreover, database facts are straightforward and definite. Typical facts found in databases include information such as "Tohru is a male," "Karen is an employee in the sales department," and "The sales department contains 30 employees."

A major strength of databases is the ability to use this type of straightforward, definite information to respond to queries such as "what are the names of all the female employees in the sales department" and "how many departments contain greater than 25 employees?" However, databases cannot deal with complex descriptions of real-world situations, rules that state causal relationships, or uncertain knowledge about the stored facts. Neither can databases handle what seems to be commonsense relationships between the stored facts.

Knowledge bases, like databases, also store straightforward definite facts. But, in addition, knowledge bases store cause-and-effect knowledge, rules, and imprecise and probabilistic information. Typical knowledge found in knowledge bases includes information such as "Smoking is bad for your health." Or else, knowledge bases handle observed or proven rules, such as "If you smoke, you are more likely to get lung cancer."

FUZZY FACTS

The latter is an example not only of a rule, but also of an imprecise, uncertain, or "fuzzy" chunk of knowledge. Fuzzy knowledge is knowledge quantified by words such as most, several, many, few, almost, unlikely, more frequently, almost impossible, very, quite, and extremely. It is difficult to describe real-world knowledge without the ability to deal with fuzzy, as well as probabilistic, knowledge because almost everything in the real world is a matter of degree.

Knowledge bases, and the inference mechanisms that manipulate and infer new information from knowledge bases, are designed to handle uncertain information. Databases are not. In the database, Karen either is or is not an employee. She is not almost an employee. She is not mostly in the sales department. Database applications understand that the sales deparment has 30 employees, not many employees.

WHO DOES THE UPDATES?

The update requirements for databases contrast sharply with those for knowledge base updates because of the differences in the type of information and in the cause-and-effect relationships contained in knowledge bases. Typical database data, such as employee name, department, and parts lists, are generic, traverse many applications, and are superficially understandable by the general populace. When new names or parts need to be added to a particular department listed in the database, a variety of people can add them.

For example, databases may be updated by workers in a data-processing department who are knowledgeable about databases. The data-processing workers do not, however, need to know about the mechanics of running a department or about the devices that will use the parts in a database.

In contrast to database information, the knowledge and rules found in knowledge bases include both data and heuristics of a professional and engineering nature, specialized for a particular application area. The application area they are specialized for determines who can update the knowledge base.

For example, one typical Mycin diagnosis rule indicates that if a blood culture shows an organism with a gram-negative stain and a rod morphology in a compromised-host patient, it suggests that the identity of an organism found in a blood culture is *Pseudomonas aeruginosa* (Figure 4-3). A knowledge base that contains this type of information needs to be modified by a doctor or expert with knowledge in this diagnostic area. Similarly, knowledge in an expert automotive troubleshooting system must be added or modified by a person with automotive troubleshooting expertise.

```
    IF The site of the culture is blood
       The gram stain of the organism is gramneg
       The morphology of the organism is rod, and
       The patient is a compromised host,
  THEN There is suggestive evidence (0.6) that the identity of
       the organism is Pseudomonas-Aeruginosa.
```

Figure 4-3 Mycin diagnosis rule

HANDLING COMMON SENSE

It is not only the ability to store general knowledge, rules, and uncertain information that differentiates knowledge bases from databases. Knowledge bases store and handle far more complex and sophisticated relationships between facts, or chunks of information, than databases can. The ability to store these interrelationships makes it possible to build and infer a great deal of causal and commonsense knowledge about the world, as well as knowledge about what is possible in a given application area.

Two things make it possible to represent causal and commonsense information in a knowledge-based system. One is the representation of knowledge symbolically. The other is the various types of knowledge base structures that have been developed to represent the knowledge and the relationships between the knowledge items in the knowledge base. These types of knowledge base structures do not exist in databases.

Most often, a database is a fairly rigidly structured set of records and items within records, comparable to what is found in a file cabinet. For example, an inventory database for corporate offices might contain a list of office desks along with their cost, location, and owners. Each office desk and the information about it is a separate database record, just as it would be a separate record on an index card in a file drawer. With such a database, users can answer such questions as "how many desks cost more than $1200?"

Interrelationships in this database are fairly simple. It is easy to represent, for example, a relationship showing that both these typewriters and desks belong to David. But certainly database structures will not contain a lot of information about what is sensible in the world. Not so for knowledge-base structures.

SEMANTIC NETWORKS

Knowledge bases represent knowledge using a system of "predicate functions" and "symbolic data structures". A function is a kind of procedure that is performed on certain input values, called arguments, and produces, or is associated with, a set of admissible values. For example, "3 plus 4," which is written in Lisp programs as (plus 3 4), is an example of the "plus" function. The function (plus 3 4) evaluates to 7. Times, Difference, Quotient, Min (to find a minimum) and Max (for maximum) are examples of other functions.

A predicate is a function that evaluates to either true or false. For example, in the function (on typewriter desk), "on" is a predicate, and the function, which states that the typewriter is on the desk, is either true or false.

A symbolic data structure is a structure that is used to represent symbolic knowledge and that can be stored in a computer's memory. One symbolic knowledge representation structure is called a semantic network.

A semantic network is a node-and-arc graphical notation that represents objects (or actions or events) and contains built-in real-world meaning, or

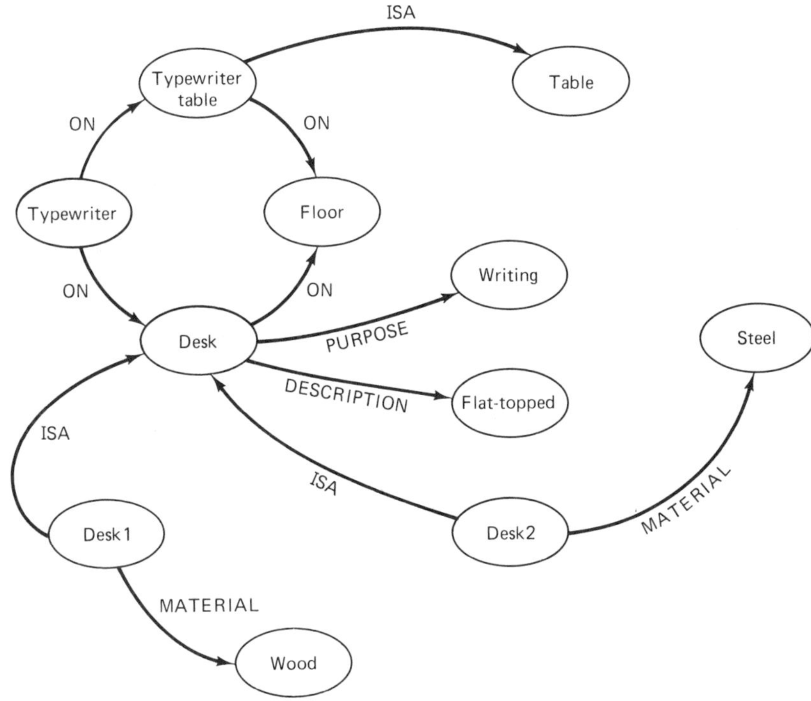

Figure 4-4 A semantic network

semantics, about the objects (Figure 4-4). The nodes represent the objects. They could also represent actions or events. The arcs between the nodes represent predicates or attributes that indicate relationships between the objects (or actions or events) shown in the nodes.

The semantic network shown in the figure uses both predicates, such as "on" and "isa," as well as attributes, such as material, to represent objects in an office and to show relationsips between the objects. A trace of the arcs that connect the nodes in this network shows that typewriters tend to sit on desks; desks do not sit on typewriters; desks tend to sit on floors; typewriters do not tend to sit on floors. This knowledge structure can infer information such as "a particular object can't be a typewriter because it has a desk sitting on it."

The semantic network also enables a knowledge system to infer information such as "a particular desk sits on the floor because, as shown, desks sit on floors." With a semantic network representation, the knowledge system can also infer that "desk 1 and desk 2 have flat tops and are used for writing because desks 1 and 2 are both examples of (instances of) desks, and desks in general have flat tops and are used for writing.

This type of inference is based on a principle called "inheritance." Here "inheritance" means that since desks 1 and 2 are instances of desks, they inherit the characteristics of that desk. Since the purpose of desks is writing and their description is flat-topped, both instances of a desk inherit the purpose of writing and the description of flat-topped.

KNOWLEDGE REPRESENTATION METHODS

There are several other methods used to represent knowledge in a knowledge base. Besides semantic networks, knowledge-based systems employ representation methods known as rules, frames, processes, logic, and scripts. These knowledge representation structures are discussed in Chapters 5 to 8, and 15.

Despite knowledge representation differences, in general anything that one representation can do can be done by the others. Ultimately, a representation choice boils down to how the chooser thinks about the knowledge in question and which representation method lends itself most efficiently to retrieval and deduction of facts.

The representation of knowledge so that a computer understands it is one of the major problems in building a knowledge-based system. It may take months to represent the relationships in a simple world such as an office. How, then, can an AI expert represent the entire building? And once the knowledge has been represented, how is it possible to search it quickly and make inferences?

RULES

Although there are many ways to represent knowledge, the most common form of knowledge representation is with "rules." A rule is a conditional statement that specifies an action to take place, or advice to follow, under a certain set of conditions. This situation-action or symptom-cause format of rules is particularly suitable for expressing knowledge that experts in the field have gained as a result of experience—their so-called rules of thumb.

In some respects, rules are similar to the conditional "if-then" statements of conventional programming languages. If-then statements are statements of the form, "IF this is the case, THEN do that" or "IF this happens, THEN do that" or even "IF this is the case, THEN that is true." For example, IF Fido is a dog, THEN Fido is an animal. Rules differ from conventional IF-THEN statements because of their extreme modularity. A set of rules is an unstructured group of IF-THEN statements that control themselves in terms of knowing when they should be applied to solve a problem.

This difference between rules and IF-THEN statements is major and has significant implications for the building of knowledge-based systems. In fact, despite their similarities, experience has shown that it is very difficult—often impossible—to develop a knowledge-based system using conventional IF-THEN statements. The difficulties exist because knowledge systems require both greater conditionality and greater need to make changes during program development than do conventional software systems.

Concerning the first requirement for conditionality, it turns out that most instructions in conventional programs are unconditional. The program executes its instructions sequentially—first one, then the next, and so on. In addition, the conditional statements that conventional programs encounter contain only a relatively small number of possible paths at each step that calls for branching to perform one or another procedure.

In contrast to the two, three, or five possibilities usual in conventional programs, the conditionality embedded in AI problems is so great that the number of paths that can be exploited grows explosively. Typical conventional programs contain a smaller number of paths because they solve problems algorithmically and therefore contain little uncertainty about what the appropriate next step is. The determination of which possible choice to take can be made on the basis of only a few critical pieces of information. On the other hand, when solving tasks heuristically, based on experience and intuition, it is not always clear what the next reasonable step is. So at every step during a heuristic problem solution, it is necessary to consider a number of alternative steps.

Unfortunately, human programmers who must specify the sequences of alternative steps that a knowledge-based system must execute are immediately confronted by the necessity to specify, at every step of a problem, several possible paths, each of which depends on several possible conditions. Each of the paths specified also necessitates further specification of several possible paths depending on a variety of conditions.

All in all, a mental picture of such a program resembles a very branchy tree with a huge number of possible paths to follow to get to a solution. It is very difficult for human beings even to visualize, much less lay out in advance and write, such branchy AI programs using conventional software methods. Because of this difficulty with the visualization and layout of programs, traditional programming methods and languages are not well suited to the development of highly conditional knowledge systems.

Even worse, conventional algorithmic programs are very difficult to change. The difficulty exists because the architecture of conventional programs is highly structured. Even in supposedly modular programs, the various modules and procedures depend on one another enough so that a change in one procedure may affect another. Most of the time, a change in one module that reflects, for example, a change in the state or strategy of a business, is a big undertaking and time consuming. As a result, once conventional programs are designed and coded, they become static.

But business activities and problem-solution requirements are not static. They often change, and computer programs based on these activities must reflect the changes. Unfortunately, conventional programs that encode all the permutations of business activities in them are not able to meet the change demand in a timely, cost-effective manner.

In fact, Digital Equipment Corp. made three unsuccessful attempts to automate its computer configuration with traditional software techniques before switching to a rule-based approach. Programs based on conventional techniques ran into difficulties because they could not keep pace with DEC's product offerings or engineering changes.

With conventional programming, every time DEC added, removed, or changed the possible mix of components in its computer system offerings, a program rewrite was needed. The conditionality expressed by the expert computer configuration system was so great that the rewrite was particularly difficult.

To compound the problem, changes occurred repeatedly within short time frames. Consequently, the conventional computer configuration program never reflected the current state of business. In the end, the firm decided that what it needed, instead, was a programming tool or language that itself considers what to do at each step of solving a problem and then selects the best alternative choice on the basis of which action is most appropriate in the context of a particular situation. In other words, for success, the tool or language, rather than the programmer, must consider and select the alternative choices.

Rule-based languages do not require programmers to specify a sequence of steps for a program. Instead, programmers need merely describe conditions indicating some situation, specify the action that should take place if that situation is true, and then dump the whole set of unstructured rules into the program.

When the program runs, a rule interpreter applies its own rules to structure the program dynamically. To apply rules, the rule interpreter uses a "pattern-matching" procedure. The rule interpreter checks to see if the conditions specified in the IF part of a rule (it views the conditions as patterns) match similar patterns in a knowledge system database set up elsewhere in the computer's memory. For example, if the database contains a pattern which states that "there is an object called a monkey and there are bananas on the ceiling," the rule interpreter looks through the "rule base" for a rule whose IF part contains the same pattern about the object called a monkey and bananas on the ceiling.

If it finds a rule with that pattern in its IF part, the rule interpreter applies the rule. "Applies the rule" means that it modifies the database to create a new pattern. A typical rule might modify the database to create the pattern, "the object 'monkey' gets an object called 'ladder'." The rule interpreter then performs this type of pattern-matching procedure all over again to handle the changed program and database state with the new pattern about the monkey, bananas, ceiling, and ladder.

The net effect of this pattern-matching technique is that each rule is fairly independent. Also, each rule is always watching the world around itself which is simulated in the knowledge system database. It watches to see if it is applicable, which means to see if it matches a database pattern. Whenever the rules sees that it is applicable, it applies itself.

Although rule languages work as described, the description given is simplistic. For example, many rules can apply at one time. There are different techniques for applying the rules. And it is unnecessary and inefficient to try out every rule every time a rule is applied. Rule-based systems in operation are discussed later in more detail.

Since the rule language does not impose any organization on the rules—the rules are applied based on pattern matches—knowledge system designers can add, modify, and delete rules with ease. In addition, since there is no need to bother about proper sequencing and consistency, system designers can explore and rapidly prototype complex, ill-specified, changeable systems.

It is important to note that although the symbolic manipulation language called Lisp is most commonly known as an AI language, most AI programming is not done directly in Lisp. What is more commonly used are a number of specialized languages, such as rule-based and frame-based languages and languages associated with knowledge system development tools. These languages operate on top of Lisp, may translate into Lisp during program execution, and use various Lisp features.

With a rule-based language, which DEC now uses for its expert computer configuration system, whenever new components are added to the DEC computer system line, the company only needs to add new rules about how the new components will interconnect. In contrast, disasters would occur if programmers moved lines of code around a program written in conventional languages such as Fortan, Pascal, or Cobol.

True, disorganized dumping of rules can contribute to the inefficiency of a system. On the other hand, it is a mistake to worry about structuring a system for efficiency and speed too early, because early structuring causes a system to become rigid. The technique in knowledge system development is to defer efficiency and speed issues until the end of the development time and give the developers as much flexibility and computational leverage as possible because the problems that knowledge systems seek to solve are so difficult. Only after the knowledge system has evolved and developed to a satisfactory point and developers are ready to freeze and deliver the system can they afford to go back and reimplement it. For example, DEC's XCON originally required $\frac{1}{2}$ hour to run a single-configuration case. That was considered fine because the goal then was to develop a program to assemble a computer system. When the developers were ready to freeze and deliver the system, the goal also became efficiency. After the reimplementation, XCON ran 200 times faster and required only a few seconds per configuration case.

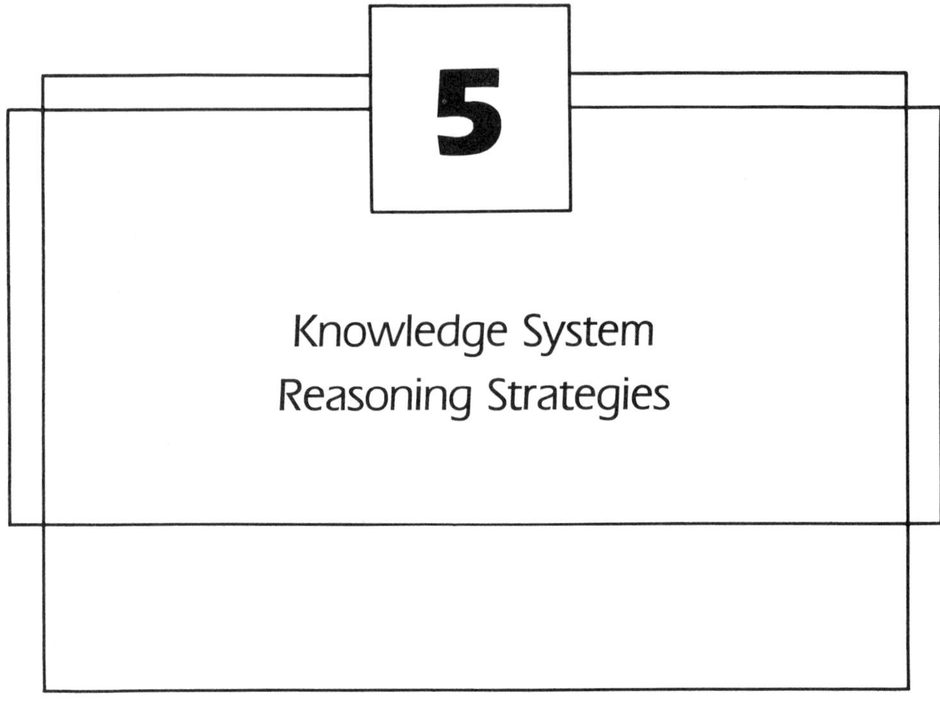

5 Knowledge System Reasoning Strategies

Since the power of a knowledge-based system is in its knowledge, a major concern of knowledge systems is the representation of that knowledge. One way to represent knowledge is in rules. Once the rules are in place, there are various ways of manipulating them to produce useful knowledge systems. A good example of rule manipulation is found in AI systems for the oil-exploration industry. Because the process of drilling a production oil well is such a complex, expensive undertaking, as measured in money, time, personnel, equipment, and materials, oil exploration companies were among the pioneer supporters of commercial rule-based expert systems.

One oil exploration system, developed by Teknowledge for the French oil company Elf Aquitaine, provides consultation services and advice on problems encountered during the drilling of oil wells. Called the Drilling Advisor, the knowledge-based system questions the drilling supervisor, who is in charge of an oil rig or set of oil rigs, in a natural language. Using the answers to the questions and its own knowledge, the Drilling Advisor then reasons about the drilling problem, identifies the cause of the problem, and finally offers, in text form, both advice on actions to solve the current problem and preventative measures to avoid a recurrence of the accident.

THE PROBLEM TO SOLVE

Sticking of the drill bit is a common oil-well drilling problem which the Drilling Advisor is designed to solve. Drill-bit sticking problems occur when the drilling assembly cannot turn, thereby preventing further drilling or the return of equipment to the surface.

Six major causes of sticking have been identified. However, it takes an expert to determine which of the six major causes of sticking is the problem in a particular drilling episode because problem determination is not done directly. There are no telemetry data from sensors at the bottom of the hole that transmit information to the surface about what is happening in the hole. Instead, by examining the drilled rock pieces, mud, and lubricant material that comes out of the drilled hole, the drilling engineer or supervisor determines the reasons that the drill bit stopped turning. This procedure is a little like archaeology techniques—we read the present to determine the past.

HOW THE KNOWLEDGE-BASED SYSTEM SOLVES THE PROBLEM

Elf Aquitaine incorporated the knowledge of its top drilling experts in a knowledge-based system aptly called the "Drilling Advisor." The knowledge-based Drilling Advisor conducts an interactive dialogue in the native language and oil-drilling terminology that is used in the field, in order to consult with the drilling supervisor and the drilling engineers on the rig. During the dialogue, the Drilling Advisor requests a small amount of data in order to seed its reasoning process. These initial data may be nothing more than the name of the well, the depth of the hole, and the type of action being performed immediately prior to the drill getting stuck. Later, the system asks more detailed questions about circumstances surrounding the onset of sticking and historical data pertaining to previous activities, conditions, problems, and treatments in the well.

Based on the knowledge incorporated in rules in its knowledge base, the Drilling Advisor offers two types of advice. The first is a diagnosis that indicates the most likely cause or causes of sticking, together with reasons to support its conclusions. The second consists of two sets of treatment recommendations aimed at alleviating the sticking condition and reducing the likelihood of its recurrence.

INFERENCE STRATEGIES

A knowledge system's advice and recommendations are produced by the system's inference strategies, which operate on the knowledge encoded in the knowledge base. Inference strategies in rule-based knowledge systems can be goal driven (a method called backward chaining) or data driven (a method called forward chaining), or a combination of these.

Backward-chaining inference strategies start off with a known goal and try to use the expert program's rules to get to that goal. In contrast to backward-chaining procedures, which plan the rules to use to reach an identified goal, knowledge systems that use a forward-chaining paradigm react to externally or internally simulated conditions or data. Some particular data or condition may cause certain rules to be invoked. The reaction, directed by the rules that happen to be invoked by the current data or conditions, may change the knowledge base or the knowledge system's environment.

The new data in the changed knowledge base or environment may cause other rules to be invoked and other changes in the knowledge base and environment. The object of a forward-chaining system is to trigger these reactions until it produces an end situation that satisfies a particular goal.

BACKWARD CHAINING

To establish its diagnosis and recommendations, the Drilling Advisor uses backward-chaining techniques to reason and interpret the knowledge encoded in its rules. For example, to determine if the cause of sticking in a particular drilling episode is sloughing, the Drilling Advisor postulates that the cause of sticking is indeed sloughing. The verification of sloughing as the cause of sticking becomes the goal at this point. Therefore, the Drilling Advisor looks for rules that lead to that conclusion, or goal.

Rule 038, a typical Drilling Advisor rule shown in Figure 5-1. is one of several rules that has sloughing as its conclusion. There are two different parts to rule 038 which are used to get to a goal: the IF part, also called the antecedent, and the THEN part, also called the consequent. The IF part, or antecedent, contains

RULE 038

[This rule applies to episodes, and is tried in order to find out about whether the cause of sticking in the episode is sloughing]

If: 1) The action being done just prior to the occurrence of the problem was either drilling or reaming,
2) There is sloughing material in the well, and
3) The upspeed of cutting is slow

Then: The cause of sticking in the episode is sloughing; the strength of evidence for this conclusion depends upon the number of stabilizers in the BHA:
a) less than 1 then (0.2);
b) between 1 and 4 then (0.4);
c) greater or equal to 4 then (0.6).

<< Comments: Reaming is a kind of re-drilling.
Sloughing material is side-wall rocks which fall into the well from layers which have already been drilled.
Upspeed refers to the rate at which the drilling fluid, containing loose side-wall material, is circulated back to the surface.
Stabilizers are elements of the drilling assembly (BHA) whose function is to keep that assembly properly centered within the whole. They also tend, unfortunately, to be places at which sloughing material accumulates, plugging the annular space around the BHA and resulting in a sticking accident.>>

Figure 5-1 Drilling Advisor rule (Teknowledge Inc.)

three clauses. The THEN part, or consequent, is true only if all the antecedent clauses are true.

The balance of the rule contains what are called "confidence factors," which tell how much evidence exists for the sloughing conclusion and therefore how much confidence should be placed in that conclusion. In this case, the evidence for the conclusion, on a scale from 0 to 1, depends on the number of stabilizers, in the bottom hole assembly, that hold the drilling assembly in the center of the hole.

As mentioned, rule 038 concludes that the cause of sticking is sloughing if all the antecedent clauses in the rule are true. So first, the knowledge system tries to substantiate the information in clause 1 (whether the action before the problem occurred was drilling or reaming) directly from some other rule in the rule base. If it cannot do that, it checks to see if this clause of the antecedent has already been concluded while the program was executing. Failing that, the system asks the user whether the action prior to the problem occurrence was drilling or reaming.

If the system cannot find support for clause 1 of rule 038, it abandons that rule, but not the goal of sloughing. It looks for another rule that also concludes that the cause of sticking is sloughing and tries to substantiate that rule. If the user types in "unknown" in response to the Drilling Advisor's question about the action prior to the problem occurrence, the Drilling Advisor goes on to check out other rules, with the aim of returning later to fill in missing information.

It is possible that clause 1 is the conclusion of a second rule. In that case, clause 1 would be true provided that the clauses in the second rule are true. This situation causes what is known as a subgoal to be established. The aim of the subgoal is to prove the clauses of the second rule. A subgoal may generate another subgoal, and so on, which is why backward chaining is often called subgoaling. The knowledge system continues to work the chain of reasoning backward until it reaches a state or clause that it knows. At that point, it about-faces and unravels itself to conclude its originally postulated goal.

If the system never finds any rules to support sloughing, it postulates a different cause (a new goal), whose applicability it tries to conclude. As can be seen, although the backward-chaining technique can solve problems that are not solvable by alternative, algorithmic methods, it can turn out to be an exhaustive search technique. If luck holds, the knowledge system runs out of items to examine at an early stage and gives up. Otherwise, it may spend a lot of time trying to prove something that is false.

CONTROL MECHANISMS

The knowledge system search picture, however, is not quite as bleak as it appears because the knowledge system does not randomly search through its rules. Instead, knowledge systems of any size generally use a control mechanism

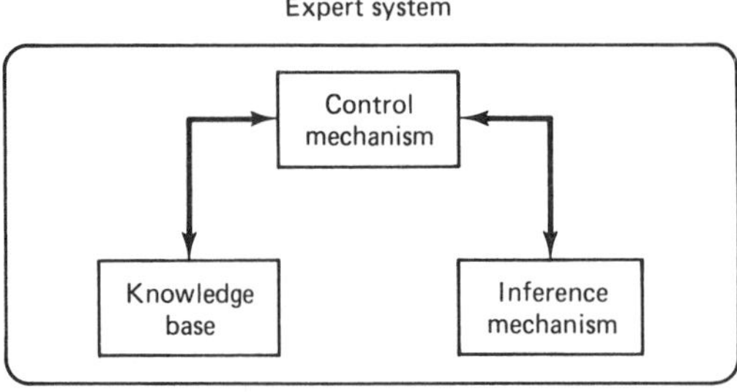

Figure 5-2 The control mechanism controls a knowledge system's search for a solution.

(Figure 5-2). The control mechanism controls the search and prevents the knowledge system from wasting its time exhaustively searching through irrelevant rules at random.

Both rules and strategies are inherent in a knowledge system's control mechanism. The rules, known as meta-rules, are rules about rules and how best to apply them, rather than about subject application knowledge. Most commonly, they are used to direct the order in which both hypotheses and different lines of reasoning should be pursued.

For example, a meta-rule might say that "to find out why a car does not start, first use the system rules to try to determine whether there is gas in the car, print the conclusions found, and only afterward check the starter motor." This meta-rule establishes system priorities. Another meta-rule might indicate that "if the starter motor turns over the engine vigorously, there is no need to check the battery or the alternator."

Meta-rules such as these facilitate knowledge system performance because knowledge systems view problem solving as a search through a space of possible solutions. Therefore, if there is a large space of possible solutions to a problem, meta-rules help narrow the search space.

In the Drilling Advisor, one way the rule-based interpreter controls searches is by selecting the most relevant rules. It determines relevancy based on its own rules about how to search rules and by building an index system based on information extracted from experts into the rules.

In another technique, some knowledge-based systems (for example, Mycin, a medical diagnosis system) avoid an exhaustive search by using heuristics to score the rules that they use to confirm the truth of a hypothesis. As the knowledge system proceeds through its search, it eliminates the highest-scoring rules from its search space of possible conclusions. It then retains and bases its further search for a conclusion only on the lowest-scoring rules that most support the goal. Thus a knowledge system uses confidence factors to direct a search through the most-likely-to-succeed rules while "pruning" unlikely paths from a problem's decision tree of possible solutions.

A common method of representing control knowledge, especially in large programs, is with conventional procedures. A control structure to diagnose a fault in a computer disk drive might look something like this:

```
Procedure
  Begin
    Display a welcome message
    Determine the disk drive symptoms
    Check that the disk drive cable plugs in
    securely
    Check the disk controller board
    ...
  End
```

CONFIDENCE IN KNOWLEDGE SYSTEM CONCLUSIONS

In rule 038, the parenthetical 0.2, 0.4, and 0.6 is a scoring or confidence factor that indicates the strength of the rule. The confidence factors range from 0.0 to 1.0. A confidence factor of 0.2 indicates very weak evidence; 0.4 indicates moderate evidence; greater than or equal to 0.6 is the strongest evidence that rule 038 allows.

Confidence factors in knowledge systems correspond to the way human experts often think about conclusions that they reach. For example, most human experts faced with the Drilling Advisor's drill bit sticking problem to solve would probably not have 100 percent confidence in their conclusion, but would act anyway. Physicians also base their conclusions on a certain probability or confidence factor; in fact, that is all the medical literature will allow.

Rule 038 is one of many rules that attempt to accumulate evidence that a particular cause is, in fact, the cause of sticking. In the Drilling Advisor, as with many knowledge-based systems, all the evidence that can be accumulated for different causes is compared in the end. At that time, the knowledge system may come up with one conclusion. Or it may decide to offer two conclusions, such as sloughing with a confidence factor of 0.6 and differential pressure with a confidence level of 0.5. This presentation of conclusions and evidence is similar to the way human experts reach conclusions and react.

Of course, it is possible that the Drilling Advisor's conclusion may turn out to be wrong, just as a human expert may reach the wrong conclusion. There are three ways that people usually deal with human experts who are wrong. One is to reexamine, or ask the human expert to reexamine, the data. A second way is to collect more data and try again. The third and last way is to get a better expert. All three ways are used by the Drilling Advisor, as well as by other knowledge-based systems.

RECOMMENDING TREATMENT

Once the Drilling Advisor has reached a conclusion about the cause of sticking, it examines a different set of rules relevant to sloughing and asks several more questions. In this manner, the system identifies what types of curative action are appropriate to correct the sticking problem and possibly prevent its recurrence.

WHAT'S THE PAYOFF?

Elf Aquitaine is an oil company whose cost of doing business illustrates the typically large payoffs that can accrue from using knowledge-based systems to alleviate knowledge bottlenecks. Elf Aquitaine drills large numbers of oil wells in scattered locations simultaneously. An offshore rig might cost an average of \$100,000 per day to operate, with a low of \$50,000 per day for land rigs and one-half million dollars per day for offshore deepwater drilling. The costs are primarily the rental of the rig itself (generally, these are rented pieces of equipment), associated operating costs for the machinery, and the cost of people on the rig. These costs are incurred 24 hours a day, seven days a week.

The number of people on the rigs varies. There are, at least, the drilling engineers with drilling backgrounds based mostly on experience, a company engineer with a general engineering background, a drilling rig captain highly experienced in drilling operations, and several "roughnecks." In addition, there is a drilling supervisor who creates and carries out the drilling program—how fast to drill, how hard, what lubricant to use—and supervises the drilling on one or a set of rigs. Depending on the company, the drilling captain and drilling supervisor may or may not be the same person.

Drilling supervisors are very experienced personnel with a high success rate at drilling wells. When the drilling rig encounters trouble that cannot be solved quickly by the drilling and company engineers, it is the drilling supervisor who gets called for help.

Drilling rig troubles are serious because they frequently cause work stoppages on the rig and require several weeks or more to correct the problem. It is not unusual for the costs attributable to forced work stoppages on drilling rigs to be about 2 percent of a company's total drilling costs.

Two percent of the total drilling costs turns out to be an enormous figure because a major oil company may be drilling as many as 100 wells at the same time. Arithmetic calculations show that it costs a company drilling 100 wells simultaneously, at \$50,000 a day per rig, \$5 million a day just for the rigs. If the rig were the only cost involved in drilling operations, a 2 percent rate would cost the company \$100,000 for one-day work stoppages, a half million dollars if a stoppage lasted for five days, and 36.5 million dollars annually. These figures are exclusive of the costs of having the drilling program delayed.

Figures this high make the drilling supervisor who can avoid or solve drilling rig problems and reduce the downtime for oil rigs a very valuable resource to an oil company. Alas, such experienced and knowledgeable drilling supervisors are a scant resource and constitute a knowledge bottleneck and therefore a potential knowledge system application candidate.

Naturally, Elf Aquitaine does not expect the Drilling Advisor to avoid all accidents, any more than a human drilling expert could. It is, however, reasonable to expect the knowledge system to avoid a lot of them because, as in so many industries, many oil rig accidents result from "dumb" mistakes. Either an expert drilling supervisor or a system such as the Drilling Advisor would be able to avoid such mistakes. Thus Elf Aquitaine's motive when it decided to develop the expert drilling diagnosis system was to reduce the downtime of its oil rigs and keep the dollars in its pockets.

GETTING THE ANSWER

An example of how a knowledge system uses backward chaining to arrive at an answer is illustrated by a crisis management expert system (developed by IntelliCorp) that diagnoses nuclear power plant accidents. The system contains nine rules (Figure 5-3) to diagnose four possible types of nuclear reactor accidents. The four possible causes of accidents are loss of feedwater, loss of coolant, steam generator tube rupture, and steam line break.

To show which of the four possible causes is the cause of an accident, the knowledge system hypothesizes each cause, in turn, and then attempts to verify the validity of each through backward chaining. The audit, in Figure 5-4, of an execution of the system shows how the knowledge-based system attempts to verify all four hypotheses. First, it hypothesizes that the accident is loss of feedwater, then it chains backwards from that goal to verify this hypothesis.

Rule 5 concludes that this first hypothesis (ACCIDENT TYPE IS LOSS-OF-FEEDWATER) is true if the first two clauses of rule 5 are true. Rule 5, clause 1's assertion (THE SECONDARY-COOLING-SYSTEM HEAT-TRANSFER IS INADEQUATE) happens to be the conclusion of rule 2. Therefore, to conclude rule 5, clause 1, it is necessary to chain backward to rule 2.

The system is able to conclude the precondition of rule 2 (PRESSURE-CONTROL-SYSTEM IS INCREASING) because, as indicated in the audit trail, that condition is known to be true for the current knowledge base state. So the system applies rule 2 and then returns to try to conclude clause 2 of rule 5.

The system cannot conclude the second clause because, as the audit shows, the knowledge system has previously determined (from sensor reading, past information, or asking the user) that the assertion FEEDWATER-PUMP FLOW IS LOW is false for the current state. Consequently, it abandons rule 5, but notes that rule 6 also concludes that ACCIDENT TYPE IS LOSS-OF-FEEDWATER. To prove the hypothesis in question using rule 6, the knowledge system chains back to rule 3, which concludes clause 1 of rule 6. Information about rule 3 is not in the rule base, nor has it been concluded previously. Therefore, the system asks the user.

Although in this example the user answers yes, the system still cannot verify clause 2 of rule 6. It therefore abandons the LOSS-OF-FEEDWATER hypothesis

```
(OUTPUT) The ACCIDENT unit
Slot: RULES      (OVERRIDE)  From ACCIDENT type: LIST Value:
[(RULE 1 (IF (PRIMARY-COOLING-SYSTEM PRESSURE IS DECREASING)
             (HIGH-PRESSURE-INJECTION-SYSTEM STATUS IS ON))
       (THEN (PRIMARY-COOLING-SYSTEM INTEGRITY IS CHALLENGED)))
 (RULE 2 (IF (PRIMARY-COOLING-SYSTEM TEMPERATURE IS INCREASING)
             )
       (THEN (SECONDARY-COOLING-SYSTEM HEAT-TRANSFER IS
                                       INADEQUATE)))
 (RULE 3 (IF (STEAM-GENERATOR LEVEL IS DECREASING))
       (THEN (STEAM-GENERATOR INVENTORY IS INADEQUATE)))
 (RULE 4 (IF (CONTAINMENT-VESSEL RADIATION IS HIGH)
             (CONTAINMENT-VESSEL PRESSURE IS HIGH))
       (THEN (CONTAINMENT-VESSEL INTEGRITY IS CHALLENGED)))
 (RULE 5 (IF (SECONDARY-COOLING-SYSTEM HEAT-TRANSFER IS
                                       INADEQUATE)
             (FEEDWATER-PUMP FLOW IS LOW))
       (THEN (ACCIDENT TYPE IS LOSS-OF-FEEDWATER))
       (UNITPUT SELF (QUOTE TYPE)
                (QUOTE LOSS-OF-FEEDWATER)))
 (RULE 6 (IF (STEAM-GENERATOR INVENTORY IS INADEQUATE)
             (FEEDWATER-PUMP FLOW IS LOW))
       (THEN (ACCIDENT TYPE IS LOSS-OF-FEEDWATER))
       (UNITPUT SELF (QUOTE TYPE)
                (QUOTE LOSS-OF-FEEDWATER)))
 (RULE 7 (IF (PRIMARY-COOLING-SYSTEM INTEGRITY IS CHALLENGED)
             (CONTAINMENT-VESSEL INTEGRITY IS CHALLENGED))
       (THEN (ACCIDENT TYPE IS LOSS-OF-COOLANT))
       (UNITPUT SELF (QUOTE TYPE)
                (QUOTE LOSS-OF-COOLANT)))
 (RULE 8 (IF (PRIMARY-COOLING-SYSTEM INTEGRITY IS CHALLENGED)
             (STEAM-GENERATOR LEVEL IS INCREASING))
       (THEN (ACCIDENT TYPE IS STEAM-GENERATOR-TUBE-RUPTURE))
       (UNITPUT SELF (QUOTE TYPE)
                (QUOTE STEAM-GENERATOR-TUBE-RUPTURE)))
 (RULE 9 (IF (STEAM-GENERATOR INVENTORY IS INADEQUATE)
             (STEAM-GENERATOR STEAM-FLOW IS HIGH))
       (THEN (ACCIDENT TYPE IS STEAM-LINE-BREAK))
       (UNITPUT SELF (QUOTE TYPE)
                (QUOTE STEAM-LINE-RUPTURE]
```

Figure 5-3 Rules from a knowledge-based crisis management system. (Program copyrights © 1983, 1984 by Intellicorp. All rights reserved).

and tries to prove the second hypothesis. ACCIDENT TYPE IS LOSS-OF-COOLANT.

To use rule 7 to prove that ACCIDENT TYPE IS LOSS-OF-COOLANT, the system chains back to rule 1, which concludes clause 1 of rule 7, which concludes that the PRIMARY-COOLING-SYSTEM-INTREGRITY IS CHAL-

```
Top level typescript window
Attempt to verify (ACCIDENT TYPE IS LOSS-OF-FEEDWATER)
Attempt to verify (SECONDARY-COOLING-SYSTEM HEAT-TRANSFER IS INADEQUATE)
Attempt to verify (PRESSURE-CONTROL-SYSTEM TEMPERATURE IS INCREASING)
(PRESSURE-CONTROL-SYSTEM TEMPERATURE IS INCREASING)
 is true for the current KB state.


(RULE 2 (IF (PRESSURE-CONTROL-SYSTEM TEMPERATURE IS INCREASING))
      (THEN (SECONDARY-COOLING-SYSTEM HEAT-TRANSFER IS INADEQUATE)))
 applied.

Attempt to verify (FEEDWATER-PUMP FLOW IS LOW)
(FEEDWATER-PUMP FLOW IS LOW) is false for the current KB state.

Attempt to verify (STEAM-GENERATOR INVENTORY IS INADEQUATE)
Attempt to verify (STEAM-GENERATOR LEVEL IS DECREASING)
Is it true that (STEAM-GENERATOR LEVEL IS DECREASING)? YES

(RULE 3 (IF (STEAM-GENERATOR LEVEL IS DECREASING))
      (THEN (STEAM-GENERATOR INVENTORY IS INADEQUATE))) applied.

Attempt to verify (FEEDWATER-PUMP FLOW IS LOW)
(FEEDWATER-PUMP FLOW IS LOW) is false for the current KB state.

Not verified: (ACCIDENT TYPE IS LOSS-OF-FEEDWATER)
Attempt to verify (ACCIDENT TYPE IS LOSS-OF-COOLANT)
Attempt to verify (PRESSURE-CONTROL-SYSTEM INTEGRITY IS CHALLENGED)
Attempt to verify (PRESSURE-CONTROL-SYSTEM PRESSURE IS DECREASING)
(PRESSURE-CONTROL-SYSTEM PRESSURE IS DECREASING)
 is true for the current KB state.

Attempt to verify (HPIS STATUS IS ON)
(HPIS STATUS IS ON) is false for the current KB state.

Not verified: (ACCIDENT TYPE IS LOSS-OF-COOLANT)
Attempt to verify (ACCIDENT TYPE IS STEAM-GENERATOR-TUBE-RUPTURE)
Attempt to verify (PRESSURE-CONTROL-SYSTEM INTEGRITY IS CHALLENGED)
Attempt to verify (PRESSURE-CONTROL-SYSTEM PRESSURE IS DECREASING)
(PRESSURE-CONTROL-SYSTEM PRESSURE IS DECREASING)
 is true for the current KB state.

Attempt to verify (HPIS STATUS IS ON)
(HPIS STATUS IS ON) is false for the current KB state.

Not verified: (ACCIDENT TYPE IS STEAM-GENERATOR-TUBE-RUPTURE)
Attempt to verify (ACCIDENT TYPE IS STEAM-LINE-BREAK)
Attempt to verify (STEAM-GENERATOR INVENTORY IS INADEQUATE)
Attempt to verify (STEAM-GENERATOR STEAM-FLOW IS HIGH)
(STEAM-GENERATOR STEAM-FLOW IS HIGH) is true for the current KB state.


(RULE 9 (IF (STEAM-GENERATOR INVENTORY IS INADEQUATE)
            (STEAM-GENERATOR STEAM-FLOW IS HIGH))
      (THEN (ACCIDENT TYPE IS STEAM-LINE-BREAK))) applied.

Verified: (ACCIDENT TYPE IS STEAM-LINE-BREAK)
^
```

Figure 5-4 The knowledge system attempts to verify four hypotheses. (Program copyrights © 1983, 1984 by Intellicorp. All rights reserved.)

LENGED (listed in the audit as PRESSURE-CONTROL-SYSTEM INTEGRITY IS CHALLENGED). Concluding rule 1 first requires the system to show that the PRIMARY-COOLING-SYSTEM PRESSURE IS DECREASING (rule 1, clause 1), and the system shows this to be true for the current knowledge base state. The audit indicates, however, that the second clause of rule 1, HIGH-PRESSURE-INJECTION-SYSTEM STATUS IS ON, has been shown to be false for the current knowledge base state, and therefore the system abandons the LOSS-OF-COOLANT hypothesis.

Attempting to prove the third hypothesis, the system tries rule 8, which concludes that the hypothesis in question (ACCIDENT TYPE IS STEAM-GENERATOR-TUBE-RUPTURE) is true if the two clauses of rule 8 are true. Rule 1 concludes clause 1 of rule 8, but the system has already been shown, when trying to verify the last hypothesis, that rule 1's second clause (HPIS IS ON) is false for the current state. Therefore, the STEAM-GENERATOR-TUBE-RUPTURE hypothesis fails and the system tries to prove the last hypothesis, ACCIDENT TYPE IS STEAM-LINE-BREAK.

With similar hypothesis verification techniques, the expert system chains from rule 9 to rule 3, discovers that clause 1 has already been verified, clause 2 is shown to be true, and finally verifies that the accident type is indeed a steam line break.

FORWARD CHAINING

The backward-chaining Drilling Advisor and nuclear reactor crisis management systems work by hypothesizing a conclusion and working backward to find existing evidence via rules or information inferred from rules. But the same results can be achieved by applying rules, noting the result, and applying other rules based on the new situation.

In the latter method, known as forward chaining, a certain true situation triggers the action or consequent part of a rule. This action may change the state of the knowledge base. It may also subsequently change the environment, where it may, for example, turn some hardware or software switch on or off. The new program situation may cause another rule to be invoked and triggered and another reaction to occur, until an end situation is reached that satisfies a particular goal.

Difficulties with a forward-chaining, reactive paradigm may occur if a rule base is large, because there is only one goal but many unproductive ways to produce irrelevant reactions. If the knowledge-based system reacts without having some goal in mind, it may go off in unfocused ways and not provide its answers efficiently.

Advantages of a forward-chaining system include the ability to react to data or conditions and not only come up with conclusions but also generate goals. In contrast, a backward-chaining system must decide on possible goals to work toward in advance. Although there are goals to work toward in a forward-chaining system, they are so general that many experts agrue that forward chaining systems merely react without having any goal in mind.

For example, the goal in a chess game is to get the opponent's king in checkmate. A forward-chaining system could react to the chessboard data and come up with several strategies of its own to satisfy the general goal. In a backward-chaining system, each strategy for getting the opponent's king in checkmate would have to be determined in advance—a difficult task considering the number of possible strategies.

SETTING UP PERSONAL COMPUTERS

XCON, DEC's computer configuration program, and several knowledge systems integrated with XCON are well-known forward-chaining systems. Similar techniques can be used to configure a personal computer.

Personal computers are not necessarily turnkey systems. PC buyers may also buy a variety of boards, peripherals, and different amounts of memory. To set up these components to form a working computer system requires that the user connect, install, and arrange the various components and then set certain switches so that both the system and the components know what components are present.

A program that uses forward-chaining techniques to configure a personal computer starts out with both a database and a knowledge base. The database contains the components in the system and some information about them. The knowledge base contains rules that embody the knowledge and constraints about PC configuration.

A typical database for configuring a PC might include, among other facts, the following items and information:

Computer	Number of slots: five Boards contained: System board Maximum system board memory: 256K Amount of system board memory filled: 256K
Mouse board	Type of mouse: mechanical
Disk controller board	Type of disks: floppy
Memory board	Maximum amount of memory: 256K Amount of memory filled: 256K
Communications board	Number of ports: two

Printer board	Type of connection: parallel
Expansion interface	Number of slots: nine
Display board	Type of display: monochrome

This is not necessarily an optimal way to buy personal computer boards because more than one of these features might be contained on one board. This simple database, however, serves to illustrate the fundamentals of forward chaining.

The rules in the knowledge base know how to put together these components to form a full-fledged PC setup. Since the rules are also known as productions, they are contained in a section of memory known as "production memory" (rule memory). The section of memory where the forward-chaining knowledge-based system does its work and keeps track of what partial configurations it has already formed is appropriately known as "working memory" (Figure 5-5).

Clearly, unless the knowledge system is physically connected to a robot, it cannot physically configure the computer. Instead, it conceptually configures it and generates a set of configuration instructions to a human configurer.

To begin the configuration process, the knowledge system loads into working memory an initial set of items from the database, as well as descriptions of the starting situation. The initial items might be the computer, the expansion interface, and the six boards. The starting situation description approximates the situation that human beings might face after having received delivery of their PCs and accompanying boards.

The PC expert configurer then examines all the rules to see if one contains an IF part, "all" of whose conditions match the items that happen to be in working memory at that instant. The knowledge system regards the items in rule memory and working memory simply as patterns. If the system finds a rule whose patterns match those in working memory, it performs the action indicated by the THEN part of that rule.

The THEN part of the rule that is matched might direct the knowledge system to add a new item or situation to working memory. The expert system then cycles through all the rules again to find another matching rule based on the

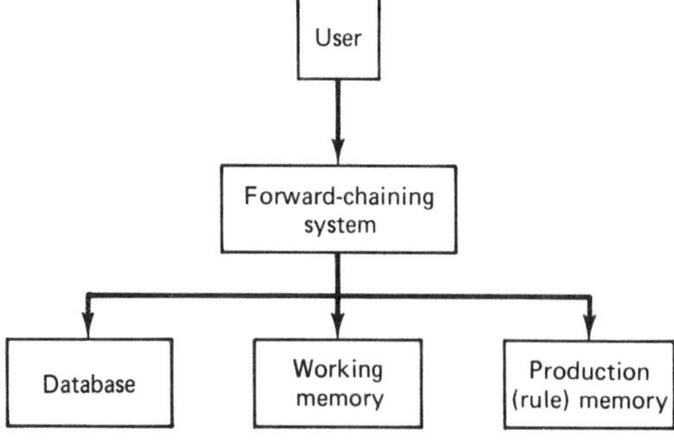

Figure 5-5 Components in a forward chaining system

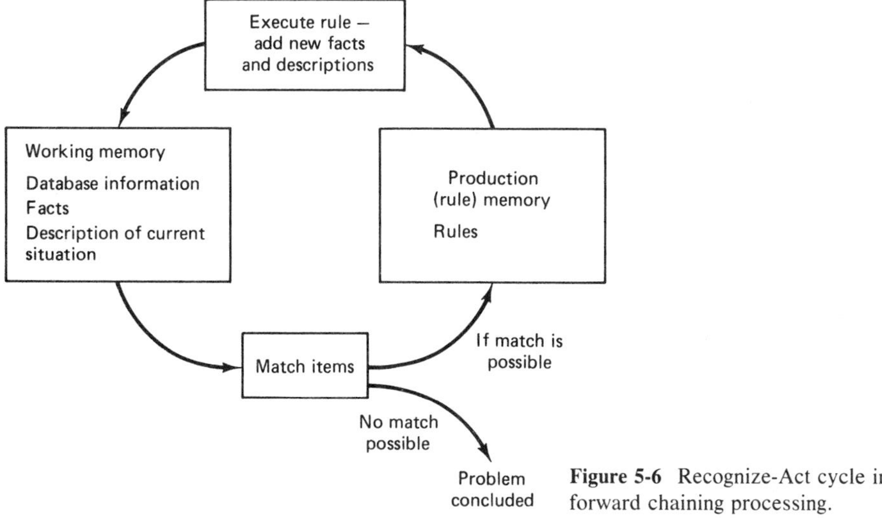

Figure 5-6 Recognize-Act cycle in forward chaining processing.

changed state of working memory (Figure 5-6). This cycle is known as the Recognize-Act cycle.

However, the rule base might contain a very large number of rules. Examining all of them, especially on a constant basis, is a very time-consuming process. Therefore, one control strategy that typical forward-chaining systems use is to partition the task into steps, called contexts.

Human beings would also likely partition a program, such as the PC-configuration task, into several different steps. One step might be to decide where in the PC to install the boards. The next step might be to set the switches to indicate the amount of memory installed. The next step might be to insert the boards; another step might test the system, and so on.

In similar fashion, the rules in a forward-chaining PC-configuration system would be divided into steps and each step given a name. One group of rules might be called STEP ASSIGN-BOARDS. Another might be called STEP CONFIGURE-MEMORY, while still another group of rules might be STEP TEST-SYSTEM. Figure 5-7 shows a rather loose English translation figure of some typical PC-configuration rules.

When the expert PC configurer loads up working memory to start, it loads the starting components and a description of the starting situation. The starting situation description includes the name of the starting step. In this program, the starting step loaded into working memory might be STEP ASSIGN-BOARDS. So when the knowledge system tries to match its rules against the items in working memory, it tests component items, but also tests the step names.

The effect of testing the step names is that the step names act as a kind of indexing structure. The knowledge system only has to examine fully the rules that are suited to each step. Generally, the problem is partitioned so that the rules for

```
PC-RULE-1
IF:      THE CURRENT STEP IS ASSIGN-BOARDS
         AND THERE ARE 5 SLOTS IN A COMPUTER
         AND THERE IS AN AVAILABLE SLOT IN THE COMPUTER
         AND THERE IS AN AVAILABLE MONOCHROME DISPLAY BOARD
THEN:    PUT THE DISPLAY BOARD IN THE COMPUTER IN AN AVAILABLE SLOT
         AND SUBTRACT ONE FROM THE NUMBER OF AVAILABLE SLOTS

PC-RULE-2
IF:      THE CURRENT STEP IS ASSIGN-BOARDS
         AND THERE ARE 5 SLOTS IN A COMPUTER
         AND THERE IS AN AVAILABLE SLOT IN THE COMPUTER
         AND THERE IS AN AVAILABLE PRINTER BOARD
THEN:    PUT THE PRINTER BOARD IN THE COMPUTER IN AN AVAILABLE SLOT
         AND SUBTRACT ONE FROM THE NUMBER OF AVAILABLE SLOTS

PC-RULE-3          disk-controller-board rule

PC-RULE-4          memory-board-rule

PC-RULE-5          communication-board rule

PC-RULE-6          color-display-board rule
                   (not applicable to this system database)

PC-RULE-7
IF:      THE CURRENT STEP IS ASSIGN-BOARDS
         AND THERE ARE 5 SLOTS IN A COMPUTER
         AND THERE IS AN AVAILABLE SLOT IN THE COMPUTER
         AND THERE IS AN AVAILABLE MOUSE BOARD
THEN:    PUT THE MOUSE BOARD IN THE COMPUTER IN AN AVAILABLE SLOT
         AND SUBTRACT ONE FROM THE NUMBER OF AVAILABLE SLOTS

PC-RULE-8
IF:      THE CURRENT STEP IS ASSIGN-BOARDS
         AND THERE ARE 5 SLOTS IN A COMPUTER
         AND THERE IS A MOUSE BOARD AVAILABLE
         AND THERE IS NO AVAILABLE SLOT FOR A MOUSE BOARD
THEN:    FIND AN EXPANSION INTERFACE AND CONNECT IT TO THE PC

PC-RULE-9
IF:      THE CURRENT STEP IS ASSIGN-BOARDS
         AND THERE IS AN EXPANSION INTERFACE
         AND THERE ARE 5 SLOTS IN THE EXPANSION INTERFACE
         AND THERE IS AN AVAILABLE SLOT IN THE EXPANSION INTERFACE
         AND THERE IS A MOUSE BOARD AVAILABLE
THEN:    PUT THE MOUSE BOARD IN THE EXPANSION INTERFACE
         AND SUBTRACT ONE FROM THE NUMBER OF AVAILABLE SLOTS

PC-RULE-10
IF:      THE STEP IS ASSIGN-BOARDS
THEN:    END THE ASSIGN-BOARDS STEP
         BEGIN THE CONFIGURE-MEMORY STEP

PC-RULE-11
IF:      THE STEP IS CONFIGURE-MEMORY
         AND THERE IS A 256K BOARD AVAILABLE
         AND THE 256K BOARD IS POPULATED WITH THE MAXIMUM AMOUNT OF MEMORY CHIPS
         AND THE SYSTEM BOARD IS POPULATED WITH THE MAXIMUM AMOUNT OF
             MEMORY CHIPS
THEN:    SET THE SWITCHES ON SWITCH-1 ON THE ADD-ON BOARD TO TELL IT
         HOW MUCH MEMORY IS ON THE ADD-ON BOARD (settings listed here)
         AND SET THE SWITCHES ON SWITCH-2 ON THE ADD-ON BOARD TO TELL IT
         HOW MUCH MEMORY IT IS BEING ADDED TO (settings listed)
```

Figure 5-7 English translation of PC-configuration rules.

```
PC-RULE-12
IF:     THE STEP IS CONFIGURE-MEMORY
        AND THERE IS A 265K BOARD AVAILABLE
        AND THE 256K BOARD IS POPULATED WITH THE MAXIMUM AMOUNT OF MEMORY CHIPS
        AND THE SYSTEM BOARD IS POPULATED WITH THE MAXIMUM AMOUNT OF
            MEMORY CHIPS
        AND THE SYSTEM BOARD REQUIRES A KNOWLEDGE OF HOW MUCH ADDITIONAL
            MEMORY WILL BE ADDED
THEN:   SET THE SWITCHES ON THE SYSTEM BOARD TO INDICATE HOW MUCH MEMORY
            WILL BE ADDED (settings listed here)
PC-RULE-13
IF:     THE STEP IS CONFIGURE-MEMORY
        AND THERE IS A 256K BOARD AVAILABLE
        AND THE 256K BOARD IS POPULATED WITH THE MAXIMUM AMOUNT OF MEMORY CHIPS
        AND THE SYSTEM BOARD HAS AVAILABLE SPACE FOR MORE MEMORY CHIPS
THEN:   FILL THE SYSTEM BOARD COMPLETELY WITH MEMORY CHIPS
```

Figure 5-7 (Cont.)

each step constitute a fairly small number and the knowledge system does not have to waste too much time fully examining and testing irrelevant rules.

In this PC-configuration example illustrated here, the first configuration step that the knowledge system attends to is to assign the various boards to slots; in another step, it sets the switches on the boards.* A full configuration example will be far more complicated, with many more steps. It is possible that two different configurers will perform some of the steps in a different order.

As the expert PC configurer begins its configuration task, it notices that all the conditions in RULE-1 correspond to items in working memory. In other words, both the IF parts of RULE-1 and working memory contain the items "current step is install-boards," "computer with five slots," "an available slot in the computer," and "an available display board." Therefore, PC-RULE-1 fires and working memory is modified to indicate that the display board has been installed in one of the computer slots. Working memory is also changed to indicate that only four slots are now available instead of five. The instructions to the human operator will direct him or her to install the display board in one of the slots.

In like manner, the expert PC configurer adds the disk controller board, memory board, communications board, and printer board to the slots in the PC and indicates the modifications to working memory. The rules for adding these four boards to the PC resemble the display board rule. In fact, all the conditions in all these rules match patterns in working memory just as well as the display board rule. Therefore, the knowledge system gathers all the rules that match working memory and could therefore fire, into a set of rules known, in the OPS5 rule language, as the "conflict set."

To choose one rule to fire, the knowledge system might use "time tags." With this technique, every item in working memory has an associated time tag. It indicates when the item was last created or modified.

*The PC-configuration example is based on techniques and a translation of the OPS5 rule language, developed at Carnegie-Mellon University by Charles Forgy.

Given a choice of rules, as happens during conflict resolution, the knowledge system chooses the rule that matches the item with the most recent time tag. The assumption here is that the most recent item is part of the process being worked on most recently and is therefore the most relevant.

Of all the boards that could be matched in this example problem, the display board was chosen first intentionally. The order in which the boards are listed is the order in which they were physically added to working memory. (The rule numbers shown are only for human readability.) The display board was the last board whose description was added to working memory and therefore has the most recent time tag. Although the time tag in this problem is trivial, the principle is a general one and has far more meaning in many other examples.

If five boards have already been added, when the expert PC configurer finally comes to PC-RULE-7, about the mouse board, it cannot apply it. Since there are no more available slots, the rule condition about "an available slot" does not match anything in working memory. PC-RULE-8, however, matches and causes the knowledge system to find an expansion interface (in the store or stock) and connect it to the PC, so the mouse board can be installed.

As mentioned, a full-fledged configuration is far more complex and must take into account several chunks of constraint knowledge, not included here for simplicity. For instance, in a real example, if an expansion interface were needed, a slot in the PC would have to be reserved for the expansion interface board.

At this point, there are no boards to be installed and it is time to go on to the next step. PC-RULE-10 is the rule that gets the knowledge system out of the step it has been working on and into the next step, which is CONFIGURE-MEMORY. At first glance, it seems that rule 10 could have fired at any time when the system was working on the ASSIGN-BOARDS step. Not so. Another conflict resolution strategy states that given a choice of rules whose conditions match those in working memory, if one rule is longer or contains more data items than the other, the longer rule should be selected. The rationale is that the rule with the greater number of data items is more specialized for the particular situation at hand. Therefore, it should be the rule of choice.

The value of this specialization strategy is demonstrated by seeing what the expert PC configurer does when it gets to the CONFIGURE-MEMORY steps. Two rules can generate a conflict in this step: PC-RULE-11, which assumes a fully populated 256K memory board and system board, and PC-RULE-12, which assumes a fully populated 256K memory board and system board but has the additional condition wherein the system board requires knowledge of how much additional memory will be added. In any situation where PC-RULE-12 matches working memory, PC-RULE-11 will also apply because it is a subset of PC-RULE-12. However, it is precisely because PC-RULE-12 is a special case of PC-RULE-11 that given the choice, the expert system will choose PC-RULE-12. By this technique, the system will be able to configure the PC properly for both situations.

Based on the specialization strategy, it is clear that PC-RULE-10 is the shortest and least specialized of all the rules in the STEP ASSIGN-BOARDS. Therefore, even though all its conditions (it only has one) match items in working memory, it fires only when there is nothing else left to fire. This makes it a general rule to deactivate one step and activate the next.

A forward-chaining system repeats this match/change-working-memory/match process until it can no longer find any rules that match anything in working memory, or until some action specifically stops the processing. At that point, it is assumed that it has arrived at a solution which, in this case, is to configure a PC properly.

An advantage that can be observed in a rule system such as this is the ease of adding new rules. The rules are self-contained and independent of each other. The order of the rules does not matter since the system repeatedly cycles through all the rules. Of course, it is possible that dependencies between rules exist because a new component to be added is dependent on components already in the database or associated with rules in the rule base. However, that same situation exists also when human beings configure systems. The issue here is to get the proper information from the expert to write the rule that expresses how he or she would handle such a situation.

FORWARD OR BACKWARD?

The different chaining paradigms are appropriate for different problem domains. For example, a forward-chaining-based medical system may react to a patient's medical data by suggesting relevant diagnosis or treatments. On the other hand, many diagnostic systems, at every step of a procedure, strive to zero in on some goal. As a result, they are often suited to backward-chaining techniques.

Knowledge-based financial systems, and many diagnosis systems profit from a combination of backward- and forward-chaining techniques. Such systems work forward from some initial database of characteristics of a company or equipment symptoms to generate some goal, such as a possible strategy or diagnosis. At the same time, they work backward to explore or prove the details of that goal. Then they meet in the middle. This is essentially the procedure that many people follow when they make decisions.

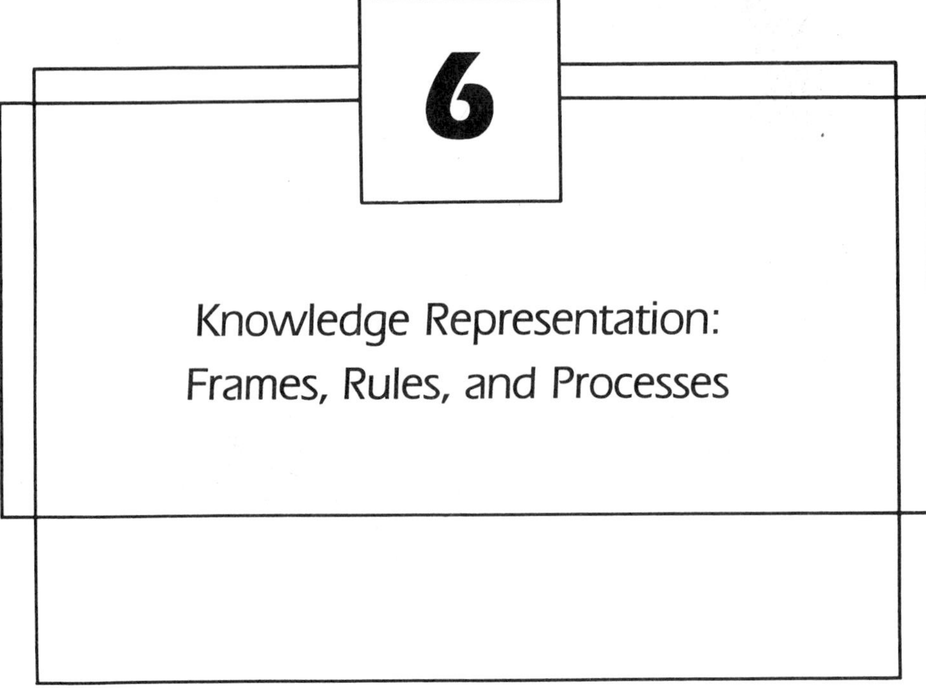

6

Knowledge Representation: Frames, Rules, and Processes

Of all the possible kinds of knowledge systems, rule-based systems win the popularity contest hands-down. They are appealing because rules are the simplest of all forms of knowledge representation to understand and to use.

Alas, like anything else, rules are not perfect. They lack variation and they are unstructured. Their format is inadequate or inconvenient to represent many types of knowledge, or to model the structure of a system. Their lack of variability in expressing knowledge also limits the representation of causal knowledge, partly because too many rules and too much effort is required to get all the effects of a causal model. This is an unfortunate inadequacy for knowledge systems because it is causal knowledge that people fall back on to solve problems when their simple rules of thumb fail.

Worse, as the number of rules in a system grows, they become difficult to manage and modify. Consequently, large rule-based systems have been known to act in some very silly ways. Even though rule-based systems are very modular, rules are not as independent as they first appear. They are independent only in the sense that they are unstructured and unsequenced. However, they assume information or actions found in other rules, and they work in conjunction with other rules. In many experts' experience, rule-based system developers cannot continue to add rules indefinitely because as they do so, they build in many assumptions about other rules and implicit relationships between rules. As a result, it becomes easy to add a new rule that violates some previously established assumption or relationship.

If a violation occurs in a rule-based system, the knowledge system does not fail or degrade gracefully. Instead, as the system approaches the limits of its knowledge, it may follow a bad chain of reasoning and make a silly inference.

If, however, the knowledge system uses a more organized representation that models the real-world system about which it is reasoning, it has a better chance to know when it is at the limits of its knowledge. Knowing its limits, it knows when it cannot make an inference, or when it is making an inference that might be based on weak evidence. Using this knowledge, the knowledge system might qualify its inferences, make partial inferences, or make an inference that could be used to reach a more helpful inference. In other words, it gracefully degrades, rather than following a bad chain of reasoning because the knowledge-system developer did not anticipate some situation.

FRAMES

One way to circumvent the weaknesses of rule-based systems and take a step closer to modeling real world systems with underlying causal knowledge is to represent knowledge in data structures known as "frames." Hypothesized by Marvin Minsky, frames are a kind of template (a generic pattern or mold) for holding clusters of related knowledge about a particular, narrow subject, which often is the name of the frame.

Since related knowledge is grouped together, frames, and the frame-based system that contains them, structure knowledge in a much more organized and manageable manner than do rule-based systems. Moreover, because related knowledge is clustered together, the frame-based organization comes closer to modeling real-world systems and mimicking the way human beings reason about the world.

Each frame contains a number of slots. Slots, which are analogous to fields in a database, are variable-length memory areas that hold different types of information associated with the frame name. For example, a knowledge-based medical diagnosis system might contain a series of frames for specific diseases. Each disease frame contains slots that describe things like disease symptoms, treatment, and morbidity rate.

The common cold frame in Figure 6-1 is a very simple one. Its information could possibly be represented in an ordinary database. For example, like the common cold frame, a disease database would contain data, attributes, and descriptions. However, slots in frames can also contain other types of information such as rules, hypotheses about a situation, questions to ask users, graphical information, explanatory information for users or programmers, debugging information, and even other frames. Moreover, they can be manipulated by knowledge-based systems' reasoning mechanism to infer new information—a feature that does not apply to traditional databases.

Constructing a knowledge system with knowledge represented in frames is more complicated than a rule-based system. Rule bases are simpler to build because it is easier to define the less complex, IF-THEN-formatted, small-sized pieces of knowledge that are rules.

Common-cold frame

Slot: SYMPTOMS value:
(stuffed nose)
(headache)
(general malaise)

Slot: TREATMENT value:
(take two aspirin)
(bedrest)
(call the doctor in the morning)

Slot: MORBIDITY-RATE value:

Figure 6-1 Typical frame

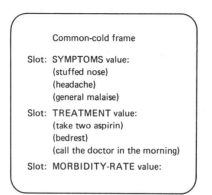

Frames are a natural, however, in some subject areas where rules, conditions, or attributes tend to cluster about a central object, concept, or event. For example, in medicine certain attributes and rules tend to cluster about particular diseases. In engineering, rules may cluster about a particular type of circuit. Such natural clustering indicates natural relationships between rules and the knowledge encoded in them.

HIERARCHIES OF FRAMES

The most important way that frames are related is hierarchically. This relationship occurs because in a frame-based knowledge system frames can contain smaller frames, called subframes, arranged in a hierarchy. An example of how this frame hierarchy works and how it is used is illustrated by some of the design information captured with Daisy Systems' Logician, Megalogician, and Gatemaster software. These contain frame-based computer-aided-engineering (CAE) expert systems for VLSI, circuit, and computer design.

Users of these systems typically might design a frame that describes a new object, such as a computer to be built. This frame would describe the computer's four major functional elements: the central processor, memory, control unit, and input/output unit. Each of these four objects is captured as a slot in the first or top-level frame and also as a subframe (Figure 6-2). At the next level down in the hierarchy, each of those frames will contain more primitive objects, which are also captured as frames. Finally, at the bottom of the hierarchy, frames describe physically realizable building blocks, such as gates, transistors, and chips.

To use the Logician to design an object, say a chip or a printed circuit board, electronic design engineers sit in front of a machine and interact with it using logic symbols. The Logician software translates the logic symbols which make up a schematic drawing into a form that can be understood by a computer program that verifies the engineer's design.

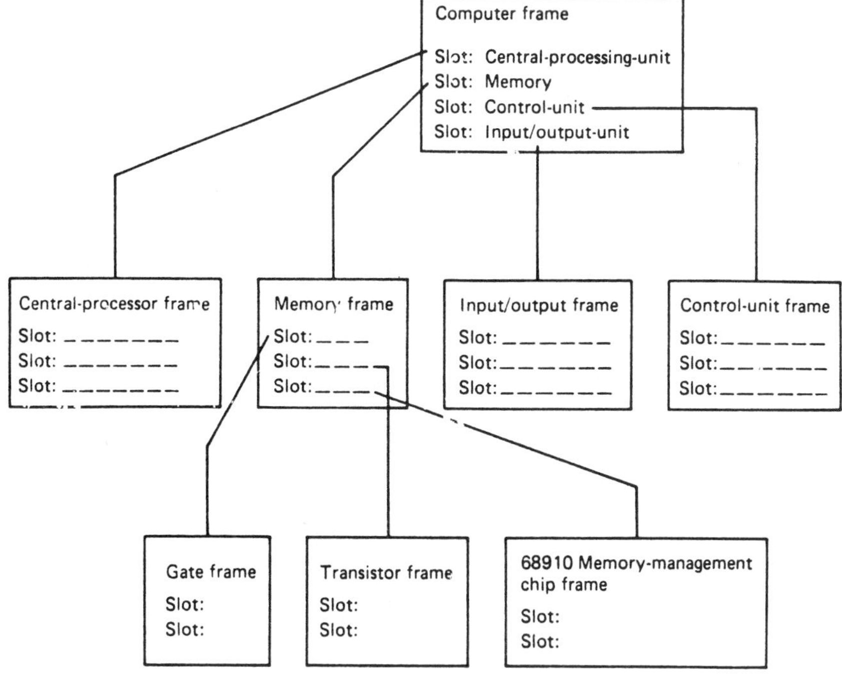

Figure 6-2 Hierarchy of frames

Frames go into action when the computer program scans the schematic diagrams as they are being composed. During the scan, the program automatically captures the schematic—both the graphical and electrical information—in the form of frames.

The frame slots describe characteristics of the objects of the system being designed, such as placement, connections, distances, data about pins, and operations that can be performed on the object. Analysis programs then manipulate—read, write, and modify—these frames.

TWO TYPES OF FRAMES

There are two types of frames: generic and specific. A typical generic frame in the Logician describes objects nonspecifically. This means that the slots of a generic frame list generic objects or information about locations, but never actually name the specific object or location (Figure 6-3).

In addition to the nonspecific information in generic frames, the Logician contains unique copies of a generic frame, called an "instance" frame, for each individual object. The unique copies of the frame have filled in slot values for

OBJECT-TYPE:	(wire, component, bus)
INSTANCE-LOCATION:	(X, Y coordinates of origin)
RECOGNITION-AREA:	(bounding box for fast selection)
INSTANCE-NAME:	(user given or default)
PARAMETER-LIST:	(type value)
REFERENCE-TO-SHARED-INVARIANT-DATA:	(component symbol description, simulation models)
CONNECTIVITY-LIST:	(wire name, component pin name)
ASSOCIATED-NOTES:	(text strings)
DISPLAY-ATTRIBUTES:	(color, brush type, highlight)

Figure 6-3 Generic frame organization (Daisy Systems)

attributes such as object type, description, electrical characteristics, connectivity rules for wire mapping, and display characteristics (Figure 6-4). Other slots might contain parameters that describe properties such as delay time through a wire, device size of a VLSI transistor, and the transistor's relationship to other components.

The generic frame in Figure 6-3 is an example of a frame containing many types of objects that could be in a database of information about a circuit. In contrast, the instance frame in Figure 6-4 contains specific information about the switch__XY (SW__XY), such as the component names, delay-time properties, and connecting signal (wire) names.

FRAME-BASED INHERITANCE

Relationships between different frames are taxonomic, similar to the relationships between grandparents, parents, and children, or between mammals and cats. The

OBJECT-TYPE:	component
INSTANCE-LOCATION:	(30, 40)
RECOGNITION-AREA:	(28, 38); (38, 48)
INSTANCE-NAME:	xcmp10
PARAMETER-LIST:	(DELAY-TIME 426325, PART-NAME 74LS02, PLACEMENT U1)
LIBRARY-REFERENCE:	LS
CONNECTIVITY-LIST:	(LEARN CLR_SCAN XSIG1)
NOTE:	"DT="
DISPLAY-ATTRIBUTES:	(COLOR red, BRUSH medium, HIGHLIGHT blink)

Figure 6-4 Instance frame organization (Daisy Systems)

taxonomic relationship indicates that similar characteristics exist in certain objects in a hierarchy, and these characteristics are inherited from corresponding objects (people, organisms, or frames) at a higher level in the hierarchy. Since frames contain knowledge, a frame lower in a hierarchy automatically inherits knowledge from its parent frames.

With this inheritance mechanism, if a top-level frame for an object contains a description and programming code, for example, of how to display certain graphical characteristics, a lower-level frame inherits that description and programming code, and therefore programmers need not rewrite it. Programs that operate on frame-based information know that frames may inherit information instead of containing it directly, and they know how to get the information from the parent frames. Because the frames are hierarchically linked, if needed information is not listed in a particular frame, the program searches up the inheritance hierarchy looking for a frame that contains the applicable information.

Consequently, as a designer adds new knowledge to a frame-based knowledge system, the subframes and the objects they describe already know how they relate to other objects and how they should behave; knowledge of these relationships and behavior has been inherited. This knowledge prevents many design errors from occurring. For example, as soon as a designer creates an object in a Logician frame, the object already knowns that it cannot accept certain kinds of inputs.

BOTH EXPERT AND APPRENTICE

The Logician is actually both an expert system and a set of traditional circuit layout and design tools. When the tools play their traditional role, they perform mundane, error-prone tasks for engineers, such as placing and connecting components and routing signals and checking for mistakes in the engineer's schematics.

These types of layout and design activities are common to many design tools available today without involving artificial intelligence. What is unique and relevant is the easy modifiability of the Logician's software and its techniques, which allow engineers, who are not professional programmers, to interface to a variety of design automation tools. These features are AI based.

The Logician incorporates AI technology in two different ways. First, its software is designed to emulate knowledge system architecture and techniques. Second, it contains a user-programmable rule base that allows engineers to compose some simple rules to extract and format information to output to other design automation tools.

KNOWLEDGE SYSTEM ARCHITECTURE IN COMPUTER-AIDED-ENGINEERING SYSTEMS

The most immportant knowledge system architectural feature that the Logician emulates is the extremely modular design of knowledge systems compared to conventional programs. Such modularity is a hallmark of knowledge systems and one of their major contributions to software engineering.

For example, the architectural design of knowledge systems separates the component parts of the system—knowledge base, inference mechanism control mechanism, and possibly database—rather than latching and interleaving them together as do conventional programs. Moreover, within the knowledge base, individual rules and frames are modularized. This modularity allows new knowledge to be added easily.

Daisy has gone to great lengths to duplicate this modular architecture in the design of its tools. For example, the Logician, Megalogician, and the Gatemaster contain, in the modularized fashion of knowledge systems, a database, two types of rule bases, and two rule base interpreters (inference mechanisms). Unlike conventional design automation programs, the database is completely decoupled from the rules that are used to manipulate it, and both are completely decoupled from the inference engine/rule interpreter. This modularity allows new information, in the form of rules that by nature are also modular, to be added without affecting other parts of the program.

The first component, the database, contains the frames, which in turn contain the schematics and the information extracted from the schematics. One rule base contains the user-programmable query rules, which, as will be seen, use AI techniques. The other rule base, used by the layout and design program, is internal to the design tools. It contains connectivity design rules for checking schematics and the different semiconductor vendors' design rules for layouts. These rules are common to many CAD tools and are not based on AI technology.

The last component in the layout and design modules in the Daisy tools are the inference engines/rule interpreters. One of these, the drawing editor connec-

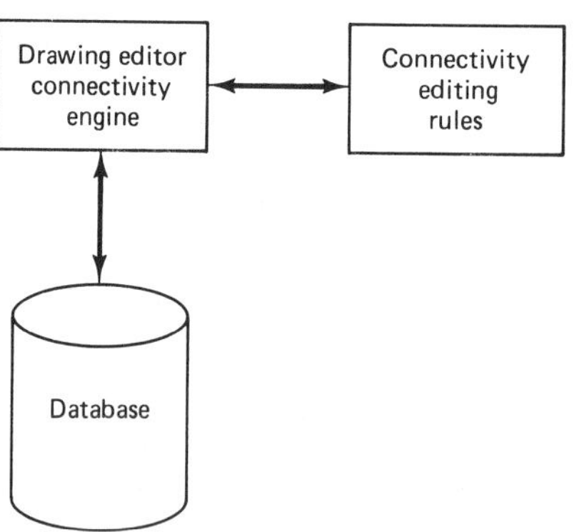

Figure 6-5 Connectivity editing assistant

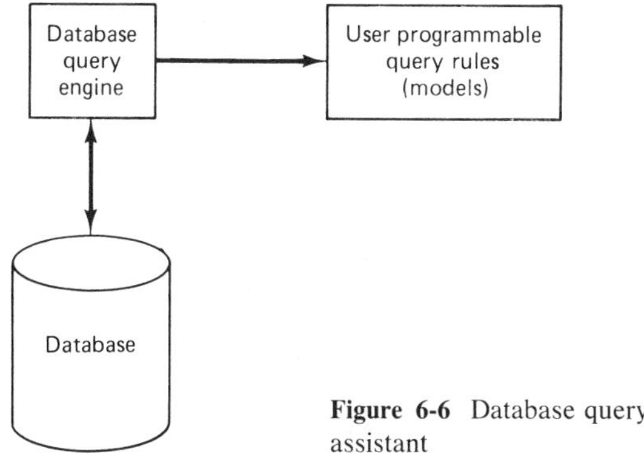

Figure 6-6 Database query assistant

tivity engine, is the link between the modules in the layout and design program. It translates the logic symbols that the engineers enter in schematic form on the CRT screen into a frame-based representation. Then it enters the frames in the database (see Figure 6-5). In addition, it interprets the design rules and uses them to manipulate the frames and to perform the design and error-checking chores. The other inference engine, called the database query engine, accesses the same database (which contains the frames) as the layout and design program modules and interprets the user-programmable rules (Figure 6-6), which are used primarily to interface to other design automation tools.

FROM ONE PROGRAM TO ANOTHER

The ability to interface to various design automation programs is important because different programs perform specialized tasks at different stages of the design process. For example, different design automation programs may perform or support printed-circuit layout, integrated-circuit layout, circuit simulation, logic simulation, or test generation.

The usual engineering procedure is to transmit information from a program that performs some stages of the design process to other programs that support other stages. Unfortunately, each design automation program has its own private language. Therefore, to interface to another design automation program; it is commonly necessary for a programmer to write a customized interface program. The customized program needs to extract the information from the first program, transfer it into a separate database, translate the information into the representation required by the targeted tool, and finally transmit that database to the second program.

ENTER AI

In contrast, with a modular knowledge-system-structured tool, which can represent information to be transferred with simple IF-THEN formatted rules, customized interface programs are not necessary. Users need only compose some simple rules to extract and format information to output to each different application on each different tool.

An example of this approach is the Logician software. Its rules typically are a few lines in length and are a relatively easy task for most engineers (see Figure 6-7). They are written in a subset of Pascal called Daisy Modeling Language (DML) because Daisy refers to the rules as "models."

The user-programmable rules are used primarily for querying and extracting connectivity information to send to other design automation tools. Typically, a user rule may request the rule interpreter to search the database, collect information from the frames in the database, and compute and format arbitrary expressions for output into specific tools. For example, the user-programmed rule in Figure 6-7 (programmed in electronic engineering terminology) requests the Logician to search the schematic database, extract delay and connectivity information, and generate the necessary reporting statements in a particular format. In addition, users can write rules that request the Logician to perform CAD tasks such as checking the connectivity in a particular circuit, finding the pin information, and making sure that distances between certain components are correct.

Other design tool databases also allow database queries. However, the Logician differs in the extensibility of the rule base and user-programmability capabilies. As mentioned, these capabilities are attributable to the simple rule format and to the modularity and independence of the rules and the components of the system. These are the architectural features that the Logician borrows from knowledge-based systems.

With this architecture and format, engineer-users can easily write a few to a dozen lines of a rule that requests a list of components and specifies a particular format for printout (or for transfer to another tool). After the user writes and adds the rules, the database query inference engine automatically interprets them.

For the interpretation, the inference engine searches the schematics' frames hierarchically to find the information that relates to the components named in the rule. Then, when it finds the appropriate instance (specific) frame, it executes the rule and produces the user-requested lists and formats. In contrast to this add-a-rule procedure, it is much more difficult for users to write an entire program for a conventionally designed system that interweaves program control and data of all kinds.

A FRAME-BASED TEACHING SYSTEM

As it turns out, the Logician and Gatemaster are actually mix-and-match systems that combine both frames and rules. Mix-and-match systems are common because different types of knowledge are more easily represented in different structures.

For example, knowledge gained as a result of experience about the best actions to take under certain conditions is well represented by rules. In contrast,

```
BEGIN

%PUT('NETLIST',%NAME||'('||%SIGNAL('O1'));     /* INSTANCE NAME WITH OUTPUT SIGNAL */

                                               /* PART TYPE WITH INPUTS, COMMA DELIMETER */
%PUT('NETLIST',') = '||%PARAM('PART_NM')||'('||%CNCT_LIST('ØØØ1',','));

IF %TEST_PARAM('DT') <> Ø THEN
   %PUT('NETLIST',') '||%PARAM('DT')||';'||CR)  .  /* GET DELAY INFO */
ELSE
   %PUT('NETLIST',') ///;'||CR);                   /* NO DELAY SPECIFIED */

END
```

```
SEL_X(AØ) = 74LSØØ(SW,X1) ///;
SEL_Y(BØ) = 74LSØØ(SW~,Y1) ///;
SW_XY(Z1) = 74LSØØ(AØ,BØ) 2 4 3 5;
XCMP9(SW~) = 74LSØ4(SW) ///;
```

This 4-line (not counting BEGIN and END delimiters), Pascal-like, user-programmed rule requests the Logician to search the schematic database, extract delay and connectivity information, and generate the necessary reporting statements in a particular format. Translating this rule yields the following:

> FOR EACH COMPONENT, PRINT ITS NAME, TYPE, AND CONNECTIVITY LIST. IF PARAMETER TYPE "DT" IS ENCOUNTERED, PRINT ITS VALUE. ELSE PRINT "///".

The percent (%) signs in the rule statements, such as in %NAME, direct the Logician to get the specified information from the frame and print it in a certain format. The result of applying this rule (model) to the schematic diagram for the circuit described is shown below the rule. The results could just as well have been sent to another design tool.

Note that while rules like this look cryptic to many readers, they are natural to electronic engineers who are their users.

Figure 6-7 Logician application rules written in the Daisy Modeling Language. (Daisy Systems)

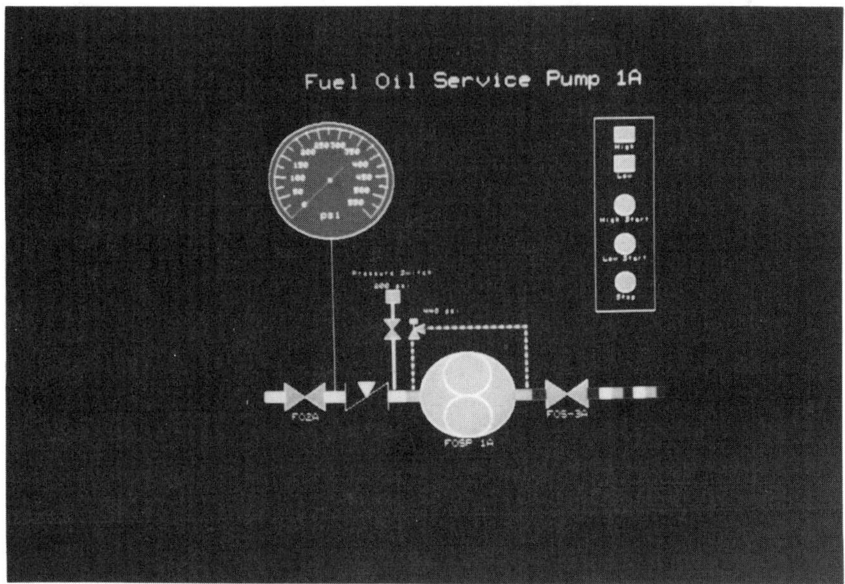

Figure 6-8 Steamer knowledge system fuel pump simulation. (Bolt Beranek and Newman, Inc.)

underlying causal models of structures and systems may be better represented by frames. Instructions to the computer to perform straightforward procedures are most efficiently represented as conventional computer programming routines. Finally, formal mathematical logic is a concise way to represent rules and facts and gain the benefits of specific procedures that check whether the represented information is true.

Steamer is a knowledge system that takes advantage of the strengths of different knowledge representations. Steamer is an educational expert system (from Bolt Beranek and Newman) that trains Navy personnel to operate steam plants on board ships. It combines frames with symbolically represented procedures written in the Lisp programming language. The frames represent knowledge of a steam plant, steam plant components, how they fit together, how they work together, and why. These frames are coupled to procedures that simulate the actual operation of a steam plant.

A third component in Steamer, coupled to its simulation procedures, is a graphical user-interface that displays hundreds of views of a working steam plant and its components (Figure 6-8). The graphic interface animation can be controlled externally by the user, who clicks a mouse to turn pumps on and off or to open or shut valves. Or the animation may be controlled by internal simulation procedures which simulate what happens in one part of the steam plant when a change occurs elsewhere.

The changes in different parts of the steam plant are shown to trainees in a variety of ways for different objects. For example, pumps change their colors, switches change their shapes, pipes change their flow rates, and indicators on gauges change their positions.

The animated graphics screen is one of two display screens that Steamer uses to instruct its students. The other screen displays a textual tutor that contains information about steam plant procedures.

Students can use the knowledge-based system's animated display and textual tutor to learn not only how to operate the steam plant, but also to explore the maze of pipes, valves, and pumps that comprise it. The purpose of the exploration is to provide a better understanding of how the different parts of a steam plant interact and the principles behind a steam plant's operation.

Toward this end, steam plant operator trainees can use Steamer's frame-based knowledge, animated displays, and textual tutor to learn about and explore the simulated steam plant in a variety of ways:

- They can use a mouse to turn pumps and valves on and off and watch the changes that occur in the animated graphical display.
- They can study a procedure presented on the screen in text form, then ask to see it execute.
- They can ask why steps in a procedure are done in a particular order and be given a textual explanation.
- They can be given a scrambled procedure in text form, unscramable it into proper order, try it out, and be critiqued.
- They can experiment with "what-if" questions. For example, "what if this pipe were to spring a leak?" or "what if the pump were turned on before the discharge valve were opened?"

Steamer answers users' questions and teaches the steam plant operation procedures based on its encoded knowledge about steam plants, its representation of that knowledge in frames, and the coupling of the frames to a numerically-oriented steam plant simulator.

The frames in the steam plant knowledge base describe both steam plant components and general concepts. For example, Figure 6-9 shows a series of Steamer frames written in the Lisp programming language. Some frames, such as "PORT," "2-PORT DEVICE," and "PUMPING-STATION" represent components. Others, such as "THERMODYNAMICS," represent concepts.

The frames contain slots, which, in turn, contain descriptions of other components or concepts. The frames may also contain subframes which represent other components and concepts. The subframes may contain still other frames, which finally contain values in the slots.

As will be seen, the frames say quite a lot about the objects they describe, both directly and indirectly. The parentheses in the frames delineate descriptions of things. The "defobject" command inside the first parenthesis of each frame is

```
(defobject PORT (flow) (thermodynamics)
           (   :types
               (flow (a quantity))))
```

```
(defobject 1-PORT-DEVICE (connection) ( )
           (   :types
               (connection (a port))))
```

```
(defobject 2-PORT-DEVICE (inlet outlet) ( )
           (   :types
               (inlet (a port))
               (outlet (a port))))
```

```
(defobject RESERVOIR (volume) (thermodynamics)
           (   :types
               (volume (a quantity))))
```

```
(defobject THERMODYNAMICS (pressure temperature) ( )
           (   :types
               (pressure (a quantity))
               (temperature (a quantity))))
```

```
(defobject STATE-DEVICE (states) ( )
           (   :types
               (states (a list))))
```

```
: : : VALVES
```

```
(defobject VALVE ( ) (2-port-device state))
```

```
(defobject STOP-VALVE ( ) (valve open-shut-states))
```

```
(defobject CHECK-VALVE ( ) (valve))
```

```
(defobject THROTTLE-VALVE ( ) (valve continuous-open-shut-states)
```

```
: : : PUMPS
```

```
(defobject PUMP (suction discharge motor) (2-port-device states)
           (   :types
               (motor (a motor)))
           (   :equalities
               ((motor attached-device) self)
               ((suction) (inlet))
               ((discharge) (outlet))))
```

```
(defobject MOTOR (attached-device controller) (states))
```

```
(defobject PUMPING-STATION (pump suction-valve discharge-valve)
                                        (2-port-device states)
           (   :types
               (pump (a pump))
               (suction-valve (a stop-valve))
               discharge-valve (a stop valve)))
           (   :equalities
               ((inlet) (suction-valve inlet)
               ((suction-valve outlet) (pump suction))
               ((pump discharge) (discharge-valve inlet))
               ((discharge-valve outlet) (outlet))))
```

Figure 6-9 Generic Frames in steamer (Bolt Beranek and Newman)

used to create or define a frame. The uppercase name (PORT, 2-DEVICE, THERMODYNAMICS, PUMPING-STATION) that follows "defobject" is the name of the frame created.

Two different sets of parenthesized information follow the frame name. The first of these is a list of slot names that are explicitly (directly) represented in that frame. For example, the 2-PORT-DEVICE frame contains two explicitly represented slots: one for inlet and one for outlet. The THERMODYNAMICS frame has a slot for pressure and another slot for temperature. Note that both of these slots describe concepts. The PUMPING-STATION frame contains three slots. These describe the pump, suction valve, and discharge-valve, all of which are components. Some frames, such as the four valve frames shown, do not contain any slots. Therefore, their parenthesized slot list if empty. Other frames may contain slots that are implicitly (indirectly) represented in that they are really slots in subframes, but the slots in the subframes also belong to the parent frames. This dual ownership of slots eliminates the need for system developers to rewrite slots, values, and code for every frame.

The second parenthetical quantity after the frame name houses the names of subframes that the frame contains. As Figure 6-9 indicates, the PUMPING-STATION frame contains two subframes: the 2-PORT-DEVICE shown and a STATES frame, not shown. A "states" frame contains information about the various states that an object can be in, such as "on," "off," "open," or "shut."

FROM THE GENERIC . . .

Frames help to organize the knowledge related to the frame names. As in the Logician system, Steamer further organizes its frames (or subframes) as generic and unique. The idea of representing knowledge in generic and unique frames allows knowledge to be explicitly represented when needed, while making it possible to represent a generalized form of the knowledge in question. Representing knowledge at different levels of specificity and abstraction simplifies the conceptualization, design, and programming of an application because certain patterns and procedures are common across many objects, events, and actions. For example, all bank accounts belonging to individuals are unique, but in any bank, in any country, people opening an account know that certain general features will be true of that account.

Similarly, in Steamer, a generic pumping station frame describes, in a general form, all pumping stations. When a knowledge engineer enters knowledge about a specific pumping station, Steamer makes a copy of that generic frame and fills in information to make it unique and specific. This specific copy of the generic frame is an instance of that frame. There is only one copy of any generic frame but lots of copies of the specific ones.

All the frames in Figure 6-10 are generic frames for system objects. But some frames are more generic than others. How generic and specific frames are related

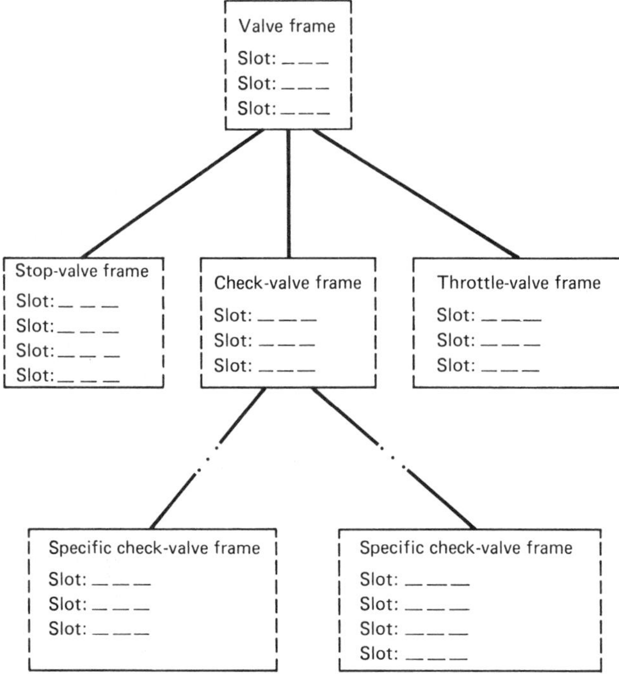

Figure 6-10 Hierarchy of generic and specific frames.

to other frames is displayed as a hierarchy. The most generic frame is at the top of the hierarchy. The most specific is at the bottom.

. . . TO THE SPECIFIC

Figure 6-11 shows instances (occurrences) of frames that represent specific components in a steam plant, such as a particular pumping station. So specific are these frames that they identify which of several existing pumps, stop valves, or ports (and frames that describe these objects) are present in the particular pumping station represented.

For example, the specific instance of the PUMPING-STATION frame contains six slots that describe a particular PUMP, SUCTION-VALVE, DISCHARGE-VALVE, INLET, OUTLET, and STATES. However, the parent generic PUMPING-STATION frame contains only the first three of these slots. Where then did the two other slots come from?

They came from the PUMPING-STATION frame, but they came indirectly. The three slots for PUMP, SUCTION-VALVE, and DISCHARGE-VALVE that were named in the generic PUMPING-STATION frame are merely those that are explicitly represented. But the PUMPING-STATION frame also implicitly con-

```
(make-instance 'pumping-station ': (identification 'psl))
#<PUMPING-STATION 32004124>

(describe (the psl))
#<PUMPING-STATION 32004124>, the MSG object known as PSl,
 has variable values:
        PUMP:                     #<PUMP 32004465>
        SUCTION-VALVE:            #<STOP-VALVE 32024323>
        DISCHARGE-VALVE:          #<STOP-VALVE 32030201>
        INLET:                    #<PORT 32034057>
        OUTLET:                   #<PORT 32035630>
        STATES:                   (STOP LOW HIGH)

#<PUMPING-STATION 32004124>

(describe (the psl pump))
#<PUMP 32004465>, an MSG object
 has variable values:
        SUCTION:                  #<PORT 32026430>
        DISCHARGE:                #<PORT 32006574>
        MOTOR:                    #<MOTOR 32010353>
        STATES:                   (STOP LOW HIGH)
        INLET:                    #<PORT 32026430>
        OUTLET:                   #<PORT 32006574>

#<PUMP 32004465>

(describe (the psl pump suction))
#<PORT 32026430>, an MSG object,
 has variable values:
        FLOW:                     #<QUANTITY 32026763>
        PRESSURE:                 #<QUANTITY 32027315>
        TEMPERATURE:              #<QUANTITY 32027647>

#<PORT 32026430>
```

Figure 6-11 Specific frames in steamer (Bolt Beranek and Newman, Inc.)

tains the slots that are contained in its subframes. The PUMPING-STATION frame contains two subframes: 2-PORT-DEVICE and STATES. INLET and OUTLET are named as slots in the 2-PORT-DEVICE frame. Therefore, they both implicitly become slots in the specific frame for PUMPING-STATION 32004124. The STATES frame has no slots, only values, such as STOP, LOW, and HIGH. These values also implicitly become part of the PUMPING-STATION frame.

Notice that the component or concept contained in a slot is treated as a variable that can take on specific values. The specific values are shown in the instance frame with their associated variables.

Similarly, the specific frame for pump 32004465 named in the PUMPING-STATION 32004124 has six slots. Three of them (SUCTION, DISCHARGE, AND MOTOR) are explicitly named. Three are implicit and are slots because in the generic PUMP frame they are subframes (STATES) or because they are slots in a subframe (INLET and OUTLET). In like manner, the PORT frame 32006430, which handles SUCTION in the PUMP 32004465 frame, gets its slots from explicit naming (FLOW) or implicitly because the slots are also slots in the PORT frame's THERMODYNAMICS subframe (PRESSURE and TEMPERATURE).

TEACHING AND EXPLAINING PROCEDURES

Slots in the lowest, most detailed level of the subframes, that describe specific components, interface to descriptions of specific steam plant procedures. These procedures are linked to corresponding procedures in Steamer's simulation model of a steam plant and to its graphical interface.

Using this integrated frame/simulation/graphical knowledge system, steam plant trainees can point to various components in the animated representation or to procedures displayed by the textual tutor. The pointing initiates the animated simulation.

Users can observe the simulation, experiment with procedures, or ask questions. But even with graphical AI-based educational tools, learning steam plant operation would normally be an ordeal, because of the overwhelming amount of material to learn. Learning is facilitated because Steamers designers generalized the material to be presented by the knowledge system.

For example, Steamer associates each generic and specific component frame with procedures that are correspondingly generic or specific. A procedure to start specific components such as "fuel oil service pump one alpha" might direct an operator to open a specific valve before turning on the pump. A more generic procedure for a more generic pump frame might be to start a positive displacement pump by opening the discharge valve before turning on the pump. At a higher level of abstraction, a procedure might indicate that for any system with an attached safety device, the safety device should always be aligned before the system is turned on.

The advantage of designing the frames in this manner is that a small number of generic devices and procedures cover the operation of a very large system. This often makes it easier to learn, remember, and understand the rationale for all the operational procedures without needing to go through all the pages of a thousand-page textbook. However, the detailed, specific information that is needed for learning steam plant operations is also explicitly available.

If during a Steamer instructional session, the trainee asks "why" about a procedure or concept, Steamer looks from the procedure or concept to the corresponding frame. Then it wriggles up the frame hierarchy until it finds a frame with explanatory information about the question.

Such a frame contains information about the constraints on each step of a steam plant operation procedure and the consequences of violating these constraints. For brevity, it stores such information as minimal English text (without articles and prepositions) in a slot. When the trainee asks questions about procedures or concepts, Steamer dynamically generates English text to flesh out the stored English sentence. In this way, trainees see syntactically correct and readable explanations as answers to their questions

Steamer can briefly respond to a trainee's question about steam plant procedures, but upon further user request, elaborate on its explanations. These

```
Current Object: Start a pump with motor


To start a pump with motor we:
   1. Align the pump.
   2. Start the motor.


To align a pump we:
   Think of it as an isolatable two port device and align it.

A pump can be thought as:
   An isolatable two port device.

   To align an isolatable two port device we:
      1. Open the outlet valve.
      2. Open the inlet valve.


      Open the outlet valve comes before open the inlet valve because one
      should always minimize the volume of downstream piping when aligning or
      securing a system since this minimizes the amount of energy released in
      case of an accident.

Therefore to align a pump we:
   1. Open the discharge valve.
   2. Open the suction valve.


To start a two speed motor we:
   1. Depress the motor controller designated start swich.
   2. Wait until operating condition is motor controller start speed.
   3. Release the motor controller designated start switch.


To start a pump with motor we:
   1. Open the pump discharge valve.
   2. Open the pump suction valve.
   3. Depress the motor motor controller designated start switch.
   4. Wait until operating condition is motor controller start speed.
   5. Release the motor motor controller designated start switch.


Presentation
```

Figure 6-12 Steamer answers trainees' questions and elaborates on explanations because it can inherit procedures. (Bolt Beranek and Newman, Inc.)

explanations and their elaboration are possible because Steamer inherits procedures as well as frame slots.

Figure 6-12 illustrates both Steamer's explanation and the inheritance of procedures. In reponse to a generic request such as "how do I start the pump," Steamer responds with a generic procedure involving aligning the pump and starting the motor. This response is too general to be of much use, so the user points to the "align the pump" statement to find out how the align procedure works.

Steamer's first response to the generic "align" question is also generic. Further probing provides more specific alignment information, such as "think of the pump as a two-port device which you align by opening a suction discharge valve."

Steamer knows the procedure for aligning the pump since it knows that the pump is an isolatable two-port device. (Isolatable means "has a valve on the inlet and outlet.") A procedure exists for aligning two-port devices and that procedure is inherited. The inheritance of procedures, as well as slot inheritance, eliminates the need to specifically encode information about how to align a pump or motor.

Every explanation given by Steamer refers to some component or concept that is represented explicitly as a frame. Therefore, users can request elaboration about any part of an explanation. For example, the two steps given to align a two-port device can be made still more specific by pointing to the individual steps in the procedure. Similarly, by pointing to other subparts of Steamer explanations, such as the "start the motor" statement, users can obtain information about any part of a procedure or the entire procedure.

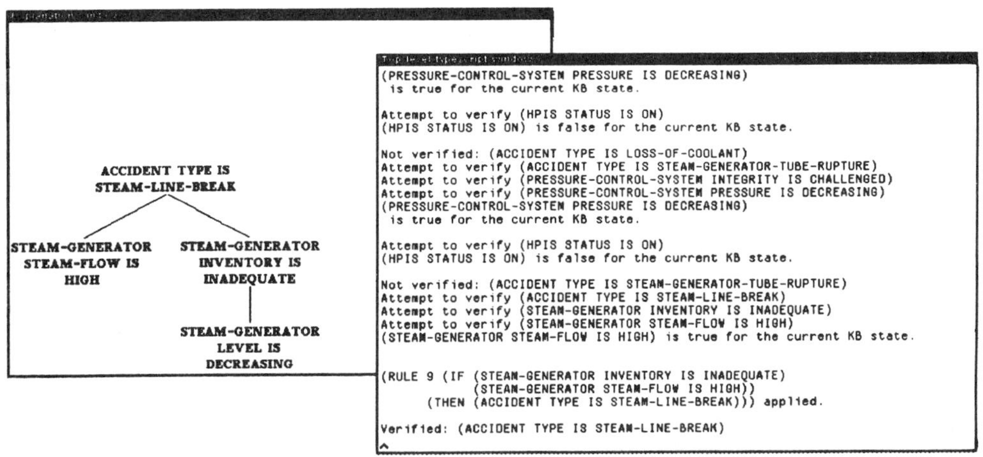

Figure 6-13 Two methods that knowledge systems use to explain their reasoning (Program copyrights 1983, 1984 by Intellicorp. All rights reserved.)

MANY WAYS TO EXPLAIN

Steamer's abbreviated-English explanations that are contained in frame slots is one of several methods to generate explanations. A different method used by one expert statistical software system responds to a request for an explanation by displaying an English-like version of the rules that it used to arrive at a conclusion in question.

Displaying an audit trail of rules used is the most common method used by knowledge systems to present reasoning explanations. Still another technique is based on a decision tree display. But some systems combine these explanation techniques.

For example, to explain its reasoning, one expert system prototype for nuclear power plant diagnosis displays an audit trail of rules it used, in addition to a decision tree (Figure 6-13). Both displays show how the system decided that the cause of a particular nuclear plant accident was a break in a steam line.

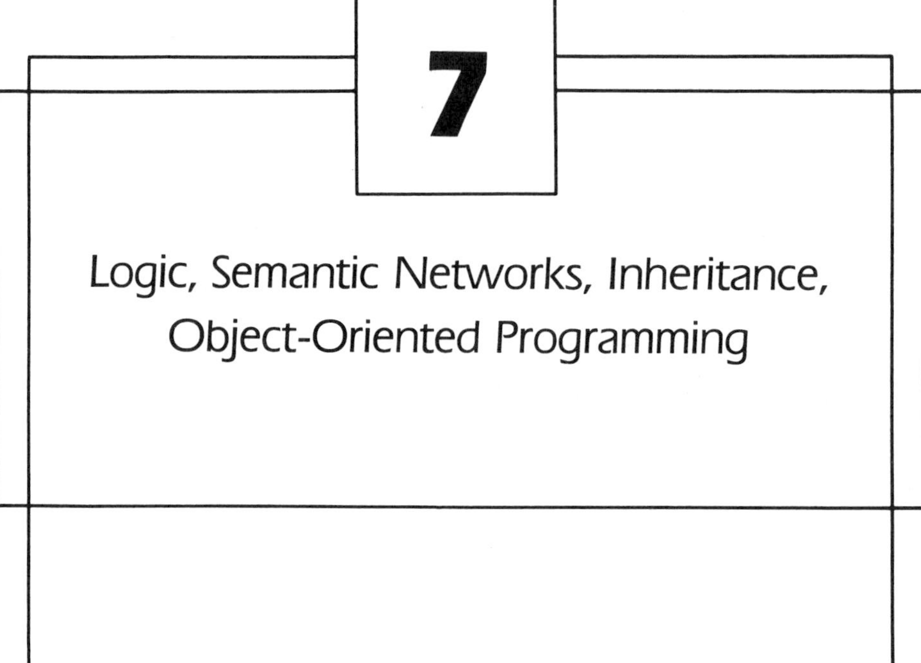

7 Logic, Semantic Networks, Inheritance, Object-Oriented Programming

The question of what is the best and most useful method to represent knowledge is still an open question in the AI community. Although rules, frames, processes, and combinations of these, discussed in the last two chapters, are common ways to represent knowledge, they are by no means the only ones.

Yet another common way to represent the type of knowledge generally used in everyday language, as well as much of modern mathematics, is formal logic. Formal logic is a technique to represent information so that it is possible to check formally whether or not the information is true. For example, whether or not Roberta is a salesperson can be represented in logic as the statement (known in logic as a proposition):

```
Salesperson (Roberta)
```

Roberta is the "argument" of the statement. The statement evaluates either to true or false.

"Predicates" in logic express relations between objects. For example,

```
Worksin (Roberta, New_York)
```

uses the predicate "worksin" to represent the fact that Roberta works in New York.

The logic system used in AI systems is known as predicate calculus. Typical predicates in these systems might be "worksin," "isa," or "earns." The predicates are defined by a programmer whereas logical connectives such as "and," "not," and "if," which are also part of logic, are predefined by the logic system. It is possible to build an entire knowledge base or relational database using formal logic.

Basic facts about and relationships between employees, inventory, and company information are entered in a manner similar to that previously shown regarding Roberta. Unlike databases, it is not necessary to store the same amount of information or type of information for each person or item in a database based on logic.

Besides expressing basic facts and descriptions, formal logic provides a built-in method for performing deduction, or correct inference. In logic, an inference can be proved correct because a logic system guarantees that if the premises of a logical declaration (called an assertion) are true, so is the conclusion. For example, the basic facts represented in two assertions such as "Lawyer(Lew)" and "Prosecute(Lawyer Court)" means that Lew is a lawyer and lawyers prosecute in court. These facts can be used to deduce new facts, such as "if Lew is a lawyer, then he prosecutes in court." This deduction is represented in logic:

```
If(Lawyer Lew) and (Prosecute(Lawyer Court))
        Then(Prosecute(Lew Court)
```

As illustrated by this logically represented, deduced fact, which is also an example of a rule, rule-based and logic-based representations grade into one another. This gradation points up an advantage of using logic to represent information in a database. Like any conventional database, a logic-based database contains facts and relationships between the facts. However, a logic-based database also contains rules. The rules are knowledge-system-types of IF-THENs that allow new facts to be inferred from original ones.

A LOGICAL APPLICATION

System Development Corp. has an expert system DADM (Deductively Augmented Data Management). Although written in Interlisp (not a logic-based language), DADM is designed around logic. DADM, which acts as a manager's assistant, interfaces simultaneously to multiple database systems. Not only does DADM generate intelligent database access strategies, it acts as a consultant to managers because it can deduce new information (based on data in the databases). Furthermore, DADM can generate explanations about the reasoning that it uses to come up with particular answers or suggestions.

To allow it to perform its deduction, DADM's knowledge base contains logic-based information about selected data stored in SDC's corporate database. The data include information about costs charged to various projects, total project costs, and standard management information systems (MIS) application data. To these logic-based data representations, DADM has added logic-based rules that

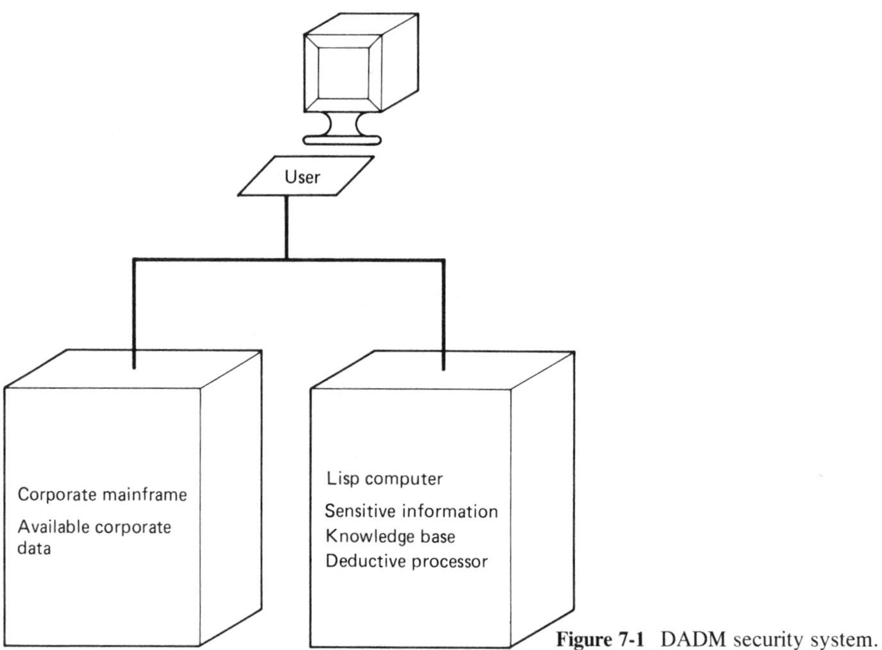

Figure 7-1 DADM security system.

the expert system calls on to answer management's sophisticated questions about projects, plans, costs, and personnel.

Knowledge engineers planned DADM's knowledge by interviewing managers to determine what kinds of questions they are most likely to ask. Symbolic WHAT-IF questions were a popular response. These questions have the form "WHAT-IF SUCH-AND-SUCH-EVENT HAPPENED" rather than the numerically oriented WHAT-IF THIS NUMBER WAS DIFFERENT, which electronic spreadsheets support. A typical symbolic WHAT-IF question might be "WHAT-IF FOX LEAVES THE COMPANY?"

DADM's response might contain information about the impact on Fox's department and the project on which he was working. DADM might even identify people with similar skills and experience levels and offer suggestions as to potential replacements.

To respond to a manager's query, DADM first chains through a series of rules that help it decide what data it needs. Then it generates a strategy to access those data. If necessary, it iterates this set of procedures until it determines the best answer to the query. Finally, it displays an audit trail or explanation of how it arrived at its answer.

As with any knowledge system, DADM's rules are modular and can be combined in many different ways. Therefore, with only several hundred rules, DADM can answer many thousands of questions that managers might generate.

There is a security aspect to a system such as DADM that potential implementers and users must consider. Security requires that sensitive information that only managers should see, such as plan information and employee salaries, must be partitioned and separated from generally available information, such as direct charges and number of people on the job per week.

To ensure company security, DADM uses two different rational database systems. The sensitive information accessible only to authorized managers resides on a Lisp machine, together with DADM's knowledge base and the deductive processor that infers information. The generally available information resides on a Britton Lee IDM 500 relational database machine (Figure 7-1).

As the DADM knowledge base and deductive processor generate multiple data access strategies to answer manager's queries, the access strategies are selectively spun off either to the Lisp machine or Britton Lee machine database systems. In many cases, DADM sends subqueries to both database systems. The partial responses that DADM received from both machines are then combined in the Lisp machine into a final answer and explanation for that answer.

TWO MORE REPRESENTATIONS

Besides formal logic and the knowledge representation techniques mentioned in the last two chapters, there are two other significant knowledge representations. One, known as a "script," is a framelike structure that describes stereotypical sequences of events that occur in everyday situations such as eating in restaurants and going to the doctor. They provide details that may not be included in people's natural-language sentences but nonetheless are needed to understand them. Scripts are discussed in Chapter 15.

Another symbolic knowledge representation structure commonly found in knowledge bases is semantic networks (discussed in Chapter 5). Recall that semantic networks are node-and-arc graphical notations that represent objects, actions, or events and contain built-in real-world meaning about the objects, actions, or events. Objects are nodes. Arcs show relationships between them. Some relationships, such as "ISA," "ON," and "MATERIAL," are commonly accepted terminology for semantic networks. Other relationships are programmer defined. Still other relationships are the result of inheritance.

OBJECT-ORIENTED PROGRAMMING

Object-oriented programming is a technique and programming style, often used for AI development because it supports exploratory programming. As discussed in Chapter 1, this is important to AI because AI programs are often built from ill-understood specifications to solve ill-understood problems. Object-oriented programming involves a different (in fact, reversed) method of handling programs and data compared to that used by other programming languages. As will be seen, it is this reversed program and data-handling method that lends itself to the exploratory programming necessary to develop AI programs.

In any language, programs have two components: a procedural part that operates on data, and the data on which the procedural component operates. The procedural component, known as the program, contains the instructions for an operation to be performed. Such components include procedures for "add," "find," "read," "write," "print," and "conditional programming statements" (such as "if this condition is true, then do that"), and so on. The data on which the program operates might typically be numbers, strings of characters, graphical shapes, documents, or files.

In conventional programming, most people consider programs as primary and the data (or objects) secondary. In object-oriented programming, the reverse is true. The data, such as a graphical shape or document to be operated on, is of primary importance.

In object-oriented programming, rather than sending the program the name of an object to manipulate (which corresponds to providing the program with data in conventional programming), the programmer sends the object (or data) a message. A message is actually the name of an operation or procedure (called a method in object-oriented programming) to be performed. Typical operations on the object "document" include open and close the document, find, print, and display it. Sending the object "document" one of these messages is like the data calling a subroutine in conventional programming.

The object is able to respond appropriately to a message because an object is defined along with a group of associated procedures that it can perform. As a result, when the object, for example, "document," receives a message, such as "display," it knows how to perform that procedure because associated with the object are the procedure instructions. To perform the same task in conventional programming, the program would call a procedure called "display," which would take the document as data, execute the display instructions, and display the document.

The object-oriented style becomes important when one operation can be performed differently depending on the object to which it is applied. Under these conditions, it is handy for each object to know how to perform its own operations. As will be seen, such knowledge avoids programming errors and allows program decisions to be made late in the program execution process. It also saves time and promotes reliability because in object-oriented programming this knowledge of procedures is inherited.

OBJECT-ORIENTED INHERITANCE

Most AI experts consider some type of inheritance mechanism crucial to AI programming. Such mechanisms are inherent in frame hierarchies and semantic networks. Lisp, the major AI language, does not have an embedded inheritance

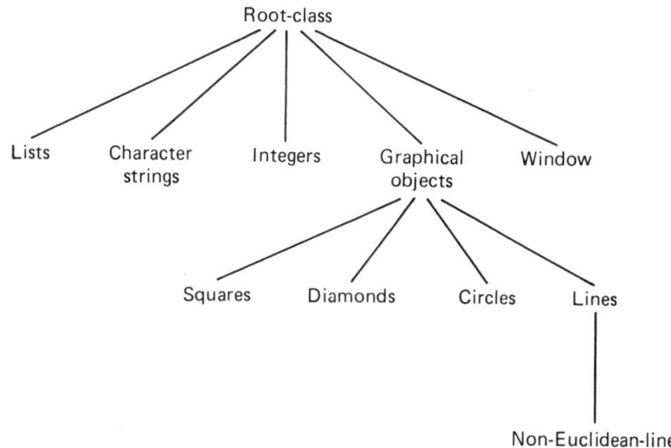

Figure 7-2 Hierarchies of classes and subclasses in object-oriented programming.

mechanism, but AI programmers usually extend Lisp to have that feature. Inheritance mechanisms, however, are found in a group of programming languages known as object-oriented languages, in addition to being incorporated in many AI development tools (discussed in Chapters 10 and 11). Inheritance is possible in object-oriented programming languages because these languages organize programs as a hierarchical arrangement of things known as classes and subclasses (Figure 7-2). Classes and subclasses are sets of the same kinds of generic objects or components. Typically, object-oriented programs might contain classes such as numbers, character strings, graphical shapes, documents, or files. Others have classes of components such as queues or frames. The highly graphical Lisp computer user interfaces are implemented with object-oriented programming techniques. These programs would likely have classes of windows, menus, and icons.

The relationships between objects in the hierarchy and those immediately below them are described as parent—child inheritance relationships, because some objects in the hierarchy are called "parents" and the related objects at the next lower level of the hierarchy are their children. The subclasses of objects lower in the hierarchy may represent a type of the parent objects. For example, in Figure 7-2, a circle is a type of graphical object. Or, as with Steamer's PUMP frames, the subclasses may represent specific objects while the parent classes describe more generic objects.

Associated with each class is a group of procedures (methods). Each subclass automatically inherits these procedures from its parents unless it has its own procedures that mask out one or more of the parent's procedures.

The highest class in a hierarchy is a single "root" class (Figure 7-3). A particular root class—for example, for a graphics program—might, at the next lower level has classes of lists, strings, integers, graphical objects, and windows.

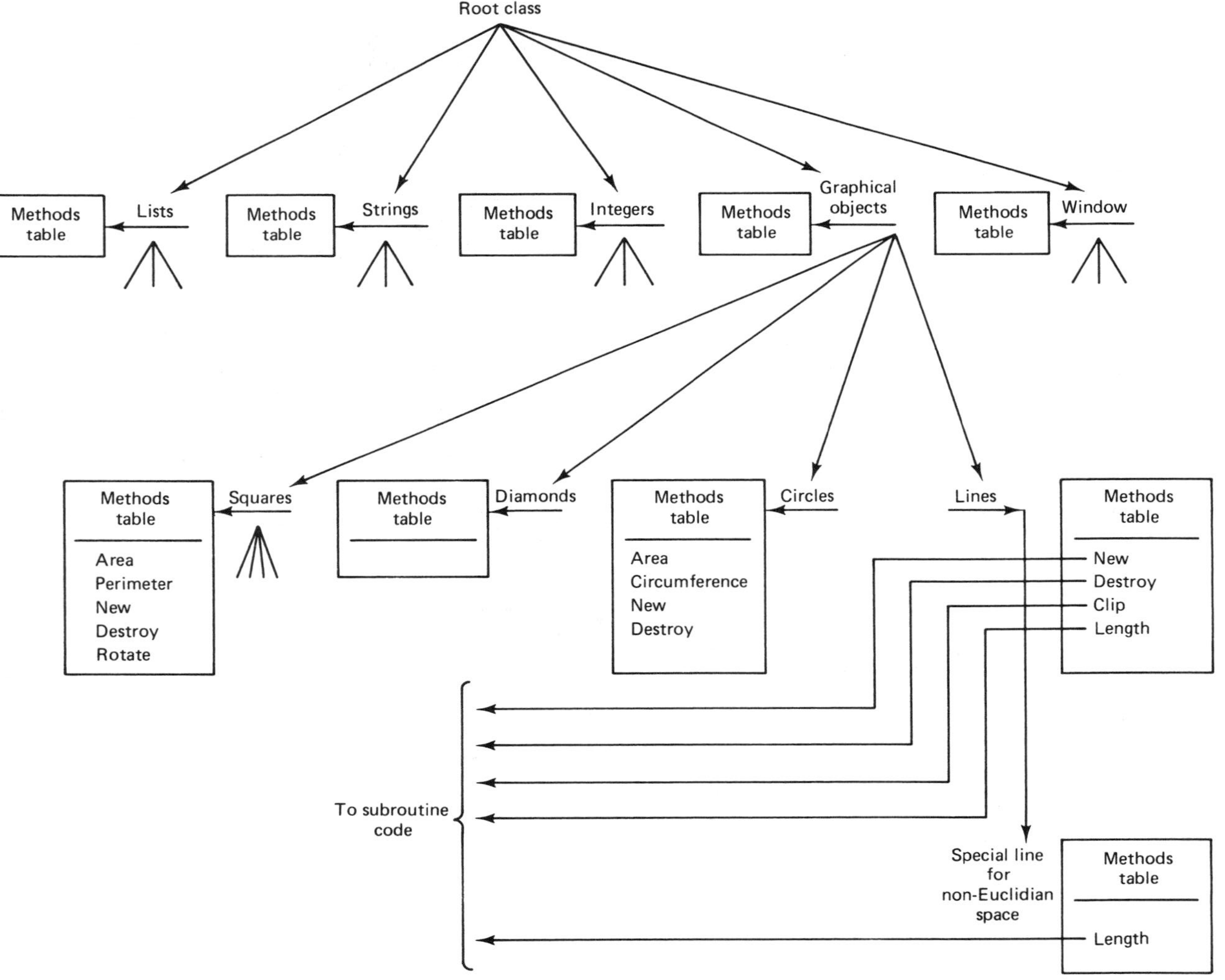

Figure 7-3 Inheritance of methods in object-oriented programming.

The graphical objects class might have subclasses of squares, diamonds, circles, and lines.

Methods associated with the subclass "lines" might include "clip" (which shortens a line), "new" (which creates a line), "destroy" which destroys a line), and "length" (which computes the length of a line). To request a program to calculate the length of a line, a user or programmer sends the message "length" to the line. To determine the length, a message routine in the object-oriented program then looks at a table of methods associated with the subclass "line" and finds the method (or routine) name "length." From there, the program follows a pointer (the address of the routine's instructions in computer memory) from the table to the routine which calculates the length of the line and then executes the routine. Similar techniques are followed for the messages "create," "destroy," and "clip."

If another special subclass of "line" is added that describes lines for non-Euclidean space, a different "length" routine must be written. Now, when a user sends the message "length" to the non-Euclidean line, the newly written "length" message initiates a call to the message routine which finds and executes the new length routine.

On the other hand, if the user sends a message to the non-Euclidean line to execute the procedure "new" or "destroy," the message routine will not find such procedures in the methods table for the non-Euclidean "line" subclass because these procedures were never written there. No matter; the non-Euclidean line subclass will execute these procedures anyway because they are contained in the methods table written for a parent class higher in the hierarchy. They need not be rewritten because, in an object-oriented program, if the message routine does not find the requested procedures in a particular methods table, it will look in the methods table of the next-higher class, which is the parent class. If the method is listed there, it is automatically executed.

What really happens is that the non-Euclidean "line" class has inherited these prewritten "new" and "destroy" routines from its "parents" higher in the hierarchy. Procedures can also be inherited from grandparents or ancestor classes. In ancestral inheritance, if a message names a particular method that is not listed in the class immediately above the one in question, the message routine will continue to look up the inheritance tree until it finds the class that contains that method, and, upon finding it, will execute it.

One advantage of this inheritance hierarchy in object-oriented programming is that the programmer does not have to change or add much system code when a new class is added. He or she only need write code to specify specialized, customized functions and characteristics that make the children unique. Children inherit the rest of their attributes from their parents. Since only code that makes the children unique needs to be written, the hierarchical relationships indicate the difference between objects at different levels.

Objects can have more than one parent. For example, an object

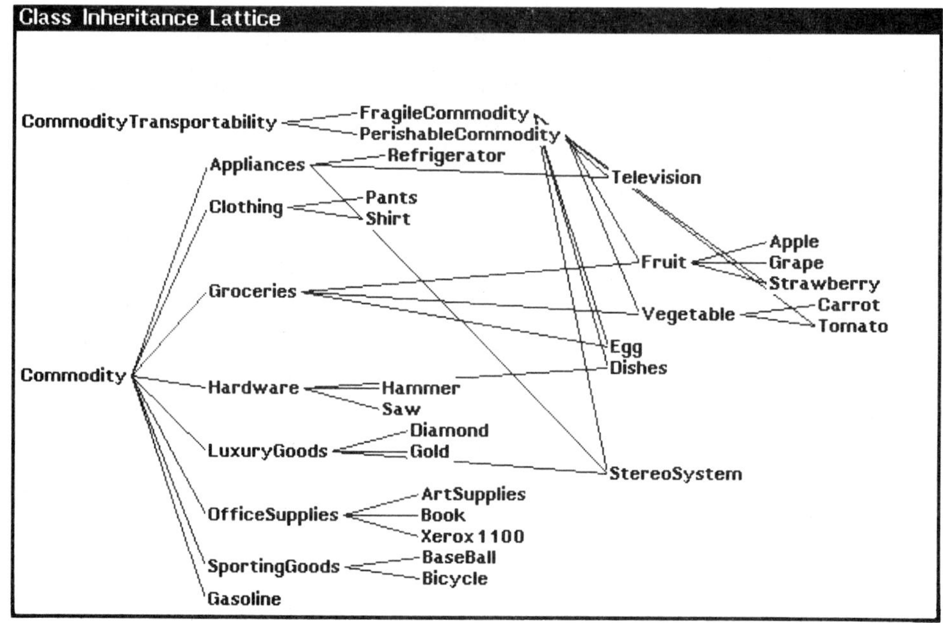

Figure 7-4 Object-oriented programming inheritance of attributes and procedures for commodity products. (Xerox Corp.)

"houseboat" in a inheritance lattice might inherit its characteristics from two parents: "house" and "boat."* The object "fruit" shown in the inheritance lattice in Figure 7-4 has three parents: Groceries, FragileCommodity, and PerishableCommodity. Therefore, "fruit" inherits from each of those parents knowledge about the characteristics and handling of groceries and fragile and perishable commodities.

This type of inheritance hierarchy would expedite the modification of object-oriented computer programs in trucking or distribution organizations as these organizations added new items to their roster of goods to be shipped. The expediting would occur because the trucking or distribution software that schedules or monitors the shipping of goods would inherit the knowledge of new goods added to the program.

So if a company undertook, for the first time, the transportation of milk, fruits, diamonds, and baseballs, and added these items to an object-oriented computer program with the class inheritance lattice shown in Figure 7-4, as soon as these items were added to the program, the program would instantly know several facts that would help prevent both programmer and human management errors. For example, the program would automatically know that diamonds do not spoil but fruits do. Moreover, the program could perform its chores knowing

*Example contributed by James Spoerl.

instantly, because of inheritance, that time is more important in shipping milk than baseballs. Therefore, a money-saving decision might be made by shipping baseballs in a truck making several stops. However, if the milk is transported for too long a time in a truck, the distributor is likely to lose money on the deal.

EXPLORATORY PROGRAMMING

Another significant feature of object-oriented programming is its ability to support exploratory programming for ill-understood AI systems. One key to exploratory programming techniques is deferring as many programming constraints and commitments (efficiency, typing of variables, and allocation of memory) as long as possible. To do otherwise imposes too heavy a burden on the programmer, who must spend time making and implementing programming decisions that are likely to need changing.

For example, implementing efficiency procedures too early makes the program inflexible before it works properly and requires massive programming changes to rework the program so that it works both properly and efficiently. An early choice as to typing variables and data structures requires the programmer to determine, compile, and make static some of the information about variables that may not be the best or most efficient representations for the program and are time consuming to change. Finally, allocating memory decisions early requires the programmer to spend much time to ensure that program information stored in memory is accessible when it should be and is eventually released so as not to fill up memory with information no longer needed (so-called "garbage" information). Deferring these commitments, on the other hand, allows the programmer to experiment with different program features.

Lisp allows some commitments to be deferred until execution time (run time). Another major factor that supports deferment is the object-oriented view of data, or objects, as the primary components in a program, to which messages are sent to perform procedures that are associated with the objects. Commitment about a particular operation and its meaning can be deferred by defining the operation generally, but having each data object provide its own definition for the operation. This technique is important because procedures often must be implemented differently depending on the object the procedure is applied to. Having each data object provide its own definition for a generic operation leads to deferred commitment because the programmer does not have to decide which specific procedure to implement. Instead, each object determines how to perform a generic procedure so that the procedure applies to the specific object. Which procedure to implement is not determined until run time.

The object-oriented technique works like this. "Print" is an operation that can be applied to many objects in a system. But there are many ways to implement "print," depending on the device associated with the procedure "print." For example, the procedure to print to a file is different from the procedure to print to a graphics screen, an ASCII terminal, or a dot-matrix printer.

For the programmer who wants a particular device to print something, it matters not which object (or device) "print" will be applied to because in object-oriented programming, "print" is a generic procedure. How to apply "print" to a particular object is determined by which object "print" is applied to. The objects determine the meaning of "print," because encapsulated within each object to which "print" can be applied (such as the file, graphics screen, ASCII terminal, and dot-matrix printer) is a procedure for "print" that is specialized for the particular object.

Consequently, during program development, a programmer who wants to print something on an ASCII terminal need only send a generic procedure message, "print," to the ASCII terminal object. How to print, and which procedure to call for the ASCII terminal to print, is determined by the ASCII terminal because, like other objects in the system, it knows how to print based on its own internal representation.

If after some experimentation, the programmer decides that it would be better to print to a graphics screen, he or she need only send the message "print" to the graphics screen instead of to the ASCII terminal. There is no need to go into the program to fiddle with procedures and procedure calls as is done in conventional programming.

Now suppose that the programmer wishes to add a new device to print to, such as a vocal synthesizer. In conventional programming, the programmer goes into the "print" procedure in the program where he or she is likely to find a big "case" statement. A "case" statement has the form "IF THE CASE IS PRINT AND IT IS APPLIED TO A FILE THEN PRINT LIKE THIS, BUT IF THE CASE IS PRINT AND IT IS APPLIED TO AN ASCII TERMINAL THEN PRINT LIKE THAT," and so on, sometimes for a relatively extended list of cases. To add directions to print to the vocal synthesizer, the programmer may further extend the case statement for the case of the vocal synthesizer. But if, in doing so, a mistake is made, the system may fail and nothing may print because there is a bug in "print."

In contrast, in object-oriented programming, the programmer defines both a new object to represent the vocal synthesizer and an associated routine that instructs the vocal synthesizer about the "print" procedure. To apply "print" to the vocal synthesizer, the programmer merely sends the message "print" to the synthesizer, which knows how to execute the procedure. Unlike with conventional programs, if the "print" procedure has a bug, all the other objects in the system still print because the "print" routines are isolated from each other and instead, encapsulated with their associated objects.

The object-oriented paradigm is particularly suited for exploratory programming in general, and is often used in human/machine interfaces. In these applications, there are specialized objects, such as a file, graphics screen, and ASCII terminal, associated with a number of device-specific operations to perform for these objects. Object-oriented programming allows the devices to be associated only with relevant procedures instead of every operation having to know about every device. At the same time, a single procedure name in an application program can be used to manage many different objects, even if the procedures corresponding to an operation are different for the different objects.

In summary, object-oriented programming allows a programmer to create easily new objects with the same name, that are similar but somewhat different, and that perform the same kinds of procedures as the original object or other children, but perform them somewhat differently.

It is important to note, however, that object-oriented programming is not as suitable for many types of applications, such as Fortran-style multimode arithmetic (arithmetic that deals with different modes, such as real and integer). Its unsuitability stems first from the lack of a single designated important object. Unlike input/output operations, which are performed on a single important object such as a file, multimode arithmetic operations deal with two operands represented in different modes, neither one of which is unique. For example, it makes no difference to an addition operation if a real number is added to an integer or an integer is added to a real number.

Conventional programming languages associate the knowledge of how to perform such mixed-mode addition with the operator "plus." To perform the addition, the language decides on a common type, generally real, maps the integer into the real-number representation, and calls the real-number addition routine. In a straightforward manner, the real-number addition routine handles addition either of integer plus real or real plus integer because the knowledge is in one place associated with the operator "plus." This type of organization is a procedural organization rather than an object-oriented one.

In object-oriented organization, the real number and the integer would correspond to objects. To perform addition of these two types of numbers, it is necessary to have routines associated with integers that know how to add real numbers and also routines associated with real numbers that know how to add integers. Such a procedural problem requires information to be represented redundantly because there is no unique object associated with the "plus" operator. In this type of situation, it is more appropriate to associate the knowledge with the operators (plus) rather than the numbers (objects).

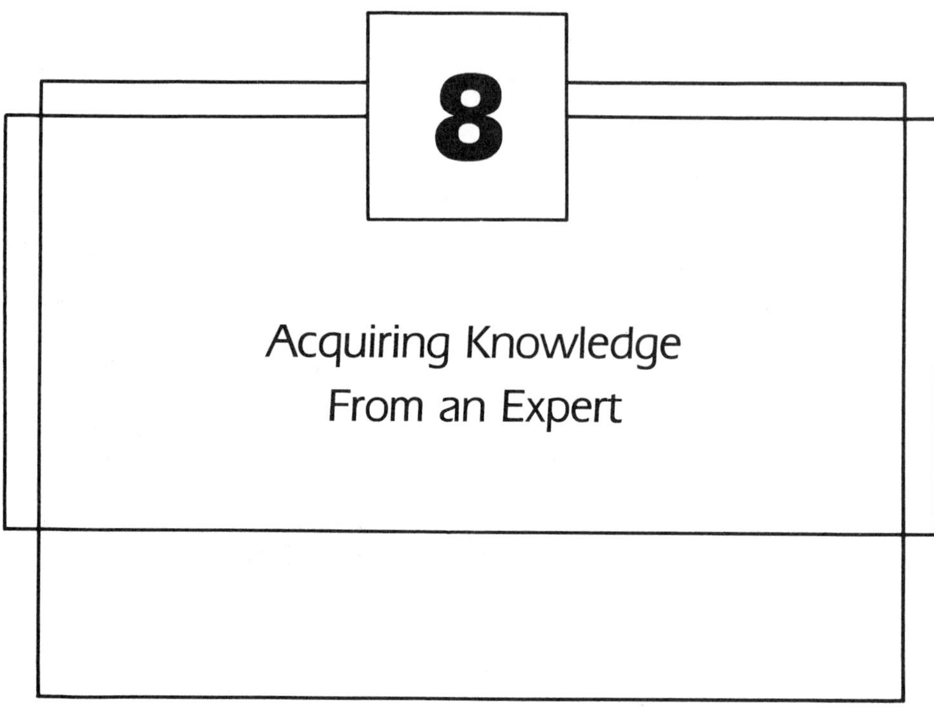

An expert system or knowledge system acts like a real expert because it has embedded in it the factual and experiential (heuristic) knowledge of a real expert. Getting that knowledge out of the real expert and into a form that can be used by a computer is a difficult job. For one thing, it requires an expert who is both cooperative and articulate. For another, it requires a person who knows something about computers, artificial intelligence, psychology, statesmanship, and the expert's application area in order to interview the expert and convert the knowledge acquired from the interviews into a computer-usable form.

The person who interviews the expert and acquires and represents the knowledge is known as a knowledge engineer. The process of acquiring the knowledge and representing it for the computer is known as knowledge engineering. As might be expected, knowledge engineering is a labor-intensive process that takes place over a long period of time. In fact, it is one of the most difficult steps in building an expert system. Furthermore, because the acquisition of knowledge is frequently dependent on only a few people—for example one knowledge engineer and one, or maybe two, experts—the process is a bottleneck in the building of a knowledge-based system.

The knowledge engineering process is arduous and long because no matter how willing experts are to communicate their knowledge, it is impossible for the knowledge engineer to get knowledge out of experts simply by asking for it. It matters not that the experts are willing to answer all the knowledge engineer's question because, especially at the beginning of an expert system building project, knowledge engineers do not yet know enough about the application to ask for the most useful knowledge. It also does not matter that the experts are willing to tell the knowledge engineers whatever they (the experts) know. Even though they know and use the knowledge, it is organized in such a way that it can only be extracted in little pieces over a fairly extensive period of time.

LIVING THROUGH ORDEALS

The length of time necessary to extract knowledge from experts can be explained by understanding what an expert really does. An expert can be thought of as a person who knows what to do in thousands of different situations. However, the mind is largely a recognition machine. Therefore, even though the experts know what to do, they cannot explain how to handle a problem unless they are immersed in the actual situation.

What knowledge engineers must do, then, is live through various situations with their experts over a long period of time. As different situations arise, the knowledge engineer systematically probes, writes, and probes again.

Although knowledge acquisition is time consuming and labor intensive, today's alternative approaches tend to be naive. Systems that learn knowledge by themselves are very rudimentary and still in the research stages. Systems that automate the knowledge acquisition process are also immature and inadequate for many applications.

There are some systems that allow experts to be their own knowledge engineers. This entails the gradual elucidation by the experts of their own knowledge, either to a standard medium such as paper or tape recorders, or directly to an expert development system. But even so, a host of difficulties attend this approach. In particular, often it happens that elucidating knowledge requires the presence of a second party to act as an observer, inquisitor, translator, and sounding board. These are some of the functions performed by knowledge engineers.

Howard Austin, one of Schlumberger's original knowledge engineers for its knowledge-based oil exploration system, notes some of the knowledge engineering difficulties typically encountered that require the presence of a knowledge engineer to resolve. For example, knowledge engineering experiences shows that if you just ask experts how they do something, what often happens is that they tell you what they believe is their procedure. Then if the knowledge engineer watches the experts in action, it turns out that they do something slightly differently.

Another common difficulty occurs when experts state what they believe is "one" procedure to accomplish some chore. Frequently, however, observation of the expert reveals that the one procedure is actually two or more separate procedures, all of which the expert performed without realizing it. Each of these procedures must be separated and clearly and explicitly identified for the knowledge system to work properly.

Achieving clear and explicit explanations at any point in the knowledge engineering process is no easy task. It is difficult for human experts to express their knowledge completely, accurately, and consistently under any circumstances. The ability to express this knowledge for use in a knowledge system is even more difficult because the language that is most natural for the expert to express knowledge is unnatural for the computer, and vice versa. Because of this gap, a knowledge engineer who knows how to represent knowledge for a computer is needed to pick out patterns in the expert's knowledge that can be converted to a form that is useful for a computer.

PRELIMINARY KNOWLEDGE ENGINEERING STAGES

The first thing the knowledge engineers did at Schlumberger when they designed the Dipmeter Advisor knowledge-based system (for oil exploration) was to make a commitment to become "mini-experts" so that they could talk intelligently to the experts and not slow down the expert's work. In pursuit of this goal, the knowledge engineers read the expert's papers and everything else they could find about the experts' application areas. As a result, they learned the terminology, general analysis patterns, and acquired a crude understanding of the experts' work. This allowed the knowledge engineers not only to help identify key concepts of a problem and to understand the experts' explanations, but to ask good questions.

IN THE FIELD

Unfortunately, the most significant heuristics that experts use are not generally capable of being verbally elucidated or written down. So after at time, the knowledge engineers need to inject themselves into the experts' daily job activities. To develop a knowledge-based oil exploration system for Schlumberger, knowledge engineers went with the experts out in the field, where they observed and recorded on tape recorders, video recorders, and paper. Similarly, for Bolt Beranek and Newman to develop Steamer, a knowledge-based system to teach Navy personnel how to operate a steam plant on board ship (Chapter 6), knowledge engineers participated in the traditional classroom and steam plant demonstration courses with other students. In developing Steamer, knowledge engineers found it helpful to know not only the typical problem-solving paths that an expert follows, but also the typical blunders that a student makes when first learning a subject.

Typically, knowledge engineers use a case study method as part of the knowledge acquisition process. For at least a few cases, they watch and record in detail exactly how an expert solves a particular problem. The experts might not follow a step-by-step analysis. They know all types of analysis and decision patterns to apply when a problem develops. They know all sorts of ways to avoid searching through a very large number of possibilities and yet come up with the correct answer or appropriate action to take. And they know all kinds of conditions that will invalidate whatever answers or actions they have determined. It is this type of knowledge that a knowledge engineer must determine in order to build a knowledge base.

Clearly, knowledge engineers must be diplomats. In fact, several companies claim that for a knowledge engineer, people skills can be as important as technical skills. Knowledge engineers must be able to listen as well as ask, and to instill confidence in, and draw out, the expert regardless of personality differences. They must understand that because so much of the expert's knowledge is intuitive and subconscious, at times there is as much to be learned from rambling as from asking direct questions.

Knowledge engineers may discover that the information the expert has exposited is inconsistent with what was exposited yesterday, what the expert is actually doing, or what another expert says. The rule of thumb is to ask questions but never directly challenge the expert. Instead, what knowledge engineers do is compare their direct observations of the expert's work and answers to questions with written words on the subject. The knowledge engineers must watch and write long enough to confirm that what the expert says coincides with what he or she is doing. Only then are they in a position to begin transferring information to a computer. If further inconsistencies remain between the expert's explanations and procedures followed, they can be resolved later in discussions or by running a sample problem using the expert's verbalized procedure.

Above all, knowledge engineers who have become familiar with an application area must beware of thinking that they know the expert's job. There is a vast difference between learning facts so that they can be recalled, understanding enough to teach them to a person or computer, and using the facts to solve a problem under pressure. Anyone who has watched and understood how an example mathematics problem was solved in a class, but later has not been able to do the homework problems, can attest to this.

CODING THE SYSTEM

When enough knowledge is acquired to write a rudimentary knowledge system, the knowledge engineers begin to segment all their transcribed knowledge into chunks that can be used in rules, frames, or whatever other knowledge representations will be used in the knowledge system in question.

At this point, the knowledge engineers encode the knowledge in an actual program. Or, as was done at Schlumberger, they give the marked-up, transcribed information to a different group of programmers to code. The actual knowledge base must be encoded using the same terminology that the experts use because it is the experts that will maintain the knowledge base when the program is complete.

How much knowledge is enough to begin coding depends on the system and the application. In general, the time to write the system is as soon as there is enough knowledge to write a very simple system to solve a simple problem. This may take months or it may happen on the first day. The technique in building expert systems is to get something running quickly, try it out, find the problem areas, fix it, run it again, and repeat the process.

Memory and time efficiency should not be considerations at this early stage of development. The issue is simply getting a prototype running. The prototype gives management something concrete to see, makes it easier to understand what a knowledge system can do for the organization, and provides a reason for continuing support. Equally important, it does the same things for the expert. The knowledge engineer and the expert then use the prototype to discover what other knowledge needs to be added.

KNOWING WHAT KNOWLEDGE LOOKS LIKE

When the knowledge engineer is ready to segment knowledge into chunks that the computer can use, it is necessary for him or her to understand the different forms of representing knowledge for a computer. A knowledge of computerized knowledge representations is also necesary in the early information-gathering stages, long before the time to begin segmenting knowledge for coding.

Starting then, knowledge engineers must interview an expert in an arbitrary and complex domain and develop a symbolic representation for that expert's knowledge so that the computer can understand it. Unfortunately, knowledge is an elusive, abstract thing. Furthermore, as mentioned earlier, verbalizing heuristic and intuitive knowledge precisely and completely is a difficult task. The difficulty is compounded by the gap that exists between the way the human expert expresses knowledge and what the computer can use.

To get the knowledge from the expert in a usable form, it is necessary to have some idea of what to look for. What to look for means much more than knowledge about an application domain. It means, also, the ability to understand what knowledge looks like in order to recognize it, organize it, and impose a picture or structure on the specific knowledge that the expert is communicating.

TRANSLATING FROM HUMAN EXPERT TO COMPUTER

The methods for organizing knowledge-based systems constitute the various knowledge representation techniques such as rules, frames, logic, and semantic networks, discussed earlier. But application domain experts do not talk in rule or frame languages. They know the procedures they perform, but they cannot necessarily articulate them in an organized form that is useful to a computer. Also, it is not realistic to figure on organizing reams of unorganized, transcribed information months after it has been given. For best results, some organization of knowledge transmitted during interviews with experts must begin at the beginning of the knowledge-collecting process, at least in the mind of the knowledge engineer. Otherwise, the organization of knowledge for encoding may be an intractable problem.

Which representation techniques to look for varies with the application, project, and knowledge engineer. Knowledge engineers visualize and translate some of an expert's knowledge exposited during interviews into forms such as "if this is the case, then do that" rules. They visualize and translate other types of information into logic representations such as "for all divisions such that profits are less than a certain amount, infer a particular strategy."

CHALLENGE THE SYSTEM

As soon as some simple examples that model the way an expert solves a few problems are understood, the knowledge engineer begins building a rudimentary prototype knowledge system. Once this rudimentary system is coded, the experts identify test cases which they try out on the system.

Clearly, the system will come to a naive conclusion since it represents only the knowledge of a novice. However, using this naive conclusion as the focus for discussion, the knowledge engineer elicits more information about the problem from the expert and uses the information elicited to improve the original system. Over many iterations, the expert points out where the program went wrong, at what point different conclusions should be made, and what new chunks of knowledge should be added to the knowledge base. Once the naivete of the knowledge system is pinpointed and the expert determines exactly what he or she would have done differently, the knowledge engineer enters a new chunk of knowledge into the knowledge base.

A good example of the adding of chunks of knowledge to an evolving knowledge system is DEC's XCON, which configures VAX-11/780 orders. The first or novice version of XCON had about 250 rules that handled XCON's original database description of 100 components. However, because the rule base knowledge was rudimentary and the VAX-11/780 could support 420 components (many more than XCON's database contained), XCON could acceptably configure only the simplest standard DEC VAX computer systems.

To extend the rule base, knowledge engineers gave XCON several orders to configure. Experts then looked at the proposed configuration and pointed out where it deviated from what was considered acceptable and what knowledge it needed to avoid the unacceptable and perform the configuration task correctly. The expert's answer in the form "IF the system knew this particular item of knowledge THEN it would know enough to do the following" was added to XCON as another rule.

By 1980, XCON grew to 750 rules, its database grew also to handle the 420 components that the VAX supported, and the expert system began to configure all VAX-11 orders, including those that involved special situations. Today, XCON has more than 5500 rules. The number of components described in the database has grown commensurate with new components supported by VAX systems. "Yet it still makes mistakes now and then," says John McDermott, XCON's principal inventor (McDermott, 1981).

Since McDermott views XCON as an expert, he expects that it will, like all experts, occasionally make mistakes. His concern is that many people view XCON (or expert systems in general) as programs and assume perfection. According to McDermott: "There is a big difference between programs and experts. Finished programs, by definition, have no bugs. When experts are finished, on the other hand, they're dead."

It is important to note that not only will knowledge systems make mistakes, they also cannot have the kind of knowledge that will not make the human expert obsolete. True, expert systems can acquire enough knowledge to make them very competent. But if an unusual situation arises, such as a potato in a tailpipe, no matter how good a knowledge-based automotive diagnostic system's prior performance, the system must fail and ask the human expert. The human expert will then add a rule to diagnose a potato in the tail pipe. But the next time, when the automobile turns out to have a turnip in the carburetor, it is back to the expert again.

9

A Guide to Building Knowledge Systems with Microcomputer-Based AI Tools

With many companies now entering the artificial intelligence business, the question "Are there enough experts to write the programs?" has been raised. The answer is that it is no longer necessary to be a Ph.D-in-AI-type of expert to write knowledge systems, because there are several expert system development tools available to build applications.

Software engineers, programmers, and data-processing professionals should have no difficulty learning to work with these tools. Some other types of engineers and application experts will also be up to the task.

General knowledge about the basic precepts of artificial intelligence, such as expert system architecture, limitations, and knowledge representations methods, is necessary to use the development tools successfully. Often, this education is provided by the AI tool companies, in courses, seminars, and contractual consulting. Educational institutions also offer AI courses, thus providing software professionals or application experts with the background knowledge to use the tools.

The incentives for acquiring tools to build knowledge system applications transcend the scarcity of AI experts; AI tools are also intended to satisfy a company's need for confidentiality. The symbolic problems that AI can solve are important to business plans and strategies and AI solutions often gives a company an edge over its competitors. Knowledge bases, however, may contain knowledge about these plans and strategies. Consequently, many companies want application development tools to build their knowledge systems in-house.

AI application development tools run on a variety of computers, from Lisp machines to microcomputers, and exhibit a range of capabilities and ease-of-use features. The application development tools that run on Lisp machines operate on top of Lisp environments, where they use the standard interactive graphics displays, editors, debuggers, and other features available there.

Another group of AI application development tools has been designed to run on microcomputers. Although microcomputer environments have less memory, processing power, graphics capabilities, and features than Lisp machines, some knowledge systems, albeit smaller ones than those built by their more expensive, microcomputer-oriented tools have the capabilities to build real-world Lisp machine-oriented counterparts.

This guide to building knowledge systems will begin with microcomputer-oriented tools because they are simpler, and it is easier to understand how to use them to build a knowledge system. Most tend to represent knowledge in easy-to-comprehend IF-THEN rules, use only one inference strategy, and support very limited control mechanisms. Once a fundamental understanding of knowledge system building principles, using simple knowledge representation and control techniques has been acquired, the next chapter will discuss how to use large-scale AI application tools, which contain a variety of AI-based features and capabilities, to build large-scale knowledge-based systems. However, the basic steps of planning, designing, building, and testing a knowledge-based system, as well as the same pitfalls, are common to microcomputer- and Lisp machine-based AI tools, and the same precautions apply.

MICROCOMPUTER-BASED AI TOOLS

AI application development tools make knowledge system development accessible to AI nonexperts. Their implementation on microcomputers has great potential to bridge the technology gap between AI experts and people who would like to explore AI and determine if it can help them in their profession. Previously, AI exploration was impractical because it required not only people with AI expertise, but also the purchase of expensive AI hardware.

PC-based knowledge system tools have a variety of capabilities and techniques for building knowledge bases. Some prompt users for knowledge base information. Some represent knowledge in tabular form or combine tabular representations with block structured procedures. Others are similar to large-scale AI tools, differing mainly in the amount of main memory available to the program, the highly graphical environments, and the sophistication of control mechanisms that can be used.

All of the PC-based AI tools are highly interactive. Some have advanced AI capabilities, such as the ability to accept incomplete and unknown answers, uncertain information, and several values for the same expression. Some can explain the system's method of reasoning used to solve a problem. Some handle meta-rules (rules about rules), which are used most often to direct the steps of a consultation.

Although AI application development tools make knowledge system development accessible to nonexperts, a number of precautions apply. In particular, it is important not to be lulled into false confidence and expectations about how easy it is to build knowledge-based systems. Tools are not a panacea for learning and hard work. As with classical software development, much of the work occurs before the knowledge system writing begins, and entails a thorough analysis of the problem, planning of the system, gathering knowledge, and organizing it to fit the knowledge system design and structures. Testing the system to ensure that needed information is not missing, does not conflict, and most important, gives correct answers or solutions, is an iterative, arduous task, involving intense, time-consuming effort. People who rush off to the keyboard and think they are going to build a knowledge system, probably will not–at least not until the preliminary planning and design work is accomplished.

In general, learning to use AI tools is similar to learning a new programming language. Within a week, the learner can build a system to perform some very simple tasks. Three months of work will render the learner able to build a reasonable-sized, practical system. But at least six months is necessary to reach virtuoso levels, where the user is facile at using all or most of the capabilities of the tool.

THE KNOWLEDGE SYSTEM BUILDING CYCLE

In general, there are four major steps to follow in building a knowledge system with microcomputer or large-scale AI tools. The steps are: analyze the problem, design the system, build a prototype, and incrementally test the prototype. These steps are equivalent to the classical engineering phases of software development: plan, design, edit and compile, and test (Figure 9-1). Only the details are changed.

AI practices		Software engineering practice
Analyze the problem	=	Plan
Design the system	=	Design
Build a prototype	=	Edit, code, and compile
Test the prototype	=	Test

Figure 9-1 Building an expert system

In the analysis step, the knowledge engineer, contractor, or user chooses a problem (Figure 9-2). Then he or she determines that the problem is suitable for AI solution, and figures out what type of expertise will be needed and who can effectively provide it. In a phase that overlaps the analysis and design phases, the knowledge engineer gathers the knowledge for the program.

Choose the problem
Determine the value of applying AI
Decide on the expert
Gather knowledge

Figure 9-2 Analysis stage

During the design phase, the knowledge engineer organizes the knowledge in a way that best corresponds to the experts' organization in working with it, and creates a skeletal structure for the knowledge system (Figure 9-3).

Organize knowledge
Gather more knowledge
Create skeletal structure

Figure 9-3 Design stage

For example, an investment planner expert might segregate criteria for recommendations to clients according to their salary brackets (Figure 9-4). Recommendations for clients in each salary bracket might be further subdivided according to preferences for secure rather than speculative investments. Under secure investments might be additional criteria for recommendations for blue-chip stocks and government certificates. A different investment planner might, instead, subdivide client criteria according to preferences for short-versus long-term gains, and then subdivide each of these categories in some way.

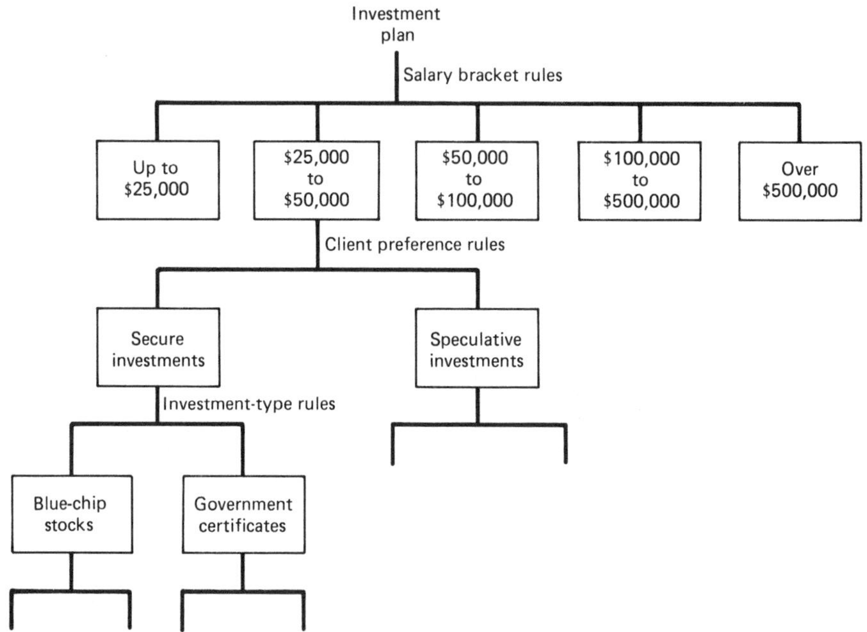

Figure 9-4 Skeletal structure for an investment advisory knowledge system.

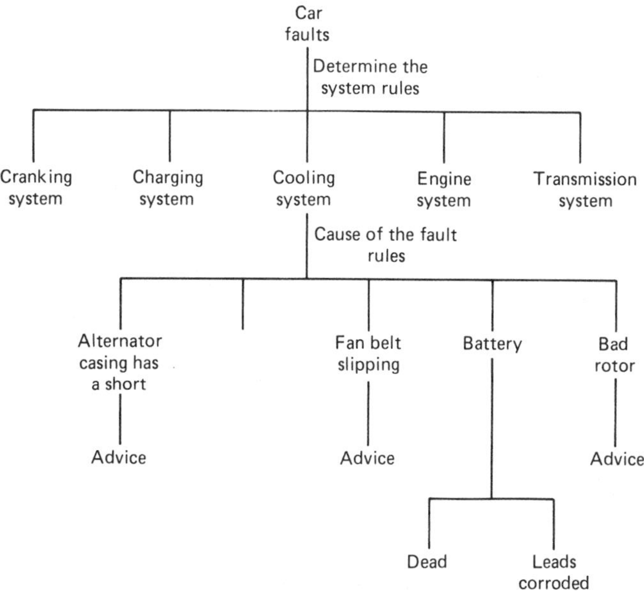

Figure 9-5 Skeletal structure for a knowledge-based automotive diagnostic system.

Automobile diagnostic experts might characterize car problems according to where the fault lies. First, they might figure out whether the fault is in the engine, transmission, cranking, charging, or some other car system (Figure 9-5). Once they pinpoint the faulty system, for example the charging system, in the next group of steps they might figure out whether the cause of the fault lies in the alternator, fan belt, battery, or other component in the charging system. If necessary, the expert, and through him or her the knowledge engineer, would further subdivide the hierarchical fault diagnostic structure until finally a sufficient level of detail is reached that supposes that the fault is that the alternator casing has a short or the battery leads are corroded.

Two types of tasks are performed during the next stage of building the prototype. In one task, the knowledge system designers fill in the detailed application information for each step of the hierarchy (Figure 9-6). Depending on the system and its knowledge representation methods, the details include diagnostic or other application rules, characteristics of physical structures, acceptable values that end users can enter, and other information necessary for the internal workings of the system. This information is written in whatever language is provided by the tool. Knowledge of these details allows the expert system to progress down the hierarchy by the reasoning strategies employed by the tool (forward chaining, backward chaining, or a combination) until it has concluded a specific diagnosis identified at the bottom of the hierarchy.

The second type of information entered during the building-the-prototype

Identify and enter goal

Code judgemental rules

Code control rules

Write user questions and allowable answers

Add more rules, questions, and allowable answers

Expand skeletal structure

Add still more knowledge

Figure 9-6 Building a prototype

phase is control information. This is contained in rules that control an actual end-user consultation by controlling the order in which both hypotheses and different lines of reasoning should be pursued and letting the system know when the problem has been solved.

Control rules are more sophisticated and more difficult to learn to use correctly than are rules about subject application knowledge, such as "IF the car won't start, THEN check to see that it has gas." For a very small or toy system, control rules are not needed because the knowledge system can simply examine every rule to see which apply to a particular problem. As the system grows progressively larger, this is impractical.

In the test-the-program step, the system designer challenges the knowledge system with several sample problems that it is supposed to be able to solve. The problems are identified by the expert (Figure 9-7).

If execution of any of the test cases produces erroneous results, it is necessary to go back to the expert. The expert can generally tell why the program produced the erroneous result and recommends what the knowledge system should know or do so as not to repeat the same mistake. This new knowledge is

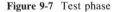

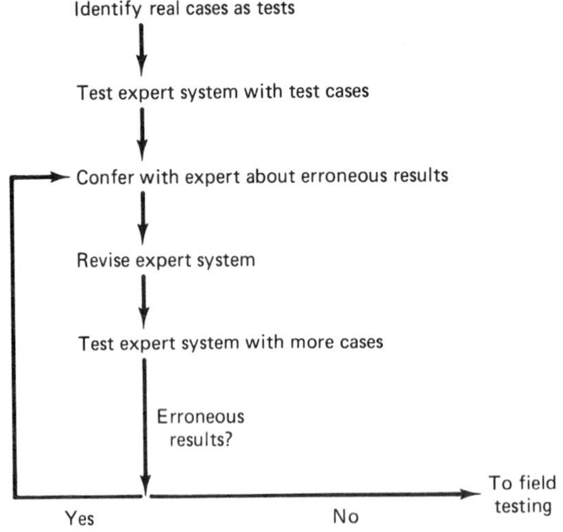

Figure 9-7 Test phase

encoded in the form of new rules and added to the system, which is tested again with more sample test cases.

When enough iterative testing, and incremental modification or addition of knowledge, produces a knowledge system that consistently provides accurate answers, advice, and diagnostics for a variety of test cases, it is ready to be tried in the field. Field testing gradually uncovers new cases that the knowledge system cannot handle, and new mistakes not previously realized. To handle the new cases and mistakes requires the addition of more rules. In this way the knowledge system gradually matures to the point where it can handle much of what human experts can handle.

BUILDING A PROTOTYPE

How to select and evaluate an application was discussed in Chapter 4, acquiring knowledge from experts in Chapter 9, and examples of successful or potential knowledge-based system applications are discussed in Volume II. In this chapter we therefore concentrate on how to build, test, and modify a prototype knowledge system using microcomputer-based AI application development tools.

To explain this development process, four different tools will demonstrate their methods of building four different knowledge systems. The tools are M.1 from Teknowledge, the Personal Consultant from Texas Instruments, Expert-Ease from Human Edge Software or Jeffrey Perrone & Associates, Inc., and RuleMaster from Radian Corp.

M.1

M.1 is a scaled-down version of certain large-scale AI tools. For the first demonstration example, M.1 will be used to built a simple prototype knowledge system, called system.car, to perform automotive diagnosis. The skeletal design for system.car is shown in Figure 9-5. The knowledge system built will consult with the user about a car's symptoms. Based on the symptoms, it will suggest the system in which the fault probably lies, and suggest tests to perform on components in that system. Depending on the test results, it will suggest the cause of the problem with the car and offer corrective advice.

Assuming that the analysis and design for a knowledge system has been completed, the primary task the tool user must perform in building the system is building a knowledge base. With M.1 any standard text editor can be used for this purpose.

The first item needed in an M.1 knowledge base is a goal. In a backward-chaining system such as M.1, the primary or top-level goal is normally a very general one, such as to provide advice to the user. During a consultation, the knowledge system looks for every rule which concludes that the advice to the user

```
M.1> list.

     kb-1: goal = cause-of-fault-in-charging-system.

     kb-2: if result-of-oscilloscope-test = straight-line
              and result-of-field-arc-test = hot-yellow
           then cause-of-fault-in-charging-system
                = alternator-casing-has-a-short.
```

Figure 9-8 Building a knowledge-based automotive diagnostic prototype

is such-and-such. Such-and-such may be a variable that stands for advice associated with the knowledge system's diagnostic conclusion identified at the bottom of the knowledge system hierarchy and concluded by several rules.

During execution, M.1 tries the different rules that conclude hypothesized causes of a fault to see which one has preconditions that can be satisfied. The conditional parts are satisfied, depending on the test results, symptoms, and the system containing the fault. By back chaining, M.1 explores the hierarchy looking for rules that conclude the symptoms and system, until finally it back-chains to a high enough point in the hierarchy to satisfy the preconditions, and therefore the conclusions, in a hierarchical path. In this way, M.1 verifies that the hypothesized cause, and advice to the user, is correct.

For simplicity in explaining, the initial prototype automotive diagnostic system illustrated will be a very small one whose goal is just to determine the cause of a fault in the charging system. This micro knowledge system will contain one goal, one rule, two questions, and two sets of acceptable values as answers to the questions. The system will then be expanded to show how a larger, more sopohisticated system might be built.

Step one in building the system.car knowledge base is to define a goal. For this micro-system, the goal defined is the cause of the fault in the charging system. To add this entry to the knowledge base the system designer types

```
>>add goal = cause-of-fault-in-charging-system.
```

Now the knowledge-based system needs some rules to help it achieve that goal. The automotive expert providing the knowledge for system.car has found that two particular tests, known as an oscilloscope test and a field arc test, performed on the charging system help determine whether or not there is a short in the alternator casing. The system designer therefore, encodes this knowledge in the form of a rule:

```
>>add if result-of-oscilloscope-test = straight-line
         and result-of-field-arc-test = hot-yellow
       then cause-of-fault-in-charging-system =
         alternator-casing-has-a-short.
```

Upon request, M.1 will list the entries in the knowledge base developed so far (Figure 9-8). To understand how interactive knowledge-based system devel-

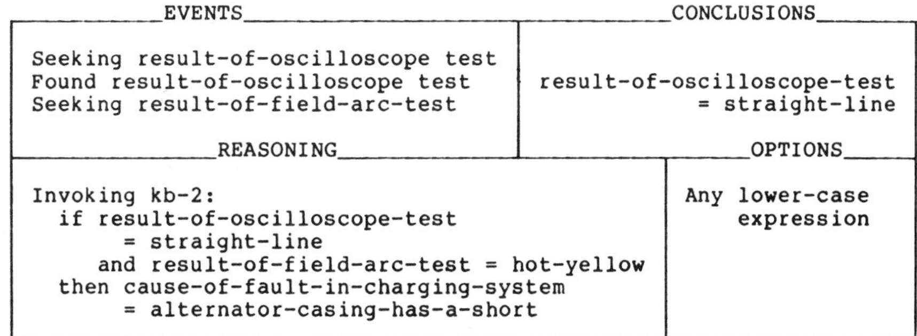
EVENTS
Seeking result-of-oscilloscope test
Found result-of-oscilloscope test
Seeking result-of-field-arc-test
CONCLUSIONS
result-of-oscilloscope-test
= straight-line
REASONING
Invoking kb-2:
if result-of-oscilloscope-test
= straight-line
and result-of-field-arc-test = hot-yellow
then cause-of-fault-in-charging-system
= alternator-casing-has-a-short
OPTIONS
Any lower-case
expression

```
What is the value of: result-of-oscilloscope-test?
>> straight-line.
>>What is the value of: result-of-field-arc-test?
```

Figure 9-9 Challenging the system

opment tools are used, how rapidly system prototypes can be built, and how easy it is to add knowledge incrementally, this automotive diagnostic knowledge system can be run right now, even though it has only two knowledge base entries. It will use its one rule to try to satisfy its goal. The M.1 tool provides a default format for asking users questions about test results, attributes, goals, or observations needed to satisfy conditions of a rule when the system cannot infer the information from other rules or facts. The default format is: "What is the value of (whatever is listed after the word *if*)?"

Execution of the one-rule, one-goal knowledge-based system is shown in Figure 9-9. As the system runs, M.1 conducts its user consultation in the lower half of the screen, while its interactive debugging environment displays a number of relevant facts in four windows on the upper half of the screen. The Events window shows significant events or occurrences such as results or attributes that M.1 has found or is seeking. The Reasoning window shows M.1's reasoning as it searches for a conclusion. Its reasoning consists of the rules currently being invoked or those that have already succeeded.

The Conclusions window displays the conclusions that M.1 has reached based on inference or answers from users. The Options window shows the answers that M.1 will accept from users.

The execution of the system reveals that based on the evidence at hand, the alternator casing has a short. Since knowledge base entry rule 2 did not specify a certainty factor in its conclusion, a certainty factor of 100 percent is assumed.

During the consultation, if the user had asked "why" the system was asking him or her a particular question, M.1 would have responded that it needed the answer to help determine if the rule being invoked was applicable in this consultation. In addition, as the M.1-based knowledge system executes, the

```
M.1> list.

     kb-1: goal = cause-of-fault-in-charging-system.

     kb-2: if result-of-oscilloscope-test = straight-line
              and result-of-field-arc-test = hot-yellow
           then cause-of-fault-in-charging-system
                = alternator-casing-has-a-short.

     kb-3: question(result-of-oscilloscope-test) ='
                Please perform a standard oscilloscope test.
                What type of pattern do you see?'.

     kb-4: legalvals(result-of-oscilloscope-test) =
               [straight-line, erratic-pattern, normal-arches,
                fluctuating-arches].

     kb-5: question(result-of-field-arc-test) =
                Turn on the ignition and pull out the filed
                connector to the alternator.  What type of
                flash do you see?'.

     kb-6: legalvals(result-of-field-arc-test) =
               [none, blue, hot-yellow].
```

Figure 9-10 Adding more knowledge base items

```
____________EVENTS______________________________________CONCLUSIONS__________
| Seeking result-of-field-arc-test      | cause-of-fault-in-charging-        |
| Found result-of-field-arc-test        |                        system      |
| Found cause-of-fault-in-charging-     |    = alternator-casing-has-        |
|                           system      |      a-short                       |
|                                       |                                    |
|__________________REASONING____________________________OPTIONS______________|
| Invoking kb-2                                        | none               |
|   if result-of-oscilloscope-test                     | blue               |
|        = straight-line                               | hot-yellow         |
|      and result-of-field-arc-test = hot-yellow       |                    |
|   then cause-of-fault-in-charging-system             |                    |
|        = alternator-casing-has-a-short               |                    |
|                                                      |                    |
|  kb-2 succeeded                                      |                    |
|______________________________________________________|____________________|

Please perform a standard oscilloscope test.  What type of pattern do
   you see?
>> straight-line.
Turn on the ignition and pull out the filed connector to the
   alternator.  What type of flash do you see?
>> hot-yellow.
   cause-of-fault-in-charging-system = alternator-casing-has-a-short
     (100%) because kb-2
```

Figure 9-11 Rechallenging the knowledge system

Reasoning window continuously changes to keep the user apprised of what the system is doing and why.

It is helpful to phrase more informative questions than the default format provides, for the knowledge base to ask the users about the results of tests or symptoms. It is also desirable to identify to the knowledge system a restricted group of appropriate answers or "legal values" the system is allowed to accept from users. Then, during a consultation, when M.1 asks questions of the users, it displays on the screen the possible answers from which to choose. Furthermore, the knowledge system checks the user's response against the list of permissible options and will not accept any other answers.

A listing of the modified knowledge base is shown in Figure 9-10. An execution of the modified system.car knowledge-based system with the programmer-phrased questions and the restrictions on users' answers is shown in Figure 9-11.

INCREMENTALLY ADDING RULES

Clearly, there are many possible causes of faults in the charging system. Therefore, the knowledge-based system will contain many rules about the different possibilities and questions and legal values for each rule.

The expert providing the knowledge for system.car knows three causes of faults in the charging system: the fan belt slipping, a short in the alternator casing, and a bad rotor. He also knows from experience that he can differentiate between these causes by observing the fan belt, noting the results of some standard tests, and examining some mechanical and electrical parts and connections in the car.

The knowledge system designer encodes these causes and the mechanic's methods for differentiating between them in the three rules listed in Figure 9-12 (kb-2, 7, and 10) and formulates questions and legal values to accompany the rules. As with the questions and legal values shown previously, the new rules and questions are simply added to the system incrementally and do not require a program redesign.

During an execution of the expanded knowledge system, M.1 checks each of the rules in numbered order. For example, it will first invoke knowledge base rule 2 and might note that the results of the oscilloscope test is a straight line but the field arc test gives no flash. Therefore, knowledge base rule 2 fails. Next, M.1 invokes knowledge base rule 7. If the user says that the fan belt does not rotate, knowledge base rule 7 fails, and knowledge base rule 10 is invoked.

The questions and legal values need not be in numbered order. Instead, once a rule is invoked and M.1 begins testing its preconditions, M.1 looks for other knowledge base entries that conclude values for the preconditions being tested or that contain the expressions in the preconditions. For example, when testing the condition "if result-of-oscilloscope-test = straight-line," M.1 will find the question asking about the result of the oscilloscope test and the entry containing the

```
M.1>  list.

      kb-1: goal = cause-of-fault-in-chargfng-system.

      kb-2: if result-of-oscilloscope-test = straight-line
               and result-of-field-arc-test = hot-yellow
            then cause-of-fault-in-charging-system
                 = alternator-casing-has-a-short.

      kb-3: question(result-of-oscilloscope-test) ='
                 Please perform a standard oscilloscope test.
                 What type of pattern do you see?'.

      kb-4: legalvals(result-of-oscilloscope-test) =
                [straight-line, erratic-pattern, normal-arches,
                 fluctuating-arches].

      kb-5: question(result-of-field-arc-test) ='
                 Turn on the ignition and pull out the filed
                 connector to the alternator.  What type of
                 flash do you see?'.

      kb-6: legalvals(result-of-field-arc-test) =
                [none, blue, hot-yellow].

      kb-7: if fan-belt-rotates
               then cause-of-fault-in-charging-system
                    = fan-belt-slipping.

      kb-8: question(fan-belt-rotates) = '
               Try rotating the pulley attached to the alternator.
               Does it turn?'.

      kb-9: legalvals(fan-belt-rotates) =
               [yes, no].

      kb-10: if result of oscilloscope-test = straight-line
                and result-of-field-arc-test = none
                and field-connector-supply-ok
                and field-connector-grounded
                and not(alternator-brushes-look-bad)
                and copper-slip-rings-connected
             then cause-of-fault-in-charging-system = bad-rotor.
```

Figure 9-12 Adding more rules and related knowledge-base items.

legal values for the result of the oscilloscope test. It will also find any other rules that conclude the result of this test.

M.1 does not go on to testing the next precondition or next rule until it has obtained all the information it needs from these related knowledge base entries, either by noting facts, inferring information, or asking the user. This persistence in one subject before going on to another promotes efficiency and is similar to the way in which human beings perform diagnosis, especially in large applications that seek many possible fault causes in many subsystems. Human beings do not generally handle different systems, seek test results, and ask questions haphazardly and randomly.

CONTROLLING A CONSULTATION

As more rules are added to a knowledge base, it becomes increasingly more inefficient to test every relevant and irrelevant rule. For example, if a problem has been determined to be in a cooling system, there is little sense in cycling through all the rules to test out parts of the transmission and engine block. To avoid cycling through all the irrelevant rules, system.car first gathers initial symptoms and determines in which system the fault probably lies. Then it performs different tasks and subtasks to test out subsystems and components within the probable faulty system. Finally, it not only determines the cause of the fault, but also displays recommended corrective action.

To ensure that the diagnostic procedures are carried out in this order, users write control rules in addition to judgmental rules. Unlike judgmental rules, control rules have nothing to do with the subject matter of the consultation. Display rules that display greetings or advice to users, as well as rules that tell the knowledge system that a consultation is over, are examples of control rules.

To provide efficiency as system.car is further expanded, a new version will be written which has a single control rule that controls the consultation, in conjunction with the knowledge base system's top-level goal and subgoals generated during system execution. A top-level goal is the overall goal of a knowledge system. A top-level goal might simply be for the consultation to be over, in which case the knowledge system will perform all the diagnostic chores necessary for the consultation to be over.

The top-level goal for system.car, listed below, is to provide advice for a consumer:

```
goal = advice-for-consumer.
```

System.car's single control rule is the following rule, which concludes advice-for-consumer.

```
if system = X
    and cause-of-fault-in-X = Y
    and recommendation-for-Y = Z
then advice-for-consumer = Z.
```

Unlike the judgmental rules seen so far, this rule contains variables: X, Y, and Z. X stands for any system. Y can be replaced by any fault in the system assigned to X. Z represents a recommendation, or advice for the consumer, for the cause-of-fault represented by Y.

To conclude the appropriate advice for the consumer, system.car must satisfy the three preconditions in the control rule, in the order in which they appear. Thus the control rule determines the sequencing of the major steps in the diagnostic process.

```
GOAL

  kb-1: goal = advice-for-consumer.

ADVICE-FOR-CONSUMER

  kb-2: if system = X
             and cause-of-fault-in-X = Y
             and recommendation-for-Y = Z
        then advice-for-consumer = Z.

CAUSE-OF-FAULT-IN-CHARGING-SYSTEM

  kb-3: if fan-belt-rotates
             then cause-of-fault-in-charging-system
                  = fan-belt-slipping.

  kb-4: if result-of-oscilloscope-test = straight-line
             and result-of-field-arc-test = hot-yellow
        then cause-of-fault-in-charging-system
             = alternator-casing-has-a-short.

  kb-5: if result-of-oscilloscope-test = straight-line
             and result-of-field-arc-test = none
             and field-connector-supply-ok
             and field-connector-grounded
             and not(alternator-brushes-look-bad)
             and copper-slip-rings-connected
        then cause-of-fault-in-charging-system = bad rotor.

FAN-BELT-ROTATES

  kb-6: question(fan-belt-rotates) = '
             Try rotating the pulley attached to the alternator.
             Does it turn?'.

  kb-7: legalvals(fan-belt-rotates) =
             [yes, no].

RESULT-OF-CRANKING-TEST

  kb-8: question(result-of-cranking-test) = '
             Try cranking the car.  What happens?'.

  kb-9: legalvals(result-of-cranking-test) =
             [dead-silence, sluggish-cranking, vibrates,
              grinds, starter-runs, cranks-normally,
              car-starts].

RESULT-OF-FIELD-ARC-TEST

  kb-10: question(result-of-field-arc-test) = '
             Turn on the ignition and pull out the filed
             connector to the alternator.  What type of
             flash do you see?'.
  kb-11: legalvals(result-of-field-arc-test) =
             [none, blue, hot-yellow].

RESULT-OF-OSCILLOSCOPE-TEST

  kb-12: question(result-of-oscilloscope-test) ='
              Please perform a standard oscilloscope test.
               What type of pattern do you see?'.

  kb-13: legalvals(result-of-oscilloscope-test) =
              [straight-line, erratic-pattern, normal-arches,
               fluctuating-arches].
```

Figure 9-13 Incrementally adding more knowledge.

```
SYSTEM

  kb-14: if symptom = car-wont-start
             and result-of-cranking-test = grinds
             or result-of-cranking-test = vibrates
             then system = cranking-system cf 80%.

  kb-15: if symptom = battery-uses-too-much-water
             then system = cooling-system cf 80%.

  kb-16: if symptom = car-wont-start
             and result-of-cranking-test = dead-silence
             then system = charging-system cf 80%.

SYMPTOM

  kb-17: question(symptom) = '
           What is wrong with the car?'.

RECOMMENDATION-FOR-X

  kb-18: recommendation-for-alternator-casing-has-a-short = '
           The casing of the alternator is shorted out.  You
           will have to replace the alternator with a new one'.

  kb-19: recommendation-for-bad-rotor = '
           The alternator rotor is bad.  Please replace the
           rotor with a new one.  For convenience, you may
           prefer to replace the entire alternator'.

  kb-20: recommendation-for-fan-belt-slipping = '
           The fan belt is loose and needs tightening.  If the
           fan belt shows signs of wear, then it should be
           replaced'.
```

Figure 9-13 (Cont.)

Each of the three preconditions–determining the system, finding the cause of the fault, and making the recommendation–are actually subgoals of system.car. To satisfy these subgoals, system.car backward chains through the rules in the knowledge base that conclude the subgoals.

For example, to determine the system in which the fault lies, system.car has a set of rules. Similarly, a set of rules and knowledge base entries are used to determine the cause-of-fault in the system.

Figure 9-13 shows system.car's knowledge base, which is a modified, expanded version of the original six-item knowledge base.* Using this knowledge base, system.car conducts the user consultation show in Figure 9-14. To consult with the knowledge-based system, the user simply types in "load system.car." This causes system.car to go looking for its top-level goal, which is advice-for-consumer. It then looks for a rule that concludes advice-for-consumer, and finds its control rule.

The control rule says that the first thing that must be done during this consultation and diagnostic process is to determine the system in which the fault

*Knowledge base entries 1-20 supplied by Teknowledge.

```
    What is wrong with the car?

>> car-wont-start.

    Try cranking the car.  What happens?

>> dead-silence.

    Try rotating the pulley attached to the alternator.

    Does it turn?

>> no.

    Please perform a standard oscilloscope test.

    What type of pattern do you see?

>> straight-line.

    Turn on the ignition and pull out the filed connector to the

    alternator.  What type of flash do you see?

>> hot-yellow.

System.car has reached the following conclusions about
advice-for-consumer:

     advice-for-consumer = '

      The casing of the alternator is shorted out.  You will

      have to replace the alternator with a new one'
```

Figure 9-14 Interactive automotive diagnosis consultation.

lies. Identification of this first required step is the result of "system = X" being the first condition that must be satisfied in the control rule. Three rules, kb-14, kb-15, and kb-16, conclude system = cranking-system, cooling-system, and charging-system.

System.car will try to satisfy the conditions in these three rules to conclude which system contains the fault. The system concluded becomes the X in the control rule.

Knowledge base rules 14 and 15 fail, but kb-16, which concludes that the fault is in the charging system, succeeds. It is possible, however, that evidence might be contradictory or might indicate that the fault could be in one of several systems. If this happens, M.1 will examine each system in turn, looking for a diagnosis.

With the faulty system now identified, system.car continues with the second precondition of its control rule, equivalent to the second step of the consultation, and tries to determine the cause-of-fault-in-charging-system. Three rules conclude the cause-of-fault-in-charging-system: kb-3, kb-4, and kb-5. Of these, kb-3 fails, but since kb-4 succeeds, the cause of the fault is determined to be a short in the alternator casing and there is no need to test kb-5.

The second precondition of the control rule is now satisfied and system.car continues with the third and final consultation step. The third precondition calls for identifying a recommendation for corrective action for Y, which has been determined to be "= alternator-casing-has-a-short." The appropriate recommendation is stated in kb-18.

With all three preconditions of the control rule satisfied, the action or "then" part of the rule is executed and system.car offers the recommendation as advice to the consumer. Like mechanics, however, a full-scale knowledge system might have less than 100 percent confidence in its diagnosis. Unless it is certain of its recommendation, M.1 repeats control rule steps 1 and 2 for other implicated automotive systems and may make multiple recommendations with varying degress of certainty.

DEBUGGING

At this point, it is important to note that although rules can easily be added, incrementally, it is not accurate to say that addition of a new rule does not affect the rest of the knowledge base. Some ways a knowledge base can be affected are illustrated by the following diagnosis of a bad battery.

Automotive mechanics know that if a car does not start, the problem may be a bad battery. Yet, during several consultations with system.car, which did not succeed in diagnosing or correcting a problem in a car that would not start, a bad battery was never suggested as a possible cause of the fault.

A sophisticated, interactive user interface and debugging tools are essential for AI environments, and M.1 is no exception. M.1's rules and other knowledge base entries are automatically indexed as they are entered in the system. Consequently, a scan of system.car's relevant knowledge base rules can be obtained by asking M.1's debugger to display on the screen all the rules which conclude that the cause of the fault is a bad battery. The display reveals that there are no rules that conclude that the cause of the fault is a bad battery. Therefore, the system designer adds the following rule:

```
kb-21: if level-of-charge = low
          and battery-loses-charge
       then cause-of-fault-in-charging-system = bad-battery.
```

A consultation with system.car is rerun but still does not conclude bad-battery as the cause of the fault. Therefore, the system designer reexamines the preconditions of the rule just added. The first precondition tests "if level-of-charge = low."

Upon request, M.1's debugger will show the value of any expression for a particular consultation and will also display all rules and facts in the knowledge base that contain information about or conclude a value for an expression in question. For this consultation, the system debugger shows that the expression "level-of-charge" had no value. Examination shows, there are no rules or questions that pertain to level-of-charge. Therefore, another rule is needed that concludes that the level-of-charge is low, so rule kb-22 is added at the end of the knowledge base.

```
kb-22: if battery-voltage-when-motor-is-off = low
          or battery-pH = high
       then level-of-charge = low.
```

Still another rule, kb-23, is needed to conclude the second condition of rule kb-21:

```
kb-23: if current-under-load-after-trickle-charge = low
       then battery-loses-charge.
```

EXPANDING THE KNOWLEDGE SYSTEM

More additions and changes must be made to the knowledge base before system.car can diagnose a bad battery. Questions are needed to ask about the battery voltage, the battery acidity (pH), and the current under load after the trickle charge. In addition, legal values are needed for each of those answers.

The addition of rules to diagnose bad batteries also affects entries already in the knowledge base. For example, the system designer must give system.car some clue about a potential battery problem and make sure it knows that the battery is part of the charging system. To provide this information, it is necessary to modify rule kb-16 that concludes that the system is the charging system.

The mechanic says that clicks heard when cranking the car is a clue to battery problems. Knowing this, the system designer asks M.1 to display rule kb-16 and modifies it to understand the relationship between clicks heard during a cranking test and a fault in the charging system. The modified rule reads as follows:

```
kb-16: if symptom = car-wont-start
          and result-of-cranking-test = dead-silence
          or result-of-cranking-test = clicks
          then system = charging system (cf 80%).
```

A scan of the question related to the cranking test shows that the original knowledge base question is still appropriate to encompass the new information. However, the question will not accept the result, "clicks." Therefore, the system designer must modify the legal values that relate to the result of cranking so that the program accepts "clicks" as an answer and shows it as an allowable choice in the options window.

At last, system.car has a complete hierarchical path in its knowledge base structure that culminates in a diagnosis of a bad battery, as well as all the related questions and appropriate legal values to handle the responses.

ADDING EXTRA FEATURES

There are several other things that knowledge system developers ought to do to make system.car as similar as possible in its capabilities to the automobile mechanic. For example, the user might not know the answer to some of the mechanic's questions. Under these circumstances, if mechanics cannot easily measure or observe the requested information, they find a way to continue their diagnosis in some other manner, without it. M.1 works similarly by looking for an alternative reasoning method so that it can continue the consultation without the requested information. For example, in addition to rule kb-22, system.car might have a second rule which also concludes that the level-of-charge-is-low:

```
kb-24: if current-under-load = low
       then level-of-charge = low.
```

If the user answers "unknown" to both kb-22's battery voltage and battery-pH questions, M.1 searches for and discovers kb-24. If it knows the current-under-load, it can use kb-24 instead of kb-22 to conclude the level of charge.

Alternatively, the user can provide a rule about what to do if an answer is unknown. Such a rule might provide several possible diagnoses, attaching a certainty factor to each. This certainty factor is not equivalent to a confidence factor as used in probability and statistics. It is the expert's expression of confidence in a diagnosis, based on his or her experience.

For example, during a consultation, a user might know that the battery charge is low, but might not know, or have the time to find out, whether the battery will hold a charge. Rule kb-25, shown below, can deal with the unknown case.

```
kb-25: if battery-hold-a-charge is unknown
    then cause-of-fault-in-charging-system =
              bad battery (cf 40%)
         and cause-of-fault-in-charging-system =
              voltage-regulator-problem (cf 20%)
         and cause-of-fault-in-charging-system =
              corroded-contacts (cf 20%)
         and cause-of-fault-in-charging-system =
              not(alternator-charging-battery) (cf 20%).
```

During a consultation, if a user answers "unknown" to the question about the current-under-load-after-trickle-charge, system.car will seek kb-25 that pertains to this unknown answer. The conclusions in kb-25 will be passed to kb-23, which will provide the user with kb-25's possible causes of the car fault, together with the attached certainty factors. In some ways, this answer is equivalent to a mechanic invoking his or her own certainty factors and telling the customer that he (the mechanic) "gave the battery, which was low, a 30 minute charge," and exhorting him (the customer) to "drive the car for a while and bring it back if it shows further problems." The again-expanded, modified knowledge base is shown in Figure 9-15.

```
GOAL
  kb-1: goal = advice-for-consumer.

ADVICE-FOR-CONSUMER
  kb-2: if system = X
           and cause-of-fault-in-X = Y
           and recommendation-for-Y = Z
        then advice-for-consumer = Z.

CAUSE-OF-FAULT-IN-CHARGING-SYSTEM

  kb-3: if fan-belt-rotates
           then cause-of-fault-in-charging-system
                = fan-belt-slipping.

  kb-4: if result-of-oscilloscope-test = straight-line
           and result-of-field-arc-test = hot-yellow
        then cause-of-fault-in-charging-system
             = alternator-casing-has-a-short.

  kb-5: if result-of-oscilloscope-test = straight-line
           and result-of-field-arc-test = none
           and field-connector-supply-ok
           and field-connector-grounded
           and not(alternator-brushes-look-bad)
           and copper-slip-rings-connected
        then cause-of-fault-in-charging-system = bad/rotor.

FAN-BELT-ROTATES

  kb-6: question(fan-belt-rotates) = '
           Try rotating the pulley attached to the alternator.
           Does it turn?'.

  kb-7: legalvals(fan-belt-rotates) =
           [yes, no].

RESULT-OF-CRANKING-TEST

  kb-8: question(result-of-cranking-test) = '
           Try cranking the car.  What happens?'.

  kb-9: legalvals(result-of-cranking-test) =
           [dead-silence, clicks, sluggish-cranking,
            vibrates, grinds, starter-runs,
            cranks-normally, car-starts].
```

Figure 9-15 Expanding the knowledge system.

```
RESULT-OF-FIELD-ARC-TEST

  kb-10: question(result-of-field-arc-test) = '
           Turn on the ignition and pull out the filed
           connector to the alternator.  What type of
           flash do you see?'.

   kb-11: legalvals(result-of-field-arc-test) =
            [none, blue, hot-yellow].

RESULT-OF-OSCILLOSCOPE-TEST

   kb-12: question(result-of-oscilloscope-test) ='
             Please perform a standard oscilloscope test.
             What type of pattern do you see?'.

  kb-13: legalvals(result-of-oscilloscope-test) =
            [straight-line, erratic-pattern, normal-arches,
             fluctuating-arches].

SYSTEM

  kb-14: if symptom = car-wont-start
            and result-of-cranking-test = grinds
                or result-of-cranking-test = vibrates
         then system = cranking-system cf 80%.

  kb-15: if symptom = battery-uses-too-much-water
         then system = cooling-system cf 80%.

  kb-16: if symptom = car-wont-start
            and result-of-cranking-test = dead-silence
            or result-of-cranking-test = clicks
         then system = charging-system cf 80%.

SYMPTOM

  kb-17: question(symptom) = '
           What is wrong with the car?'.

RECOMMENDATION-FOR-X

  kb-18: recommendation-for-alternator-casing-has-a-short = '
           The casing of the alternator is shorted out.  You
           will have to replace the alternator with a new one'.

  kb-19: recommendation-for-bad-rotor = '
           The alternator rotor is bad.  Please replace the
           rotor with a new one.  For convenience, you may
           prefer to replace the entire alternator'.

  kb-20: recommendation-for-fan-belt-slipping = '
           The fan belt is loose and needs tightening.  If the
           fan belt shows signs of wear, then it should be
           replaced'.

BAD-BATTERY

  kb-21: if level-of-charge = low
          and battery-loses-charge
         then cause-of-fault-in-charging-system = bad-battery.


LEVEL-OF-CHARGE

  kb-22: if battery-voltage-when-motor-is-off = low
            or battery-pH = high
         then level-of-charge = low.
```

Figure 9-15 (Cont.)

```
BATTERY-HOLD-A-CHARGE

   kb-23: if current-under-load-after-trickle-charge = low
             then battery-loses-charge.

LEVEL-OF-CHARGE

   kb-24: if current-under-load = low
             then level-of-charge = low.

UNCERTAIN ANSWER

   kb-25: if battery-hold-a-charge is unknown
          then cause-of-fault-in-charging-system =
                    bad-battery (cf 40%)
               and cause-of-fault-in-charging-system =
                    voltage-regulator-problem (cf 20%)
               and cause-of-fault-in-charging-system =
                    corroded-contacts (cf 20%)
               and cause-of-fault-in-charging-system =
                    not(alternator-charging-battery) (cf 20%).

BATTERY-VOLTAGE-WITH-MOTOR-OFF

    kb-26: question(battery-voltage-with-motor-off) = '
              Measure the voltage of the battery with the motor off.
              What is the voltage?'.

    kb-27: legalvals(battery-voltage-with-motor-off) =
                [low, okay].

BATTERY PH

    kb-28: question(battery-pH) = '
              Measure the acidity of the battery?  What is it?'.

    kb-29: legalvals(battery-pH) =
                [high, okay].

CURRENT-UNDER-LOAD-AFTER-TRICKLE-CHARGE

    kb-30: question(current-under-load-after-trickle-charge) = '
              Charge the battery for 10 hours.  Measure the current
              that it can deliver.  What is it?.

    kb-31: legalvals(current-under-load-after-trickle-charge) =
                [low, regular].

CURRENT-UNDER-LOAD

    kb-32: question(current-under-load) = '
              Measure the current the car can deliver under load?
              What is it?'.

    kb-33: legalvals(current-under-load) =
                [low, regular].
```

Figure 9-15 (Cont.)

LARGER KNOWLEDGE SYSTEMS

Building the knowledge system prototype with application development tools is not a cryptic, abstract experience. As seen, however, it entails a lot of logistics work when entries are added to the knowledge base—more as the system becomes larger because more entries are relevant. Worse, adding new knowledge base entries may require more knowledge acquisition to satisfy new rule conditions. Or it may require the system designer to act the role of automotive mechanic (or other domain expert) in order to add enough knowledge to coordinate all the new and existing rules with each other.

The large amount of logistics and knowledge coordination is one reason for partitioning the knowledge system into small, manageable blocks and then dealing with each block separately. In addition, not only do system designers find it more efficient, but so does M.1, and that enhances performance.

As a knowledge-based system becomes much larger, even partitioning the system does not make it manageable enough. The embedding of control of the program in the rules is one reason. Some rules are solely control rules such as system.car's kb-2, and specify the order of a consultation. But for large, complex systems, control embedded in rules is inadequate because it may be desirable to change the order of the consultation based on the way the consultation is proceeding. With a large knowledge system, the ability to change the order of the consultation avoids cycling through a lot of rules that the system has determined during a consultation to be irrelevant. In a large system, this avoidance makes a big difference in system efficiency and user boredom (the time required to cycle through rules is perceptible).

With M.1, control information that changes the order of a consultation midstream is interwoven in the rules. Unfortunately, this means that the rules that previously contained nicely described pieces of knowledge now also contain additional information to force control to happen in a certain way. Combining control and application information makes the rules less understandable, and maintaining the knowledge base becomes correspondingly more difficult. In addition, building control knowledge into a rule and subject matter limits the various ways and situations in which the rules might be used.

Frequently, AI programmers control their knowledge systems by escaping into the underlying language, which usually is Lisp. Lisp allows them to write code that directs the program to do this, then do that, then loop on some step and perform it iteratively a certain number of times.

Lisp has the disadvantage, however, of being a language less easily understood by nonexperts than the English-like language of AI tools. Also, setting up explanation facilities for the user to understand why some Lisp code performed a certain way requires a translation between Lisp and English, which is inefficient.

Confronting this control problem, some AI tools, among them S.1 (also from Teknowledge), have added a special procedural language for programmers to specify control for large programs in a conventional, block-structured manner.

This "control block language," as it is called in S.1, contains block-structured statements such as BEGIN-END, IF-THEN, and LOOP.

M.1 had a top-level goal and a top-level control rule. S.1 has a top-level control block. Like M.1's top-level control rule, the top-level control block specifies a sequence of actions to perform. The control block, however, may invoke rules, examine facts, execute other control blocks, and modify the order of the consultation.

Similar control sequences can be performed with M.1, by coding control in rules. Experience has shown that programmers do not mind writing 10 to 20 control rules in a small- to medium-sized system such as M.1 handles. As the knowledge base grows, however, especially to 500 rules or more, many programmers prefer a more procedural programming language for control rules. In particular, the ability to write conventional loops and condition-branch statements directly saves them much time and planning.

THE PERSONAL CONSULTANT

Like M.1, Texas Instruments' Personal Consultant is a scaled-down version of large-scale AI application development tools. It comes in three varieties: PC Easy, and two versions of Personal Consultant Plus. PC Easy, is a simplified PC-based version for learners. Learners can graduate to the more sophisticated PC-resident Personal Consultant Plus. The other version of Personal Consultant

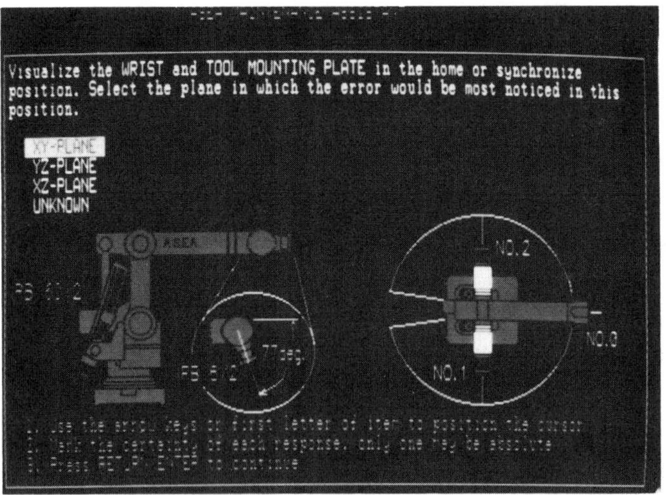

Figure 9-16 Personal Consultant is a menu- and window-oriented knowledge-system development tool that prompts users for rules, parameters, properties, and other information required.

Plus runs on the Explorer (TI's Lisp machine) where it provides access to Lisp machine features. All three Personal Consultant versions are compatible, however, allowing users to move between the versions depending on whether they need a delivery environment or more extensive capabilities.

In many ways, the Personal Consultant Plus and M.1 are similar. Both tools support an English-like rule-entry language, multi-valued parameters (parameters that can have multiple values), certainty factors, explanation facilities, and legal values (for restricting the values that the knowledge system will accept). Both systems provide access to Ashton Tate's dBase II and dBase III. And both systems are primarily rule-based, backward chaining knowledge systems.

The systems are also different. For example, Personal Consultant is a menu- and pop-up window-oriented system. It prompts users for the IF and THEN parts of rules, parameters, properties, user prompts, and other information required. As Figure 9-16 shows, the Personal Consultant also supports bit-mapped graphics, which Ford Motor Company uses extensively in its knowledge system that diagnoses problems with ASEA robots. In addition, the Personal Consultant supports several features, such as meta knowledge (knowledge about how to apply knowledge), and active values (procedures that automatically execute when a parameter acquires a certain value), that previously were characteristic of Lisp machines.

PC TOOLS GET SOME LISP-MACHINE-LIKE FEATURES

Besides being rule-based, Personal Consultant is a frame-like system. It is frame-like in that it satisfies Marvin Minsky's original definition of frames which is a structure that organizes and groups together related knowledge. However, it does not support many of the inheritance and inference techniques that AI developers have come to expect of frame-based systems.

With frame-based inheritance techniques, AI developers can define frames to be generic, somewhat specific, or an instance (a specific occurrence). The more specific frames inherit attributes from more generic frames. This allows a knowledge system to infer a lot about an instance frame as soon as the system developer defines the generic frame.

For example, a truck is a vehicle, therefore a truck has a motor in it. This fact need not be explicitly stored because the truck frame inherits the property of "motor-in-it" from the vehicle frame. Furthermore, a frame-based knowledge system infers that a Ford pick-up truck has a motor in it, because the Ford truck is an instance of the more generic truck frame. Many other types of information can also be inferred because frame-based knowledge systems allow system developers to specify that an instance frame inherit only certain attributes, override others with its own unique attributes, or inherit attributes from multiple parent frames to get a frame with the behavior of all the parents.

Personal Consultant does not support this kind of inheritance for frames. All frames defined for Personal Consultant are generic. The frames have parameters, which are the equivalent of slots. During a consultation, parameters acquire values, based on a situation. As a parameter acquires different values, it essentially becomes a dynamically-created instance of the frame.

Suppose, for example, system.car (developed with M.1) was developed with Personal Consultant. The system might have a generic frame about problems starting a car. During a consultation, system.car would ask the user about the type of car problem occurring. If the user responds, a "start" problem, Personal Consultant then creates an instance of the start frame. Parameters (or slots) in this instance will have the values that the user enters during the consultation.

The Personal Consultant-based system.car then chains through all its rules to satisfy the goal in that frame. After system.car offers its repair advice, it again asks the user if there still is a start problem. If the answer is yes, system.car creates another instance of the start problem and fills in all the parameters in the instance with new values.

BUILDING A KNOWLEDGE SYSTEM

The first step in building system.car (or any application) using the Personal Consultant is to decompose the problem into frames. The same skeletal design used for the M.1-based system.car, also defines the frames to be used for the Personal Consultant-based system.car (see Figure 9-5).

For each frame created, the developer must also define a group of properties to describe the features of the frame and to control various aspects of the consultation (Figure 9-17). Frame properties include goals, user prompts, INITIALDATA (data that the user should supply when a frame is first activated), TRANSLATION (a phrase to describe the frame), and DISPLAYRESULTS (which specifies whether or not to do so).

Rules, parameters, and their properties also must be defined for each frame. "If", "Then", and TRANSLATION are among the properties that rules have. TRANSLATION is the programmer-defined translation of a rule or parameter from a language that the system understands into English that will be displayed to the user. That translation is particularly important because it is used to debug the knowledge system interactively with a domain expert who does not understand computer language. A parameter's properties include TYPE (the kind of values a parameter can have, such as single-valued, positive number), TRANSLATION, PROMPT, HELP, EXPECT (or legal values), active values, and access methods.

Active-values and access methods are features normally found in large-scale tools. An active-value monitors a parameter and whenever the parameter takes on a new value, the active value triggers the execution of a specified procedure. Typically, the procedure, called an access method, forces the value of another parameter to change. The advantage of active values and access methods is that they allow developers to write knowledge systems in which data changes, rather than rules, control the execution of the specified procedures.

Although active-values and methods are often used for tasks such as debugging a knowledge base, most commonly they are used to graphically display

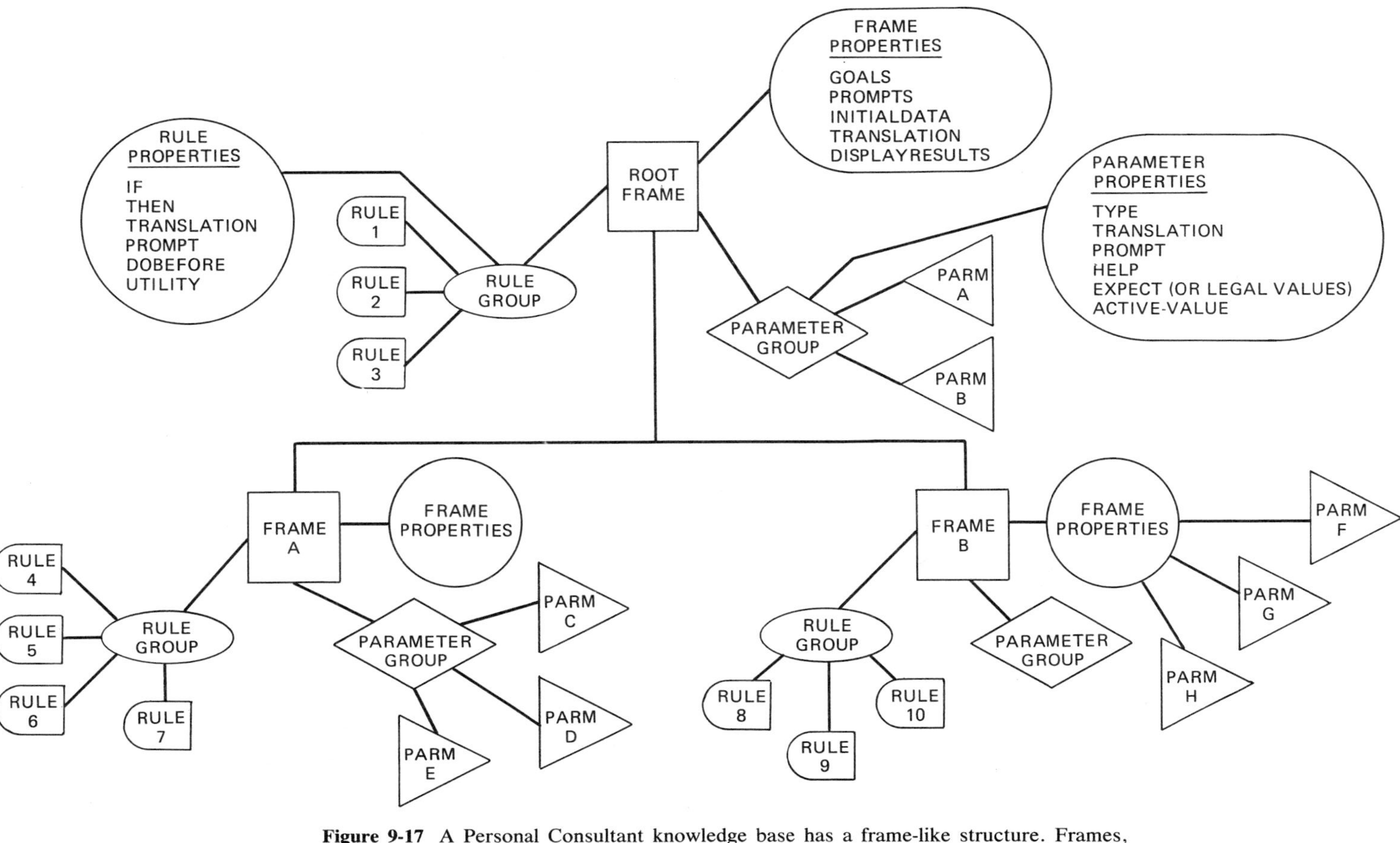

Figure 9-17 A Personal Consultant knowledge base has a frame-like structure. Frames, parameters, and rules each have their own sets of properties.

changing data in a system. For example, an active value might monitor a parameter such as temperature, a stock trading price, or the angular position of the robot arm shown in Fig. 9-16. These parameter values might be displayed graphically in a thermometer icon, bar graph, or robot arm diagram, respectively. Then whenever the value of the temperature, stock-trading price, or robot arm position changed, the active value would trigger execution of a procedure to change the graphical display accordingly.

ONE REASON WHY SOME KNOWLEDGE SYSTEMS FAIL

A process-control expert and a knowledge engineer developed a knowledge-based, real-time process-control application to troubleshoot a critical, very complex, plating operation. The system was completed and made operational. From the expert's viewpoint, however, trouble began early in the troubleshooting process when it was realized that the knowledge system required large amounts of questions and time to get the information that the expert gathered in a few minutes. Similar problems continued through the entire data entry process because the knowledge system asked a lot of questions and required an answer to every one. Still other problems were the lack of a direct connection to shop-floor machines and poor performance, because the knowledge system had to check every permutation of the rules.

Although this knowledge system was operational and worked successfully, in the end it was abandoned. The expert considered the use of the expert system more effort than doing the job traditionally, so he revamped the process and solved the problem with hard wired techniques. Among the conclusions drawn from the post mortems was the probability of minimizing the expert's effort if the knowledge system could control the sequence in which questions are asked and ask only for the information needed to solve the problems.

Such a capability requires "meta knowledge." Large-scale tools support meta knowledge. So does the PC-based GoldWorks (from Gold Hill Computers) and Personal Consultant.

Metaknowledge, in Personal Consultant, consists of meta-rules and two rule properties: DOBEFORE and UTILITY. Meta-rules determine how to modify the list of ordinary knowledge rules (called object-rules) so Personal Consultant can use the knowledge base more efficiently. The DOBEFORE property is a list of rules the system should try before trying the current rule. The UTILITY property value for a rule is a rating of how important the rule is in satisfying a goal.

When Personal Consultant tries to solve a problem, it retrieves a list of rules relevant to a current goal. It also determines if any meta-rules are relevant to that goal. The following are two Personal Consultant meta-rules from a TI assets and liabilities knowledge system.

If 1) determination how to acquire the asset is known, and
2) put any OBJRULES which meet the condition: lease is to

be a modifiable option lease is mentioned in the rule
into SET-1, and
3) put any OBJRULES which meet the condition: lease is to
be a straight lease is mentioned in the rule into SET-1,
Then DOBEFORE is assigned the values: (VALUE-OF-SET-1)

IF: CANNOT-BORROW AND PRESERVES-CREDIT AND PRESERVES-CASH
THEN:
FINANCE-IT = TXTG1
UTILITY: 5

These two meta-rules either reorder the rules that Personal Consultant considers so that it reaches the most relevant rules first, or they decrease the number of rules Personal Consultant needs to consider to satisfy a goal. Either way, they increase the efficiency of the knowledge base and, in that way, increase performance.

TABLE-BASED AI TOOLS

The accuracy and completeness of the knowledge base determine how well a knowledge system performs. In many business and industrial knowledge systems, not only the cost but also the timeliness of acquiring the knowledge base dominates other knowledge system building factors.

The AI application development tools discussed so far require a person to act as a knowledge engineer and, over an extended period of time, to interview experts, iteratively extract knowledge, organize it, and code it. The knowledge acquisition process is human-intensive, time-consuming, and in some fields where the knowledge changes rapidly, the knowledge base may be partially obsolete before the knowledge system is completed. The problem is that the knowledge acquisition process constitutes a bottleneck.

One way to improve the efficiency of knowledge acquisition is to characterize various aspects of knowledge in spreadsheet-like tables from which the knowledge system induces its own rules. There are several advantages to the spreadsheet table format. People are familiar with it. It is easy to use and consequently, nonprogrammers, rather than knowledge engineers, can rapidly build or modify the knowledge base instead of extracting knowledge over time. The system that is produced from the tables is a dialogue system which, like other expert consultative systems, conducts a dialogue with the user and suggests advice based on questions and answers.

To develop a knowledge system with a table-based tool, users enter straightforward facts and resulting decisions that arise during their routine work. For example, a real-estate agent recommends that a client buy a four-bedroom, colonial-style house located in the Beverly Hills section of California and costing

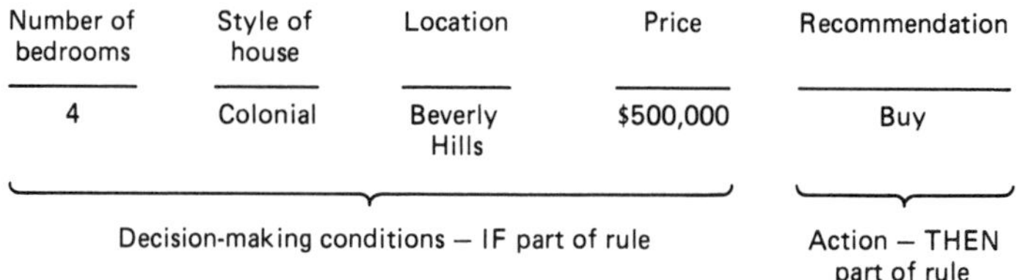

Number of bedrooms
Style of house
Location
Price
Recommendation
4
Colonial
Beverly Hills
$500,000
Buy
Decision-making conditions – IF part of rule
Action – THEN part of rule

Figure 9-18 Partial table for real-estate knowledge system.

$500,000. The agent then enters the number of bedrooms, style of house, location, and price of that house, together with the buy recommendation, into a table (Figure 9-18).

This real-estate application is an example of a decision-making situation based on certain criteria. In the table, all the cell headings except the last represent the criteria, equivalent to the conditional parts of a knowledge system rule. The last cell heading represents the action, recommendation, or diagnosis part of a rule. Thus, each row of the table has the same information as a knowledge system (production) rule.

Every time another situation arises and the real-estate agent makes another decision, the facts of the situation and the resulting decision are entered in the table. After a time, the table contains a large record of situations and consequent decisions.

A person new to the business might regard these facts and decisions as examples to learn from, especially if experience shows the decisions to have been successful. Often, there is a pattern contained within the examples that, if recognized, could provide a clue or suggestion for the less experienced person's action.

The idea behind the table-based AI tools is to find that pattern and transform it into a decision. The decision tree then guides the questioning of the user and the eventual suggested decision. The real-estate application was developed with Expert-Ease, a general-purpose AI tool that will be used, in the next section, to illustrate the use and limitations of table-driven AI application tools.

EXPERT-EASE

Since Expert-Ease works by finding a pattern in the examples provided to the system, clearly it will only work for a problem or decision where there is such a pattern. Since it uses past examples as a guide to what action to suggest for a problem, the examples must be representative of the problem and decisions, and must be as complete a set of examples as possible. The developed system is only as good as the examples from which it is built. How many examples are enough depends on the user's desired accuracy. The greater number of examples, the more accurate the results are likely to be. If past examples do not serve as a precedent for future actions, a table-based tool may not be suitable.

BUILDING A SYSTEM WITH A TABLE-BASED TOOL

There are four steps to creating a knowledge system application with Expert-Ease. First, the user defines the cell heading, called attributes, for an application. Second, the user enters examples of real or hypothetical situations and the consequent action or decision. Third, the user asks Expert-Ease to "induce" a rule from the examples entered. Fourth, the system developed is tested by running a dialogue and test case.

In step one of Expert-Ease system development, users analyze their problem and identify a set of attributes that pertain to the problem. These attributes and their values define the criteria or conditions for a decision. For example, in one partially completed system that could help automobile-insurance agents determine what type of insurance company and plan to assign to clients, facts about a client's personal and driving record are attributes. These facts include why the client is calling for insurance (whycalling), age, marital status, age of car, number of minor violations within four years (minor.viol), number of accidents within four years where the client is at fault or not at fault, number of major violations within 10 years and supporting business with the insurance company (Figure 9-19).

Attributes can have many possible values, and the values are either logical or integer. Logical values are specified as names containing up to 10 letters, such as at.fault.1 (one accident, driver at fault), notfault.1, dwi (driving while intoxicated), leave.acc (leaving the scene of an accident), and veh.homcid (vehicular homicide). Integer values are integers between 32,766 and −32,766.

The values for the attributes are the conditions used to make the recommendation for an insurance company assignment. These conditions correspond to the IF parts of knowledge system rules. The last column of the table is called the result column. It contains the recommended assignment attribute whose values are the possible decisions or actions. In this example, the values are one of five types of insurance companies/plans referred to by numbers. These companies/plans are (1) assigned risk plan distributed among many companies, (2) highest rate substandard company, (3) standard company, (4) preferred, and (5) super-preferred. The result column values correspond to the THEN part of a rule.

Once the attributes and values have been defined, system developers enter values for actual or hypothetical examples of situations that pertain to the application in question.* Figure 9-20, for instance, shows in tabular form 26 examples where clients were assigned to different insurance companies and plans. The first nine columns consist of the personal and driving records of insured clients, or else an asterisk (wild-card symbol) which indicates that the value in that

* Insurance examples supplied by Joseph Mione.

EXPERT-EASE Attribute Listing, Problem: INSURANCE Date: 5-oct-84

	whycalling	age	marital.st	car.age	car.type	accidents	minor.viol	maj.viol	supprt.bus	ins.cmpany
	logical	integer	logical	integer	logical	logical	logical	logical	logical	logical
1	dropped		single		conservtiv	none	none	none	none	company.1
2	rateshopng		married		high.perf	at.fault.1	one	leave.acc	life	company.2
3	recommend				sports	at.fault.2	two	veh.homcid	busines	company.3
4	brok.retir				luxury	at.fault.3	three	dwi.lt5yrs	health	company.4
5						notfault.1		dwi.gt5yrs	homeowners	company.5
6						notfault.2		dwi.gt8yrs	two.or.mor	
7						notfault.3		dwi.10yrs		

Figure 9-19 Table of some possible attribute values for an automobile insurance advisory system.

Problem file name

Attributes

Type of Attributes

EXPERT-EASE Attribute Listing, Problem: INSURANCE Date: 5-oct-84

	whycalling	age	marital.st	car.age	car.type	accidents	minor.viol	maj.viol	supprt.bus	ins.cmpany
	logical	integer	logical	integer	logical	logical	logical	logical	logical	logical
1	rateshopng	28	married	6	conservtiv	none	one	none	life	company.3
2	dropped	*	*	*	*	*	*	*	*	company.1
3	*	17	*	*	*	*	*	*	*	company.1
4	rateshopng	30	married	3	conservtiv	none	none	none	homeowners	company.5
5	recommend	40	married	5	conservtiv	none	one	none	homeowners	company.4
6	recommend	42	married	5	conservtiv	at.fault.1	none	none	homeowners	company.3
7	recommend	36	single	12	conservtiv	none	none	none	none	company.2
8	*	18	*	*	*	*	*	*	*	company.1
9	rateshopng	45	married	2	conservtiv	none	none	dwi.gt8yrs	two.or.mor	company.1
10	brok.retir	50	married	1	luxury	notfault.1	none	none	homeowners	company.4
11	recommend	50	married	1	luxury	notfault.1	one	none	homeowners	company.2
12	recommend	30	single	10	conservtiv	none	none	none	none	company.2
13	recommend	30	single	2	conservtiv	none	none	none	none	company.4
14	rateshopng	60	married	5	conservtiv	none	two	none	none	company.1
15	rateshopng	70	married	5	conservtiv	none	none	none	none	company.1
16	recommend	40	married	2	sports	*	*	*	*	company.1
17	brok.retir	31	married	3	sports	*	*	*	*	company.1
18	recommend	27	married	5	conservtiv	none	one	dwi.10yrs	*	company.1
19	rateshopng	35	single	3	conservtiv	none	one	none	none	company.2
20	recommend	44	married	2	luxury	none	two	none	none	company.2
21	recommend	46	married	4	conservtiv	notfault.2	none	none	none	company.2
22	recommend	25	single	4	conservtiv	notfault.2	one	none	none	company.1
23	recommend	47	married	1	luxury	none	one	none	none	company.3
24	brok.retir	38	married	2	luxury	none	one	none	homeowners	company.4
25	brok.retir	40	married	2	luxury	none	one	none	none	company.3
26	recommend	41	married	3	conservtiv	notfault.1	none	none	none	company.3

Numbered Examples

Editing examples

Input line prompt → why calling: dropped, rateshopng, recommend, brok.retir? ← Menu of possible attribute valves

Figure 9-20

column does not matter because it does not affect the final result. The last column is the recommended insurance company associated with the first nine attribute values.

The examples and attributes can be added or modified at any time. Expert-Ease prompts the users for the values and attributes. Also, a simple text command allows system developers to define questions to ask users and synonyms for cryptic, maximum ten-character attributes in the tables.

INDUCING RULES

After sufficient examples have been given, the user can command Expert-Ease to induce a rule by typing the ! key. Expert-Ease examines the examples, searches for an underlying pattern, and produces a rule, or "decision tree," which corresponds to this pattern. Expert-Ease then uses this rule to guide the questioning of users and to predict results, suggest decisions, diagnoses, and actions.

The decision tree, which can be displayed and inspected with Expert-Ease's "rule" command, consists of a nested, branchy group of nodes containing attributes and values (Figure 9-21). All the values of attributes form branches of the decision tree; their branches may be other attributes, and so on. The values at the leaf nodes, or ends of each branch, are drawn from the results column, so that any path through the tree produces an answer.

Sometimes a branch of the decision tree may be marked "null." For example, a null recommendation is given next to the insurance company rule node that handles cases where a potential client had two accidents in which he (or she) was at fault (at.fault.2). Such a recommendation means that Expert-Ease has not been given an example that covers this case. For Expert-Ease to produce an answer that handles the case marked null, it is necessary to generate a new example to provide the knowledge of how to make the decision.

If two given examples contradict one another, for example two identical sets of attributes values have different result values, the system will be unable to induce a consistent rule that covers all examples. The rule inducer flags the situation and informs the user which examples are contradictory and prevents Expert-Ease from deciding between result values. The user can delete the contradictory examples or put them in reserve store, where they will be remembered for some possible future use, but ignored when the rule is induced. If the user wants the contradictory example to be included in the decision system, he or she must add new attributes or change some values to show the system how to make decisions between the contradictory examples.

If an attribute is type "integer," Expert-Ease produces a tree that branches on conditional tests of the value. For example, nodes in Figure 9-21 contain values of ≥35 and <46, indicating clients 35 years of age or older or less than 46 years old.

```
EXPERT-EASE Rule Listing, Problem: INSURANCE      Date:  5-oct-84

age
        <28 : company.1
        >=28 : whycalling
          dropped : company.1
       rateshopng : supprt.bus
                    none : age
                           <48 : company.2
                           >=48 : company.1
                    life : company.3
                business : null
                  health : null
              homeowners : company.5
              two.or.mor : company.1
        recommend : car.type
             conservtiv : accidents
                          none : car.age
                                 <8 : company.4
                                 >=8 : company.2
              at.fault.1 : company.3
              at.fault.2 : null
              at.fault.3 : null
              notfault.1 : company.3
              notfault.2 : company.2
              notfault.3 : null
         high.perf : null
            sports : company.1
            luxury : age
                   <46 : company.2
                   >=46 : age
                          <49 : company.3
                          >=49 : company.2
 brok.retir : age
              <35 : company.1
              >=35 : supprt.bus
                    none : company.3
                    life : null
                business : null
                  health : null
              homeowners : company.4
              two.or.mor : null
```

Figure 9-21 Decision tree induced from examples in automobile insurance advisory system.

The decisions made by this sample insurance knowledge system are limited because the number of attributes and examples that fit in Figure 9-20 are limited. In the real world, insurance plan and company assignments are based on many more attributes, such as residential stability, employment stability, type of occupation, and interest of the insurance company and agent in obtaining new clients. In addition, assignments and rates are determined by statistically large numbers of cases.

The complexity of a multiple-attribute/multiple-value system can be great. Expert-Ease often finds a rule that restricts this complexity and produces an answer by asking only a few of the questions implied in the attribute sheet. Thus, if the first question in the insurance knowledge system is "why calling" and the answer is "being dropped by current insurance company," Expert-Ease need not ask any further questions to conclude the assigned risk plan. Unfortunately, the major place where Expert-Ease falls slightly short of knowledge system expectations is seen in the query facility. It cannot give explanations of how it reached its conclusion or why it is asking a question.

Testing of an Expert-Ease system is similar to testing any other knowledge system. If incorrect results are found, it is necessary to add more knowledge, in the form of new attributes, values, or examples, after which the system is tested again. This cycle is repeated until a desired level of performance is reached.

The table-based tools have been criticized by some members of the AI community as not producing true knowledge systems. It is fair to say at this point, however, that the table-based tools can be used by people with the least expertise or training. Certainly, also, they have many limitations which their larger-scale cousins do not have. Yet the ability to produce models of processes requiring specialized knowledge and the ability to be used by nonprogrammers gives them a niche of their own, especially if they are combined with other programming techniques.

PROCEDURE AND TABLE TOOLS

An example of a tool combining table-based knowledge representation facilities with other programming techniques is RuleMaster, an integrated table-based knowledge tool and block-structured procedural tool. The tool has two components. One is Radial, an English-like, structured, recursive programming language with constructs of finite state machines. The other is RuleMaker, which induces rules and decision trees from examples of cases represented as knowledge in tables. Written in C, RuleMaster runs under Unix on machines such as Sun Microsystems, Apollo, Gould, IBM's PC AT, AT&T's Unix PC, Perkin-Elmer, and VAX computers.

A Radial program is a collection of related modules which can call one another. Each module defines one or more states which change to another state either in the same or another module. The modules also contain an action which can be an executable procedure, advice, or a piece of data.

```
/* The purpose of this module is to determine the status of the WD500
   disk drive based on a combination of indicator lights.  First, the
   user is given directions to power up the unit, then questioned about
   the state of the indicator lights.  The rule that is generated from
   these examples is structured in such a way that the problem can be
   determined with the fewest number of questions asked about the lights. */

module: ti.device.disk_drive.wd500
declarations:
[  intent: "\the WD500 disk problem\"
    child: power_up         win_term
           formatter        flex
           p_bus_id         p_bus_loop
           win_1            no_lights
           win_2
]
state: directions
  [( power_up, check )]

state: check
actions:
    formatter   [ formatter ]   /* problem with disk formatter */
    p_bus_id    [ p_bus_id ]    /* peripheral bus id problem   */
    win_1       [ win_1 ]       /* problem with winchester disk # 1 */
    win_2       [ win_2 ]       /* problem with winchester disk # 2 */
    win_term    [ win_term ]    /* problem with winchester terminators */
    flex        [ flex ]        /* flexible drive or cable problem */
    p_bus_loop  [ p_bus_loop ]  /* peripheral bus loopback test failure */
    no_lights   [ no_lights ]   /* fuse, power, connections, cable, etc. */

conditions:
  light_1 [ ask2 "What is the status of LED indicator 1?" "on,blinking,not_on"
            "LED indicator 1" "on,blink,off" ] {on,blink,off}
  light_2 [ ask2 "What is the status of LED indicator 2?" "on,blinking,not_on"
            "LED indicator 2" "on,blink,off" ] {on,blink,off}
  light_3 [ ask2 "What is the status of LED indicator 3?" "on,not_on"
            "LED indicator 3" "on,off" ] {on,off}
  light_4 [ ask2 "What is the status of LED indicator 4?" "on,not_on"
            "LED indicator 4" "on,off" ] {on,off}
  light_5 [ ask2 "What is the status of LED indicator 5?" "on,not_on"
            "LED indicator 5" "on,off" ] {on,off}
  light_6 [ ask2 "What is the status of LED indicator 6?" "on,blinking,not_on"
            "LED indicator 6" "on,blink,off" ] {on,blink,off}

examples:
/*  1       2       3       4       5       6                          */

    off     off     off     off     off     on      => (formatter,goal)
    off     off     off     off     off     blink   => (formatter,goal)
    on      on      on      on      on      on      => (formatter,goal)
    off     on      on      on      on      blink   => (formatter,goal)
    off     blink   off     off     off     blink   => (p_bus_id,goal)
    off     on      off     off     off     on      => (win_1,goal)
    on      on      off     off     off     on      => (win_1,goal)
    off     off     on      off     off     on      => (win_2,goal)
    on      off     on      off     off     on      => (win_2,goal)
    off     on      on      off     off     on      => (win_term,goal)
    off     off     off     on      off     on      => (flex,goal)
    on      off     off     on      off     on      => (flex,goal)
    off     off     off     off     on      on      => (p_bus_loop,goal)
    on      off     off     off     on      on      => (p_bus_loop,goal)
    off     off     off     off     off     off     => (no_lights,goal)
```

Figure 9-22 A RuleMaster knowledge system module containing states, actions, user-questions, and a table of example criteria and consequent actions, in this or other modules, from which a decision tree is induced. (Radian Corp.)

The RuleMaker table-based component allows users to enter rules from examples. An example of this capability is seen in Titan, an expert system that trains and aids Radian Corp.'s service technicians in troubleshooting faults in the TI 990 minicomputer system. A diagnostic feature of the computer's WD500 disk drives is a set of six LED indicator lights, each of which has three possible states: on, off, or blinking. Different combinations of lights and states indicate the probable cause of a failure. A fifteen page troubleshooting flowchart for the disk drive, which deals mostly with the information contained in the LED indicators, normally provides the procedural knowledge and advice for troubleshooters to follow.

With RuleMaster, however, the various LED indicators, probable cause of the failure they indicate, and the appropriate action to take is entered in a table (Figure 9-22). Such tabular knowledge is an example of declarative knowledge. Generally it is easier for experts, technicians, and knowledge engineers to work with declarative than procedural knowledge. RuleMaster converts the declarative knowledge into the more difficult-to-work-with procedural knowledge represented in the form of rules or a decision tree.

Although a table-based tool, RuleMaster differs from Expert-Ease in several respects. In Expert-Ease, an action is only advice; in RuleMaster, it can be advice or executable code. RuleMaster's knowledge-based advice can be based on partial certainty using multi-valued logic, Zadeh's fuzzy set operators, or heuristic uncertainty defined by the expert. Unlike Expert-Ease, RuleMaster has a "next_ state" capability and also can explain its reasoning. In addition, programs in languages, such as Pascal, C, and Fortran are callable from RuleMaster. In fact, because RuleMaster runs under Unix, it can interface to Unix-based languages through the Unix "pipes" facility (which allows the output of one program to be the input to another). Finally, RuleMaster allows users to define their own compound data types (like Pascal records) or abstract data types, and supports consistency, completeness, and data type checking.

AI TOOLS INTEGRATED WITH TRADITIONAL APPLICATIONS

One other type of knowledge-system development tool deserves mention at this point. This type of tool embeds value-added AI capabilities in conventional applications. In the next generation of AI systems, these tools are likely to become prevalent.

Guru (from Micro Data Base Systems, Inc.) is an example of such a tool. It embeds knowledge system techniques in an environment that supports integrated spreadsheet processing, text processing, relational database management, forms management, report generating, graphics, communications, and business computing. Guru users and developers can use a simple English-like language and knowledge-system development facilities to develop a rule-based, backward-chaining system. Guru-developed knowledge systems, however, differ from traditional knowledge systems in that Guru's rules are more versatile.

In most knowledge systems, the premise, or IF part refers to working variables; the conclusion of a rule supports assignment statements, advice, or procedures. Guru, however, allows rule premises and conclusions also to refer to spreadsheet cells; perform spreadsheet processing; create, access, or update databases; handle graphics generation and remote communications, and perform a variety of built-in functions for business processing. Such capabilities allow the development of knowledge systems that, for example, might dial a remote machine, read financial information, combine the information with database data, and then base the remainder of a program's reasoning process on the information that it dialed up from remote storage or accessed from a corporate database.

Approaching integrated knowledge system processing from another view, Guru allows users to define a cell of a spreadsheet to be a knowledge system consultation. So when the user reevaluates the spreadsheet, the value of that cell is not determined just by an arithmetic formula, but also can be the result of a rule-based consultation.

Applications built with Guru include CitiBank's telecommunications troubleshooting system, Raymond Chabot's (a Canadian investment house) tax investment advisor built by William Blair & Co.'s Investment Bank and Client Information system, More From Less Inc.'s (a Honolulu-based legal firm) legal case management system, and Soft Computing Inc.'s (Paris, France) Gas Station Site Advisor system and Building Cost Estimator system. It is currently being used to develop a medical claims insurance system for Allstate Insurance. This insurance system is further discussed in Chapter 19.

10

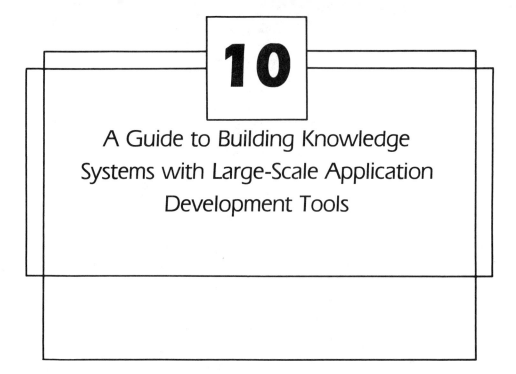

A Guide to Building Knowledge Systems with Large-Scale Application Development Tools

The microcomputer-based AI tools discussed in Chapter 9 are useful for many knowledge system applications. Moreover, they promote AI exploration and take a giant step toward bridging the AI technology gap because of their low price and the fact that they run on microcomputers. But, large-scale knowledge systems often need integrated development environments, an assortment of knowledge representation and reasoning techniques, and special AI capabilities that are characteristic of large-scale tools.

The different knowledge representations and reasoning strategies accommodate different ways of thinking about, formulating, and solving complex problems. The graphics environments visually show the different structures of the knowledge system and the relationships between them, making it easier to understand the developing knowledge system.

MULTIPLE PARADIGMS

Many of the large-scale tools incorporate, within one tool, multiple AI paradigms such as object-oriented programming, logic programming, and reasoning in parallel about hypothetical situations. Several tools can represent knowledge in frames, rules, and logical assertions. They can reason by backward-chaining and forward-chaining, or some combination of these. Some support gauge-like images, on the terminal screen, that access and monitor changes to data during program execution. For efficiency, several tools also incorporate conventional programming procedures. Sometimes these control a consultation for a large system—a tiresome task to accomplish exclusively with rules, the dominant knowledge representation on micros—and, other times, they implement algorithms.

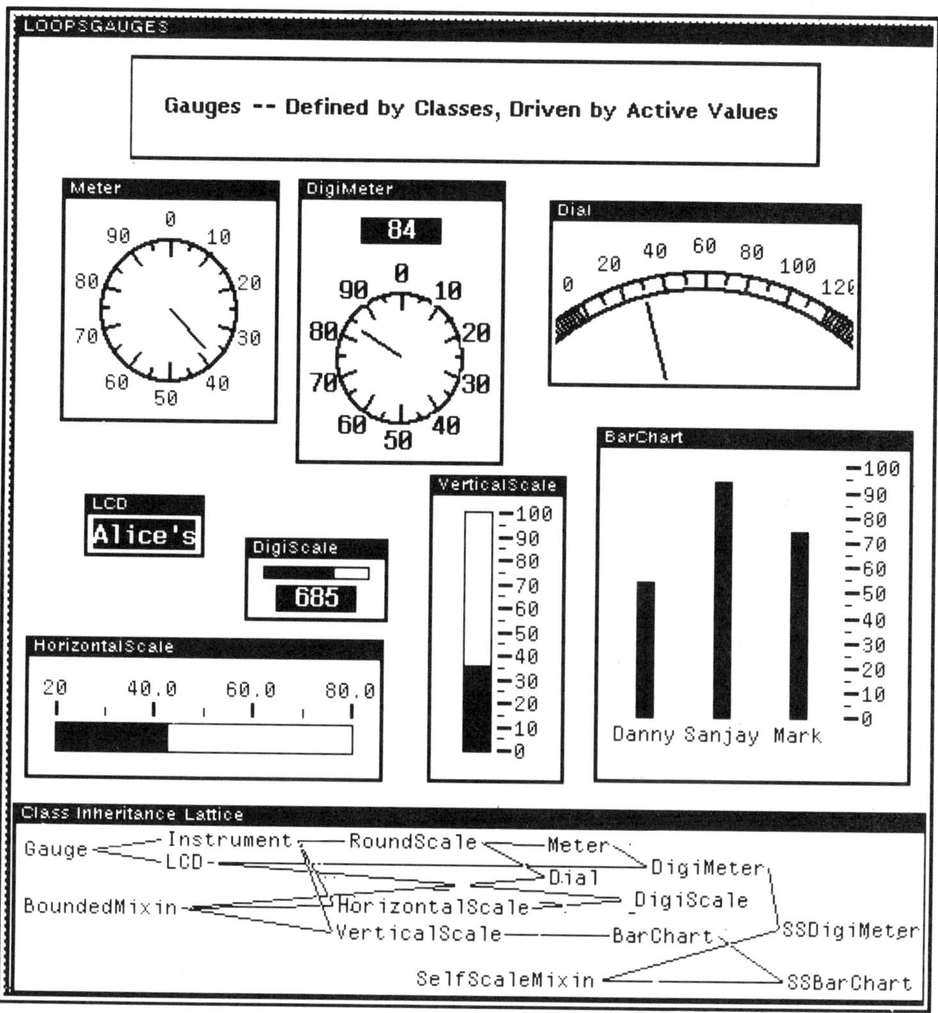

Figure 10-1 Loops' gauges attached to program variables are responsive to changes in these variables (Xerox Corp.)

Typical of the multiple paradigm tools is Xerox's Loops, which features four programming paradigms: object-oriented, procedure-oriented, rule-oriented, and data-oriented. The object-oriented paradigm lets users view programs as collections of objects with associated (encapsulated) procedures that send and receive messages to execute these procedures. The objects are organized in a class hierarchy, where each class describes one or more similar objects, such as gauges (Figure 10-1 bottom). Traveling down the hierarchy, the classes are subdivided into subclasses like instruments and LCD's, which may be further subdivided, until a specific object is reached. Subclasses and instances lower down in the hierarchy inherit both attributes and procedures from those higher in the hierarchy.

The rule-oriented paradigm is specialized for specifying knowledge in the form of condition-action rules. The procedure-oriented paradigm, allows users to build classical procedures in Lisp.

Data-oriented programming is supported by many large-scale tools under a variety of names such as access-oriented programming, active values, and procedural attachments. With data-oriented programming, procedures can be attached to variables or frame slots designated as active. Whenever these designated variables or slots are accessed or changed, the program automatically invokes attached specified procedures. In this way, data-driven control of these procedures is supported.

Although the attached procedures may be used for a variety of purposes, often users of data-driven programming tools attach variables or slots to graphically represented physical devices and measuring instruments such as gauges and meters. Associated with the attached devices and instruments are routines to handle them. Many procedural attachments supported by Loops, and as will be seen, by IntelliCorp's KEE (Knowledge Engineering Environment) tool, are straightforward to use because Loops and KEE also supply knowledge bases of prewritten graphical devices and corresponding handling routines.

In Loops, for example, variables can be designated to be active. Whenever an active variable is accessed or changed, a procedure invoked drives the attached gauge, meter, or other graphics icons to display the new values (Figure 10-1 top). This allows users to monitor programs, during program development and debugging as well as during application execution.

ENVIRONMENTS FOR TOOLS

Many large-scale AI application development tools run on dedicated Lisp computers and also on traditional computers such as the DEC VAX and Sun, Apollo, and Hewlett-Packard workstations. Traditional workstations are often less flashy than the highly graphically-oriented Lisp machines. But, they have several very practical advantages. They already exist in corporate environments. Corporate data and programs reside on these machines. Personnel are accustomed to working on them. And the per user cost is less than that for a dedicated Lisp machine.

Lisp machines also have several important advantages. The integrated AI and graphical environments found on Lisp computers makes program development easier. The graphical environments allow AI application developers to move about within the framework of the program under development, view the structures they have built and, simultaneously, in another window on the computer screen, graphically display and manipulate the relationships between them. This increases the chances of knowledge system success.

To accommodate both the AI development environment and traditional computing world, some tool companies have developed tools that allow programmers to develop an application on a Lisp computer, but transport the completed knowledge system to a conventional computer. This allows companies to justify smaller numbers of higher cost Lisp machines for program development, but use standard, less expensive computers for the production environment.

WHO USES THE TOOLS?

A new question arises: "If large-scale tools have so many sophisticated capabilities, how easy are they and their documentation to use?" Some insight into the ease-of-use of these application development tools can be gleaned from a knowledge of what kind of people are using the tools. For example, with basic knowledge and training provided by AI tool vendors, management consultants at companies like Arthur D. Little Inc. have been using KEE (Knowledge Engineering Environment) to help provide AI systems and services for its clients. Some Lawrence Livermore Laboratories chemists used KEE to develop intelligent interfaces that help tune Triple Quadrapole Mass Spectrometers.

Newspaper publishing professionals and software engineers at Composition Systems, Inc., developed a knowledge-based editorial layout and typesetting program using ART (Advanced Reasoning Tool) from Inference Corp., while electrical engineers and software engineers at Hughes Radar Systems used ART to build the AI-based diagnosis program for manufacturing systems. And chemical engineers from Chevron used Knowledge Craft (from Carnegie Group, Inc.) to build a metal-working fluid consultant program that helps decide on the best drilling fluid to use in a particular situation. These examples support the notion that AI nonexperts can successfully build knowledge systems, with the help of AI application development tools.

Further insight into the training needed to use these commercial AI application development tools can be gained by looking at two end-user companies who build operational AI applications with large-scale tools. One application is a knowledge-based design system, developed with a VAX-based version of S.1 and operational at Delco Products, Division of General Motors. (S.1 is discussed in Chapter 9.) Built by project engineers with mechanical and electrical engineering backgrounds, the Delco system consults with designers of brushes (for motors), and specifies the information sent to a computer-aided-design system to make the production drawing for these brushes.

As preparation for this project, one engineer enrolled in a Teknowledge two-week training course and then trained other Delco engineers in basic AI concepts and the use of the tool. It required about four months' of development to make the brush design system operational. Delco subsequently developed knowledge systems to design other parts of DC motors.

The second system, a Babcock & Wilcox (B&W) knowledge-based weld scheduler developed with KEE on a Symbolics machine, illustrates tool use and required training, and also points out a major economic concern in commercial AI deployment. The B&W weld scheduler automates the generation of weld schedule information, including selection of the proper weld procedure and determination of specific preheat, postheat, and NDE (nondestructive examination) requirements. The AI system incorporates engineering data, the detailed industry code requirements, and welding heuristics.

To build the system, B&W engineers used a mixture of frames, rules, object-oriented programming, and KEE's forward chaining mechanism (Figure 10-2). They received a week of on-site training and consultation after KEE was delivered (February 1985). During the initial week, the application designers put together a first cut of the weld-scheduler project; thereafter, they worked independently.

By June 1985, the weld scheduler was functional at B&W's Lynchburg Research Center and initial system development was scheduled for the next year. But how to deploy the system was an issue that had first to be resolved.

B&W admits that the graphical interfaces supported both by KEE and B&W's Symbolics machine were productivity aids during knowledge system development, and that they are also an adjunct to run-time versions of many graphically-oriented programs (e.g. knowledge-based simulation systems and intelligent interfaces to scientific instruments or complex control panels). But the input (a matrix of engineering design data) and output (a schedule) for B&W's run-time system is alphanumeric text and seldom requires expensive graphics. Consequently, B&W considered two more-economic options: a centralized Symbolics machine with remote access via modems, and less-expensive computers in the company's field offices to run the weld scheduler. Pending its deployment decision, B&W was clear about its desire for hardware and software vendors to provide run-time support of AI software on hardware costing between $25,000 and $35,000, without requiring users to perform any code translation.

Vendors have responded to users' run-time needs in several ways. For example, Teknowledge and Inference Corp. have translated S.1 and ART into the C programming language so that both the development and delivery systems can run on conventional programs. Carnegie Group, Inc., has always run a Common Lisp implementation of Knowledge Craft on traditional computers, such as the DEC VAX.

For its part, IntelliCorp has developed a nongraphics version of KEE for conventional, time-shared computers that do not support extensive graphics capabilities, as well as a Common Lisp implementation that runs on Lisp machines, minicomputers, and technical workstations. In addition, it has designed a run-time version of KEE that allows KEE-based applications to be developed on a Lisp machine, but executed on any conventional machine that supports Common Lisp. Very little translation is needed because most of the application (including the graphics interface and object-oriented programming) is in KEE

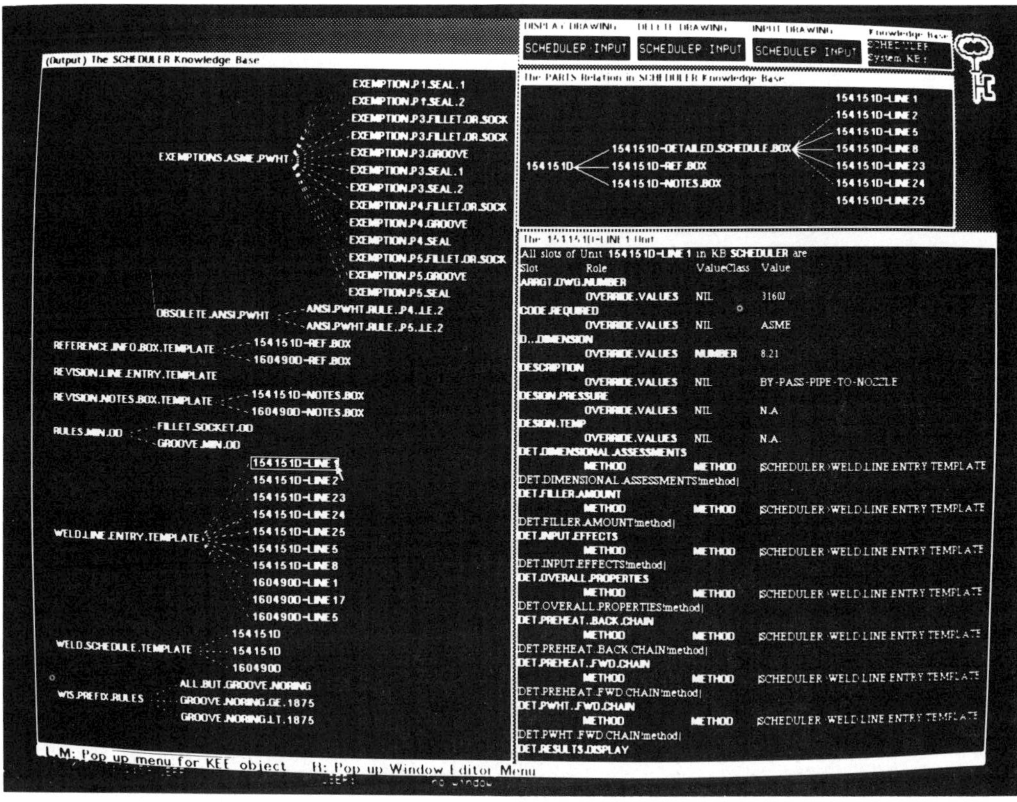

Figure 10-2 The left window displays part of the Weld Scheduler knowledge base, using KEE's graphical format for objects associated via either a class-subclass or class-member relationship. The objects in the knowledge base range from conceptual objects used as templates for creating new objects, specific objects instantiated from these templates, as well as numerous rules (both industry code standards as well as heuristic rules-of-thumb) organized into appropriate rule classes.

The upper right window displays a typical instantiated weld schedule using KEE's graphical format for whole-part object relationships.

The lower right window displays details of relevant slot information associated with one of the objects in the knowledge base. (Babcock & Wilcox)

code, which is common to both the development and run-time machines. A KEE scanner flags the places where Common Lisp differs on the development and run-time machine.

The run-time KEE distributes its capabilities across a large-scale host computer and a PC. The PC runs a piece of the KEE graphics interface. More than a dumb user interface, it allows users to downline-load the local knowledge base, browse through it, modify values, and delete or add members to the knowledge base structure. However, it does not allow users to make changes to the knowledge-base architecture.

The knowledge base and the core of KEE, such as the rule system, inheritance mechanism, inference mechanisms, and object-oriented programming capabilities reside on the host computer. The host computer provides high-performance and large-memory capacity for the knowledge base and knowledge system processing, and access to company databases.

BUILDING A LARGE-SCALE KNOWLEDGE SYSTEM

Learning from second hand stories of other company's experiences is limited. To understand what can be done with knowledge system development tools, the potential user needs to take a close look at an AI application development tool and how it works, both from the knowledge system end-user and the developer points of view. KEE, and a KEE-developed knowledge system called Reactors, which interfaces to the controlling instrumentation for a nuclear power plant, provides a good example of both a tool and application, with information transferable to other applications.

The control panels that normally interface to the controlling instrumentation of nuclear power plants, as well as to many types of equipment, industrial processes, and so on, are extremely complex. Their fifty to several hundred meters, gauges, digital readouts, and various kinds of alarms produce an information overload under the best of conditions and can cause total confusion on the part of the system operators during a crisis.

A reactor performs status and monitoring functions for a nuclear power plant, analyzes the plant's behavior, indicates its status, reports when unusual events have occurred, and provides maintenance and diagnostic advice in routine and crisis situations. Although few people have nuclear reactors, the application illustrates the different steps, design, knowledge base organization, and defining of related and interacting details to build a large-scale knowledge system with a knowledge system development tool.

Before understanding how to build a knowledge system using KEE, it is necessary to understand the basic components from which a KEE-based knowledge system is built. These components are KEE's frames, rules, hierarchies, and inheritance mechanisms. System builders must understand what is in a frame, how to write and modify a rule, how a hierarchical structure is organized, why it is important, and how system components inherit knowledge from others. Once these fundamentals are understood, the frames, rules, and hierarchies can be combined to build the knowledge system that accomplishes specific goals and performs "intelligent-like" tasks.

WHAT'S IN A FRAME?

KEE organizes knowledge in knowledge bases. Each knowledge base contains frames. In KEE, frames are called units. They may contain knowledge about components, rules, or combinations of the two.

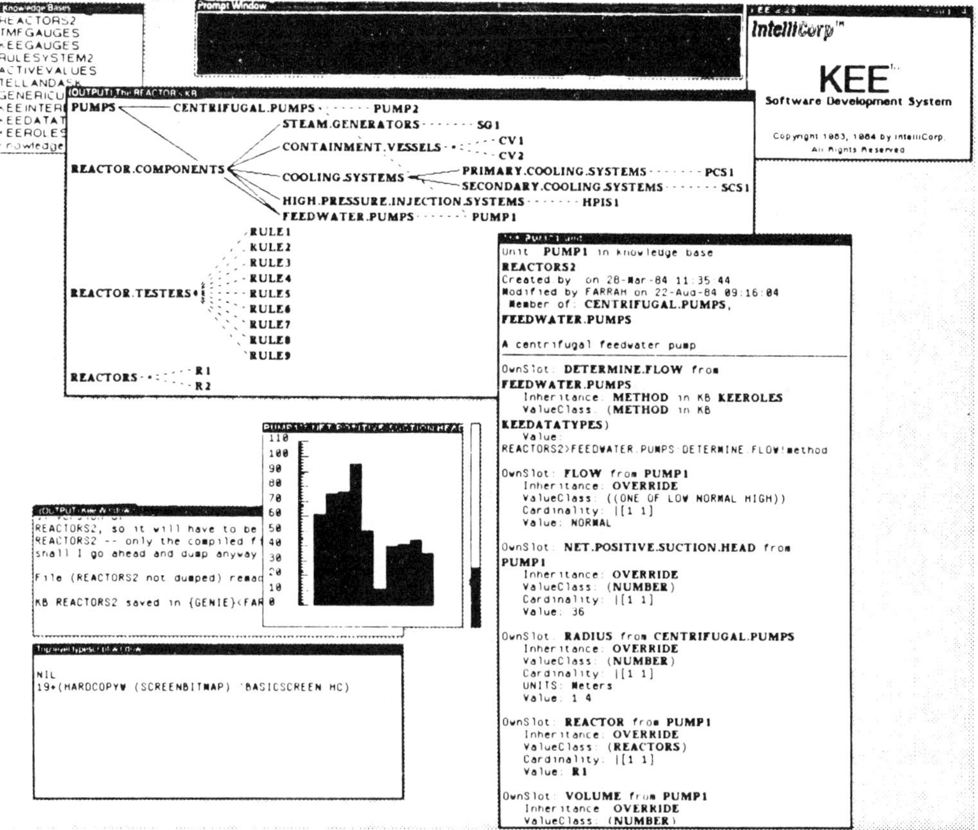

Figure 10-3 Hierarchical relationships between units in the Reactors system. (Program copyrights © 1983, 1984 by IntelliCorp. All rights reserved.)

The partial frame, or unit, shown in Figure 10-3 is named PUMP1 and contains knowledge about a particular component. As indicated, it is located in the REACTORS2 knowledge base. This is one of several knowledge bases on a KEE system, some of which are supplied with KEE for tasks such as building guages or interpreting rules and some of which are built by application designers.

Units are composed of slots. Slots may contain, among other things, descriptive attributes, rules, methods (procedures that execute when they receive a "message"), textual information, logical assertions, and other units. The PUMP1 unit contains more slots than Figure 10-3 shows.

In the PUMP1 unit, which is typical of component units, some slots contain observable or measurable characteristics of the component. Other slots contain general information or knowledge of how to obtain needed information. For example, the slot named FLOW describes PUMP1's flow, which is allowed to be low, normal or high. NET.POSITIVE.SUCTION.HEAD and RADIUS are

```
The RULE4 unit
Unit: RULE4 in knowledge base REACTORS2
Created by  on  4-Feb-84 14:56:22
Modified by FARRAH on 21-Aug-84 16:23:51
 Member of: REACTOR.TESTERS

OwnSlot: ACTION from RULES
   Inheritance: APPEND
   Value: Unknown

OwnSlot: ASSERTION from RULE4
   Inheritance: APPEND
   AVUNITS: (WFFINDEX)
   Value: (|Wff:(AN INTEGRITY OF ?A.VESSEL IS CHALLENGED))

OwnSlot: BACKCHAINER.BREAK from RULES
   Inheritance: OVERRIDE
   ValueClass: ((ONE.OF T))
   Cardinality: |[0 1]
   Value: Unknown

OwnSlot: EXTERNAL.FORM from RULE4
   Inheritance: SAME
   ValueClass: (LIST)
   Value: (IF ((?A.VESSEL IS IN CLASS CONTAINMENT.VESSELS)
                AND
                (THE RADIATION OF ?A.VESSEL IS HIGH)
                AND
                (THE PRESSURE OF ?A.VESSEL IS HIGH))
               THEN
               (THE INTEGRITY OF ?A.VESSEL IS CHALLENGED))

OwnSlot: PARSE from RULES
   Inheritance: METHOD in KB KEEROLES
   ValueClass: (METHOD in KB KEEDATATYPES)
   Value: DEFAULT.RULE.PARSER

OwnSlot: PREMISE from RULE4
   Inheritance: APPEND
   AVUNITS: (WFFINDEX)
   Value: (|Wff:(?A.VESSEL IS IN CLASS CONTAINMENT.VESSELS)
                          |Wff:(A RADIATION OF ?A.VESSEL IS HIGH)

                           |Wff:(A PRESSURE OF ?A.VESSEL IS HIGH))
```

Figure 10-4 KEE Unit containing rule-based knowledge. (Program copyrights)

measurable quantities. The slot named VOLUME contains the volume of fluid flow per unit time of PUMP1. Slot DETERMINE.FLOW contains a Lisp function which calculates what the flow of this pump will be, depending on parameters contained in slots in this and other units. Slot REACTOR points to the particular reactor unit—R1 or R2—that PUMP1 belongs to.

Another unit, shown in Figure 10-4, is called RULE4. It contains knowledge about a rule. Its slots contain various versions of a particular rule, mechanisms for debugging the rule, and the means for manipulating and reasoning about parts of the rule. One RULE4 slot, named EXTERNAL.FORM, contains an IF-THEN version of the rule. For KEE's internal purposes, however, and also to allow knowledge system designers as great an ability as possible to reason about, manipulate, and restrict parts of the rule, the rule is broken down into structural parts. These structural parts are identified in individual slots, as is the parser which breaks down the rule into its parts or puts them back together again, and the rule debugger.

For example, the slot named PREMISE contains the IF part of the rule. The ASSERTION slot contains a statement, or assertion, which happens to be the THEN part of the rule. The ACTION slot is a trap door to the Lisp system and enables the programmers to write Lisp procedures to execute some action other than those indicated by simple assertions. The BACKCHAINER.BREAK slot controls a program debugging mechanism. If the programmer defines the value in the slot to be T (or True), then whenever rule 4 fires, the program breaks (stops) and prints out values that are in the system at that time. This allows the programmer to uncover errors by tracing what happens as the system executes.

A question mark in front of a character or string of characters, as shown in some rule slots, indicates a variable. For example, one condition clause of the rule (shown in the EXTERNAL.FORM slot) states that "THE RADIATION OF ?A.VESSEL IS HIGH." The term "?A.VESSEL" represents some variable vessel in the system.

The term "wff" contained in the assertion and premise slots stands for "well-formed formula." A wff is a legal sentence in the language of predicate calculus. Most commonly, programmers or users enter rules into the knowledge system in the external (IF-THEN) rather than the wff form. The parser decomposes the rule, translates it into the logical form, and stuffs the appropriate wffs into the premise, assertion, and action slots for the knowledge system internals to execute. Programmers can, however, if they wish, enter, edit, and manipulate rules in logical form. Upon request, the parser can translate the wff structures into an IF-THEN rule form for display to the user.

HIERARCHICAL RELATIONSHIPS

Different units in a KEE knowledge base are related hierarchically (Figure 10-3). And the knowledge in the units is inherited down the hierarchy.

The most conceptually abstract or general frame, such as REACTOR.COMPONENTS, is at the top of the hierarchy. Units that describe specific objects, such as CV1 and CV2 (Containment Vessels 1 and 2), PCS1 (Primary Cooling System 1), HPIS1 (High Pressure Injection System 1), and PUMP1 are at the bottom of the hierarchy.

A unit that is connected to another unit one level down in the hierarchy is called the parent of that unit, and the lower unit is the child. Children in turn are also parents.

A KEE-created knowledge system is organized into not one, but several different hierarchies. For example, the Reactors system shows four hierarchies. They are the Pumps hierarchy, the Reactor Components hierarchy, the Reactor Testers hierarchy, and the Reactors hierarchy.

Frames within any one hierarchy are interconnected by two different types of parent-child links: class-subclass links and member links. Class-subclass links, shown by solid lines in the diagram, connect a parent and child, where the parent represents a general group or category of objects called a "class" and the children represent different types, or subsets, of the parent objects.

For example, in Figure 10-3, PUMPS is a general class of objects, while its children CENTRIFUGAL.PUMPS and FEEDWATER.PUMPS are types of pumps that form subclasses of the class of pumps. Similarly, five types of reactor components which are subclasses of REACTOR.COMPONENTS are shown: STEAM.GENERATORS, CONTAINMENT.VESSELS, COOLING.SYSTEMS, HIGH.PRESSURE.INJECTION.SYSTEMS, and FEEDWATER.PUMPS.

The other kind of parent-child link is a member link, shown by a dashed line. It connects parents and children, where the child is the same type of object as the parent, but is a specific instance (or example) of the parent. Thus, in the nuclear power plant to which the Reactors knowledge system interfaces, there are two centrifugal pumps, two containment vessels, nine rules, and two reactors. PUMP1 and PUMP2 are each specific instances of centrifugal pumps. CV1 and CV2 are instances of containment vessels. R1 and R2 are instances of reactors.

The different hierarchies can be related. As the hierarchy diagram shows, PUMP1 is an instance in both the PUMPS and REACTOR.COMPONENTS hierarchies.

INHERITANCE

There are two major advantages to arranging objects in a knowledge system hierarchically. For one, a display of this hierarchy allows knowledge system designers to determine how to move from unit to unit within the knowledge system and see, at a glance, how the various units are related.

The second advantage is the inheritance capabilities made possible by the hierarchical links. Attributes and procedures associated with units that represent classes of objects are inherited by the subclasses and members of these units. This makes it unnecessary for programmers to rewrite already written characteristics and procedures. Instead, they can concentrate on specifying changes and additions that make children unique, letting them inherit the rest of their attributes and procedures from their parents.

Inheritance in KEE takes place according to certain rules. Children may inherit all attributes (such as structure of the slot, characteristics, values, and procedures), override some attributes with their own values, append values from multiple parents to get an object with behaviors of all the parents, or they may be unique and take no values from parents. There are other inheritance mechanisms and users can also write their own.

For example, the PUMP1 unit inherits some slots from FEEDWATER. PUMPS and others from CENTRIFUGAL.PUMPS, which makes PUMP1 a centrifugal-feedwater pump. The external form of the rule in the RULE4 unit has been created at the RULE4 level of the hierarchy, and therefore it does not take information from its parent. Similarly, the CURRENT.STATE slot in the R1 unit in Figure 10-7, and the ASSERTION, PREMISE, and ACTION slots in the RULE4 unit, use knowledge created for their own units, but such slots could append knowledge from other units.

As Figures 10-3 and 10-4 show, slots themselves contain attributes called "facets" that determine allowable values for the slots. Rules for inheritance are determined by an Inheritance Role facet. Another facet, ValueClass, places programmer-defined restrictions on the types of values that a slot may contain. For example, the NET.POSITIVE.SUCTION.HEAD, RADIUS, and VOLUME slots in the PUMP1 unit has a Value Class of NUMBER. This means that the value of the slot must be a number. The REACTOR slot has a ValueClass of REACTORS. This specifies that the value of this slot must be a member of the class, REACTORS. With this value restriction capability, a KEE-created knowledge system will check input values and reject unacceptable ones, whether the values are explicitly input or inplicitly obtained during program execution.

The Cardinality facet determines the number of values that a slot may contain. Cardinality is specified as a range. The REACTOR slot in the PUMP1 unit has a Cardinality of [1 1]. This means that there must be between 1 and 1 (i.e., exactly 1) values in this slot. This makes sense, since a particular pump should be a component of only one reactor. If a user entered two reactors for PUMP1, KEE would flag it as an error.

There are other system-defined facets and the user may define still other facets. For instance, the UNITS facet of the RADIUS slot is a user-defined facet that describes the units of measurement for the pump radius.

BUILDING THE KNOWLEDGE SYSTEM

Building any knowledge system involves a certain amount of planning before rushing to the keyboard—and the larger the knowledge system to be built, the greater the amount of planning necessary. System designers must know, first, the expected behavior of their system and the types of objects it will contain. They must be able to draw at least a minimal hierarchical diagram showing the relationships between these objects. The hierarchy can be expanded incrementally as the system evolves.

System designers also need to know some details about the knowledge system objects in order to begin defining both their attributes and behavior. These details are acquired from interviews with experts. More details are added, also incrementally, as the system evolves. And the knowledge system designers must know the knowledge bases available to them so that they know what slots, procedures, and features they can inherit from these knowledge bases.

When the planning stage is completed and enough knowledge of details has been acquired to build a minimal working system, the programmer is ready to begin constructing the knowledge-system prototype. To build a knowledge-system prototype using the KEE tool, in step 1, system builders first select a menu option to create a blank knowledge base, and second, select an option that asks KEE to create a frame or unit in the knowledge base. Selection of the "Create-Unit" option causes KEE to query the user about information necessary to create the unit, such as name of the unit and who its parents are. Based on the answers, KEE hooks up the created unit in its proper place in the knowledge base hierarchy so that it will inherit the values and procedures due it.

If the knowledge system will contain rules, according to KEE's designers, the desirable first unit to create should be a subclass of the unit RULES and a member of the unit RULE.CLASSES. Both the RULES and RULE.CLASSES units are located in knowledge bases that are supplied with KEE. A subclass of RULES automatically inherits its "rule-methods." System builders can then specialize the new unit for their own purposes.

The specialized unit that the system builder creates is a "rule class" and its member units are individual rules. In the Reactors knowledge system in Figure 10-3, REACTORS.TESTERS is an example of a rule class. It has nine members, each of which represents a single rule. The rules are written in an English-like language. A set of rules being modified in the unit editor is shown in Figure 10-5.

The first specialization steps require the addition of knowledge system rules to the rule class, REACTOR.TESTERS. Once there are enough rules to make the system look like a knowledge system (albeit a novice one), the designer creates other units to represent the object referred to in the rules, and fills in their slots.

KEE's designers recommend that "novice" system builders develop a knowledge system in this order, because the rules already written guide the user in deciding what units and slots to create. For example, RULE4 concludes "THE INTEGRITY OF ?A. VESSEL IS CHALLENGED." This statement suggests that vessels should be units in the system hierarchy, that INTEGRITY is a slot name, and that CHALLENGED is a possible value for the slot.

KEE's rule system is logic-oriented. Premises make use of a full set of logical and set operators, such as AND, OR, NOT, ONE.OF, and SUBCLASS.OF. Rules can contain variables, which allow a single rule to apply in more than one situation. For example, RULE4 contains the variable ?A.VESSEL. This variable can be replaced with the name of any unit that has the slots RADIATION, PRESSURE, and INTEGRITY (slots indicated by the rule) and that is in the class CONTAINMENT.VESSELS. In the REACTORS2 knowledge base, the units CV1 and CV2 qualify for replacement.

```
Edit of Unit REACTOR.TESTERS
(MemberOf (RULE.CLASSES RULESYSTEM2))
(Comment "Rules for determining the current state of a reactor.")
(Rules (RULE1 (IF ((?A.PRIMARY.COOLING.SYSTEM IS IN CLASS PRIMARY.COOLING.SYSTEMS)
                   AND (THE PRESSURE OF ?A.PRIMARY.COOLING.SYSTEM IS DECREASING)
                   AND (THE STATUS OF (THE HIGH.PRESSURE.INJECTION.SYSTEM OF (THE REACTOR OF
                                                                              ?A.PRIMARY.COOLING.SYSTEM))
                            IS ON))
                THEN (THE INTEGRITY OF ?A.PRIMARY.COOLING.SYSTEM IS CHALLENGED)))
       (RULE2 (IF ((?A.SECONDARY.COOLING.SYSTEM IS IN CLASS SECONDARY.COOLING.SYSTEMS)
                   AND (THE TEMPERATURE OF (THE PRIMARY.COOLING.SYSTEM OF (THE REACTOR OF
                                                                         ?A.SECONDARY.COOLING.SYSTEM))
                            IS INCREASING))
                THEN (THE HEAT.TRANSFER OF ?A.SECONDARY.COOLING.SYSTEM IS INADEQUATE)))
       (RULE3 (IF ((?A.GENERATOR IS IN CLASS STEAM.GENERATORS) AND (THE LEVEL OF ?A.GENERATOR IS DECREASING))
                THEN (THE INVENTORY OF ?A.GENERATOR IS INADEQUATE)))
       (RULE4 (IF ((?A.VESSEL IS IN CLASS CONTAINMENT.VESSELS) AND (THE RADIATION OF ?A.VESSEL IS HIGH)
                   AND (THE PRESSURE OF ?A.VESSEL IS HIGH))
                THEN (THE INTEGRITY OF ?A.VESSEL IS CHALLENGED)))
       (RULE5 (IF ((?A.REACTOR IS IN CLASS REACTORS) AND (THE HEAT.TRANSFER OF (THE SECONDARY.COOLING.SYSTEM OF
                                                                                ?A.REACTOR)
                                                      IS INADEQUATE)
                   AND (THE FLOW OF (THE FEEDWATER.PUMP OF ?A.REACTOR)
                            IS LOW))
                THEN (A CURRENT.STATE OF ?A.REACTOR IS "Loss of Feedwater Accident")))
       (RULE6 (IF ((?A.REACTOR IS IN CLASS REACTORS) AND (THE INVENTORY OF (THE STEAM.GENERATOR OF ?A.REACTOR)
                                                      IS INADEQUATE)
                   AND (THE FLOW OF (THE FEEDWATER.PUMP OF ?A.REACTOR)
                            IS LOW))
                THEN (A CURRENT.STATE OF ?A.REACTOR IS "Loss of Feedwater Accident")))
       (RULE7 (IF ((?A.REACTOR IS IN CLASS REACTORS) AND (THE INTEGRITY OF (THE PRIMARY.COOLING.SYSTEM OF
                                                                            ?A.REACTOR)
                                                      IS CHALLENGED)
                   AND (THE INTEGRITY OF (THE CONTAINMENT.VESSEL OF ?A.REACTOR)
                            IS CHALLENGED))
                THEN (A CURRENT.STATE OF ?A.REACTOR IS "Loss of Coolant Accident")))
       (RULE8 (IF ((?A.REACTOR IS IN CLASS REACTORS) AND (THE INTEGRITY OF (THE PRIMARY.COOLING.SYSTEM OF
                                                                            ?A.REACTOR)
                                                      IS CHALLENGED)
                   AND (THE LEVEL OF (THE STEAM.GENERATOR OF ?A.REACTOR)
                            IS INCREASING))
                THEN (A CURRENT.STATE OF ?A.REACTOR IS "Steam Generator Tube Rupture")))
       (RULE9 (IF ((?A.REACTOR IS IN CLASS REACTORS) AND (THE INVENTORY OF (THE STEAM.GENERATOR OF ?A.REACTOR)
                                                      IS INADEQUATE)
                   AND (THE STEAM.FLOW OF (THE STEAM.GENERATOR OF ?A.REACTOR)
                            IS HIGH))
                THEN (A CURRENT.STATE OF ?A.REACTOR IS "Steam Line Break"))))
```

Figure 10-5 Reactors system rules. (Program copyrights © 1983, 1984 by IntelliCorp. All rights reserved.)

ATTACHING GRAPHICAL IMAGES

Values that are of particular interest can be displayed and manipulated graphically using a set of predefined images, such as plots, pie charts, thermometers, pipes, and valves. For example, in Figure 10-3 a graphic image of a histogram has been attached to the NET.POSITIVE.SUCTION.HEAD slot of PUMP1. This particular histogram, which simulates the monitoring of the pressure on the inlet side of the pump over time, changes as the value of the NET.POSITIVE.SUCTION.HEAD slot changes. Conversely, the user can change the value of the slot by pointing to the histogram image with the mouse.

This histogram is one of many graphical images that are predefined in the ACTIVEIMAGES AND KEEGAUGES knowledge bases. Programmers select and place graphical images on the screen via menu choices, attach the images to particular slots by pointing with a mouse, and then edit or specialize the image for their own purposes.

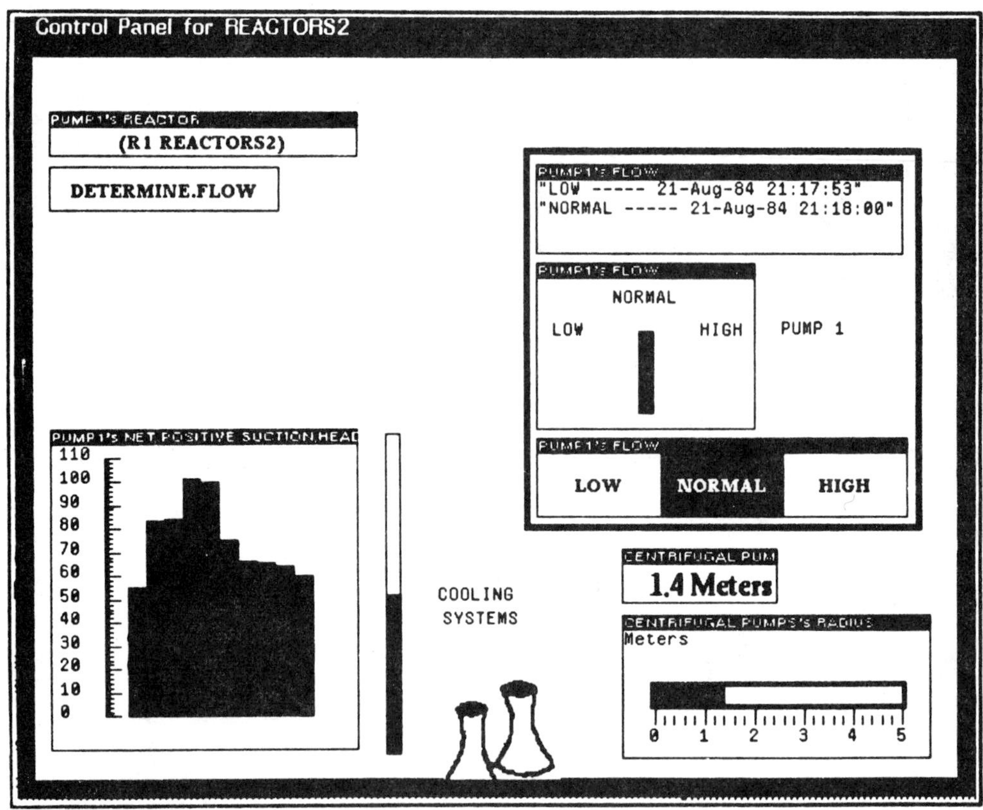

Figure 10-6 KEE images, attached to frame slots, form a miniature control panel to monitor pump activity. (Program copyrights © 1983, 1984 by IntelliCorp. All rights reserved.)

Collections of images can be created for different applications, as illustrated in Figure 10-6. Here the knowledge system designer built a miniature control panel to monitor pump activity. The control panel contains the NET.POSITIVE-.SUCTION.HEAD histogram, a meter resembling a metric ruler, digital readouts, two cooling towers, and a levelometer. Within the control panel, the programmer has also designed a composite gauge, with its own border. The composite gauge consists of a group of gauges that display flow measures determined according to a method gauge button called DETERMINE.FLOW. When pointed at, this button carries out a specified action. DETERMINE.FLOW is a slot in the PUMP1 unit. The FLOW that it determines is also a slot in that unit. Because of the restricted flow values indicated in that slot, the meter readings can be only LOW, NORMAL, or HIGH.

Once the initial objects, hierarchies, units, and rules are created, KEE users can use the unit editor to add or modify units, their slots, values, or children in the inheritance hierarchy. Much like all knowledge system designers, they will engage in short, tight, repetitive cycles of modify and test—in other words, exploratory programming and rapid prototyping. This REACTORS2 knowledge base is an example of what a knowledge system designer might construct in a day or two as the first development cycle of a large system.

USING THE KEE-CREATED KNOWLEDGE SYSTEM

To operate this KEE-developed expert system, users may respond to knowledge system prompts for symptoms. Or, they may use an English-like assertion/retrieval language to make statements or to ask questions about the system.

For example, to enter into the system the fact that the flow of the feedwater pump of reactor R1 is low, the user can enter the assertion

```
(ASSERT (THE FLOW OF (THE FEEDWATER.PUMP OF R1) IS LOW))
```

The system will figure out that the value of the slot FEEDWATER.PUMP of the unit R1, shown in Figure 10-7, is PUMP1. It will then respond to the assertion by setting the value of the FLOW slot of PUMP1 to LOW.

After a system parameter has been altered, the user might want to know the current state of the reactor. Using the assertion/retrieval language, the user enters

```
(QUERY (THE CURRENT.STATE OF R1 IS ?WHAT) 'ALL 'REACTOR.TESTERS)
```

This query is shown in the Top Level Typescript window (bottom left window) of Figure 10-7. The hypothesis in this query contains a variable, ?WHAT. KEE's rule system will backward-chain through all rules with conclusions that match this hypothesis, allowing arbitrary substitutions for the variable ?WHAT. The argument 'ALL tells the rule system to test all the hypotheses that

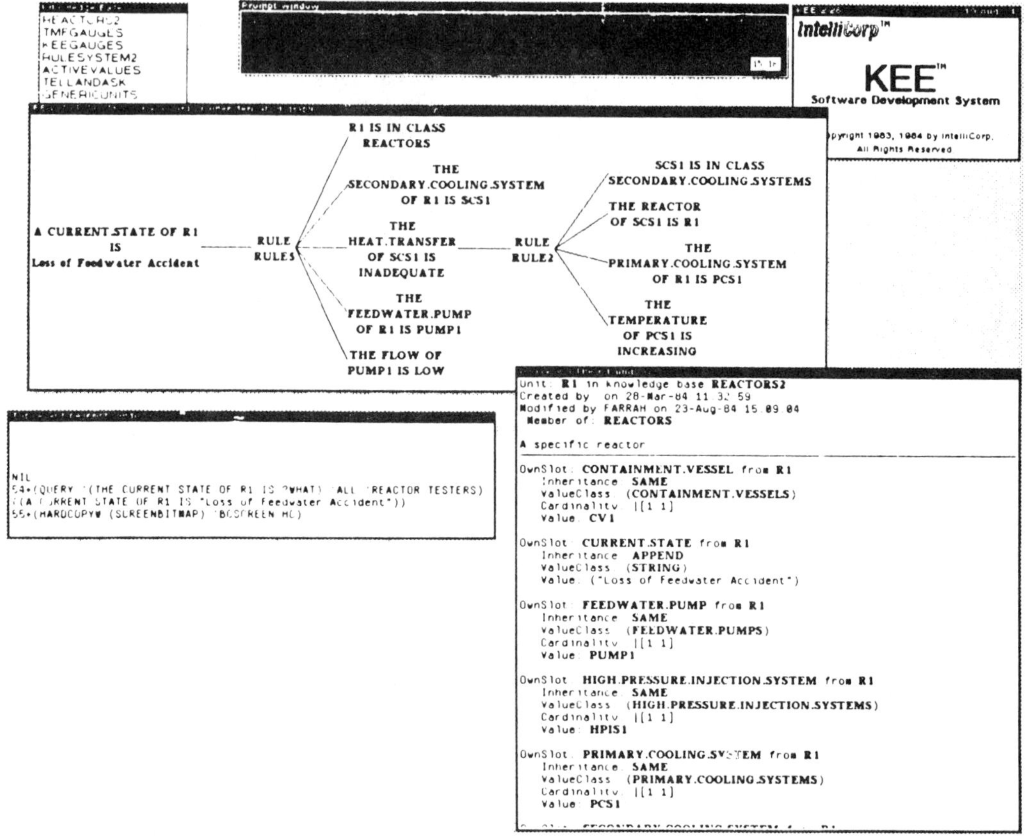

Figure 10-7 The Reactors knowledge system solves a problem and explains its reasoning. (Programs copyright © 1983, 1984, by IntelliCorp. All rights reserved.)

conclude THE CURRENT.STATE OF R1 IS ?WHAT, continuing even after one has been found to be true. The argument 'REACTOR.TESTERS tells which rule class to use.

Rules 5 through 9 in Figure 10-5 have conclusions that make statements about the current state of a reactor. KEE concludes, however, that the CURRENT.STATE OF R1 IS LOSS OF FEEDWATER ACCIDENT. The decision tree in Figure 10-7 is KEE's explanation of how it arrived at this conclusion.

KEE hypothesizes first that the current state is Loss of Feedwater Accident. It then attempts to verify this hypothesis. Rule 5, which concludes this hypothesis, has five clauses which must be satisfied. KEE tries to satisfy each of the clauses in several ways. It scans the list of facts in the units contained in the knowledge base, and those that have been concluded by other rules, to verify whether the clauses are already known to be true or false. Failing these clause verification techniques, KEE scans the conclusion of each rule to determine whether the clause in question can be inferred by at least one other rule.

To conclude a rule, it is sometimes necessary to back-chain recursively. In such a case, KEE evaluates a clause in the premise of one rule to use that rule's conclusion to satisfy a premise of a second rule to use the second rule's conclusion to satisfy the premise of a third rule, and so on, until the desired conclusion is inferred. Finally, when a necessary fact is not listed in a unit and cannot be directly inferred by a rule, KEE requests information from either the user or a sensor.

The first clause in rule 5 hypothesizes that ?A.REACTOR IS IN CLASS REACTORS. ?A.REACTOR is a variable, and therefore KEE looks through its knowledge base for reactors. It finds two, R1 and R2. The unit R1 states that R1 is a member of REACTORS, and therefore the first clause of rule 5 is satisfied.

The rule listing shows the next two clauses on the explanation graph written as a nested statement. The clause THE SECONDARY.COOLING.SYSTEM OF R1 IS SCS1 is a known fact, because a slot in the R1 unit indicates that the value of SECONDARY.COOLING.SYSTEM is SCS1. This slot is scrolled off the portion of the R1 unit shown in Figure 10-7 and therefore is not visible.

The third clause, THE HEAT.TRANSFER OF SCS1 IS INADEQUATE is not a fact, but a conclusion of rule 2. So, to conclude inadequate heat transfer, KEE chains back to rule 2 and tries to satisfy rule 2's conditions. The first three clauses in rule 2 are facts found in the SCS1 and R1 units. The fourth clause, the TEMPERATURE OF PCS1 IS INCREASING, is known to be true because the value in a slot of the PCS1 unit says so. The information in the PCS1 slot comes from sensor readings.

Having concluded the conditions of rule 2, KEE can now conclude the third clause of rule 5 about the heat transfer of SCS1 being inadequate. Rule 5's fourth clause is satisfied because the value of the FEEDWATER.PUMP slot from the R1 unit is PUMP1. The PUMP1 unit in Figure 10-3, whose readings correspond to the explanation graph, shows the value of the FLOW OF PUMP1 IS LOW.

After backward chaining in this way, KEE responds with

```
THE CURRENT.STATE OF R1 IS LOSS OF FEEDWATER ACCIDENT
```

KEE automatically enters this fact into the knowledge base by adding LOSS OF FEEDWATER ACCIDENT to the list of values for the slot CURRENT.STATE in R1. There it is accessible for further reasoning and decision making on the part of either KEE or the user.

MANY VIEWPOINTS

A range of capabilities and features characterize the various knowledge system application tools. One feature, for example, that became popular in Inference

Corp.'s ART (Advanced Reasoning Tool), and was subsequently added to KEE, is a mechanism known as "viewpoints" (called "Worlds" in KEE). As will be seen, it is particularly useful for reasoning with processes that change with time, and for reasoning with various alternative solutions to a problem.

In database terms, viewpoints are analogous to a logical user view—the view that different users, such as a personnel manager and department manager have of a database. Similarly, viewpoints are essentially different views of the world about which the program is reasoning.

Each viewpoint created in a knowledge system contains a subset of the facts in that system. Typically, knowledge system developers create viewpoints to represent different situations, one situation at different times, hypothetical situations, or alternative courses of action.

Like objects in object-oriented programming, the viewpoints are organized into an inheritance hierarchy. Viewpoints lower in this hierarchy inherit facts and conceptual information from the higher level viewpoints.

During program execution, knowledge systems use the different viewpoints to reason, in parallel, along independent paths and to explore various solutions or the consequences of several possible decisions. Once ART identifies a relevant viewpoint to reason with, it can view only those facts that have been created or asserted for that viewpoint, or are inherited; other information is excluded.

For example, system developers might create viewpoints to represent analysts's different estimates of a market or their competing explanations for observations made about a business. The analysts would then use the viewpoints to reason about and compare competing estimates or explanations in order to choose one that best fits a situation or observation. As the knowledge system reasons about each analyst's market estimate, it sees all the facts and assumptions leading up to that estimate, and only those facts and assumptions. The same viewpoint mechanism could just as well apply to the signal processing domain where there is input data with a lot of uncertainties, noise, and conflicting interpretations of what is occurring.

Another benefit of having a viewpoint mechanism is its ability to reason about different partial solutions in parallel instead of committing to one solution until it is proved wrong. More commonly, knowledge systems do not reason in parallel, but approach problem solving in knowledge systems through a mechanism called backtracking. With backtracking, a program selects a rule, applies the rule which changes the database, applies another rule against the new database, and so on until a problem solution is reached.

Alas, it may happen that a solution is not reached and that the program must backtrack to some decision point to begin again the process of selecting and applying rules in a new decision path. Needless to say, a large search space can result in an exponentially large computation.

The viewpoint mechanism reduces the amount of backtracking necessary by creating several viewpoints representing alternative reasoning paths. As the program reasons, it proceeds along different reasoning paths in parallel. Since one of the parallel paths generally leads to a solution or decision, while others may lead to a dead end along the way, parallel reasoning about viewpoints avoids the need for sequential, exhaustive consideration of all options.

Geese can be used to illustrate the benefits of viewpoints. In a signal-processing application, incoming data may suggest either bombers approaching a country's borders or a flock of geese. With a viewpoints mechanism, a knowledge system need not assume bombers and travel all the way down the path of reasoning until it uncovers a contradition, and then backtrack and try out the flock of geese hypothesis. Instead, the viewpoints-based system can assume the bombers in one viewpoint, the flock of geese in the other, and explore in parallel the ramifications of each.

One knowledge system, developed with ART, schedules helicopters (but could be designed to schedule any vehicle or machine) in response to reservation requests and route availability information. Designers of the ART-based scheduling system created the system with two levels of viewpoints that are each used differently. One level, called the hypothetical level, uses them for hypothetical reasoning. Viewpoints that the system creates at this level represent hypotheses about the different ways to satisfy routing requests. A level within the hypothetical level, called the state level, contains vehicle-related state information. The scheduling system creates viewpoints at this level to represent the state of vehicles at different times during a journey.

During the scheduling process, the scheduling system dynamically creates new hypothetical and state viewpoints. Because some journeys entail multiple hops (they are not nonstop), the system may create multiple hierarchical chains of hypothetical viewpoints to represent possible ways to satisfy reservations at different legs of a journey, as well as hierarchies of state viewpoints to represent reservations satisfied during the legs of the journey.

Child viewpoints created in these multiple hierarchies inherit information from their parents. However, the hierarchies are separate. Once the scheduling system identifies a particular viewpoint to reason about, it can see only the information that has been asserted for that viewpoint or inherited by it; other route information is invisible to it.

The system designers placed global scheduling and routing information in the root viewpoint at the hypothetical level. Initial system information, such as what vehicle routings are desired and the current location of each vehicle in the system, are placed in the root viewpoint at the state level.

When a vehicle reservation requires movement of the vehicle from its current location to another, the system creates one or more children of the root viewpoint at the hypothetical level. Each represents possible reservations, and each contains inherited information about routing and previous reservations. Rules reason, in parallel, about each of the hypothetical viewpoints created. As the different route and reservation viewpoints are explored, unsatisfactory ones are rejected. Rules then update the state viewpoint by creating child viewpoints that indicate the state, or partial schedule, that results after the first reservation has been satisfied.

The system then repeats this set of procedures. By doing so, it reasons about the partial schedule viewpoints, creating viewpoint hierarchies until it has found a way to satisfy all reservations and produce a completed schedule.

Another ART-based knowledge system helps portfolio managers construct a portfolio based on the amount of money available to invest, general economic and market conditions, the portfolio manager's profile, and the instruments available for investment. The available instruments are found in various financial databases that the knowledge system accesses. To construct a portfolio, the Portfolio Manager uses six levels of viewpoints, representing views of different money managers, economic scenarios, assets, transactions, holdings lists, and possible portfolios.

As with the scheduling system, each level of viewpoints is used differently. To quote one example, at the holdings-list level, the Portfolio Manager system generates all the possible combinations of various percentages of potential investments. Each combination is represented by a viewpoint. If the combination does not represent 100 percent of the money allocated for a portfolio, the system merges two or more viewpoints to build a new combination. Since the number of possible combinations is too large for a computer to handle in a reasonable amount of time, as the viewpoints are being built the knowledge system uses constraints and criteria, embodied in rules, to eliminate those it considers unsatisfactory. The Portfolio Manager knowledge system is discussed in detail in Chapter 20.

A KNOWLEDGE BASE TOOL WITH DATABASE FEATURES

Another knowledge system tool, Knowledge Craft (from Carnegie Group, Inc.), has distinguished itself not only by its knowledge engineering features, but also because it implements some features normally associated with database management systems. Its knowledge engineering features include multiple, embedded knowledge representation languages to represent knowledge in whatever way is best for a problem at hand, an "agenda" mechanism that keeps track of queues of events, and a viewpoint mechanism. Its database features are important because they give to knowledge-based systems some of the database management capabilities taken for granted in database applications.

Unlike databases, most knowledge bases are limited in size and performance because they require the complete program and knowledge base to be contained in main memory during program operation. Knowledge-based systems have gotten by, until now, with these main memory requirements because most knowledge systems have been small enough to be able to rely on virtual memory techniques. With virtual memory, program parts that do not fit in main memory remain temporarily on a disk but are swapped with program parts already in main memory in order to be used. It goes without saying that as a program becomes very large, the increasing number of disk accesses required to page material into main memory cause performance to suffer. This, in turn, limits the size of programs. In addition, the handling of virtual memory by the operating system environment interferes with knowledge base control over such functions as buffering and transaction handling. Removal of this control, in favor of the operating system, further limits performance as well as the ability to ensure data integrity.

Databases do not encounter these problems because they come equipped with a disk storage management system which allows them to store, access, and manipulate large amounts of data on a disk without first needing to load it into main memory. Handling data directly on disk permits further increases in performance through sophisticated indexing of the disk data and fine tuning of the layout of the databases on the disk.

Knowledge Craft provides such disk storage management capabilities for its knowledge bases. With a knowledge-based management system (the knowledge system counterpart of a database management system), gone is the time wasted while hundreds of frames are loaded into memory in order to start program execution. Gone also is the time spent waiting while no longer useful or accessible frames are garbage-collected (a technique used to remove useless information from memory) to make room for other frames needed by the program. Performance is gained because the inefficiencies of virtual memory are eliminated. Also, the knowledge bases can be tuned for optimized performance. Since knowledge-based management systems manage knowledge on disk, they can support very large knowledge-based applications without requiring huge amounts of memory.

Knowledge Craft is not new, nor are its undertakings in building large knowledge-based systems. Developed at Carnegie-Mellon University, in its precommercial days the system was named SRL (Schema Representation Language) and was used in a number of large-scale, knowledge-based manufacturing projects. Subsequently, SRL was enhanced and renamed.

SRL was designed to model organizations at different levels of abstraction. At a concrete level, it models machines, tools, materials, and people. At a more abstract level, it models departments, tasks, goals, events, communications, authority interactions, and time. The organization models developed are used by assorted knowledge system processes to perform analyses and make decisions.

Three design goals influenced Knowledge Craft's model-building decisions. First, the system should be able to model many types of organizations (continuous and discrete). Second, managers and engineers, who are the prime users of such systems, should be able to easily learn, peruse, modify, and understand the model, preferably because it uses the same terms that people use to think about the organization and its problems. Third, all objects, system features, and program capabilities must be integrated. Since no single problem-solving or knowledge representation technique has yet proven adequate for all problems, Knowledge Craft's designers endowed the system with several integrated problem-solving and knowledge representation techniques, which may be combined in a single application.

For example, the system contains three embedded AI languages: OPS5, Prolog, and SRL (also called CRL). OPS5 is the rule-based language used to build commercial applications such as XCON, DEC's knowledge-based computer configuration system, and XSEL, the sales representative's version of the application. Prolog is a logic-based language which has rule-based and inference capabilities in addition to relational database characteristics. SRL is a frame-based language (a frame in the CMU systems is called a "schema"). It was used to build ISIS, a CMU/Westinghouse factory scheduling system, and a variety of other planning, factory management, and monitoring systems developed for DEC, Westinghouse, and the U.S. Air Force.

These languages, and their associated knowledge representation techniques (rules, logic, and frames), allow knowledge system designers to describe different types of organizations in whatever manner is most natural for that organization, for different users, and preferred by the designer. Further flexibility, and funtionality, in problem solving is provided because conventional programs may be associated with slots in frames.

The agenda mechanism keeps track of multiple queues of events and manages the scheduling of the events for execution. Such a mechanism helps adapt Knowledge Craft for applications such as simulation and scheduling. In simulation systems, the agenda mechanism is instrumental in tracking and simulating events. In scheduling systems, it manages and schedules events for execution on a critical or specified time basis.

Coupled with the rule-based mechanism, the agenda mechanism can provide a viewpoint mechanism. The rules can sprout new contexts (subdivisions of a problem). The agenda mechanism then keeps track of the multiple contexts. The result is a viewpoint mechanism that can explore alternative problem-solving paths, simultaneously.

Further details about building knowledge systems with Knowledge Craft are discussed in Chapters 15 to 18 in the context of the manufacturing systems it was used to develop.

MORE ABOUT DATABASES

Even though knowledge system development tools are essential elements in commercializing knowledge systems, it is the practical issues that will pace their penetration into industry. Only as the knowledge systems developed become compatible with existing computers and software applications, and the knowledge base size and performance constraints are overcome, can AI technology really catch on.

Carnegie Group, Inc. addressed some of these problems via Knowledge Craft's database management capabilities and ability to run on a variety of time-sharing systems, in addition to AI workstations. To varying degrees,

Teknowledge, Inference Corp., and IntelliCorp are transporting their knowledge-based tools to conventional computers so that knowledge systems developed with these tools can execute on relatively inexpensive computers and be integrated with conventional applications.

Silogic, Inc. is in agreement with this kind of thinking. So it designed its Logic Workbench with database capabilities and standard-computer compatibility. The Logic Workbench is a Prolog application development system that addresses several issues important to commercial knowledge system acceptance. Available on 68000-based Unix machines, which are common in standard operational environments, the Logic Workbench stores and manages its knowledge bases on disk rather than in main memory. As a result, like Knowledge Craft, the Logic Workbench's knowledge-based management system supports enhanced performance and very large knowledge-based applications.

The Logic Workbench carries its database and compatibility capabilities even further in that it interfaces to ordinary Unix databases. Consequently, AI programmers and users need not rekey information already present in their corporate databases. Because Prolog has many characteristics of relational databases, including query and database representation capabilities, they can use the same Prolog commands to access and manipulate both database and knowledge base information. This single, consistent interface across the database and knowledge base contributes to ease of use of knowledge systems developed with such a dual access tool.

MENU-DRIVEN TOOLS FOR VERTICAL MARKETS

Most large-scale tools discussed have been general purpose tools. However, there is a developing trend toward specialized tools, with generic knowledge applicable to a particular application domain. For example, Escort, a shell developed by London, England's PA Computers and Telecommunications for machine fault diagnosis (as part of an interface to process plant instrumentation), knows about process plant things like stop valves, control loops, and sensor switches. This kind of knowledge forms part of a precanned, generic knowledge base, applicable to any process plant. Users need add only specific company process-plant knowledge.

Some vertical-market AI tools know about specific industrial or financial areas, such as factory monitoring, real-time, and loan approval. Others are more general and contain knowledge about solving certain classes of problems.

The best-known examples of vertical knowledge-based shells that know about factory monitoring are Simkit from IntelliCorp, and Simulation Craft from Carnegie Group, Inc. Simkit is built on top of KEE; Simulation Craft is built on top of Knowledge Craft.

Both Simkit and Simulation Craft are graphical, menu- and icon-based simulation systems. Their precanned knowledge bases contain generic-factory knowledge, for example about factory components, scheduling, assembly operations, materials flow, and factory goals. However, the knowledge bases do not contain specific knowledge, such as about a particular manufacturing facility or the products manufactured there. Users of these systems—typically non-programmers—add this knowledge by combining plant-component icons to represent their plant and by picking textual choices from menus.

The knowledge system uses its generic factory knowledge to prompt the users for specific knowledge. Based on this knowledge, the application simulates factory production. During the simulation, it uses its knowledge of manufacturing to detect where bottlenecks will occur and to recommend corrective action.

It is important to note that shells like these are not limited to factories. They are being built with knowledge about any system that a user wants to model and simulate.

Having even more general aims in mind, Teknowledge is building Copernicus, a modular tool, upward compatible from S.1, and with modules containing pre-canned knowledge about broad classes of applications. For example, different Copernicus modules will contain knowledge about application classes such as diagnostics, planning, design assistance, and decision support. Knowledge-system developers can select the modules applicable to their application and also select modules to tailor the tool for development or delivery.

A diagnostics module's knowledge base would contain knowledge that applies to all diagnostic problems. This includes knowledge about things like hypotheses, tests, measurements, and explanations. The knowledge base acts like a template or shell on top of the core Copernicus system. Programmers can start their applications with this knowledge base and then modify it or add more knowledge about a specific problem to complete the application.

It is possible to build layers of shells on top of shells. With this in mind, Teknowledge is looking to build layers of application-specific shells on top of these general problem-solving shells. The application-specific shells would be built using the vocabulary of the vertical market applications. They would draw on the general knowledge of the underlying shells. But they would address specific diagnostic or decision-support applications such as commercial loan approval and financial risk management.

All in all, tools are alleviating many problems limiting widespread acceptance of knowledge systems. A problem remaining can be solved only with time; users must gain experience in building and running a variety of applications.

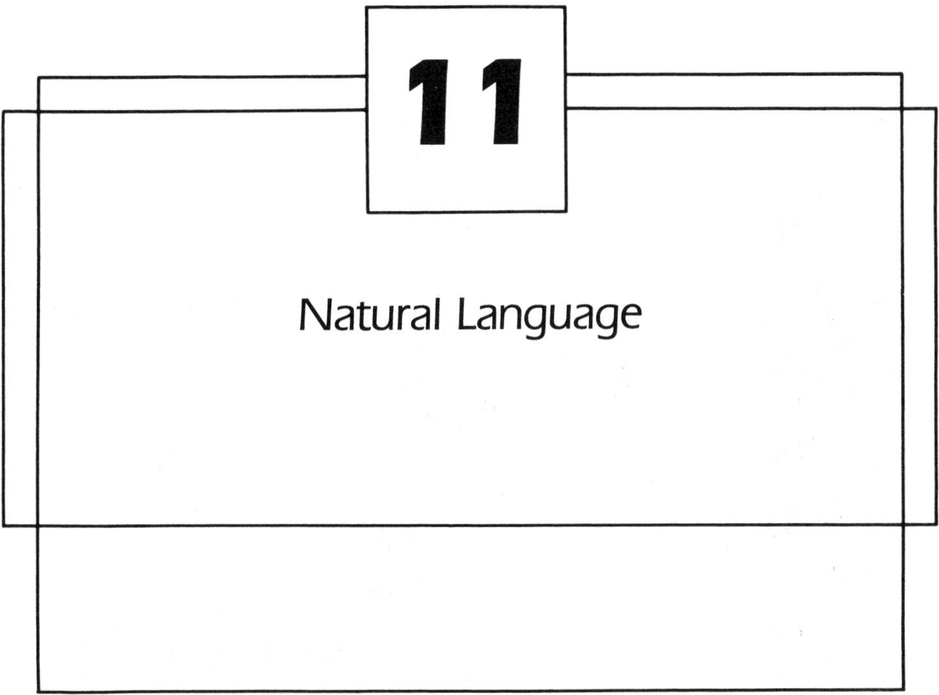

11 Natural Language

Natural language is the communications medium of people everywhere in the world, and exclusively of people. In an attempt to change that exclusivity, in the 1970s a number of experiments were performed to teach natural language to chimpanzees. Of course, the chimps could not speak. But they could understand American Sign Language (the language developed for the deaf) and they could understand felt material symbols for words on a felt board.

One chimp, named Sarah, had a vocabulary of 130 word symbols. Another chimp, named Washoe, could sign 130 words with her fingers and hands. These vocabularies were less than that of a small schoolchild. Nonetheless, Sarah's trainer could, for example, say "Sarah insert apple pail banana dish" in symbols and Sarah would respond by putting the apple in the pail and the banana in the dish. As another example of what the chimps could do, Washoe could put together the words and sign "Roger you tickle" and "come hug" and Roger would respond by tickling or hugging Washoe.

Despite these and similar communications examples, the success of the natural language and chimpanzee experiments were always controversial. Proponents said that Sarah understood the trainer because she gave the appropriate response, which was to put the apple in the pail and the banana in the dish. Furthermore, they said, Washoe was able to map her needs and desires into the trainer's natural language. That natural-language communications occurred was evidenced by the fact that Washoe elicited the appropriate response from her trainer, who responded by tickling or hugging her. Critics, however, argued that the responses were nothing more than conditioning.

Since we do not know how or why people understand natural language, the

Figure 11-1 Toddler indicates understanding of natural language by her response. (Photo courtesy Erik Keller)

appropriate response or action is the usual measure of natural-language understanding and often the only point of interest. For example, we know that students have understood a teacher's natural-language communications if they give the appropriate responses on a test. We also know that a toddler has developed to the point where the toddler understands language when that toddler can respond to a request such as "show me the new car" by producing a toy (Figure 11-1). On the other hand, if we said the same thing to an automobile salesperson, the salesperson will have understood if he or she goes into a sales pitch.

With the success of the chimp language experiments still undetermined, natural language remains the communications medium solely of human beings. Recently, however, a new candidate—the computer—has emerged that appears to be able to communicate in natural language. Consider, as evidence, the following office scenario that took place on one of those days when nothing seems to go right.

On that day, Joe NewManager, very concerned with rising to the responsibilities of his new position, arrived at the office late because of traffic, only to be informed that an emergency marketing meeting had been called for 20 minutes hence. Losing no time, Joe turned to his assistant and said, "We need to find where the money's going. Get me a list of the last two months' total expenses for each department and a piechart of total salaries in each department."

Ten minutes later, Joe had his figures and graphs and was off to the meeting. His assistant stayed behind on the desk. Yes, on the desk, because Joe's assistant was a computer, not a person. Nonetheless, his nonhuman assistant understood his humanoid, ungrammatical, natural-language requests.

How do we know the computer understood him? We know because it performed the appropriate actions; it fetched the data from the database and made up Joe's graphs.

The nice thing about Joe (or anyone else) being able to speak natural language to a computer is that natural language is so natural to human beings. It stands in marked contrast to formal computer languages, such as Basic, Fortran, and Cobol. Such formal languages are ideal for expressing algorithms and data structures so that they are easily understood by computers. Unfortunately, because they are complex and highly structured, they are not as easily understood by noncomputing professionals who require or desire access to computers, but for many reasons, may not wish to learn a formal language.

For this reason there is a growing movement to put natural-language systems on computers. The most popular of the natural-language systems, which address the most immediate need, are database front ends that understand database queries phrased in unconstrained English (or other native language) rather than formal query languages. Other natural-language systems solve problems based on users' English language requests or act as advisory and consulting systems that converse with the user.

Typically, natural-language systems can handle a range of queries, phrased differently. They can understand sentences with missing parts and they can deal with users who do not speak correct English.

Despite this flexibility, natural-language systems have several limitations. Most important, they are inherently limited to handling queries about a specifically designed narrow domain of knowledge that pertains only to their own database. Similarly, most commercial natural-language systems can only recognize vocabulary that is encoded in their dictionaries. Some of the natural-language companies are alleviating this problem by automating the acquisition-of-knowledge process so that users can easily extend the dictionary and some of the database definitions themselves. Adding vocabulary of different databases by moving the natural-language interface from one database to another is a more difficult problem that requires knowledge of natural language and databases.

Computer programs that understand natural language must also be able to resolve the problems associated with ambiguous sentences. Most natural-language systems handle ambiguities by using sentence structure, grammatical and dictionary knowledge, and sometimes, also, a knowledge of what is in the database. But these are only partially adequate solutions. Human beings typically resolve ambiguity by understanding sentences in the context of their knowledge of the real world. Only a few sophisticated natural-language systems can imitate this method, and then, only to some degree.

For example, consider the classified ad

> DOG FOR SALE. VERY FRIENDLY. NOT FEROCIOUS. WILL EAT ANYTHING. ESPECIALLY FOND OF CHILDREN.

Although amusing, this ad points out a real problem. Few people would misinterpret this ad as describing the dog's preferred diet. Natural-language systems could be misled. And, although possible, representing the knowledge of the context of the advertisement on a computer is a difficult task.

Motivation analysis is a difficult capability to computerize, but it is necessary to fully understand and interpret natural language. Motivation analysis is the reason that telephone callers who say "HELLO, CAN I SPEAK TO SONIA" or even "HELLO, IS SONIA THERE," are not generally given a simple yes-or-no answer. Similarly, an ideal natural-language-based tax assistant advisory system that helps a client fill out tax forms could use motivation analysis to respond to a question such as "What is a 1040?" Instead of a dictionary-definition response, a more valuable answer (based on the probable motivation for the question) is "It is the form that says 1040 in block letters at the top."

Finally, pronouns, and determining what they refer to, often cause natural-language-system developers grave woes. For example, human beings interpret sentences such as "STEVE WENT TO THE STORE, FOUND A BASEBALL GLOVE ON THE SHELF, PAID FOR IT AND LEFT" in light of common sense knowledge of real-world situations. Unfortunately, the average natural-language system relies on more mundane techniques. For example, if the sentence represents information contained in an interfacing database, the natural-language system commonly determines the referent by interrogating the database to see whether the glove or the shelf has an associated price. Otherwise, it determines the referent with the help of grammmatical rules. These rules associate the pronoun with the closest noun, which, in this case, is clearly incorrect.

Despite these limitations, several successful natural-language systems, particularly natural-language interfaces to databases, have been built. In fact, a number of database companies and analysts contend that competitive pressures will drive every serious database company to provide natural-language front ends to all its operations.

There is another school of thought. Some firms will not plan a natural-language interface for their databases because there are still too many limitations and problems left to solve. They point out that natural-language interfaces to databases are not general-purpose interfaces. Instead, they are suitable for specific database applications. They also claim that it is still too difficult for end-user companies to set up a lexicon (dictionary) for new applications.

NATURAL-LANGUAGE-SYSTEM INNARDS

There are three basic natural-language techniques: pattern and keyword matching, a mixture of syntax (grammar) and (some) semantics (meaning) directed, and systems containing knowledge base representations of real-world information and scenarios. One of the earliest natural-language programs, ELIZA, which simulates the behavior of a psychologist (Rogerian therapist) and a patient, is a pattern-matching system. Considered a very primitive system today, ELIZA carries on a doctor—patient dialogue but does not really understand the meaning of any input sentences (Figure 11-2). Instead, the ELIZA system tests for keywords and phrases. But it fools users into thinking that it is intelligent because it responds to the user—patient input with associated canned responses and because it echoes the user's sentence but substitutes personal pronouns such as "your" for "my" and "you" for "I".

Most of the current natural-language programs are more useful than ELIZA and employ more intelligent techniques. The dominant technique (although not the most flexible) is to use a formal grammar that contains rules of the English language to help understand a user's sentence. These rules describe the structure of English sentences. Typical rules state that a sentence is made up of a noun phrase followed by a verb phrase, and a verb phrase is a verb followed by a noun phrase. No system, however, can be totally syntax-based because such a system would understand only whether the structure of a sentence is legal. Clearly, this capability would not satisfy users' needs.

For a natural-language system to be useful, it must also be able to deal with semantic information. In the most common type of natural-language system, semantic as well as syntactic information is contained in a lexicon (dictionary). The natural-language system then uses the information in the formal grammar and the lexicon to generate some representation or translation for the input sentence.

```
P.  I FEEL UNHAPPY LATELY.

D.  Do you often feel unhappy lately?
P.  YES.

D.  Is there something bothering you?
P.  MY MOTHER HATES MY SCIENTIFIC STUDIES.

D.  Is it important to you that your mother hates your scientific studies?
P.  I WANT HER TO APPROVE OF ME.

D.  What would it mean to you if you got her to approve of you?
P.  I WOULD FEEL PLEASED.

D.  You say you would feel pleased?
P.  YES, IT IS NICE WHEN PEOPLE ADMIRE YOU.

D.  Is there any other time?
P.
```

Figure 11-2 An Eliza dialog

The representation or translation is necessary to map the natural language of the user to the language of the computer. For a user's natural-language database query that asks for, say, "the numbers and names of the employees that make more than $300 per week," the representation may be a formal database query, such as, "SELECT EMPNO, LASTNAME FROM DSN8.TEMPLE WHERE (SALARY/52) > 300". For a story-reading program, the representation or translation of a UPI newpaper article might be a paraphrase of an input paragraph. If the users' goal is to trigger some action or response, the users' input might be represented as computer instructions to perform a task.

RECOGNIZING WORDS

The most common way to respresent the rules of grammar is to use what is known as an "augmented transition network." To understand an augmented transition network, it is first necessary to understand simpler transition networks. A transition network (also called a finite-state automaton) is a node-and-arc graph. The nodes represent "states" of some system, such as "starting state" or the "state of having recognized a noun phrase or a verb phrase." The arcs represent rules to apply, or tests to perform, to get to those states.

For example, the transition network in Figure 11-3a is a graphical way of showing that a sentence is composed of a noun phrase followed by a verb phrase. The starting state of the transition network is S1. The arc that leads out of S1 indicates that to get from "state 1" to "state 2" it is necessary to find a noun phrase. To get from "state 2" to "state 3" it is necessary to find a verb phrase.

Other transition networks show the structure of other language constructs, such as noun phrases, verb phrases, and prepositional phrases. Figure 11-3b shows that a noun phrase is composed of either a determiner (such as "the" or "an") or a proper noun or an adjective, followed by any number of adjectives (or no adjectives), followed by a noun, and possibly followed by a prepositional phrase. The arc labeled "jump" indicates that it is possible to jump over this arc without satisfying any rules or matching any words or phrases. Using the jump arc, a noun phrase can also be just a single noun.

These transition network rules can be used to string together words to produce several types of sentences. For example, according to these rules, the phrase "the opera" is a noun phrase because it is composed of a determiner followed by a noun. The phrase "the good opera," which contains a determiner followed by an adjective and then a noun, is also a legal noun phrase, as is the phrase "the magnificently great opera," which is made of a determiner followed by two adjectives followed by a noun. Similarly, "the opera in the park" is a noun phrase because it is composed of a determiner followed by a noun followed by a prepositional phrase. The single noun "opera" also fits the noun phrase definition because jumping from state 4 to state 5 shows that a single noun is allowed.

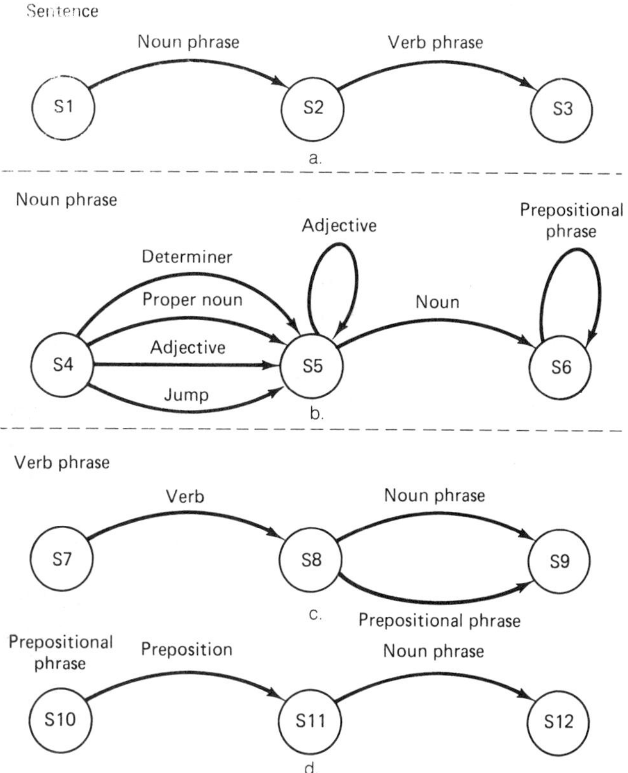

Figure 11-3 Augmented transition network

By the same reasoning, Figure 11-3c shows that a verb phrase is composed of a verb followed by either a noun phrase or a prepositional phrase. Figure 11-3d shows that a prepositional phrase is composed of a preposition followed by a noun phrase.

A parser is a natural-language mechanism that takes a sentence apart word by word. Its goal is to get from one end of a transition network to another in order to recognize sentences. To move from end to end, the parser goes from one node to another by finding the construct specified by the arc. When it has reached the end, in this case by finding a noun phrase followed by a verb phrase, it knows that it has found a sentence.

However, to get from end to end, rules must be able to call other transition networks as subroutines. For example, in Figure 11-3a, to get from state 1 to state 2, the transition network that specializes in sentences must be able to call the noun-phrase specialist. This ability to call different transition networks, like a computer program calls subroutines, is one way that simple transition networks have been augmented—hence they are called "augmented transition network," usually abbreviated to ATN.

ANALYZING SENTENCES

For a parser to parse a sentence and get through a transition network, it must obtain syntactical (grammatical) information about the words in the sentence. Such information is stored in the natural-language system's lexicon.

Typically, the lexicon contains not only information about parts of speech, but also semantic information (Figure 11-4). The semantic information includes the meaning of a word, whether it is a name or a cardinal or ordinal number, an interrogative word, and whether it is contained in a database. Irregular nouns and verbs have separate entries for singular, plural, and irregular forms. Otherwise, plurals and various verb forms are usually generated from the corresponding root entries.

If a word is contained in an interfacing database, the lexicon contains a pointer to (a computer address for) that word's entry in the database. On the other hand, if the word has a representation in some semantic network, the lexicon contains a pointer to the relevant node in that semantic network.

To analyze the sentence "Sparkle fruit stores purchase forty orange crates," the parser begins with the sentence transition network and looks for a noun phrase. To determine if it has found one, the parser must call the noun phrase network.

There are four possible paths in the noun phrase network: determiner, proper noun, adjective, and jump. The parser examines the first word of the sentence to see if it corresponds to its list of determiners, such as the, a, one, and each. Since the lexicon shows that it does not, the parser proceeds to check the next, or proper noun, path.

Since "Sparkle" is both a proper noun and a verb, the parser now has two different choices. At this point, however, the transition network will accept only a determiner, proper noun, or adjective, or it will accept a noun if the jump path is used. Therefore, the parser rules out the possibility that Sparkle is a verb and there is no ambiguity involved in the first noun phrase. The parser takes the proper noun definition of Sparkle and continues.

However, when the parser comes to the next word, "fruit", a temporarily ambiguous situation occurs. "Fruit" is both an adjective and a noun, and the transition network node coming up accepts both an adjective and a noun.

In situations like this where the natural-language system does not specify how to choose, many systems generate two sentences, one based on each possible choice. They then proceed to examine the rest of the phrase and defer their final decision until they find some information that allows them to make a choice.

In the "Sparkle fruit" noun phrase under consideration, only one choice (fruit as an adjective) leads to eventual success in getting through the network.

Word	Category	Features
A	Determiner	Number: singular
Banana	Noun	
Be	Verb	Transitivity: intransitive
Been	Verb	Form: past participle; Type: be
Cat	Noun	
Caught	Verb	Form: past, past participle
Crate	Noun	
Fish	Noun	Number: singular, plural
	Verb	Transitivity: intransitive
Fly	Noun	
	Verb	Transitivity: intransitive
Forty	Adjective	
Fruit	Noun, Adjective	
Like	Verb	Transitivity: transitive
	Preposition	
	Conjunction	
Orange	Adjective, Noun	
Purchase	Noun	
	Verb	Transitivity: transitive
Sparkle	Proper noun	
	Verb	Transitivity: intransitive
Store	Noun	
	Verb	Transitivity: transitive
That	Complementizer	
	Determiner	
	Pronoun	
	Relative	
The	Determiner	
To	Complementizer	
	Preposition	
We	Pronoun	Number: plural; Person: first; Case: subjective
Which	Determiner	Question: yes
	Relative	
Whom	Pronoun	Case: objective; Question: yes
	Relative	
With	Preposition	

Figure 11-4 Some dictionary entries

Thus the system resolves the ambiguity by waiting before it chooses, and choosing when it discovers that there is only one possible successful choice. Sometimes, however, a system may need to wend its way through several transition networks before it can finally make a choice.

This type of scheme, where the natural-language system does not choose until it is certain, but instead tries all the arcs at a particular network node and generates and tests all possible sentences, is called a "nondeterministic" scheme.

PARSE TREES

It is not enough to recognize sentences. A natural-language system also must represent the syntactic structure of a sentence in a way that shows how words and phrases in a sentence relate to one another. These relationships are usually represented in a form known as a "parse tree" (Figure 11-5).

The parse tree for the sentence "the cat caught a fish" looks like an upside-down tree with a single root representing a sentence. The first level of branches decompose the sentence into a noun phrase and a verb phrase. The next level of branches decompose the noun and verb phrases into their component parts. The final level, called the "terminal branches" or just "terminals" or "leaves," contain the results of repeatedly decomposed sentence parts until only single words in the sentence remain.

The syntactic structure, so conveniently displayed in a parse tree, acts as a guide to merging the small chunks and phrases that comprise a sentence into a meaningful representation of the complete sentence. The parse tree can provide information necessary for a meaningful representation because, for one thing, when it is built, it incorporates knowledge about which words modify others. In addition, the parse tree identifies the sentence as an active rather than a passive one. Therefore, the parse tree shows facts such as the cat caught the fish instead of the fish catching the cat.

It is possible to generate a parse tree because a notation known as a "context-free" grammar is used to represent English-language syntax. A context-free grammar is one of four types of grammars defined by Noam Chomsky (at MIT) in the 1950s. The grammars range from very general to highly restricted in terms of the rules that allow sentence components (such as "prepositional

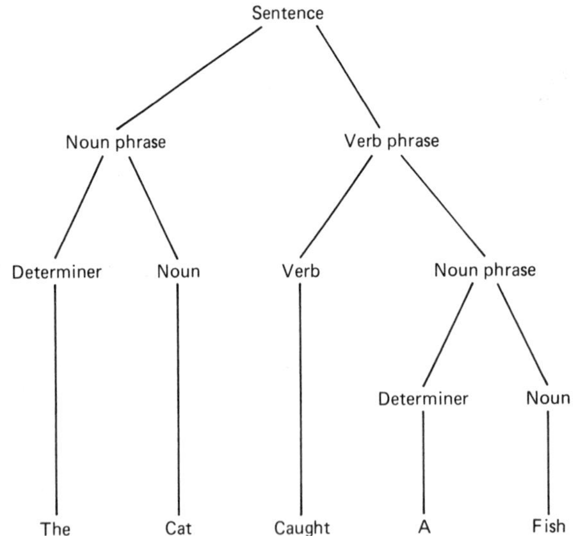

Figure 11-5 A parse tree

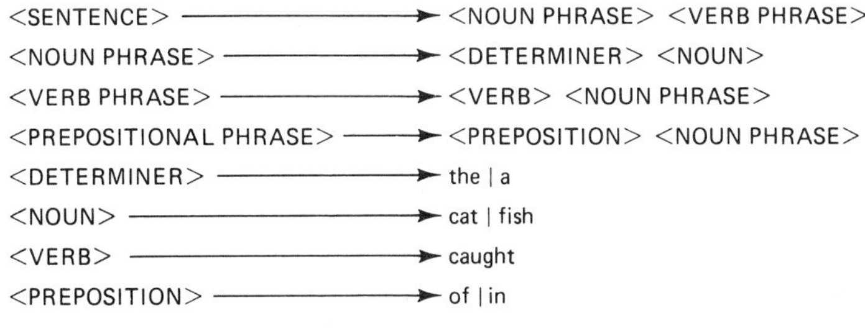
<SENTENCE> → <NOUN PHRASE> <VERB PHRASE>
<NOUN PHRASE> → <DETERMINER> <NOUN>
<VERB PHRASE> → <VERB> <NOUN PHRASE>
<PREPOSITIONAL PHRASE> → <PREPOSITION> <NOUN PHRASE>
<DETERMINER> → the | a
<NOUN> → cat | fish
<VERB> → caught
<PREPOSITION> → of | in

(*Note*: | means "or". For example, a determiner can be "the" or "a.")

Figure 11-6 Production rules for a small subset of a context-free English grammar

phrase'') to be replaced by other sentence components (such as ''preposition follwed by a noun phrase'') in order to generate well-formed sentences in a language.

Basically, Chomsky's grammars consist of a series of rewrite rules (also called production rules) to rewrite a sentence in terms of the sentence parts of which it is made. A typical production rule states that a sentence can be rewritten as (or produces) a noun phrase and a verb phrase. (Figure 11-6).

Production rules replace parts of a sentence with their component parts, down to the terminal branch level, where replacement is no longer possible. For example, the second production rule in Figure 11-6 states that ''a noun phrase can be rewritten as a determiner followed by a noun.'' This rule allows a noun phrase in a sentence to be replaced by a determiner and noun. Determiner and noun can be further decomposed. As other production rules in the figure show, ''a determiner can be rewritten as either the words 'the' or 'a''' and ''a noun can be rewritten as either 'cat' or 'fish'.'' The words ''the,'' ''a,'' ''cat,'' and ''fish'' cannot be further decomposed. To indicate that the decomposition process is at an end, terminal symbols are written in lower case letters.

To generate a parse tree, it is necessary to follow this process and replace the left side of each rule with the appropriate symbols on the right side. What makes a context-free grammar suitable for generating parse trees is that, by definition, the left side of each rule consists of only one symbol to be replaced.

PARSE TREES ARE NOT A BED OF ROSES

ATNs and production rule grammars fail their users when they verify a sentence to be legal and parse it correctly, but the sentence turns out to be illogical. For example, the statement ''IT'S 24 PARTLY CLOUDY DEGREES TODAY'' is a syntactically correct statement. Yet the statement is meaningless.

Worse, grammars can encounter ambiguity difficulties when there is more than one way to build a parse tree with the same sequence of leaf nodes. One of the best known examples is the sentence ''FRUIT FLIES LIKE A BANANA,''

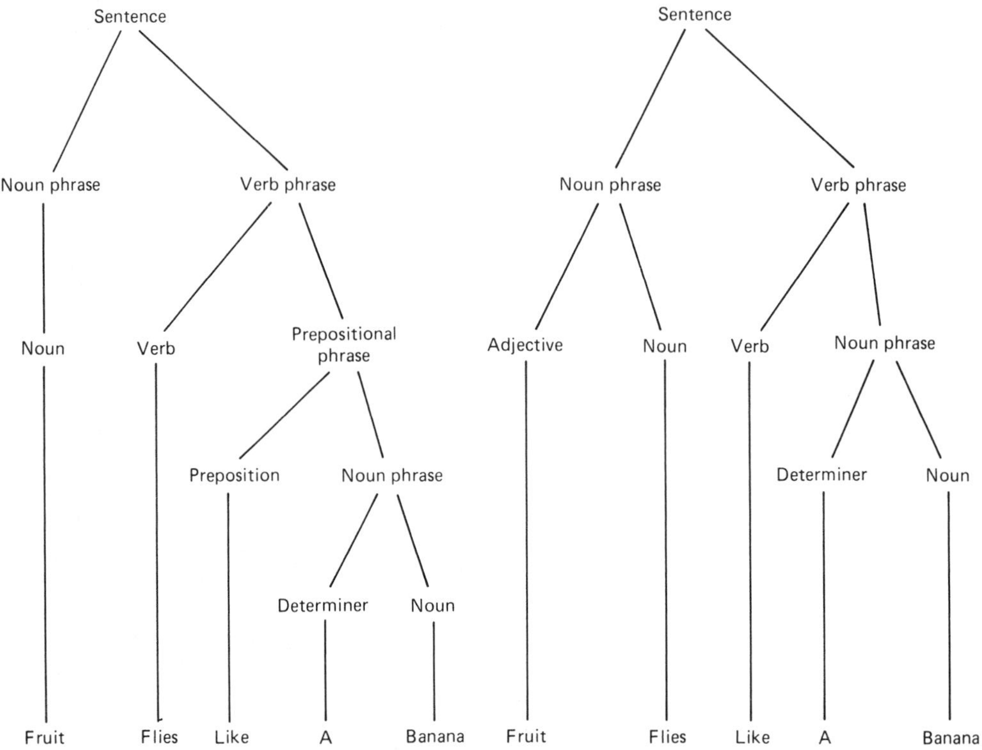

Figure 11-7 Two successful parses of a sentence result in ambiguity.

which clearly has two successful parses (Figure 11-7). The two successful parses occur because "fruit" functions as both a noun and an adjective, while "flies" is a noun as well as a verb, and "like" functions as a verb, preposition, and conjunction. Based on the same sequence of words, in the same order, the parser can traverse the ATN taking the path either of noun-verb-prepositional phrase, or adjective-noun-verb-noun phrase. In cases of true ambiguity, such as this one, in order to clarify meaning, a natural-language system usually must ask the user which choice is the intended one. Although this example is meant to be amusing and educational, similar types of ambiguities occur in newspapers, textbooks, advertisements, and everyday language (Figure 11-8).

There are existing natural-language systems (discussed in Chapter 14) that attempt to resolve ambiguity by incorporating real-world knowledge in their systems. Such a system might interpret Barnum's original ad that read "PAY 25 CENTS AND SEE A MAN EATING CHICKEN" because it would know that few people would pay to see a man chomping on a chicken but people might pay money to see a chicken eating a man. But even a system with real-world knowledge could not decipher the grammatically correct sentence, "FLYING

```
Commuter Tax
On New Yorkers
 Killed in Jersey
```
The New York Times 6/9/81

```
3 Arrested in Slaying
Of Economist for FTC
```
The Washington Post 1/12/83

```
2 Teen-Agers Indicted
For Drowning in Lake
```
The New York Times 10/10/82

Figure 11-8 Everyday ambiguities are resolved by using knowledge of what makes sense.

PLANES CAN BE DANGEROUS." This sentence has two correct parses with the same sequence of leaf nodes, and unfortunately, both of them make sense.

UNDERSTANDING WHAT IS SAID

If there were no correlation between the structure of a sentence and its social and fuctional meaning, the sentence analyses discussed until now would be of interest only to a linguist. Clearly, this is not the case. In the end, the structure of a sentence is correlated with meaning, by identifying the roles that component words and phrases play in a sentence and the relationships between these roles. For example, the sentence "Reynold jumped over the moon" contains information about the action "jumped," who jumped, and where Reynold jumped. Similarly, to respond to the statement "List the employees who work in Chicago," it is necessary to know how "employees" and "Chicago" relate to the verb "work" and how all these words relate to the verb "list."

Most commonly, a system of "grammatical cases," which denote relationships between agents of an action, the action, and states, is used to identify these roles. Researchers have proposed a number of different cases to identify roles and relationships in English. In various theories, these identify, for example, the causal agent of an action, the coagent, counteragent, instrument or means by which an action is performed, location, source, destination, theme, object of the action, experiencer, and result of the action.

Natural-language systems use syntax as an aid to determining the roles of words and phrases in a sentence. For example, the agent is almost always the subject of the sentence, as in "Tony ate green cheese." However, the logical subject may be an entire noun phrase, as in "Sparkle fruit stores ordered 40 orange crates." Similarly, the instrument is likely to be an indirect object, as in "Tony ate green cheese with a fork."

EXCEPTIONS ABOUND

Since English is a large and difficult language, there are more rules that provide for exceptions that determine the probable cases. One major exception occurs if the sentence in question is a passive rather than an active one. In a passive sentence, the subject, and therefore the agent, is usually the word in the "by" phrase instead of the first noun phrase. Consequently, in "Green cheese was eaten by Tony," Tony remains the agent.

However, even here there are exceptions, depending on the verb. Some verbs, for example, allow an instrument in the subject position. Thus, in the sentences "Richard broke the window with a brick" and "A brick broke the window," "brick" is the instrument and not the agent.

As these examples show, it is dangerous to make automatic assumptions about roles of sentence parts in order to understand underlying meaning. Attempts to do so lead to misconceptions about scenarios such as "Juana is cooking" and "The meat is cooking." Pointing up the same difficulties are "He made Robert a soda" and "He made Robert the engineering director."

Similarly, syntactically-oriented systems cannot differentiate between the meaning of two sentences such as "Helen ordered a frankfurter with mustard" and "Helen ordered a frankfurter with soda." Since Helen is not likely to want the soda on her frankfurter, a different type of natural-language system that contains a knowledge-based mechanism is necessary to determine what is likely and plausible in the real world. Finally, even such a knowledge-based mechanism fails for a legitimate legal sentence such as 'the duck is ready to eat." Only examination of the sentence in the context of a larger story, which reveals whether the sentence in question is about a dinner or a farm, may indicate whether the duck is performing the action of eating or is being acted upon and thus eaten.

Natural Language Goes Commercial for Mainframes and Minicomputers

Most of the present natural-language systems are interfaces to databases. They allow users to issue randomly phrased requests to get data out of the database. An example is

> "HOW MANY COOKS WORK AT THE COMPANY? HOW MANY BAKERS? HOW MANY COOKS ARE BAKERS?"

Since natural language is not yet well understood, and because the nature, interpretation, and representation of meaning is far from an exact science, computerized natural-language systems are subject to the ever-present danger of misinterpretation. For example, the query "HOW MANY COOKS WORK AT THE COMPANY?" might have a different meaning if the company is a restaurant or law firm. Even if the company is a restaurant, misinterpretation is still possible because cooks, named Cook, could work for a restaurant. Cooks could also be bakers, and people named Cook could be bakers.

Despite the dangers of misinterpretation, several vendors have created fairly robust natural-language interfaces to databases. The greatest number of these systems use variations on the syntactic/semantic type of language analysis, described in Chapter 11, as their underlying technology.

Most commercial natural-language systems have four components (Figure 12-1). One component contains knowledge about syntax (grammar) to tell the natural-language system how to put together, take apart, and analyze a user's sentence. A second component has knowledge of the meaning of words (semantics) and their roles and relationships to each other in a sentence. The third component of a natural-language system internally represents the user's natural-

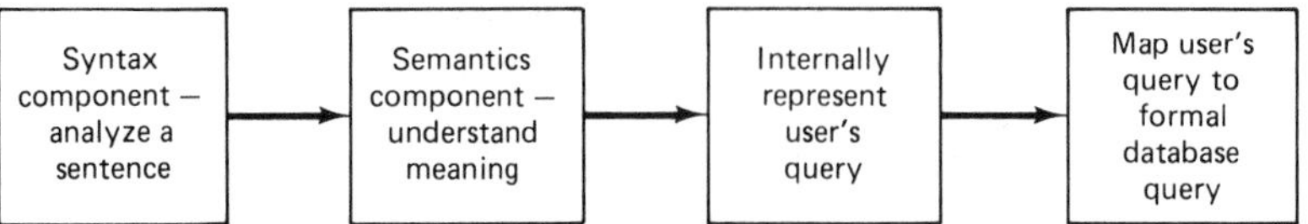

Figure 12-1 Natural-language database interface components.

language input in some language form that the computer can understand. The fourth component, which is common to all types of natural-language systems, maps the user's natural query into some formal database query, programming language instruction, or sentence paraphrase.

Although natural-language systems based on a syntactic/semantic type of analysis are the most common ones, they are by no means the only type. For example, another type of natural-language system uses expert system-like rules and heuristics, in conjunction with syntactic and semantic components, to interpret users' queries (Chapter 13). A very different type of natural-language system seeks to understand users' input sentences almost exclusively through meaning. To achieve this goal, the system contains encoded knowledge about particular subject areas of interest that correspond to people's stored-up past experiences. Like human beings, the natural-language system can refer to this stored subject knowledge to help understand, interpret, and anticipate new situations (Chapter 14).

CHOOSING A NATURAL-LANGUAGE SYSTEM

Larry Harris, founder of Artificial Intelligence Corp. and designer of the natural-language system called Intellect, defines four key issues that natural-language interfaces to databases must handle (Figure 12-2). The issues are density of language coverage, ambiguity, navigation of a database, and references to database fields with long descriptive names (particularly containing time-related information) (Harris, 1984). Users must understand these issues to evaluate natural-language systems.

DENSITY OF COVERAGE

Contrary to many people's first impressions, density of coverage does not refer to how large a subset of a natural language a system can cover. Instead, it means how densely a natural-language system covers the portion of the language it is designed to handle.

To evaluate natural-language system, check:

– Density of coverage
– Handling of ambiguity
– Database navigation
– Series information (multiword field names)

Figure 12-2 Key issues for natural language interfaces to databases.

This definition is actually another way of saying that a system with dense coverage is tolerant to minor alterations or rewording of a request. In contrast, a system with sparse coverage may fail if the user drops an article or a preposition.

Unfortunately, it is difficult to determine whether or not a system provides dense coverage just from viewing a demonstration. By choosing the right examples, a system with sparse coverage can be made to look good. Then when the users get the system back in their home office, they discover that it behaves erratically.

Users will swear that the same query that the system understood yesterday, is no longer understood today. In reality, the system is not behaving erratically. It only seems so because yesterday's query is not phrased exactly the same as today's. Today's query may be reasonably similar, except that it is lacking, say, the article "a" or the preposition "of." Although this lack is not significant to users, some natural-language systems may cover the language too sparsely to understand the many different ways of wording a request.

Users can gain some clues to the density of coverage characteristics of a natural-language system by taking note of a demonstrator's sample queries. Harris advises users to be suspicious if the samples chosen consistently show a stylized form of English. For example, the query (Harris, 1984)

SHOW TOTAL SALES FOR EACH STATE FOR EACH CITY

is clearly stylized because repeated use of "FOR EACH" is not very natural. Systems that require such stylized queries have sparse coverage. In contrast, a natural-language system with dense coverage would understand each of the following wordings (Harris, 1984):

SHOW THE TOTAL SALES IN EACH STATE AND CITY.
WHAT ARE THE SALES OR TOTALS FOR EACH CITY WITHIN EACH STATE.

AMBIGUITY

The second key issue that natural-language systems must handle is ambiguity, because natural languages are ambiguous. Formal computer languages, in contrast, do not have an ambiguity problem because they are carefully designed to be unambiguous.

As Chapter 11 indicated, the ambiguity in natural languages stems from several sources. For example, natural-language systems often find it difficult to determine which noun a pronoun refers to. Consider the following set of queries (Harris, 1984):

"LIST THE TOP 10 COMPANIES IN THE UNITED STATES"
"WHICH OF THEM ARE LOCATED IN THE WESTERN UNITED STATES?"
"WHICH OF THEM ARE LOCATED IN THE EASTERN UNITED STATES?"
"WHICH OF THESE ARE HIGH-TECHNOLOGY FIRMS?"

(From New York Times, Jan. 6, 1983)

CUOMO TO FREEZE
HOSPITAL BUILDING

Possible subheads:

Lack of volunteers for cryogenic
experiments cited by officials

Governor criticized for not
emptying the building first

Part of new program to stem
decay of aging city buildings

Figure 12-3 Ambiguity can result from words that have different meanings in different contexts. (Subheads courtesy Ronald Schneiderman)

The problem with this sequence is that clearly the pronoun "them" in the second and third queries refers to the "top 10 companies" mentioned in the first query. It is not clear, however, whether the pronoun "these" in the fourth query refers to the original top 10 companies or only the companies in the eastern region.

Ambiguity in natural language also occurs because words have different meanings when they are used in different contexts. The *New York Times* headline in Figure 12-3 illustrates the problem with different meanings in different contexts. A natural-language interface to a newspaper-story database might receive a query that refers to this article. The query might ask for the date that Cuomo, governor of New York State at the time of the story, froze New York's hospital building. The natural-language system might become perplexed, however, trying to determine whether to search the index for newspaper-story subjects pertaining to cryogenics, disasters, or building preservation programs.

Still another source for ambiguity is conjunctions. For example, determination of meaning is difficult in the following query because the conjunction "and" has four different meanings (Harris, 1984):

FOR OHIO AND IOWA, PRINT THE NAME AND AGE OF ANYONE WHO
EARNS BETWEEN $30,000 AND $50,000 AND IS MARRIED.

In its first occurence, "AND" implies search union. Search union means that the final printout will contain the names of everyone who lives in Ohio as well as (AND) everyone who lives in Iowa, as long as they meet the stated conditions.

The second occurence of "AND" specifies a list of fields to be retrieved. The two fields, which are equivalent to lines to be filled out on a paper form in a file cabinet, are "name" AND "age."

The third occurence of "AND" specifies a range search. In other words, the user wants information about people who earn salaries between the range $30,000 AND $50,000.

The fourth occurence of "AND" implies what is known as search intersection. This query calls for information about people who meet two conditions. They must earn between $30,000 and $50,000 AND they must be married.

NAVIGATING THE DATABASE

The third key issue, the ability to navigate through the database, is necessary because the purpose of most natural-language systems is to allow users to retrieve database information without knowing anything about database structure or database access languages. Since users are permitted to be naive about database structure and access, the natural-language system must be knowledgeable in these areas and assume the responsibilities of the sophisticated database user.

To perform accordingly, natural-language systems must know how to map the user's natural-language requests into a formal database query. They also need knowledge of the underlying database architecture. With these kinds of knowledge, natural-language interfaces interpret and translate user queries into formal database queries. In addition, they know how to instruct the formal database system to relate or join files. This knowledge permits the handling of complex queries which require the retrieval of requested data scattered in several files.

SERIES INFORMATION

The fourth issue that a natural-language system must handle successfully is the understanding of randomly phrased queries that refer to a database field name. This is not a problem when database fields are named with a single word such as NAME or ADDRESS. Difficulties in fluency of expression may be encountered in this area, however, when database fields are named by a series of words, such as "ACTUAL YEAR TO DATE SALES."

The difficulties arise if the database field name is directly coupled to lexicon words and phrases via a 1:1 association. Under this condition, a user query about a database field must contain the name of that database field exactly as it appears in the database. A multiple-word database field name such as NEW YORK will not generally cause trouble because few people are likely to refer to "YORK NEW." But a field name such as "1985 ACTUAL YEAR TO DATE SALES" may present a problem because the probability of users always typing these words in that order is slim. Words such as *actual* and *year to date* are concepts in the users' heads and they are therefore likely to refer to them in random orders. To allow fluency of natural-language expression, a natural-language system must contain definitions for each word in a database field name and be able to put these words together linguistically, rather than in the database field name order, and retrieve the data items referred to.

It turns out that this issue of series data is particularly pertinent to time-related information. The ability to handle time-related information is an important issue because so many types of database information have minimal usefulness unless compared with the same or similar information in a previous or estimated future time period. Consequently, the areas of time-related information are so replete with long descriptive field names such as ACTUAL YEAR TO DATE SALES or ESTIMATED YEAR TO DATE SALES that the term "time series" has been coined to refer to the coupling (or decoupling) of these fields with lexicons.

Second only to the problem of word order in trying to achieve natural-language fluency is the problem of awkward, repetitious qualifiers and modifiers. It is unlikely that people would use their native language to ask questions such as "SHOW ME THE 1985 ACTUAL YEAR TO DATE SALES AND THE 1985 ESTIMATED YEAR TO DATE SALES without being taught to do so. It is more natural to ask for "THE ACTUAL AND ESTIMATED YEAR TO DATE SALES." Therefore, to be maximally useful, a natural-language analyzer must be able to determine that "year-to-date" sales has been factored out of the names of the two fields. It must also recognize if a particular year (often different for the actual and estimated information) has been defaulted.

COMMERCIAL SYSTEMS

Mainframes, minicomputers, and micros can all boast of hosting natural-language interfaces to databases. Some of these natural-language interfaces allow users to input free-form queries, phrased any way they want. The system then attempts to figure out what the user really meant.

Other natural-language systems operate more like multiple-choice questionnaires. They allow the users to string together selected words and phrases from choices that the system presents on a screen.

Finally, some natural-language database interfaces are extensions of fourth-generation database languages. These are English-like languages that are too stylized and structured to be considered natural. Since their structure and style are oriented toward computer capabilities, it is often easier for knowledgeable users to express complex formatting directions and some database update requests in the fourth-generation language than in a true natural-language. However, fourth-generation languages with natural-language extensions allow users to switch between the two language applications, depending on the functions they wish to perform.

These commercialized natural-language systems can be bought as off-the-shelf packages. However, they generally contain some means to allow users to customize the system for their own company's applications and to accommodate their own personal or company terminology.

To avoid misinterpretation and ensure robustness, after analyzing user's queries, most natural-language systems check their interpretations for correctness by paraphrasing the query back to the user. Users view the paraphrase to check that the computer's understanding of a query corresponds to what they meant to say.

A good example of a natural-language interface is Intellect from Artificial Intelligence Corp. The grand-daddy of commercial natural-language systems (marketed since 1980), Intellect uses classic natural-language syntactic and semantic techniques, described in Chapter 11. It interfaces to major databases, graphics systems, and statistical analysis tools to allow computer operators to use natural language to request not only data but graphic and statistical analyses.

Licensed by IBM, Cullinet (who markets Intellect under the name On-line English), and Information Builders, Inc., Intellect draws on five different sources of information to help analyze users' queries. The sources are two types of lexicons, a grammar, knowledge both of database structure and the information in the database, and as a last resort, the user (Figure 12-4).

Intellect's knowledge of English words comes from three of these sources: the root lexicon that is built into the system, the application-specific lexicon that is constructed at the site by the users, and the database system itself.

The root lexicon, which is delivered with Intellect, contains syntactic and semantic information about generic English words (such as who, is, and but) that can be used in any subject domain.

In contrast to the root lexicon, the application-specific lexicon is created locally by a person who is building an application. This person is typically a data-processing person who knows the application and is trained to work with the lexicon. He or she defines the words that are unique to the application that will interface to Intellect. Rather than being linguistic in nature, the definitions in the application-specific lexicon map between the way the user views the data (user's conceptual schema) and how the database views it (logical database schema).

Some of the information in the application-specific dictionary is either contained in or related to information in the database system's data dictionary. The data dictionary is an organized listing of specifications and descriptions of data in database fields. Because its information overlaps that contained in the application-specific lexicon, Intellect can automatically generate parts of the application-specific lexicon from a user-company's data dictionary.

The database system, the last source for English word knowledge, includes the database schema information and all the indexed fields within the database. Armed with this information, Intellect can correlate the type of information in the database and the names of the database fields with the data requested by a user's query.

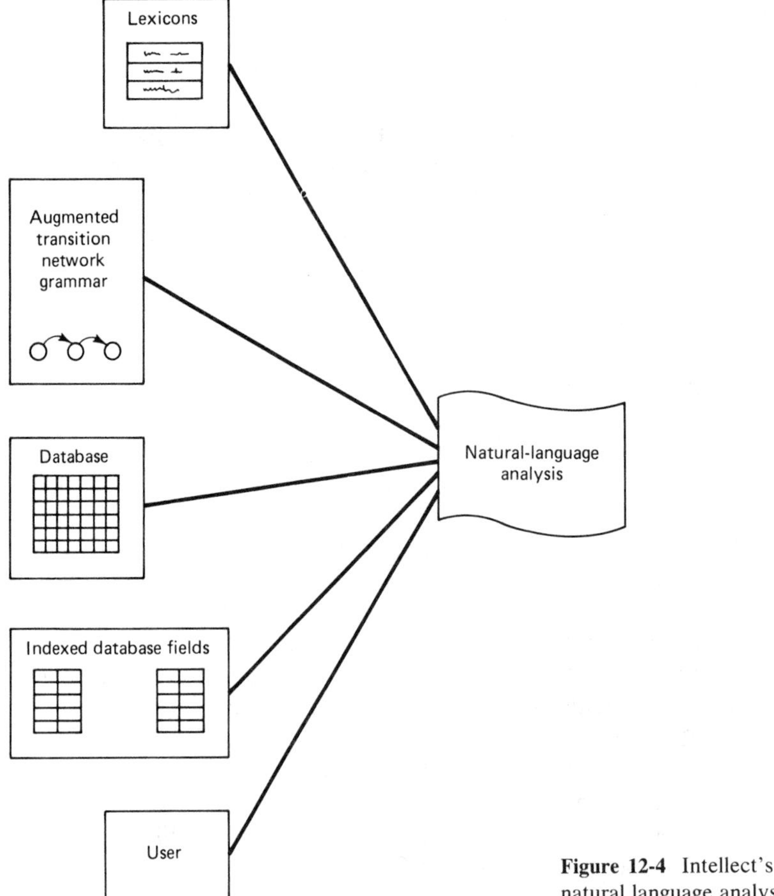

Figure 12-4 Intellect's sources for natural language analysis.

But Intellect does not require a one-to-one relationship between its field names and user phrases. Instead, it handles a user request that refers to the field named "ACTUAL YEAR TO DATE SALES" by providing separate definitions for the field name components, such as "ACTUAL" or "YEAR TO DATE."

These individual definitions, combined with knowledge of the context in which the words are used, allow Intellect to understand more naturally worded references to database fields. For example, Intellect responds to the request to "COMPARE THE ACTUAL SALES FOR JUNE TO THE ESTIMATES" by printing the current year's ACTUAL JUNE SALES, the current year's ESTIMATED JUNE SALES, and the absolute and relative differences between them.

Intellect's second source for natural-language analysis is its ATN-based English-language grammar. This grammar contains the means to build up parse tree—level information from input words and eventually map this information into database queries.

```
User:       How many cooks are in the company?

Computer:  YOUR REQUEST IS AMBIGUOUS TO ME.  DO YOU WANT:
            1): CURRENT JOB TITLE = COOK.

            2): LAST NAME = COOK.

           PLEASE ENTER THE NUMBER OF THE INTERPRETATION YOU INTENDED
User:      .2

Computer
Paraphrase: COUNT THE EMPLOYEES WITH LAST NAME = COOK.

Computer   ANSWER:  1                                              (A)

Computer:  NEXT REQUEST.
```

Figure 12-5 Intellect's final source for resolving ambiguity is the user. (Artificial Intelligence Corp.)

To provide density of coverage, Intellect has more than one ATN. It uses its primary ATN to parse requests that it assumes are phrased in proper grammar. If the primary ATN fails to understand the user's request, Intellect calls a second ATN that helps understand sentence fragments and ungrammatical requests.

Intellect's third source of query analysis is knowledge about how the data are structured in the database. This knowledge is necessary because unlike queries posed by data-processing professionals, typical natural-language users' queries are not phrased in any way that indicates the data's location. Therefore, the natural-language system must know how the data are organized in order to project a high-level English representation onto a particular database structure and to navigate that database. The fourth query analysis source is knowledge of the indexed fields of the database. Intellect uses this information to minimize the likelihood of errors that stem from ambiguity.

To resolve ambiguity using the database, if more than one interpretation of a query is possible, Intellect's parser, which is nondeterministic, generates multiple interpretations. It then assigns a preference rating to each interpretation. The preference ratings are based on how easily the query fits the grammar rules or whether the grammar rules had to be stretched to fit the query.

If the preference ratings are different and one interpretation has a high rating, Intellect chooses the high-preference interpretation. However, if the preference ratings are approximately equal, Intellect looks in the database to see which interpretation makes more sense.

If one interpretation makes more sense in light of the database information, Intellect will prefer that interpretation. However, it checks with the user anyway. If the preferred interpretation is not the user's intended one, Intellect prints out all possible interpretations. Thus the database is actually a heuristic rather than absolute deciding factor.

If the database system treats both interpretations equally, Intellect goes to its fifth source of query analysis information, which is the user (Figure 12-5). For example, in the query "HOW MANY COOKS ARE IN THE COMPANY?",

Intellect will first use its ATNs to determine that the query makes equal sense whether "cooks" refers to a person's name or a job title. If both queries are valid, Intellect will check the database for clues to the user's meaning. If the database indicates that the company has no job title of "cook" but several people by that name work there, it will assume that the user wants to know about people of that name. However, it will warn the user by asking "Is this the meaning you intended?" If the database indicates that the company has people named "Cook," as well as people with the job title of "cook," it will confront the user with both interpretations and ask the user to choose the intended one.

Natural-language database interfaces are not limited to database query systems. For example, Intellect users can use English to count the number of employees or to request a spreadsheet or graph. The system will echo back its understanding of the user's directions to make sure that its interpretation is correct. Then it will perform the task.

Intellect is written in the PL/1 programming language rather than Lisp, the language most commonly used for AI, for a very practical reason. Most commercial databases support Cobol, PL/1, and Fortran interfaces, but not Lisp. However, there are so many Lisp capabilities important to AI but lacking in PL/1 that in designing Intellect, it was necessary first to build up some of the Lisp environment under PL/1.

NATURAL LANGUAGE AND FOURTH-GENERATION LANGUAGES

The natural-language database front ends described so far are limited to retrieval capabilities only. Martin Marietta Data Systems has partially circumvented this limitation by adding "English," its natural-language interface, to Ramis II, its fourth-generation programming and database language.

Both languages are very-high-level English or English-like languages. Fourth-generation languages, however, require much more stylized and constrained English than natural-language systems. For example, a typical "English" (the natural-language extension) query is "TELL ME HOW MANY SALESPERSONS ARE IN THE NORTHEAST." English might respond with "17." The user can then say "LIST THEM." The system will remember the previous query, flesh out the missing sentence parts, and list those seventeen salespersons. Moreover, users can specify their queries in various ways, including Ramis II, that will all be understood by "English" (Figure 12-6). The more constrained English of Ramis II requires a user to phrase the same query as "PRINT NAME IF REGION IS NORTHEAST AND IF JOB TITLE IS SALESPERSON."

It is important at this point to note that although fourth-generation languages are more stylized and constrained than natural languages, they are, as mentioned, English-like. True, they require more training to use than natural language. However, they bear no resemblance to the more cryptic, difficult-to-learn formal programming languages such as Cobol, Fortran, or PL/1.

Suppose gross equals units times listprice. Let mfgcost = units * ucost.
Now show me total gross, mfgcost, and profit for each product.

PRODNUM	PRODNAME	GROSS	MFGCOST	PROFIT
15PUM21	PUMP	3,772,200.00	3,460,364.80	311,835.20
21TRA12	TRANSMISSION	9,088,065.00	8,179,258.50	908,806.50
42PUL29	PULLEY ASSEMBLY	763,423.30	598,125.90	165,297.40
42PUL65	FRAME	450,240.00	256,208.00	194,032.00
50PUL64	HARDWARE KIT	176,280.00	89,496.00	86,784.00
54PUM89	PUMP, CORROSIVE	16,465,320.50	14,591,980.50	1,873,340.00
59DRA73	DRAWINGS	70,256.95	14,122.00	56,134.95
66MOT37	MOTOR,ELEC.,MOD1	2,357,752.32	2,094,048.00	263,704.32
71MOT07	MOTOR, ELEC.,MOD2	11,609,593.60	10,468,951.68	1,140,641.92
87DUM93		.00	.00	.00
87PUM93	HOSE ASSEMBLY	2,313,647.00	2,235,036.60	78,610.40

Show me the total, average, maximum and minimum units sold to each customer.

What are the total, ave, max and min units that have been purchased by every customer?

I need to know the total, ave, max and min units purchased by each customer. Please give me the answers I need.

Give me the total units sold to each customer. What were the average units also? Include the max and min units as well.

Table file sales sum units and ave units and max units and min units by customer end

CUSTOMER	UNITS	AVE UNITS	MAX UNITS	MIN UNITS
COMP. DEVELOPMENT, LTD.	57911	742	2300	127
ENGINEERING ASSOC.	11753	133	464	24
MOD MODELLING, LTD.	5373	89	282	19
ROYAL MFG CO.	55040	519	2075	117
SOFT PROCESSING INC.	19122	285	1500	45

Figure 12-6 Ramis can specify database queries in various ways, using natural language or a fourth generation language. The first four queries are equivalent English language versions. The fifth, also equivalent, query is written in Ramis II. (Martin Marietta Data Systems)

Which system—natural language or fourth-generation language—is most effective depends on the type of user. Applied Data Research (ADR) has identified three classes of users: expert, frequent, and infrequent or naive. According to ADR, for the expert or frequent user, the more structured systems are the most efficient. Whatever the user types in has been explicitly specified by the language. There is no need for structured language systems to try to interpret what the user really meant. Consquently, they provide the least ambiguity and the most reliable results. Natural-language facilities, however, make the computer accessible to the infrequent or naive user, even though it may cause more ambiguity, and costs more overhead to provide the service.

The advantage of combining Ramis II and "English" into one system, or for that matter extending any fourth-generation database language with a natural language, is the ability to switch between the two. It is not only that users can switch to the more stylized Ramis to update the database and to the more natural "English" to query it. Users can also switch between the languages to avoid problems that may arise when users try to use natural language for detailed operations such as complex printouts of reports. In addition, novices can use "English" as a start-up query language and as an aid to the gradual learning of Ramis since, upon request, the combination system will display the Ramis II equivalent of an English-language query.

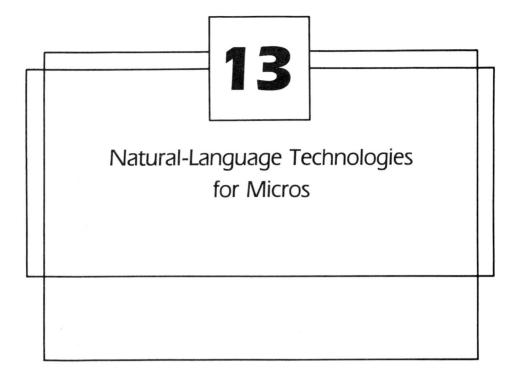

13 Natural-Language Technologies for Micros

Years ago, only computing professionals used database management systems to manage and access data stored in computers. But it is human nature to rapidly get used to new developments. So, soon, noncomputing professionals also wanted to manage and access their data on a computer.

Natural-language database interfaces provided the opportunity for them to do so. Economics, however, dictates that noncomputing professionals are more likely to store their data on microcomputers rather than on larger mainframes or minicomputers. And while some natural-language systems designed for large-scale computers have been shoe-horned into micros, many natural-language system developers feel that different techniques are needed for personal computers in order to maximize natural-language understanding in a scaled-down environment.

With microcomputer users pushing for easy access to their databases, two new microcomputer-oriented commercial approaches to natural language are emerging. One approach requires users to select query words and phrases only from those offered in computer windows, instead of allowing free-form queries. This multiple-choice technique prevents users from asking invalid questions. It also eliminates the need for the natural-language system to interpret the same question asked many different ways. As a result, the system requires less memory to interpret users' queries accurately and unambiguously. This makes it easier to implement the natural-language interface on personal computers.

The other approach uses knowledge-based system heuristic techniques to interpret user queries. This approach has not eliminated the traditional syntactic/semantic approach to natural language. The traditional approach is particularly effective for certain tasks, such as resolving ambiguities and handling conditions in queries (limitations placed on data to be selected such as "sales between $10,000 and $17,000" or "last name begins with Mc"). So borrowing the best of different worlds, designers of this type of microcomputer-oriented natural-language system have integrated traditional natural-language methods with techniques borrowed from knowledge systems. This integrated approach provides greater microcomputer language-understanding power with less memory.

TRUST THE USER

It has often been said that we learn from our mistakes. However, it is a good thing that we do not learn only from our mistakes because Texas Instruments has gone to great lengths to design a natural-language database query system that ensures that database end users, and even the systems analysts who define specific database interfaces, do not make any.

Called NaturalLink, the TI natural-language query system guarantees correct user queries because at every step in the query-building process it offers users a choice of all the valid words and phrases they can select. Since users can select only from the choices that NaturalLink offers, they are never given the opportunity to make an invalid selection.

NaturalLink runs on PCs and interfaces to company databases on mainframes and minicomputers. It differs from other natural-language systems because they usually require users to generate a natural-language query and the computer to understand it. NaturalLink works in reverse. The computer, under guidance from the user, creates the natural-langauge query. The user understands it.

To create a query, NaturalLink offers the user a screen divided into windows. Each window contains a different type of word, phrase, or other query element (Figure 13-1).

For example, one window may contain generic nouns from a database, such as parts, shipments, or suppliers. Other windows may contain attributes, qualifiers, connectors (e.g. and, or), comparison operators (e.g. greater than, equal to), and database operations (e.g. find).

Words and phrases from the different windows can be strung together to make up just about any kind of query that is valid for a particular database. With natural-language query systems that allow users to key in free-form words and phrases, they can also be strung together to make up a number of invalid queries.

The difference between NaturalLink and other natural-language query systems is that while covering all valid database items and allowable operations, NaturalLink restricts user choices of elements that formulate a query to only valid ones.

Users can make their choices only from certain windows which NaturalLink terms "active" windows. The choice of an item from a window may cause that

COMMANDS: Find	Find the	Find all	
FEATURES: part number part name quantity supplier name supplier address supplier number color weight	CONNECTORS: and or of the average NOUNS: parts shipments suppliers	QUALIFIERS: which are supplied by whose colors are whose weight is whose shipment number is whose name is whose address is who supply	COMPARISONS: between >= = < > <= <> ATTRIBUTES: <part number> <quantity> <supplier> <weight> <color>
QUERY OPERATIONS: BUILD RECALL SAVE DELETE EDIT SHOW EXECUTE			

Figure 13-1 NaturalLink offers the user a screen of windows, each containing a different type of word, phrase, or other query element. As the user builds a query, NaturalLink echoes it in the blank window below the selection windows. (Texas Instruments)

window to become inactive and determines which windows will become active next. Thus NaturalLink enforces the stringing together of valid choices in a valid order. This guarantees that every query that users ask is valid in the context of the referenced database.

The guarantee of correct queries, however, is only as good as the choices that are offered to the user. These choices depend on both the content of the database that NaturalLink interfaces to and the formal database query language. As with other natural-language database interface vocabularies, the database interface choices are defined not by a linguist or natural-language developer, but by a person knowledgeable about the database and its contents. Such a person could be an end user, a data-processing professional, or a system analyst.

To eliminate as many mistakes as possible in defining the choices, as well as to simplify the process of defining a database interface, TI provides a toolkit of interface definition tools. The tools prompt the system analyst or user for database items, phrasing or choices that are offered to users, and database access permissions. They also check the analyst's entered information for completeness and errors. Finally, the interface definition tools manage NaturalLink's windows. This window management function is a particularly important function because, as will be seen, NaturalLink's windows perform query building as well as display functions. Thus, if the wrong window is made active, the user will be able to build an incorrect query.

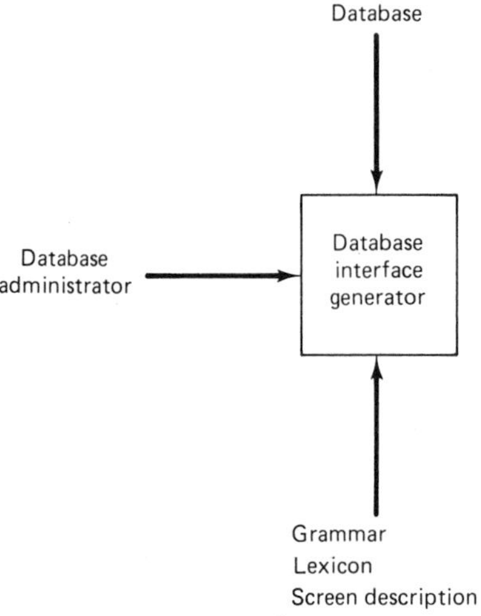

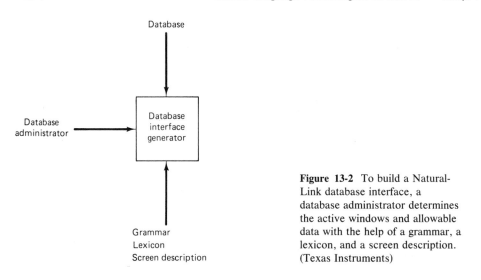

Figure 13-2 To build a NaturalLink database interface, a database administrator determines the active windows and allowable data with the help of a grammar, a lexicon, and a screen description. (Texas Instruments)

INTERFACING A NATURAL LANGUAGE TO A DATABASE

To guarantee that the user can make only valid selections, the natural-language query system needs at any time to know two things: which windows should be active and what data should be displayed in each active window. To determine the active windows and their data requires three types of input: a grammar, a lexicon, and a screen description (Figure 13-2).

The first component, the grammar, contains the formal rules that specify how words and phrases can be combined correctly. It also contains some information that affects how these words and phrases map into a target database query language. The second, or lexicon, component contains the rest of the

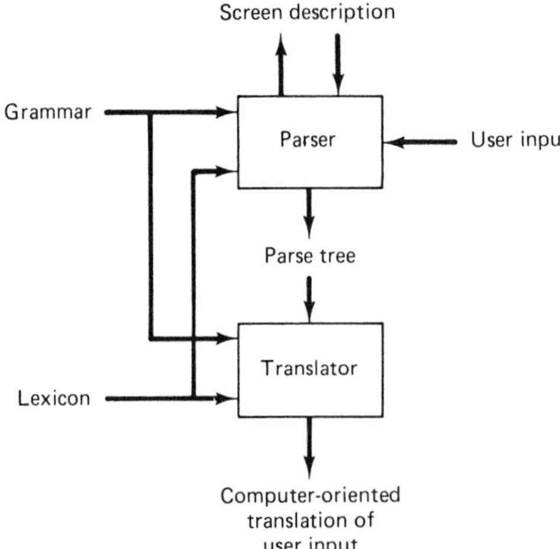

Figure 13-3 NaturalLink's parser and translator accept inputs from the grammar, lexicon, screen description, and user and generate a query translation for a target database query language. (Texas Instruments)

information necessary to translate a natural-language query into a target database query language. It also defines the text to be displayed in the screen windows. The third component is the screen description that specifies the placement and content of all windows that are presented to the user.

Information from these components is input to a parser and translator (Figure 13-3). The parser and translator parse a sentence into its grammatical elements and perform the translation into the target database query language.

The translation from user query to database query proceeds as follows. First the user selects an item from an active window. Every time the user selects an item, the parser continues to resolve the input into grammatical elements.

HOW TO WRITE A GRAMMAR

To resolve the sentence into grammatical parts, the parser uses formal rules defined in the natural-language grammar. The grammar rules describe the structure of sentences. Specifically, they describe all the grammatical sentence components, such as noun, verb, and prepositional phrase, down to ordinary words that can be put together in a certain order to form a legitimate sentence. The systems analyst who knows the database and application defines this grammar by determining the sentences that best fit a particular application.

For example, a partial grammar (often called a semantic grammar) shown in Figure 13-4 is defined for the database interface language shown in Figure 13-1. This grammar may be read as follows:

- A sentence may consist of the terminal symbol "find" followed by NP (Noun Phrase).
- NP may consist of SHIPMENTS_NP OR PARTS_NP.
- SHIPMENT_NP may consist of an optional element of the SHIPMENT_ ATTRIBUTE followed by SHIPMENTS_NOUN.

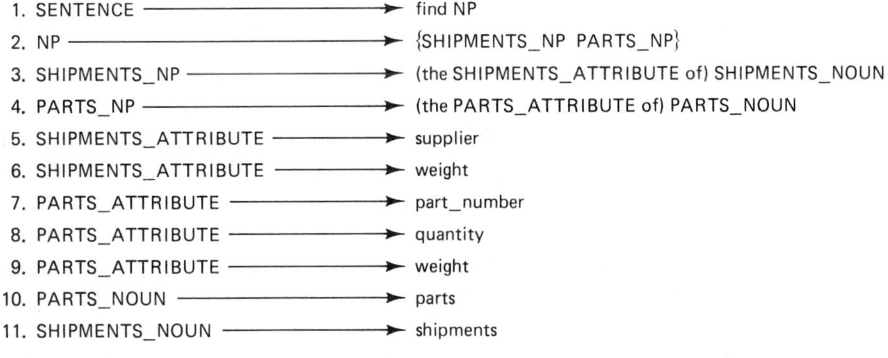

1. SENTENCE → find NP
2. NP → {SHIPMENTS_NP PARTS_NP}
3. SHIPMENTS_NP → (the SHIPMENTS_ATTRIBUTE of) SHIPMENTS_NOUN
4. PARTS_NP → (the PARTS_ATTRIBUTE of) PARTS_NOUN
5. SHIPMENTS_ATTRIBUTE → supplier
6. SHIPMENTS_ATTRIBUTE → weight
7. PARTS_ATTRIBUTE → part_number
8. PARTS_ATTRIBUTE → quantity
9. PARTS_ATTRIBUTE → weight
10. PARTS_NOUN → parts
11. SHIPMENTS_NOUN → shipments
Note: NP means Noun Phrase

Figure 13-4 A partial grammar for a database interface.

- SHIPMENT_ATTRIBUTE may consist of the terminal symbol "supplier."
- SHIPMENTS_NOUN consists of the terminal symbol "shipments."
- And so on.

The left side of each of these rules, called production rules, consists of only one component. Each rule can be rewritten by replacing the left-hand element by the right side of the rule. Therefore, production rules are also called "rewrite" rules or "replacement" rules.

The uppercase symbols shown indicate that those symbols are compound symbols and can be replaced by more fundamental symbols. The lowercase symbols, called terminals, are the most fundamental symbols and cannot be decomposed any further. By performing the replacements indicated by these production rules, the partial grammar shown in the figure can generate and recognize legal sentences such as "Find the suppliers of shipments" and "Find the quantity of parts."

For example, to generate the first sentence, it is necessary first to use rule 1, which says that a sentence can be replaced by "find" followed by a NOUN PHRASE. Rule 2 says that a NOUN PHRASE can be replaced by something called "SHIPMENTS_NP" (shipments noun-phrase). Rule 3 says SHIPMENTS_NP can be replaced by (the SHIPMENTS_ATTRIBUTE of) followed by SHIPMENTS_NOUN. Applying these three rules gives us, at this point, a partial sentence that reads

"Find the SHIPMENTS_ATTRIBUTE of SHIPMENTS_ NOUN."

To generate more of the sentence, it is necessary to apply rule 5, which states that SHIPMENTS_ATTRIBUTE can be replaced by the word "supplier." The sentence now reads

"Find the supplier of SHIPMENTS_NOUN."

One sentence component, SHIPMENTS_NOUN yet needs to be resolved. Rule 11 tells us the SHIPMENTS_NOUN can be replaced by the single word "shipments." With SHIPMENTS_NOUN resolved, the sentence "Find the supplier of shipments" is complete.

When the user issues a natural-language database query, NaturalLink follows a similar procedure to the manual one above. Every time the user selects a word or phrase from an active window, NaturalLink uses its production rules to resolve the query into its grammatical components. From these grammatical components, NaturalLink builds a query sentence which it displays to the user. Ultimately, NaturalLink parses this sentence, analyzes it, and maps it into a formal query that it submits to the underlying database system.

THE GRAMMARIAN

There is nothing particularly difficult about writing a grammar, but the process is error prone. It is easy to overlook errors that range from missing parentheses and leaving out some rules that represent allowable sentences to inconsistencies with the query system lexicon.

To avoid mistakes, the TI natural-language toolkit contains a Grammarian that assists the system analyst by checking a grammar for several kinds of errors. First, it checks for formal errors such as use of proper syntax to form rules, balanced braces, and the inclusion of only valid characters.

Second, the Grammarian checks to see if the grammar contains any hanging parts that are not reachable. For example, a rule in the Figure 13-14 grammar such as "ORDER_ATTRIBUTE→quantity" cannot be reached from any sentence generated by this grammar. It is unreachable because although the word "quantity" is part of the grammar, "ORDER_ATTRIBUTE" is not.

A third check tests whether or not two or more rules have a common replacement. Such a situation would create an ambiguous situation. The fourth check, for inconsistent translation, tests each grammar rule for well-formedness of the translation information. Finally, the fifth check makes sure that the grammar does not contain a sequence of rules that permit an infinite number of parses.

LEXICONS . . .

The NaturalLink parser plays a number of nontraditional as well as traditional roles. On the traditional side, it uses the grammar and user input to build a tree structure (called a parse tree) that describes the syntactical relationships of the user input.

The parser passes this parse tree to the translator. The translator examines the tree to identify the newest grammatical component. It then uses the lexicon to get the text needed to map the new grammatical component to a database query language. Since the lexicon contains the translation text for the terminal symbols that reside in the grammar, information in the grammar and lexicon must be consistent.

The parser also requires other, less traditional information that is generally stored in the lexicon, such as information about NaturalLink's windows. For example, the information in the grammar and the lexicon, as well as the progression of phrases selected by the user from active windows, constrains which windows and contents of windows the users can choose from to construct a query. Based on the system grammar, lexicon, and previous user selections, the parser modifies the presentation of active and inactive windows, and decides which window contents should appear or be removed.

To control these windows and therefore ensure correct user queries, the parser must know both the window and the location within the window of each "terminal" component of the user language. This information is contained in the lexicon.

. . . AND THE LEXICOGRAPHER

As can be seen, the creation of a lexicon can be a messy task. It normally requires the system analyst or programmer to understand, and remember, the details of the internal structure of the lexicon and manually format the data using a text editor.

The Lexicographer that the natural-language toolkit provides eliminates much of the mess and detail by either simplifying or actually performing some of the normal user tasks. For example, the Lexicographer prompts the analyst for information about the data items contained in the database that the interface will reference, the target language phrases that the English selections map to, and the screen description.

The Lexicographer also checks the lexicon against the grammar to make sure that the complete set of "terminal" grammatical components is matched by translation text in the lexicon. This frees the analyst from the burden of checking the lexicon for completeness by inspection.

THE SCREENBUILDER

Since screens containing groupings of windows that each hold various kinds of information influence NaturalLink's query understanding process, the screens and windows need more careful specification than a system that uses them solely for display purposes. So the TI natural-language toolkit contains a ScreenBuilder tool that helps the analyst specify window descriptions.

The window descriptions include window characteristics such as display coordinates, size, and contents of each window. To facilitate quick and easy changes to a window, ScreenBuilder keeps the window descriptions in a file rather than embedded in program code. This allows system analysts to add new window descriptions easily to the file and modify and delete existing windows.

PUT IT TOGETHER

For a natural-language interface to work correctly, its components must be coordinated and compatible with one another. A NaturalLink toolkit utility called the Coordinator helps the analyst to coordinate the various functional parts of the interface.

Coordination is necessary because the various functional parts of the interface—grammar, lexicon, and window—depend on each other. For example, the contents of the lexicon is a function of the grammar. Both the grammar and the lexicon determine the contents of the windows.

In addition, the set of currently active windows and the set of selectable items within the windows are a function of the grammatical components currently selected by the user. If the parser determines from the grammar that a specific window is to be made inactive at a stage of a parse, and if that window is not defined, an error will result.

Among its functions, the Coordinator ensures that if changes are made in one component, all possible affected components will be checked and the corresponding changes also made. It also checks the specification of the grammar and lexicon and notifies the analyst if any windows are referenced but not defined, or defined but not referenced. Finally, the Coordinator can, from a completed grammar, construct a set of statements that can be used to test all grammatical paths.

INTEGRATING KNOWLEDGE SYSTEMS WITH SYNTAX ANALYSIS

A different microcomputer-oriented approach to natural-language is illustrated by Clout (from Microrim). A natural-language program, Clout uses a combination syntactic/semantic and rule-based knowledge system approach to interface to Microrim's R:Base series of general-purpose relational database management systems. A relational database management system is a database system that views its data as a collection of tables or files, called relations (Figure 13-5). Rows in a relation correspond to individual records in a file. Columns are analogous to fields in a file or individual types of information on a file card.

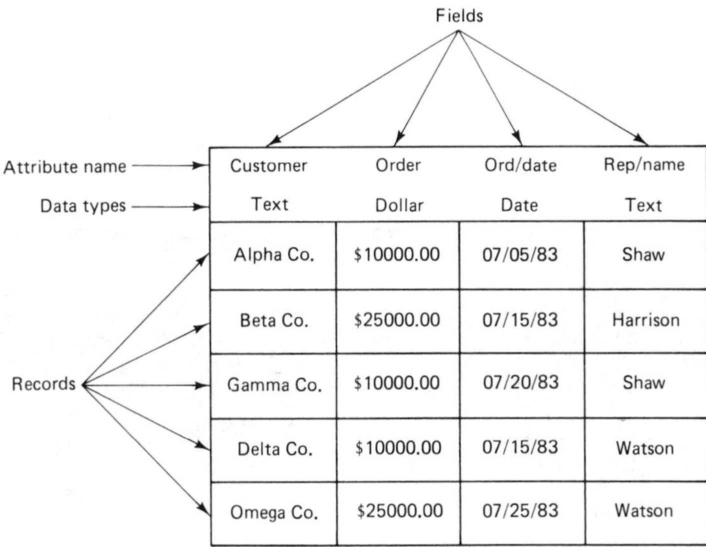

Customer	Order	Ord/date	Rep/name
Text	Dollar	Date	Text
Alpha Co.	$10000.00	07/05/83	Shaw
Beta Co.	$25000.00	07/15/83	Harrison
Gamma Co.	$10000.00	07/20/83	Shaw
Delta Co.	$10000.00	07/15/83	Watson
Omega Co.	$25000.00	07/25/83	Watson

Figure 13-5 A single relation

```
                    Current Query Context
 list the salespeople with salary greater than average
 which of those are in california

salespeople                  salary       TERR
--------------------------   ----------   ----------
LAKE                          $30,000.00  CA

 average: $29,600.00
Enter query or [ESC] to return to main menu.
R>_
```

Figure 13-6 Clout understands query fragments in the context of previous queries. (Microrim, Inc.)

Clout accepts users' unconstrained English-language queries. Queries need not all be stand-alone, complete sentences. As in human conversation, Clout can understand query fragments in the context of previous queries (Figure 13-6). With such queries, pronouns provide one clue to the possibility that a query refers to a previous request. So does the determination of whether the query makes sense as a stand-alone query. Finally, if Clout encounters an unfamiliar term in a user's query, it interrupts its dialogue with the user and asks for a temporary or permanent dictionary definition (Figure 13-7).

Interactive definition capabilities are particularly useful in natural-language applications where computer professionals are not on-hand to define new lexicon words. Such situations are particularly relevant to microcomputer users. In departments of large organizations, the overburdened data-processing department frequently prefers microcomputer users to attend to this task independently. Small businesses may not have a data-processing department, in which case microcomputer users are on their own.

However, the interactive definiton capability can have an annoying side. Although words such as "LIST," "GIVE ME," and "HOW MANY" are

```
                    Current Query Context
 list the salespeople with salary greater than average
 which of those are in california
 are there any poor performers

Did not understand: poor.performers
Please enter a synonym or change spelling.
R>salespeople with sales less than plan

Do you want to make this a permanent definition? (Y/N)...............
```

Figure 13-7 Clout asks the user for definitions of unknown words. (Microrim Inc.)

standard database vocabulary words, many other words are peculiar to individual users. Consequently, the first few weeks of working with a natural-language system can turn into a guessing game where the language system seems to understand nothing and prompts the user to define everything. The situation is similar to translating a foreign-language document where the meaning of almost every word must be looked up.

A recommended procedure for new natural-language system users, which avoids this guess-what-I-mean situation, is to inaugurate the dictionary by defining as many synonyms and definitions as they can think of the first time they use the system. The procedure results in the system instantly knowing a large percentage of the user's vocabulary. After this, it is a matter of convenience to be able to interactively define other new words as they occur.

MICROCOMPUTER PROCESSING

Three design features of Clout help make up for the scaled-down environment of micros. Clout sparingly uses syntactic/semantic techniques which are processing-intensive. It parses sentences into components such as database attributes (names of fields or records in a relation, such as "employee" or "address"), comparison operators (greater than, equal to), and values (in the database fields), rather than into grammatical components. It uses knowledge sytem rules and heuristics (rules of thumb) to understand bad grammar, and queries worded in different ways, to navigate through the database, and to limit the searching of databases for information.

NONGRAMMATICAL ATNs

Clout uses augmented transition networks (ATNs) to parse a user's request into possible interpretations (Chapter 11). ATNs are groups of node and arc graphs, called transition networks. The arcs are labeled with sentence components that must be found to get to the next sentence parsing state, represented by nodes (Figure 13-8). These transition networks are augmented with registers that give the natural-language program the ability to store and remember information about the components it has found. The program uses the stored information to construct phrases from individual components, sentences from phrases, and to make decisions about the grammatical role of a new component, based on previous components found and the partial sentence already constructed. (Without registers, once the program used a component to move to a new node, it would forget the component, and when it reached the end of the transition network, it would be able to say only that it parsed the input sentence successfully and therefore the sentence was legal.)

ATNs in Clout differ from classical ATNs in that Clout's arcs do not specify grammatical components. Instead, they specify database information such as attributes, comparison operators, and values.

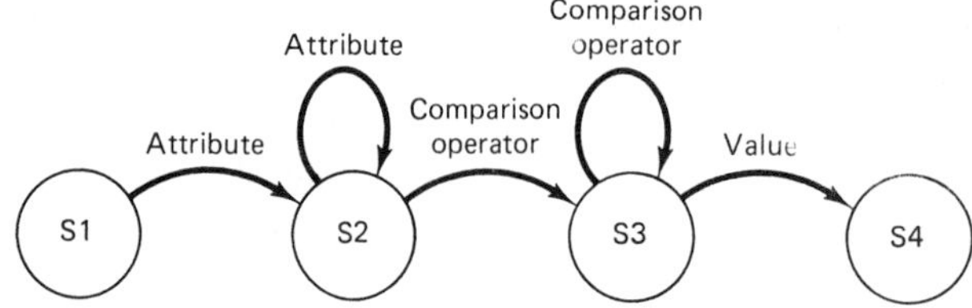

Figure 13-8 Localized augmented transition network to handle a simple comparison. This net catches comparisons such as, salaries greater than 40K, and names beginning with Mc. (Microrim Inc.)

Using these arc labels to parse and interpret the query "SHOW ME THE EMPLOYEES WITH SALARIES GREATER THAN $40,000," Clout first identifies the word SHOW from its lexicon as equivalent to a command to list something.* To find out what to list, Clout examines the rest of the query and looks for database attributes. Finding two of them consecutively, it moves first from state 1 to state 2 on the attribute "EMPLOYEES," and from state 2 again to state 2 on the attribute "SALARY." The next arc in the transition network specifies a comparison operator, and thus Clout moves to state 3 based on the requested comparison "GREATER THAN." The sentence parse and the transition network traversal are both complete as Clout moves to state 4 when it finds the value of $40,000.

In the case of a compound sentence, such as "SHOW ME THE EMPLOYEES WITH SALARIES GREATER THAN $40,000 AND LAST NAMES THAT BEGIN WITH A," Clout parses the first segment of the query that ends with $40,000 and stores the information from that ATN in table form. Then it takes a similar pass through the lexicon and other (or same) ATN to parse the second segment of the query. With the query parsing complete, Clout combines the information obtained from its lexicon and ATNs in order to translate a complete query into a formal database request.

LIMITS OF ATNs

Neither the database query translation, nor the full query parsing necessary for the translation, is wholly accomplished by ATNs in Clout. Knowledge-based heuristic rules also play a large role in these tasks because they reduce the amount of time and processing needed to analyze the complex structures of natural-language.

Some of the difficulties in an exclusively ATN-based approach to natural-language on microcomputers become clear by pointing out the large number of ATNs needed to fully interpret queries. Multiple ATNs are needed to translate each of the many different grammatical constructions that express the same query. Multiple ATNs are also needed to handle incomplete or badly phrased queries.

* Clout examples supplied by Geoffrey von Limbach.

For example, "LIST THE SECRETARIES IN CHICAGO" and "LIST THE CHICAGO SECRETARIES" both translate to the same formal database inquiry. Yet they each require different transition networks for their translation.

Even the existence of multiple ATNs to handle all legitimately phrased queries is inadequate to provide full natural-language understanding because people's queries are not always grammatically correct or stated in complete sentences. There are two ATN-based approaches to handling bad grammar and incomplete sentences. With one, the natural-language system tries to parse a query with the normal ATN rules. If that proves impossible, it relaxes the rules and tries again.

With the second approach, the natural-language system has two types of ATNs. One type is a full set of ATNs for parsing legitimately phrased sentences. The other includes ATNs for parsing sentence fragments and grammatically poor constructions.

Clout's approach is comparable to human beings who instinctively recognize the various sentence constructions that express the same query. Clout has encoded some of these instinctive recognition methods in knowledge system rules. The system's developers admit that the rules are not perfect but say they work often enough to be useful. In addition, the modularity of knowledge system rules allows them to be continuously refined and new rules added to cover exceptions. Finally, incorporation of knowledge system rules eliminates much of the time needed to analyze syntax. This rule-based approach makes the natural-language system more efficient for microcomputer applications.

A KNOWLEDGE SYSTEM APPROACH

A typical Clout heuristic rule that avoids much syntax analysis states that

IF: A QUERY HAS A DATABASE ENTRY
AND IT IS NOT NEXT TO SOME SORT OF CONDITION
(SUCH AS SALARIES GREATER THAN $12,000)
THEN: INSTEAD OF PARSING THE SENTENCE WITH AN ATN,
PICK OUT THE ROWS IN THE DATABASE THAT CONTAIN
THE REQUESTED VALUE.

Clout uses this heuristic to process the queries "LIST THE SECRETARIES IN CHICAGO" and "LIST THE CHICAGO SECRETARIES." It does not matter whether SECRETARIES and CHICAGO are nouns, adjectives, or parts of prepositional phrases because they are both database entries. Therefore, following the direction in the rule, Clout discontinues its ATN processing and heads for the database. There it notes that "SECRETARIES" is found in the database job title field, and "CHICAGO" is in the city field, and the requested values are available for the asking.

A more difficult-to-handle example occurs in the analysis of the similar queries "SHOW ME THE PARTS OF THE PUMP THAT WERE FIXED BY

JOE" versus "SHOW ME THE PARTS OF THE PUMP THAT WAS FIXED BY JOE." The first of these sentences (parts that were) refers to the parts that Joe fixed. The second (pump that was) refers to the pump that Joe fixed.

An ATN-based approach requires much syntax analysis to resolve the agreement between the verb (fixed) and the referent (which could be parts or pumps) in order to translate this sentence to the intended formal database inquiry. A heuristic rule might direct Clout to bypass the ATNs if it finds that the referenced database contains fields either for parts or for pumps. This would eliminate the need to resolve the verb and referent agreement issue, thus saving time and processing.

The ATN approach, however, has proven the most useful method of parsing queries with conditions because it requires a relatively simple set of ATNs. The ATN in Figure 13-8 is typical. Similar simple ATNs suffice for complex conditions involving expressions, lists of attributes, and sorting of information into unusual orders. In contrast, a heuristic approach to identifying conditions usually results in a system with a lot of heuristics. Therefore, Clout uses ATNs for identifying conditions, selecting lists for output, and sorting. It reserves heuristics for resolution of ambiguities, database searches, joining parsed sentence segments, and translation of user queries into formal database inquiries.

DATABASE SEARCHES

Clout employs heuristics to limit database searches because the heuristics guide it first to the most likely relations (tables) that contain the requested information. This reduction of processing becomes increasingly important in cases where the data that users requested are scattered in many relations.

A request for data that are contained in one relation, such as "LIST THE PRODUCTION WORKERS IN THE NEW YORK CITY DIVISION," is a simple matter, However, a personnel manager might want a one-time answer to the question "WHICH PRODUCTION WORKERS HAD LESS THAN 20 TOTAL TRAINING HOURS IN 1985?" The training records and department information might be in two separate relations or files. Other requests might require data that span, for example, five relations.

The process of retrieving data located in multiple relations involves finding the data requested in two relations with a common field. The two tables are then joined, using the common field, to form a new relation that contains the desired data and the common field from each of the original tables. Other tables containing other desired data are similarly joined with each other, and with the newly formed relation, until finally a relation is formed that contains all the desired data. The user's data are retrieved from this relation. Unfortunately, the searching and linking of multiple relations in this way are time consuming. Heuristics in Clout optimize and speed this process.

For example, Clout heuristics may direct Clout to look in relations where some things mentioned in the user query are already known. Another heuristic may guide Clout to count how many facts are known about various relations and first examine the relations about which the most information is known. Still other heuristics may favor looking in short relations first or in relations that were involved in a recent user query.

These heuristics are some of the instinctive techniques of human beings that are encoded in the program. Most people, for example, would find the salespeople that work for the IBM Corp. in a Hong Kong office by first accessing the files of the Hong Kong office and then searching for salespeople. The alternative, examining the files of all IBM salespeople, then determining which ones work out of Hong Kong, is likely to result in a search of far more voluminous files.

DISPLAYING THE APPROPRIATE DATA

To a computer, a request for the top three salespeople in Hong Kong could refer to an alphabetical listing, or a listing by sales, salary, or other criteria. Deciding how to display the requested data to the user entails deciding how to handle the conditions imposed, how to sort the data and by what, and whether to group the data together and by what. This is a complex problem that human beings handle through common sense and experience and which is driven by Clout's heuristic, rather than syntactic, techniques.

How heuristics handle data display is too involved a subject to discuss here in great detail. Typically, however, a rule-based natural-language system might perform some tasks and use the following heuristics to decide on ranking criteria (von Limbach and Taylor, 1984). For example, the request

SHOW ME THE TOP 3 SALARIES

implies ranking the output by some criterion. An appropriate heuristic might be

Heuristic 1: THE RANKING CRITERION FOLLOWS THE "TOP N" PHRASE.

This heuristic directs the natural-language system to rank the requested database values by salaries, because in the query, the attribute SALARY follows TOP N (top 3).

However, the request

SHOW ME THE TOP 3 SALESPEOPLE RANKED BY SALES

requires a modification of the original heuristic. The modification is necessary because SALESPEOPLE follows the TOP N phrase. There are many ways to rank salespeople, but in this query, the ranking criterion is specifically mentioned in the query. A possible refinement might be

Heuristic 2: THE RANKING CRITERION FOLLOWS THE TOP N PHRASE UNLESS THE CRITERIA ARE SPECIFICALLY MENTIONED ELSEWHERE.

Further refinement, or a new heuristic, is needed for the query that asks

SHOW ME THE TOP 3 SALESPEOPLE.

From experience we know that the user probably does not want the people whose last name begins with an "A" (alphabetical ranking). In the real world, people have a greater tendency to rank by numerics. Therefore, a heuristic might say the following:

Heuristic 3: UNLESS PEOPLE EXPLICITLY STATE IN THEIR QUERY, "RANKED BY SALESPEOPLE," THEN ASK THE USER "RANKED BY WHAT?"

FROM QUERY TO RESPONSE

Heuristic 3 points up one method that Clout employs to cope with unknown information necessary to respond to a user's query—it asks the user. However, the user is only one source of information toward understanding natural-language queries and building a formal database request. Clout also uses information from its internal dictionary, a user dictionary, the database schema, and the database itself.

Clout begins its natural-language processing tasks by matching query words and phrases with those in its application dictionary and then in its internal dictionary (lexicon). The application dictionary contains user-defined words such as synonyms for database attributes, user defintions (including arithmetic expressions) such as profits equals sales minus expenses, and general vocabulary, for example to initiate standard reports. In contrast, the internal dictionary is factory defined, shipped with the natural-language system, and contains standard database request words. These include prepositions, articles, pronouns, arithmetic operators, comparison operators, and subtotal phrases. Other generic lexicon vocabulary includes request words such as "list," phrases that indicate sorts such as "by" or "for each," and conjunctions such as "and," "or," and "not." Synonyms for these words may be defined in the application dictionary. When matching query with dictionary words, if a choice exists, Clout selects the longest expressions first. For example, given the choice of "west coast" and "west coast salespeople," Clout replaces the longer phrase with its dictionary meaning. Although Clout expands users' queries by replacing words with longer defintions, it still retains knowledge of the original query words. For example, if Clout replaces the term "profits" with "sales minus expenses," it can still handle queries that refer to profits. In addition, Clout understands various tenses and inflections of words such as plurals and present and past participles.

After matching query and dictionary words, Clout seeks out information it needs from both the database schema and the database. The schema refers to the structure and organization of the database, the types of information contained, and the relationships between the data. The database is the set of tables that contains the data.

Both types of knowledge are necessary to select and process database fields and retrieve the specifically requested data. As explained, for this type of processing, Clout uses both parsing and heuristic techniques. Parsing, for example, is the choice to identify conditions. Clout uses heuristic rules to bypass the parser and resolve ambiguity with database help or to efficiently search the database.

When all else fails, Clout assumes that the user request is a legitimate one that happens to include a new word or phrase. Therefore, it asks the user to identify unrecognized words or phrases as data from the database, retype the word or phrase, omit the word or phrase from the request, or define the word to the language program.

Once the terminology and context are resolved, the user's request must be converted into a formal database inquiry, the requested data retrieved from the database, and the retrieved data displayed for the user. Conversion to a formal database inquiry is an internal mapping procedure. The task of displaying data in listed, grouped, sorted, totaled, or subsetted formats, however, is performed mostly by heuristic rules.

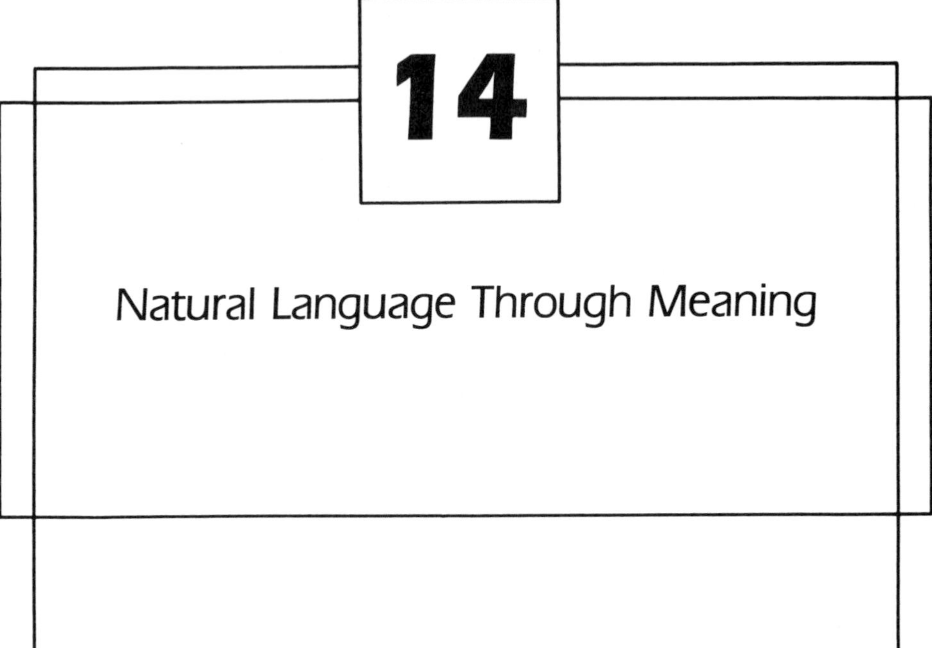

14

Natural Language Through Meaning

Compared to human beings, most natural-language systems underachieve. True, they can parse an English-language query and respond to it. They can even understand a partial query, such as "List them," if "them" is related to a prior query such as "How many clerical employees work here?" And to some degree, they can resolve ambiguities.

Yet natural-language systems cannot demonstrate even a fraction of the natural-language competence of three-year-old children. Average three-year-olds not only understand their native language but know that differently phrased sentences can have identical meanings. In addition, they can translate one meaning or concept into several differently phrased sentences. By five years of age, children can recognize long sequences of sentences, comprehend them, fill in gaps with information that was implied but not spoken, draw inferences, and generalize some things. In addition, they can perform actions or paraphrase information based on their realization of analogies between a language sequence and some previous event or observation.

Many of these capabilities are possible because children approach language through meaning, not structure. To help decipher meaning, they rely on a broad range of experiences, observations, and general knowledge which they can refer to and apply whenever necessary. For example, as soon as children are told that a book's name is *The Three Bears*, they instantly anticipate some of the material in the book because they already know a lot about bears. They know that bears are living creatures, big, furry, and either brown or black. They know that the bears like honey, live in woods, and sleep in caves. Part of the book's appeal stems from the children's knowledge that bears do not live in houses, sit on chairs, sleep in beds, and cook porridge.

The fact is that children stand a better chance of understanding and answering questions about stories than computers do, because the children can retrieve a variety of associations from past experiences and reconstruct the general context of knowledge in which some event occurred. This reconstructed knowledge is available to help interpret meaning for a specific story or conversation. When grandma says "I'm cold," children know that it means "You put on a sweater." Similarly, children are not misled by a phrase such as "With the passage of time, the jacket grew too small to fit." Children invariably know that "the jacket didn't grow small; the child grew bigger."

UNDERSTANDING MEANING

Unlike children, most modern natural-language systems cannot reconstruct and bring to bear past experiences. They generally use a combination of syntax, language structure mechanisms, and semantics to interpret language. Much is known about the syntactical and structural components of natural-language systems. Unfortunately, little is known about the semantic components and methods for interpreting meaning. Consequently, greater emphasis in most natural-language systems is placed on syntax and structure.

For Roger Schank, computer science department chairman at Yale University, however, to have even a small child's understanding of language, it is necessary to approach natural language in the same way that human beings do—through meaning. Taking this approach, Schank has built not only natural-language interfaces to databases, but conversational advisory systems and systems that can comprehend and paraphrase newspaper articles. Schank's systems differ from previous natural-language systems in that their internal techniques emphasize, almost exclusively, the representation of meaning.

Another approach to language through meaning, taken by Carnegie Group, Inc., emphasizes meaning, but less exclusively, and focuses on different sorts of meanings than Schank's systems. Positioned in-between Schank's exclusive emphasis on meaning and more limited syntactic-oriented techniques, one of Carnegie Group's goals is to build interfaces to knowledge acquisition systems so that programmers can use their natural language to enter knowledge to knowledge-based systems.

With either approach, the emphasis on meaning gives natural-language systems the humanlike ability to infer varying amounts of information that is implied but not said. For example, Schank's systems realize that a simple statement such as "Harvey went to Burger King and bought a hamburger" implies eating. Yet nowhere in this statement is eating mentioned.

Furthermore, Schank's language systems can check that the facts in a series of sentences and the inferences drawn from them are consistent. So it would interpret a simple statement such as "Andrea took the train" in terms of cities and time schedules. However, the system would reinterpret the statement about Andrea in terms of the more consistent domain of children and toys if the next statement in a sequence turned out to be "Eric grabbed it back."

STEREOTYPES AND SCRIPTS

Schank's natural-language systems recognize both ambiguous and implied information because, like human beings, they contain internal representations of stereotypical situations and events. The stereotypical situations are represented in framelike templates called scripts. This stereotypical knowledge helps the programs interpret new situations because the stored stereotypical situation tells them what to expect.

A stereotypical situation might be a story of a prince who saves a princess after a two-hour fight with a dragon. A Schank script represents a generalized form of this stereotypical story, including the anticipated ending wherein the prince marries the princess and lives happily ever after.

UNDERNEATH SCRIPTS

Scripts are made of fundamental unambiguous representations of meaning called "conceptual dependencies." These conceptual dependencies consist of 11 primitive acts (defined by Schank) to represent actions and state changes (such as who has, owns, or transfers something) that languages handle (Figure 14-1). They include primitives for physically or mentally transferring objects or ideas. There are also primitives for movement, grasping, and applying force. Still other primitives pertain to sense organs, ingestion by animals, and thinking types of acts such as "decide" and "imagine."

Like human beings, conceptual dependency primitives can translate the many different sentences that have the same meaning into one unique representation. For example, PTRANS is an action that means the transfer of the location of a physical object. Thus, whether a sentence is written "Manny gave Trudy a book," "Trudy got a book from Manny," or "Manny put a book in Trudy's hand," a conceptual dependency template in a computer represents the sentence as "Manny PRTANSed the book to Trudy."

Conceptual dependency primitives can, to some degree, infer information—a capability they use to help interpret sentences. The inference capability is partly due to the many relationships between objects, actions, and concepts that become apparent when different sentences are translated into the same conceptual dependency representation.

For example, "Marianne likes reading" and "Marianne likes books" have the same representation. This sameness allows the natural-language system to

PTRANS:	The transfer of location of a physical object, such as Manny PTRANSed the book to Trudy, or to "go" is to PTRANS oneself to a place
ATRANS:	The transfer of an abstract relationship, such as possession, ownership, or control. For example, "buy" is made of two conceptualizations that cause each other. One is an ATRANS of money. The other is an ATRANS of the object being bought.
PROPEL:	The application of physical force to an object.
MOVE:	Movement of a body part.
GRASP:	The grasping of an object by an actor.
INGEST:	The taking in of an object by an animal to the inside of that animal. This includes food, liquid, and gas.
EXPEL:	The expulsion of an object from the body of an animal into the physical world. This includes sweat, spit, and cry.
MTRANS:	Memory or mental transfer between animals or within an animal. This includes "tell," which is MTRANS between people; "see," which is MTRANS between eyes and consciousness; and think, remember, forget, and learn.
MBUILD:	The construction by an animal of new information from old information. This includes decide, conclude, imagine, and consider.
SPEAK:	The actions of producing sounds. This includes say, purr, play music, and scream.
ATTEND:	The action of attending or focusing a sense organ toward a stimulus. For example, ATTEND ear is listen. ATTEND eye is see. But "see" is treated as MTRANS to consciousness by instrument of ATTEND eye to object.

Figure 14-1 The primitive acts of conceptual dependency. (Roger Schank, Yale University)

infer that reading and books are related. Another example shows that a conceptual dependency-based language program can infer that the sentence "Ellen likes apples" is related to eating. The relationship is inferred because the conceptual dependency representation for "Ellen likes apples" requires the primitive INGEST, which involves eating (Figure 14-2). Thus the system can infer that "Ellen eats apples."

Inferences can also be made based on the actual information incorporated in the definition of some conceptual dependency primitives. For instance, in the earlier PTRANS example (Manny gave Trudy a book), the computer infers that the book is now possessed by Trudy, it is no longer in the location it was when it was possessed by Manny, and it is located wherever Trudy put it.

The slightly different sentence "Manny sold Trudy a book" still involves the physical transfer of a book. However, the sentence meaning is changed because

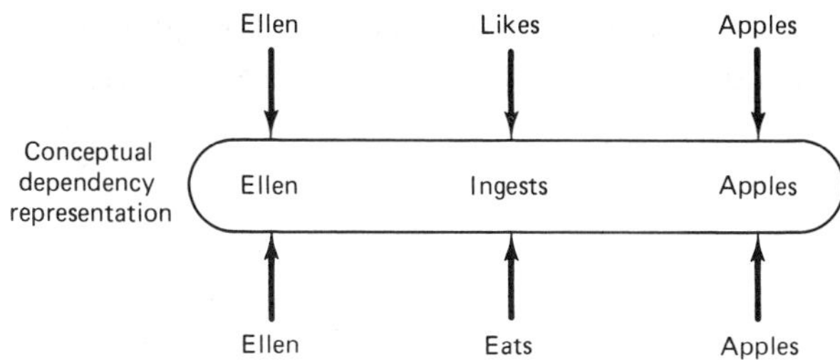

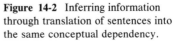

Figure 14-2 Inferring information through translation of sentences into the same conceptual dependency.

the definition of "sold" involves not only the transfer of a book, but also the transfer of a second physical object—money. A conceptual dependency primitive called ATRANS describes this two-concept action. Although similar to PTRANS in that both primitives involve some sort of transfer, ATRANS entails a different set of inferences. For example, after Manny ATRANSed the book to Trudy, not only does Manny no longer have the book, but Trudy has less money while, unless he spent the money received, Manny is richer.

UNDERSTANDING WITH CONCEPTUAL DEPENDENCIES

Unlike the natural-language systems discussed in previous chapters, when conceptual dependency-based sentences interpret users' sentences, they do not look for syntactic sentence elements such as nouns, subjects, and verbs. Instead, they read a sentence from left to right to look for elements such as the primitive action, its actor, an object transferred, and the direction of transference. So to interpret "Manny sold Trudy a book," the natural-language program first understands "Manny" to be a human being. That information conveys little knowledge, so the language program moves to the next word. It understands the next word, "sold," to be an ATRANS. As soon as the language program recognizes the ATRANS, it realizes that Manny is probably the actor who is doing the ATRANS (Figure 14-3).

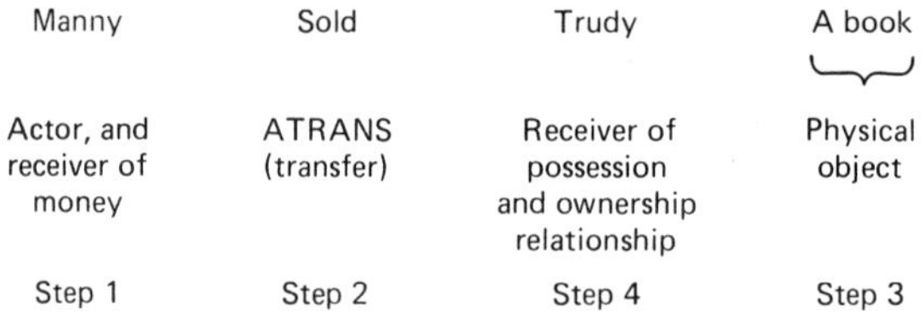

Manny	Sold	Trudy	A book
Actor, and receiver of money	ATRANS (transfer)	Receiver of possession and ownership relationship	Physical object
Step 1	Step 2	Step 4	Step 3

Figure 14-3 Understanding with conceptual dependencies.

Besides creating expectations about an actor doing the ATRANS, the word "sold" also creates expectations about what else the sentence contains. For example, the computer expects to hear what was sold and to whom it was sold. However, when the computer reaches "Manny sold Trudy," it must wait for more of the sentence because the sentence could read "Manny sold Trudy to the slavedrivers."

Once the computer reads the words "a book," it makes its final inferences. It realizes that people usually sell physical objects. Moreover, they do not sell objects or people to physical objects. Therefore, the computer eliminates these possibilities and concludes that the book is the object that was sold and that it was sold to Trudy.

UNDERSTANDING WITH SCRIPTS

Interpreting events, objects, and descriptions by literally analyzing stories or dialogues word by word or sentence by sentence is difficult at best and can result

Script:	Restaurant		
Track:	Diner	Roles:	Customer
Props:	Tables Chairs Menu Food Check Money		Waiter, waitress Cook Cashier Owner
Entry conditions:	Customer is hungry. Customer has money.	Result conditions:	Customer has less money. Owner has more money. Customer is not hungry.
Scene 1:	Entering Enter restaurant (Customer PTRANS into restaurant) Wait to be seated . . . . . . Decide where to sit . . . . . . Move to table . . . . . . Sit down		
Scene 2:	Ordering Menu on table, or waiter brings menu, or customer asks for menu Read menu Choose food Signal waiter Order food Waiter transmits order to cook → Cook tells waiter no food Waiter tells customer Customer rechooses food or customer goes to scene 4 at the "no pay path." → Cook prepares food		
Scene 3:	Eating Cook gives food to waiter Waiter gives food to customer Customer eats food		
Scene 4:	Exiting Waiter writes check Waiter gives check to customer Customer gives tip to waiter Customer pays cashier		
(no-pay path):	Customer leaves restaurant		

Figure 14-4 Translation of an abridged eat-at-restaurant script. (Roger Schank, Yale University)

in some weird pitfalls. Human beings generally avoid the pitfalls because they bring their past experiences, observations, and general knowledge to bear on their understanding of natural-language sequences.

Consider, for example, the following two sentences from the same laboratory manual: "Take turns sanding a piece of wood with your partner" and "You will need a classmate for this experiment." Although not well written, these directions give the laboratory students no cause for alarm because they interpret the directions based on knowledge about what students do in laboratories. To provide computerized language programs with these capabilities, Schank invented the concept and structure called "scripts."

Scripts, as the name suggests, are a sequence of events (stored in a computer) that illustrate a stereotypical situation. Schank has developed scripts for going to a restaurant, to a theatre, riding on a bus, and visiting the doctor.

Natural-language programs use these scripts as though they were previous experiences that can help interpret new situations. Like human beings, when script-based natural-language systems encounter a new situation (similar to one described in a script), they start with strong expectations about what will happen. The expectations allow the language systems to understand implied information and fill in missing information.

For example, a restaurant script describes entering the restaurant, waiting to be seated, sitting at the table, reading the menu, choosing food, ordering from the waiter or waitress, paying, tipping, and leaving (Figure 14-4). The script acts as a reference guide that can supply missing details needed to understand a dialogue and answer questions about it. So in the story "Eva went to a restaurant, ordered some chicken, and left," a script-based system would assume that she was served, ate the chicken, and paid for it. In fact, it would assume that she left a tip even if the chicken was not very good. Yet the story does not mention waiters, eating, or money.

USING SCRIPTS AND MOPS

To know which existing script (for example, geology, banking, airlines, fast-food establishment) is appropriate for a sentence, a Schank system scans the sentence in question from left to right. In the sentence "The sergeant ordered a lobster to go," the system gathers as much information as possible from the words, *the*, *sergeant*, and *ordered*. The word *ordered*, in this example, signifies an action that requires an actor. Although the system realizes that *the sergeant* is the actor, it does not yet know what type of script to instantiate. *Ordered* may require the restaurant script, but it could require a military script, as in "The sergeant ordered the soldier to go."

Since the sergeant clearly does not want a soldier wrapped like a lobster, the system must postpone its script decision until it has more information. Only after the system reads "ordered a lobster" does it guess that the story pertains to buying food. At that point it instantiates the restaurant script.

Although scripts for different domains are different, in some ways they are repetitive. For example, a visit to a doctor, dentist, or lawyer contains many

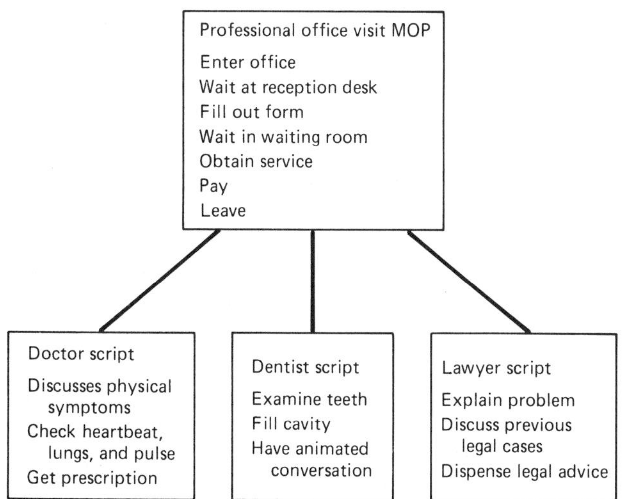

Figure 14-5 One MOP can be invoked by several scripts.

similar experiences. To accommodate the similarities and make the natural-language programs more efficient, scripts with shared experiences have been structured into a hierarchy called MOPS (Memory Organization Packages). Just the organizing of information in this way facilitates faster inferencing in less memory space.

With MOPS, instead of having to handle separate scripts for every situation, a Schank system calls upon a Professional Office Visit MOP, whether it is conversing about doctor, dentist, or lawyer visits. This MOP describes the sequence of events that occurs when a person enters a professional office, waits at a reception desk, fills out forms during the first visit, waits in a waiting room, gets a service (generically), pays, and leaves (Figure 14-5). For the particular service, however, the Professional Office Visit MOP calls on the specific script.

SCRIPTS GO COMMERCIAL

Like all other natural-language systems, script-based systems apply only to a narrow domain described by the script. Yet their ability to understand implied meaning and fill in missing conversational details in these domains makes them tolerable to human beings who expect and get such capabilities in their people-to-people conversations. The potential for natural-language systems with these capabilities and advantages has led Schank to form Cognitive Systems, Inc. to commercialize script-based systems for a variety of applications. Applications include natural-language database interfaces that are tailored to highly specialized domains of knowledge, and also advisory systems.

For example, one natural-language database interface, called the Explorer, contains geological knowledge that pertains to oil-well operations. The Explorer interfaces to a graphics package that retrieves information from a database and produces maps that help determine where to drill for oil. The database contains geological data and information about thousands of oil wells. The graphics program uses these data and information to prepare maps that display both geological data and oil-well information.

The difference between the Explorer and classical natural-language interfaces to databases is the amount of geology and oil exploration information that the Explorer contains in its scripts. The Explorer is not a general-purpose interface to a general-purpose database. Its script-based knowledge allows geologists and geophysicists to converse and interact not only in ordinary unconstrained natural language, but to use geology and oil exploration jargon to specify the geological maps that they need generated. Its oil exploration knowledge base also allows the Explorer to anticipate some of the geologists' geological needs and be flexible in its understanding of their geologically oriented input.

A script-based language system's ability to understand meaning and implied information also makes it suitable for advisory systems, say in bank and company lobbies, and in shopping malls. An automated will writer, estate planner, tax assistant, financial planner, and insurance advisor are among the script-based systems developed or under development.

A typical script-based advisory system in a bank lobby will converse in unconstrained English with untrained users to advise customers about the fine points of opening bank accounts. Normally, knowledgeable white-collar workers perform these account advice chores. They explain the different types of bank accounts and their options. Based on their knowledge of customer needs, they provide suitable advice. Although not a difficult task, advice giving is time-consuming. Banks claim that customers who consult with bank employees for ten minutes and then deposit only $100 cost the bank more than the worth of their accounts.

For computers to perform this advice-giving job, they must be conversant with the task domain, be able to choose a client's intended meaning, and answer questions without requiring clients to express every last detail. A system that asks about a client's occupation and then misinterprets syntactically correct responses such as "I'm a criminal lawyer," can only give exasperating, inappropriate advice. Script-based natural-language systems, however, can retrieve scripts that pertain to the subject at hand and choose the correct meaning in light of what makes sense in a particular situation.

BETWEEN SYNTACTIC ANALYSIS AND SCRIPTS

Despite their advantages, script-based natural languages have their limitations. For example, some companies and research institutions consider scripts static, limited only to stereotypical situations, and inadequate for full language understanding. Script-based systems depend too much on knowledge of a domain. If a script happens to exist for a subject area, the system understands in-depth and implied information; without this specialized information, the system understands almost nothing. Clearly, it would be impractical for a language-understanding system to contain scripts for every conceivable subject and contingency that could arise during a query or dialogue session. Even building scripts is a cumbersome process because it requires construction of a parser program to process the semantics for each new area of subject knowledge.

Part of the reason for these problems is simply that the script-based approach to language understanding is a state-of-the-art, still-evolving technique. But as is often the case, while the evolution is in progress, a simultaneous search is on to improve language-understanding systems by combining the best of the old with the most feasible of the new.

One such combination evolved into Language Craft (from Carnegie Group, Inc.), a language-understanding system and natural-language development environment that combines syntactic analysis with scriptlike semantics. Language Craft is a frame-based system with a general purpose parser that works across all frames in the system.

The parser operates similarly to script-based system parsers. It sifts through the words and phrases in a sentence to discover semantic components such as actions and agents performing the action. If necessary, it can query a knowledge base to get its semantic information. It may also look for traditional grammatical components, such as noun phrases or verbs. But unlike syntactic analysis systems, it does not build a grammatical parse tree. The parser's goal, instead, is to find words or patterns that indicate which frame to instantiate (activate).

The frames, called "case frames," contain both worldly and linguistic knowledge. As will be seen, the world knowledge in case frames is more general than subject knowledge scripts. This knowledge may be represented as declarative knowledge, or embedded in rules that can infer new information while a system is running.

The linguistic knowledge, also used by case frames to help understand meaning, comes from two different sources. One source is a data structure known as a "sentence structure." It contains information about possible legal syntactic combinations of words that conform to different types of sentences, such as imperative, declarative, or interrogative. For example, the sentence structure indicates that an imperative sentence contains a central verb, usually conjugated in the present tense, has no subject field, may have a direct object, and so on.

The second source of linguistic knowledge is dictionary entries. These indicate all of the words, in various forms, that signify a particular topic and therefore should activate relevant case frames.

When a user inputs a sentence, Language Craft performs a syntactic and semantic analysis simultaneously. For example, it looks up the words in the dictionary and assigns syntactic categories to them. If words fall into more than one syntactic category, the parser generates interpretations for both categories and then uses semantic information to determine the correct one. With this combination of syntactic and semantic analysis, if the system semantics understand that crocodiles are not normally part of people's dietary habits, the system interprets the ambiguous phrase "man eating crocodile" to be a phrase containing a noun compound (man eating) that describes the crocodile, instead of a sentence about a man who happens to be eating a crocodile.

The dictionary entries consist of various semantic constraints which, if satisfied, indicate the appropriate case frame to instantiate. For example, in the following three sentences, the word *ordered* has different meanings: commanded, purchased, and put in a particular sequence.

The sergeant ordered the soldier to go.
The sergeant ordered a lobster to go.
The sergeant ordered the list of names alphabetically

Separate case frames—call them A, B, and C—exist for each definition of "ordered." All point to the same syntactic structure, which defines "ordered" as the main point, warranting a direct object. But each case frame contains different semantics.

In examining these sentences, the parser ignores phrases like "the sergeant" and "to go" because the sentence structure indicates that "ordered" is the central verb and central point of the sentence. "Ordered" therefore becomes the key to decisions about which case frame to instantiate.

Case frame A, where "ordered" means "command," indicates that a human recipient of "ordered" is required, as well as an action that the human being can perform. Since the first sentence is consistent with these inputs, case frame A is instantiated.

The second sentence requires a particular food, packaged in a particular way. Since the soldier does not qualify as food, case frame A would not be instantiated. The system therefore continues looking for an appropriate case frame, and it finds case frame B, containing syntactic and semantic information about the definition "purchase." Similarly, the dictionary indicates that case frame C, containing knowledge about sequencing, should be instantiated if the direct object consists of (or refers to) a list of items.

This frame-based approach differs from Schankian scripts in that frame instantiation is not tied to a stereotypical situation. One problem with stereotypical script systems is that they may require a good deal of information to be explicitly stated in order to reliably instantiate the correct script. For example, the sentence, "the sergeant ordered a lobster to go" might incorrectly cause a restaurant script to be instantiated unless the sentence was extended to read "the sergeant went to the restaurant and ordered a lobster to go." Just the word "lobster," or any other food item, is insufficient because the next sentence could say "the fish store manager wrapped it and gave it to him."

Language Craft operates differently because "ordering to go," meaning "purchase," is not confined to a restaurant. Instead, it is tied to a particular activity that can be performed in many different places, wherever it is possible to purchase the thing ordered.

Another major difference between Language Craft's frame-based approach and Schankian scripts is that script-based systems require a separate script for every stereotypical situation rather than one for central words or points. For example, a Schankian system would have separate scripts for a military, classroom, warehouse, and hospital environment for the following four sentences:

The sergeant ordered the soldier to go to the office.
The teacher ordered Olga to do her homework.
The boss ordered Mickey to load the truck.
The doctor ordered Sara to set up an intravenous feeding.

Yet all four sentences are built around the idea of issuing a command, and much information can be gleaned just by understanding what it means to command someone to do something. Taking a different approach from Schankian scripts, only a single Language Craft case frame is instantiated for all these sentences, and it focuses on the meaning of issuing a command rather than the stereotypical situation in which the command is issued. The case frame is created with skeletal information about a command situation. This skeletal information, represented by slots in the frame, sets up general expectations about things involved in issuing a command, such as a command giver, recipients of the command, actions to take, and a number of other ramifications of commanding not present in most syntactic analysis-based language systems. These expectations are the same for all contexts of the command definition of the word, "order," or any other word synonymous with command. The meaning of a particular command situation becomes more specific as the slots are filled in with the information contained in the sentence.

If additional detailed information is needed, frames akin to Schankian scripts are required. This information does not come from Language Craft's basic language understanding system, but from knowledge representation frames found in a knowledge system development tool called Knowledge Craft (also from Carnegie Group, Inc., and discussed in Chapter 10). Since Knowledge Craft is used to build knowledge-based applications, it contains detailed information about the application domain. Language Craft interfaces to Knowledge Craft, so this detailed information is available, resulting in a specialized scriptlike language system.

Without the tie-in to Knowledge Craft, Language Craft becomes a general-purpose language understanding system, more fluent in understanding meaning than syntactic analysis systems, but less so than Schankian script programs. Unlike script-based systems, even if Language Craft does not have specialized, thorough understanding of a subject, it still can understand a good deal of immediate meaning.

This mixed paradigm approach gives Language Craft a unique niche. Like other natural-language systems, Language Craft can interface to a database or application, and it has also been used to develop interfaces to operating systems. But its method of understanding meaning also equips it to be an interface to a knowledge acquisition system. In this capacity, the language-understanding system allows programmers to build new scripts, frames, and other knowledge representations, for knowledge systems, by communicating in their native language. To achieve the level of comprehension necessary for this purpose, clearly the system needs to be able to understand the meaning of the users' input sentences without having a preexisting script (because the frames and scripts are first being built).

Language Craft interfaces to the Knowledge Craft knowledge system development tool and allows a variety of types of people to use Knowledge Craft to build knowledge-based systems. Experts entering first-time knowledge into a knowledge base use their natural language to type in rules or assertions pertaining to a particular topic. Language Craft then creates the frames corresponding to the new knowledge that has been typed in. In doing so, it builds an internal network. This network indicates relationships, as well as missing relationships, between frames and other knowledge pieces. As Language Craft spots the missing relationships, it asks the user how to connect new knowledge to previous knowledge. Once these initial relationships between pieces of knowledge are established, when the system is used, it can infer the information itself.

NATURAL-LANGUAGE SYSTEMS TELL TALES

Could a computer program ever read, skim, summarize, highlight, or answer questions about the vast amount of information generated by today's information-processing society? Maybe, but such programs would require not only knowledge of language and of the subject being read, but also knowledge of why people do things.

Some such programs—mostly script-based—exist, although they are still in their infancy. One of these programs is known as Sam (Script Applying Mechanism). In addition to processing scripts, Sam works with a program called Pam (Plan Applying Mechanism), which contains information about human goals, plans, beliefs, motivations, and how people achieve what they want.

With Pam's help, Sam can read and analyze stories such as the following: "John wanted some money. John got a gun and walked into a liquor store. John told the owner he wanted some money. The owner gave John the money and he left." (Nelson, 1978).

This story does not explain what John planned to do in the store or why the owner gave him money. But using knowledge that Pam supplies about people's plans, motivations, and behavior, Sam infers that John probably did not go to the store to buy liquor since a purchase requires money but does not normally require a gun. Sam therefore switches to the knowledge structure about robbery motives.

It interprets the statement "John got a gun" as part of a plan to get some money. It knows that people fear harm when confronted with a gun. From these facts and movitations, Sam deduces that the store owner gave John the money because he was afraid.

Another story-understanding program, called Frump (Fast Reading Understanding and Memory Program), funded by the Navy, reads and summarizes UPI (United Press International) stories. Unlike Sam, Frump does not read the news stories very carefully. It reads in a more sketchy fashion, similar to the way a person skims a newspaper. When skimming a newspaper, people read very quickly, catching key words and phrases that attract them. They often have preconceived ideas of what to look for, what an item of interest is, and how much they want to get out of a story. Based on these ideas, they stop to carefully read only certain articles of interest.

To skim a story as people do, Frump uses what are called "sketchy scripts." These differ from ordinary scripts in that sketchy scripts have room for far fewer conceptual dependency representations. As a result, they only represent facts, concepts, and events that the script designer considers the most important.

Newspaper-reading programs are particularly suited to a sketchy script approach to understanding because the important facts to look for in news stories, such as "who," "what," "when," "where," and "how," are easily represented by sketchy scripts. Frump uses the sketchy scripts as templates of expected facts, concepts, and events to look for when reading a story. Each type of newspaper story has its own defined list of expected facts. The collection of all the expectations for one type of story constitutes the sketchy script for that type of story and is equivalent to the preconceived ideas that people use when reading that story type.

Sketchy scripts have been defined for a number of story types. Newspaper-reading programs use these sketchy scripts to read stories, for example, about automobile accidents, earthquakes, and visiting dignitaries, international terrorism, oil spills, and heads of state.

For example, the vehicle-accident sketchy script used for the newspaper story shown in Figure 14-6 defines four types of expectations (called requests in the script) for Frump to look for (Figure 14-7). The first request is the type of vehicle involved in the accident, the object that the vehicle collided with, and the location of the accident. The second type of request is the number of people killed. The third is the number injured. The fourth is who was at fault in the accident.

But Frump is not perfect. Stephen Slade, assistant chairman of the computer science department at Yale, recalls that Frump, which also reads UPI earthquake stories, once sent out a message stating that an earthquake had occurred in the United States (O'Connor, 1981). In reporting this disaster, it left out information normally included, such as the quake's exact location, the scale of the quake, and any damages or casualties. Moreover, no other media were able to confirm an earthquake anywhere in the nation. When AI researchers checked the UPI

```
INPUT: A PASSENGER TRAIN CARRYING TOURISTS, INCLUDING SOME AMERICANS, COLLIDED
WITH A FREIGHT TRAIN IN THE RUGGED SIERRA MADRE OF NORTHERN MEXICO, KILLING AT
LEAST SEVENTEEN PERSONS AND INJURING 45, THE POLICE REPORTED TODAY.

THEY SAID THAT AT LEAST FIVE OF THE INJURED WERE AMERICANS, AND THERE WERE
UNOFFICIAL REPORTS THAT ONE OF THE DEAD WAS FROM NEW YORK CITY.

SOME OF THE PASSENGERS WERE TRAVEL AGENTS, MOST FROM MEXICO CITY, MAKING THE
TRIP AS PART OF A TOURISM PROMOTION, THE POLICE SAID.

THE AMERICAN SOCIETY OF TRAVEL AGENTS HAD BEEN MEETING IN GUADALAJARA, THOUGH
IT WAS NOT KNOWN WHETHER ANY OF THE GROUP WERE ABOARD THE TRAIN.

ONE OBSERVATION CAR ON THE RAILROAD TO THE PACIFIC TUMBLED INTO A 45 FOOT
CANYON WHEN THE PASSENGER TRAIN SMASHED INTO THE FREIGHT YESTERDAY AFTERNOON
NEAR THE VILLAGE OF PITTORREAL ABOUT 20 MILES WEST OF CHIHUAHUA CITY AND 200
MILES SOUTH OF THE UNITED STATES BORDER, THE POLICE SAID.

THEY SAID THAT RESCUE WORKERS WERE STILL TRYING TO PRY APART THE CAR'S
WRECKAGE TO REACH PASSENGERS TRAPPED INSIDE. THE RESCUE SQUADS COULD NOT USE
CUTTING TORCHES ON THE WRECKAGE BECAUSE SPILLED DIESEL FUEL MIGHT IGNITE, THE
POLICE REPORTED.
```

Figure 14-6 Vehicle accident newspaper story (Roger Schank, Yale University)

original copy, they found the headline that Frump interpreted as an American earthquake: "DEATH OF POPE SHAKES U.S."

Despite its overly literal interpretation (Frump makes humanlike mistakes), Frump has an action-packed history. During the Carter administration, (U.S. presidential) Frump was connected to another program called Cyrus (Computerized Yale Retrieval and Updating System). Cyrus, the given name of the Secretary of State at that time, kept track of news events that involved the diplomatic life of Cyrus Vance. The Cyrus text-understanding program remembers the contents of the stories that it reads because it stores these contents in its equivalent of a database. It uses this remembered information as an aid in analyzing future stories.

The Secretary of State was chosen as the subject to track for two reasons (Kaarsberg, 1981). For one, such a high-ranking diplomat is likely to be in the news often. This means that Cyrus's database is continually updating itself. Since Cyrus's data processes and memory organization are modeled on the techniques that some psychologists believe are akin to human organization, storage, and retrieval of information in long-term memory, this continuous updating gives Cyrus's developers a chance to observe how Cyrus actually stores its new information.

The second reason the Secretary of State was chosen as the subject for the

```
SELECTED SKETCHY SCRIPT $VEHACCIDENT
SATISFIED REQUESTS:
((SCRIPT ($VEHACCIDENT VEH $V-VEH OBJ $V-OBJ
LOC $V-LOC)))
$V-VEH
       CLASS       (PHYSOBJ)
       TYPE        (*VEHICLE*)
       SROLE       ($V-TRAIN)
       SCRIPT      ($TRAIN)
$V-OBJ
       CLASS       (PHYSOBJ)
       TYPE        (*VEHICLE*)
       SROLE       ($V-TRAIN)
       SCRIPT      ($TRAIN)
$V-LOC
       CLASS       (LOCATION)
       LOCALE      (*MEXICO*)
((ACTOR $V-HURTGRP TOWARD (*HEALTH*VAL (-LT10))))
$V-DEADGRP
       NUMBER      (17)
       CLASS       (PERSON)

((ACTOR $V-DEADGRP TOWARD (*HEALTH*VAL (-10))))
$V-HURTGRP
       NUMBER      (45)
       CLASS       (PERSON)

CPU TIME 4.504 SECONDS
SUMMARY: A TRAIN HIT A TRAIN IN MEXICO. 17 PEOPLE DIED. 45
PEOPLE WERE INJURED.
```

Figure 14-7 Facts extracted from a newspaper story to produce a summary of the story. (Roger Schank, Yale University)

program is that the reported activities of a diplomat are all of the same sort. Since these similarities in activities exist, it is possible to represent diplomatic activities in scripts.

As it turned out, besides summarizing news stories, Cyrus was able to make some interesting inferences. For example, it was asked whether Vance's wife had ever met the wife of the then Israeli Prime Minister Menachem Begin. Although that information was never explicitly stated in any story it had read, Cyrus discovered that Vance and Begin attended a couple of state banquets together. Since it also knew that wives were often present at such affairs, it deduced that Mrs. Vance and Mrs. Begin had met. And, indeed, they had.

A similar newspaper reader story, called IPP (Integrated Partial Parser), uses MOPs to store and organize knowledge about international terrorism (Kaarsberg, 1981). Like Cyrus, IPP remembers the contents of stories it has read and uses them to analyze future stories. It differs from Cyrus in that instead of answering questions about specific events, it uses its updating database to make generalizations.

For example, IPP read several stories about businessmen who were kidnapped and held for ransom in Italy. Based on information gleaned from these stories, IPP generalized that "when there is a kidnapping in Italy, the victim is usually a businessman."

Another state-of-the-art, script-based natural-language program argues. Called Abdul-Ilana, it contains subject knowledge about the Middle East and it argues about the responsibility for wars there. Abdul, in the program, represents the Arabic side. Ilana is the Israeli. Each arguer in the program tries both to understand the arguments produced by the opposing side, to refute them, and to look as good as possible at the opponent's expense. Here is a fragment from an Abdul-Ilana argument (Kaarsberg, 1981).

1. Arab: Who started the '67 war?
2. Israeli: The Arabs did, by blockading the Straits of Tiran.
3. Arab: But Israel fired first.
4. Israeli: According to international law, blockades are acts of war.
5. Arab: Were we supposed to let you import American arms through the Straits?
6. Israeli: Israel was not importing arms through the Straits. The reason for the blockade was to keep Israel from importing oil from Iran.
7. Arab: But Israel was importing arms and that's because Israel is trying to take over the Middle East.

The Abdul-Ilana program, the true frontier of current research, transcends just ordinary natural-language understanding. The program deals also with understanding the opposing arguer's claims and motivation analysis for these claims, and it plans rebuttals. Part of the goal of this program is to provide some insight into how our own minds work and how they handle the process of argumentation.

For example, rebuttals are not preplanned. Researchers discover that the program often finds the rebuttal it is seeking while it is trying to understand the opposing argument. According to Lawrence Birnbaum, one of Abdul-Ilana's developers at Yale, this technique "accords more with our intuition and experience that argumentation is a combination of plan and fortuitous discovery" (O'Connor, 1981).

An examination of the arguments shows that statement 1 begins the argument (Kaarsberg, 1981). Statement 2 is generated by an argument rule that assumes that the opponent in the argument is responsible for any bad events. In statements 3 and 4, both the Arab and the Israeli search their memories to find a possible cause of war that could justify their positions. In statement 5, the Arab program component changes its tactics. It calls on its knowledge of Israeli importation of arms from the United States and updates some pertinent facts in its memory to attempt to justify the blockade. However, in statement 6, the Israeli counters the argument by showing that the Arab's facts were mistaken and states the actual reason for the blockade. Backed into a corner, in statement 7, the Arab program-component shifts the focus of the argument away from the question of whether or not the blockade was justified. It mentions the factual basis for its assumption as an excuse for it and then proceeds to change the subject.

It is important to note that in this program, both arguers use the same techniques of argumentation, and both arguers share the same historical facts. Thus, the program can easily take either side in an argument.

Abdul-Ilana is only one of many state-of-the-art AI programs under development. Many projects are under way in developing systems that learn, see, and hear, and that probe theories of the structure of the human mind and how it works.

These systems are part of the distant future. Meanwhile, language-understanding programs are available to make computer-based data and applications accessible to large numbers of noncomputing professionals. All in all, natural-language systems have the potential to be one of the most important types of AI systems because they are geared to the layperson in the entire world community.

15

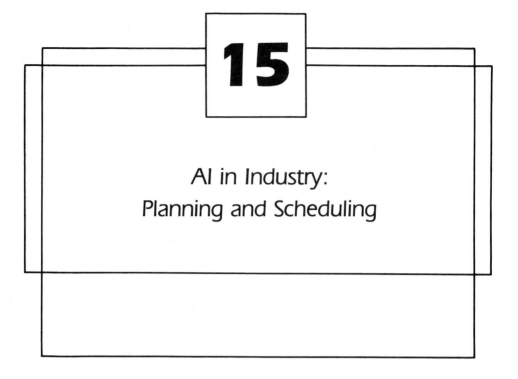

AI in Industry: Planning and Scheduling

Since the invention of the cotton gin, we have been striving to automate as many of our industries as possible. So far, automation of manufacturing processes has been able to increase only certain kinds of productivity—particularly, the productivity concerned with the actual production processes and the blue-collar worker.

But the manufacturing cycle encompasses white- as well as blue-collar involvement in a series of steps starting with customer or company specification, and going through product design, planning of the manufacturing process, making and assembling a product, and selling and distributing it. Industrial automation has traditionally addressed only steps in the manufacturing cycle concerned with machines, assembly lines, robots, and processes that can be reduced to a series of well-defined, repetitive operations, performed and supervised by blue-collar workers.

For much manufacturing, the percentage of time consumed by these machine operations is often small compared to total manufacturing time, as is the percentage of time and costs attributable to blue-collar workers. Instead, the specification, design, planning, and selling, which are the professional and management functions performed by white-collar workers, consume the bulk of the manufacturing cycle and costs.

There are many examples of this phenomenon. For example, observations show that ''in many small batch-oriented factories, white collar labor accounts for a large fraction of total labor costs and in some cases exceeds 50 percent'' (''Machine Tool Technology,'' 1980). Lest it be thought that small batch-oriented factories are the exceptional case, note that ''small batch-size production accounts for 50 percent to 75 percent of the dollar value of durable goods produced in the United States.''

Also, in ''metal-cutting job-shop production environments, it has been found that only 20 percent of the time an order is in a factory, is it actually mounted on a machine. And, during only 5 percent to 10 percent of its time on the machine, are value-added operations being performed.'' (''Machine Tool Technology,'' 1980).

Clearly, considerable savings would be realized if more computer-based industrial automation technology focused on white-collar activities and productivity. These activities are not amenable to traditional automation because they involve symbolic processing rather than the repetitive or number-crunching activities at which computers excel. AI technology, however, addresses the white-collar professional and management functions of the manufacturing cycle.

A number of AI systems have been developed to increase professional and management productivity in industry. These systems address all phases of the manufacturing cycle not previously automated, and many have begun use in production facilities.

For example, knowledge-based systems that perform computer configuration and provide diagnostic consulting about many kinds of mechanical equipment have become popular. Other expert systems that perform tasks such as specification of product at points of sale, planning sequences of operations, scheduling, organization, and facility layout are also in the process of demonstrating their feasibility in various production plants. Still other manufacturing tasks that expert systems perform are monitoring, project management, and distribution of products to resellers and customers.

A trend is afoot to integrate knowledge programs to reflect the relationship and interactions between different stages of manufacturing. Toward this end, some companies have linked groups of these knowledge programs together so that the output of one automatically feeds into the program that handles the next manufacturing phase.

As with many other fields involved with AI technology, the manufacturing companies do not expect knowledge systems to generate revenues directly. Instead, they expect the programs to reduce project costs and time, increase the number of projects that can be done in a certain time, and make available, to more people, the knowledge of how to manufacture better quality, more reliable products. In this way, the knowledge-based system increases a company's competitive edge.

ISSUES IN MANUFACTURING

Carnegie–Mellon University, which has been working with many large manufacturers to develop knowledge-based systems, defines four major manufacturing issues which AI could benefit by increasing knowledge and quality while reducing costs and time. These issues are disappearing expertise and interdependence of decisions; complexity of decisions, control, and information; and required fast reaction times.

These issues are dependent on, and compounded by, each other. For example, the problem of disappearing expertise is compounded by more complex equipment to design, operate, maintain, and diagnose. Similarly, the use of more complex equipment requires more complicated decisions to be made more quickly.

The disappearing expertise problem stems partly from recent recessions and seniority policies, and partly from a change in societal values that affect craftsmanship and many skilled types of jobs. Concerning recessions and seniority, several organizations claim that their best hourly design people or diagnosticians are retiring in two years. Unfortunately, these firms do not have enough younger people coming up through the ranks whose skill and experience level is sufficient to replace the retirees.

Observers attribute the lack of upcoming expertise to the cutting of junior-level people during the recessions, while senior-level people who remained have now reached the age of retirement. As a result, a sizable percentage of a generation of skilled people were lost. At the same time, job values have changed to favor jobs with greater status and remuneration expectations. Consequently, insufficient numbers of people are entering certain fields.

To address the disppearing expertise issue, knowledge-based manufacturing programs aim to provide consulting services for newer workers. The expert knowledge is acquired from the old-time, experienced experts, encoded in a knowledge system, and made available for the competent but less experienced workers to consult just as they would consult a human expert.

The interdependency issue arises because decisions that must be made in different manufacturing stages are really interdependent. For example, product distribution is dependent upon sales and field services organizations. The design decisions made at the engineering level may drastically affect what happens at the manufacturing level. This interdependency means that one cannot do the best job of designing a part without knowing how it will be assembled, manufactured, tested, or debugged in the field. Yet many decisions are made in a vacuum without considering interdependent tasks. One goal of AI-based manufacturing programs is to move knowledge concerning many stages of manufacturing cycle into the engineering stage. This will help engineers determine what the effects of their design decisions will be.

The complexity issue in manufacturing affects many aspects of every manufacturing stage. For example, with the greater use of flexible automation and versatile machines, alternative methods of manufacturing items are increasing. Consequently, the issue of deciding "what to do next" and "what machine to do it on" is becoming correspondingly more complex.

Unfortunately, existing software does not do that good a job of considering all the necessary knowledge to schedule our current complex manufacturing operations. And the increased complexity makes planning, control, scheduling, and maintenance decisions that much more difficult for human beings.

It is not just individual equipment that has become more complex and difficult to control and maintain, it is the entire factory. The advent of computerized environments has resulted in increasing numbers of terminals on the factory floor and sensors on machines, all providing information. Although the information is helpful or necessary, so much of it is provided that the computerized environment may be counterproductive. The question, then, is how to manipulate this information so that the information that a person sees is greatly reduced but still pertinent and sufficiently informative.

Knowledge-based systems can address the complexity issue because they know how to use the power of the computer to apply user- and sensor-generated information to determine and weigh more possible decisions than people could. Furthermore, knowledge systems can easily be modified to account for new information, such as changes in orders, new strategies, or new company policies.

The issue of fast-reaction-times arises as an outgrowth of the benefits of progress. Flexible automation offers many manufacturing method alternatives. Also, since the machines that perform the manufacturing processes are programmable, the amount of time necessary to set up a machine to satisfy one of the alternatives is drastically reduced.

An unanticipated consequence of this time reduction is a corresponding reduction in the amount of time that decision makers have to react to plant events or crises, such as choosing a new machine to run a job when the original one breaks down. Automated production processes have increased their chances of making a mistake because a greater number of more complex decisions must be made in a shorter amount of time.

A wrong choice, especially after company value is added—for example, after one-half-hour of cutting metal—may cause substantial cost penalties. Knowledge-based systems can address this issue. They contain knowledge of manufacturing processes, different machines, their versatile capabilities, and ramifications of alternatives which they use to determine and weigh the possible decisions and made suggestions at computerized speed, before the wrong choice has a chance to be made.

PLANNING SYSTEMS: MANUFACTURING PRINTED CIRCUIT BOARDS

One important industrial function performed by professionals or managerial personnel is planning. Planning involves deciding what operations are to be performed and in what sequence they are to be performed.

Planning systems typically fall into two categories. One type of system plans operations on a small scale, such as planning the sequence of procedures necessary to put together a part of a product. The other type operates on a more

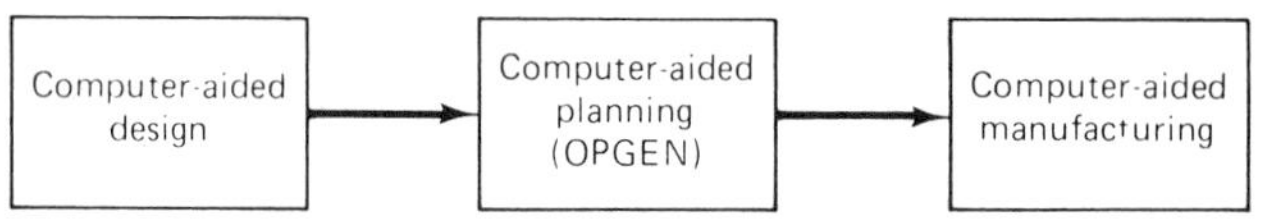

Figure 15-1 *Opgen*: A computer-aided planning program.

macro scale, where it sequences operations, schedules resources, and plans the route that a product travels through a factory during its manufacture.

The feasibility of the first type of expert system that can plan (not consult about) the sequence of operations to assemble a product part gains substance from several existing systems, particularly one developed at Hazeltine Corp. There, a knowledge-based system called Opgen performs the planning chores for printed circuit (PC) board assembly. These are normally tedious, time-consuming activities performed by industrial engineers (IEs). Planning requires the IEs to use their manufacturing and parts knowledge and experience to plan and prepare instruction sheets, called *operations sheets*, for technicians. Operations sheets contain detailed instructions that indicate who does what, in what work center, which parts get installed by hand, which by machine, which parts must be installed before others, and so on.

If a large number of PC boards are produced by traditional manual IE planning methods, this process is relatively efficient. However, for a firm that deals with low-volume, nonstandard PC boards, the planning procedure, normally performed by industrial engineers, constitutes a knowledge bottleneck for that organization.

With the aim of removing this production bottleneck, Hazeltine Corp. has installed a knowledge-based artificial intelligence system, called Opgen, in its printed circuit board production facility. Opgen plans the sequence of instructions that technicians follow to assemble a PC board. This computer-aided-planning stage occurs between the design and assembly/manufacturing stages (Figure 15-1).

The design stage, usually performed with the aid of a computer-aided-design (CAD) program, produces a schematic and PC board layout drawing. During the assembly/manufacturing stage, either a technician or a machine follows the drawings to pop the components shown into the positions indicated on the PC board.

Opgen fills the gap between the design and manufacturing processes by automatically generating the operations sheets (Figure 15-2). It typically requires about 20 hours of IE time for an assembly that contains fifty different parts. However, given a parts list and a PC board layout drawing, Opgen requires less than 90 seconds to generate the same operations sheets, as long as it knows all the parts it encounters.

A goal in Hazeltine's factory integration program is to interface Opgen to many hardware and software systems. This integration allows Opgen to get its parts and design information directly from business and CAD programs. It will also allow the instructions generated by Opgen, for machine insertable parts, to be sent to autoinsertion machines for machine insertion at the appropriate time.

ASSEMBLY NO.: 124323 DESCRIPTION: RF Control Board Assembly

OPER. NO.	WK. CTR.	ITEM NO.	QTY.	OPERATION DESCRIPTION
50 (cont.)	902			Hand install the following TRANSISTORS as per figure # :
		14	1	2N2219 TRANSISTOR (note the polarity) with:
		60	2	the AN960C3 WASHER-FLAT
		49	2	the MS35338-134 WASHER-LOCK
		59	2	the MS51957-3 SCREW
		73	1	the 340354 HEAT-SINK
		14	5	2N2219 TRANSISTOR (note the polarity) with:
		17	5	the 670078 PAD
		13	4	2N2222 TRANSISTOR (note the polarity) with:
		16	4	the 670099 PAD
		63	8	2N2369A TRANSISTOR (note the polarity) with:
		16	8	the 670099 PAD

Figure 15-2 An *Opgen*-generated operations sheet (Hazeltine Corp.)

Opgen's knowledge capabilities go even further. If Opgen encounters a part that it does not know about, it does not require a knowledge engineer to extend its knowledge base. Instead, it asks the IE a number of pertinent questions, and then assimilates the responses to acquire, automatically, knowledge of new parts and manufacturing operations. An Opgen execution in which Opgen encounters unknown parts that it must learn about from the IE requires minutes, rather than seconds, to generate the operations sheets—still resulting in productivity increases of several orders of magnitude.

Hazeltine felt that it was important to take its first AI step in this direction because although Opgen does not directly result in a salable product that generates new revenues, it reduces support costs per PC board, thus giving the firm a competitive edge. The firm opted for a PC board planning application for its entry into AI because the application is a finite, well-definable problem and therefore amenable to developing a successful knowledge-based system.

FUEL TO START

To peform its planning operations, Opgen needs the PC board layout drawings output from CAD programs, plus a list of the parts that comprise a PC board assembly. The PC board layout drawings, which are based on the original PC board schematics, graphically describe PC-board part placement (Figure 15-3). They also contain installation procedures for special cases and define those parts on the parts list that must be installed as a set. (For example, a transistor must be installed with a heat sink, pad, and screws.)

The parts for a particular circuit board, determined at design time, are stored in a database on an IBM 4341 computer (Hazeltine's business computer). The parts list includes information relevant to the preparation of operations sheets, such as part numbers, names, and quantity used, as well as irrelevant information such as prices and commodity codes. Opgen filters out the irrelevant information and retains only what it needs.

THE KNOWLEDGE BASE

To do its job, the Hazeltine system contains heuristic knowledge used by the IE. For example, to instruct human assemblers in installation procedures, the IE must know the proper installation time and procedure for each part contained in the assembly. This includes information such as which parts are heat-sensitive and the necessity for installing heat-sensitive parts after soldering operations.

Necessary heuristic knowledge also includes knowledge of which parts are insertable by machine and which by hand, as well as knowledge of parts that are used "as required." These are parts such as solder, solder flux, adhesive, and various compounds and lubricants for mechanical linkages whose installation time

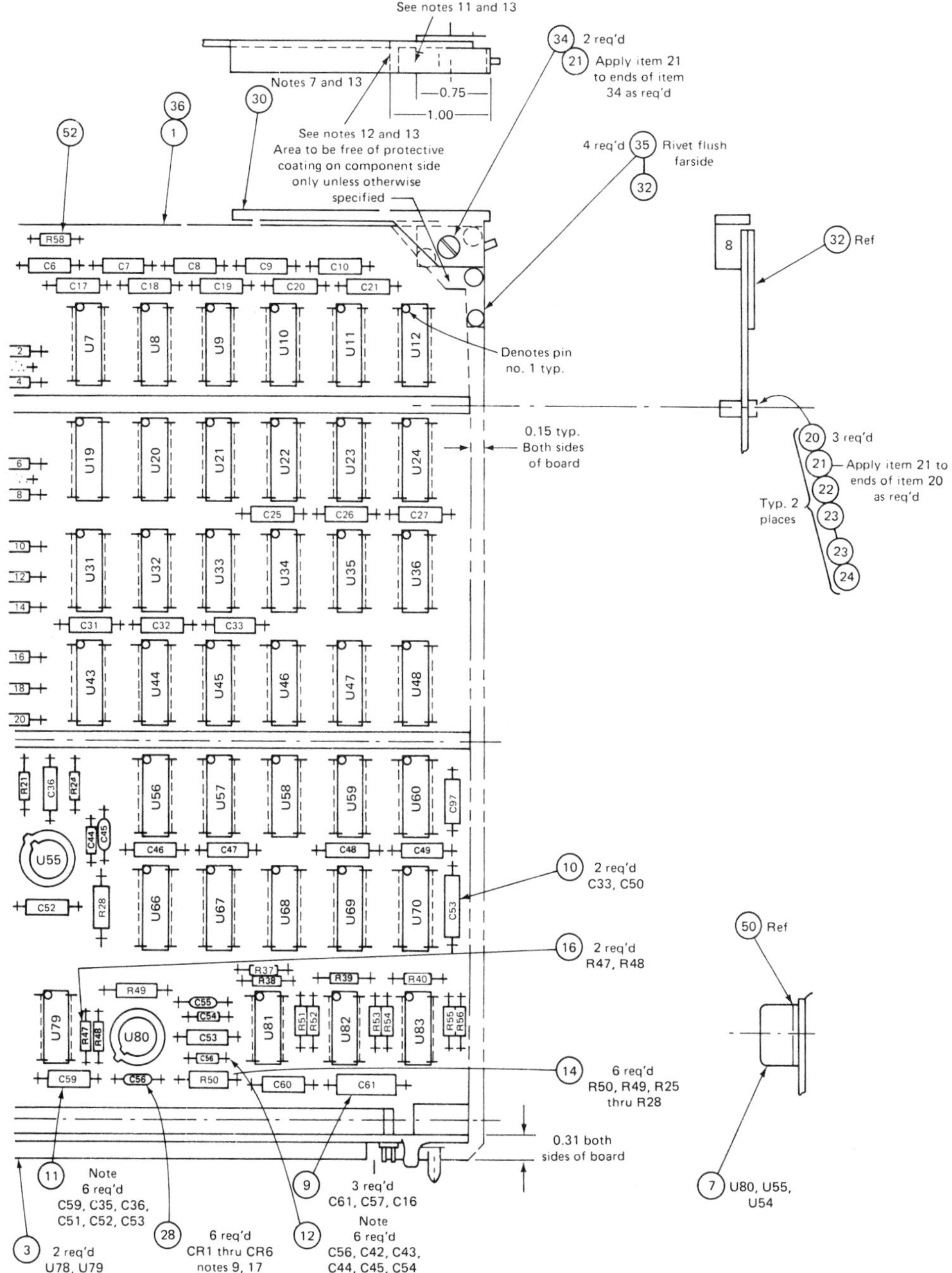

Figure 15-3 *Opgen* inputs: Printed circuit board layout drawing (Hazeltine Corp.)

is flexible. IEs must know which assembly operations imply the use of "as required" parts.

Opgen uses both frames and rules to represent knowledge. Its frames organize related information about specific subjects. Its rules are typical conditional statements. Opgen uses rules to represent general planning knowledge and frames to represent knowledge specific to each manufacturing operation.

Frames, located in an operation-specific knowledge base, describe a single manufacturing or part installation operation. Their slots indicate when and where the operation is to occur and if conditions must be satisfied before a frame's operation description is to be generated. An English-like example of a mechanical components frame contained in the operation-specific knowledge base for PC board assembly is:

DESCRIPTION: Hand-install mechanical components
WHEN: After the installation of axial lead components
WORK CENTER: 941
CONDITIONAL OPERATION: Yes

Rules, located in a general planning knowledge base, represent general planning knowledge about how to extend the operation sequence of an assembly based on the time and sequence constraints contained in the operation-specific knowledge base. An English-like representation of a rule, in the general planning knowledge base, used for installing sets is:

```
IF it is time to install sets
     AND there is an uninstalled set member
     corresponding to a part on the parts list
THEN
   write installation instructions on the
     operations sheets
     AND prepare to install the other members
     of this set
```

HOW IT WORKS

For Opgen to generate operations sheets, its general-planning rules are applied to appropriate slots in the specific-operation frames, located in a specific-operations knowledge base. For example, the mechanical-components frame just shown indicates when and where the installation of mechanical parts is to take place. To determine whether or not to instantiate (make active) this frame, Opgen must first determine whether a part in question is a mechanical one. For this determination, rules in the general-planning knowledge base refer to another group of frames that associate a part with its type (mechanical, electrical, heat-sensitive).

If the part in question is determined to be mechanical, Opgen can generate the mechanical-components frame's description of installation "when's" and "where's" in an operations sheet. But it generates these installation instructions only if the conditions referred to in the conditional slot are satisfied. To determine satisfaction, rules in the general planning knowledge base access the conditions associated with a particular operation. Based on satisfying these conditions, Opgen generates the operation description.

LEARNING UNKNOWN PARTS

Upon loading the PC board layout diagrams and parts, Opgen begins to grind away to generate installation instructions for various parts. Should it encounter a part about which it has no rule, it initiates an English-language interactive dialogue with the IE to acquire knowledge of the installation procedures for the unknown part.

This interactive knowledge acquisition process is possible because of the knowledge base. The general-planning knowledge base contains generic knowledge about how to install parts; the operation-specific knowledge base contains generic information about manufacturing and installation. Because the generic knowledge contained in both knowledge bases provides a general case of any specific PC board, almost every part that Hazeltine uses in its PC boards fits into some generic category that is covered.

Opgen's questions in the interactive dialogue with the IE are geared toward determining this category. Once the category is determined, Opgen instantiates the appropriate frame and permanently records the new information, as a specific example, or instance, of the generic frame, in the operation-specific knowledge base. In this way, the IE educates Opgen about installation procedures for new parts.

RULE SYSTEM EVOLVES TO FRAMES

Opgen evolved from Hazeltine's earlier knowledge-based PC-board planning program called HAIL-1. HAIL-1 provided the same functionality as Opgen. It differed in that it was exclusively rule-based. Opgen's developers switched to frames to avoid memory and computational overhead inefficiencies, and to increase the ease with which the IEs could add knowledge.

For example, for 50,000 parts, at an average of six rules per part, 300,000 rules would be necessary to cover all parts in the domain. In addition, HAIL-1's technique of using meta-rules (rules for constructing new installation rule groups based on information acquired from the IEs) for knowledge acquisition procedures required much computation overhead.

Finally, HAIL-1 required the IEs to know a rule language in order to add a new rule. In contrast, Opgen users need only interact in English to provide the necessary information for Opgen to instantiate a frame.

THE MILITARY-BUSINESS VIEWPOINT

Opgen's combination rule and frame system went into production use first in a controlled environment test basis, and later across the board. In the controlled environment, changes to the knowledge system are made by the research and development group, with users acting as consultants. Once the users take over the program, they maintain it and make all changes with the research group acting as consultants.

Despite the ease of making changes, "when the system goes into full production, we don't want many changes," said Sal Nuzzo, Hazeltine's president and chief executive officer when the system was adopted. "The reason is the same as for any production environment; changes entail costly, constant training."

Nuzzo describes the benefits that Hazeltine expects to derive from Opgen as requiring less industrial engineering time for each PC board setup and, therefore, lower support costs per manufacturing project.

These benefits are particularly important for many manufacturers dealing with the military because the military business often involves small runs of many kinds of nonstandard PC boards. In addition, the military business demands lots of changes because new technology is evolving very fast and technology is the name of the game in the defense industry. The evolving technology requires the military-industrial complex to constantly make changes in its designs.

Subtle as they may be, almost every change necessitates a change in a PC board. The PC board changes, in turn, require new operations sheets in order to be able to assemble and test the boards correctly.

FACTORY SCHEDULING: PLANNING ON A LARGE SCALE

In a modern factory environment, numerous parts, such as resistors, PC boards, motors, compressors, fuselages, or taillights, are either manufactured in-house or subcontracted outside, and ultimately assembled to make a whole product. But planning and scheduling the sequence of operations necessary to make a whole product from start to finish are difficult tasks, largely because of complexity, competition, and constraints.

The problem is that often a factory is producing many different models of what is considered as one item. There are many different ways of manufacturing each item. All the orders for the items are competing for the same resources, such as machines, personnel, tools, and materials. Also, the various orders are constrained by due dates, stipulated costs, and availability of resources at any particular time.

Consequently, each product model can travel many alternative paths through the factory to get from start to finish of its manufacture. Which route to take is constrained by the availability of resources and the relative importance of time and cost. Furthermore, schedules generated must be able to change dynamically as new constraints arise during manufacturing operations. Typical constraints that might occur after supposed final schedules are generated include machine breakdowns or a virus epidemic that takes large numbers of workers out of action.

Normally, factory scheduling is done manually with the help of computerized scheduling programs. The problem with existing scheduling systems is that they are static. They tend to schedule based on a model that assumes close to infinite capacity of all of a company's machines, tools, and human resources rather than those that happen to be available at a particular moment. Moreover, as factory conditions and the number of resources actually available change, which they do often, existing scheduling programs cannot be modified easily enough to keep up with the changes.

More important, experience has shown that a good deal of the scheduling information produced by computers tends to be ignored. The reason is that current computer scheduling systems ignore too many of the constraints that human schedulers take into account when manually constructing schedules. They focus instead on start and finish times based on scheduling machines that are ideally available. Meanwhile, they ignore a lot of information about the environment that could affect and constrain that schedule.

ENTER ISIS

A knowledge-based system called ISIS, which attempts to account for all imaginable constraints in job shop scheduling, was put together by a team from Carnegie–Mellon University (CMU), supported by Westinghouse Corp. and the Air Force Office of Scientific Research (AFOSR). It is in pilot operation at the Westinghouse Turbine Component Plant in Winston-Salem, North Carolina, a plant that manufactures steam turbine blades. As a first goal in developing ISIS, a Westinghouse/CMU group set out to identify everyone and everything in a company that could affect a factory schedule.

"Interviews with schedulers and other factory personnel have shown that they receive information from more than 20 sources in the plant, such as forging, tooling, numerical control programming, materials, marketing, forecasting, and sales," says Mark Fox, principal investigator of ISIS's development. In other words, potentially every department in a plant has some impact.

The relevant scheduling information from the various departments takes the form of constraints on the schedule. Typical constraints include (Fox et al., 1983a):

- Start dates
- Due dates
- Cost
- Operation alternatives

- Operation preferences
- Operation precedence
- Machine alternatives
- Machine preferences
- Resource requirements
- Possible resource substitutions
- Existing resource reservations
- Machine physical constraints (such as product form and length)
- Personnel requirements
- Order sequencing
- Priority of orders
- Work-in-process (desirable to reduce because it requires inventory levels whose costs are not recoverable until delivery)
- Shifts available
- Machine downtime and maintenance
- Machine productivity
- Quality

Like human beings, the ISIS system generates a schedule by attempting to satisfy all these and other constraints. However, the scheduling process is complicated, because different departments and orders may have conflicting constraints. For example, marketing wants to meet an early due date for its good customers, while advanced planning wants to use a slower, less expensive machine in order to reduce overhead.

Because they conflict, it is not generally possible to build a system that satisfies all constraints. When conflicting constraints occur, human beings typically weigh the trade-offs, juggle the constraints, and bargain with the departments that originated the constraints, to alter them. Similarly, ISIS is able to "relax" the constraints if they cannot be satisfied and then generate a schedule based on the relaxed constraints.

To do its constraint bargaining, ISIS must know all the constraints that may affect a scheduling system and their importance. If they cannot be satisfied according to importance, ISIS must then be able to decide when and which constraints should be relaxed and how to relax them. Finally, it must be able to evaluate the schedule it generates based on the constraints and relaxations, and then tune or regenerate a schedule if it considers that its first attempt resulted in a poor schedule.

HOW ISIS WORKS

ISIS gets its knowledge of orders and constraints from users who input this information into their computers. The system then either automatically generates

```
{ { operation
    { IS=A act
        NEXT·OPERATION: "operations which follow this"
        PREVIOUS·OPERATION: "operations which directly precede this"
        ENABLED·BY "state which enables this action"
        CAUSES: "states caused by this action"
        DURATION: "time of this action"  }    } }
```

Figure 15-4 Generic manufacturing operation schema (Mark Fox, Carnegie-Mellon University).

the schedule or works interactively with its users to evaluate the constraints, forecast their impact, and suggest methods of satisfying them.

New constraints, however, may be defined dynamically as the production process proceeds. For example, if a machine breaks down, users can update the status of the plant's resources and orders and ISIS reschedules the affected orders.

REPRESENTING CONSTRAINTS

How intelligent any system can act is limited by knowledge of its task and environment. To provide ISIS with the maximum intelligence to generate its schedules, ISIS's developers equipped it with a knowledge base that uses a frame-based system to model the relevant job shop production environment at all levels of detail.

The frames, dubbed "schema" (plural "schemata") by CMU, describe all products, resources (such as machines, tools, and personnel), operations and processes, departments, and plant layout. The frame-based scheduling system was built using a frame representation tool, an environment, and a language called SRL (Schema Representation Language), which was subsequently enhanced by Carnegie Group, Inc. and renamed Knowledge Craft. Objects such as machines, as well as actions, constraints, and goals, are stored in the schemata. Besides its schema-based language and organizational modeling capabilities, Knowledge Craft uses what is called an "agenda" mechanism to help it perform its scheduling chores. The agenda mechanism manages multiple queues of events and can therefore be used to keep track of, or simulate, events being handled at different times.

Figure 15-4 illustrates a schema (frame) that describes a manufacturing operation generically. This description states that an OPERATION IS-A type of ACT (a more generic activity than an operation). The schema contains slots for the NEXT-OPERATION and PREVIOUS-OPERATION (which establishes precedence relationships), states (or conditions) that must exist to ENABLE a particular operation, states that are CAUSED by the action, and the DURATION of the action.

Frames are related to each other hierarchically, with frames lower in the hierarchy applicable to more specific operations, products, resources, or departments than the generic frames at higher levels in the hierarchy. For example, a more specific frame in an operation schema hierarchy might describe a milling operation. Besides containing the same slots as the generic frame, the specific frame would also contain slots for work-center and required resources. In addition, it would have specific filled-in values for slots such as NEXT-OPERATION and ENABLED-BY. Most important, constraints may be attached to any schemata or slots defined in the schemata.

The constraints themselves are represented as separate schemata. Typical slots in constraint schemata include the importance of the constraint, the context of applicability, and the obligation by the system to use the contraint. Other slots describe duration of applicability of constraints over time and during operations, relaxation of the constraint if it cannot be satisfied, interactions among constraints, and the utility of their satisfaction (usefulness for an intended application or step of an application).

Since all constraints are not of equal importance, they can, to some degree, be ranked according to importance. Clearly, the due date constraint associated with a high-priority order is more important than an operation preference constraint. However, other constraint importance rankings are not as clear cut and, worse, vary from order to order. For example, in one order, the due date is most important, whereas in another cost is of top priority.

Fortunately, ISIS's constraint representation has the ability to express absolute measures of importance for each constraint. And it can also express importance rankings based on scheduling goals, such as low cost or rapid-turnaround service. This knowledge guides ISIS in its choice of which constraints to relax.

Interaction among constraints occurs because the satisfaction of one constraint may have an adverse effect on the ability to satisfy other constraints. For example, removing a machine's second shift may decrease costs but may also cause the order to miss its due date. To determine what alternatives to generate

```
{ { due-date-spec
    {IS=A range-constraint
         IMPORTANCE:
         CONTEXT: t
         DOMAIN:
            range: (type IS=A lot)
         RELATION: due-date
         CONSTRAINT:
            range: (type IS=A due-date-constraint)     }
    PRIORITY=CLASS:     } }
```

Figure 15-5 Generic due-date schema (Mark Fox, Carnegie-Mellon University).

```
{ { due-date-constraint
   {IS=A continuous·constraint
        CONSISTENCY: exclusive
        DOMAIN: dates
        PIECE=WISE=LINEAR=UTILITY: }      } }
```

Figure 15-6 Due-date-constraint schema (Mark Fox, Carnegie-Mellon University).

for consideration and which constraints to relax, ISIS uses a measure called *utility of satisfaction*. Utility of satisfaction is a preference measure associated with each relaxation (alternatives, such as different dates or machines) that indicates the preferred relaxations among those available.

An example of how a constraint used to generate a factory schedule is applied is illustrated by the "due-date-spec" schema (Figure 15-5). This is a generic schema that indicates that a due-date constraint exists for another schema that represents lots (a lot is a group of orders which are run through the plant as a unit). The slot within the "lots" schema that will be constrained is the "due-date" slot (a relation is a slot).

The type of constraint to apply to this slot is described by the "due-date-constraint" schema shown in Figure 15-6. This schema says that a due-date-constraint is-a continuous-constraint. A *continuous* constraint restricts the value of a slot to a particular domain—in this case the domain of dates—generally within certain bounds (as opposed to a restriction that indicates a discrete value or set of values).

Another slot describes an attribute called *consistency*. Consistency pertains to situations where multiple alternatives exist. For example, if a plant has more than one shift, it can meet its due date by scheduling work to be done by both shifts (inclusive) or by one or the other (exclusive). The "domain" slot states that the due date constraint applies to the domain of dates. The due-date-constraint schema also specifies a function, called a piece wise-linear function, to be used to determine the utility (preference) of any particular value chosen.

CONSTRUCTING A SCHEDULE

The idea behind ISIS (and also behind manual scheduling) is its view of the generation of a job shop schedule as a search through a space of all the possible schedules. As mentioned, there are many alternative routes for a product to travel through the factory, depending on the availability of resources and the relative importance of factors such as cost and time. Because there are so many routes, there are too many possible schedules to search—unless a method can be found to narrow the search space.

ISIS uses the constraints generated by many different departments to narrow the search space. Since satisfaction of a constraint eliminates an entire class of possible schedules, to construct a job shop schedule, ISIS searches the space of possible schedules hierarchically, by trying to satisfy all the constraints, beginning with the most important ones.

As ISIS finds constraints that it cannot satisfy, it generates alternatives—possibly many. The alternatives represent relaxation of the constraints.

For example, an important constraint to satisfy pertains to the sequencing of operations, such as milling before drilling. If it turns out that the milling machine is unavailable at the requested date because it is preassigned, ISIS generates alternative times.

Each application of a constraint generates a utility (preference measure) that indicates how good the alternatives are. The utility ranges from 0 to 2 with 0 signifying that the alternative is not admissible, 1 signifying indifference, and 2 signifying maximal support. So an alternative due date that makes a product one day late might be acceptable; one that makes it three weeks late has a poor utility rating and is unacceptable.

Only the highest-rated alternatives are selected to be encoded as constraints which are considered at the next level of search. However, rejection of the partially generated schedule because the utility ratings are too low may lead to an alteration of the search space at the current or even at a higher level by relaxing other constraints. Thus the constraints, the ability to satisfy them, the alternatives generated, and their ratings direct the search. For this reason, ISIS is considered a constraint-directed reasoning system.

ISIS begins its scheduling at any point—start date, due date, or in the middle—and then schedules either backward or forward from that point, or both. The ability to start any place and schedule in any direction allows ISIS to anticipate bottlenecks in a plant by equating bottlenecks with constraints that are particularly important to satisfy first. For example, if there is an important but scarce resource to acquire, ISIS will schedule that resource first and then generate the rest of its schedule both forward and backward from that resource scheduling point. This is a technique aptly known as *opportunistic scheduling*.

Figure 15-7 shows a partial display of ISIS in the process of generating a schedule. The schedule applies to an order for turbine blades at Westinghouse's Winston-Salem turbine component plant. Each rectangle in the figure represents an operation, such as drilling, milling, or inspection. Operation numbers at the top left of each box indicate the operation. The numbers at the top right of each box refer to particular machines, such as one or more models of milling or grinding machines. Several operation rectangles show the same operation being done on different machines. The sets of numbers on the second and third lines of the rectangles indicate the start (S) and finish (F) times generated at this point in the scheduling process, in terms of week, day, and hour.

The operation rectangles generated by ISIS are color coded. Colors range from green to red, with the darkest green indicating the highest utility rating and the darkest red having the worst utility.

The lines linking the operation rectangles show sequences of steps (operations, machines, and dates) that ISIS could recommend at a certain point in the schedule. As the figure shows, one operation can generate several alternatives. However, some alternatives lead to dead ends because their average utility ratings are too low to continue along a certain path. But not all red rectangles lead to dead

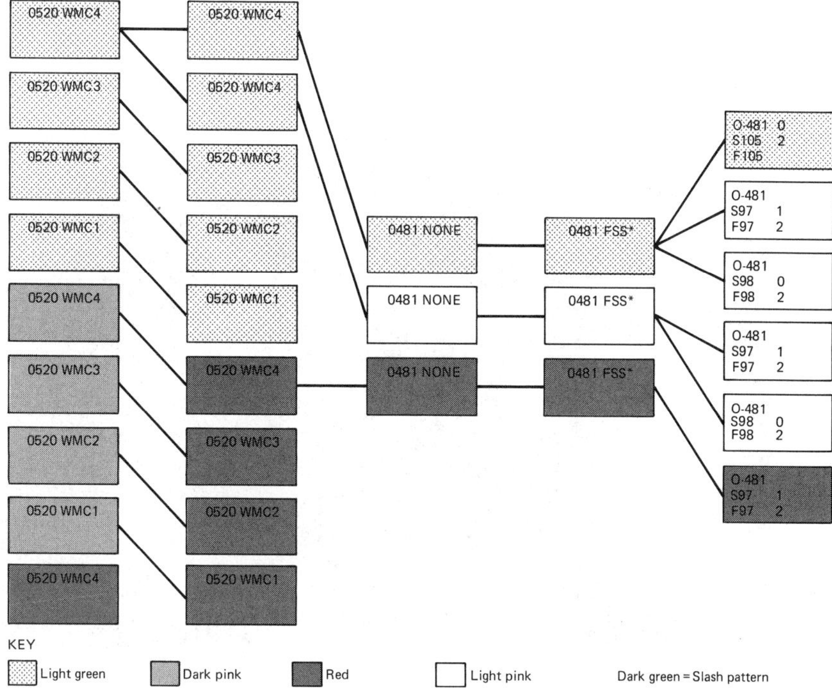

Figure 15-7 ISIS generating a schedule (Mark Fox, Carnegie-Mellon University).

ends, because the utility ratings are averaged. So choices with low utility ratings at one point in the schedule may, after averaging with choices later in the schedule, wind up in the green.

EVALUATING ITS OWN SCHEDULE

ISIS's constraint-directed search proceeds in this manner until finally the system has defined a complete path from beginning to end in the schedule's search space. The alternatives generated during schedule generation do not converge to become only a single complete path; multiple alternative schedules may be found. Under these conditions, ISIS will determine the schedule with the highest utility rating.

Once ISIS has generated a candidate schedule, it assesses the quality of that schedule. If it decides that it has generated a poor schedule, it determines where repairs should be made and then retries the schedule generation process. ISIS can tell if a schedule is acceptable by checking the constraints to see if enough of them have been satisfied and by checking their utility ratings. In a poor schedule, the average utility ratings of the relevant constituent constraints (which range from 0 to 2) will be low.

Detailed Machine Schedule

Machine	Blade Section	Blade Style	Material	Color-code	Mfg. Quantity	Shipping Quantity
208c	ts1016	743J868-001		pink	68	68
	ts1061-6	744J078-061		green	53	53
208d	ts1063-6	728J737-001		purple	62	62
	ts1063-6	728J737-003		white	59	59
	1-1	0567283-000		pink	141	141
	ts1482	771J987-001		pink	118	118
	ts1484	771J989-001		yellow	142	142
	ts1485	771J990-001		purple	142	142
	ts1408	771J943-001		pink	120	120
	ts1393	751J483-001		pink	144	144
208e	ts1482	771J987-001		pink	118	118
	ts1484	771J989-001		yellow	142	142
	ts1485	771J990-001		purple	142	142
	ts1408	771J943-001		pink	120	120
	ts1393	751J483-001		pink	144	144
208f	ts804a	752J348-008		green	203	203
	ts801b	731J712-008		pink	180	180
	ts802a	731J709-016		gray	180	180
	ts802a	731J709-016		gray	180	180
	ts803a	731J710-016		yellow	180	180

Figure 15-8 ISIS report indicating a schedule (Mark Fox, Carnegie-Mellon University).

Further utility-rating analysis may show that poor utility ratings at the later stages of schedule generation may be directly traceable to a poor constraint decision at an earlier stage. Since a poor decision at a higher level can adversely affect the utilities of constraints at a lower level, ISIS will choose an alternative value and regenerate a schedule from that point based on the new value.

In the final stage of ISIS's scheduling process, ISIS performs two tasks. One task is to output its recommended schedule to the user in the form of a report. The first five columns of the report in Figure 15-8 show the parts (turbine blades) and color-coded orders scheduled to be machined in different machines, identified by machine numbers. The last two columns of this report show manufacturing and shipping quantities to be the same. Sometimes, however, the manufactured quantity is greater to ensure sufficient quantity for shipping should damage occur. Other reports generated by ISIS indicate the breakdown of a large order into smaller orders for scheduling on different machines and the status of orders at various times during the manufacturing process.

ISIS's second task is to refer to the process routing, resource, and time decisions it has made for the order under consideration and then formally reserve each required resource in its schedule. The resulting resource reservations are added to the existing shop schedule and act as additional constraints for use in scheduling subsequent orders.

AI in Industry: Project Management, Factory Simulation, Long-Term Planning, and Integration of Knowledge Systems

The ISIS scheduling system described in Chapter 15 is actually only one part of a much larger series of manufacturing-oriented expert systems called the Intelligent Management System (IMS). Still under development at CMU's Intelligent Systems Laboratory (part of the Robotics Institute) is the development of AI technology to build an integrated manufacturing system that extends to the process, production, engineering, and management levels in a typical manufacturing organization.

Such an integrated manufacturing system is really a very long-term goal. Implementation of such a system must await, first, continued advances in AI technology so that AI systems can address increasingly more complex manufacturing problems, Second, it must wait until more factories are designed with fully computerized and networked environments so that the individual AI systems can communicate. Third, full integration must wait for more automation of materials handling.

In the absence of these prerequisites, CMU is concentrating on developing and using AI techniques to automate the individual manufacturing activities in such a way that they can be integrated at a later date. Currently, IMS contains individual expert systems that perform tasks such as resource scheduling (discussed in Chapter 15), monitoring, project management, scheduling of floor capacity, planning of system assembly and testing, corporate distribution analysis, long-range planning, and diagnostics. In addition, CMU has related expert systems, also amenable to integration within the IMS framework, in the areas of specification, design, computer configuration, and natural language.

It is not CMU that will integrate these systems, because they are being developed as separate joint ventures with commercial firms and government

* What is the effect of changes in engineering specifications: designs, materials, process specifications, etc?

* What is the proper inventory level at various levels, i.e., raw, work in progress, finished parts, etc?

* What if the jig grinder goes down with maintenance problems?

* Based on downtime, cost of maintenance and cost of replacement parts, how do I determine when to buy a new piece of production equipment?

* Charlotte moves one (1) BB72 rotor two (2) months ahead of schedule and Lester moves two (2) BB22 rotors back in schedule.

  1. How are all promised dates for next six months affected?

  2. What staffing changes are needed by cost center to accomplish changes?

  3. What material delivery changes need to be made?

* How do I select the process to be used? What if the shop changes the plan and needs to perform a particular job on a different machine from the standard?

* Not enough information concerning the current state of production on the floor, orders in process, problems etc. is communicated quickly and succinctly to interested parties within the plant.

* Changes to products or tools by the engineering division are not adequately communicated and coordinated with changes taking place in the factory.

* If I have a database containing lamp prices, sales volume, ics (internal product cost) transportation cost, overhead allotment, . . for all lamp types, what will the profit be if I change transportation, or change the source of manufacturing?

* Predict machine failures and prescribe preventative maintenance by sound vibration, machine timing, shrinkage trends, and end of normal part life.

* Determine correlations between gas, fill, temperature, stack up, and shrinkage.

Figure 16-1 Results of a questionnaire: Issues industrial managers most frequently face in their jobs (Mark Fox, Carnegie-Mellon University).

research agencies. What is important is that the means and the technology will be developed and the individual pieces will exist and be transferable to other applications.

The choice of expert systems to develop within IMS was determined as a result of an analysis of professional and managerial needs and by questioning more than thirty managers from three Westinghouse plants about the problems they face most frequently during the performance of their jobs. The replies, a few of which are shown in Figure 16-1, indicate problems in the areas of status of activities, communications and coordination, and machine failure. However, most problems are in the area of decision support.

To solve these problems, the IMS incorporated techniques to allow it to automatically sense information, model the organization, provide expert assistance, schedule, monitor, answer status questions, and analyze how the structure and processing of the organization should be changed to optimize such criteria as cost, throughput, and quality. The sensing capabilities include the ability to sense machine signals, locate objects, and determine the status of activities both on the plant floor and in supervisory areas. Modeling capabilities include the ability to model an organization at many levels of abstraction, ranging from concrete entities such as machines, people, materials, orders, and departments, to the more abstract operations, authority, interactions, time, beliefs, goals, and constraints. For modeling purposes, some IMS systems represent their knowledge in SRL-based schemata (frames) as ISIS does. Others use a more traditional rule-based approach, while still others are built on simulation techniques based on schemata representations.

FACTORY AUTOMATION ARCHITECTURE

Although integrated, the IMS is designed to be a distributed (not necessarily hierarchical) system where a lot of activities are performed in parallel in a distributed, multiprocessing factory environment. The ultimate goal is for employees in this environment to have what CMU calls a User Interface Process (UIP). A UIP is composed of a computer workstation, graphics display, keyboard, microphone, and network interface.

Software systems will provide the UIP with the intelligence to interpret and implement user requests and queries. Natural-language capabilities are important to these systems because the level of education of people in many areas of manufacturing is often low and not conducive to learning complex program execution methods. However, while some tasks, such as specification of constraints for the ISIS scheduling program, are most easily expressed in natural language, many programs are more easily driven with menu systems, which IMS will also contain.

All UIPs must be interconnected via a communication network in order to integrate the expert systems so that they can cooperatively interact to solve problems and communicate information. Some IMS systems on the network will provide expert advice and assistance to users. Others will carry out many tasks automatically.

Each machine will have a Machine Supervisory Process (MSP) that monitors and controls it. The MSP is connected to the network, so it can reply to queries and commands initiated by other MSPs or UIPs on the network. Finally, Task Management Processes (TMPs) will perform some of the more mundane task monitoring and control, freeing managers to do the more complex decision-making tasks.

A USER INTERFACE FOR FACTORY SYSTEMS

An aim of IMS is to integrate a user interface, with IMS systems, that answers "WHAT-IF" and "TELL ME WHEN" questions and issues "YOU'VE GOT PROBLEMS" communiques. Unlike numerically oriented spreadsheets' WHAT-IF questions, IMS's WHAT-IF's are symbolically oriented and cover such problems as "should we buy another machine or subcontract the order."

An IMS user query, targeted at the symbolic WHAT-IF facility, might be "WHAT ARE THE EFFECTS ON ORDERS OVER THE NEXT SIX MONTHS IF WE BUY ANOTHER MACHINE X?" (Fox, 1981). The system then enters into a dialogue with the user to determine the information required to analyze the question. It gathers information it needs from other IMS systems, alters the factory model to contain the user's premise, runs a simulation with the new premise, analyzes the output, and provides the manager with the answer and explanations.

The TELL ME WHEN capability allows a marketing manager who is under heavy pressure to ship a large order to tell his or her machine "INFORM ME WHEN ORDER X IS SHIPPED." The IMS User Interface Process (UIP) translates this English-language request into a rule that says "IF ORDER X IS SHIPPED THEN SEND MESSAGE TO MANAGER Y." The IMS expert system then sends the translated message to an IMS shipping Task Management Process (TMP), which interprets the rule, monitors the system, and when the rule condition occurs, sends the message to the manager.

IMS's YOU'VE GOT PROBLEMS communique capabilities take over under conditions such as a machine failure during a production process that results in damage not only to the machine but also to a high-priority order. The machine's sensors transmit the information to its Machine Supervisory Process (MSP).

The MSP analyzes the problem, shuts down the machine, and informs all responsible and affected personnel, as well as the integrated control and management expert systems. For example, it informs the floor supervisor and the scheduler TMP of the breakdown; the scheduling TMP reroutes orders. It informs the maintenance TMP, which allocates a maintenance person to fix the machine.

Finally, the MSP checks the importance of the order and informs all personnel that might be affected by the breakdown, such as the marketing staff, who must inform a client that an order must be delayed.

KNOWLEDGE-BASED PROJECT MANAGEMENT

Even though some of the goals of the IMS have already been implemented in production facilities, it will require many years of work before all the long-term goals can be satisfied. Only as the expert systems are tentatively tried and tested, so that they can acquire sufficient field experience to gain credibility and become competitive with the traditional combination of programs/people/manufacturing machines, will AI technology catch on in industrial, business, or scientific domains.

Still, with the rapid progress being made in commercial AI technology, attention is shifting from the more theoretical aspects to how to use AI to avoid some of the manufacturing headaches that plague managers. Project delay is a major headache. In an age when companies are trying to reduce product development time in order to enter the market as early as possible, problems with project management and technical support are causing critical delays.

Most often, project management is performed manually, by people, with aid from computerized critical path methods (CPM) and PERT techniques. CPM and PERT techniques are concerned with finding a path, through an activity network, which contains no slack. The network is made up of nodes which represent activities and lines which define precedence. A delay in an activity on the critical path results in the entire project's being delayed. Therefore, it is desirable to find the critical path in order to know which activities are most important to keep on time.

Although CPM and PERT techniques are standard project management techniques, the problem with these methods is that they indicate a theoretical critical path, but they do not manage projects. People manage projects.

When people manage projects, it is often the case in manufacturing that complexity and interactions between the various aspects of a project underlie the management and technical support delays. Callisto, a CMU/Digital Equipment Corp. pilot knowledge system–based project management system that takes into account the interactions that occur during different phases of the manufacturing cycle, is currently being tested at DEC.

A constituent expert system of IMS, Callisto schedules activities to accomplish some task, monitors the status of parallel activities to ascertain both plan and schedule changes required to meet project goals, and manages engineering change orders (change in part of a production cycle because of new information, such as a new component or procedure). To account for the complex interactions that invariably occur, and to avoid the resulting project delays, Callisto's knowledge base uses two methods to represent its knowledge. One is a schemata-based representation, similar to ISIS's, which models the factory resources, products, activities, and constraints that Callisto uses to infer general information about the production environment. In addition, Callisto uses a rule-based language to represent managerial rules and heuristics in order to analyze the interactions between activities. These rules do such things as notice resource conflicts, delays in activities, and interactions among activities. With this combination modeling technique and rule language, Callisto, which is designed for use by the engineer/designer as well as manager, can catch the following typical type of problem at an early stage.

It often happens that an engineer designs a component for a larger product—say a computer—whose prototype building is planned for six months hence. What happens in terms of ordering and delivery if the designer uses circuits that have a year's lead time?

Normally, there are managers whose job it is to examine the parts list generated by the designer to determine the lead times and feasibility of building the computer with the designer's specified parts. The problem is that when only people are involved, the managers cannot examine the specified parts list until

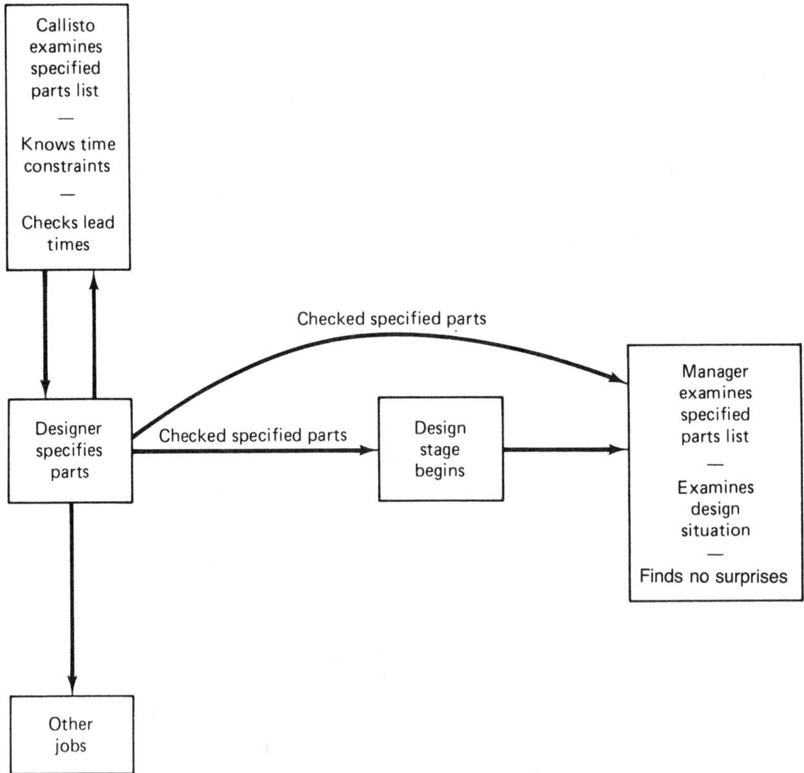

Figure 16-2 Computerized project management.

some period of design work has passed. Before that there is little to see and design ideas are still changing. After that, there are normal, unavoidable delays in communications between designer and manager and in interpreting the design situation.

Unfortunately, by the time it is determined that some parts cannot be ordered in time, the designer has frequently gone on to another job. Even if the designer is available, the newly discovered lead time of the purchased part requires rethinking and redesign of the engineer's component, followed by a repetition of the same cycle.

By putting Callisto in the hands of the designer as well as the manager, designers can find out the time constraints on their tentatively specified parts while they are still thinking out the design. Simply put, designers enter their parts lists into the computer as they are considering them (Figure 16-2). Callisto, with its model of planned project activities and interactions, determines that the choice of a particular part is constrained because the prototype is scheduled to be built in six months. Next, it checks the lead time through its knowledge of vendors, either via a database or by notifying the manager of the need to check. In this way, both the designer and the project manager are provided with instantaneous feedback across different phases of manufacturing.

INDUSTRY INTEREST

All these performance and delay avoidance capabilities add up to a technology in which just about all manufacturers should be interested. And they are. AI offers them the ability to conserve human resources, and to amplify the abilities of those who are available.

Alcoa, for example, is looking into using AI to discover new aluminum alloys. In the Alcoa project, given a set of criteria for a new aluminum alloy, an expert system called Aladin tries to determine the composition of elements used to make up the alloy that meets these criteria and the process by which to produce the actual metal. Some of Aladin's suggestions are based on the analysis of related industrial systems and designs that can be altered to form a new system or design that meets different specifications. The alloy analysis and new alloy suggestion process is currently performed by highly skilled metallurgists to which Aladin would act as a consultant and recommend compositions and thermal mechanical processing.

The Delco Products Division of General Motors has an operational knowledge system, which consults with designers of brushes (for DC motors), and specifies the information to make the production drawing for these brushes. The specifications are sent via network to an Intergraph computer-aided-design system, which converts the output of the consultation into Intergraph system commands and makes a complete drawing of the brush.

Engineers at Delco developed the knowledge system using Teknowledge's S.1 application development tool. Subsequent Delco knowledge systems design other motor components such as the spring that holds the brushes against the commutator.

Hewlett-Packard has a knowledge system that advises how to manufacture integrated circuits, and Fairchild is developing knowledge systems to monitor its semiconductor-wafer fabrication production line. A General Telephone & Electronics knowledge system consults with data communication managers and network engineers to design least-cost telecommunications networks. It was developed by GTE engineers using Teknowledge's PC-based M.1 application development tool. Babcock & Wilcox has a weld scheduler that automates the generation of weld schedule information currently being done manually. The weld scheduler was developed by B&W engineers using IntelliCorp's KEE application development tool. (Details are in Chapter 10.)

An example of the economic leverage that AI can provide is Digital Equipment Corp.'s knowledge system that performs job dispatching for the assembly of printed wire boards. Developed by Carnegie Group Inc., the knowledge system runs on VAXs and has been operational since August 1985. Essentially, it consists of a large amount of conventional real-time job-dispatching code, along with some value-added AI that makes the conventional system work smarter. As for how much smarter, Digital says that the job-dispatching knowledge system has increased its throughput by 100 percent and saves the company $25 million a year.

FACTORY SIMULATION

Knowledge-based simulation programs that represent the behavior of factory machines and floor space simulate the consequences of various events, and provide advice to correct factory problems that may arise. Litton Industries uses such a program to simulate the flow of materials in some of its factories.

Unfortunately, although the number of people that can build such customized AI programs is growing, it is still less than the number needed. And turnkey systems are not so likely to be found in manufacturing domains because factories are not generic.

A compromise—customized turnkey systems—is turning up in some manufacturing areas. These systems are essentially knowledge system development tools that are supplied with some generic knowledge applicable to certain application areas. Users then add company-specific knowledge via a menu-based interface.

Two good examples of such systems are off-the-shelf knowledge-based simulation systems from IntelliCorp and Carnegie Group Inc. These programs require users to know about the system, factory, or network they want to model and the knowledge-based simulation system's functionality, but not about knowledge engineering, AI techniques, or programming.

Both companies' systems are visually oriented and frame-based. The frames contain knowledge of system components, such as machines, material handling

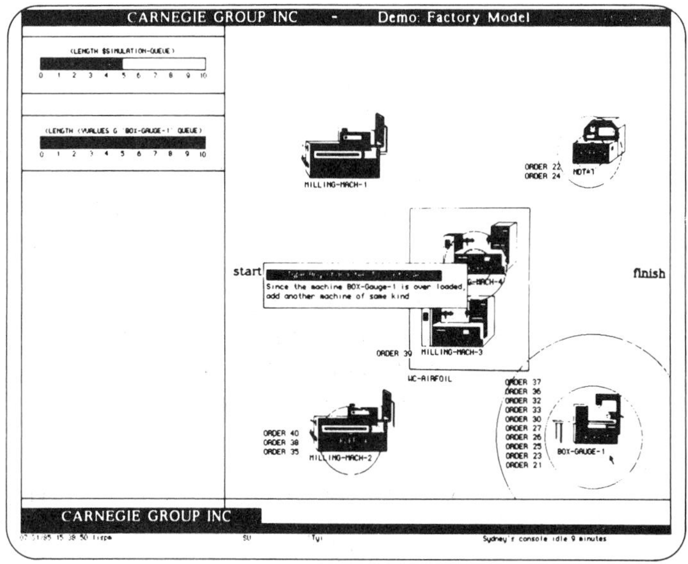

Figure 16-3 Industrial engineers and managers use a model editor and icons that represent physical system objects to build models of a factory. The knowledge-based simulation system analyzes the flow of materials in the factory, issues reports, indicates the build up of orders at different stations, and offers advice to correct bottlenecks. (Carnegie Group Inc.)

systems, parts, events, goals, constraints, scheduling, and rules about how to recognize bottlenecks. As the Carnegie Group Inc.'s system shows (see Figure 16-3), a model editor and icons that represent physical system objects, together with a library of frames that contains knowledge about these objects, allow users to visually build models of the system.

The simulation system then uses its knowledge of manufacturing parameters to ask the user about application-specific parameters such as orders to be run, the set-up time, and run-time. This concludes most of the user's job, because the frames have pointers to predefined, related frames that contain knowledge about generating standard reports, analyses germaine to the manufacturing world, constraints on various machines, gauges that monitor machines, how to schedule an order, and so on.

The simulation facility allows users to run the simulation, define break points, and generate real-time screen displays of events and build up of orders at different stations. The analysis-management system uses frames that define constraints, reports, and rules to analyze the simulation, compare alternative models, generate reports, recommend changes, and feed the changes back into the simulation process. For example, as Figure 16-3 shows, the simulation facility indicates the build up of orders at different stations in a factory and proposes a solution to correct the bottleneck.

LONG-RANGE PLANNING

The planning involved in the project management and scheduling systems described so far is for the short term. Long-term planning is frequently based on information obtained from computerized financial planning models. These models generally do little more than calculate and display results. They do not check for reasonble outputs for a situation in question, detect anomalous input or output values, verify that the data satisfy the assumptions of the model, explain what the outputs represent, or understand what consequences they imply. Such tasks are normally performed by human analysts who intelligently apply a programmed model to answer managerial questions.

To circumvent the limitations of traditional financial planning systems, an expert system called ROME, developed by CMU and DEC, and undergoing testing at DEC in Marlboro, Massachusetts, provides "intelligent" decision support for long-range planning because it contains knowledge of what the variables in the financial models mean. ROME is similar to electronic spreadsheet programs in that it uses a row-and-column format and handles quantitative (numerical) information. It differs in that it uses AI techniques to perform analyses of the quantitative information that would be impossible with traditional, numerically oriented programs.

For example, ROME represents, in schema form, information such as the meaning of the input or calculated variables in terms of the real-world entities they represent, user-specified expected values for the variables and deviations from these expectations, and corporate goals. It uses this knowledge to detect and diagnose deviations and explain what may have caused them.

It often happens that what is normal in one situation may be abnormal in another. In such cases, ROME can use its knowledge to differentiate good from bad consequences based on the goals of the organization.

17

AI in Industry: Sales, Design, Manufacturing, Distribution, Field Services, and Expert System Integration

Pioneer knowledge-based planning, scheduling, monitoring, and management systems, such as those described in the last two chapters, have aroused industry-wide interest. So encouraging are the benefits gained from these systems that they have lent credibility to the development of others, in manufacturing and military environments.

One of the most successful knowledge programs that has been applied to different kinds of systems in many companies is Digital Equipment Corp.'s XCON. XCON, prototyped at Carnegie–Mellon University (the history of its development and acceptance is presented in Chapter 2), is Digital Equipment Corp.'s expert system that is used daily in a number of manufacturing plants in the United States and in Europe to configure VAX-11 and some PDP-11 computer systems. Configuration means ensuring that computer components and options are correctly connected so that a customer's order is buildable by manufacturing. Given a customer's order, which might consist of as many as 30 to 40 different line items (there could be several of each), including a central processor and a number of peripherals, such as different styles of disks, printers, terminals, tape systems, communications options, and cabinets, XCON decides what, if any, modifications or additions have to be made to the order to provide a functioning system. The problem is even more complicated because each line item is actually a bundle of configuration-level components, and there is an expansion factor of about 10 to go from line items to configuration-level items. So a customer order of 10 line items becomes a configuration-level order of about 100 items.

The configuration output sheets generated by XCON indicate the customer's

```
DEC-NUMBER: SAMPLE        CUSTOMER-NAME: FRED
XCON RELEASE AS OF V3.4
FULL SYSTEM CONFIGURATION

PASS  1

COMPONENTS ORDERED
LINE  QTY   NAME           DESCRIPTION                        COMMENT
  1    1   780CA-AE      11780 QE001-DZ 2MB 64K 120/6
  2    1   MS780-FC      6MB ECC/64K/MOS 11780 EXP ME
  3    2   RA81-AA       456MB 16B DISK, 120V/60,NO CA
  4    1   LA120-DA      LA120 UNIV PWR SUPPLY NUM PA
  5    1   FP780-AA      FLT PT PROC 11/780 120V
  6    4   DMR11-AP      NETWRK LINK EIA RS232-C/423
  7    1   DEUNA-AA      UBUS TO ETHERNET CONTROLLER
  8    1   RA60-CA       RA60-AA, H9642-AP, 60HZ
  9    1   QE001-AZ      VAX/VMS INSTAL/WARR/TRAIN  CR
 10    1   QE001-HM      VAX/VMS UPD N/S 16MT9
 11    1   DMF32-LP      MULTIFUNCTION 8ASYN,1SYN,LPD
 12    1   TEU78-FB      11780 SINGL ACC TAPE SYS 60H
 13    1   VT125-BA      PACK OF 4 VT125-AA

COMPONENTS ADDED
LINE  QTY   NAME           DESCRIPTION                        COMMENT


 14    1   BA11-KU       10 ½ INCH EXPANDER BOX 120         NEEDED TO PROVIDE BOX
                                                              SPACE FOR THE UNIBUS
                                                              MODULES
 15    2   DD11-DK       DD11-D 2-SU FOR BA11-K             NEEDED TO REASONABLY
                                                              PLACE UNIBUS MODULES


ITEMS NOT CONFIGURED: TO BE USED AS SPARES, ON ANOTHER CONFIGURATION,
                      OR FOR TESTING

  1   H7100-A       POWER SUPPLY 115V
```

Figure 17-1 The expert configurer indicates the customer's original order and additions, deletions, and substitutions along with explanations for the changes. (Digital Equipment Corp.)

original order, any additions, deletions, or substitutions of items, and associated explanations for the changes (Figure 17-1). A series of diagrams, also generated, show the layout of the system and spatial relationships as well as the placement of components within the cabinets (Figure 17-2). In addition, the system figures out the exact lengths of the cables between components; vector addresses, which are the physical addresses of devices on a bus (the data highway that links together and transmits data between devices and other components); direct-

```
CABINET LAYOUT
                         |--------------------|------------|
                         |11780-FE            |H9652-MF 1  |
                         |                    |            |
                         |                    |            |
                         |                    |            |  |------------|
                         |                    ||----------||  |H9642-AP 1  |
                         |                    ||BA11-KU 2 ||  ||----------||
    |------------|       |                    ||UBA 0     ||  ||RA60-AA   ||
    |CONSOLE     |       |                    ||----------||  ||UNIT # 2  ||
    |LA120-DA 0  |       |                    |            |  ||----------||
    |            |       |                    ||----------||  ||RA81-AA   ||
    |            |       |                    ||BA11-KU 1 ||  ||UNIT #1   ||
                         |                    ||UBA 0     ||  ||----------||
    |            |       |                    ||----------||  ||RA81-AA   ||
    |            |       |                    |            |  ||UNIT # 0  ||
    |------------|       |--------------------||----------||  ||----------||

                                      |------------|
                                      |TU78-AF 0   |
                                      |            |
                                      |            |
  |------------|   |------------|     |            |
  |SC008 0     |   |HSC50-AA 0  |     |            |
  |            |   |            |     |            |
  |            |   |            |     ||----------||
  |            |   |            |     ||TM78-AB 1 ||
  |            |   |            |     ||0 MBA 0   ||
  |            |   |            |     ||----------||
  |            |   |            |     |            |
  |            |   |            |     |            |
  |            |   |            |     |            |
  |            |   |            |     |            |
  |------------|   |------------|     |------------|     NO FREE
                                                         STANDING
                                                         DEVICES
  11780-FE
  |-----------------------------------|   SC008
  | F | K | | D |MS780-EC | C | R | M|   |------------|
  | P | A | | W |8192 KB  | I | H | 9|   |PATH A      |
  | 7 | 7 | | 7 |         | 7 | 7 | 0|   |NODES 0-7   |
  | 8 | 8 | | 8 |         | 8 | 8 | 4|   |------------|
  | 0 | 0 | | 0 |         | 0 | 0 | 3|   |            |
  | - | - | |   |         |   |   |  |   |            |
  | A | A | | 0 |         | 0 | 0 | E|   |------------|
  | A | A | |   |         |   |   | N|   |PATH B      |
  |   |   | |   |         |   |   | D|   |NODES 0-7   |
  |   |   | |   |         |   |   |  |   |------------|
  |-----------------------------------|   |            |
  |                                   |   |            |
  |-----------------------------------|   |------------|
```

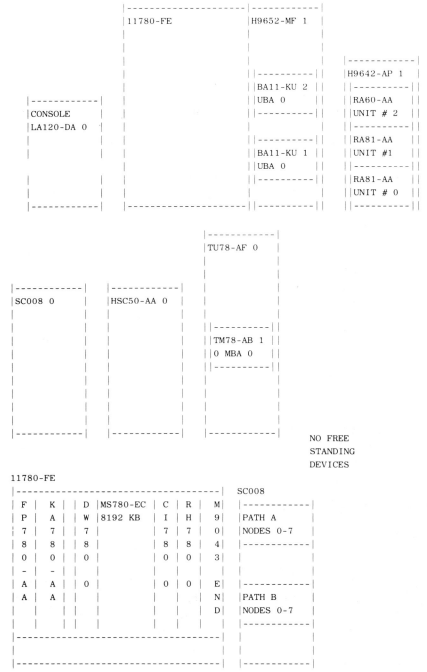

Figure 17-2 Partial expert configurer output indicating the layout of a computer system, spatial relationships, and placement of components in cabinets. (Digital Equipment Corp.)

current (DC) loads on the bus; used and unused power; and the exact unused memory capacity.

For example, Figure 17-1 indicates that two components were added because there was insufficient space for the Unibus (one of DEC's computer buses) modules specified in the original customer order. Figure 17-2 is a partial XCON printout showing the layout of modules within cabinets. The original customer order sheet contains a description of some of the model numbers shown. For example LA120-DA is a hard-copy terminal, BA11-KU is an expander box, RA81-AA are disk units, the 11780-FE is the central processor, UBA is the Unibus adapter, and MBA is the Massbus adapter.

A detailed view of the CPU cabinet shows the actual central processor boards (KA780-AA), the memory controller, and the memory. Further XCON printouts (not shown) indicate length and load information and unused capacity, such as how many more bytes of memory could be installed if necessary and how many more controllers, tape drives, disk drives, or data channels can be supported. They also indicate calculated cable lengths and vector addresses.

Configuration at DEC is particularly complex because DEC offers its customers a menu of over 5,000 components, supported by VAX-11 systems, to choose from. Previously, trained technical configurers in DEC's manufacturing group required twenty to thirty minutes per system order to generate a substantially less detailed configuration than XCON's.

Now, however, as the manufacturing group at DEC receives customer's orders, it enters them into the XCON process. In 2½ CPU minutes, XCON configures extremely complex orders and generates configuration output sheets, which are then used directly on the manufacturing floor by technicians to assemble the equipment. When the equipment is assembled and shipped, the same output sheets are included with the billing materials for the field service people to use when installing the system.

THE CONFIGURATION SYSTEM*

To perform its configuration tasks, XCON, like a human configurer, needs two kinds of knowledge: component knowledge and configuration constraint knowledge. Component knowledge is knowledge about each of the components that a customer might order. It includes information about each component's properties that are relevant to computer configuration, such as voltage, frequency, how many devices the computer can support, and how many ports it has.

A description of each of the components supported by a VAX system is contained in an XCON database. Figure 17-3 shows four typical database items each of which contains the name of a component and a set of attribute/value pairs that indicate the properties of that component relevant to the configuration task. For example, the RK711-EA is a bundle of components. It contains a 25-foot

*This discussion is based on McDermott (1980).

```
RK711-EA
    CLASS: BUNDLE
    TYPE: DISK DRIVE
    SUPPORTED: YES
    COMPONENT LIST: 1 070-12292-25
                    1 RK07-EA*
                    1 RK611
RK07-EA*
    CLASS: UNIBUS DEVICE
    TYPE: DISK DRIVE
    SUPPORTED: YES
    FLOOR RANK: 8
    DEPTH: 28 INCHES
    WIDTH: 24 INCHES
    HEIGHT: 42 INCHES
    UNIBUS MODULE REQUIRED: RK611*
    PORTS: 1
    VOLTAGE: 120 VOLTS
    FREQUENCY: 60 HERTZ
    CABLE TYPE REQUIRED: 1 070-12292 FROM A DISK DRIVE UNIBUS MODULE
                      OR 1 070-12292 FROM A DISK DRIVE UNIBUS DEVICE

RK611
    CLASS: BUNDLE
    TYPE: DISK DRIVE
    SUPPORTED: YES
    COMPONENT LIST: 3 G727
                    1 M9202
                    1 070-12412-00
                    1 RK611*

070-12412-00
    CLASS: BACKPLANE
    TYPE: RK611
    SUPPORTED: YES
    NUMBER OF SYSTEM UNITS: 2
    LENGTH: 2.0 FEET
    NUMBER OF SLOTS: 9
    SLOT TYPES: 3 SPC (1 TO 3)
                6 RK611 (4 TO 9)
```

Figure 17-3 Part of an XCON database (John McDermott)

cable (70-12292-25), a disk drive (RK07-EA), and a bundle of components (RK611), which itself consists of other components.

Configuration constraint knowledge, in the form of IF-THEN rules, indicates what classes of components can (or must) be associated to form first a partial and then a full computer system configuration and what constraints there are on forming these associations. Typical constraints limit the size of the backplane (a container for boards) based on the box it will be placed in, the number of devices that can be assigned to a Massbus, the position of boards and devices, and the total amount of power that can be drawn from a regulator. Other constraints might determine how the number, size, and type of boards in a module affect its placement. Still other constraints require the presence of certain components to either house or be associated with other components, require a repeater if the length of, or load on, a Unibus exceeds a certain limit, or require certain devices to precede others on a bus.

Considering that there are many types of each basic component (such as four-slot and nine-slot backplanes or dual-port or single-port disk drives) and many have several options, they can be combined to form an unimaginable number of possible configurations. XCON uses its constraint knowledge to limit the combinations in order to form a functionally acceptable computer system.

All of XCON's rules incorporate a piece of its constraint knowledge. Since there are more than 4000 rules, to avoid having to consider irrelevant rules, they are partitioned into separate tasks or configuration steps. These steps reflect the way that human experts approach the configuration task. Six major tasks have been identified:

- Determine whether there is anything grossly wrong with the order, such as mismatched or missing items.
- Put the appropriate components in the processor and processor expansion cabinets.
- Put boxes in the Unibus expansion cabinet and put the appropriate components in these boxes.
- Put panels in the Unibus expansion cabinets.
- Lay out the system on the floor.
- Do the cabling.

These major tasks (and rules) are further partitioned into subtasks, called *contexts*. Contexts correspond to more specific steps that human configurers perform. Typical steps, or contexts, are "assign-power-supply," "check-voltage-and-frequency," "verify-SBI-and-Massbus-device-adequacy," "assign-Unibus-modules-except-those-connecting-to-panels," and "check-for-Unibus-jumper-cable-changes." (An SBI module is the main bus on the VAX-11/780 computer).

Figure 17-4 shows an English translation of four of the nine rules associated with the context of assigning power supplies to SBI modules. The first rule adds a power supply to the order if one is needed and if all the power supplies ordered have already been configured. The second rule indicates what SBI module the power supply should be connected to and where in what cabinet it should be put. The fourth rule is similar to, but is a special case of, the second rule. It contains

```
ASSIGN-POWER-SUPPLY-1

    IF: THE MOST CURRENT ACTIVE CONTEXT IS ASSIGNING A POWER SUPPLY
        AND AN SBI MODULE OF ANY TYPE HAS BEEN PUT IN A CABINET
        AND THE POSITION IT OCCUPIES IN THE CABINET (ITS NEXUS) IS KNOWN
        AND THERE IS SPACE AVAILABLE IN THE CABINET FOR A POWER SUPPLY FOR THAT NEXUS
        AND THERE IS NO AVAILABLE POWER SUPPLY
        AND THE VOLTAGE AND FREQUENCY OF THE COMPONENTS ON THE ORDER IS KNOWN
  THEN: FIND A POWER SUPPLY OF THAT VOLTAGE AND FREQUENCY AND ADD IT TO THE ORDER


ASSIGN-POWER-SUPPLY-2

    IF: THE MOST CURRENT ACTIVE CONTEXT IS ASSIGNING A POWER SUPPLY
        AND AN SBI MODULE OF ANY TYPE HAS BEEN PUT IN A CABINET
        AND THE POSITION IT OCCUPIES IN THE CABINET (ITS NEXUS) IS KNOWN
        AND THERE IS SPACE AVAILABLE IN THE CABINET FOR A POWER SUPPLY FOR THAT NEXUS
        AND THERE IS AN AVAILABLE POWER SUPPLY
  THEN: PUT THE POWER SUPPLY IN THE CABINET IN THE AVAILABLE SPACE


ASSIGN-POWER-SUPPLY-6

    IF: THE MOST CURRENT ACTIVE CONTEXT IS ASSIGNING A POWER SUPPLY
        AND A UNIBUS ADAPTOR HAS BEEN PUT IN A CABINET
        AND THE POSITION IT OCCUPIES IN THE CABINET (ITS NEXUS) IS KNOWN
        AND THERE IS SPACE AVAILABLE IN THE CABINET FOR A POWER SUPPLY FOR THAT NEXUS
        AND THERE IS AN AVAILABLE POWER SUPPLY
        AND THERE IS NO H7101 REGULATOR AVAILABLE
  THEN: ADD AN H7101 REGULATOR TO THE ORDER


ASSIGN-POWER-SUPPLY-7

    IF: THE MOST CURRENT ACTIVE CONTEXT IS ASSIGNING A POWER SUPPLY
        AND A UNIBUS ADAPTOR HAS BEEN PUT IN A CABINET
        AND THE POSITION IT OCCUPIES IN THE CABINET (ITS NEXUS) IS KNOWN
        AND THERE IS SPACE AVAILABLE IN THE CABINET FOR A POWER SUPPLY FOR THAT NEXUS
        AND THERE IS AN AVAILABLE POWER SUPPLY
        AND THERE IS AN H7101 REGULATOR AVAILABLE
  THEN: PUT THE POWER SUPPLY AND THE REGULATOR IN THE CABINET IN THE AVAILABLE SPACE
```

Figure 17-4 English translation of four XCON rules (John McDermott)

extra knowledge that says, when the SBI module that needs a power supply is a Unibus adapter, a particular regulator (the H7101) must be associated with the power supply. The third rule adds the appropriate regulator to the order if all the conditions required to satisfy the fourth rule are satisfied except the availability of a regulator.

HOW XCON CONFIGURES

XCON's rules, called *productions*, are located in a section of computer memory aptly called *production memory*. Another section of memory where the configuration work is actually performed is equally appropriately called *working memory*. At any random time, working memory contains descriptions of both certain database components and of partial configurations that have been determined so far.

XCON's approach to configuration can be thought of as a search through all its rules to find one all of whose conditions, or IF parts, match the items that happen to be in working memory at that moment. When it finds such a rule, it performs the action indicated by the THEN part of that rule. The new situation described by the action performed by that rule is then added to working memory.

XCON repeats this process until no more rules can be satisfied or until some action stops the processing. At that point, it has arrived at a solution and configured a computer system. This rule-based approach is an example of forward chaining.

Before showing an example of how this works, it is important to understand certain of XCON's methods. First, although XCON cycles through all the rules every time it performs an action, it does not thoroughly search, investigate, or try out every rule every time, any more than a human configurer does. Like a person who focuses only on the information needed to perform a particular step currently being worked on, XCON focuses only on the rules relevant to the most active context, or step.

Second, besides rules that contain configuration knowledge, XCON has other types of rules that activate contexts and deactivate contexts. As a general procedure, XCON activates a context, does all that it can within a context before leaving it, and then deactivates that context and activates another.

Third, it is possible that at any one time two or even several rules can be satisfied. In such a case, XCON relies on several conflict resolution strategies (which are actually part of OPS5, the language in which XCON is written) to determine which rule to apply. The most important of these is known as the *special case strategy*.

This strategy assumes that the rules have been written so that some are general and some are specialized. Given a choice of two rules, with conditions that all match items in working memory, if one rule's IF part is a superset of the other, XCON will select the rule that has more data items, on the assumption that it is specialized for the particular situation at hand.

WALKING THROUGH XCON

XCON begins its configuration by loading into working memory an initial set of components from the database and descriptions of a starting situation. The initial

```
ACTIVE CONTEXT = ASSIGN-POWER-SUPPLY
COMPONENT = SBI-MODULE OF TYPE = ANY-KIND IS IN CABINET
CABINET POSITION COORDINATES FOR COMPONENT SBI-MODULE = KNOWN
   (coordinates listed)
CABINET SPACE AVAILABLE FOR POWER-SUPPLY WITH COORDINATES = KNOWN
   (coordinates equal to those listed above)
COMPONENT = POWER-SUPPLY IS NOT AVAILABLE (not configured)
VOLTAGE AND FREQUENCY OF ORDERED COMPONENTS = KNOWN (listed here)
```

Figure 17-5 Part of a working memory

components and situation description reflect the initial components and starting situation that a human configurer faces.

XCON then begins its matching process as described above. At some point during the configuration process, when a certain amount of information about the computer system is known, it is time to assign a power supply. At that point, XCON activates the "ASSIGN-A-POWER-SUPPLY context."

To fire rule ASSIGN-A-POWER-SUPPLY-1, working memory must contain information that corresponds to each of the conditions in this rule. Figure 17-5 shows an English translation of the six items whose presence in working memory would be necessary to fire this rule.

Since all the conditions in rule "ASSIGN-POWER-SUPPLY-1" are matched by elements in working memory, XCON executes the action or THEN part of the rule. The action part of this rule directs XCON to add a new element to working memory: a power supply of the voltage and frequency of the components in the order (Figure 17-6).

Actually, rule ASSIGN-POWER-SUPPLY-1 ordinarily does not fire because all the appropriate power supplies are usually on a customer's order. This rule handles the exceptional situations when for one reason or another the customer has neglected to order a required power supply. Sample executions show that XCON uses only about one-third of its knowledge to configure a typical system. It contains a lot of other knowledge whose function is just to be on hand in case exceptional situations are encountered.

Rule ASSIGN-POWER-SUPPLY-2 is almost the same as rule ASSIGN-POWER-SUPPLY-1. But the condition requiring an available power supply is different.

```
ACTIVE CONTEXT = ASSIGN-POWER-SUPPLY
COMPONENT = SBI-MODULE OF TYPE = ANY-KIND IS IN CABINET
CABINET POSITION COORDINATES FOR COMPONENT SBI-MODULE = KNOWN
   (coordinates listed)
CABINET SPACE AVAILABLE FOR POWER-SUPPLY WITH COORDINATES = KNOWN
   (coordinates equal to those listed above)
VOLTAGE AND FREQUENCY OF ORDERED COMPONENTS = KNOWN (listed here)
COMPONENT = POWER-SUPPLY IS AVAILABLE (not configured)
```

Figure 17-6 Part of a working memory

```
ACTIVE CONTEXT = ASSIGN-POWER-SUPPLY
COMPONENT = SBI-MODULE OF TYPE = ANY-KIND IS IN CABINET
CABINET POSITION COORDINATES FOR COMPONENT SBI-MODULE = KNOWN
   (coordinates listed)
COMPONENT = POWER-SUPPLY IS IN CABINET WITH COORDINATES = KNOWN
   (coordinates equal to those listed above)
VOLTAGE AND FREQUENCY OF ORDERED COMPONENTS = KNOWN (listed here)
COMPONENT = POWER-SUPPLY IS AVAILABLE (configured)
```

Figure 17-7 Part of a working memory

After instantiating rule ASSIGN-POWER-SUPPLY-1, however, working memory now contains an available power supply. Consequently, all the patterns in the condition part of ASSIGN-POWER-SUPPLY-2 can be matched by patterns in working memory. Rule ASSIGN-POWER-SUPPLY-2 therefore fires.

This firing adds a new item to production memory that indicates that the power supply is in the cabinet in the available space, while also deleting the available cabinet space item (Figure 17-7). In addition, the previous working memory element that says "POWER-SUPPLY IS NOT CONFIGURED" is replaced with an element that says "POWER-SUPPLY IS CONFIGURED."

CONFLICTS

It is possible that working memory contains all the items shown in Figure 17-6, in addition to an item that indicates that the type of SBI module that needs a power supply is a Unibus adapter, and another item that indicates that an H7101 regulator is available (Figure 17-8). In this case, all the conditions of both ASSIGN-POWER-SUPPLY-2 and ASSIGN-POWER-SUPPLY-7 can be satisfied. Therefore, both rules are applicable.

However, XCON will choose rule ASSIGN-POWER-SUPPLY-7 because it is a special case, and XCON (actually, OPS5) always prefers special-case rules over more general rules. In this case, XCON would change working memory to

```
ACTIVE CONTEXT = ASSIGN-POWER-SUPPLY
COMPONENT = UNIBUS-ADAPTER SBI-MODULE OF TYPE = UNIBUS-ADAPTER IS IN
   CABINET
CABINET POSITION COORDINATES FOR COMPONENT SBI-MODULE = KNOWN
   (coordinates listed)
CABINET SPACE AVAILABLE FOR UNIBUS-ADAPTER POWER SUPPLY WITH
   COORDINATES = KNOWN (coordinates equal to those listed above)
VOLTAGE AND FREQUENCY OF ORDERED COMPONENTS = KNOWN (listed here)
COMPONENT = POWER SUPPLY IS AVAILABLE (not configured)
COMPONENT = H7101 REGULATOR IS AVAILABLE (not configured)
```

Figure 17-8 Part of a working memory

show that both a power supply and an H7101 regulator were added to the cabinet. It would also delete the available space item, and it would replace both the unconfigured power supply and the unconfigured H7101 regulator items with corresponding configured items.

As seen, every time XCON instantiates a rule, it adds, deletes, or modifies an item in working memory. The changes in working memory indicate increasing progress in configuring computer systems, just as every new component that human configurers hook up, to or plug into, a cabinet brings them closer to their configuration goals.

As a result of the changes to working memory, the next time XCON cycles through its rules, it finds new matching patterns plus old ones that no longer match. Sooner or later a point is reached where working memory is so changed that the only rules with IF patterns that can be satisfied are XCON's most general rules, which have the least number of data items.

The IF part of these general rules says nothing more than "IF THE MOST ACTIVE CONTEXT IS ASSIGN POWER SUPPLY." This rule finds a match in working memory because the active context has not yet been changed. However, the action part of this rule would direct XCON to deactivate the context ASSIGN-POWER-SUPPLY and activate the next context, such as the context FILL-MEMORY-SLOTS or the context ADD-UNIBUS-ADAPTERS.

In this way, XCON progresses from configuration task to task or context to context. It begins with a starting state that contains a description of the components in the customer's order. It progresses through a series of intermediate states that describe partial configurations and the as-yet-unconfigured components. Finally, it reaches a solution state, in which the entire computer system is configured.

At each decision point during the computer configuration process, the constraint knowledge about what steps to take next in order to form a new partial configuration is provided by XCON's rules. Because of the large amount of knowledge contained in XCON and the way the rules are written (from very general to highly specialized), XCON always has enough knowledge to match some rule with the items in working memory.

A consequence of this pattern-matching technique is that XCON almost never generates any dead-end paths. Therefore, it rarely has to backtrack (retrace its steps) to an earlier situation in order to find the true path. As long as there is at least one possible computer system configuration based on a customer's order, even though it may require adding some components, XCON's pattern-matching procedures will find a path from the initial state to the solution state without generating any false paths.

The ability to avoid backtracking evolved during XCON's development. At that time, whenever the expert system hit a dead end and would have needed to backtrack, human experts were always able to suggest how XCON could have recognized in advance that the false path was not an appropriate one. New knowledge was then added so that in the future XCON could avoid this dead end and the need to backtrack.

An interesting observation by XCON's inventor, John McDermott, is that human beings do not solve the computer configuration task by the straightforward pattern-matching techniques that XCON uses. Instead, he says, "they use a more general (weaker) heuristic; that is, they engage in backtracking. This is true of novices and to a lesser extent true of experienced configurers. Novices in particular frequently make decisions in the wrong order or neglect to preserve information needed for future decisions" (McDermott, 1980).

One reason that human beings are more likely to make the wrong decision and generate false paths is their lack of thoroughness in analyzing the possible implications of a choice of a particular path. To be as thorough as XCON requires more time per configuration step. However, more careful analysis might avoid the need for backtracking, resulting, in the long run, in less overall configuration time.

WHY BOTHER?

The advantages of an expert system computer configurer encompass more than just savings of time. According to Dennis O'Connor, director of expert systems projects at DEC, "the artificial intelligence methodologies of expert systems is a new and innovative way of helping manage change, complexity and exceptions in the DEC business operations." O'Connor points to the large portion of system orders that in the past were scheduled to the factory floor although they had numerous configuration errors and lacked completeness. Now, with the use of XCON, thousands of complex VAX orders scheduled to be built have very accurate configurations 98 percent of the time (O'Connor, 1983, p. 4).

The automated, more reliable configuration process increases the throughput order rate, decreases shipment delays due to system configuration errors, and provides better utilization of materials on hand. As for change and exception management, XCON can easily and quickly handle line-item changes on customer orders already scheduled in the manufacturing process.

All told, DEC's plant management professes extreme satisfaction with the emerging artificial intelligence methodologies for manufacturing. And small wonder, since the firm claims that the expert systems save time, increase output per person (even when customer change orders arise), and lower manufacturing costs, about $40 million per year. Since XCON has (the firm says) increased technician productivity, DEC has now redeployed its highly trained senior technicians, thus allowing them to address more technically difficult tasks and resulting in better utilization of the firm's people assets.

A KNOWLEDGE NETWORK

XCON is now firmly entrenched and routinely used at DEC. Since its acceptance, the DEC AI group is integrating a series of other expert systems, with XCON.

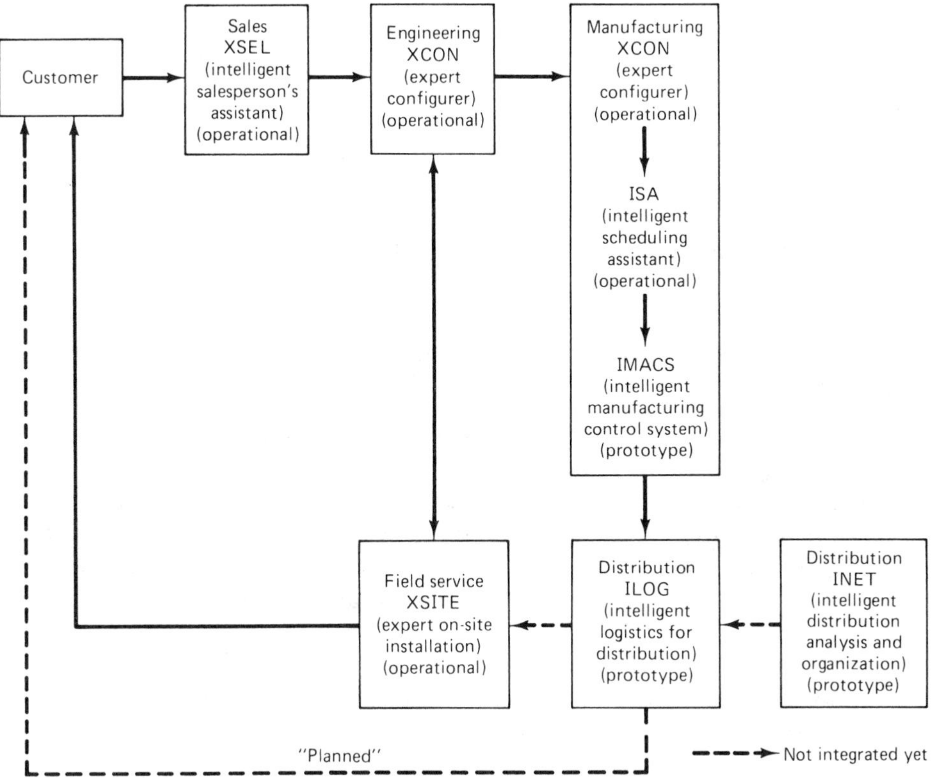

Figure 17-9 Expert knowledge network at DEC

These integrated expert systems will eventually form what DEC calls a Knowledge Network to integrate sales, engineering, configuration, manufacturing, distribution, installation, and field service (Figure 17-9).

SALES

Computer configuration is necessary both for the manufacturing group to assemble a system and for the sales staff to quote prices. However, in the form just described in this chapter, XCON has limited usefulness for DEC's sales representatives because it is a batch-oriented system (a system that in one fell swoop processes a job that has collected and entered all its data in advance) rather than an interactive system. As a result, it cannot directly answer "WHAT-IF" questions, a feature that sales representatives find very convenient when they need to quote prices and describe systems to customers who want to know WHAT-IF they ordered the system with more or less features.

Therefore, the DEC/CMU team developed an interactive expert system called XSEL (Expert Sales Person's Assistant), which sits on top of XCON and interfaces to it. XSEL helps salespeople quote prices on multiple versions of configured computer system orders at their point of sale.

To explore options, XSEL, like XCON, takes a customer's order and works out a valid, working configured computer system. However, it configures at a less detailed level than XCON. It does not bother with details such as the cable lengths, module placements, and vector addresses that XCON includes for the manufacturing and installation groups. Instead, it focuses on an interactive user interface that lets a salesperson request and question a configuration that includes only line-item-level products.

To sell a computer system, the DEC sales representative can take a briefcase-size portable computer/line printer with an attached modem to the customer's site. The modem plugs into an ordinary telephone and accesses XSEL via the phone lines.

The customer specifies his or her requirements to the sales representative, who types them into XSEL. XSEL then initiates a dialogue that assists the sales representative in filling out a complete order. As XSEL asks questions, the sales representatives, depending on their sales experience and knowledge of DEC computers and their experience in using computers, can enter answers directly. If they are novices, they can get XSEL to display all the possible choices on the computer screen.

XSEL then interacts with XCON to produce a configuration based on the customer's requirements. In only a few minutes, XCON feeds back the configuration results to XSEL.

After an XSEL session, the sales representative leaves the customer with not one or two, but a series of computer-generated quotes and configurations. Each quote and configuration is XSEL's response first to a basic-system request, and then to questions such as "WHAT-IF I added two megabytes of memory?"

SHARING EXPERT SYSTEMS

XSEL feeds the customer's final ordering decision into XCON for the detailed configuration. Various groups in engineering, manufacturing, and field services then use the product information that is resident there.

XCON is used in engineering because XCON depends on the engineering knowledge to be encoded in the products and systems offered. Manufacturing technicians use XCON to assemble a configured computer system. Field services use the output of XCON for installation purposes.

SCHEDULING MANUFACTURING

Other expert systems in DEC's knowledge network schedule computer system orders against the available material and schedule floor capacity, create a flexible build plan, manage distribution of the product, and help lay out the computer system at the customer site.

DEC's Intelligent Scheduling Assistant (ISA) is the first manufacturing expert system directly integrated with XCON and XSEL. Prototyped in early 1982, ISA is a rule-based system that schedules customer system orders against the current and planned material allocations. It can schedule orders at the rate of "orders per minute." Traditional manufacturing order schedulers require at least 10 to 15 minutes per system to perform the same task.

The initial version of ISA is an extension to DEC's corporate Common Scheduling System. Each night, ISA reads two files produced by the Common Scheduler that day: the order transaction file and the cancellations transactions file (O'Connor, 1983, p. 4).

After ISA deals with cancellations, it tentatively schedules, at the customer's requested time, all new orders and change orders that do not have either material shortage problems or credit-line-insufficiency problems. It passes these schedules to the Common Scheduler and produces a report containing a one-line notification of the month in which each of these orders has been scheduled.

With the easier work out of the way, ISA approaches the scheduling of problem orders by applying the constraints (which are embedded in its rules) that deal with material shortage and credit-line-insufficiency problems. It tentatively schedules each of these orders for a month that satisfies these constraints. Then, in an effort to schedule closer to the desired date, ISA relaxes some of these constraints and tries again to find an alternative date. The strategies that ISA uses to select a scheduling date or alternatives include partial shipments, roll forward by quarter, suggested substitutions, and speculative orders.

ISA produces brief reports that contain its proposed schedules for problematic orders. Human schedulers, however, have the final say. Upon request, ISA assists them by displaying screenfuls of information that indicate the proposed schedule, the scheduling problems, and any alternative proposals for when the order might be scheduled.

SCHEDULING THE SHOP FLOOR

Both XCON and ISA information feeds into the Intelligent Management Assistant for Computer Systems Manufacturing (IMACS). As the next in the chain of integrated expert systems in DEC's knowledge network, IMACS is a rule-based manufacturing control system that pays attention to all manufacturing activities that happen inside the four walls of a factory. These "four-wall" activities include scheduling the floor capacity for the system being built, inventory management, diagnosing and managing of problems that arise during the manufacturing process, and managing exceptions. IMACS is actually a series of cooperating expert systems. Each of these subsystems is an expert in one aspect of the system manufacturing and plant management task.

IMACS' major job is to construct a flexible build plan for each system, which determines when the system should begin to be built and where it should be placed on the floor, and plans the assembly and testing of the computer system. IMACS' input is the flow of orders from the order processing group.

With knowledge of the delivery date, that has been assigned, IMACS first constructs a skeletal build plan which enables it to estimate roughly the resource requirements for the order. If any of the plant's projected resources are significantly off, IMACS alerts the people responsible for materials acquisition to possible impending shortages and consequent problems.

Then, several weeks before the system is scheduled to be built, IMACS constructs a detailed build plan. It monitors this build plan with the goal of minimizing the disruptive effects of unexpected events, resources, or time constraints.

As part of its monitoring activities, IMACS draws the attention of the appropriate personnel to potential shortages or surpluses. It also alerts the order administration staff to the dates by which order administration issues must be resolved. Finally, IMACS generates reports that summarize various aspects of plant performance.

In contrast to ISIS (Chapter 15), which is a job shop scheduler, IMACS performs scheduling activities known as *flow shop scheduling*. The difference is that job shops contain alternative ways to produce a product, whereas in a flow shop there is generally only one way. Therefore, the complexity of a search for a scheduling solution in a flow shop is much less.

DISTRIBUTION

The next planned integrated expert system, the Intelligent Logistics System (ILOG), helps manage the distribution of the computer products and systems from the plant to the customer. Given an order, ILOG uses its knowledge, for example of plant locations, truck routes, and delivery times, to attend to the logistics concerned with coordinating shipments of products. Typically, the components and subassemblies of these products are manufactured and warehoused at geographically separated locations, assembled at different plants, and from there distributed to geographically disparate customers.

ILOG gets its knowledge of the organization structure and the corporate distribution system from INET, a strategic analysis expert system (ILOG is considered a tactical system) which helps make organizational structure and distribution management decisions. These decisions concern transportation, warehousing, manufacturing, and order administration policies. Especially in a large manufacturing organization, well-thought-out distribution decisions help the company assure adequate market penetration and retention for its products. Unfortunately, the decisions that must be made often have far-reaching, conflicting consequences.

For example, low transportation and warehousing costs facilitate aggressive pricing. High inventory levels promote on-time deliveries that are not held up because of customer stockouts. This promotes customer satisfaction. However, these policies conflict because a high inventory level will minimize stockouts and reduce the cost of transportation but will increase warehouse costs and exact cash flow penalties.

To avoid problems, distribution decisions that must be thought out include the location of manufacturing centers, warehouses, and distribution centers. They further include the capacities of these centers, the choice of merging products at distribution centers or at customer sites, the choice of transportation modes and schedules that can affect customer stockouts, and the possible consolidation of manufacturing and distribution facilities.

These distribution decisions are complicated by factors such as the location of vendors that supply components, seasonal demands, varying lead times to build or expand manufacturing facilities, the need to maintain uniform production levels, contractual agreements with vendors, and the effects of weather and labor problems on transportation schedules.

Clearly, the distribution problem involves countless possibilities and enormous complexity. Because of the possibilities and complexity, the available mathematical techniques are limited in their ability to adequately handle corporate distribution systems.

Therefore, INET uses a simulation system (Knowledge-based Simulation—KBS—developed at CMU) that simulates various scenarios in the corporate distribution network at several different levels of detail. The simulation techniques allow managers to describe their organization in the terms familiar to them rather than in alien mathematical terms.

Simulation systems are common in many fields. The INET simulation system, however, contains artificial intelligence capabilities that automate the analysis of simulation results and detect interesting and out-of-line phenomena.

FIELD SERVICES

Another expert system to be integrated in DEC's knowledge network is XSITE, which, as the name suggests, contains information that pertains to the customer's site. As such, it is targeted towards the field service people, who use it for site preparation and site management. In fact, the field service staff, who perform both the installation and servicing of systems, use XSITE in addition to the XCON printouts that are shipped with computer system orders.

XSITE will interface to both XCON and ILOG. Its knowledge encompasses environmental aspects of customer sites, such as physical spacing, arrangements, power, and air conditioning. XSITE closes the loop of DEC's knowledge network, which begins and ends with the customer.

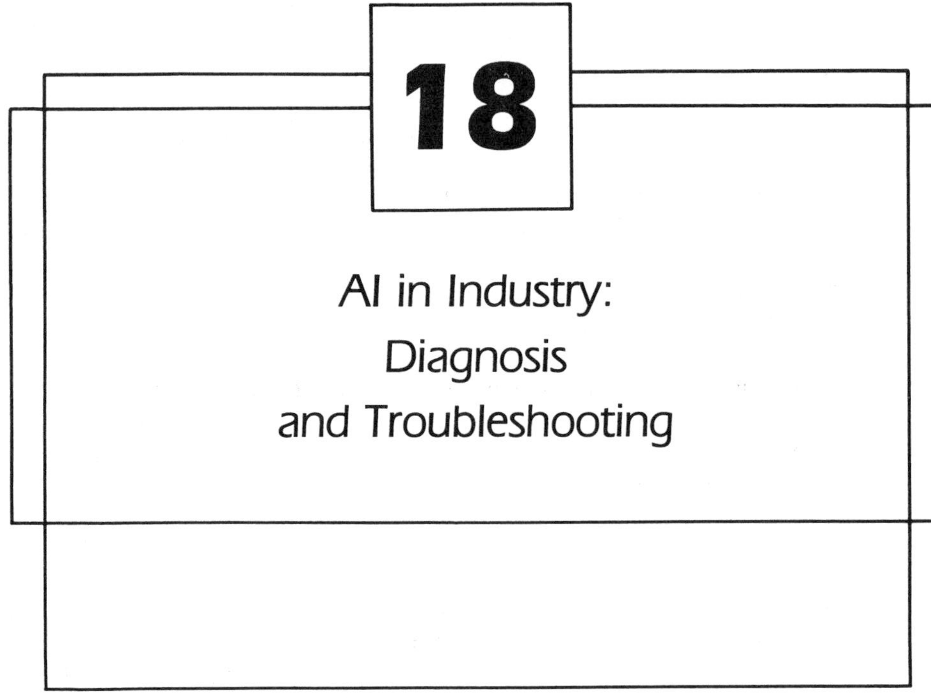

18 AI in Industry: Diagnosis and Troubleshooting

In 1967, the New York Citizens Committee for Metropolitan Affairs altered the distributor-point setting of a 1966 Oldsmobile station wagon from the manufacturer's recommended specification, and then requested a mechanic's diagnosis from 19 automobile repair garages. Their survey found that only five mechanics accurately diagnosed the minor engine defect and that the repair cost estimates ranged from no charge to $40 (equivalent to $60 to $80 in the 1980s).

The garages surveyed were selected with standard market sampling techniques that the committee believes "gave a cross section of garages that was representative of automotive repair centers for the entire New York State."* The point setting that was altered regulates the firing of the spark plugs in the engine. The alteration produced a rough engine with loss of power and difficulty in starting. According to the president of the committee, "this alteration should be recognized by a kid in a high school mechanics class as being caused by an improper point setting."†

As it turned out, only one of the five mechanics who correctly diagnosed the problem did so immediately and corrected it without charge. Most of the mechanics consulted recommended a full tune-up (a cover-all diagnosis), either from lack of knowledge, lack of desire to investigate, or in some cases from lack of ethics. Some mechanics gave bizarre, irrelevant diagnoses. Others were completely baffled, even though the committee's report contended that "the car's engine was running so badly that an experienced mechanic could not have failed

*_The New York Times_, Sept. 17, 1967, Sec. 1, p. 1.

†Ibid.

to suspect improper ignition timing which could have been corrected by a simple adjustment."

The committee president concluded that, among other things, the survey had shown "a shocking scarcity of well-trained mechanics."*

Similar scarcities of skilled diagnosticians and troubleshooters have been noted in many other industries—and this in a time when equipment and machinery are becoming increasingly complex and require more skill, and often time, to troubleshoot.

This is unfortunate because malfunctions of electrical and mechanical equipment cause loss of money, loss of life, inconvenience, wasted time, and customer dissatisfaction. For example, airline reservation systems report a loss of $30,000 for every minute a failed computer reservation system is out of order, and utilities report millions of dollars in lost revenues every time a failed machine causes loss of power generation. Faulty machines that monitor hospital patients or chemical or nuclear plants may cause death. Yet fast and accurate diagnosis requires a skill that is often difficult to come by nowadays.

THE DIAGNOSIS PROBLEM

What makes diagnosis difficult is the large amount of knowledge and experience it requires. First, it requires knowledge of the equipment and how it operates normally. Second, it requires gathering some information about the failed equipment and its fault symptoms. Third, it requires knowledge of what type of equipment information it is necessary to gather that is relevant to the fault. Fourth, it requires the ability to use the knowledge about the equipment and the information gathered to explain how the fault could have occurred. Fifth, it requires the ability to form a hypothesis and perform some tests to get back more information that either confirms or denies the hypothesis.

The process of gathering information and formulating and testing hypotheses may need to be done several times if the hypotheses formulated turn out negative (Figure 18-1). Only at the end of this process can the diagnostician repair the fault or replace the malfunctioning part.

Unfortunately, few people appear to have this body of knowledge necessary to make them good troubleshooters. Those that do tend to be promoted so that they do not use their troubleshooting expertise anymore. The remaining troubleshooters may be competent, but they lack the spark and instincts that made the expert unique.

THE DIAGNOSIS SOLUTION

Knowledge systems offer a way to preserve and protect a troubleshooter's expertise and to make that expert troubleshooter a consultant to many people.

*The New York Times, Sept. 17, 1967, Sec. 2, p. 1.

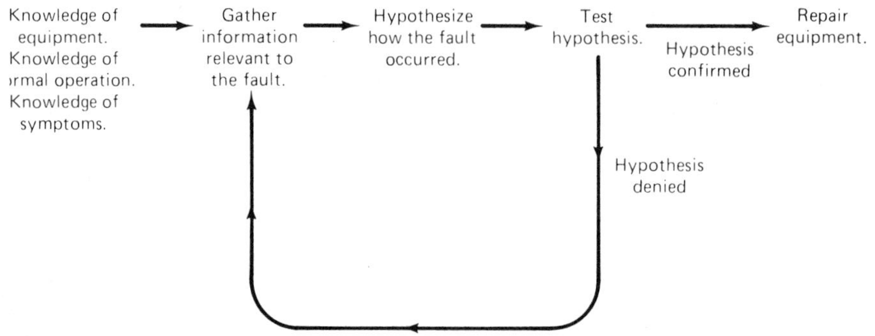

Figure 18-1 The diagnosis process

The idea is to encode as much as possible of the expert's wisdom, judgments, and decision-making techniques in a representation that can be understood and manipulated by a computer that is accessible to other troubleshooters. In this manner, the knowledge and skills of the expert can be used to advise and amplify the knowledge of less experienced personnel.

A decision to develop knowledge systems for diagnosis requires the consideration of certain hardware and software factors that are relevant to the system's cost-effectiveness. For example, several equipment diagnosis systems are likely to be needed at many locations rather than the one or a few needed at a centralized site. This multisystem requirement limits the amount of money that is likely to be allocated for dedicated AI computers to run (as opposed to develop) the completed systems.

In addition, the diagnosis process often requires a good deal of ancillary information about many equipment components and related previous troubles. Since such information is usually present in company databases, companies with knowledge-based diagnostic systems would like them to be able to access the relevant databases automatically, instead of repeatedly rekeying needed information into a knowledge base.

RELIABLE TRAINS

A flurry of AI-based equipment diagnostic activity has produced several knowledge systems than can diagnose locomotives, automobiles, steam generators, networks, computers, disk drives, circuit boards, and telephone cable troubles. General Electric's (GE) experience with CATS-1 (Computer-aided Trouble Shooting), a knowledge system designed to be used at locomotive minor-maintenance repair shops, is typical of what can be gained by applying expert system techniques to diagnosis problems.

GE makes, among other products, diesel-electric locomotives which it sells to railroads. Each railroad is responsible for the maintenance of its locomotives.

If the locomotives are easy to maintain and service, it reduces the buyer's operational costs and increases the seller's advantage. Therefore, GE took a hard look at how to increase productivity of the railroad maintenance shops.

The first level of maintenance that the locomotive sees is in railroad "running repair shops," the equivalent of fancy gas stations for locomotives. They have the tools and people skills to handle faults that require about two hours for diagnosis and repairs, such as checking dirty fuel strainers and clogged fuel lines, and adjusting governors.

Otherwise, the locomotive is sent to a major repair shop, where it remains for some time while it is scheduled for overhaul. GE developed CATS-1 because too many technicians in the running repair shops were tying up $1 million worth of gear by scheduling for major overhaul locomotives that had minor problems.

As often happens, GE had an expert troubleshooter, Dave Smith, who could accurately isolate locomotive faults greater than 90 percent of the time. Smith spent a lot of time troubleshooting over the phone. People called from different parts of the country to ask his advice about their diagnoses and subsequent repairs that did not fix the fault in question, or repairs that fixed the equipment only to have it break down again.

Troubleshooting manuals proved unsuccessful in increasing productivity. So GE decided to have a try at expert system technology in order to capture the knowledge of its key expert and make it available at remote locations.

GETTING STARTED

In late 1981, GE put together a small rule-based (45 rules) troubleshooting system, written in Lisp, just to show that it was feasible to tackle the troubleshooting problem with expert system techniques. The feasibility demonstration resulted in permission to complete the system, but with certain constraints. To achieve the most widespread use, GE wanted its knowledge systems used in the field to be resident on small, inexpensive (about $10,000) computers rather than on more expensive, dedicated Lisp computers or on a mainframe system. To achieve this requirement, the system needed to be written in a relatively portable programming language rather than in a specialized AI language.

Consequently, CATS-1 was rewritten in the Forth programming language and implemented on a DEC PDP-11/23 computer (a desktop minicomputer). It requires 1/2 megabyte of memory, a 10-megabyte Winchester disk, a graphics board to access computer-aided design (CAD) files as well as alphanumeric files, and communications facilities to connect to other computers and devices. In addition, CATS-1 can read external information from sensors that will be available in new model locomotives.

By July 1983, the first field prototypes went into the GE's locomotive operations training center for testing, and in September 1984 testing began in the field at various railroads around the United States. This prototype contained about 550 rules. Of these, roughly 350 were devoted to fault diagnosis and repair procedures. The other 200 rules formed a Help system which, on demand, provided additional information for the user.

TESTING THE SYSTEM

The first problem chosen to be a test diagnosis case illustrates the difficulties that confront troubleshooters and how a knowledge-based troubleshooter can be constructed to handle these difficulties. To choose the test problem, GE asked its troubleshooters to identify the most recurrent problem that their running repair shops have to face.

According to the CATS-1 inventors, questioning of the repair shops' troubleshooters revealed that "something called 'not loading properly' accounted for about 30 percent of reported symptoms." The problem with this symptom is its vagueness. "Not loading properly" means that the locomotive is not pulling the load the way it should, or in other words, there is something wrong with the locomotive. Clearly, this symptom could result from several causes, including mechanical faults, electrical problems, transmission difficulties, or human error.

To narrow the field of possible causes for the locomotive problem, the CATS-1 knowledge base is taxonomically divided into a series of different

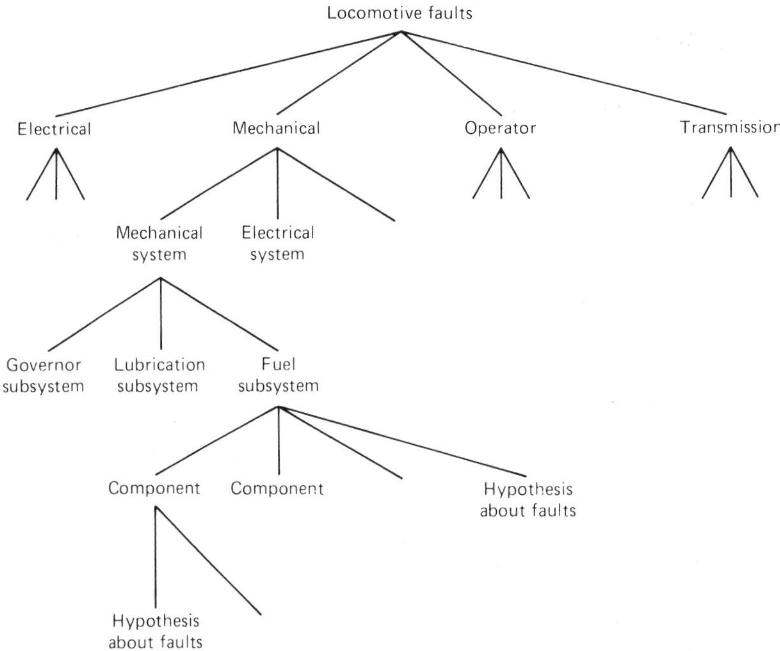

Figure 18-2 CATS-1 knowledge about faults

knowledge and locomotive systems areas (Figure 18-2). For example, CATS-1 knowledge, in the form of rules, is first divided according to faults, such as electrical, mechanical, transmission, or operator problems. These faults could apply to different types of diesel locomotive systems, such as the mechanical or electrical systems. The system areas are further partitioned into subsystems. For example, the mechanical system is composed of subsystems that include the governor system, lubrication system, and fuel system. Each of these subsystems has components. Finally, within each subsystem division, rules are subdivided according to hypotheses about faults such as operator error and engine unable to make power.

DIAGNOSING

During a troubleshooting session, CATS-1 starts by collecting background information and problem symptoms. Upon startup, the system asks a number of questions about the locomotive model number, model year, and reported symptoms (Figure 18-3). CATS-1 tables provide additional information, such as the

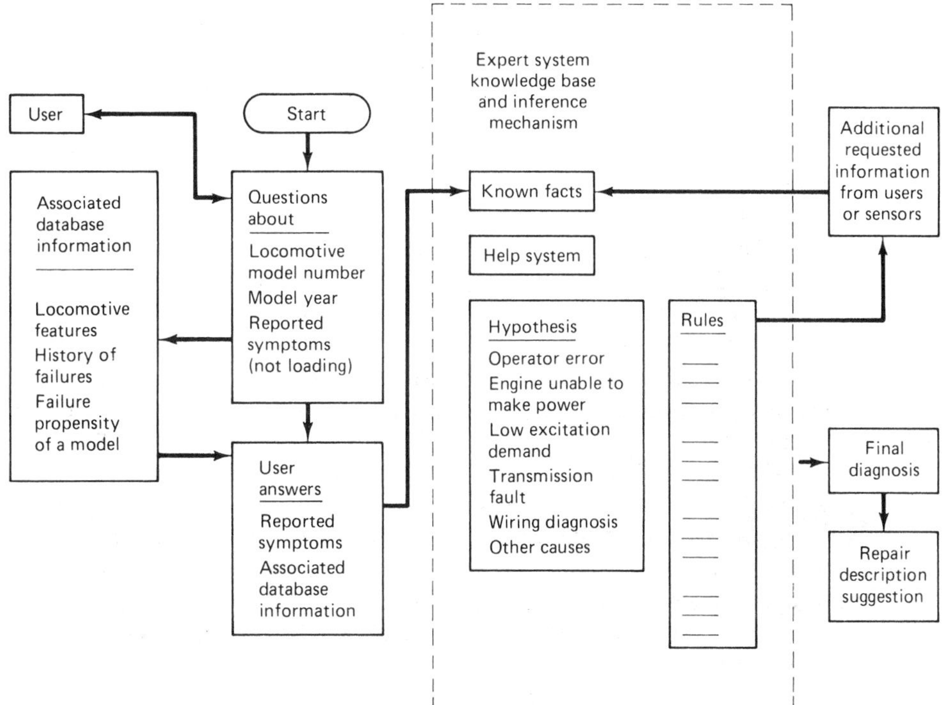

Figure 18-3 Expert troubleshooting system architecture (General Electric)

locomotive's standard features, history of failures, and that model's propensity for failures.

The loading of the reported symptoms and background information into the knowledge system triggers its diagnostic procedures, which culminate not only in a diagnosis but also in recommended corrective actions. The diagnostic procedures involve both backward and forward chaining techniques for reasoning. To perform its deductions and diagnosis, CATS-1 uses information input by users or sensors, in addition to its own knowledge in the form of IF-Rules; IFF (if-and-only-if) Rules; WHEN Rules, which activate new procedures associated with newly inferred facts; and Meta Rules, which control, reorganize, and reorder the reasoning processes.

The diagnostic process begins with backward chaining. Based on the initial symptoms input by the user and the possible causes that the expert has suggested, the backward chainer proposes a likely hypothesis for the particular problem area in question. Then it attempts to find rules which substantiate that hypothesis.

A typical CATS-1 question to the user, to determine the symptoms and hypothesis that start the backward-chaining process, might be: "Is the governor steady?" If the answer is no, CATS-1 knows five possible causes. The order in which these causes are proposed as hypotheses for evaluation are in order of increasing cost of the test to prove or disprove the hypothesis. In the case of factors that could make an unsteady governor, the simplest thing to check first is whether there is enough oil; second is a test to determine whether or not the oil is clean. If neither of these solves the problem, CATS-1 tries out the next, more complex, least expensive hypothesis.

Determining a specific faulty component may involve interaction with several rules and with the forward chainer. For example, while the backward chainer is active, CATS-1 rule 760 might hypothesize that a locomotive has a fuel system fault (Figure 18-4). Loosely translated, rule 760 says: "IF the engine is set at idle AND the fuel pressure is below normal AND the readings were taken from the locomotive gauge AND we are sure that the gauge is accurate THEN we can conclude that the fuel system is faulty (1.00)." The number 1.00 associated with the action part of the rule is a certainty factor. Defined by the experts, it can range between -1 and 1 and indicates the strength of the implication or conclusion of the rule.

For rule 760's hypothesis to be true, each of the conditions in the rule must be true. To prove this hypothesis, for each condition CATS-1 first scans the system facts to see if that premise is already known. If so, it goes on to the next condition. If not, it tries to infer that condition by evaluating a second rule that concludes the condition in question. If conditions in the second rule are all true, then evaluation terminates, the conclusion is true, and CATS-1 continues its deductive process with the next condition in rule 760.

However, CATS-1 may have to recursively evaluate still a third rule (or more) to conclude a condition in the premise of the second rule.

Finally, if CATS-1 does not know, and also cannot infer, the sought-for

```
Rule 760
   there is a fault in the fuel system at idling speed
   and readings were taken from locomotive fuel pressure gage
IF:
   EQ  [ ENGINE SET IDLE ]
      Is the engine at idle?
   EQ  [ FUEL PRESSURE BELOW NORMAL ]
      Is the fuel pressure below normal? {Less than 38 psi?}
   EQ  [ FUEL-PRESSURE-GAGE USED IN TEST ]
      Did you use the locomotive gage?
   EQ  [ FUEL-PRESSURE-GAGE STATUS OK ]
      Is locomotive gage known to be accurate?
THEN:
   WRITE  [ FUEL SYSTEM FAULTY ]  1.00
      establishes that there is a fuel system fault.
End of rule 760
```

Figure 18-4 A sample CATS-1 IF rule (General Electric)

information, as a last-ditch effort, it requests the information from either the user or a sensor. To ask the user, CATS-1 requests the information by displaying on the computer screen the lowercase text that is associated with the clauses in the rule. But it may not be necessary to bother the user. In many cases, CATS-1 can get its information, such as the rpm of the engine, by directly interrogating one of the locomotive's sensors.

During this deductive process, users and sensors input new information; at the same time, the backward chainer infers other new information. The new input or inferred information changes the facts that CATS-1 knows, just as new discoveries about the locomotive problem or completion of repairs made to some locomotive parts change the way a mechanic views the state of a locomotive system.

THE FORWARD CHAINER

In contrast to the backward chainer, which is goal directed (tries to prove a goal), the forward chainer simply reacts to changes. Whenever the forward chainer spots new facts that have been added to the known ones, it scans the CATS-1 rules to see if its known information is now sufficient to execute the THEN parts of any rules that contain the new facts as their conditions. The execution of these rules allows CATS-1 to infer still more facts, which the forward chainer uses to try to execute other rules. Some of the information inferred, and subsequent rules executed, causes the forward chainer to submit a new hypothesis to the backward chainer.

WHEN rules may be used to submit new hypotheses. Used only by the forward chainer, they take the form, "WHEN this is true THEN do that" or

```
Rule 1460
   there is at least one faulty fuel system component
WHEN:
   EQ  [ FUEL SYSTEM FAULTY ]
      The fuel-system is faulty
THEN:
   DISPLAY  [ FUEL SYSTEM FAULTY ]

      There is a fuel system fault.

   WRITE  [ FUEL PROBLEM SOLVED ]  -1.00
      establishes that the fuel problem is not solved.
   EVAL-ALL  [ FUEL SYSTEM-COMPONENT FAULTY ]
      is evaluating for a faulty fuel system component.
End of rule 1460
```

Figure 18-5 A sample CATS-1 WHEN rule (General Electric)

"WHEN this is true THEN that is also true." For example, a translated version of rule 1460 in Figure 18-5 says WHEN the fuel system is faulty, THEN there is at least one faulty fuel system component. The −1.00 number in the THEN part of rule 1460 indicates a nil probability that the fuel problem has been solved. The EVAL (for evaluate) function in the next statement is the function that generates, reorders, and allows CATS-1 to submit a new hypothesis that will refocus the search and gradually pinpoint the fuel system fault.

When the forward chainer cannot find any more rules to react to and execute, it returns control to the backward chainer. The backward chainer continues its deductive process until it has proved a hypothesis or has exhaustively evaluated and either proved or disproved all its hypotheses.

DON'T STOP AT JUST ONE FAULT

CATS-1 does not assume that only one component is at fault, because the GE engineers do not consider that realistic. Instead, every time CATS-1 finds a fault at any level of the locomotive system, it expects it to be fixed immediately. It then reevaluates the locomotive symptoms to see if the fix resets the system to normality or if there are more faulty components.

HELP

Upon request from the user, a CATS-1 Help system provides additional information, such as location and identification of locomotive components, replacement parts classification, and description of repair procedures. Since typical users are skilled blue collar workers, the Help system is organized so as not to intimidate the user in terms of spelling or excessive choices. The user is either offered a menu or prompted for information that requires a vocabulary consisting mostly of "YES," "NO," "I DON'T KNOW," "HELP," and "WHY." If the system contains information about the exact situation on which the user is currently working, the Help system displays it. Otherwise, the Help system chooses the closest, most relevant information to display.

The Help information can be displayed in the form of textual information, CAD diagrams (schematics), or video pictures of components and repair sequences that are stored on a laser video disk. Sometimes, troubleshooters can only tell if something is running satisfactorily by the sound it makes. Simply put, if it sounds okay, it is. For such information, which cannot be measured or seen, the CATS-1 Help system interfaces to audio disks to provide examples of normal sounds for comparison purposes.

The GE diagnostic system will play a role in repair and maintenance training, as well as in the troubleshooting process. It will also allow its on-the-job technicians to incorporate in the system their own knowledge and experience. In its original form, CAT-1 confines its troubleshooters to the ideas and disciplines of the expert whose knowledge was professionally embedded in the system. This is considered by GE to be a "quasi-optimal" rather than an "optimal" situation.

GENERATING POWER RELIABLY

CATS-1's conclusions are limited by the accuracy of the gauges providing the technicians with input data. So CATS-1 provides another set of rules to guide users in checking the accuracy of gauges or other measuring instruments. However, in the new model locomotives, CATS-1 can bypass users and interrogate sensors directly. Unfortunately, sensor-based diagnosis systems can be problematic because often there are more false sensor readings than there are malfunctions in equipment being monitored by the sensors.

For this reason, Westinghouse's Process Diagnosis System (PDS), developed by CMU, is designed with the knowledge to diagnose its diagnoses and decide whether a sensor malfunction reading is due to a real malfunction or other extraneous event.

PDS diagnoses faults in stream turbine generators. Currently licensed and in production use for seven steam turbine generators at a Texas utility company, PDS directly accepts readings from a variety of chemical, electrical, and temperature sensors.

The initial PDS implementations revealed two sources of sensor-related problems. First, over a period of time sensors tend to degrade, thus reducing their diagnostic value. Second, even properly operating sensors produce spurious values intermittently either due to external factors or to sensor malfunctions.

Conventional diagnostic systems generally detect and filter or smooth out spurious readings before they reach the diagnostic system. Such an approach may not be desirable in expert systems because system designers use the unaltered sensor data to relook at the signals, perform unanticipated analyses, and infer new information which can be used to refine the knowledge base.

To get around the false-sensor-reading problem, PDS has, in addition to its steam turbine diagnostic rules, another set of rules to analyze the sensors in order to distinguish the false from the real signals. If these sensor rules find a sensor malfunction, they alter the rule base that diagnoses the steam turbine generator so that PDS no longer considers any input from the malfunctioning sensor it has discovered. Until the malfunctioning sensor is fixed, PDS bases its diagnosis only on other system sensors. In this way, PDS monitors its own diagnosis and adapts its rule base to a new, error-causing situation.

KNOWLEDGE SYSTEMS FIX MANY FAULTS

The diagnostic process is unusual among intelligent human activities in that it is understood well enough to build knowledge-based systems that leverage troubleshooters of all sorts of equipment. It therefore comes as no surprise that diagnostic knowledge systems are the most common AI systems in use today.

Bolt Beranek and Newman, for example, has an expert system to monitor and diagnose computer networks and network nodes. Campbell Soup also is using an expert system. It was developed on a PC using Texas Instruments' Personal Consultant application development tool, to diagnose malfunctions in cookers that sterilize many canned foods.

Meanwhile, Gould, Inc. is developing knowledge-based equipment and system diagnosis applications. These programs could be mounted on its Unix-based superminis. But Gould is also looking to run these knowledge programs on Lisp processor boards that plug into its programmable controllers. The boards will perform an initial knowledge-based diagnosis. However, they will also hook up to Lisp machines, via a MAP network, in order to perform further expert analysis, clarification, and symbolic decision support.

Some diagnostic knowledge systems have already demonstrated payback. For example, Spear, a remote tape-drive diagnostic system that contains an AI component, saves Digital Equipment Corp. $50 million a year, according to Digital. Spear is usually run periodically for preventative maintenance. During system execution, Spear calls the remote system and reads its error logs. The AI component uses the error log data and its own knowledge to detect causes of intermittent failures and to predict hard failures before they occur. In the case of an existing failure, Spear determines, in advance, the bad component and then dispatches a repairman.

Another example of AI leverage is Ford Motor Company's knowledge system that diagnoses problems with Asea robots. The problem with traditional diagnostic procedures for robots, or other high-technology gear, is their complexity. Technicians are given intensive training in the maintenance of this equipment.

Unfortunately, unless the equipment malfunctions often enough so they can practice what they learned, they forget many of the details.

The knowledge-based robot maintenance system was developed on a PC, using Texas Instrument's Personal Consultant tool. The tool's graphics support is used extensively to pinpoint problematic areas with the robot and show, rather than just tell, exactly what course of action to take (Figure 9-16). The knowledge system has proved so successful that Ford sent a videotaped demonstration of the knowledge system, along with a sample of its knowledge base, to its equipment suppliers. The videotape promised future purchase preference to suppliers who delivered knowledge-based maintenance with their high-technology equipment.

TELEPHONE REPAIR

Considering the technological advances in the telecommunications industry and the geographical dispersion of its networks, an AI-based diagnostic system was a natural for AT&T Bell Laboratories to develop. AT&T and some of the telephone operating companies are using AT&T Bell's ACE (Automated Cable Expertise), a knowledge-based, cable-trouble analysis system to find and diagnose cable troubles in Dallas and Houston.

The ACE system aids the manager of a telephone network center who is responsible for maintenance (both preventative and rehabilitation) of cables and their associated telephone poles, terminal boxes, and outside plants (the collection of cables that hang from telephone poles or reside underground). A variety of electrical faults and environmental conditions persistently cause cable problems, especially in the outside plants. These problems include pinholes in the cables, moisture in the cables, loose ends that corrode, insect infestations in terminal boxes, rodents that gnaw on cables, and cars knocking over poles.

Clearly, it is not feasible to check every telephone cable every day. Instead, for diagnostic and maintenance performed, the operating companies traditionally rely on customer and employee reports generated from a database by an automated complaint tracking system. These reports, which provide important information for identifying trouble spots in the local network, contain a history of where and when the complaint occurred and how it was fixed.

Highly trained specialists routinely peruse and analyze these reports to identify trouble spots and prevent further disruption of customer service. The problem is that the database/complaint tracking system produces large volumes of detailed information that a limited number of specialists must analyze in order to make an informed selection of candidates for rehabilitative maintenance.

This large amount of information to analyze prevents timely identification and analysis of persistent problem areas that need rehabilitation. The rehabilitation backlog prevents the identification and analysis of prospective areas for preventative maintenance. However, this knowledge bottleneck created makes the telephone cable maintenance problem a candidate for expert system solution.

The ACE expert system automatically peruses the large volumes of daily complaints and maintenance reports and helps the managers digest the data that are output from the automated complaint system. For this purpose, it analyzes and correlates them with related cable problems and geographical characteristics of cable locations to pinpoint where to send work crews.

ACE is practical because it integrates AI rule-based, forward-chaining techniques into conventional computing environments. Although ACE runs in a high-level AI language called OPS4, under a version of the Lisp programming language called Franz Lisp, it runs on a standard DEC VAX-11/780 computer under the readily available Unix operating system. A user interface is not necessary because no one feeds information into ACE.

To get its starting information, the ACE knowledge base interfaces to a traditional database and report-generating system that contains the details and history of cable trouble for an area (Figure 18-6). Every night, ACE dials this database using a traditional Unix network program, UUCP (Unix to Unix Communications Protocol).

ACE pours over the data and digests, analyzes, and correlates it. If during the course of its analysis ACE decides that it needs more data, ACE dials up the database again and asks for more.

To analyze the data and spot correlations, ACE contains knowledge in the form of rules. Knowledge engineers collected its rule-based knowledge from four sources (Stolfo and Vesonder, 1982 p. 14). These are:

- Textbook knowledge obtained from primers on telephone cable analysis
- Advice from developers of the automated complaint tracking system
- Expert advice from theoreticians of cable analysis at both Bell Telephone Laboratories and the local operating companies
- Local analysts from the operating companies and users of the complaint tracking system who perform the actual analysis

Although an automatic system, the user or telephone maintenance center can itself define a threshold. The threshold is a minimum rating for some problem quantity below which the problem is considered negligible and not worth scheduling at the present time.

Outside of setting thresholds, the ACE user does very little. Every night the system retrieves reports from the database of the day's trouble complaints and asks for the history of cable trouble for the area if it needs it. It chains through its knowledge rules, infers information, and performs analyses. By morning, analysis reports and suggestions, in conversational English, are stored in ordinary Unix mailboxes where they wait for the cable maintenance managers. The suggestions indicate the trouble spots that require the dispatching of work crews to inspect the cable. They also indicate appropriate preventative maintenance or repair.

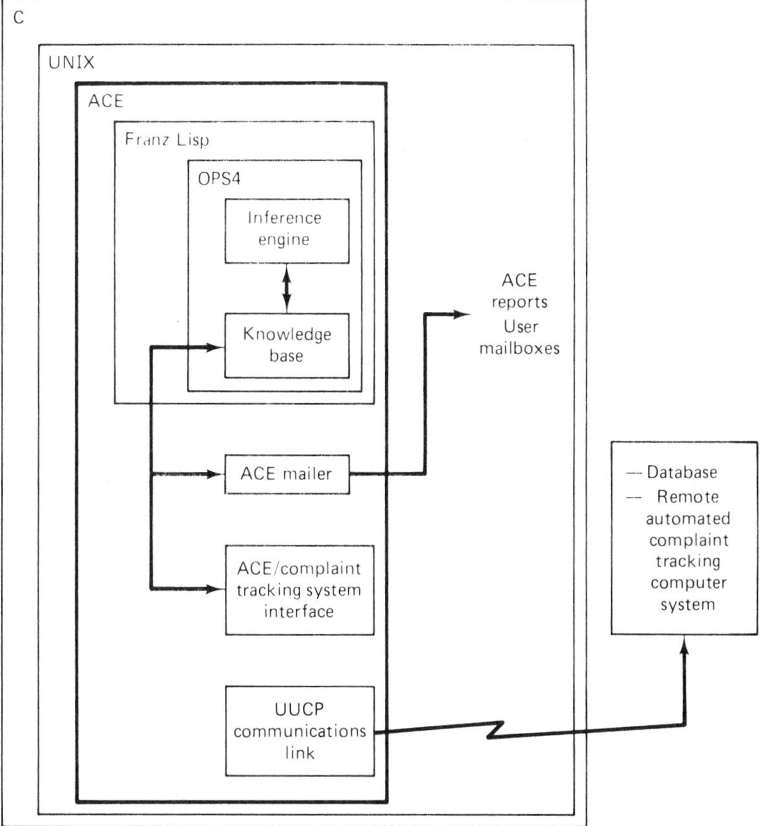

Figure 18-6 The organization of ACE and supporting systems (AT&T Bell Laboratories)

A TOOL FOR BUILDING DIAGNOSTIC SYSTEMS

Most diagnostic knowledge systems described in this chapter were built by AI experts. Since they were built, AI companies have designed tools that simplify AI programming so people with no AI expertise can build knowledge systems. But before these tools can be widely used for troubleshooting systems, some problems need to be solved.

For example, most tools focus on acquiring knowledge and representing it in rules or frames. However, interviewing experts and representing their knowledge in a knowledge base is too time-consuming to be used to develop the large number of diagnostic systems wanted. Also, human troubleshooters do not talk in rule or frame languages.

A new type of shell further simplifies AI programming so that troubleshooters can be their own knowledge engineers. The Troubleshooting Expert System

Tool (TEST) from Carnegie Group Inc. is a good example of such a tool. TEST, designed specifically for building diagnostic knowledge systems, uses a problem-solving strategy that matches the way troubleshooting technicians think about diagnosing failures. It is being used to develop knowledge systems at Ford Motor Company, Digital Equipment Corp., and Texas Instruments, in several machine diagnosis domains, including car audio, vehicle powertrain, semiconductor manufacturing equipment, and computer system diagnosis.

Two key things make TEST easy to use by troubleshooters. For one, TEST directly maps the knowledge that the troubleshooter provides into the representations that the knowledge system understands. Since the user's knowledge is used in the knowledge system exactly as the user provided it, the system avoids the problem of having to interpret the user's intent when it maps the user's inputs to the underlying representation. Also eliminated is the problem of the user being mystified as to the results of providing the knowledge.

The second thing that makes TEST easy to use by troubleshooters is the editor used to enter knowledge. For example, although TEST represents knowledge in frames (called "schemata") and rules, troubleshooters need not understand anything about schemata, slots, or any other AI things. They merely enumerate the possible causes of a failure in a system, the tests that could confirm or disconfirm a failure or cause of a failure, and other diagnostic-related factors. They add this information to the knowledge base by either moving icons into windows or responding to prompts for keyboard entry.

TEST'S APPROACH

TEST models the way troubleshooters diagnose equipment, rather than modeling the way equipment operates. CGI's studies showed that troubleshooters tend to diagnose equipment by determining which low-level failures can cause higher-level failures. To emulate the troubleshooter, TEST is designed around a hierarchy of failure modes. The failure modes are connected via "due-to" and "always-leads-to" relationships. For example, observable failures of a unit, such as a car failing to start, are at the top of the hierarchy. This failure-mode is connected to the ignition-system failure mode and the fuel-system failure because the car failing to start might be due-to a failure in the ignition system or the fuel system. The ignition-system failure mode is connected to failure-modes of components at the bottom of the hierarchy, such as a dead battery or bad starter. Tests, which might confirm or disconfirm a particular failure mode, as well as repairs, and rules are associated with the failure modes.

Knowledge about failure-modes, tests, and so on, is represented in "schemata." The schemata act as a template for entering diagnostic knowledge. For example, all failure-mode schemata have slots such as "due to" and "has-tests." Thus, while troubleshooters may have to learn some syntax for entering knowledge, they do not have to design an entire knowledge system architecture.

For example, the following informal description for diagnosing performance problems in multi-user computer systems was provided by a domain expert.

> A CPU limitation can be caused by one or more processes monopolizing the CPU, excessive interrupt stack activity, the quantum being set too low, or the CPU being at full capacity. The way I tell if there's a problem with the CPU is by looking at the idle time. If it's 10% or less, I know I've got a problem. If it's 25% or more, the CPU may or may not be the problem, but I'd go ahead and investigate its possible causes anyway.

This knowledge was represented in the following schema:

```
(defschema FM-CPU-LIMITATION
  (instance failure-mode)
  (due-to
    fm-process-monopolizing-cpu
    fm-excessive-interrupt-stack-activity
    fm-quantum-set-too-low
    fm-cpu-at-full-capacity)
(has-tests
    T-IDLE-TIME
    (:meta nil
      (confirming-results (in-range 0 10))
      (disconfirming-results (in-range 25 100)))))
```

This schema says that "cpu limitation" is a failure-mode, lists the possible causes of a cpu limitation, indicates the name of a test for determining whether or not a CPU limitation is occurring, and states what values to use in making that determination. T-IDLE-TIME is the name of the test schema and contains all the information necessary for performing the test.

When the knowledge system executes, it attempts to determine if an observed or suspected failure-mode has occurred by using the tests specified in the has-tests slot of the failure-mode frame. Test results are obtained by querying the user, checking a file containing test data, or checking a sensor directly. The possible causes of a failure-mode are investigated in the order specified in the knowledge base, which is based on the way a human expert would diagnose them.

Rules can be used to modify the order of investigating the possible causes of a failure-mode. Rules were used, for example, when a troubleshooter said, "normally, when I suspect a memory limitation, I'll check for excessive paging and then look for a problem with swapping. But if the average process size is very large, I look at swapping before paging." The ability to alter the order in which failures are investigated solves the problem more quickly.

Much more could be said about TEST's capabilities. However, the discussion here was intended only to provide an idea about the continuously increasing ease-of-AI programming. Teknowlege also has an AI shell, oriented toward diagnostics (see Chapter 10). Other similar shells are expected to be developed, and all are expected to evolve for some time in terms of speed, accuracy, and still greater ease of knowledge system development.

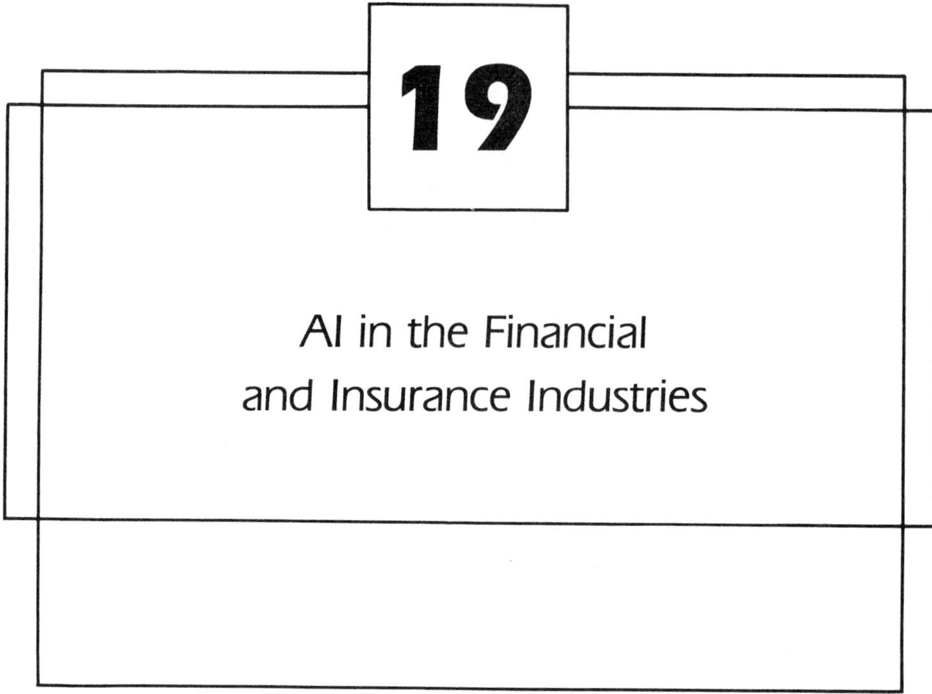

19 AI in the Financial and Insurance Industries

Many financial and insurance companies are looking toward AI to aid them in increasing the quality, efficiency, and competitive leverage of their operations. Shearson/Lehman Brothers/American Express, Coopers & Lybrand, and Allstate Insurance Company, not to mention Arthur Anderson, Travelers Insurance Company, CitiCorp, William Blair & Co., and the American International Group, are but a few.

Corporate profits are the reason. To quote one example, of the $15 million received in fees over a two-month span for its interest-rate-swapping services (matching of partners who wish to swap interest rates), Shearson/Lehman Brothers/American Express claims that $1 million would not have been received without the help of an artificial-intelligence program. The program was developed by one of its former senior vice-presidents.

WHY AI CAN INCREASE PROFITS

Interest-rate swapping illustrates what AI can do for certain business applications that traditional numeric processing cannot. To understand fully the potential benefits that AI can provide, it is necessary to first understand something about the application.

Interest-rate swapping is a multimillion-dollar procedure that takes place when two organizations decide that the interest rates are greener in each other's backyard. For example, a bank might borrow a large sum of money in a fixed-rate interest market, but would benefit more from a floating-rate loan. Or a trucking business might have borrowed a large sum of money in a floating-rate interest market but prefer a fixed-rate loan.

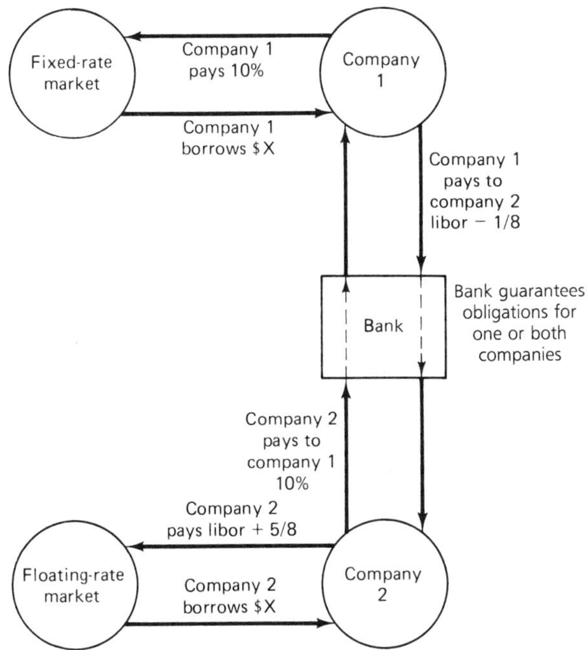

Note: Libor is an international interest rate, comparable to the U.S. prime rate. Libor −1/8 or Libor +5/8 are "going rates," subject to change depending on time and conditions.

Figure 19-1 How an interest rate swap works

These companies might call a brokerage house, which would match up their needs and arrange a deal whereby they could swap interest payment obligations without exchanging principal-payment obligations. Since banks can generally obtain fixed-rate loans at low rates, while attractive floating-rate terms are likely to be available for a trucking business, the swap allows both parties to reduce their effective borrowing costs (Figure 19-1). The savings to both parties involved in the swap are approximately 3/8 to 7/8 of a point. That can add up to an enormous amount of money for loans that range from $100 million to $500 million, even after brokerage fees are paid. However, all monies saved or earned hinge on whether suitable partners can be found.

AI comes into action when partners must be matched. When a client calls and wants to swap interest rates, the broker must search a large amount of information in order to match requirements and find a suitable swapping partner. If the brokers attempt to do this manually, based on personal contacts and experience, they generally will be able to contact only two or three candidates. The problem is too big and beyond the bounds of normal manual manipulation. Databases are also inadequate as match-up tools because they contain only facts, not the reasons and trade-offs for making a match.

The kind of information needed to choose swapping partners is based on broker experiences. Such experiential knowledge as judgments and intuition is symbolic in nature and can be encoded in a knowledge-based system. It is AI's abilities to represent symbolic knowledge, discern complex relationships between knowledge and information, and reason with and infer new knowledge, that allow AI programs to handle the symbolic aspects of interest-rate swapping and other business activities.

It is important to note that even though computational processing is a necessity for most companies to carry on their operations, most of what people do in their daily business lives (reasoning, understanding, discussing, making judgments) is symbolically—rather than numerically—oriented. In that sense, AI is very suited to business operations, as Lehman Brothers realized early.

Lehman Brothers reports that it services two to three swaps a month. Each swap nets the firm $500,000 to $700,000. So if it can match up the partners and service even one extra swap each month, it is satisfied. And since in a two-month period, two swaps, in addition to two mergers and acquisitions, were directly attributable to its AI-based program, the firm feels that the AI capability was worthwhile.

COMES THE EVOLUTION

AI's penetration into the financial and insurance industries is just beginning. Many market analysts believe that in the next decade or two, the financial and insurance industries are going to become very dependent on AI.

However, today's knowledge-based financial and insurance applications tend to be very much under wraps, rather than openly studied like expert systems for high-technology applications. The difference-in-secrecy policies occur because the high-technology applications originated in universities where the policy is to share information and publish achievements. In contrast, business people with ideas that will leverage their companies are not likely to publish those ideas for the competition to know. In addition, in these early days of commercial AI, companies tend to be very conservative about publicizing the use of a new technology to manage the data and money whose integrity is at the heart of their business.

However, the outlook is changing rapidly as corporate decision makers see and evaluate knowledge system success stories in other fields. High-technology oriented, academically developed expert systems were the pioneers. The next decade is expected to see banks, insurance companies, public accounting firms, investment houses, and management consulting houses, using AI to offer new services, improve the quality of their old ones, save money, and gain leverage.

That AI technology should gravitate into the financial and insurance industries is a logical evolution. These industries already recognize the strategic importance of high technology to business applications; in fact, they were among the pioneers in computerized business data processing. In addition, the English-like fourth generation database query languages and the electronic spreadsheets developed for personal computers have given many corporate decision makers personal experience with computer capabilities. Consequently, many of these decision makers are ready for AI-based opportunities.

FUZZY BUSINESS-REQUIREMENTS

Another requirement in several application fields, but particularly in business applications, is the ability to deal with what are called *fuzzy concepts*. Fuzzy concepts include approximate quantifiers and qualifiers, such as most, several, few, frequently, almost always, very likely, and almost impossible. Fuzzy concepts also include vague or fuzzy descriptions, such as high, low, tall, short, reasonable, fairly high, adequate, and near.

A form of logic called *fuzzy logic* (originated in 1965 by Lotfi Zadeh, professor at the University of California, Berkeley) was developed to reason with approximate or fuzzy concepts.

Fuzzy logic is not, however, equivalent to probability theory. Probability is concerned with imprecision in a specified event which can take on specific values. A statement such as "a 75 percent chance that oil is present" is a probabilistic statement. It is the values themselves, as well as the degree of truth, which are vague in fuzzy logic. Most programming systems do not handle such fuzzy reasoning.

Fuzzy logic is important for expressing statements about real-world conditions because in the real world most conditions are not true or false, nor are they exactly this or that, but are somewhere in between. Fuzzy logic is particularly important for creating corporate models because these models are generally descriptive in nature and are not well suited to the precise mathematical descriptions found in most computer models.

Standard computer models are better suited to responding to a database retrieval request, say, of "companies with profits greater than $100 million," which the program can then use to set up a table of candidate companies for some purpose, such as acquisition evaluation. The figure for profits is sharply defined as "greater than $100 million" and the queried database will return a list of companies with that attribute.

But this list may not adequately reflect the motivation of the user. It is not likely that the user is uninterested in the company with profits of $99 million. It is more likely that the user is interested in companies with "reasonable" or "high" profits and cannot easily express this in a computer program that does not handle fuzzy concepts.

AI IN THE FINANCIAL INDUSTRY

There is a problem with applying AI to financial and insurance activities. Many of these activities are performed by experts who rely more on instinct than on systematic expertise. How much knowledge can be extracted from experts in these intangible business areas is not known. Companies are willing to try, though. For example, in the financial area:

- American Express has a knowledge-based system to aid in credit checking. CitiCorp is developing one too.
- Arthur Anderson is using knowledge systems for planning audits and picking appropriate audit techniques.
- Arthur Anderson and Arthur D. Little use AI technology for organizing, analyzing, assimilating, and presenting management information.
- The U.S. Government Securities and Exchange Commission (SEC) extends its conventional data processing systems with a frame-based natural-language knowledge system that analyzes financial statements, submitted to the SEC via a conventional processing system, to spot suspicious filings made by public companies.
- Coopers & Lybrand has a knowledge system, ExperTAX, for supporting corporate tax accrual (the process of identifying and explaining tax-book differences between statutory and effective tax rates) and planning processes. Its frame-based system functions as an intelligent questionnaire that guides staff accountants through the information gathering process. During the process, it notes relevant issues, points out the importance of information requested, and analyzes information to identify relevant issues to be brought to the attention of audit and tax managers.
- The Athena Group has developed advisory systems for institutional portfolio management and foreign-exchange trading strategies for a number of Wall Street Investment banking firms.
- First Financial Planners, a subsidiary of Travelers Insurance Company, uses a knowledge-based system called PlanPower (from Applied Expert Systems) to perform comprehensive personal financial planning. It is designed for financial planners who can interact with it, control it, or run it in an automated mode.

AI IN THE INSURANCE INDUSTRY

As for the insurance business, a 1986 Coopers & Lybrand survey showed that 30 percent of the top 100 insurance companies in the United States were already using or developing knowledge systems and 50 percent of the remaining companies expected to begin development by 1988. Areas of high development activity within insurance companies include not just pure insurance applications, but also investment and personal financial planning.

Underwriting, in the areas of group life and health insurance, investment-related individual life insurance, and commercial property and casualty insurance are boasting considerable knowledge system activity. Claims management support systems that aid in the early detection of problem claims, help evaluate the soundness of a claim, and recommend the action to be taken by a claims adjuster are also favored application areas. Still another type of system is designed to support the clients of a professional reinsurer in the analysis and underwriting of the financial and medical data required to evaluate life insurance cases that cannot be rated with normal actuarial tables. The goals of this system include not only enhanced quality and consistency of the decision-making process, but also reduction of the cost associated with the exchange of case documentation between insurer and reinsurer.

USER CONCERNS AND REQUIREMENTS

Cost, training, risk, portability, language, hardware, security, user interfaces, and integration with traditional hardware and software are concerns for any AI project. They are major concerns in the financial and insurance industries where AI is generally intended to be used to enhance and improve existing computerized operations.

The market is already full of solutions that alleviate these problems. Many vendors have translated their AI application development tools to Common Lisp or C language and subsequently ported these tools to a variety of machines from mainframes to PCs. The second generation of PCs can efficiently cope with processing-intensive and memory-intensive AI programs. Also a second generation of PC-based AI tools has been emerging that are scaled-down versions of multiple-paradigm Lisp machine tools, or are integrated with business and productivity software.

An easy-to-use interface is another requirement for knowledge system acceptance. A knowledge system interface should, as closely as possible, approximate users' normal business styles and techniques.

Security is, of course, a requirement, with knowledge systems in general and with the financial and insurance industries in particular. Knowledge-base software contains the accumulated knowledge of a firm that is necessary to a company's plans and strategies. Clearly, misappropriation or unauthorized use or transfer of this software can have grave effects. At the same time, it is necessary to maintain an environment that does not constrain authorized application users or developers. Accordingly, organizational and hardware and software controls assume a greater significance in knowledge systems than in many other types of software.

It is because of security requirements that a number of companies are undecided as to whether their knowledge systems should reside on a workstation or mainframe, or, in some way, be distributed across the workstation and mainframe. Workstations are generally regarded as the more convenient vehicle for AI, while AI on mainframes can degrade other users' processing. However, many people who view knowledge as a corporate asset do not wish to distribute that asset so that one day their knowledge base can walk out the door and go to a competitor.

HOOKING UP TO DATABASES

One problem on its way to being solved is the integration of knowledge systems with traditional software. Most of the serious AI tool vendors allow programs written in conventional programming languages to be incorporated into their tool-based applications. Most of the tools also have some kind of connection to SQL databases.

There are two major ways that AI tool companies are addressing database integration. One, illustrated by IntelliCorp's KEE Connection, focuses on transparent database access. KEE Connection reads the relations and field names from a relational database's data dictionary. It creates a mapping between the database's relations and fields and KEE's classes of objects, object attributes, and frame slots, and it graphically displays this mapping. Without programming, developers can use mouse and menu tools to modify and transform the mapping so it is more appropriate for an AI application. When the application executes, KEE Connection uses the mapping to dynamically generate the SQL query and transparently access and retrieve the data.

Transparent access is often incompatible with optimized performance. Therefore, the other major focus in AI and database integration is performance. For optimum performance in a high-volume transaction environment, database transactions depend heavily on intelligent programming strategies that take into account database access methods, the organization of the database(s), the application that needs the data, and knowledge of the data and its validity.

Inference Corp.'s ART is a good example of the performance-oriented database-integration approach. With performance in mind, Inference Corp. developed a programmatic interface to SQL databases for ART. The interface provides language constructs within ART that allow developers that use the SQL query language to program and optimize specific accesses, updates, and other database operations. However, the database interface does not require them to navigate the data.

THE HARDEST PART

Some of the biggest cost concerns are related to choice of hardware for an AI project. However, the many financial and insurance companies involved in AI are far from agreed on the best hardware path.

Frequently, companies get started on PCs and grow their application until they have to move to large machines. For some companies, the machine can be one of a variety, as long as it is a type that exists on premises.

A common ploy is to develop AI programs on specialized Lisp machines, but deploy the production system on standard machines, such as a company minicomputer or PCs, which are often pervasive throughout a company. The economic advantages are many, and the increasingly sophisticated generations of PCs, which tend to blend with workstations, will make this technically more feasible. Other companies cleave to a Lisp machine, even for delivery, because of its memory size, flexibility, and capabilities. The ever-increasing VLSI support for Lisp machines, with resulting decreasing prices will make this economically more practical.

First Financial Planners' PlanPower, for example, runs on Xerox Lisp machines. A large-scale system, PlanPower performs comprehensive financial planning. It differs from a number of similar, but smaller systems, including some on PCs, primarily in scope. PlanPower's developers claim that PlanPower covers all the details, analyses, and planning that the major education bodies in the financial industry define as necessary for comprehensive financial planning. Most smaller systems, although useful, bite off only a small part of the problem. However, PlanPower needs a lot of memory and processing power to tackle such a comprehensive problem.

Coopers & Lybrand and Allstate Insurance Company, however, took different approaches. As part of a proof of concept project, Coopers & Lybrand used ART (an AI application development tool from Inference Corp.), running on a Symbolics Lisp machine, to develop an expert system for underwriting marine liability umbrella insurance policies. Then they redeveloped the same system on a PC using GoldWorks. GoldWorks, developed by Gold Hall Computers, is an AI application development tool for 80286- and 80386-based PCs. It incorporates multiple paradigms, including rules, frames, backward and forward chaining, object-oriented programming, graphics, and active values.

Allstate Insurance is looking to a knowledge system that processes medical insurance claims. Allstate, however, looked to develop its knowledge system at the outset on PCs using Guru (from Micro Data Base Systems, Inc.). Guru is a PC-based application development tool integrated with PC spreadsheet, database, graphics, forms management, and other business-computing programs.

The implementation of useful AI systems on PCs is controversial. That these systems have been implemented on PCs is proof that it can be done at all. Whether it can be done well can only be answered with time. Meanwhile, the Coopers & Lybrand and Allstate systems are good examples of types of knowledge systems likely to be found in the insurance industry and of what can be done with insurance systems on PCs. So we will discuss them in some detail. In particular, we will focus on some of the technical and nontechnical factors that experience is showing make the difference between the success and failure of a knowledge system.

KNOWLEDGE-SYSTEM DEVELOPMENT PROBLEMS

ExMarine, the Coopers & Lybrand underwriters' knowledge system, collects information about applicants and their insurance brokers, underwrites the risk, and suggests a premium. To write the initial system, the firm developed a tool, called FFAST, which runs on top of ART. (ART is described in Chapter 10. Development of an ART-based application is discussed in Chapter 20.) FFAST was designed to bridge the gap, to some degree, between knowledge engineers and financial (or insurance) experts, and, at the same time, decrease the time and cost required to build a knowledge system.

Knowledge engineers know that incremental development and exploratory programming are fundamental to AI software design. They know that system designers rapidly build simple prototypes and run test cases in order to determine what knowledge needs to be added.

Financial and insurance experts don't necessarily know this. So they tend to be impatient with the conclusions drawn by early, incomplete prototypes and, as a result, are suspicious of the knowledge system. Worse, a lengthy amount of time is required for financial or insurance experts, whose knowledge is needed for the knowledge system, to transfer useful knowledge.

SOLVING THE PROBLEMS

What Coopers & Lybrand felt was needed to solve these problems was a series of specialized software shells and environment to be used in entering knowledge and building prototypes. The software shells would reduce the prototype development time and strain on client's patience because they closely emulate the usual methods that the insurance experts are accustomed to using to enter data, assess a situation, and come up with a premium.

It is human to distrust what we don't know. Therefore, another important feature of the knowledge prototyping environment is clear displays that let users see how the application is structured and exactly what it is doing to arrive at a final answer. The environment must allow users to access and alter system-generated data and solution strategies easily. It also must support multiple test cases, retaining all data for incomplete or interrupted cases. And to develop the optimal system, the environment needs to be able to use as many expert system techniques as possible.

FFAST, essentially a knowledge acquisition tool, was designed with such an environment and software shells. At the heart of the tool is an interactive application editor. This editor can be used by a knowledge engineer for structuring applications using data fields, forms, form schedules, folders, and decision-process flowcharts. Knowledge engineers can use this structure to capture the system's intended behavior through rules.

Coopers & Lybrand says that this shell cuts about two months from the conventional prototype development phase, bringing the time required for a highly functional prototype to be ready for review to about one month after a project begins. Depending on the application, this time reduction yields $50,000 to $100,000 in cost savings. Consequently, when ExMarine was migrated to the IBM

PC-AT and the PC-based GoldWorks, the same methodology was used for application development there.

KNOWLEDGE-BASED INSURANCE UNDERWRITING

Overall, the PC-based insurance underwriter acts in the same way as a human underwriter. Given a minimal description of an applicant provided by a broker, ExMarine will underwrite the risk and suggest a premium. If the broker disagrees and volunteers more information about the applicant, ExMarine will reassess the situation and suggest a different premium.

As will be described, to arrive at its premium, ExMarine represents knowledge in frames and rules. It uses GoldWorks' object-oriented programming capabilities and reasons with its rules using forward-chaining techniques.

Users see none of these paradigms. They see a filing cabinet paradigm. The first screen in the system contains four boxes, each representing a folder (Figure 19-2). Selecting any of the folders produces the forms within it. Selecting one of the forms produces a form screen that displays all the fields in which the underwriter usually enters data.

The information that the underwriter normally collects during an initial telephone conversation with the broker appears in a form appropriately called

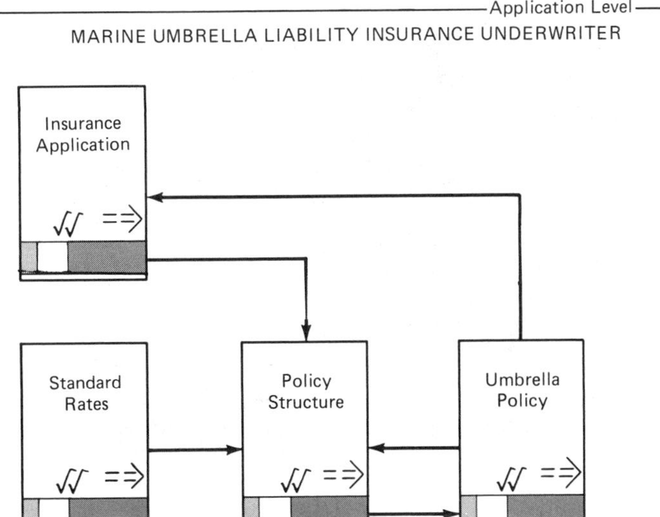

Figure 19-2 Human insurance underwriters using the knowledge-based insurance underwriting system see folders of forms that resemble those that the underwriters are accustomed to using to enter data, assess a situation, and come up with a premium.

"Preliminary Information." As soon as ExMarine sees the applicant's name, it looks it up in a database of applicants to access other information that it needs. Only if the database does not know about the applicant does the underwriter have to fill out the rest of the form.

There are six other forms in this folder. The Preliminary Information form is the only one, however, which must be filled in. Information in the other six is given default values, which can be overridden by the underwriter or filled out later if needed. The default values are generally conservative guesses.

The information filled in on the screen triggers rules in the forward-chaining mode. As with any forward-chaining system, the program reasons forward from a set of known facts and rules by applying other rules and inferring new information until it finally arrives at a solution. So when the underwriter has filled in enough information, ExMarine forward-chains through its rules until it arrives at the suggested premium.

THE KNOWLEDGE SYSTEM'S PREMIUM

To find out the suggested premium, the underwriter closes the Preliminary Information form and returns to the first screen containing the folders. One folder, called "Insurance Policy" is, as expected, the policy folder. Inside it are two forms: the premium, and the policy endorsements.

The premium form lists four different ways that the system can arrive at a premium, but suggests only one. The suggested premium is the base premium. ExMarine then adjusts the base premium by various factors such as loss record, exposures inherent to the applicant, competition, and accommodation in order to arrive at the quoted premium.

Graphics is used in this application to help give underwriters some quick perspective on the suggested premium. The graphics consists of three color-coded "risk meters" in the shape of arrowheads drawn on the premium form. Their color, graded from red to green, provides underwriters with a quick feel for the risk involved in underwriting the application. (Red is riskiest.)

Below the "quoted premium" field is a field called "target premium." Target premium, the premium that the broker says the client deserves, gives the broker a chance to disagree with the underwriter. The disagreement triggers other rules that direct the broker to fill in some of the defaulted information. Based on the new information, ExMarine reevaluates the risk and recalculates the premium.

WHO CARES ABOUT ALL THOSE AI PARADIGMS?

A preliminary version of ExMarine was built using only a rule-based language. It guided underwriters through all the detailed information about the applicant that could ever be needed in order to come up with a premium. And the underwriters hated it because it took so long to get an answer. It required them to find out all the detailed information that the broker probably would never supply.

The second version eliminated the problem by using multiple paradigms including rules, frames, forward and backward chaining, and object-oriented programming to better organize ExMarine's knowledge and activities. The different AI paradigms help to reduce the effort required for experts in an application area to use a knowledge system. For example, the different paradigms allowed ExMarine to handle many underwriting tasks automatically, based on data entered or the knowledge system's intermediate conclusions.

(Users should understand that there is by no means agreement as to the value of the different AI paradigms. There is evidence that use of multiple paradigms decreases the effort needed both to build and use a knowledge system. On the other hand, rule-based systems are the easiest to learn and the least intimidating, and therefore provide the greatest benefit with the least risk, especially for people who are not experienced in AI. Furthermore, anything that can be built with a multiple-paradigm system can also be built with a rule-based system. Numerous developers who have used rule-based tools to build serious AI systems claim never to have been at a loss. However, when it comes to using rules only to build large, complex knowledge systems, experience is showing that the amount of effort is so great that developers often get tired and tend not to build the systems.)

To understand how the different AI paradigms made the difference between ExMarine's success and failure, it is necessary to understand a bit about ExMarine's organization.

ORGANIZING THE FRAMES

ExMarine classifies and represents applicant and policy knowledge in frames. Folders, forms, fields, and primary insurance are examples of ExMarine's frames. These frames differ markedly, but they are related in two major ways.

For one, as is typical with frame-based systems, ExMarine's frames are related hierarchically. To gain the inheritance and organizational benefits of this relationship, the different types of frames are grouped into hierarchies (Figure 19-3). The application developer decides on the most convenient way to group the frames to achieve the goals of the knowledge system.

The most generic frames are always placed at the top of an individual hierarchy. Specific occurrences of a frame, (called "instances,") are located at the bottom.

Frames and instances inherit attributes from their parent frames. Examples of inherited attributes include icons, pre-defined displays, data types, input methods, certainty, and some frame slots. Inheritance capabilities make system development easier because system developers do not have to redefine those attributes that are inherited.

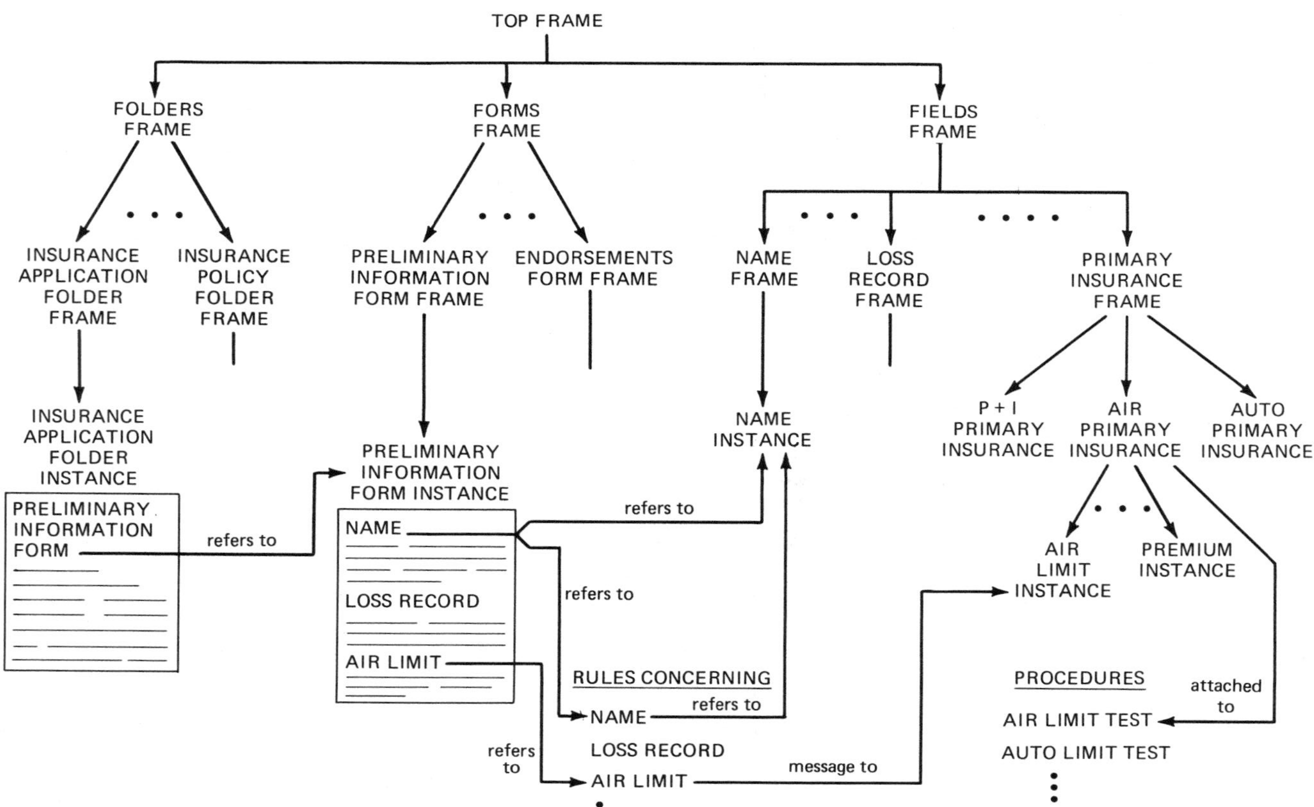

Figure 19-3 Architecture of a knowledge-based insurance underwriter system.

Clearly, frames in the different subhierarchies are also related, since folders contain forms and forms contain fields. Instances of such frames are related through their slot values, and this is the second way in which frames are related.

For example, as Figure 19-3 shows, the slot "name" in the applicant information form refers to a name value in an instance of a field. The field values "Primary Insurance" and "Loss Record" are associated with other slots in the applicant information form.

Slots can contain a variety of values besides text and integers, such as procedures, and even other frames and instances. Therefore, giving a value of "Preliminary Information Form" to a slot in the "Insurance Application Folder" frame, causes the "Preliminary Information Form" (an instance itself in another hierarchy) to seem to be inserted in the "Insurance Application Folder."

BETTER USE OF RULES

ExMarine's rules can refer to instance slots and values. Therefore, filling in an instance slot with a value causes certain forward-chaining rules to fire.

For example, a rule might say something like:

IF an applicant's name = ?name
THEN retrieve applicant data from the database for ?name

(Note: "?" in a rule refers to a variable. The rule antecedent, "If an applicant has ?name" means "if some name is entered for the applicant." The variable is bound in the antecedent, or IF part of the rule, and its value is used in the consequent, or THEN part.)

The database might contain applicant information because the applicant has other insurance with the company or because the policy requested is a renewal.

As soon as the underwriter enters a value for the name, this rule's antecedent is satisfied and the rule fires. The information retrieved might refer to other slots in the form. This information is automatically entered in the appropriate instance slots without the underwriter's having to do anything.

Entering one of these new values might cause another rule to execute. In this way, ExMarine chains through a series of rules until it either has a solution or comes to a dead end.

It might come to a dead end if the knowledge system doesn't find the applicant information in the database. If that happens, other rules do not fire and the forward chaining stops. Then the underwriter would have to enter another value into the form, which might cause the system to chain through another series of rules.

WHAT OBJECT-ORIENTED PROGRAMMING CAN DO FOR UNDERWRITERS

Besides supporting frame- and rule-based capabilities, GoldWorks also integrates object-oriented programming with the frames and rules. ExMarine uses all these capabilities. A major value of object-oriented programming is that it further automates the performance of many of ExMarine's tasks so that underwriters do not have to get bogged down in data entry. Instead, a minimum of data entry may not only cause a series of rules to fire, but it also may cause various procedures to automatically execute. Here is why.

First, because GoldWorks' object-oriented programming capabilities are integrated with its frame capabilities, each of ExMarine's frames is viewed as an object as well as a frame. Second, the integrated object-oriented programming capabilities allow application developers to attach procedures (called "handlers") to frames. Third, in object-oriented programming, sending a message to an object triggers execution of attached procedures.

One area where ExMarine uses these automated execution capabilities is to perform a "limit test." A limit test is used to help insurance companies assess an applicant and determine the premium for an umbrella policy that provides blanket coverage for named and unnamed exposures. Before issuing a blanket policy, the insurance company requires the applicant to buy primary insurance in various areas for up to (meaning "for a limit of") a certain amount of money. The limits the insurance company requires are different in each area. The limit test determines if the applicant has enough primary insurance in those areas.

Among the primary-insurance areas that must be tested to see if applicants have sufficient coverage are protection and indemnity (P&I), air, and auto. To reflect the natural organization of insurance information, as Figure 19-3 shows, ExMarine has a field frame with generic information about primary insurance. Further down the frame hierarchy are more specific frames with information about types of primary insurance: P&I, air, and auto. Underneath each of these are the primary-insurance field instances. These fields include the "premium" and the "limit" for the particular type of primary insurance in question.

Procedures can be attached to the field frames. For example, ExMarine's primary insurance frames have procedures attached that perform limit tests for different types of primary insurance.

Using these methods is automatic. As Figure 19-3 shows, as soon as an underwriter enters an air-limit value into the form instance (for example, one-half million dollars), the "air-limit" rule associated with that instance slot fires. The air-limit rule sends a "message" saying "perform a limit test" to the air-limit field insurance that is grouped under the air-primary-insurance frame.

The air-primary-insurance frame knows how to perform the air-limit test because it has attached to it the air-limit-test procedure. The air-limit instance inherits this test from the air-limit frame. So when the instance receives the "perform-test" message, ExMarine finds the test, executes the procedure to perform the test, and compares it to the limit value that the underwriter entered. In this way, ExMarine decides whether or not the limit value in each primary-insurance area is sufficient for the applicant to qualify for the blanket coverage provided by an umbrella insurance policy.

REALITY THERAPY

Some of Coopers & Lybrand's experiences in developing ExMarine are common among application experts providing expertise for knowledge systems in many fields. There are certain facts that can be learned from these experiences:

- Application-domain experts will not be data entry clerks;
- Knowledge systems that require more time and effort than performing the same task with traditional methods are not worthwhile to the experts using them.

NO-FAULT

Allstate's knowledge system is intended to process the no-fault medical insurance claims that are based on the New York State Workman's Compensation Board Schedule of Medical Insurance Fees. The schedule in effect when Allstate began negotiating for the knowledge system contained about 3,000 rules. The newer version, released at the end of 1986, contains 6,000 to 10,000 rules. Typically, rules will define reimbursements for specific amounts, for example if a claim is received for three X-rays, but will reduce the reimbursement if the X-rays are contiguous—that is they overlap in some area of the body.

So when Allstate receives a claim, it must review the claim to insure that the requested, or seemingly appropriate, reimbursement conforms to the schedule. Since the insurance schedule is so complex, Allstate sends out about 70 percent of their claims to two service bureaus. The service bureau maintains a staff of professionals who are experts at processing claims. Allstate feels it is too costly to retain sufficient experts in-house. (This situation is not unusual for insurance companies.)

What Allstate wants to do is to use AI capabilities to turn this situation around, at least to some degree. It wants to get a handle on the 30 percent of the claims that it processes in-house. These are the simplest claims, but Allstate needs to make sure that it processes and pays them in a timely manner; otherwise it is penalized by the state. Allstate also wants to ensure that it does not overpay on claims, where overpay means that the reimbursement it pays for a claim is not conformant with the schedule. Finally, Allstate wants to be able to reduce expenses by bringing the percentage of claims that it processes in-house up to 50 percent.

The Allstate bottleneck occurs because its managers have claims-processing expertise, but there are too few of these managers. The idea of a knowledge system is to spread this expertise among clerks. If the knowledge system delivers what it promises, clerks would be able to enter verbatim the information on the claims forms that they receive in the mail. The knowledge system would then peruse its knowledge base, which would contain a subset of the rules in the compensation schedule. With this knowledge base, the system would be able to determine the proper compensation reimbursement under the schedule.

There are periodic addendums to the schedule. And once every six years or so, there is a major update. Clearly, Allstate would have to maintain the knowledge-based representation of the schedule periodically. For Allstate's knowledge system developers, the issue is what kind of software lends itself to this application, how easy is the software to use, and how easy is it to maintain.

Vision Systems Inc. (Hackensack, New Jersey), the firm that developed the Allstate knowledge system, chose Guru as a cost-effective development tool and delivery vehicle because of Guru's integrated capabilities. Guru's most important features for this claims processing system are its database, communications system, and rule-base knowledge system and inference mechanism and the fact that they are integrated.

The Guru-based claims-processing system uses the database to store rules and data. Essentially, the system consists of a rule-based knowledge system that can retrieve information from the database, use the data in conjunction with rule-based reasoning to infer new knowledge, and put back information into the database.

Not all the rules in the schedule need to be incorporated in the system. The system only requires enough rules to give it the level of expertise that Allstate needs in order to do its in-house processing. However, Guru can handle almost unlimited rules because they can be grouped into different rule sets. The system uses one rule set at a time. But each rule set used can call other rule sets.

Communications is an integral part of the Allstate system too since the database containing the data needed may not be local. In fact, Allstate would store the knowledge base on its central computer. Then whenever the knowledge base is updated, it would have to transmit the updated knowledge to all its sites.

Of course, the system developers could have chosen any AI application development tool and planned on writing their own database interface. However, the problem with doing that is practicality and cost.

Unfortunately, practicality and cost often result in an AI application's database interface only being able to perform file transfer, but not the finely grained data access needed by many applications. Another problem with systems that are not fully integrated is performance and control in switching between applications. The problem occurs because the most commonly used database-access technique used on PCs is a multiple-stage process where a file or portion of a file is transferred into PC memory and then converted into a format that can be read by the application. However, the need for intermediate stages slows down application processing and provides less flexibility and control than a fully integrated system.

It's clear that many financial and insurance firms are capitalizing on AI to acquire competitive leverage. AI's techniques won't be perfected overnight. Also, the concerns mentioned in this chapter will have to be solved. However, there is no doubt that the financial and insurance industries are moving forward with AI.

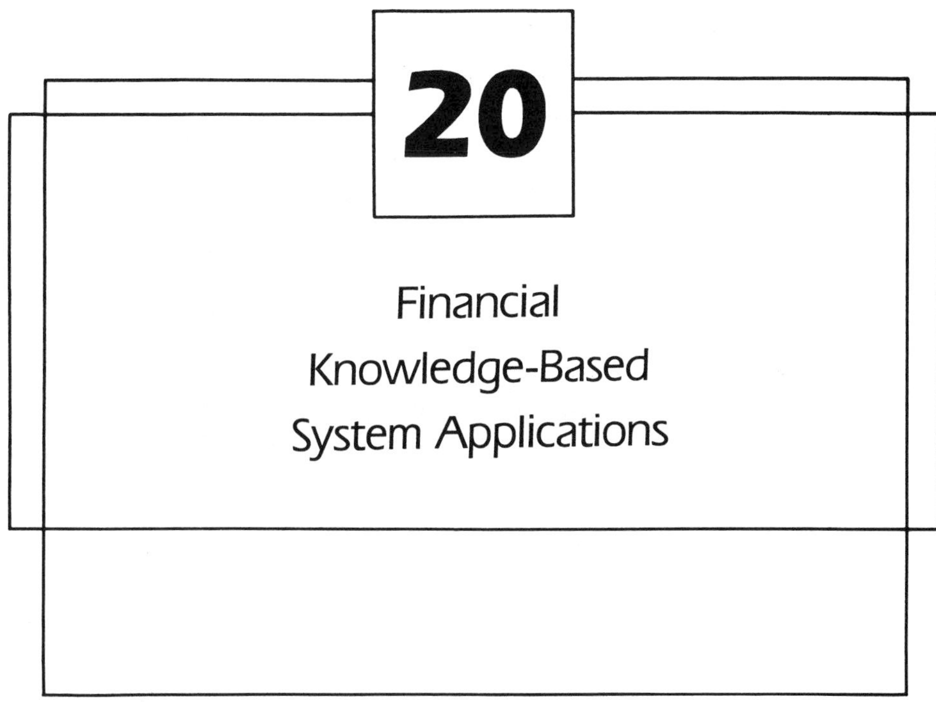

20 Financial Knowledge-Based System Applications

As indicated in the last chapter, financial companies are increasingly recognizing the importance of AI to business and opting to commit their companies, at least to some degree, to using AI in business operations. The extent to which AI technology can be turned into leverage for financial services companies depends very much on choosing appropriate applications.

Financially oriented knowledge system applications can be categorized into several types of systems (Figure 20-1):

- There are business-oriented advisory and consultation systems that are meant for specialists in some application area. For example, a tax accountant, investment planner, or auditor might be likely to consult with an expert system to acquire tax advice, compute the financial consequences of investment planning alternatives, or help assess a company's bad-debt allowance.
- Another type of business-oriented advisory or consultation system is for nonspecialists who need information about an application area to make some decision. Such a system might be in a bank or insurance company and help potential customers make up their minds about which bank services, account types, or insurance policies best meet their needs. These types of systems are particularly valuable when customers want low-cost but high-quality services or accounts. There is a tendency for companies to turn down this business even though they want the fee because it is not cost-effective to tie up a bank officer to acquire $100 worth of business.
- Still another type of knowledge system intelligently selects, explores, and

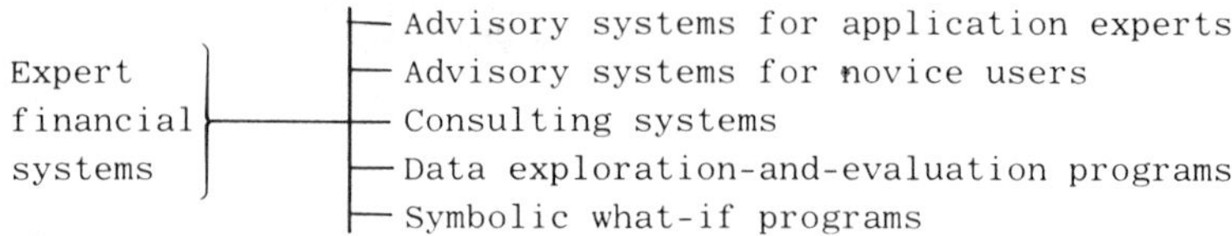

Figure 20-1 Types of knowledge system applications in business

evaluates a lot of data—far more than a person can manually examine and often far more than a computer can consider within a requisite amount of time. A case-in-point is a symbolic decision support system. It allows users to ask WHAT-IF questions. These are not the WHAT-IF questions associated with electronic spreadsheets. Electronic spreadsheets respond to questions, such as "WHAT IF the sales were $8,000 more," by recalculating many numbers. In contrast, AI-based decision support systems use knowledge and symbolic processing to respond to such questions as "WHAT IF we decided to buy instead of lease this equipment?"

As with any other decision support system, the knowledge system only provides support. In the end, the decision maker makes the decision. However, because AI-based decision support systems can intelligently select which data to explore and offer suggestions based on their exploration, they have moved beyond the traditional WHAT-IF type of system into something better described as a HOW-CAN-I system.

APPLICATION TYPES

Certain financial applications, amenable to knowledge system solutions, have already become popular examples of the role that AI can play in financial organizations. Among these are financial statements analysis, portfolio management, assets and liability management, credit and loan review, and financial

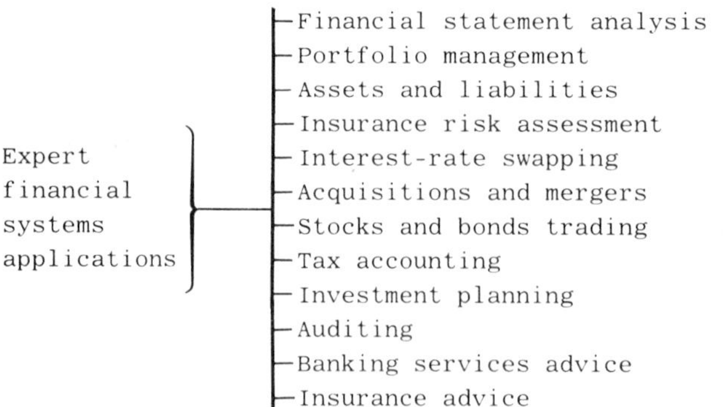

Figure 20-2 Knowledge-based financial applications

planning (Figure 20-2). Three of these will be discussed here because they are representative of what knowledge systems can do for the financial industry and because their techniques are transferable to different financial application areas.

FINANCIAL STATEMENTS

The financial statement, published annually by most companies, describes the heart of the business worthiness of a company. It contains information about a company's income, current assets, current liabilities, expenses, revenues, accounts receivable, long- and short-term investments and debts, property, plants, equipment, leases, stocks, and more. In addition, it contains an overview statement of the company's financial position compared over a two-year period. In short, the financial statement is a historic record of a firm's financial position and strength.

The reading and interpretation of a company's financial statements is crucial to anyone doing business with, investing in, loaning money to, or acquiring that company or even valuing its stock. It is crucial because financial statements are designed very judiciously, by management, to represent to the world only what they would like to represent, and to do it in such a fashion as to make the financial presentation comply with a very comprehensive set of accounting rules and principles known as Generally Accepted Accounting Principles (GAAP). As a result, the interpretation of these financial statements by the people who will take risks for the corporation has been developed to a high art by people who have a great deal of experience with financial statements.

The ability to read and interpret financial statements well is not widespread. Yet there are certain people who are extraordinarily good at it. These people's skill is generally characterized by their ability to read a financial statement's "footnotes."

Footnotes are explanations of the criteria used to prepare the statement. Their purpose is to make the statements clearer and more comprehensive and, as such, they are almost always given. In fact, footnotes to a financial statement are required by GAAP for full and fair disclosure and to ensure that statements are not misleading.

Financial analysts read the explanations in the footnotes to mentally adjust the variables in financial statements in order to get an accurate picture of a company, relative to companies that used different criteria to prepare their financials. For example, acquisitions, divestitures, and depreciation may be accounted for in different ways. Certain parts of a business's activities may or may not be included in a financial statement.

Contingent liabilities, such as pending lawsuits, generally need to be interpreted from a financial's footnotes. The amount a company is being sued for may exceed the assets on the balance sheet; it is important to consider such contingent liabilities carefully. Also, obligations such as leasing arrangements may or may not be considered debt. Clearly, they are a debt in that they are an obligation of the company and may total several million dollars in unique financing arrangements. But because of the accounting rules used, they may show up on a balance sheet as near-term debt (because it is necessary to make the year's lease payments) rather than as long-term or short-term debt; or they may be buried in operating expenses.

The point is that companies, to a limited degree, can put forth different faces because financial statement presentation is an art, not an exact science. The criteria used change from one financial statement to another because financial officers who need to represent a certain view of a corporation to the world can be very creative. The creative process even has a name; it is called financial statement design.

READING FINANCIALS

The ability to interpret financial statements requires a large body of financial, general, and heuristic knowledge. The financial knowledge concerns the many criteria for preparing financial statements and the ways a company can operate. General knowledge needed to interpret financial statements includes qualitative information about the industry a company is in, and knowledge of the shape of the national economy. It also encompasses comparative quantitative information about other companies and trends among the companies.

Financial statement experts use this general knowledge in conjunction with their own ideas and heuristics to govern the clues they look for in a company's financial statement, their view of exceptions, and the emphasis they place on particular portions of a financial statement. Putting all the knowledge and financial information together, they interpret the important issues that pertain to a certain company and make a judgement about the firm's financial health.

The ideas and heuristics of these experts in reading and interpreting financial statements can be characterized and incorporated in a knowledge-based system. Dissemination of this knowledge system as a personal consultant to others in the field offers a number of benefits to business users. For one, the knowledge system is a tool to help business people better discern a statement's realities. For another, the chances of missing information are lessened dramatically. Finally, the time involved in making sure that everything in a financial statement is properly evaluated is shortened.

FINANCIAL STATEMENT KNOWLEDGE-BASED SYSTEMS

Financial statement knowledge systems can be designed to run in two modes: diagnostic or interactive. In the diagnostic mode, users input a firm's financial statements and the particular interests, goals, and reasons for evaluating the statements. The knowledge system then asks questions based on the information the user is trying to derive. In this type of system, the knowledge system takes the initiative, examines the input financial statement, and decides to run particular simulations to determine what the financial statement would look like if certain parts were prepared differently or if certain criteria were different. The key to such a system is its incorporation of knowledge that would allow it to determine what questions are relevant in order to accomplish some fairly high-level goal by evaluating certain kinds of companies financially.

In the interactive mode, a financial statement knowledge system allows the more expert user to ask various WHAT-IF questions based on a company's financials. These are symbolic WHAT-IFS, such as, "WHAT IF THE COMPANY DID NOT INCLUDE THIS ASPECT OF THE BUSINESS IN ITS FINANCIALS?" or "WHAT WOULD THE CONSOLIDATED FINANCIALS LOOK LIKE IF THE COMPANY ACQUIRED THIS OTHER COMPANY?" or "WHAT IF THE COMPANY ACCOUNTED FOR DEPRECIATION DIFFERENTLY?"

The amount of "what-ifing" a financial statement knowledge system user can do with a company's financials is often limited only by the what-ifer's imagination. The idea in an interactive financial statement knowledge system is to have the knowledge system use its own heuristics to ask some questions of the user, run some simulations that it determines, and come up with some answers of its own based on its examination of, and experimentation with, the financial statement. At the same time, the knowledge system allows users to specify some of the things to be examined and tested. At all times, the expert system can explain what it did (and why). Based on these explanations, the user can tell the knowledge system not to be as harsh on certain points (or be more harsh) and to modify the knowledge system's analysis.

PORTFOLIO MANAGEMENT

As with financial statement interpretation, some people are better than others at recommending the best suited industry groups or stocks for a client's portfolio. Consequently, several companies are working with these experts with the aim of encoding some of their knowledge in knowledge systems.

Whether or not a knowledge system can do a good job of managing monies and investments is unknown. Opponents of the idea claim that it is not possible to represent properly the behavior of a very good money manager. On the other hand, these opponents admit that most people do not deal with the top-notch experts. Instead, they go to the average money-market manager, who is faced with an overwhelming number of portfolio possibilities. In view of the time needed to sort out all this information, which limits the amount of information that can be considered, many opponents admit that a portfolio management knowledge system can help the average money manager perform better.

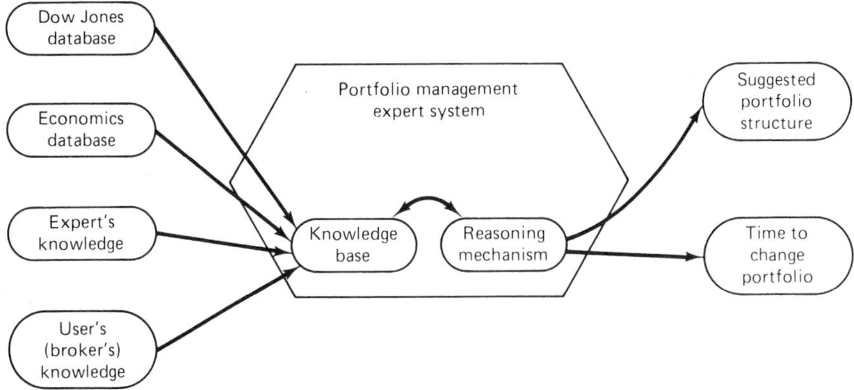

Figure 20-3 Knowledge-based portfolio management systems provide advice using inputs from many sources.

One problem in portfolio management is the large amount of information to consider. It is easy to tap into databases such as the Dow Jones database and obtain too much information about companies on the New York, American, and over-the-counter stock exchanges.

Portfolio management knowledge systems, with their symbolic processing capabilities, knowledge bases of facts, goals and heuristics, and ability to examine many possible portfolio items rapidly are suited to this type of problem. They help users (who are knowledgeable about the application) select and structure portfolios to meet certain criteria. The knowledge base of such a knowledge system contains, among other information, the user's criteria for structuring a portfolio. The knowledge system portfolio management system handles variables such as "conservativeness," "maximum return on investment," "cash-on-cash basis," "paying on dividend," or "coupons on the bond." More elaborate criteria can be encoded, such as a requisite certain percentage of a portfolio in high-growth or new-technology stocks.

An advantage to portfolio management knowledge systems is their ability to provide consulting based on information from many sources (Figure 20-3). One source, of course, is their encoded expertise, obtained from an expert in the field. Another source derives from the fact that they can tap into multiple databases.

The third source is the knowledge system users, such as investment analysts, who can enter their own rules into the knowledge system. The user-written rules define what they (the users) believe will happen when various interest fluctuations (indicated by the database) occur, and what type of action to take. Depending on the users' criteria and the types of conclusions they want their knowledge system to draw from different kinds of database data, a knowledge-based portfolio management system advises users on how to structure their portfolios. Based on the criteria specified, the knowledge system also flags for them the appropriate time to change their portfolio.

Furthermore, because knowledge systems are built from independent modular components, users can easily change their goals and add new rules and criteria. As a user's goals and criteria change, the knowledge system restructures itself and advises users how best to meet their changing goals.

The advantages of applying expert system technology to portfolio management are time and thoroughness in evaluating the database of industry group stocks and bonds. Without AI, given the complexity of the problem and the number of companies on the various stock exchanges, many companies go unevaluated and unconsidered.

A PORTFOLIO MANAGEMENT KNOWLEDGE SYSTEM

One knowledge system, popular on Wall Street, illustrates how thorough a knowledge-based portfolio management system can be. Designed by New York City's Athena Group and targeted at large institutional portfolios, the Portfolio Manager knowledge system makes ranked recommendations about how to structure an optimal portfolio. It also can perform ongoing portfolio correction.

Much like a human portfolio manager, the knowledge system bases its portfolio recommendations and its buy and sell decisions on knowledge of the underlying fundamental and technical aspects of the market and the economy, the policies and preferences of an institution, the profile and selection methods of the institution's human portfolio managers, and generic knowledge about how to select a portfolio. Such information is partly numeric and partly symbolic. To make sense out of such diverse and complex information, the Portfolio Manager knowledge system contains and integrates both a quantitative and qualitative understanding of modern portfolio theory.

This integrated information in the system allows human portfolio managers to use the Portfolio Manager knowledge system in two ways: as an assistant and advisor. When it acts as an assistant, like a human assistant it carries out intelligent tasks needed to determine a portfolio with minimal or no direction, complete direction, or anywhere in-between. In the advisor mode, the system suggests portfolios using knowledge of how the human portfolio manager would select a portfolio, as well as its own knowledge.

The Portfolio Manager knowledge system takes as input the names and data about possible instruments for investments obtained from databases, as well as parameters entered by the portfolio manager. The database information comes from any quotation source such as the Value Line Information database or the Dow Jones database. The parameters that the portfolio managers enter include a definition of their risk aversion, the total dollar amount to be invested, investment targets in terms of the desired annual investment rate of return and fundamental risk (known as the fundamental beta), and asset selection criteria and constraints such as asset rate of return, price-to-book value, price/earnings ratio, and beta. Many or all of the initial parameters can be set up as defaults. Using menus and a mouse, portfolio managers then specify only those that they wish to override.

The knowledge system outputs the recommended portfolio and its specific contents, and a histogram displaying breakdown of the portfolio by business sector. A graph of a capital asset pricing model is also output (Figure 20-4a). This graph shows the annual rate of return versus risk, the capital market line, and the recommended portfolio relative to the capital market line. Any portfolio on the capital market line is, by definition, an indexed portfolio. Clearly, any portfolio manager has to operate above the capital market line, which is why this display was considered important for the output.

Very high-level languages are more understandable than formal programming languages—they make it easier for application developers to design and maintain applications. The Portfolio Manager designers therefore designed their knowledge system using ART (from Inference Corp.), one of several knowledge system application development tools that are sometimes termed "fifth-generation languages."

WHAT'S IN THE PORTFOLIO MANAGER KNOWLEDGE SYSTEM

Central to the Portfolio Manager knowledge system is a mechanism, found in ART, known as "viewpoints." A viewpoint is a collection of facts that are appropriate to a particular situation, time, course of action, or interpretation of data. A major advantage to a viewpoint mechanism is that it allows users of applications to hypothesize various situations, one situation at different times, or competing situations. The ART-based system then reasons about the hypothesized viewpoints, in parallel, in order to choose those which best fit some particular conditions.

In the case of the Portfolio Manager, the goal is to choose the optimal portfolio from among all the possible portfolios. But before it gets to that point, the system uses viewpoints, rules, factual data and expectation analysis, to evaluate the instruments in the financial databases that it accesses so it can narrow down the number of potential holdings it will consider for a portfolio. It uses viewpoints, and rules concerning an institution's restrictions and constraints on transactions, to reason about the transactions that occur to make up a holdings list. It also uses viewpoints to hypothesize and reason about different holdings lists.

The selection and combinations of instruments to make up holdings lists, and selection of a holdings list for a portfolio, are affected and determined by more general viewpoints that model what it means to be a portfolio manager, as well as economic forecasts. The manager-viewpoints contain the views that individual portfolio managers have of managing their aspects of a portfolio. Additionally, the system maintains internal generic knowledge of how it would approach the problem of managing a portfolio.

The economic forecasts are based on the knowledge system's very detailed models of the economy, the markets (equities, bonds, stocks, commodities,

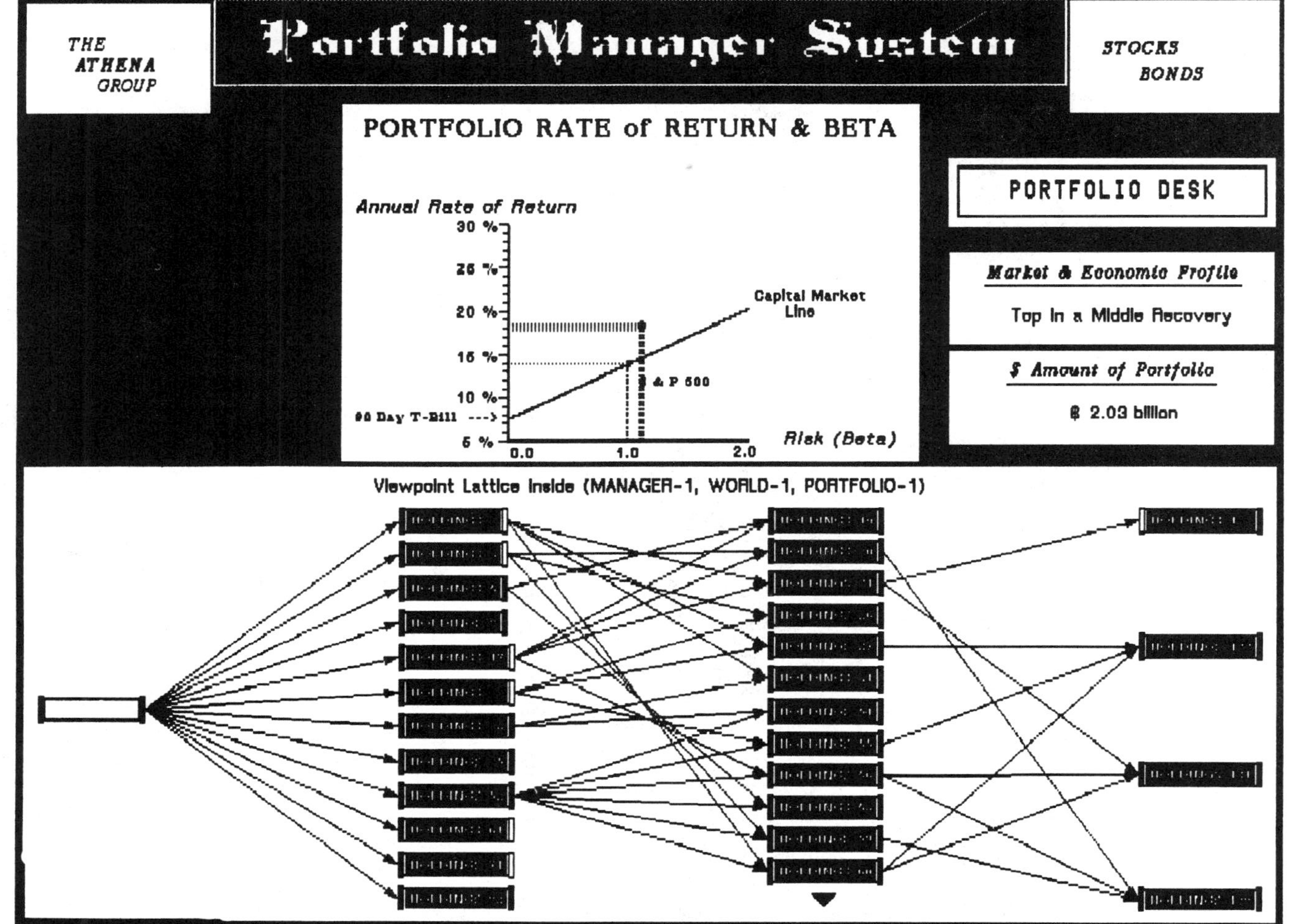

Figure 20-4 The knowledge-based portfolio manager displays (a) its recommended portfolio relative to the capital market line and (b) a lattice showing the combinations of different percentages of various assets that the portfolio manager considers, reasons about, and eliminates in order to construct a portfolio.

options, etc.) the portfolio is to be drawn from, and a qualitative specification of the relationship between the market and economy (currently implemented as cycle analysis). The Portfolio Manager then uses viewpoints to perform hypothetical reasoning, over time, using either scenarios defined by individual portfolio managers or scenarios predefined by the internal system.

HOW THE KNOWLEDGE SYSTEM WORKS

The process of selecting holdings lists illustrates what a knowledge system can do for portfolio management. In particular, it shows the thoroughness with which a knowledge system can consider and evaluate the maximum number of potential assets and portfolios. This relatively exhaustive approach would be difficult, if not impossible, to accomplish with either manual processing or traditional numeric processing.

To create the various holdings lists to be considered for a portfolio, the system creates viewpoints representing all of the possible combinations of different percentages of instruments that have already been determined to be potential assets (Figure 20-4b). It begins with one viewpoint that represents an empty folder of holdings, as seen by the single box in the first column. Each box in the second column represents a viewpoint containing different percentages, but of only one potential asset. Those viewpoints boxes with no arrows emanating represent situations where 100 percent of a portfolio has been allocated toward one type of investment.

If less than 100 percent is allocated, then, as seen in column 3, the Portfolio Manager merges two viewpoints to make up a third viewpoint which contains two types of investments. For each new viewpoint that still does not represent a completed potential portfolio, using the viewpoint merge operation, the system constructs new viewpoints containing combinations of different percentages of three holdings. This process is repeated until all the holdings percentages add up to 100 percent.

The actual viewpoint lattice generated is many times larger than shown in the figure. If the process of generating holdings lists was not controlled, too many combinations would be generated to construct a portfolio in a reasonable amount of time.

To restrict the number of viewpoints that can be generated as the system's processing proceeds, the system refers to its constraints and criteria. The constraints and criteria are embodied in rules that can reason with each of the viewpoints. A typical rule used to eliminate holdings-viewpoints might state that "IF it has been determined that interest rates are going up steeply with the time horizon in question, THEN companies whose primary products are heavily reliant on interest rates should not be combined in one holdings list."

By the time the holdings level has finished its processing, the Portfolio Manager has generated all the combinations of holdings, eliminated many, and retained the legal combinations of holdings. ''Legal'' is defined by actual legal constraints, diversification rules, analysis of the economy, government restrictions, investor policies, and a number of other factors. However, numerous holdings lists satisfy these constraints. To construct an actual portfolio, the ''best'' of these holdings lists must be selected.

A PORTFOLIO AT LAST

To construct a portfolio, the Portfolio Manager uses viewpoints to reason about the different holdings lists, and finally creates a portfolio as defined by the human portfolio manager. ''Best'' could have a number of different definitions, which vary with the institution and portfolio managers. To determine ''best,'' the human portfolio manager specifies a particular definition for selection of a portfolio. The definition includes parameters such as rate of return on a portfolio, risk of a portfolio, diversification across business sectors, transaction costs, and tax considerations. The knowledge system evaluates these parameters for each holdings list and comes up with a preferred measure called the ''portfolio utility,'' based on quantitative and qualitative reasoning. The best portfolio is then determined by the portfolio with the maximum utility.

However, the choice is not always clear. In these cases, the portfolio manager can ask for an ordered list of portfolios, based upon specified criteria to maximize rate of return, minimize risk, minimize transaction costs, minimize tax considerations, utility, and more. The knowledge system would then output an ordered list according to each of these constraints and the human would make the final selection.

ASSETS AND LIABILITIES

Another application considered for a knowledge-based expert system is assets and liability management for an institution. Currently, assets and liability management is a time-consuming, human-intensive process. Most commonly it involves making up a model to simulate different strategies a financial institution can take (under varying conditions) to maximize its net interest margin, minimize variability in its net interest margin, and avoid liquidity traps.

The limitation of this technique is the tediousness and lengthiness of the model-building process. It requires about six weeks to generate the simulation model from the raw data collected and come up with a strategy recommendation. As a result, many banks must operate on a six- to eight-week strategy-review time frame. This means that non-money center banks (they trade 10 to 20 percent of their asset base per day) and money center banks (they may trade greater than 100 percent of their asset base per day—billions of dollars) review their strategy every two months. By having a knowledge system do a lot of the strategy synthesis for the simulation model, the time can be reduced to a few days or a week. Moreover, the knowledge system can consider many more alternatives and many more risk scenarios, and do this on a more timely basis.

THE WAY IT IS DONE NOW

The current high-technology techniques used for assets and liabilities management involve manual generation of simulation models. The model's information is determined from raw data in the economic world, such as interest rates, the institution's financial position, the types of securities that are available to be manipulated, desired goals and constraints, and legal regulations. Typically, the models contain the various ways that interest rates might vary for the different types of notes and instruments with which the institution deals. They also contain information about how the institution expects its customers to react to these interest-rate variations.

Generally, an institution builds three alternative models of possible interest rate scenarios: rising, falling, and stagnant interest rates. The institution also develops corresponding customer behavior models that affect where an institution thinks its funds will be, both for assets and liabilities. Finally, for each of these possible proposed future interest rates and customer behavior scenarios, the institution develops a corresponding model for actions it might take and transactions it might perform. These actions and transactions encompass the various ways an institution might invest its money or raise money.

Once the models are built, they are simulated, or evaluated. The numerical result of each simulation indicates the financial performance of a possible action or strategy the institution might take. Based on these scenarios and the simulated results, a decision matrix is built. The matrix—typically 3 by 3—contains the three interest rate/customer behavior scenarios (for rising, falling, and stagnant interest rates) and the three actions or portfolio strategies the financial institution might take (see Figure 20-5). The matrix indicates the financial return on money for three portfolio strategies for each of the interest-rate scenarios.

The simulation model and matrix development process is performed by highly trained professionals in a financial institution's treasury department. An executive committee evaluates the matrix and makes the final decisions. The decisions include how to trade the institution's securities, whether to take long-term or short-term positions, what to keep liquid, what to tie up, and what interest rates to charge.

Normally, the simulations are done automatically, by computers, but the development of the strategies and customer scenarios for the simulation model and the strategy decision matrix is done manually.

Unfortunately, the analysis of asset and liability management strategies is limited by the parts of the process that are not automated. In particular, the simulation model-building process is not normally computerized because the

Interest rate/customer scenarios (ICs)
versus
portfolio strategies (PSs)

	PS_1	PS_2	PS_3
IC_1			
IC_2			
IC_3			

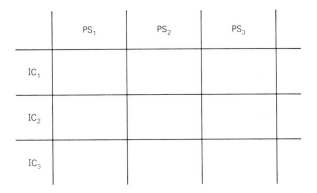

Figure 20-5 A typical assets and liabilities management decision matrix

process involves uncertain, judgmental, experiential (heuristic) information which does not yield to conventional algorithmic computerization. There are uncertainties involved in determining many aspects of the financial state of an institution and the environment. Uncertainty, judgment, and experience are also involved in estimating how future interest rates might vary for all types of financial securities, determining what interest rates should be set on an institution's products, and assessing customers' reactions to the varying interest rates.

Because of all this heuristic information, together with large amounts of raw economic data, regulations, and policies that must be taken into account, it takes weeks to develop the simulation models manually. As a result, it is possible to consider only a very small number of actions that the institution can take. The model builders must, therefore, use very restrictive heuristics to narrow the search space of the possible actions they can consider and put into the decision-making matrix.

WHERE KNOWLEDGE-BASED SYSTEMS FIT IN

A knowledge-based assets and liabilities system does not make decisions. However, it can help in the manually intensive, lengthy model-building process by automatically generating sensible scenarios and corresponding strategies.

Inference Corp. describes such a system as needing to contain a knowledge base with knowledge of a particular institution, its assets and liabilities goals, and the constraints on these goals. Constraints include regulations, conflicting goals that might require trade-offs to be made, and relationships to factors that affect the goals. Raw financial market data and data pertaining to the institution's financial position also need to be input to the knowledge system, together with general heuristic knowledge concerning the financial market, competing institutions, customers' reactive behavior to various decisions, and portfolio mixes. As expected, the knowledge system needs an interface that allows the institution managers and analysts easily and interactively to modify the system's data, knowledge, goals, preferences, and expectations.

With the raw data and heuristics contained in its knowledge base, an assets and liabilities knowledge system can generate "sensible" scenarios and strategies for the simulation model. Using its knowledge, it infers the likely interest-rate fluctuations, corresponding customer behaviors, and associated actions that satisfy the institution's goals and produce a desirable portfolio and set of interest rates. As with other knowledge-based systems, its knowledge and heuristics are based on the expertise of the people in the financial institutions experienced in building the simulation model manually.

An additional feature of the system is a symbolic WHAT-IF capability. Potential WHAT-IF questions of a knowledge-based assets and liabilities system include queries about how to handle new business demands to conform to certain strategies, the impact of a particular security or adverse condition or modification in the model, or whether a particular goal is attainable. It then suggests the best financial instrument transaction for a particular strategy.*

KNOWLEDGE-BASED ASSET AND LIABILITY BENEFITS

The effect of a knowledge-based assets and liabilities management system is to reduce greatly the amount of human effort required to build the simulation models and decision-making matrix. Automating the building of the simulation models may allow the exploration of hundreds of alternative financial institution actions instead of the usual three. This feat makes it possible to do a lot more and deeper analysis. Also, a knowledge system can reduce the model and matrix building time from weeks to days.

Consequently, the financial institution can review its strategies almost as often as desired. Bank officers know this is useful because interest rates fluctuate daily. Until now, banks have been forced to smooth out interest fluctuations over one or two months.

A conservative approach is the usual reaction to an enforced long waiting time to make a change in an institution's strategy. This approach is appropriate. When the waiting time is long, no institution wants to be involved in a high-risk situation, even though the return may be high. However, if it is easy to change a strategy quickly, then the degree of risk taken in the high-risk situation is less. Therefore, if the institution wishes, it can take a more aggressive posture with its assets and liabilities (or profit) planning.

There is both a tangible and an intangible benefit associated with the ability to review frequently the cash position and financial strategies of a company. On

*"The Application of Focus to Asset/Liability Management" (internal document, Inference Corp., 1983).

the tangible side, the greater number of cases that can be considered and the frequent review permitted by a knowledge system approach to assets and liabilities management can go directly to the bottom line. The frequent review and increased number of cases considered allow more intelligent manipulation and management of the spread between the interest rates paid out and the interest rates charged, thus increasing the chances of greater profits.

The intangible gains occur because the more often financial institution officers know the cash position and profit-and-loss position of the institution whose finances they manage, the more comfortable they feel in making their decisions about how to run that institution. Out of that comfort may come sounder decision making and smoother performance by the company.

Assets and liabilities management as a knowledge system application has been slow in catching on because the application is so central to a financial institution's operations and profits. Because AI and commercial knowledge systems are still in the early stages, many institutions consider assets and liabilities management too major a project for an expert system to undertake. They prefer to begin their entry into AI with small steps and get comfortable with the technology.

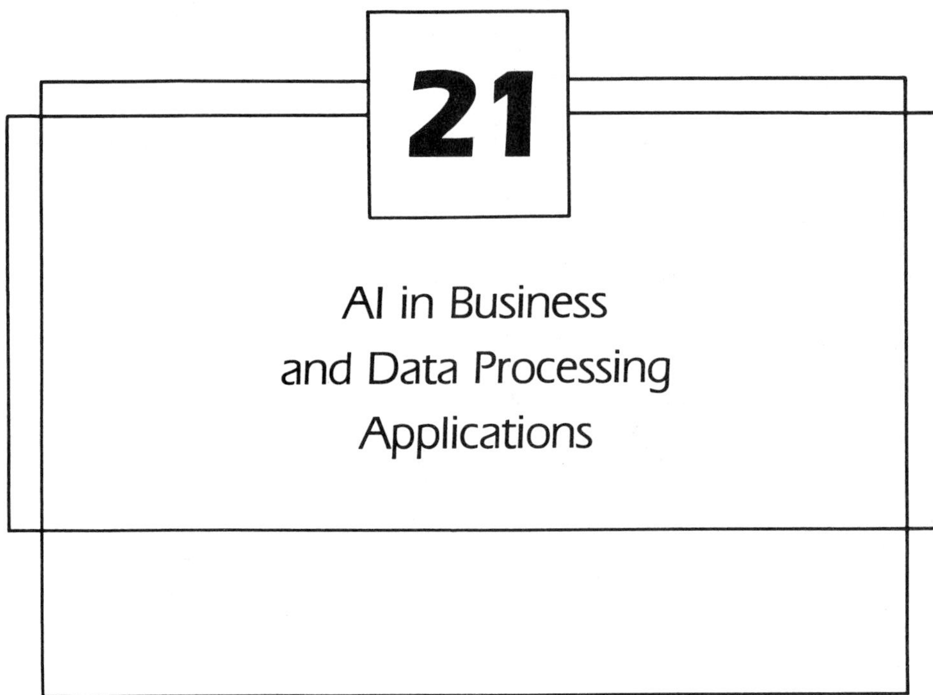

21

AI in Business and Data Processing Applications

The computer has always been hailed for its ability to increase productivity. Nowhere is this truer than in business organizations where computers are at the heart of fundamental business operations and recordkeeping.

Recently, a lot of companies have been looking to further boost productivity by merging standard programs and AI technologies. For example, almost every reasonably sized organization has a database and a backlog of applications waiting to be developed. The productivity of the database users can be enhanced by a knowledge-based database assistant. The productivity of data processing professionals can be enhanced by using AI's exploratory programming and rapid prototyping capabilities to develop applications, and AI's modularity and modifiability capabilities to maintain them.

Knowledge-based database assistants are still leading-edge technology. A number of MIS departments, however, have begun to use knowledge system development tools to solve some of their software development problems and develop conventional MIS applications.

EXPERT DATABASE SYSTEMS

A computer can store lots of information in its databases. Getting the information out of its databases, easily, quickly, and upon demand, is a different matter.

Natural-language database access programs were the first step toward simplifying database access. The next step is intelligent database assistants.

Intelligent database assistants combine knowledge of database content, database access methods, general business information, and reasoning capabili-

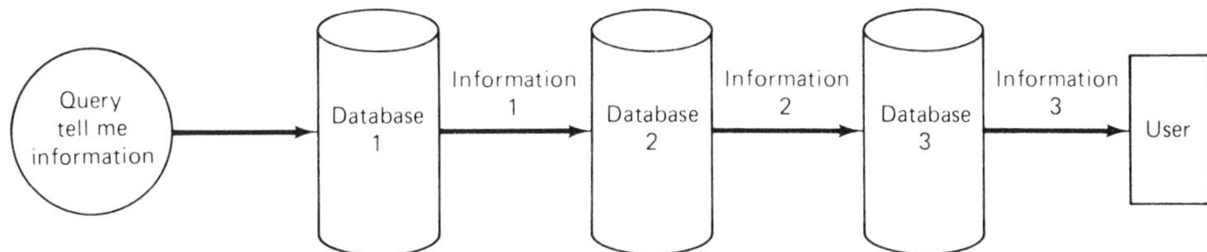

Figure 21-1 Database assistants use information retrieved from one database to retrieve information from others.

ties. They use this knowledge for two purposes: to determine the best and fastest strategy to get information from one or more databases, and to try to provide answers that make sense.

Among other things, database assistants aim to be able to query multiple databases to respond to a user's request. For example, they might use their knowledge of database content and access methods to generate a query to retrieve data from one database, then use that data to retrieve other data from a second database. This retrieved information may be used as an index into still a third database (Figure 21-1).

Fred and Minet are examples of a database assistant. Fred knows how to access multiple medical information databases (Minet). Minet, which was developed at General Telephone and Electronics (GTE) in conjunction with the American Medical Association (AMA), contains databases of medical information such as a drug database, an adverse reactions database, and a disease database. Fred, under development at GTE, can generate database strategies to search more than one of the databases to answer queries such as "Is there a drug and a disease for which a symptom is common to both?"

UNDERSTANDING HUMAN MOTIVATION

Another goal of intelligent database assistants is to use general and database knowledge to make sense out of users' requests by understanding not only the request, but also the users' motivation for the request. Database access programs today do not perform motivation analysis. They return to users the information they requested, but often in such a way that the database programs appear to be noncooperative, even smart-alecks, and they practice a technique that database experts call "stonewalling."

For example, users who query an automobile dealer's database as to how many new model cars were sold in July might receive an answer of "0" (zero). The user then might conclude that July was a bad month for new car sales, or that this particular automobile dealership is having sales problems. It happens that a similar query that asks how many new model cars were for sale in July might also

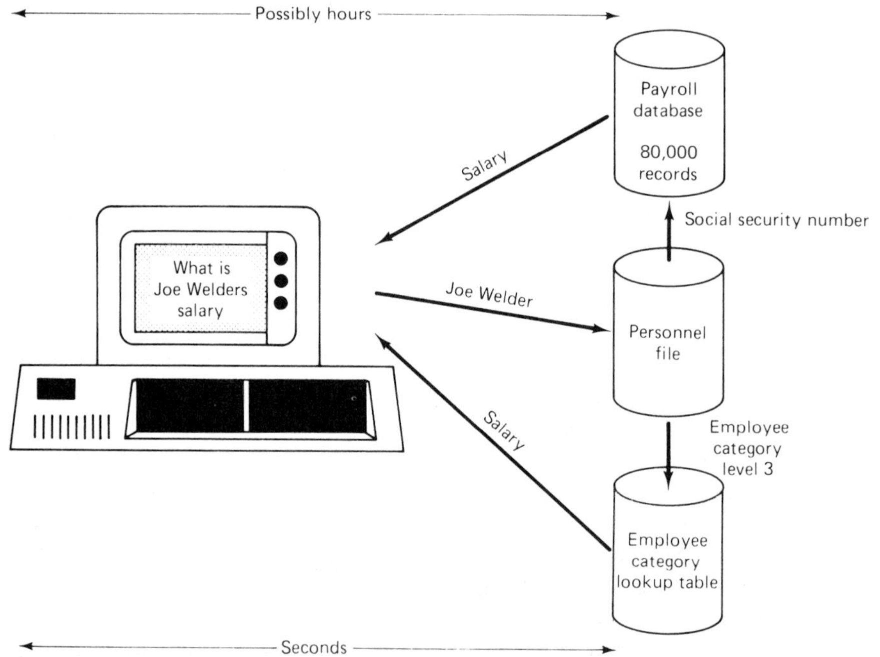

Figure 21-2 A knowledge-based database interface uses knowledge about databases to find the shortest, fastest path to answer a user query.

result in an answer of "0" because July is too early for dealerships to receive new model cars.

If database interfaces sometimes stonewall users by providing too little information, they may act equally uncooperatively by providing too much. For example, an Austin, Texas, nightclub owner that queries a national musician's organization database for names of guitar players to form a three-piece band probably does not want a listing of 12,000 musicians across the country. More likely, the nightclub owner would appreciate a response based on a few, well-chosen questions such as, "Are you interested only in the musicians within a 50-mile radius of Austin?"

Database searches tend to be time-consuming. So a third goal of intelligent database interfaces is to reduce this search time by using their knowledge and heuristics to generate an "intelligent" rather than a "brute force" search strategy. For example, a database querier who needs Joe Welder's salary might decide that the payroll database is the logical place to obtain it. However, the payroll database is large and complex to search. Worse, the payroll database generally does not contain employee names. Access is by means of social security numbers, which must first be obtained from the personnel file.

A human database expert or an AI-based database interface both have the knowledge to realize that the user query is about a salary, and the database says that salary is an attribute of people. They infer that only people have salaries, so Joe Welder must be an instance of the object category "people." Therefore, they proceed to the personnel file, which they know has people information. The personnel file is simpler than the payroll database because it has fewer items, fewer relationships, and less volume.

The personnel file might directly list Joe Welder's salary. However, there is even an easier way to find Joe Welder's salary. Many institutions assign different types of employees to salary categories. The categories are listed in the personnel file; the salaries for the categories are then listed in a separate look-up table. Upon discovering that Joe is an employee in category welder level number 3, and knowing that this employee category commands a fixed salary, an expert database assistant can look up the fixed salary for welder level 3 in the brief, easy-to-search lookup table (Figure 21-2).

SEARCHING FOR SHIPS

A database with these kinds of smarts was jointly developed at Stanford University and SRI International. Called Quist, the database contains information about 34,000 merchant ships (3,000 of which are tankers), and interfaces to a knowledge-based system. The knowledge system generates database access strategies of a type normally attributed to human intelligence. The strategies generated are based on knowledge of database content and general heuristic knowledge about the items contained in the database.

An oil-shipping example illustrates Quist's capabilities. Normally, a database system requires that a user, who wants to know how much oil is exported from China, look through all of the bills of lading for each ship in the database in order to find out when oil was loaded in China. This is a time-consuming search because every ship makes about a dozen trips and goes into at least a dozen ports each year. Furthermore, each bill of lading can have hundreds of items on it. Therefore, a response requires a search of millions of records.

Quist uses its knowledge to narrow its search. It ignores vessels such as grain ships, ore ships, coal ships, freight ships, and fishing boats, because it knows that oil is normally carried in tankers. Therefore, it only has to search the records of 3,000 tankers, instead of 34,000 ships. As a side benefit, a tanker is an invariant attribute of a ship. Invariant attributes allow construction of an index, which in this case allows 3,000 tankers to be found very quickly. Each tanker found, for each port, has a single bill of lading with one entry. Quist uses the bills of lading only to compute how much oil was loaded by the number of tankers that went to a port in China (Figure 21-3).

Under some circumstances, the difference might be seconds versus hours for the search. To be sure, such a search might miss oil that was carried out of China in barrels on freighters or by pipeline.

However, a knowledge-based interface would be less likely to flunk this query than a conventional database interface because the knowledge base would

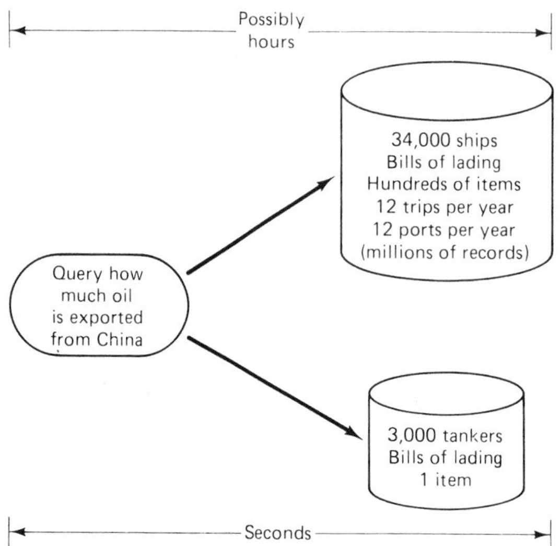

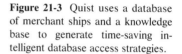

Figure 21-3 Quist uses a database of merchant ships and a knowledge base to generate time-saving intelligent database access strategies.

contain heuristics about what it is logical to assume in shipping oil. Quist rules and heuristics, for example, were developed after collaboration with Exxon, and they incorporate general knowledge about shipping procedures and ships.

AI BOOSTS DATA PROCESSING PRODUCTIVITY

No one needs to tell data processing professionals that they are in the midst of a software crisis. The application backlog, and the large amount of software that is delivered late and over budget proves that. Furthermore, much software never quite performs its intended function. Therefore, the most important use that data processing professionals see for AI is to facilitate application development.

THE SOFTWARE DEVELOPMENT PROBLEM

The application backlog is created by the growing number of software applications in almost every industry and organization. The increasing demand for software applications is so great that it is literally impossible for the limited number of good software designers to keep up with it. The problem is compounded by the software maintenance time and costs.

Software "maintenance" refers to the modifying, redesigning, and rewriting of software that has already been produced. Maintenance today is the largest cost of software. It averages about 70 percent of the life-cycle of a software system according to a General Motors' study.

There are two major reasons for this maintenance expense. Either users' needs change and, therefore, applications based on those needs must change, or the user's specification of the software requirements was faulty, and the application design conformed to the faulty requirements.

If a completed application must be modified after it is in production, the cost of making changes is, according to several companies' estimates, up to 25 times the cost of developing it. Moreover, sometimes the software cannot be properly fixed. There are two noteworthy cases: United Airlines and the U.S. Air Force Logistics Systems each cancelled its software system after spending $56 million and $200 million, respectively, in development.

One reason for these software problems is that traditional software development methods do not support ways for users to see what they are getting until the software is completed. Few people would buy a car or contract for a house without first looking at models, pictures, or blueprints. Unfortunately, there are no similar models, pictures, or blueprints to show users what their software looks like. Worse, the abstract nature of software, together with the rapid growth in software's ability to solve complex problems, makes it difficult for users to accurately foresee how their application will turn out.

To ease this problem, the software engineering community recommends that users build prototypes just as airlines and other industries do. A software prototype is a scaled-down version of the final program that focuses on the functions that the user requires. It is studied by users to see if it meets requirements, needs additional options, and can be modified to meet future business changes. The real software package built is based on the prototype.

Alas, traditional software development methods do not permit rapid prototyping except for small applications, nor do they allow easy, inexpensive software modification.

WHAT AI CAN DO FOR TRADITIONAL SOFTWARE DEVELOPMENT

Traditional approaches to designing applications produce full-scale programs based on requirements that were decided on and then frozen. The traditional programs produced are very difficult to modify because a change to one part of an application affects other parts of the application.

AI programs are produced incrementally, so small-scale executable programs are always available. Furthermore, AI programs are easily modifiable because of their modular architecture. Most important, AI technology is not limited to producing AI programs. It can be used to create conventional applications that have the rapid prototyping and modifiability characteristics of AI programs.

Consequently, a number of large user and vendor companies expect AI to ultimately be widely used to bridge the communications gap between end-users and data processing professionals who develop applications for the end-users. Toward this end, AI tools and languages would be integrated with procedural languages used in Management Information Systems (MIS) departments. The emphasis in the systems built with AI technology would be less on knowledge acquisition of scarce or disappearing expertise, and more on changing the economics of ordinary programming systems.

Initially, knowledge system tools and shells will be used for MIS application development. Eventually, AI-like extensions to conventional languages could also be a solution. For example, an IBM research effort into the use of AI in conventional MIS programming employs an IBM tool called YES/L1. YES/L1 is an extension of PL/1 that adds AI rules and capabilities based on the OPS5 language to the conventional, procedural PL/1. YES/L1 acts as a PL/1 preprocessor and outputs compilable PL/1 code.

Users will not be aware of any AI in the applications developed. The only difference between the applications developed via conventional and AI techniques is in the way the programmer approaches the program.

For example, either conventional or AI techniques can be used to write a simple routine that merges two sorted files into a single ordered file. On a conventional computer, the best way to merge the files is to successively compare the first items in each file and output the record with the smallest key into a third table, repeating the process until both files are empty.

A conventional program that implements this algorithm typically requires three dummy variables to serve as indices into the files, an initialization step for these variables, two if-then-else control constructs nested in a while loop with compound conditions, and various declarations. Furthermore, these constructs and all other program statements and expressions must be sequenced in a specific order.

The same problem can be solved with a rule-based system containing five rules. Rules might encode knowledge such as the following:

1. If the item read in the first file is less than the item in the second file, then pick that smaller item, write it to a third file, and fire this rule again.
2. If the item read in the second file is less than the item in the first file, then pick that smaller item, write it to a third file, and fire this rule again.
3. If the first file is empty, write the items in the second file to the third file.
4. If the second file is empty, write the items in the first file to the third file.
5. If both files are empty, say "goodbye."

The rules are unsequenced, so the order in which the rules are added doesn't matter. Rules can be changed without affecting other rules. The system can be expanded just by adding more rules, also in any order. It is not necessary for programmers to declare variables because the inference mechanism in most AI tools identifies and manages data types. Initialization steps and dummy variables are not needed either. All in all, the algorithmic application built with a rule-based tool produces an application that is easily modifiable, expandable, and shorter and simpler to develop than a traditionally-programmed implementation of the same algorithm.

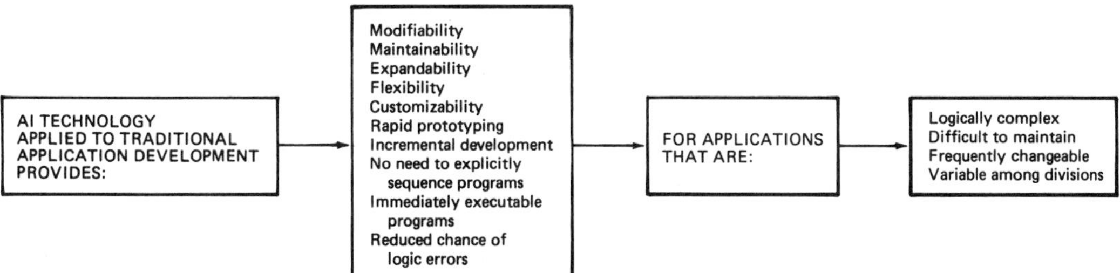

Figure 21-4 Time it takes to prepare to do AI work (Arthur D. Little, Inc.)

WHEN TO USE AI FOR TRADITIONAL SOFTWARE DEVELOPMENT

Programmers will probably not use AI to code algorithmic problems like the merge application because it is more cost-effective to design such a program using traditional techniques. There are two cases, however, where it makes sense for data processing professionals to use AI technology to develop conventional applications, in order to gain AI architectural benefits (Figure 21-4).

One example occurs when the logical analysis required for a program is sufficiently complex to make defining and coding of a specific set of sequential statements for implementing the logic very error-prone and, therefore, very costly. An analysis application from Boole & Babbage will be described that illustrates this situation. Another example occurs in cases when the modification or customization rate of an application is expected to be high. MIS applications developed at Data General and Northern Telecom illustrate this.

AI SIMPLIFIES PROGRAMMING OF LOGICALLY COMPLEX APPLICATIONS

Boole & Babbage used Aion Corp.'s Aion Development System (ADS), running on IBM computers under the MVS operating system, to develop a response manager package for the systems management people who optimize computer execution in computer centers. The response manager package measures, analyzes, and reports on the storage utilization characteristics of Direct Access Storage Devices (DASD) in a multiple, large CPU environment so that disk storage utilization can be optimized.

Computer center performance is dramatically impacted by how the DASD is affected by factors such as channel bottlenecks, control unit bottlenecks, path bottlenecks, rotational position sensing bottlenecks, and how much data is on any particular device. In the past, many companies have gathered information about these factors and produced system reports that were too voluminous to be read or acted on properly. What Boole & Babbage envisioned was a system that could evaluate the data and come up with consolidated reports and recommendations, based on rules of thumb, as to what the different characteristics of the bottlenecks meant.

Boole & Babbage DASD experts were able to analyze the data characteristics measured and describe what the various combinations and permutations of symptoms meant. The impossible problem was using traditional software technology to code a system that represented and analyzed all these characteristics.

Therefore, Boole & Babbage decided to write the program in the ADS rules language. Using the rule-based tool for program development had several benefits. First, Boole & Babbage application developers were able to write down their knowledge of device characteristics, and the performance implications of these characteristics, in the form of the rules-of-thumb with which the experts normally understand their task. The rules-of-thumb are of the form "if condition A and condition B then take action A and action B."

Second, the developers could specify their rules-of-thumb as they came to mind, without having to pre-analyze and specify a sequence for execution of the rules. They just wrote down their understanding of the DASD analysis and optimization process, without programming it, and let the ADS inference engine figure out the sequence for execution. The same application running multiple times, with multiple sets of data inputs, might follow several different sequences based on the differences in the data. However, the developer did not have to worry about defining the different control sequences based on the different types of data input. ADS's AI technology sorted out the data and the appropriate execution sequences.

Third, as the rules-of-thumb were added to the program, they were immediately executable. This made it easy to quickly discover program problems and immediately modify the rules to fix the problem. At the same time, the rule-based technique and incremental development capability eliminated the need to first write a pseudocode sequence and then a formal code sequence.

It took about three months for the application developers and DASD experts to write down, without any order, their understanding of device characteristics, performance implications, and optimization actions. Because the knowledge was written in a rules language, however, the unsequenced knowledge was also the executable program. Boole & Babbage estimates that if its application developers had to go through the normal process of fully analyzing, sequencing, and writing in English what they knew about DASD problems, and then programming that knowledge, it would have taken another sequential year to develop the application.

AI SIMPLIFIES MIS APPLICATION MAINTENANCE

The Boole & Babbage response monitor is an example of a logically-intricate application. The use of knowledge system tools, which could dynamically sequence and synthesize the program, simplified application development and reduced the chances of programming errors.

Knowledge system tools are also being used to develop applications that have a high probability of needing modifications in order to meet changing (or division-specialized) business requirements. The cost of changing the applications if they are built in typical third-generation languages is very high, and sometimes, applications simply become unmaintainable.

The treasury department at Data General had such an almost unmaintainable application, which it rewrote using rules and frames. Called a *Transfer-Pricing* application, the application was originally written in Cobol and it assisted treasury and marketing people in implementing the pricing policies and procedures associated with transferring Data General equipment (products, parts, etc.) to international subsidiaries. However, this kind of application, (which is common to any organization that ships products internationally) must be modifiable because the factors on which a company's pricing policy depends, such as the product, exchange rate, and government regulations, change or fluctuate fairly rapidly. Hence the transfer-pricing policy changes quite often.

Unfortunately, when written in Cobol, Data General's Transfer-Pricing program was a typical software maintenance horror story. The program contained thousands of lines of code. It was written by one group of people, but maintained by another. It was difficult to understand. Compromises made because Cobol did not provide an easy way to model the data the application handled (such as categorizing anything that didn't fit easily into tables of hardware or software parts as hardware) made it difficult to verify whether the policy was being applied correctly or completely.

The treasury department people finally used AI tools to design the new application because they felt that another Cobol program would also develop maintenance problems. If the program was written, instead, using AI paradigms, the program would be easily modifiable. Moreover, the organization imposed on the program by an AI tool would make the program easier to understand.

In the end, the new Transfer-Pricing application was developed with Gold-Works (from Gold Hill Computer), a multiple paradigm tool that runs on 80286- and 80386-based PCs. The application runs on the Hummingboard (an 80386-based single-board computer, also from Gold Hill Computer, that plugs into PC-ATs and XTs) and accesses the corporate bill of materials database.

About 35 rules and 25 frames were required to design this application. From an AI perspective, this isn't a lot of rules. From a business environment perspective, however, major applications with a small number of rules are not unusual because, in some ways, the business world is the inverse of the AI world. In the AI world, programs tend to have a lot of rules and a small amount of data. This contrasts with the business world where very productive applications tend to have large amounts of data but not too many rules.

AI SIMPLIFIES APPLICATION TAILORING

Northern Telecom used the ADS knowledge system tool to develop an engineering change control application that manages engineering change administration and implementation processes. It chose an AI tool to develop this application because the probability that this application would need modification was very great. Northern Telecom is a manufacturing company with a continuously changing product line. The engineering change application would have to reflect these changes. Moreover, changes are constantly proposed by different divisions, each of which have their own procedures for evaluating and approving the changes. The application would have to be tailored to reflect each division's engineering change control procedures.

Northern Telecom's application developers felt that designing the application with an AI architecture and paradigms facilitated program maintenance. The AI technology also provided the simplest way to design an application that allowed different divisions to easily customize it for their requirements.

Overall, engineering change control is an administrative process management application, needed in every engineering and manufacturing company. It is needed because there are numerous evaluation steps between proposal of a product change and the implementation of a product change.

For example, before any proposed product change can be implemented, the effect on every component, subassembly, and assembly impacted by the change must be determined. The change must be justified economically. It must be analyzed for manufacturability. Approvals for the change must be obtained from the many departments affected by the change. If the change is approved, preparation work must be performed before the change can be implemented. This includes checking materials on hand, purchasing materials, establishing new schedules, updating design files and databases, and notifying the people affected.

Before selecting the automated engineering change control system from the MIS application backlog, Northern Telecom primarily used a paper-based system. It was based on a form that was walked from department to department, along with a few on-line systems used for certain tasks.

In 1985, Northern Telecom began work on an automated system. Shortly after, work ground to a halt because the company's various divisions could not agree on a common process to drive the automated engineering change control system. After numerous discussions, it became clear that for the engineering change system to be useful in all divisions, it had to be tunable by each division.

At first, Northern Telecom figured on satisfying this tunability requirement by creating a special language, based on a traditional language. While pursuing this goal, Northern learned of the possible match between its requirements and available AI tools.

The consideration of AI tools introduced an application constraint. The tool selected, and system developed with the tool, had to be compatible with Northern's existing applications. These were written using conventional languages that ran on IBM's VM operating system. The tool and system also had to be compatible with data stored in the SQL/DS database. ADS, the AI tool selected, runs on IBM mainframes under VM, as well as on PCs.

During development, Northern Telecom constructed a prototype system both on PCs and under VM. The ADS-based prototype was tested for its ability to talk to existing applications and to SQL. The user-programmability features were also tested since one application goal was to send a basic model of the engineering change control system to every Northern Telecom division, along with some end-user tools, so each division could tweak the engineering change process to meet its own business requirements. After testing, Northern Telecom decided that, the knowledge system tools provided a more cost-effective way to build a user-tunable application than did conventional techniques.

Joseph Sura, manager of computer-aided manufacturing at Northern Telecom and chief designer of the engineering change control system, points out that to operate any of the knowledge system shells (he investigated most of them) requires some computer knowlege and programming experience. "The AI technology makes the programmers' jobs easier, compared to conventional languages, and provides about a 30 to 40 percent productivity advantage. However, at this point in AI tool evolution, anyone who uses AI for conventional projects will wind up wanting to do little things not accommodated by the tool. That takes knowlege of the computer environment, operating system features, database access methods, and so on."

DEVELOPING THE TRADITIONAL APPLICATION WITH AI TOOLS

Northern Telecom's AI-designed engineering change control system, and the task of developing it, was unlike anything in most people's traditional or AI programming experiences. From the end-user's perspective, the application appears to be a menu-driven system with conventional functions such as on-line queries, on-line documentation reports, and data entry screens (Figure 21-5). The system asks the users a minimum number of questions, designed to be as intelligent and relevant as possible. Which questions to ask are determined by switching blocks of code on and off, based on previous answers given to questions. Users can also query the system and see the composite of the change information assembled so far.

To system managers, who implement and maintain the application in various divisions, the system appears quite different. The underlying system consists of a different set of functions and easy-to-use developer interfaces for example, for defining rules, screens, authorized users, and knowledge bases. When the application is designed, engineering change modules, which include both the system manager and end-user functions shown in Figure 21-4, are associated with all engineering, manufacturing, and business departments that have the potential to create or approve changes.

To acquire the knowledge for the knowledge base, the Northern Telecom application developers went through a dialogue that spanned a two-week period

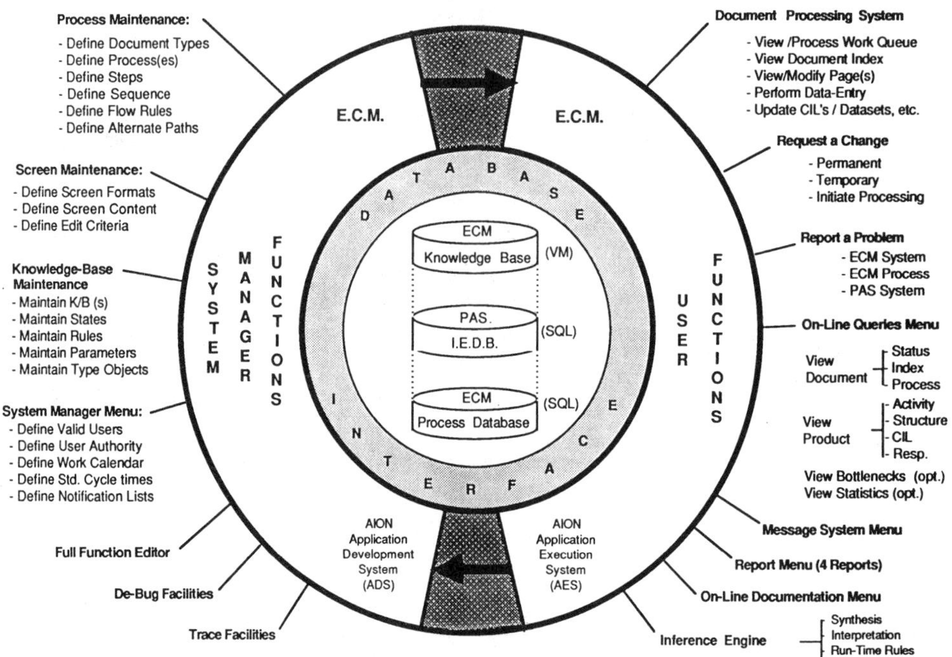

Figure 21-5 Contents of Phase 01 ECM System.

and 15 departments. As they proceeded, the developers grew an intelligent dialogue and knowledge about product changes. The dialogue and knowledge encompassed every stage in the engineering change process, beginning with the proposal of the change, through the stages where the change is evaluated, qualified, economically justified, and implemented. The dialogue and knowledge gained about each stage in the engineering change process were incrementally added to the application at each step.

The dialogue was incorporated in the on-screen, menu-driven questions to be asked of the appropriate departments. The knowledge was encoded in rules related to the departments and to each stage of the engineering change process. The rules encode knowledge about economic justification, expected benefits, materials, manufacturability, test fixtures, implementation, and more.

As the system executes, these rules determine whether or not to approve a change, as well as when to implement an approved change. When the system executes, a series of initial questions is asked of the person proposing the change. The answers to the initial questions, along with rules associated with those questions, are used to characterize the nature of a proposed change.

Once the change is characterized, the system sets up the rest of the process flow. The proposed change, with the knowledge characterizing it, is mailed, electronically, to the next department. When that department completes its data entry requirements, it electronically mails the engineering change information to the next appropriate department.

To prevent information and questions from getting lost in someone's electronic in-basket, the system developers designed the system with many features of a manufacturing monitoring system. These include time allocations for data entry about a proposed change, exception reporting, bottleneck reporting, and the ability to issue snapshot queries that show the location and status of everything in the engineering change process.

The coding of the engineering change system was completed in October of 1987. Implementation then began with a user acceptance testing phase. Production operation is scheduled for the first quarter of 1988 at Northern Telecom in Santa Clara, followed by rollout of the system to 17 other divisions.

MORE KNOWLEDGE NEEDED

It's partly the sheer unfamiliarity of AI, in addition to its still high perceived risk, that will delay the widespread adoption of this commercially new software technology in traditional data processing. Potential users need a better understanding of what AI can do for them, and MIS managers need to overcome their resistance to change—much as an earlier generation did in making the switch from assembly language to high-level languages.

Remedying this state of affairs will take time. The need for time is pretty much normal since commercial adoption of new technology is almost always an evolutionary rather than revolutionary, process. However, there is no doubt that, for logically intensive applications and for applications that are highly susceptible and costly to change, AI technology can provide very large, rather than incremental, productivity improvements. Over time, these benefits will make AI a practical alternative to third generation languages.

22

AI in Science and Real-Time Process Control

With every blessing, there is a curse. The newest blessings are the advanced technology gadgets and gear that have pervaded commercial, industrial, scientific, and military organizations. They help perform many tasks for these organizations better, faster, and cheaper than ever. In the case of scientific organizations, they help perform tasks and achieve goals never previously possible at all.

The curse is the complexity of these gadgets and gear, as well as the huge amount of information they produce. Scientific- and technology-oriented organizations have developed instruments to collect data—from underground to detect oil, from space and underwater to distinguish threatening objects and distant galaxies, and on earth where they determine chemical, biological, and medical information about subatomic particles and life processes.

The flaw in this wizard technology is that to use the data-collecting instruments correctly requires a degree of training and expertise that few people possess or have time to acquire. Once collected, the data must be analyzed and interpreted. The experts who perform such analyses and interpretations are scarce, hard to get, and very expensive. Moreover, the amount of information collected for analysis and interpretation are frequently too massive for human information-processing capabilities to cope with. There are software tools to help analyze the data. Unfortunately, the software is often very difficult to use properly and, consequently, may be used incorrectly or infrequently.

AI can help companies and organizations in diverse fields deal with the complexity of equipment, and with information overload in several different ways. For example, knowledge-based systems can act as intelligent interfaces to equipment. In that capacity, the knowledge systems assume some of the burdensome tasks necessary to use the equipment. They also call attention to the most important gauge and meter readings, which they differentiate from the less significant ones. Another type of knowledge system helps experts analyze data. Still other types of knowledge systems can act as guides to the proper use of software.

CONFUSION

The importance of knowledge-based systems in equipment complexity and information-overload situations becomes clear from experiences of engineers in several types of organizations, such as in the nuclear reactor power plant at Three Mile Island. There, a pipe, in a peripheral system to a nuclear generator, sprang a leak and resulted in radiation leakage to the atmosphere. In less than a minute, more than 400 different alarms went off at once, signaling to the control room operators that multiple systems and components were malfunctioning and required their instant attention.

Similarly, a control room system operator in an oil refinery was also confronted with the problem of alarm overload. In an oil refinery which breaks down crude petroleum into the refined gasoline products that make internal combustion engines run, every step in the process must have a certain yield. But when the control room operator received a dozen signals at once, telling him that a dozen yields were below par, and each demanding an instant decision, the operator only felt confused and helpless.

Control panels, which form the human-operator interface to the controlling instrumentation for generators, test equipment, industrial processes, dams, outer-space missions, and so on, contain between fifty and several hundred gauges, meters, digital readouts, buzzers, and flashing lights. Should an emergency occur, human operators, acting under pressure, are expected to read, interpret, and act on this large quantity of displayed data. At Three Mile Island, for example, decisions that needed to be made instantly included specific actions to isolate the leak, in addition to more cosmic decisions such as whether to evacuate the area adjacent to the plant.

In such a high-pressure situation, it certainly would be human for a person to miss, misread, or misinterpret something. Compounding the problem is the fact that one malfunction in a system may cause about twenty other things to appear to be wrong.

SMART CONTROL PANELS

One purpose of knowledge-based-system interfaces to complex control systems is to indicate only true malfunctions and distinguish between their primary and secondary causes. To do this, they contain knowledge of the instrument-controlled system.

Reactors is an example of a knowledge-based intelligent interface system, built for the electric power and utility industry, under the auspices of the Electrical Power Research Institute (EPRI) (members of which generate about 70 percent of the country's electrical power). Designed with IntelliCorp's KEE knowledge system application development tool, Reactors interfaces to the controlling instrumentation in a nuclear power plant and performs status, monitoring, and diagnostic functions in emergency and routine situations. Its knowledge base contains knowledge of the machines it is monitoring, what happens when a fault occurs in one of them, and how the different components, machines, and subsystems in the nuclear plant interact. The knowledge is contained in frames and rules. The frames contain knowledge about all the components in a nuclear power plant. The rules contain knowledge of faults in the plant and their possible causes.

Reactors also contains graphical representations of meters, dials, gauges, alarm indicators, and some objects in the nuclear power plant. The graphical indicators are associated with frame slots that describe allowable operating values for measurable or observable physical parameters of components of the plant. In addition, the Reactors control panel includes sets of NORMAL—CAUTION—ALARM indicators that describe the operating status of the plant, reactor subsystems, and plant component parts. The knowledge system uses these graphical representations to simulate a control panel and to help explain events in the plant (Figure 22-1).

To perform its analysis and diagnostic functions, Reactors uses its knowledge of allowable attribute values for plant components, and a concept known as "active values." Active values means that if the attribute values an expert system designer has designated "active" are changed, certain procedures are automatically invoked, thus providing data-driven control of the Reactors' system operation.

Some of these procedures update the values displayed on the graphical control panel for users to examine. Other procedures check to see whether certain events have occurred. What events to check for is governed by Reactors' rules. Significant events are recorded in Reactors' memory. The rule interpreter then performs backward or forward chaining to propagate the effects of these events and to reason about their implications.

For example, the forward chainer is invoked when an event occurs, such as the coolant level in a reactor containment vessel becoming low. This "low-coolant-level" event will cause the preconditions of some rules to become true. The THEN part of these rules may designate some consequent action to be taken, or the new value to be stored in an appropriate frame slot for an object associated with the value. Changing this value invokes KEE's active value mechanism which invokes other procedures, one of which is to report the new value to the user, via the graphic display.

Backward-chaining strategies are invoked to analyze the new plant state,

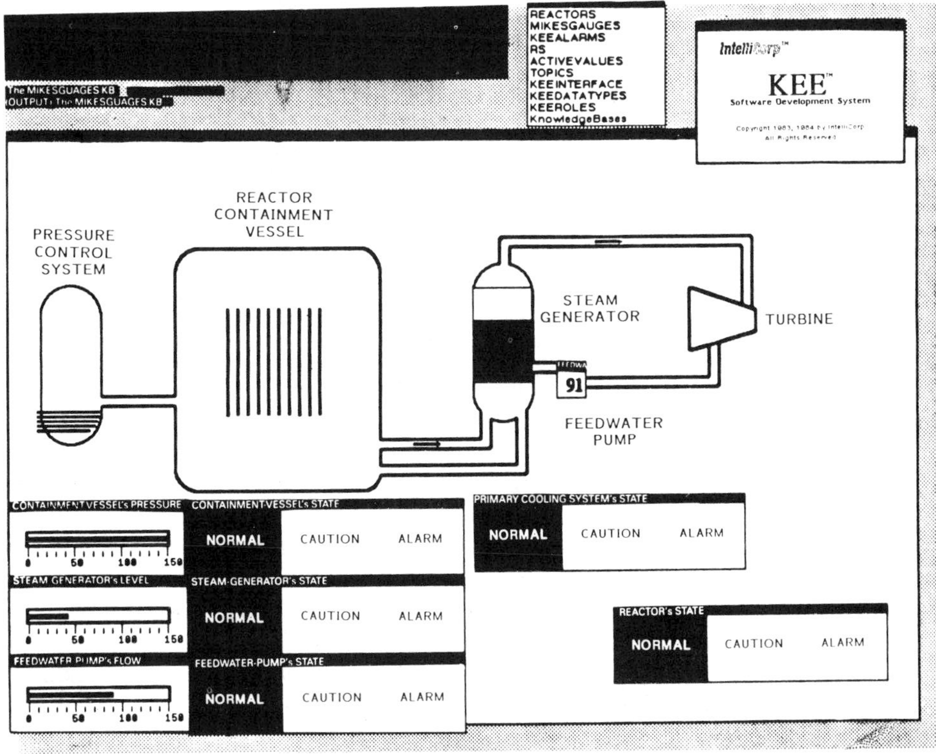

Figure 22-1 Reactors knowledge-based control panel (Program copyrights © 1983. 1984 by IntelliCorp. All rights reserved.)

based on new values. Interaction between forward and backward chaining allows a mixed bottom-up and top-down analysis of data.

For example, to find out the current state of the plant, reactor subsystems, or components, users type a pseudo-English query into the Reactors program. Reactors responds to this status request not only by graphically presenting simulated control panel readouts and a displayed status and diagnosis, but also an explanation graph showing how it reached its conclusion. The explanation graph in Figure 22-2 shows the current state of R1 (Reactor 1) is loss of feedwater. To reach this conclusion, Reactors examines its knowledge base. There, it finds that rule 5 has the five conditions shown in the middle of Figure 22-2. It obtains its knowledge about whether these conditions are satisfied either from facts in frames, sensor data, previously concluded information, the user, or by inferring new knowledge through other rules. In this case, to infer whether the heat transfer of SCS1 is inadequate, Reactors chains backward to rule 2.

Rule 2 has four conditions, as shown. They are shown to be true by the same methods used to test rule 5. Therefore, rule 5 is satisfied and Reactors displays

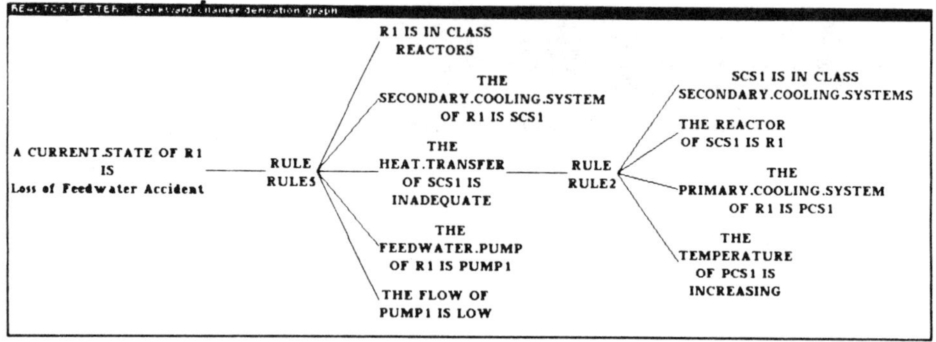

Figure 22-2 Reactors explanation graph (Program copyrights © 1983, 1984 by IntelliCorp. All rights reserved.)

and explains to the user the status of the power plant, which also can be the cause of an accident.

Armed with this knowledge and reasoning capability, a knowledge system interface is not likely to be misled by false malfunction alarms that are set off by malfunctions elsewhere. Therefore, it can filter out some of the irrelevant warnings before it communicates with the user.

However, the knowledge system does not totally eliminate what it considers to be irrelevant warning data from the information presented to system operators. Instead, it calls attention to certain gauges and presents to the operator a hypothesis that states what it believes to be the major problem and how this assumption of the main problem explains all the other warning indicators. But it makes sure that the operator is aware of the other warning indicators since they could indicate either other minor problems or even a knowledge system error.

KNOWLEDGE-BASED PROCESS CONTROL PROGRAMS

Few companies have to worry about nuclear reactors. However, process control industries, which are at the heart of industrial America, also have highly elaborate control systems. As with nuclear power plants, knowledge-based interfaces to these control systems can help monitor the thousands of process variables and the constant stream of information delivered to the control room. Knowledge-based interfaces also can help handle multiple alarms when a crisis occurs. This helps keep the process control companies operating at peak efficiency.

Exxon Corp., Johnson Controls Inc., Leeds & Northrup Co., and Texaco have operational knowledge-based interfaces to process control systems. They developed these interfaces using LMI's Picon, a menu- and graphics-oriented tool with a partially precanned knowledge base containing process-control knowledge.

Picon became the model tool of its kind and it spurred the addition of real-time and menu capabilities to a number of diverse application-development tools. Alas, Picon's future turned uncertain when LMI's future turned uncertain. Meanwhile, a second generation of process-control development tools arose that had greater knowledge capabilities and emphasis on application portability.

Gensym Corporation's G2, for example, is an AI application development tool for building knowledge-based interfaces to large, real-time applications where hundreds or thousands of variables are monitored concurrently. It was developed for the process control industry, but it can just as well be used for such applications as financial trading, network monitoring, and automatic testing. Not intended for programmers, G2 contains a knowledge base with generic process-control knowledge and menu and graphical aids to help application-oriented professionals enter the knowledge specific to their process plant.

G2 has two major components: a knowledge-analysis program and a real-time communications-gateway module. The knowledge-based component receives data from the gateway program, reasons about the data, and offers advice about critical process-control points of interest, multiple alarms, and diagnosis of trouble spots. The gateway module communicates with a network of data acquisition equipment, sensors, alarm systems, work-cell controllers, and factory minicomputers. The gateway receives data in real time from these devices and computers and passes the data to the knowledge program for knowledge analysis.

FOCUS ON THE RELEVANT THINGS

Data gathered for analysis is generally sampled from many machines, perhaps 10 to 100 times a second, and results in vast quantities of data. Neither humans nor computer programs can efficiently handle this amount of data.

Human operators attempting to monitor a large, real-time system do not continuously evaluate all this data. They maintain peripheral awareness of the system, but respond to key changes by selectively focusing their attention on certain areas of the system.

Early knowledge systems were not so selective. Backward- and forward-chaining were their major inferencing techniques. These techniques work by exhaustively searching large segments of the system's knowledge and data for certain patterns. Each time they find a pattern match, they repeat the process based on new intermediate conclusions and patterns established. Exclusive use of this technique is inherently slow for large, on-line, real-time problems. Knowledge systems can achieve greater performance and efficiency, however, if they support "metaknowledge." Metaknowledge is knowledge about knowledge, such as when different types of knowledge should be applied, and what knowledge should be invoked to handle certain situations.

For example, most of the time G2 uses only a subset of knowledge—the equivalent of peripheral knowledge. During its reasoning process, G2 uses heuristic rules, frames, and time-dependent dynamic analytic models to determine what disturbances are significant, which are cause for alarm, and what components in the process control plant are critical to developing problems. Other heuristics, including metaknowledge, then cause G2 to focus attention on the critical process nodes surrounding an actual or possible disturbance. At that time G2 decides what knowledge is necessary to analyze and diagnose the problem. It invokes the appropriate knowledge, reads relevant sensors, and chains through the rules concerning only the trouble spot on which it is focusing.

To help ensure the validity of analyses and diagnoses, G2 supports what is known as a "truth maintenance" system. A truth maintenance system is one that maintains the truth of a knowledge system's conclusions because whenever some data (or knowledge) changes, then the system changes the conclusions that are based upon that data. Without such a system, the programmer must attend to this chore.

Truth maintenance is more important for real-time systems than static systems because lots of real-time data can change rapidly. Furthermore, in a real-time system, it may be necessary to change the conclusions even though data has not changed. This may happen if the conclusion is based on old data. Therefore, to ensure the validity of a conclusion, real-time knowledge systems must change their conclusions not only when data changes, but also based on whether the data gathered is new enough to represent the truth.

Determining whether the data, and the inferences, and final conclusions based on the data, are still valid takes time, and time is a scarce resource in a real-time system. A focus mechanism, such as G2's, can optimize this time because it allows the knowledge system to concern itself with updating only conclusions that are the current focus of interest. This is analogous to people's lack of concern with the cross traffic for the street they just passed because that street is no longer their focus of interest.

PORTABILITY AND COMMUNICATIONS

Knowledge-analysis benefits notwithstanding, it is G2's design for portability and communications that makes its knowledge-based applications practical. They are practical because G2's design allows users to integrate new knowledge capabilities with existing process-control applications.

With a world emerging where manufacturing plants are demanding standards, communications compatibility, and software transportability, Gensym implemented G2 in standard Common Lisp. G2 runs on a variety of Lisp machines and traditional computers. These include Symbolics' Lisp machines, Texas Instruments' Explorers, DEC VAX (under VMS), Hewlett-Packard's 9000, Sun Microsystems' Sun 3 Workstation, and Gold Hill Computers' Hummingboard (plugged into PC-XTs and ATs). The gateway module can run in the same computer as the knowledge program or in a separate processor. Running in the same computer has the advantage of lower cost; the separate processor approach, however, provides higher performance.

Communications between knowledge systems across a network is via public-domain or industry standard protocols such as TCP/IP, MAP, and Decnet. Communications is via shared memory if the two processors run on the same bus (e.g. the Lisp and Unix processors in the Explorer LX). A network can be configured with multiple gateways, each linked to multiple knowledge systems. With such a setup, any of the knowledge systems can access any of the gateways.

INSIDE THE PROCESS-CONTROL KNOWLEDGE SYSTEM

G2 uses schematic diagrams, frames, heuristic rules, and dynamic models to represent an application expert's process-control knowledge. The beauty of using schematics in the knowledge system is that they are a well-recognized, widely-used way to represent a process. However, in several ways, G2's schematics are more than a drawing of components and connections.

For one, the schematics are tightly integrated into the knowledge base. This means that as a process engineer draws the schematic on the computer, the knowledge base automatically understands the connectivity between the components. Second, frames representing knowledge about the components in a schematic are attached to the schematic. This means that as the engineer adds components to the schematic, the knowledge base automatically knows about those components.

Third, rules are also integrated with schematics. This allows the engineer to define rules with general knowledge, but the knowledge system will use the schematic to determine which specific components in a process system are appropriate for applying the knowledge. An example is a general statement of knowledge that might say:

> If any valve has changed more than 10% in the last minute
>   And if there is a flowmeter in the same line
>   And if it has not changed in the last minute by at least 2%
> Then consider that possibly the valve is stuck

The knowledge system uses the schematic to trace components and connections in order to locate and interpret each specific valve and flowmeter. If necessary, the knowledge system will feed values from one component to another.

A fourth type of knowledge that can be attached to schematics in G2 is dynamic analytic models. This type of knowledge is needed because real-time systems must be able to represent behavior over time. Differential equations are the basic dynamic analytic model for representing timed behavior in real-time process-control applications because differential equations provide continuous time analysis.

Process control systems use the dynamic analytic models to compare expected performance to observed performance for the purpose of detecting problems with the measurements or with the process itself, such as unexpected reactions. A continuous (dynamic) rather than discrete (static) model is necessary in process control applications to predict heat, temperature, and pressure, etc., changes over time. If monitoring of sensors shows deviations from expected behavior, these deviations can be detected before alarm limits are reached.

Unfortunately, there is no practical way to represent continuous timed behavior with heuristic rules. Knowledge systems that represent time usually do so in a static way, for example, by defining certain rules or frames for a discrete time period or by programming a state machine where the state of the machine changes with ticks of a timer.

HOW TO WRITE A REAL-TIME KNOWLEDGE SYSTEM

Since G2 is intended for use by process engineers and operators without extensive AI knowledge, G2 has a number of programming aids for application development. The programming aids consist of a natural-language, menu- and icon-driven, interactive graphics system, and G2's ability to capture knowledge directly from schematics.

To develop an expert application, process engineers begin by drawing a schematic to represent their system. For example, the schematic in Figure 22-3 represents part of Reliable Water Company's (Boston, Mass.) reversible osmosis water purification system that is controlled by a G2-based knowledge system. The schematic shows valves, pumps, process units, filtration units, and flow lines. As Figure 22-3 (bottom) shows, users can zoom in on any part of the schematic.

As the process engineer draws the schematic, G2 captures the component/icon information, its type, connections, and relationship to the process control plant. It then programs the necessary information in Lisp to represent the entire process plant schematic as a data structure.

At the same time, the process engineer defines a frame for each component in the system. As the engineer draws the schematic, G2 automatically captures information about the components to enter in the appropriate frame. This captured information forms part of the knowledge base. Similarly, a high-level interface allows process engineers to specify dynamic analytic models. For example, time-based properties of variables, such as rate of change and time series statistics are expressable in structured natural language.

The last part of the knowledge base is composed of rules. A menu-oriented interface interactively guides process engineers in entering and editing rules. The syntax and grammar in the menus are appropriate to real-time applications, and the grammer can be customized to specific application domains. This technique for constructing rules is similar to that used by Picon, and is becoming a standard concept in the knowledge systems industry.

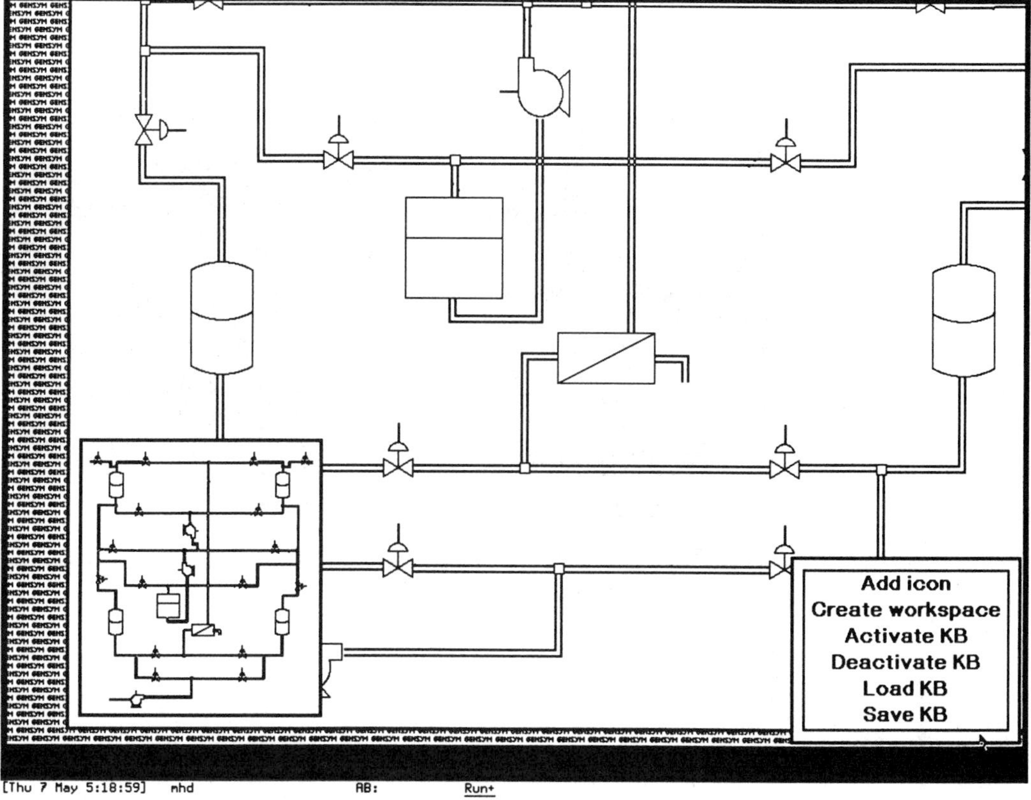

Figure 22-3 G2 captures knowledge from schematics to build models of process control plants (Gensym Corp.).

A BUG-FREE WAY TO CONSTRUCT RULES

To help the process engineer or knowledge system designer capture the system rules, Picon provides a menu which contains word and phrase choices that are strung together to form conditional clauses and consequences of a rule (Figure 22-4). The program knows the legal grammar for the knowledge system rules and will not accept anything but a grammatical sentence (although it will accept nonsensical physical constants).

Users begin all rules by choosing IF with the mouse. As the rule is built up, it is shown in the readout section (middle) of the screen. Next, users pick a process unit—in this case, furnace. Similarly, they pick from the menu building blocks a variable and logical operator and then type in a constant, using the math package—in this case, 60. Information such as messages, focus information, possible diagnoses, or actions to take are entered in the system by application experts.

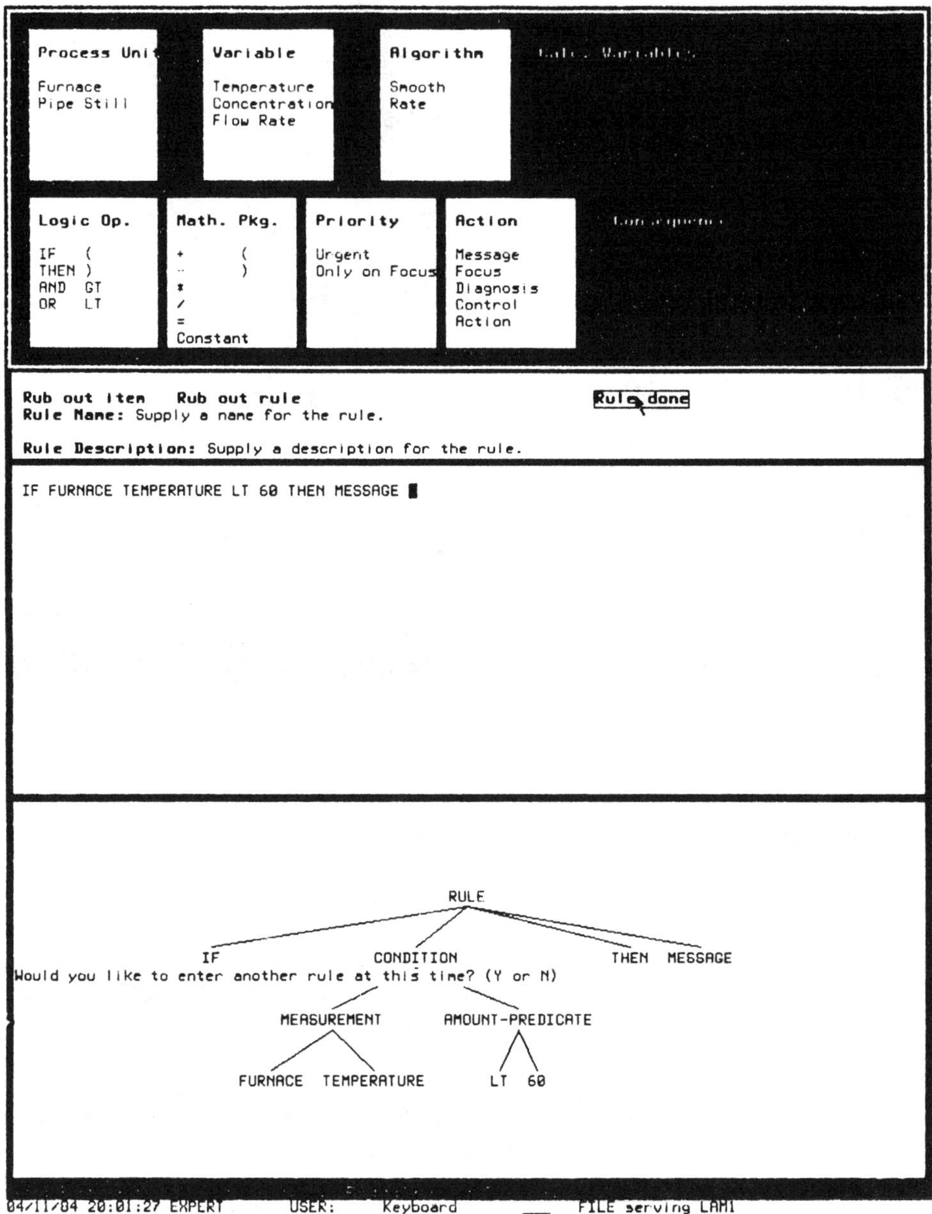

Figure 22-4 Picon provides a menu of choices to construct rules (LISP Machine Inc.)

The bottom window in Figure 22-4 is a graphical parsing window that shows, graphically, Picon's understanding of the rule. Once the rules are formed or modified, they can be executed. If a rule is added or changed, it is not necessary to recompile and relink the knowledge system. Lisp systems handle all that dynamically. Consequently, users can evolve their own knowledge systems. They begin with the rules they know. As the system performs, it is challenged with new tasks, and makes errors. Users determine that the error would not have been made if the system knew about this-and-this under that-and-that condition. Then they use the Picon programming tool to guide them in adding the new information, in rule form, without having to call in programmers.

SMART INSTRUMENTS

An innovative intelligent software interface helps individuals in any field to use complex instruments, but is particularly important in scientific organizations. These organizations have a number of expensive, complex, nongeneric instruments that are not only difficult to use, but difficult to set up for use.

Lawrence Livermore Laboratories has made life easier for its scientists by using the KEE application development tool to build an intelligent interface to a Triple Quadripole Mass Spectrometer (TQMS). A mass spectrometer analyzes chemical structures by bombarding a chemical with energetic electrons, separating the resulting fragments according to their mass-to-charge ratio, and plotting the relative intensities of the signals (which corresponds to the abundance of the ions that impinge upon a collector plate) versus the mass-to-energy ratios. The plot, called a mass spectrogram, is highly characteristic of a particular compound with a particular structure.

The TQMS requires special tuning procedures for different experimental situations. To tune the instrument, users need to know both the characteristics of the experiments and of the components of the instruments. Each experimental situation requires a multistep tuning procedure and manipulation of a large number of interactive controls to optimally tune the instrument. Unfortunately, the manual tuning of one set of controls to optimize certain characteristics during one stage of the tuning process is likely to influence and upset other characteristics of the machine optimized during a prior tuning stage.

When that happens (and such a happening is a rule rather than an exception) the tuner must backtrack to the upset, prior stage and start over from there. Compounding this tuning problem is the difficulty of immediately telling whether the machine is truly optimally tuned for a particular experimental situation.

Typically, the user/expert/tuner adjusts controls until an attached display device produces a desired curve shape. Through experience, the user develops a heuristic insight into how the instrument components interact in order to produce the desired curve shape. The problems of tuning complex instruments are exclusive of whether the instrument is applicable to a chemical, electrical, or physical domain.

WHAT'S IN THE INTERFACE?

The knowledge system/intelligent interface to the TQMS at Lawrence Livermore Labs is a combination rule and frame base system whose knowledge base contains the different types of knowledge necessary to tune the instrument. For example, there are several classes of experimental situations whose characteristics the interface knows about. In addition, for each of these classes, it knows what the approximate initial tuning is and how to go about performing it.

Each component of the TQMS has an underlying frame-based knowledge representation in the TQMS knowledge system. This frame representation (called "units" in KEE-based systems) provides the basic structure for building models of the various aspects of the tuning process.

Besides frames to represent components, rules in the TQMS expert system interface encode the tuning heuristics of the expert. And to make it easier to develop, debug, and use the knowledge-based tuning system, a graphical interface displays, on a computer screen, schematic diagrams of the actual graphical devices used to tune the TQMS manually (Figure 22-5).

The menu in the top window and a mouse are used to attach and detach gauges and actuators to various slots and display them. For example, the thermometer and digimeter in Figure 22-5 is attached to the Q1 unit's BIAS-

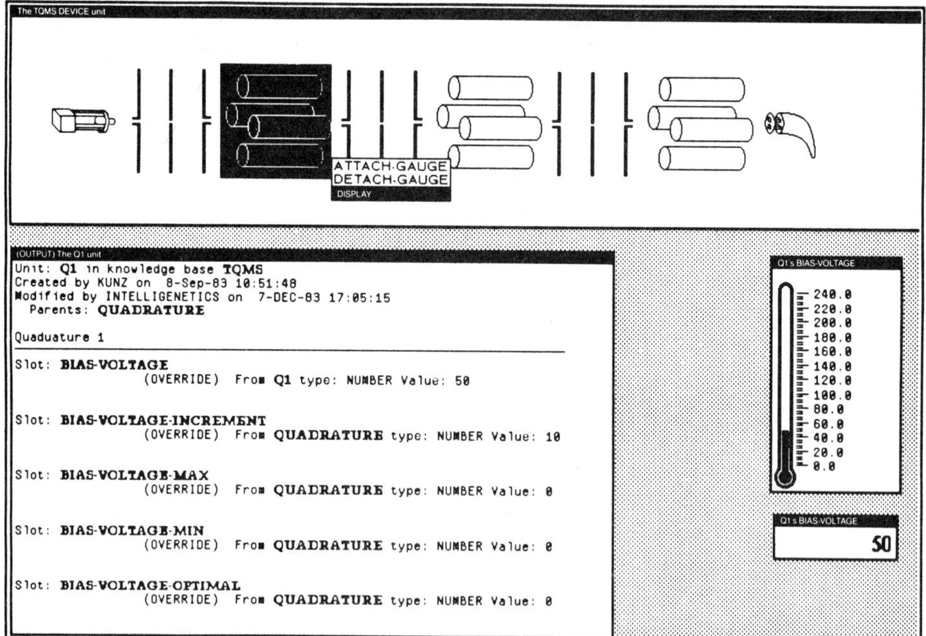

Figure 22-5 Knowledge-based system allows users to interact with graphical gauges and actuators to tune a mass spectrometer (Lawrence Livermore Laboratories)

VOLTAGE slot. When the physical gauges attached to the relevant parameters of the instrument being tuned change, active value procedures are invoked which change the corresponding value in the frame slot. They also update the graphics icons to show the new parameter values. Reversed interactions are also possible. Users may interact with the individual slots of the underlying units by changing these graphical devices with a mouse.

Through these graphical gauges and user interactions, as the system conducts a calibration, operators can monitor device performance, set new parameters, and analyze tuning situations. As with manual tuning procedures, the graphical interfaces are invaluable aids in providing feedback to the operator. The feedback is used to observe the consequences of alternate tuning strategies and thereby add more tuning knowledge to the TQMS intelligent interface knowledge base.

The rule base, which contains the tuning heuristics, makes the TQMS knowledge system, to some degree, capable of tuning the of TQMS itself. Toward this end, the knowledge system queries the instrument as to its current parameters (various machine readouts) and also queries the knowledge system frames about whether or not the TQMS is optimally tuned.

The knowledge system can tell when the tuning is optimal because the parameters are connected to slots in frames which contain calculation procedures involving these parameters and rules about optimal tuning. The rules encode the expert's knowledge about how to tell if individual parameters are maximized and, based on maximized parameters, whether the TQMS is optimally tuned. If it is not, the knowledge system interface adjusts a parameter, tries to maximize it, and iterates this procedure until it is convinced that the TQMS is optimally tuned.

USING COMPLEX SOFTWARE

Complex equipment was once a matter of hardware, but it is rapidly also becoming a matter of software. Worldwide commitment to software is very great indeed. Large, complex software systems have a major influence on running companies, projects, and making technical and business decisions. It is therefore important that companies, managers, and engineers (all types such as civil, electrical, mechanical) who use or depend on the software become familiar now with the available software and the proper way to use it.

Unfortunately, the newness of software and the fact that it is more abstract than hardware have led to several problems in its use. These problems often occur in engineering and oil exploration companies because they employ very large, complex software systems for data analysis or interpretation. The size and complexity of these software systems make them difficult to use correctly and efficiently.

Only a small handful of experts understand this software well enough to obtain its full benefits. Most users do not understand it, and worse, they tend to operate it in a trial-and-error mode. Since a number of companies that are confronted with the how-to-use-complex-software problem have hundreds of engineers applying trial-and-error techniques daily, the time wasted adds up to a significant amount.

The office world does not tolerate this. There, users want windows, prompts, and menus to ensure that they know what to do next. A guidance strategy is also needed to use data analysis and interpretation software optimally. These programs are generally composed of many different modules that offer all kinds of options and methods to model and analyze the problem in question. For example, one structural analysis software package that uses finite-element analysis techniques to simulate the mechanical behavior of a physical structure under various mechanical loading conditions is described as having so many options that a year is required to learn how to use them proficiently.

Several companies are getting around the complex-software problem by developing a knowledge-based system which acts as an intelligent interface to the software. The interface contains knowledge of the application domain in question (geology, oil exploration, structural analysis, mathematics), as well as knowledge of the software system and the modules that comprise it. It uses this knowledge to guide users through the maze of possible ways to link together modules and to suggest which modules to use next.

STRUCTURAL ANALYSIS

A prototype knowledge-based system, Sacon, functions as an intelligent interface to a general-purpose software package for structural analysis which contains a large number of options and subroutines. The structural analysis software package is a simulation program that knows the governing equations for various stress-strain analyses of physical structures. Structures that can be analyzed by the structural analysis program include aircraft wings, reactor pressure vessels, rocket motor casings, bridges, and buildings.

Engineer-users provide inputs to the structural analysis program about a structure to be analyzed and its expected loading conditions. Typical inputs are internal forces such as weight and external forces such as wind or forces experienced during breaking or banking an airplane. Other inputs include substructures of a structure, structural properties, material characteristics, construction information, and the geometry of the substructure. Engineers decide how to decompose the structure into substructures to determine the most aggravated stress and displacement behaviors. The analysis program then outputs resulting behaviors.

Matters are sufficiently complex that well-educated, experienced engineers must choose an appropriate analysis strategy and software subroutines to implement it. Analysis strategies vary from very sophisticated to very crude, depending on the desired accuracy of an answer and how much the engineer knows a priori about a structure. For example, the equations describing a structural situation may be nonlinear differential equations. An analysis technique can attempt to solve these directly (a sophisticated, difficult problem), or it can approximate the solution with linear differential equations.

The structural analysis program is flexible and contains options that account for all kinds of situations, exceptions, and strategies. But it is so complex that it requires the engineers who are experts in designing and analyzing structures to have a greater degree of expertise in using computer programs than they normally have.

The Sacon knowledge system alleviates the software expertise problem by

```
The following analysis classes are relevant to the
analysis of your structure:

general-inelastic

The following are specific analysis recommendations
you should follow when performing the structure
analysis:

Activate incremental stress - incremental strain analysis.

Model nonlinear stress-strain relations of the material.

Solution will be based on a mix of gradient and Newton methods.

Special code should be written to scan stress at each step, and
evaluate fatigue. A single cycle of loading is sufficient for
fatigue estimates.

Special code should be written to scan stresses, smooth stresses,
and compare with allowable stresses (with appropriate safety factors).

Special code should be written to scan deflections,
calculate relative values, and compare with standard code limits.

Cumulative strain damage should be calculated.

Analysis should include two or more load cycles (if cyclic)
with extrapolation for strain acculumation.

Special code should be written to perform shakedown
extrapolation.
```

Figure 22-6 The Sacon Knowledge system guides engineers in the proper operation, options, and subroutines so they can efficiently use a complex structural analysis software program (Teknowledge Inc.)

recommending an analysis strategy (such as linear or nonlinear), the program options to use, the sequence of analysis steps, and special code to be written (Figure 22–6). Its recommendations are based on its internal factual and heuristic knowledge of the engineer's application, the software, and the information obtained from the engineer-user desiring the structural analysis. Sacon's knowledge base includes knowledge about methods for determining stress and behavior based on various criteria, heuristic mathematical models that estimate stress and behavior, and rules for determining analysis strategies. The engineer-user information is obtained through a dialogue that Sacon conducts with the users.

During this dialogue, Sacon asks the engineers to input information similar to that required by the structural analysis program, but less of it and in less detail. Other questions ask whether a macroanalysis is desired (such as whether the Golden Gate bridge will withstand certain storm forces) or whether the analysis must provide information about the behavior of individual bridge components in response to various stresses and strains, and the degree of analysis precision required.

The Sacon prototype, now in the public domain, was never fielded. There are several reasons. Among them, after Sacon recommended the analysis strategy, options, and step sequences, the engineer-users still had to select the structural analysis program subroutines that implemeneted the recommendations and they had to rekey information in order to have the structural analysis program do its processing. Several subsequent programs, however, now alive in civil engineering and other domains, have taken Sacon a step further. They contain knowledge of their domain, user requirements, and of the subroutines in the conventional analysis program that interfaces to the knowledge program. With this knowledge, they both select the right subroutines in the appropriate order for the problem at hand, and then invoke them automatically.

STATISTICAL ANALYSIS PROGRAMS

Commercial statistical analysis packages have widespread applicability, but when inexperienced people use them, they frequently turn out poor-quality results. Knowledge-based system interfaces to statistical packages know the reasons and avoid them. Such knowledge-based interfaces provide interpretation advice and instruction in addition to guidance for using the statistical routines included in these packages.

Consequently, knowledge system/intelligent interfaces to statistical analysis software can enable that software to be more widely used, optimally. Many people feel that a trend toward greater automation of white-collar jobs is certain to create the need for intelligent interfaces to all statistical routines.

AT&T Bell Laboratories, for instance, has a frame-based knowledge system called REX (Regression Expert) that interfaces to the regression analysis routine in a commercial AT&T statistical package (called S). Regression is a widely used statistical technique for fitting a straight line through a bunch of points. Traditional regression analysis software makes a number of assumptions. Among them, it assumes that the bunch of points are somewhat compact and the differences between the line that is drawn and the original points is approximately normally distributed. To produce a high-quality regression, it is necessary to check that these assumptions are not violated.

An experienced regression expert checks the assumptions. A less experienced one may blunder and violate one. So REX interfaces to the regression routine, checks all the assumptions, analyzes the results, and if it finds something wrong, figures out how to correct the situation in order to produce a quality regression.

AT&T Bell Labs says that its goal in developing REX is to increase productivity and double the number of people at Bell and elsewhere that can do a quality regression. Without REX, training in statistics is required to use S, examine the plots that S has made, perhaps decide that a graph is not really linear, and to apply a transform.

REX lowers the requirements for use of S, thus making regression analysis capabilities available to people who could not handle it previously. This is possible because REX's frames each contain a slot with an average of five rules that encode the statistical heuristics of a statistician. Another slot in each frame contains hypotheses to prove in order to decide on the best course of checking or fixing action.

AT&T Bell pictures REX's most common user as someone who has had one statistics course ten years ago. Normally, to do a good regression takes a couple of courses (one in regression) or equivalent knowledge gained through experience.

SOLVING MATH PROBLEMS

AI programs such as SMP (from Inference Corp.) and Macsyma (developed at MIT and marketed by Symbolics) solve symbolic (as opposed to numeric) mathematical problems. These include problems in algebra, differential and integral calculus, manipulation of matrices, vector and tensor analysis, and solution of linear and nonlinear equations.

These types of problems are not amenable to ordinary computer automation, which is deft with computational problems. They are normally solved by hand with pencil and paper and by using various approximations where possible.

AI-based computer algebra programs can succeed where traditional computer methods fail because besides having traditional computational capabilities, they bring to the problem domain a knowledge base that contains knowledge about mathematical relationships, rules for simplifying mathematical expressions, and knowledge about how to solve various types of mathematical problems. The knowledge is expressed in the form of rules.

But AI knowledge is not the whole story because computer algebra programs also contain algorithmic programming procedures. Both rules and programming procedures can be written in an AI language such as Lisp. Inference Corp., however, opted for a hybrid approach in its SMP program. With this approach, SMP rules are written in a proprietary rule-based language. Some of its procedures are written in an SMP programming language akin to Lisp. But others are packaged in ordinary programming procedure subroutines, written in the standard operational C programming language.

It is the modularity of AI languages that allows SMP users to easily extend SMP's mathematical knowledge. Mathematicians and engineers can define new mathematical notations, new problem-solving paradigms, and new rules for manipulating their own notation in SMP's rule-based language or in its Lisp-like procedural language without worrying about the impact on the rest of the program.

However, Inference Corp. considers it unreasonable to rely only on AI langugages for an algebra system's procedures because many algorithmic procedures already exist in conventional languages. Therefore, SMP also uses C programming language routines to do the algorithmic job. Such hybridization allows users to choose the best solutions to a problem, rather than be locked into a single technique because it has an AI label.

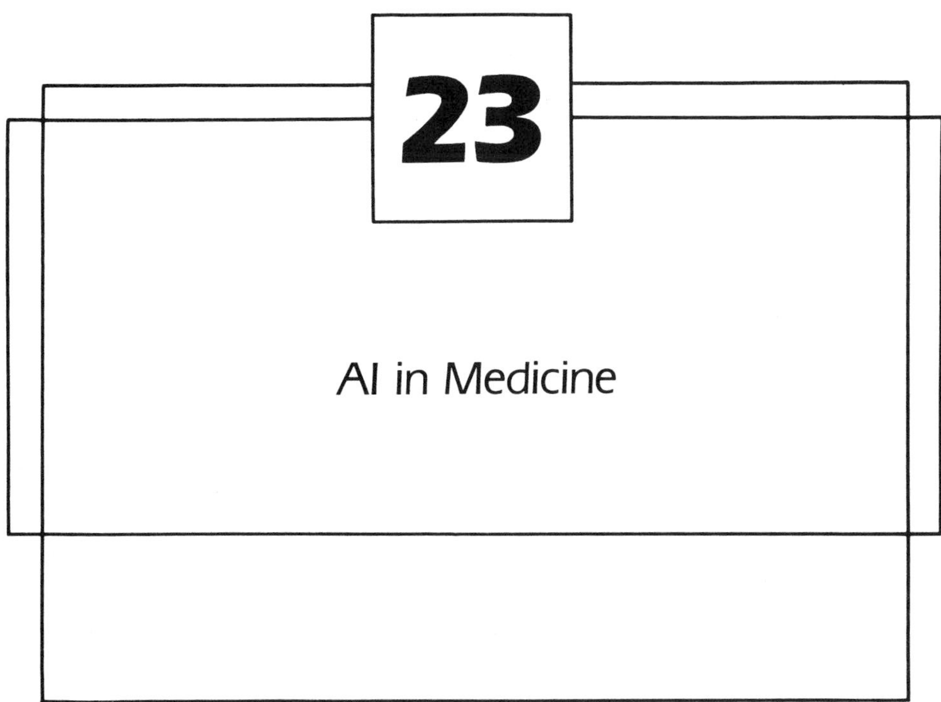

23

AI in Medicine

It is a decision that could mean the difference between life and death. How should a physician react to each new test result? Does it signify a change from the last one? Is it abnormal? If so, can it be explained by a known diagnosis? By drug toxicity? Does the diagnosis indicate that a particular drug should be prescribed, and how much of it? Is the patient allergic to the drug of choice? Do any of the patient's other ailments or current treatments show a contraindication for the prescribed treatment?

The information to answer these questions is based on experience or comes from information sources such as medical records, laboratory reports, textbooks, and documented case histories. The experience, of course, is the physician's. The information sources are readily available. The answers mostly require simple list searches and comparisons. But the amount of data to search, compare, and remember is enormous.

Clement J. McDonald, doctor of internal medicine at the Regenstrief Institute for Health Care, points out that "individually the data examination tasks consume minuscule amounts of time; collectively, they take up much of the physician's day. What is worse, they add significantly to the information processing load of the physician and cause, in computer terminology, intermittent information channel overload and its companion, errors" (McDonald, 1981). But some hospitals are reducing the chances of error by providing a round-the-clock consultant for every physician.

The consultant is a computerized medical knowledge-based system that links medical records, the hospital testing facilities, pharmacy, patients' rooms, and outpatient clinics. By putting together this information, along with the factual and heuristic medical knowledge in its knowledge base, the knowledge system can interpret instrument readouts, suggest what the patient's illness might be, and advise about the proper drugs and treatment.

Such consultant systems have been in use since the middle to late 1970s at the Pacific Medical Center (San Francisco, California), Regenstrief Institute of Health Care (Indianapolis, Indiana), and LDS Hospital (Salt Lake City, Utah). Puff, the Pacific Medical Center system, is a diagnostic system for pulmonary diseases. The Regenstrief knowledge system called Care, and the LDS Hospital knowledge system named Help, are both consultants that handle a more comprehensive range of physicians' chores.

These knowledge-based systems are not limited to their hometown hospitals. The Help system, for example, has been adopted by Arnot-Ogden Memorial Hospital (Elmira, New York). The University of Utah Hospital in Salt Lake City and Rex Hospital in Raleigh, North Carolina, have contracts to install it. Control Data Corp. is marketing it. Even patients at remote locations have received the Help system's benefits over the phone lines—among them Barney Clark, the recipient of the first artificial heart.

PUFF

Puff (for Pulmonary Function) was developed originally at Stanford University by AI experts, in conjunction with a pulmonary physician (Robert Fallat) from Pacific Medical Center whose knowledge is encoded in the program. Puff's emphasis was on representing symbolic knowledge and using symbolic processing techniques to make decisions.

Puff's medical task is to interpret respiratory tests administered to patients in the pulmonary function laboratory at Pacific Medical Center. Its interpretation is based on historic and symptomatic information as well as test results and general medical knowledge. As output, Puff typically produces a natural-language explanation of its interpretation, proposes a diagnosis, and includes a confidence factor that indicates the system's confidence in that diagnosis (Figure 23-1).

The test measurements in the top of Figure 23-1 are collected by laboratory technicians using a variety of equipment. The measurements are given as a percent of the predicted values for a normal patient of the same sex, height, and weight. These measurements are followed by interpretation statements and a pulmonary function diagnosis.

Although earlier experimental expert systems could produce such reports competently, they generally did not include historic and symptomatic information or the variety of tests included in the Puff program. Inclusion of this type of data required a great deal of professional time dedicated to data-entry chores, on an interactive basis, at system execution time. Puff differs from these prototypes in that it produces its interpretations automatically, with minimum need for user interaction. The laboratory test results, patient's history, and symptoms that

```
PRESBYTERIAN HOSPITAL OF PMC            SCHULZ                          PUL
 CLAY AND BUCHANAN, BOX 7999            P186455.
 SAN FRANCISCO, CA. 94120               DR. CLARENCE BLOG
   PULMONARY FUNCTION LAB

WT 69.0 KG,   HT 182 CM,   AGE 66   SEX M
REFERRAL DX-
****************************************************TEST DATE 06/28/82
                                   PREDICTED                POST DILATION
                                    (+/-SD) OBSER(%PRED)     OBSER(%PRED)
INSPIR VITAL CAP (IVC)  L       4.5(0.6)  3.2   ( 71)     3.3   ( 73)
RESIDUAL VOL        (RV)  L       2.4(0.4)  2.4   ( 99)     1.9   ( 78)
TOTAL LUNG CAP   (TLC)  L       6.9(0.7)  5.6   ( 81)     5.2   ( 75)
RV/TLC                  %       35.       43.               37.

FORCED EXPIR VOL(FEV1)  L       3.3 (0.5) 2.2   ( 66)     2.3   ( 69)
FORCED VITAL CAP (FVC)  L       4.5 (0.6) 3.2   ( 71)     3.3   ( 73)
FEV1/FVC                %       76.       69.               70.
PEAK EXPIR FLOW  (PEF)  L/S     9.1 (1.7) 4.1   ( 45)     4.8   ( 52)
FORCED EXP FLOW  25-75% L/S     3.3 (0.8) 1.4   ( 42)     1.6   ( 48)
AIRWAY RESIST(RAW) (TLC  5.6) 2.5         3.5               1.2

DF CAP-HGB= 0.0    (TLC  5.1) 25.        18.1   ( 72) ( 56%IF TLC= 6.9)

ARTERIAL BLOOD GASES       PH     PCO2   PO2    SAT%   HCO3    BASEX.
    REST ROOM AIR          7.48   40.0   77.0   96.0   30.0    7.0
**********************************************************************
INTERPRETATION:  THE  REDUCED TLC AND IVC INDICATE A MILD RESTRICTIVE
DEFECT.  THE FORCED VITAL CAPACITY, FEV1/FVC RATIO AND MID-EXPIRATORY
FLOW  ARE  REDUCED AND THE AIRWAY RESISTANCE IS INCREASED, SUGGESTING
MODERATE  AIRWAY OBSTRUCTION.  FOLLOWING BRONCHODILATION, THE EXPIRED
FLOWS  SHOW ONLY SLIGHT IMPROVEMENT.  HOWEVER, THE DECREASE IN AIRWAY
RESISTANCE  INDICATES  SOME  REVERSIBLE COMPONENT.  THE LOW DIFFUSING
CAPACITY  INDICATES  A  LOSS  OF ALVEOLAR CAPILLARY SURFACE, WHICH IS
SEVERE.

WHEN  CORRECTED FOR AGE, ARTERIAL PO2 AND PCO2 ON ROOM AIR ARE WITHIN
NORMAL  LIMITS.   THE  ARTERIAL  PH  IS  SLIGHTLY INCREASED.  THIS IS
CONSISTENT  WITH  A  MILD  METABOLIC  ALKALOSIS  WITHOUT  RESPIRATORY
COMPENSATION.

CONCLUSIONS:  THE  REDUCED  DIFFUSING CAPACITY IS CONSISTENT WITH THE
COMBINATION OF DISEASES.  IN VIEW OF THE RESPONSE TO BRONCHODILATORS,
CONTINUED USE WOULD BE RECOMMENDED.

PULMONARY FUNCTION DIAGNOSIS:
1. MODERATE OBSTRUCTIVE AIRWAYS DISEASE.
2. SEVERE DIFFUSION DEFECT.
3. MILD RESTRICTIVE LUNG DISEASE.
4. MILD METABOLIC ALKALOSIS.
```

Figure 23-1 Pulmonary function report generated by PDP-11 version of PUFF. (Pacific Medical Center)

relate to pulmonary diseases are entered into the computer by technicians as part of the normal laboratory routine.

Since the domain of pulmonary physiology is a relatively circumscribed field, other large bodies of knowledge are not required to produce accurate diagnoses of pulmonary disease in the patient. This bounded domain minimizes not only the data-entry problem, but also the problem of misdiagnosis that stems from lack of knowledge about related diseases that are also present in the patient. Such misdiagnosis was a problem in Mycin, an early prototype expert system for diagnosing infectious diseases and prescribing therapy.

Physicians are not bound by Puff's diagnoses. They are suggestions to the physicians, equivalent to calling in a second opinion. Nonetheless, physician-users have acquired confidence in Puff's accuracy and indicate support for the system, as seen by their acceptance of its diagnoses.

Puff has been routinely used in the Pacific Medical Center's pulmonary function laboratory since 1978, and during its first six years of use, interpreted the results of more than 6,000 cases. Currently, Puff generates lung test interpretations for about ten patients daily. Fallat claims that about 85 percent of Puff's diagnoses and reports are now accepted without modification by the hospital's pulmonary staff. Changes made to most other reports are minor. Typically, they "add a statement suggesting that the patient's physician compare the interpretation with previous tests taken" (Aikens and others, 1983).

PHYSICIAN'S MANAGEMENT SYSTEMS

In contrast to Puff, whose origins are in the academic AI community, doctors rather than AI specialists pioneered the Care and Help systems at the Regenstrief and LDS medical institutions. Two major pionts of emphasis differentiate Care and Help from Puff. These are the ability to perform the spectrum of medical chores (although some more thoroughly than others) and, most important, their integration with databases.

Besides performing medical diagnoses, Care and Help act as comprehensive physician's management systems, as well as assistant interpreters of instrument-based tests and data derived from X-rays. In their managerial role, the knowledge-based systems attend to the little nonglamorous medical things with which physicians must contend.

CARE

Care, for example, issues reminders about the day-to-day chores that physicians must remember. These include reminders about follow-up tests, drugs, preventative care, immunizations, and Pap smears.

Each night, a program automatically checks the records of all patients who have appointments at the general medicine clinic the next day. Based on this check, it issues three types of patient reminder/reports.

The first is a physician's flowsheet summary for each scheduled patient. This is a cumulative report, in the flowsheet format that most clinical laboratory systems use (Figure 23-2). In keeping with the way that physicians maintain flowsheets manually, the Care flowsheets are densely printed with ten to fifteen results across a page. This dense reporting allows physicians to visualize important time trends.

The second form that Care produces is a Patient Encounter Form, divided into four areas (Figure 23-3). The upper right-hand area contains the problem list recorded at the previous visit. The upper left-hand area has a list of flowsheet observations, such as weight, systolic and diastolic blood pressure, and pulse. The middle section is the orders area where the computer provides a menu of frequently ordered diagnostic tests. The bottom section presents the prescriptions

WISHARD MEMORIAL HOSPITAL ¦SAMPLE.PATIENT #9999999-7

DX & COMPLAINTS

DX & COMPLAINTS

DX & COMPLAINT 01-NOV-82 DIABETES MEL, CARDIOMEGALY, SURGERY S/P OTHR/NOSE SURG, SKIN ABN OTHR/SCAR ON FACE
12-SEP-77 DIABETES MEL, ARTHRITIS NOS, HYPERTENSION
19-SEP-75 JOINT PAIN, HYPERTENSION, DIABETES MEL, OBESITY, CHF

CLINIC DATA	19-NOV -79	23-OCT -79	18-JUN -79	12-JUN -79	19-APR -79	09-FEB -79	22-JAN -79	08-JAN -79	07-JUN -78	11-NOV -77	09-FEB -77	16-MAY -76
CLINIC DATA												
ENCTR SITE	MED CL		MED CL	MED CL	MED CL	DIAB CL	OTHER E	MED CL	DISCH	MED CL	MED CL	MED CL
DR ID	.	.	401	401	401	.	.	401	.	.	.	.
VITALS												
PULSE									.	.	.	85
SYS BP SITTING	.	.	140	135	130	150	135	145	.	140	135	155
DIAS BP SITTIN	.	.	80	75	85	70	60	78	.	85	70	95*H
HEIGHT(IN)	.	.	64						.			
WEIGHT LBS	.	.	240*H	230*H	225*H	215*H	230*H	224*H	.	217*H	228*H	208*H
GLUCOSE TESTS												
GLUCOSE FASTIN	.	.				400*H			.	.		.
GLUCOSE RANDOM	.	.	190*H	200*H	232*H	220*H	170*H	170*H	.	.	180*H	.
HRS PP	.	.	4.0	4.0	4.0	.	4.0	4.0	.	.	4.0	.
TREATMENTS												
AMPICILLIN	.	.				.	.	.	D/C	2000	.	.
ASPIRIN	.	.	3900	3900	3900	.	3900	3900	.	3900	.	3900
CHOLINE SAL LI	.	.	.	.	.	.	.	.	D/C	20	.	.
DEXAMETHASONE	.	.	.	.	.	.	.	.	D/C	1.00	.	.
DIAZEPAM	.	.	.	.	.	.	.	.	.	20	.	.
DICLOXACILLIN	.	.	.	.	.	.	.	.	.	1000	.	.
DIGOXIN	.	0.250	.	0.500	.	.	.	.	.	0.500	.	0.250
DYAZIDE	.	.	.	2	2	.	2	2	.	2	2	2
EPINEPH BOR 1%	.	.	.	.	.	.	.	.	.	2	.	.
EPINEPH [illegible]	.	.	.	.	.	.	.	.	.	1	.	.
ERYTHROMYCIN L	.	.	.	.	.	.	.	.	.	1000	.	.
EUCERIN ONT	.	.	.	.	.	.	.	.	.	3	.	.
HYDROCHLOROTHI	.	.	.	.	.	.	.	.	.	50	.	.
LENTE U 100	.	.	.	D/C	10	15	25	35	.	.	15	50
MAALOX	.	.	120	.	.	.	.	.	.	90	.	.
PHENOBARBITAL	.	.	.	.	.	.	.	.	.	260	.	.
PHENYTOIN	.	.	.	.	.	.	.	.	.	300	.	.
PILOCARPINE 4%	.	.	.	.	.	.	.	.	.	8	.	.
PNEUMO VAC	.	.	.	.	0.5	.	.	.	.	.	.	.
TEST TAPE	.	.	.	2	2	.	.	.	.	.	2	.

CARDIOPULMONARY	16-MAY -76	18-NOV -75	19-SEP -75	19-AUG -75	24-JUN -75	08-APR -75	23-JAN -75	17-OCT -74	
CARDIOPULMONARY									
ANGINA(#/MO)	.	0.0	.	.	.	0.0	.	4.0*H	#/MO
EDEMA PERIPH	0	0	0	0	2*H	0	0	1*H	0-4
S3 GALLOP	.	0	.	.	0	.	2*H	.	0-4

EKG 16-MAY-76 NONSP ST-T CHNG
23-JAN-75 LVH BY VOLTAGE, MI OLD ANT'

* ABNORMAL RESULT

RHC SUMMARY 07-Dec-82

SAMPLE.PATIENT
#9999999-7

PAGE 1

PLACE IN FRONT OF CHART

Figure 23-2 Partial Care cumulative report (Regenstrief Health Center)

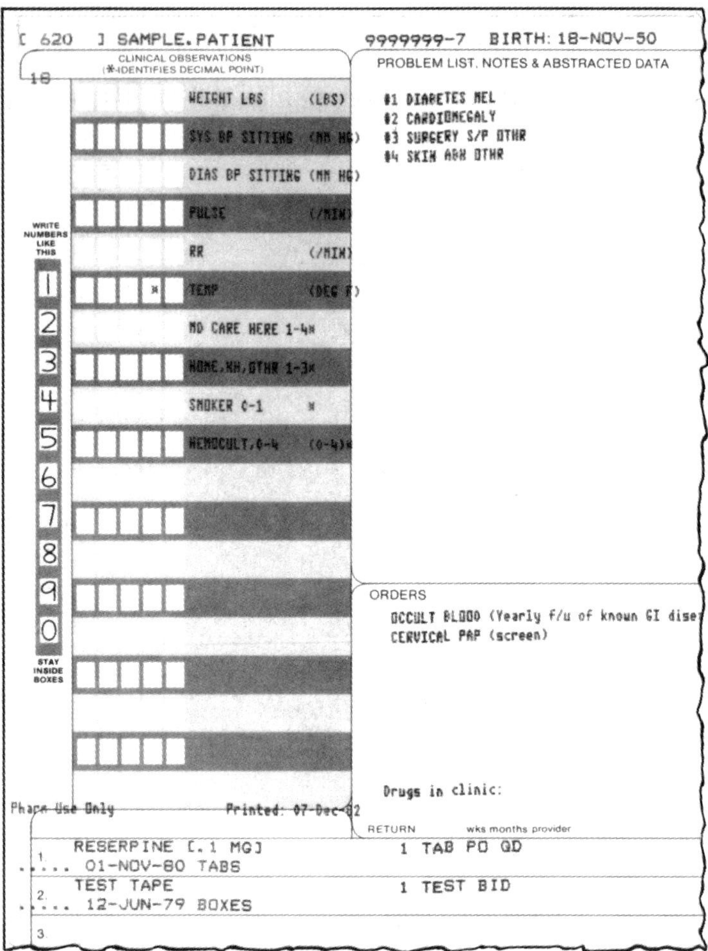

[620] SAMPLE.PATIENT 9999999-7 BIRTH: 18-NOV-50

CLINICAL OBSERVATIONS
(*IDENTIFIES DECIMAL POINT)

18

WEIGHT LBS (LBS)
SYS BP SITTING (MM HG)
DIAS BP SITTING (MM HG)
PULSE (/MIN)
RR (/MIN)
TEMP (DEG F)
MD CARE HERE 1-4*
HOME,NH,OTHR 1-3*
SMOKER 0-1 *
HEMOCULT,0-4 (0-4)*

WRITE NUMBERS LIKE THIS
1 2 3 4 5 6 7 8 9 0
STAY INSIDE BOXES

PROBLEM LIST, NOTES & ABSTRACTED DATA

#1 DIABETES MEL
#2 CARDIOMEGALY
#3 SURGERY S/P OTHR
#4 SKIN ABN OTHR

ORDERS

OCCULT BLOOD (Yearly f/u of known GI dise
CERVICAL PAP (screen)

Drugs in clinic:

Pharm Use Only Printed: 07-Dec-82

RETURN wks months provider

1. RESERPINE [.1 MG] 1 TAB PO QD
..... 01-NOV-80 TABS
2. TEST TAPE 1 TEST BID
..... 12-JUN-79 BOXES
3.

Figure 23-3 Patient encounter form (Regenstrief Health Center)

that were active as of the last clinic visit. Physicians may continue, discontinue, modify, or order a new prescription by simply writing in the amount of medication to be dispensed at this visit, writing "D/C" or writing a different or new name.

The third Care report produced, prior to a patient's visit, contains the reminders or recommendations to the physician (Figure 23-4). The reminders and recommendations are based on a search through the patient's record for conditions requiring physician attention. Working in this manner, in one year Care generated over 70,000 reminders on a variety of subjects, ranging from cardiology, neurology, psychiatry, and gynecology, for 30,000 patient encounters.

```
07-Dec-82 "ENTRY_CTL: C02"

            Please return to Regenstrief Institute, do not chart.

                         TIDBITS FROM THE COMPUTER
              These suggestions are based on incomplete data;
                    your judgment should take precedence.


SAMPLE.PATIENT   #9999999-7  AGE:32  SEX:F  RACE:  PHONE:000-0000
Scheduled to  MCDONALD,CLEMENT on 19-DEC-83 at 01:30 PM (1)

 Consider yearly screen of stool for occult blood to monitor GI tract
bleeding risk in patient with BULB DEFORMED

 Consider getting chest x-ray every 2 years to follow CARDIOMEGALY
reported on 01-NOV-80.

 All women should have at least 2 annual cervical pap tests on record.
It has been more than a year since this patient's first test, dated
15-NOV-80. R:2232.
```

Figure 23-4 Care reminders to physicians (Regenstrief Health Center)

HELP

Help performs tasks similar to Care's, but it performs them interactively. For example, Help checks the patients' records and generates on-the-spot physician's prompts and second opinions about physician's decisions, ranging from mundane issues such as the price of drugs, to critical issues affecting patients' care.

In one Help scenario, an LDS Hospital doctor making ward calls may leave a patient prescription for Meperidine at the nurse's station. The hospital pharmacist enters the prescription into the patient's file through a computer terminal at the nurse's station.

As the prescription enters the file, the Help system automatically checks its information about the drug and then checks to see if any circumstances surrounding the patient might make Meperidine a dangerous drug in the dosage prescribed. A typical Help message might indicate that the patient is also using Mao inhibitors, which, if used concurrently with Meperidine, can result in severe agitation. The Help system might also suggest that under the circumstances, low doses of morphine or pentazocine are preferable (Figure 23-5).

The doctor is not bound by the knowledge-based system's suggestion. However, "80 percent of the time LDS physicians follow the knowledge system suggestions," says Homer Warner, head of LDS Hospital's department of medical biophysics, chairman of the department of biophysics and computing at the University of Utah's school of medicine, and chief developer of Help. When

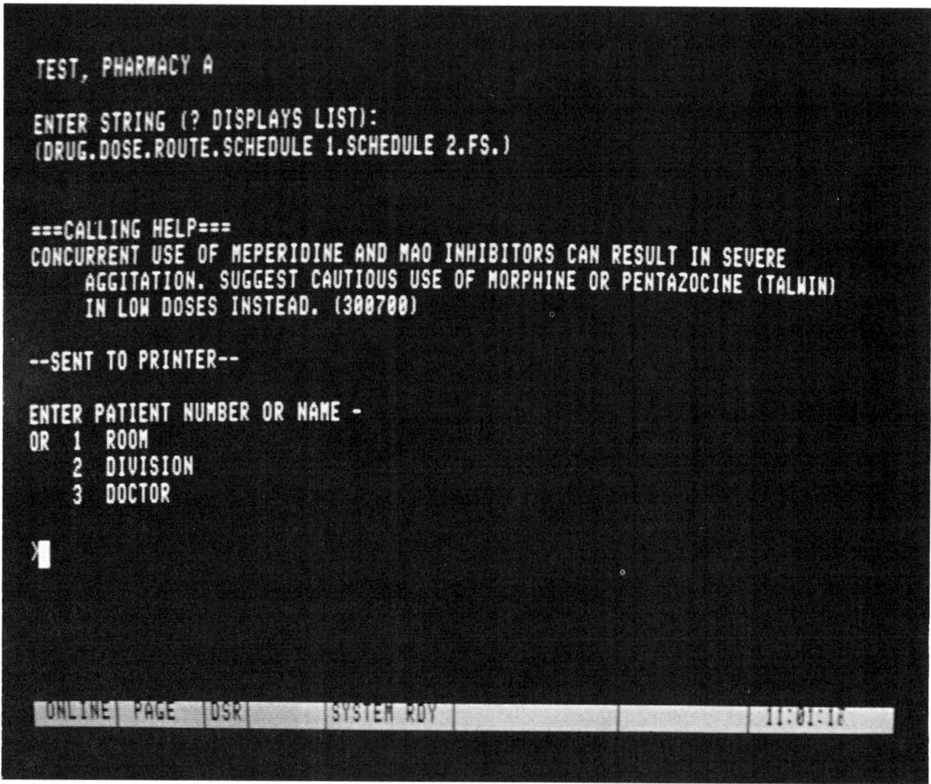

TEST, PHARMACY A
ENTER STRING (? DISPLAYS LIST):
(DRUG.DOSE.ROUTE.SCHEDULE 1.SCHEDULE 2.FS.)
===CALLING HELP===
CONCURRENT USE OF MEPERIDINE AND MAO INHIBITORS CAN RESULT IN SEVERE
AGGITATION. SUGGEST CAUTIOUS USE OF MORPHINE OR PENTAZOCINE (TALWIN)
IN LOW DOSES INSTEAD. (300700)
--SENT TO PRINTER--
ENTER PATIENT NUMBER OR NAME -
OR 1 ROOM
2 DIVISION
3 DOCTOR
ONLINE
PAGE
DSR
SYSTEM RDY

Figure 23-5 A HELP drug alert prompt to physician (LDS Hospital)

they wish to override the advice because they feel there are other considerations, they are free to do so. For medical legal purposes, they document their decision and reasons in the record.

In another role as instrumentation assistant, the Help system reads and interprets, for example, all the hospital electrocardiograms, blood gas measurements, spirometry (breathing) data from the respiratory lab, and data from the cardiovascular lab. Typically, physicians take an EKG machine with an attached modem into the patient's room. They hook it up to the patient's telephone and the EKG date is transmitted to the computer in which the knowledge system resides (Chapter 1, Figure 1-1).

Meanwhile, at the Intensive Care Unit (ICU), patients are physically connected from the electrocardiogram at their bedsides to a small computer in the ICU. The ICU computer performs all the preliminary pattern recognition and feeds its output into the hospital's central computer where the record storage and decision making is done.

As test data—whether EKGs, bacteriological cultures, X-rays, or other—are transmitted to the central computer, the knowledge system interprets the test results in the light of other patient laboratory data, observations made by the physician and the nurse, and its own general factual and heuristic knowledge. The Help system then makes its therapeutic recommendations, suggests the next stage of tests to work up, recommends changes in drugs or drug dosages, prescribes less expensive generic antibiotics, or proposes diagnoses.

THE DATABASE FACTOR

Care has been used on a routine basis by the staff of a general medicine clinic (Regenstrief Institute for Health Care) that is affiliated with the 580-bed Wishard Memorial Hospital since 1975. Help has been used by the staff of the 550-bed LDS Hospital since 1973.

Key to Care's and Help's acceptance by physicians, is these systems' focus on integrating medical data in ordinary databases with knowledge in knowledge bases. Examples of data include all the information in a patient's chart, hospital records, pharmacy databases, and diagnostic laboratory reports. To get these data, both Care and Help have direct access to the time-oriented hospital and patient databases, clinical computerized laboratory systems, or computerized pharmacy systems.

Doctors also need knowledge to make decisions. Knowledge includes medical textbook information and heuristic knowledge acquired from experience (Figure 23-6).

Most knowledge-based systems concentrate on the knowledge half of the problem—how to gather it, represent it, and reason from it. This type of knowledge is necessary but not sufficient for doctors to make medical decisions.

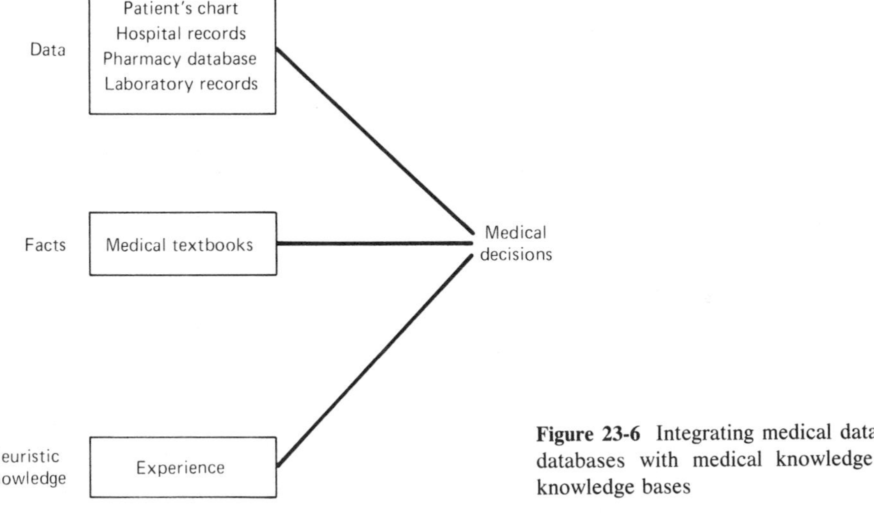

Figure 23-6 Integrating medical data in databases with medical knowledge in knowledge bases

Diagnosis and treatment of patients also require information about the patients themselves.

Traditionally, most knowledge systems depend on human beings to input manually the data they need about the case at hand, rather than automatically getting their data from existing databases. Human data entry is a cost-effective technique when the information to be input to the knowledge system can be described succinctly, the cost of the human data-entry time is low, the knowledge system advice concerns difficult matters, and the value of the advice given in response to the data entry is very high.

For example, the data-entry costs compared to the possible payoffs are considered reasonable in the oil exploration business, where companies may spend $1 million drilling a well. However, in medical environments, low-cost, succinct data entry that provides high-value advice about difficult matters is rare. Medical knowledge, in general, is low-density knowledge. This means that it is necessary to tell a knowledge system a great deal of information to characterize a patient so the knowledge system can do useful work. This information includes simple facts that the physician sees at a glance.

A knowledge system, for example, has none of the gestalt information that is available to the physician, such as how the patient looks—the patient is walking, talking, not staggering, and has no blood on his chest. Neither does it contain information about the patient's detailed medical history, physical information, and objective diagnostic studies.

There are, of course, medical problems that require small amounts of data for their resolution. However, these cases do not need knowledge system consultation; once aware of the problem, physicians make the decision as fast as they gather the data.

A case in point is diabetes. According to C. J. McDonald, chief developer of the Care system, patients with new diabetes are usually easy to recognize. They have a family history of diabetes. They have frequent urination and great thirst. The diagnosis can generally be made by testing the urine for sugar.

Unfortunately, cases that are complex enough to pose difficulties for the physician and warrant the use of a knowledge system also tend to require burdensome amounts of data entry. For this reason, both McDonald and Warner insist that medical knowledge-based systems will be useful only if they are integrated with the medical records and have automatic access to all the data contained therein.

This automatic access eliminates the need for doctors to enter manually lots of patient data every time they see a patient or wish expert system consultation. Automatic access has another advantage. It makes it possible for the knowledge system to search the records and offer advice and reminders when, because of an oversight concerning some relevant information, the physician is least likely to request a consultation.

Several doctors insist that the lack of database access is a major reason that Caduceus (originally called Internist) is not currently used in practice. Caduceus is a standalone, experimental, diagnostic expert system that knows about 100,000 symptomatic associations and 350 disease manifestations for 500 different diseases and can also diagnose multiple simultaneous diseases. It is accepted by many in the AI and medical communities that Caduceus' expertise encompasses about 85 percent of internal medicine and the medical diagnostic system displays expert performance in three-fourths of major known diseases. Unfortunately, despite the knowledge, doctors insist that the usefulness of Caduceus is limited because Caduceus requires a twenty to thirty minute data-entry dialogue for physicians to describe a patient.

When that twenty to thirty minutes per patient session is multiplied by twenty to thirty patients per day, the resulting time obtained, which is necessary to converse with a machine, is not tolerable to physicians. To be routinely useful, a medical knowledge-based system must be sufficiently intelligent not only to use knowledge to make decisions and diagnoses, but also to automatically gather and remember data about the patient in question. To provide these functions, it is necessary to couple a database to the knowledge system.

For this reason, the physician teams at the Regenstrief Institute and LDS Hospital spent a good proportion of their expert system development time occupied with problems of how to capture, code, represent, and reduce data so that expert system rules could understand and reason from it. These problems largely solved, both Care and Help interface with, and can obtain most of their data directly from, computerized medical records.

PHYSICIAN ACCEPTANCE

There are two advantages to integrating the database and the knowledge base. One is the elimination of most of the physician/knowledge system dialogue. The other pertains to getting the full staff of physicians to accept and use the knowledge systems.

Knowledge system acceptance at the Regenstrief Institute and LDS Hospital has to occur because the knowledge systems at these institutions are bundled with the medical record system, so physicians cannot get one without the other.

The bundling causes no problems. The physicians do not balk (and never did) at using a computerized medical record system. They learn to use a terminal when they come to the hospital because it is the quickest way to find data and get lab reports. If the medical records and knowledge systems are bundled together, each time the physicians get their lab results or patient data, they also automatically get their reminders, interpretations, and advice, generated by the knowledge system (Figure 23-7).

There is no special opposition to the advice offered. In fact, a positive attitude is prevalent among the LDS Hospital physicians. At the Regenstrief Institute, some physicians like the computer system but are wary of the reminders. The wary doctors are mostly residents.

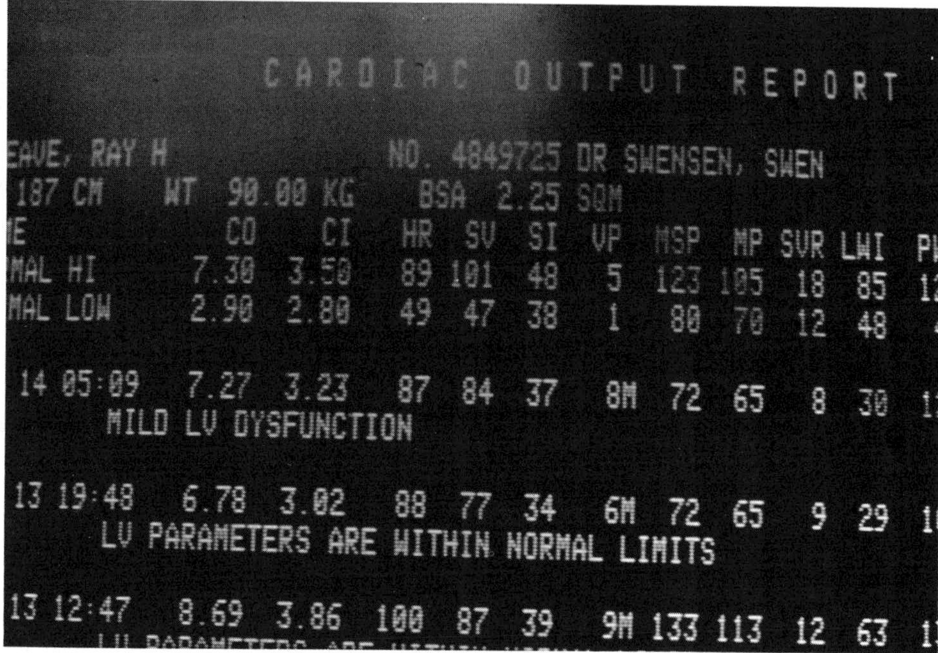

Figure 23-7 Partial laboratory data bundled with HELP reminder (LDS Hospital)

Doctors at the Regenstrief Institute were asked to rate the Care system on a 5-point scale. A 3 rating was neutral. Above 3 indicated that they liked the use of the system, while below 3 constituted dislike.

On average, the doctors scored all system functions about 4.8 except the reminders for the expert system, which they scored 3. Further investigations indicated that the staff physicians were enthusiastic about the system. The residents, according to McDonald, "are a little unsure of themselves and feel threatened by the system." Their feelings are exacerbated because they did not have any input into the system.

But that is because it has not been practical to have 110 relatively transient residents each tuning the rules in a centralized system for their own requirements. Some rule changes, however, were made at the request of staff physicians who wanted to make the system conform to their ways of practicing medicine. Since they had a say in the knowledge system rules, they had more confidence in the system.

Plans are to personalize Care for still more doctors. The Regenstrief Institute is installing microcomputers linked to the hospital mainframe system. The micros will act as physicians' workstations and make it possible for physicians to tune the rules to their own requirements. Then, rather than someone telling the physicians what to do, it will be like the physicians telling themselves what to do—a much less threatening situation.

```
            L D S   H O S P I T A L   B L O O D   G A S   R E P O R T

          ESTHER E          NO.  61534 DR          DANIEL          RM 5N79
FEB 03 82   PH   PCO2 HCO3   BE   HB  CO/MT PO2 SO2  O2CT %O2  PK/ PL/PP MR/SR
NORMAL HI  7.45  40.0 25.0  2.5 17.0  2/ 1  85  95  22.7
NORMAL LOW 7.35  34.0 19.0 -2.5 13.0  0/ 1  68  93  17.4

03 09:41 V 7.28  52.3 24.0 -3.0 13.4  1/ 0  44  76  14.2 100  32/ 25/ 0 12/ 0
03 09:40 A 7.29  48.2 22.7 -3.9 13.1  1/ 1  70  93  17.2 100  32/ 25/ 0 12/ 0
          SAMPLE #  51, TEMP 35.2, BREATHING STATUS : IMV
          MODERATE ACUTE RESPIRATORY ACIDOSIS
          HYPOVENTILATION (PREVIOUSLY NORMAL)
          CONSIDER DIABETIC KETOACIDOSIS (URINE: GLUCOSE 4+,KETONES 0+)
          O2 CONSUMPTION 176 ML/MIN - CO  5.29 L/MIN
          AV O2 CONTENT DIFF  3.32 (HB 13.25) O2 EXTRACT RATIO  2%
          R-TO-L SHUNT  44%+/-3%
          A-A GRADIENT 482, A/A  13% (EST ALV PO2 552)

03 06:01 V 7.35  45.8 24.9 -0.5 12.7  1/ 0  37  69  12.2  40  26/ 22/ 6 11/ 0
03 06:00 A 7.37  41.3 23.5 -1.1 12.5  1/ 1  49  84  14.8  40  26/ 22/ 6 11/ 0
          SAMPLE #  50, TEMP 35.6, BREATHING STATUS : IMV
          MILD ACID-BASE DISORDER
          O2 CONSUMPTION 163 ML/MIN - CO  5.93 L/MIN
          AV O2 CONTENT DIFF  2.75 (HB 12.60) O2 EXTRACT RATIO  2%
          R-TO-L SHUNT  52%+/-3%
          A-A GRADIENT 144, A/A  25% (EST ALV PO2 193)
          SEVERE HYPOXEMIA  **CONTACT MD OR RN!!!!

03 01:43 V 7.36  48.3 26.9  1.3 13.8  1/ 0  40  69  13.3  41  29/ 23/ 6 11/ 0
03 01:42 A 7.39  42.7 25.5  1.0 13.5  1/ 1  55  86  16.4  41  29/  3/ 6 11/ 0
          SAMPLE #  49, TEMP 36.4, BREATHING STATUS : IMV
          MILD ACID-BASE DISORDER
          O2 CONSUMPTION 209 ML/MIN - CO  6.27 L/MIN
          AV O2 CONTENT DIFF  3.33 (HB 13.65) O2 EXTRACT RATIO  2%
          R-TO-L SHUNT  45%+/-3%
          A-A GRADIENT 142, A/A  28% (EST ALV PO2 197)
          SEVERE HYPOXEMIA BREATHING OXYGEN **CONTACT MD OR RN!!!!

02 22:25 A 7.44  35.3 23.8  0.9 14.1  1/ 0  58  89  17.5  41  32/ 26/ 6 10/ 0
          SAMPLE #  48, TEMP 37.1, BREATHING STATUS : IMV
          NORMAL ARTERIAL ACID-BASE CHEMISTRY
          ESTIMATED R-L SHUNT 73,46,33% (AT AV DIFF OF  0.90, 2.90, 4.90)
          A-A GRADIENT 147, A/A  28% (EST ALV PO2 205)
          SEVERE HYPOXEMIA BREATHING OXYGEN **CONTACT MD OR RN!!!!

02 21:11 V 7.45  37.1 25.6  2.6 14.0  1/ 1  38  70  13.8  41  30/ 23/ 4 10/ 0
02 21:10 A 7.47  35.5 25.7  3.2 13.7  2/ 1  49  85  16.4  41  30/ 23/ 4 10/ 0
          SAMPLE #  47, TEMP 36.9, BREATHING STATUS : IMV
          MILD ACID-BASE DISORDER
          AV O2 CONTENT DIFF  2.90 (HB 13.85) O2 EXTRACT RATIO  2%
          R-TO-L SHUNT  50%+/-3%
          A-A GRADIENT 156, A/A  24% (EST ALV PO2 205)
          SEVERE HYPOXEMIA BREATHING OXYGEN **CONTACT MD OR RN!!!!

   PRELIMINARY INTERPRETATION -- BASED ONLY ON BLOOD GAS DATA.
      ***(FINAL DIAGNOSIS REQUIRES CLINICAL CORRELATION)***
KEY:A=ARTERIAL, V=MIXED VENOUS, C=CAPILLARY, E=EXPIRED CO2, W=WEDGE
    CO=CARBOXY HB, MT=MET HB, O2CT=O2 CONTENT, PK=PEAK, PL=PLATEAU, PP=PEEP
    MR=MACHINE RATE, SR=SPONTANEOUS RATE
            TIME OUT: FEB 03 82 10:11
```

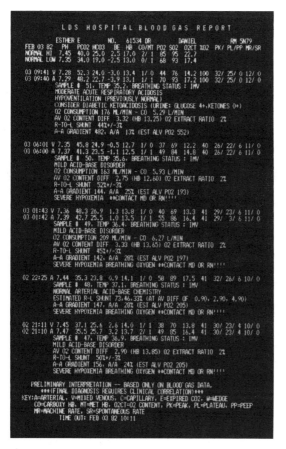

Figure 23-8 A HELP blood gas alert (LDS Hospital)

At LDS Hospital, most early opposition to the expert system has been overcome. The biggest opposition concerned the interpretation of tests such as the ECG (EKG), on the grounds that ECG interpretation rightfully belonged to the cardiologists.

A recent independently conducted survey of physicians at LDS Hospital revealed that physicians found the HELP system valuable and supported its use (Pryor and others, 1983). The highest proportion of enthusiasm came from specialists in surgery and internal medicine. The system is also a favorite among nurses and pharmacists, especially in the care of critically ill patients. In addition, physicians indicated that of Help's various on-line, specialized laboratory modules, the pulmonary function laboratory module was a particularly valuable and time-saving service. In one year, it performed more than 62,000 blood gas analyses and over 1200 pulmonary function tests (Figure 23-8). The knowledge-based system gathered data, interpreted them, generated reports that were printed at the appropriate nursing division, provided laboratory management and quality control information, and even generated billing information.

Responses from physicians in the intensive and critical care units, which have been computerized the longest, indicate several benefits. These physicians feel that the knowledge system organizes data so that they are more easily reviewed for clinical decision making. It makes the data available faster where needed, and provides data interpretation and alarm functions. The knowledge system's reports and alarms focus attention of personnel on the treatment and management of most of the problems of the critically ill patient. In addition, the knowledge-based decision-making system provides an excellent basis for teaching logical decision-making skills to house staff and staff physicians.

Results from the pharmacy, incorporated into the Help system since 1975, indicate some dramatic, life-saving benefits (Pryor et al., 1983). In the pharmacy, the Help system monitors drug usage and issues drug alerts. The importance of computerizing the alert function is demonstrated by the fact that only about 5 percent of the patients in a hospital have an alert. Only 20 percent of these alerts are truly life-threatening or require physician interaction or changing of a drug or procedure. This means that a large amount of uninteresting data must be reviewed to find and flag the few patients, and drugs ordered, that represent problems. This increases the chances of missing something.

LDS Hospital shows "a 94 percent compliance rate for those action-oriented, life-threatening alerts. Therefore, about 50 patients each month are helped in some dramatic way by having the computer monitor the drugs ordered. (Pryor et al., 1983).

An unexpected advantage to medical knowledge systems is the removal of some of the drudgery from medicine. Many of a physician's tasks are simple and repetitive. Most tests results are straightforward. With a knowledge-based medical consultant around, physicians feel they can have the challenge of looking at the more interesting cases and concentrating on the more difficult ones.

ADVICE FOR FUTURE DEVELOPERS

Care and Help have been in operation so long that physicians at the Regenstrief Institute and LDS Hospital have essentially grown up with the knowledge systems and accept them automatically. However, despite their demonstrated advantages, general acceptance of medical knowledge-based systems is by no means assured. The Regenstrief and LDS knowledge system development teams have identified certain requisites that are necessary for a medical knowledge system to be accepted by physicians. One requisite is the bundling of the knowledge system with the medical databases. The reasons concern more than just saving the time that physicians would otherwise need to input information. The concern is that if the knowledge systems and medical databases were separated, doctors would resist the idea of abstractly asking a computer system for advice. In addition, if the systems were separate, doctors would not learn to rely on the knowledge system. It would become an experiment and eventually would be neglected.

Another factor necessary for acceptance of the new technology also applies to many other fields. To make significant inroads it is necessary to get the medical institution's top physicians personally involved in the project. For example, even though the Help system was developed by doctors at LDS Hospital, it was not until the team got one of LDS's top cardiologists sufficiently involved in the project that he became enthusiastic enough to be able to sell the idea to the other cardiologists in the hospital. Before that, the knowledge system could barely even be considered for implementation because the people who developed the knowledge system were outsiders.

ANATOMY OF A MEDICAL KNOWLEDGE-BASED SYSTEM

Like all classical knowledge systems, Care, Help, and Puff separate data, knowledge, and control. They incorporate physicians' heuristics. All use or simulate some form of backward chaining.

They differ from classical knowledge systems in that Lisp has not been the language of choice. Care is written in VAX Basic, a compiled, extensive superset of Basic that offers recursion, reentrant subroutines, separately compiled subroutines, a map file record structure, and a variety of structured programming constructs. Help is programmed in TAL, a Pascal-like language for Tandem computers. Puff is programmed in Basic but is being rewritten in Pascal.

The programming of these knowledge systems in conventional programming languages allows the systems to run on conventional computers, and in the cases of Care and Help, interface to databases. For example, Care runs on the DEC VAX-11/780 computer. Help runs on the Tandem Nonstop II computer. Puff ran, in Basic, on the DEC PDP-11 but was translated into Pascal. The translated version, renamed Micropuff, runs on a Tektronix 5200 computer and is being targeted at a variety of microcomputers.

Although Basic and Tal are the programming languages underlying Care and Help, both Care and Help are high-level programming languages in their own rights and they are the languages in which medical expertise for each system is encoded.

Both the Care and Help languages have incorporated a few Lisp features. Unlike Lisp, however, the Care and Help languages support conventional procedural components (ordinary subroutines and control constructs, such as IF-THEN-ELSE), as well as knowledge-based types of nonprocedural components (rules and frames). In addition, both Care and Help are English-like languages understandable by physicians and other members of the medical community not trained in computer science.

Puff's development grew out of work done on the infectious disease expert system, Mycin. The first version of Puff, before it was translated to Basic and then Pascal, was written in Emycin, a generalized form of Mycin. Emycin consists of certain of Mycin's components, such as its rule interpreter, inference mechanism,

```
RULE011
-------

If:   1) A: The mmf/mmf-predicted ratio is between 35 and 45, and
         B: The fvc/fvc-predicted ratio is greater than 80, or
      2) A: The mmf/mmf-predicted ratio is between 25 and 35, and
         B: The fvc/fvc-predicted ratio is less than 80
Then:   1) There is suggestive evidence (.5) that the degree of
           obstructive airways disease as indicated by the MMF
           is moderate, and
        2) It is definite (1.0) that the following is one of the
           findings about the diagnosis of obstructive airways
           disease:  Reduced mid-expiratory flow indicates
           moderate airway obstruction.
```

Figure 23-9 A typical PUFF rule (Pacific Medical Center)

and knowledge acquisition modules. These can be applied to a knowledge base in any domain. Emycin and the Emycin version of Puff are written in Interlisp.

Puff's knowledge is written in the form of rules and clinical parameters. Clincial parameters represent pulmonary function test results, such as total lung capacity and residual volume; patient data, such as age, smoking history, pulmonary symptoms, and referral diagnosis; and data that are derived from the rules, such as findings associated with a disease. The clinical parameters may be associated with information, such as a list of expected values and an English translation used to communicate with the user.

Puff's rules, written in classical expert system format, consist of one or more conditional clauses followed by one or more action clauses (Figure 23-9). In 1983, Puff had 400 rules and 75 clinical parameters (Aikens et al., 1983).

To come up with its diagnoses and interpretations, Puff employs goal-directed, backward chaining techniques. Its goal at any time is to determine a value for a given clinical parameter. To conclude this value, it chains backward through the rules whose actions conclude clinical parameter values.

As with other classical backward chaining systems, Puff employs three methods of concluding a value. It looks to see if the value is immediately present. If not, it tries to infer the value from backward chaining through the rules. Failing this, Puff asks the user. An exception is for parameters labeled ASKFIRST. Since these represent parameters generally known by the user (such as the results of pulmonary function tests), Puff asks the user first, rather than trying to infer the information from the rules.

PHYSIOLOGY OF CARE

C. J. McDonald, Care's chief developer, describes Care as both "more and less than Mycin" (McDonald, 1984a). It is less because it deals with a large variety of topics, but it deals with these topics at a more shallow level than Mycin deals with diagnosis and treatment of infections. Care provides no automatic weighting of conclusions and no means of selecting the best of a series of competing conclusions. In addition, it has no explanation facility other than the text embedded in the program's conclusions.

On the other hand, Care is more than Mycin, particularly because it uses database, as well as knowledge base, systems. Care can obtain the data needed for its decisions directly from the medical record, as well as from dialogues with the physician or other health practitioner. It can deal with the time dimension—a necessary medical capability. It also has arithmetic and algebraic capabilities.

The Regenstrief Medical Record System coupled to Care is a time-oriented computerized medical database. It contains objective data gathered during patients' visits to the emergency room, the medicine clinics, or admissions to the hospital. This includes all medical treatments, diagnoses, laboratory, and imaging studies in an encoded form.

This medical record system is large and contains records for more than 60,000 patients—some of whom the Regenstrief Institute has followed for more than ten years. The total database occupies more than 300 million bytes and has approximately 22 million separate results. Meaning is encoded into the system by means of a dictionary with over 8,000 different items.

Medical expertise in Care is written in the Care language, a rule-based language for representing medical knowledge and making decisions about patients. Care contains approximately 1491 rules, which take up about 120 pages of computer printout and can generate 751 different reminder messages. These numbers are actually less than cited for earlier versions of the system because the Care language has been modified to make it more succinct than previous versions.

Like Mycin, Care stores its medical knowledge as conditional-type statements. A typical Mycin statement looks like this:

```
IF:    1) THE SITE OF THE CULTURE IS BLOOD, AND
       2) THE GRAM STAIN OF THE ORGANISM IS GRAMNEG, AND
       3) THE MORPHOLOGY OF THE ORGANISM IS ROD, AND
       4) THE PATIENT IS A COMPROMISED HOST
THEN:  THERE IS SUGGESTIVE EVIDENCE (0.6) THAT THE IDENTITY
       OF THE ORGANISM IS PSEUDOMONAS-AERUGINOSA
```

A typical Care statement has a similar form (McDonald et al., 1984a):

```
IF"HCT DROP" OCCURRED ON AFTER "MOST RECENT VISIT"
  AND (NO "OCCULT BLOOD DX" WAS BEFORE "ANEMIA ONSET"
  OR "OCCULT BLOOD DX" WAS BEFORE "ANEMIA ONSET")
THEN consider testing stool for "occult blood" unless
     recent HCT drop has been explained.
```

As seen, both Mycin and Care statements contain one or more clauses in their IF (premise) and THEN (action) parts. In addition, both expert systems describe the possible subjects of their clauses in the parameter dictionary.

```
DEFINE "CV RISK" AS 100/(1 + EXP(-"CV RISK INDEX"))

DEFINE "CV RISK INDEX" AS
"AGE" IS GT 35  LT 75
        AND ("MALE PATIENT"
               AND EX:  0.3743*"AGE"
               -0.0021*"AGE"*"AGE"
               +0.0258*"CHOLESTEROL LAST"
               +0.0157*"SYS BP SITTING LAST"
               +1.0530*"LVH DX" {TVAL}
               +0.6020*"DIABETES DX1"  {TVAL}
               -0.00036*"CHOLESTEROL LAST"*"AGE"
               +0.5583*"SMOKER" {TVAL}
               -19.771)
        OR ("FEMALE PATIENT"
               AND EX:  0.267*"AGE"
               -0.00127*"AGE"*"AGE"
               +0.016*"CHOLESTEROL LAST"
               +0.014*"SYS BP SITTING LAST"
               +0.039*"SMOKER" {TVAL}
               +0.874*"LVH DX" {TVAL}
               +0.682*"DIABETES DX1" {TVAL}
               -0.00022*"CHOLESTEROL LAST"*"AGE"
               -16.460)

DEFINE "DIABETES DX" AS "DX LAST" WAS = "DIABETES
MEL" OR "DIABETES MEDS USE"

DEFINE "DIABETES DX" AS "DX LAST" WAS = "DIABETES
MEL" OR "DIABETES MEDS USE"

DEFINE "DIABETES MEDS USE" AS "INSULIN USE" OR
"ORAL HYPOGLYCEMIC USE"

DEFINE "PATIENT SEX" AS
        "SEX" IS = 'M'
        OR
        "SEX" IS = 'F'
        OR
        (LOAD {PARAMETER} WITH "SEX VALUE"
        AND LOAD {DATE} WITH TODAY
        AND ASK {VALUE} WITH 'Sex')

DEFINE "AGE" AS
        EX:(TODAY - "BIRTH")/365
        OR
        (LOAD {PARAMETER} WITH "TIME VALUE"
        AND LOAD {DATE} WITH TODAY
        AND ASK {VALUE} WITH 'Age')
```

Figure 23-10 Typical DEFINE statement knowledge in CARE (Regenstrief Health Center)

Mycin is a backward-chaining system that tries to accomplish a goal by chaining backward through the rules whose action parts conclude a premise of the rule currently in question. Care chains backward through a series of DEFINE statements which may contain reference to other rules and/or logic for asking user questions directly.

Care's DEFINE statements are analogous to the knowledge rules in Mycin. Like Mycin rules, they are nonprocedural. They provide a means of defining a variable by searching the computer database to see if the information is available. If it is not, Care tries to assert or infer the variable by chaining through its DEFINE statements. If that fails, Care asks the user.

Figure 23-10 shows a series of DEFINE statements. They differ from Mycin rules in that they only contain conditions. They (and the Care system in general) further differ from Mycin in that evaluation of the define statements is initiated by

```
IF "AGE" IS GE 35  LT 75 AND "CV RISK" IS GT 15
    IF SMOKER THEN
         REMIND Patient's Framingham CV risk (risk
         of stroke, MI or claudication in next 8
         years) is "CV RISK"  VALUE  percent.
         Cessation of smoking would decrease these
         risks.
    ELSE IF "CHOLESTEROL LAST" WAS GT 300 THEN
         REMIND Framingham CV risk (risk of stroke,
         MI or claudication in the next 8 years) is
         "CV RISK" {VALUE} percent.  Reducing the
         patient's cholesterol ("CHOLESTEROL LAST"
         {VAL} on {DATE} would reduce these risks.
```

Figure 23-11 Control statements in CARE (Regenstrief Health Center)

procedural statements that are part of Care. Mycin allows no conventional-type procedural statements.

Care however, has three kinds of procedural statements: organization, control, and action. The organizational statements are BEGIN BLOCK and END BLOCK. They mark the beginning and end of a group of logically related statements, such as those that deal with ordering hematocrit determinations or starting digitalis therapy.

Control statements determine the order in which statements are processed by the computer. Examples of control statements are traditional IF-THEN-ELSE constructs (Figure 23-11). Typically, they are found just inside each block and they determine whether the system should skip all the succeeding statements in the block, perform the indicated action and stop, or continue processing with the next procedural statement that appears.

Action statements are found in the THEN or ELSE part of IF-THEN-ELSE statements. The action statements may generate one or more reminders. Alternatively, they may be control actions that affect the order in which statements are processed. These include actions such as EXIT, which direct the computer to exit from a block either before or after a reminder is generated. Finally, the action may be a retrieval action that tells the computer which variable to save and where to save it.

As with any knowledge-based system, to perform an action in Care, it is necessary to satisfy all the conditions in the IF part of IF-THEN-ELSE statements—the equivalent of classical expert system rules. The variables (enclosed in quotes) in these statements invoke the evaluation of DEFINE statements. When all the conditions in the DEFINE statements are evaluated or satisfied in some way, Care's logic instantiates the value of the variable for use in control, action, or other DEFINE statements.

As Figure 23-10 shows, the DEFINE statements also contain variables, in quotes, to be evaluated. Some are evaluated by searching the medical record database. Others require the evaluation of equations. The first DEFINE statement, for example, contains the Framingham Cardiovascular Equation (CV RISK). This is a logistic regression equation to compute the cardiovascular risk based on the Framingham study of cholesterol, smoking history, diabetes, blood pressure, age, and a number of other variables. Different equations apply to males and females.

Still other quoted variables in the DEFINE statements must be evaluated by invoking other DEFINE statements. To evaluate the quoted CV RISK equation in the first DEFINE statement, it is necessary to invoke the second DEFINE statement to evaluate the quoted CV RISK INDEX. The invocation of other DEFINE statements may require the invocation of still others, or even trigger a cascade of invoked DEFINE statements. This cascading of DEFINE statements is equivalent to backward chaining.

For example, the DEFINE statements in Figure 23-10 just lie fallow until the quoted CV RISK in the procedural statement in Figure 23-11 invokes the first DEFINE statement. To satisfy this statement, it is necessary to evaluate the CV RISK equation defined in this statement. To evaluate this CV RISK equation, it is necessary to invoke the CV RISK INDEX in the second DEFINE statement. Satisfaction of the CV RISK INDEX DEFINE statement requires the evaluation of patient AGE, SEX, and several other variables. These variables are the subject of still other DEFINE statements that must be invoked.

Some of these DEFINE statements may require computations, as with the AGE equals (TODAY - "BIRTH")/365. Quoted variables such as BIRTH may be obtained from the database. Alternatively, AGE may be obtained by asking the user. Other variables, such as the presence of diabetes in the patient, may be inferred by knowing that the patient is on Insulin.

The text in the reminder message may also contain variables. As with IF clause variables, text variables may be raw data in the medical records, data computed algebraically, or data inferred from other data.

Printing of the reminder message incorporated in the action clause is a fairly dumb text processing activity. Yet by the time the reminder is generated, it is highly specific to the patient in question. For example, Figure 23-11 indicates that if the patient's age is greater than 35 and less than 75 and the Cardiovascular Risk is greater than 15, it means that there is a 15 percent chance of something bad happening in eight years. Therefore, if the patient is a smoker, Care suggests that the doctor tell him to quit.

What to suggest in the reminder messages has been the subject of much discussion. Doctors at the Regenstrief Institute point out that there is little sense in telling patients about risk factors that they cannot control. For example, telling patients that they are at risk because they are 75 years old, or that they will die early because they are male, at the least causes worry, and at the most may be harmful. Therefore, the physician team at the Regenstrief Institute has limited Care's reminder messages to constructive actions.

Figure 23-12 shows separate control blocks that trigger backward chaining through a series of DEFINE statements to conclude information and provide reminders about depression and influenza vaccines. The large cascade of DEFINE statements required by these blocks are not shown here.

Almost always, Care uses an exit condition at the beginning of the block. This eliminates much unnecessary processing for certain conditions that pertain to that block. With this in mind, the first statement in the Figure 23-12 Begin-End

```
BEGIN BLOCK "ANTIDEPRESSANTS"

IF "ANTIDEPRESSANT USE" OR "PREMATURES DX" OR
"ANGINA DX" THEN
    EXIT

!Tests for symptoms or drug use which suggests the
possibility of depression.

IF "DEPRESSION SX" EXISTS SINCE 1 YEAR AGO
    AND ("BENZODIAZEPINES USE" WAS SINCE 6 MONTHS
    AGO OR "PAIN MEDS USE" WAS SINCE 6 MONTHS AGO)
    THEN
        REMIND The patient has been described drugs
        ({PARAMETER}) and has symptoms ("DEPRESSION
        SX" {VALUE}) suggestive of background
        depression. Look for sleep disturbances,
        especially early wakening, multiple somatic
        complaints, the 'blues', flat affect, and
        loss of interest in vegative functions.
        Many of these symptoms will abate with
        tricyclic treatment.  R:4009
    AND EXIT

END BLOCK "ANTIDEPRESSANTS"


BEGIN BLOCK "FLU SHOT"

IF TODAY IS NOT AFTER 10/1  BEFORE 12/31 OR "FLU
SHOT LAST" IS AFTER 8/1 OR LAST "REFUSED FLU INJ"
WAS = 1  SINCE 1 YEAR AGO OR "DRUG ALLERGIES" WAS
= "SERUM ALRGY" V "VACCINE ALRGY" OR "ALLERGY HX"
WAS = "SERUM ALRGY" V "VACCINE ALRGY"
    THEN EXIT

IF "DX'S" WAS = "ASTHMA" V "COPD" OR "CXR LAST"
WAS = "COPD" THEN
    REMIND Consider giving Flu Shot AB if there
    is no egg allergy because lung disease
    ( {PARAMETER} = {VALUE} on {DATE} ) places
    patient in high risk category.  R:2124
    AND EXIT

END BLOCK "FLU SHOT"
```

Figure 23-12 Procedural statements in CARE (Regenstrief Health Center)

block directs the Care system to quit the block immediately if angina has been diagnosed in a patient because there is some risk in using antidepressants for people with heart disease. The symbol ! after the first EXIT indicates a comment in the statement.

The depression reminder accompanying the block's second statement does not make an explicit recommendation. It suggests that the physician only be aware of certain tests and symptoms because depression is not a condition that is diagnosed objectively. Instead, depression is a diagnosis which depends very strongly on symptoms that individual physicians string together and weigh against what they see in the patient.

The symptoms in this statement, which are defined as "having had to exist from within the past year," illustrate the reason that any knowledge-based system must evolve for some time. It is taken for granted that if a patient does not report certain symptoms for a year, the symptoms may have disappeared without the patient saying so. However, it is these types of details that knowledge engineers and experts frequently fail to even think of in the initial versions of a knowledge system.

Two amusing examples of tuning requirements occurred in the initial version of Care. One was the printing of the patient's age to six decimal places (47.619201 years). In a second case, the patient's sex was printed as "none of the above."

The last message in the block's second statement reminder notice is the cryptic number after R:. This is a citation to the relevant medical literature.

The second block, also shown in Figure 23-12, is part of a more conventional reminder block about conditions that pertain to fall flu shots. The block requires computation of the date and accounts for patients who already received a flu shot (they do not need it again), who refused one, or who have a variety of allergies or lung disease.

Two different kinds of allergies are covered. For one kind, the vaccine is recommended; for the other it is not. The checking for disease conditions, such as asthma, may require Care to cascade through symptoms of communicable diseases in order to reach a diagnosis and prove that the patient has (or does not have) asthma.

When the conditional part of an action rule is satisfied by the patient record or information inferred by Care, the reminder text is saved in a file for inclusion in that patient's reminder report. The reminder report is given to the physician at the time he or she sees the patient.

A two-year controlled study revealed significant health care advantages to the medical knowledge-based reminder system (McDonald et al., 1984b). For example, twice as many physicians performed preventative actions, such as cancer detection and immunization, when they received the reminders as when not ($p<0.0001$). Results were less significant for therapeutic actions, among other reasons because these actions tend to be patient-complaint driven. In other words, when the patient says "something hurts," the physician reacts.

HOW HELP WORKS

Other medical institutions with similar systems report similar results. It is because of these results that LDS Hospital's Dr. Warner calls the Help medical knowledge system a quality control tool that acts as an adjunct to physicians' own knowledge base and helps them act in accordance with their goals.

Like Care and Mycin, Help can use straightforward, deterministic IF-THEN logic. It differs from both these systems in three important respects: its interactive capabilities (discussed earlier), its ability to use probabilistic logic, and its knowledge organization.

Help is one of the first medical knowledge systems to use Bayesian statistics. To be sure, many classical expert systems express their answers with an appropriate certainty factor. But this factor is usually empirical and depends on the experience of the expert whose knowledge is encoded in the expert program.

Carrying the weighting factor criteria a step further, Help can express decision criteria as conditional probabilities (where the probability of an event occurring is dependent on prior events or observations). Its probabilistic calculations depend on the algebraic expression known as the Bayes formula. As data input, among other factors, the Bayes formula uses measured frequencies of occurrences of data or events (such as symptoms). It therefore produces answers that are more exact than those that can be produced by expert systems with predetermined probability factors.

However, the Help system is not purely Bayesian oriented. It also uses independent probability calculations. Which method is chosen depends on the events in question. For example, given that a patient has a disease, the presence of one symptom may have no bearing on the presence of another (independent probability). On the other hand, the presence of symptoms may be dependent on the presence of the associated disease (Bayesian probability).

Knowledge in Help is organized in a form called a *sector*, which is similar in some respects to a frame-based representation. Each sector corresponds to a single modular decision. It can have up to 52 different statements. The statements can consist of, or handle, IF-THEN rules, Bayesian probability logic, arithmetic or regression equations, and instructions that direct the search of the patient's record. Other sector statements contain the criteria for evaluating the patient's data, messages that are displayed when the sector criteria are satisfied, and references to other Help sectors.

Help has 2147 sectors which encompass a wide variety of applications. The most popular are involved with EKG interpretation, blood gas interpretation, pharmacy alerts, predicted X-ray findings, and clinical laboratory alerts. The sectors that pertain to these applications are invoked at the appropriate time during the normal course of hospital activities. For example, a cardiologist might leave a prescription of digitalis at the nursing station. When the pharmacist enters the prescription into the nursing station terminal, the entry activates any help sectors that relate to digitalis.

Typical statements in these Help sectors might cause Help to examine laboratory data and medical records to see if the patient has an active prescription for digitalis. The next search item might require a medical record search for the patient's serum potassium value. Next might be to find out if the patient is getting a potassium supplement. These search items might be followed by an IF-THEN rule like the following:

```
IF THE PATIENT IS ON DIGITALIS
  AND THE SERUM POTASSIUM IS LESS THAN 2.4
    MILLIEQUIVALENTS PER LITER
  AND THE PATIENT IS NOT GETTING A POTASSIUM
    SUPPLEMENT
THEN THE SECTOR IS TRUE
```

The sector might then print a message suggesting that digitalis is dangerous in this dose because the patient has a low serum potassium and recommend that the physician give a potassium supplement with the digitalis.

WALKING THROUGH A BAYESIAN SECTOR*

Figure 23-13 shows a sector to predict the presence of pleural fluid by radiograph. This sector is activated whenever a physician orders a chest film for a patient.

The physician's X-ray request is sent to the radiology department, where technicians key it in. This triggers the activation of all help sectors that relate to possible interpretations of the X-ray. The Help system processes these sectors to advise the radiologist about what he or she is likely to find.

The items in the sector may be search items. For example, item A causes the computer to search through the patient database for a doctor-ordered chest examination of a specific type that has not yet been processed by Help. If it exists the value of item A is set to a code between 1 and 8 depending on the type of examination that was ordered.

Item B sets the initial a priori probability of having pleural fluid (probability of pleural fluid on the chest X-ray before anything else is known about the patient) at 1 percent (10/1000). This figure is specific to inpatients at LDS Hospital on whom chest films are ordered. Items C through E change the a priori probability (value of item B) depending on the specific procedure (value of item A) that was ordered.

Items F through O cause the patient's record to be searched for data that affect the likelihood of pleural fluid. Other items set a priori probabilities to be used in subsequent Bayesian probability calculations, which are performed in other items.

The final likelihood of pleural fluid is the value of line II and reflects the influence of clinical data such as laboratory tests and prior radiology findings as well as reasons for ordering the examination. As mentioned, numerous other Help sectors that relate to chest film interpretations have also been activated, processed, and the probability calculated when the physician orders a chest film for a patient.

The Help system picks the five most likely interpretations and prints them on the X-ray requisition that is sent to the radiologist. The goal is to facilitate interpretation by the radiologist by telling him or her what the likelihood is of particular interpretations, based on clinical and statistical data. It turns out that about 80 percent of the time, the radiologist's interpretation correlates with the one predicted. This provides the reinforcement of a second opinion and the physician then need only check the correct box.

*This discussion is based on Pryor and others (1983).

```
                    Pleural Fluid          Final Evaluation II
A             X-ray, chest, specific exam
B             10
C             If (A EQ 7) then B=524
D             If (A EQ 1) or (A EQ 2)  or (A EQ 3) then B-150
E             If (A EQ 56) then B=79
F             Chest pain (reason)
G         ?   Pleural effusion (reason)
H             Pre-op (general reason)
I             Followup known disease (general reason)
J             Chair (transportation)
K             Post op (general reason)
L             Walk (transportation)
M         ?   Pneumothorax (reason)
N             Coronary artery disease (reason)
O         ?   Pulmonary embolus (reason)
P             Pleural fluid reported in last 2 days
                   (ITEM)        (PRIOR PROB.)        P(S/D)            P(S/D)
Q       Prob binary   F               B                .022              .070
R                     G               Q                .193              .029
S                     H               R                .009              .150
T                     I               S                .210              .146
U                     J               T                .546              .420
V                     K               U                .395              .255
W                     L               V                .004              .084
X                     M               W                .059              .021
Y                     N               X                .004              .030
Z                     O               Y                .053              .018
AA                    P               Z                .243              .036
BB            (A) SMA-12, Albumin GM%
CC            (A) CBC, Hemoglobin GM%
DD            (A) SMA-12, Calcium MG%
EE            (A) Age
                   ITEM  (P)  MIN   MAX  (1)   (2)    (3)     (4)     (5)     (6)    (7)    (8)
FF      Prob dist   BB   AA   1.1   5.4  6/2   13/4   16/8    23/13   22/19   12/25  6/17   2/12
GG      Prob dist   CC   FF   4.7  18.0  5/2   14/7   18/9    23/11   18/19   13/23  6/16   2/14
HH      Prob dist   DD   GG   6.8  11.0  6/2   12/4   15/10   21/15   18/28   18/27  6/10   3/3
II      Prob dist   EE   HH   0    100   1/1    4/6    5/11    8/11   25/24   34/31  18/13  5/3
```

Figure 23-13 HELP sector logic for calculating likelihood of pleural fluid in a patient (LDS Hospital)

HELP AND CARE CONTINUE GROWING

Besides extending and enhancing the logic of Help, its physician/developers are concentrating new development efforts in the areas of efficiency and distribution of the system.

The database is a candidate for efficiency enhancement. The Help database, on average, is accessed about seven to eight times a second, twenty-four hours a day. Moreover, every decision requires multiple accesses to the database. Therefore, the database must be organized in such a way as to optimize the response time and ease of getting at the data.

An effort will also be made to increase Help system performance and efficient use by distributing the database processing throughout the hospital. Toward this end, centrally stored database and knowledge-base information, and centrally processed Help decisions, will be transmitted to microprocessor-based systems located at each nursing station where local processing needed for speedy review will be performed. This distribution will decrease the load on the central database and increase the speed of Help processing at the centralized location, as well as the speed of review by medical personnel at local stations.

Still another way planned to extend the knowledge system is to place microprocessor-based Help systems in doctor's offices. These local systems will communicate with the central databases and knowledge bases. By so doing, they will provide Help capabilities for follow-ups of patients from the doctor's office.

At the Regenstrief Institute, micros are being integrated with the mainframe computers, with the aim of extending Care's user base. Despite its advantages, Care's physician/developers see some deficiencies in the system. For some decisions, for example, the information contained in the medical record is insufficient. More data are needed, particularly because Care is a batch mode rather than an interactive system and therefore, knows nothing about the observations obtained at the patient's scheduled visit.

Another disadvantage is the large number of rules in the system. Efforts are currently under way to reduce the number of rules by expressing them in more general terms. Toward this end, the Care development team is looking at tabular representations and studying the possibility of switching to Prolog as the underlying programming language.

Prolog is under consideration because it allows medical data to be represented in a relational database form. So far, Care's developers have converted the syntax of Care into a Prolog parse definition. They claim to be impressed with the resulting performance but are still learning the subtleties of declarative programming.

24

AI in Engineering

Wherever the eye turns, there is evidence of unceasing activity in the fields of very large-scale integration (VLSI)/large-scale integration (LSI) chips. Microprocessors, memories, and controllers are turning up not only in computers and technologically advanced equipment, but also in washing machines, typewriters, toys, automobiles, and television sets.

Once conceived of, a variety of computer-aided design/computer-aided engineering tools exist to draw the circuits that the engineers designed, check them for errors, and prepare blueprints of the engineers' ideas for production processes. Between the conception of the idea by the engineers and the manufacture of a piece of silicon that transforms the idea into physical reality, there is a long, tedious process. During this time, engineers find a combination of circuits that perform the functions they conceived of, that also meet performance standards in terms of speed and low error rates, and that fit into a minimum amount of area (real estate) on a piece of silicon.

Finding the right combination is a difficult task because the requirements are often contradictory. To satisfy spatial requirements it may be necessary to sacrifice performance. Performance may require the sacrifice of functionality. Power and size may be incompatible.

In addition, VLSI design problems are particularly complex, involving two different types of complexity. One type of complexity results from the problems of interconnecting a very large number of objects involved in a task or thing. Chip layout and routing problems are included in this category. The other type of complexity stems from the object involved having very complicated descriptions and behaviors. Chip design synthesis problems fit into this second complexity category.

CHIP LAYOUT

Layout refers to laying out the specific blocks of circuits in a chip. Routing is the problem of interconnecting all these circuits.

Chip layout complexity results from the sheer number of microelectronic components that make up a ½-inch by ½-inch chip. A 64K RAM might have 100,000 transistors; a 32-bit microprocessor may have 500,000. Automating the layout of a 64K RAM is a problem whose complexity is roughly equivalent to automating the layout of the streets of New York City, block by block, house by house, and fire hydrant by hydrant. For the 32-bit microprocessor, it is equivalent to laying out the streets in several states in the southwestern United States. The complexity of the routing task for the RAM and the microprocessor corresponds to wiring such cities or regions.

AI is not yet able to handle these large, complex layout tasks, not only because of the large number of components, but because there are so many constraints to be satisfied. Again, a city layout makes a good analogy. Warehouses should not be located next to apartment buildings. Fire hydrants must be located near all buildings. And so on.

Similarly, for very large-scale integrated circuits, the problem of constraints and the propagation of these constraints (constraints on one part of the circuit propagate and affect other parts of the circuit) is unmanageable for the present state of AI programs. It is not even that a knowledge system could not be (or has not been) built to lay out a chip design. In the case of a simple controller with only 30,000 transistors, such as for an industrial application, Texas Instruments (TI) has built knowledge-based systems that automate layout and routing functions. The problem, says George Heilmeier, TI's senior vice president and chief technical officer, is that designs produced by knowledge systems are not generally optimized enough to be commercially competitive; they are inferior to a human-designed chip in terms of chip area and speed.

The importance of speed is self-explanatory. As for area, VLSI economics dictates that as the area of the chip becomes larger, the chip yield for a given diameter wafer decreases, and, consequently the cost per chip increases. Moreover, the cost increases exponentially. The difference in cost between a chip that measures 50,000 square mils (1 mil = 1/1000 inch) compared to a 100,000-square mil chip is not 2:1 but closer to 10:1.

For this reason, commercial VLSI designs must be optimized to occupy minimal space. Unfortunately, knowledge systems have not been very successful in capturing human heuristics to perform this spatial optimization because it involves a lot of pattern recognition. Human beings are adept at pattern-recognition tasks. They can look at a variety of objects and decide the best way to pack clothes in a suitcase or objects in the trunk of a car. However, it is very difficult to explain to a computer how they did it.

Similarly, engineers can visualize how to arrange tens of thousands of circuits to minimize the amount of area they occupy. When laying out a type of circuit known as a programmable logic array (PLA), engineers may notice that some of the rows in the PLA are nearly empty. At the same time, some clever geometrical and topological ideas may occur to them that enable them to do some clever folding of the layout to make the overall layout more compact. The folding may have some side effects, propagated to the circuits surrounding the PLA, which the engineer will also have to reconcile. But it is not yet understood what types of topological rules to specify to a knowledge system for VLSI design layout, nor is much known even about how to specify these types of rules.

DESIGN SYNTHESIS

The area of VLSI that AI experts feel will be most susceptible to AI help is the area of design syntheses. Here, knowledge-based systems can be constructed to act as a designer's assistant or design consultant. Still largely in the research stages, VLSI design consultants provide advice and suggestions for VLSI designers, just as various diagnostic advisory systems and oil exploration and manufacturing consultants do for troubleshooters, geophysicists, and project managers. A typical AI-based VLSI design consultant understands the purpose of various chip components, such as memory and arithmetic-logic units, and contains knowledge of how engineers design integrated circuits. Using this knowledge, the consultant can look at descriptions and specifications for a circuit and decide the best way to implement them. To make its decision, the consultant might examine the possibilities of making discrete connections between components using multiplexers, buses, or point-to-point links, weigh trade-offs, and propose an architecture that satisfies various constraints.

Checking out a design is another major function of a knowledge-based VLSI consultant. But checking out a design does not mean checking for legal inputs and connections, such as CAD and CAE systems do. It means, rather, critiquing the design decisions made by examining their ramifications and the trade-offs, like designers do.

For example, a design consultant might critique a design and suggest that a particular decision is not the best one because it costs the system speed. Or for a particular task, it might suggest that a different class of logic or class of registers would be a better choice. For another design, the consultant might hypothesize using a bus, then determine how expensive it would be to compile a design using that bus, and finally decide how the proposed bus and its cost relate to power, area, and speed constraints.

The knowledge and reasoning necessary to provide such design advice must not be underestimated. Like VLSI design layout, VLSI design synthesis is a large-constraint problem with a lot of conflicting constraints. It is not known a priori how many components are to be connected where they might go, or how to connect them. There are vast numbers of alternative paths to be exploited and no fixed architecture to strive for. Simply put, a VLSI design system creates a never-before-created architecture, on the fly, from circuit descriptions and specifications. Consequently, the search space of possible solutions tends to be huge.

Besides complexity, a major problem in designing a knowledge-based system for VLSI design is a lack of understanding about how engineers do VLSI design. This lack is illustrated by the experiences of a group of AI researchers at MIT who set up a computer-aided design project with the goal of building an intelligent computerized assistant for a human chip designer.

As it turned out, the group never built the intelligent chip designer. Instead, they ended up designing a microprocessor using traditional techniques and taking notes of what types of thinking processes they performed in order to make their design decisions. This analysis of the human design process was necessary because the MIT researchers discovered that the types of informal reasoning that people do when designing chips had never been formalized and was ill-understood.

WHAT AI DOES NOT DO

Although the informal reasoning needed for VLSI design activities is not yet sufficiently clarified for commercialization, a number of algorithms for routing and placement of circuit elements (the production end of the VLSI design process) and the mathematics of the circuit-theory domain (the analytical side of the process) are both well understood and formalized. This understanding makes possible a large number of sophisticated computer-aided design (CAD) and computer-aided engineering (CAE) tools. These are powerful, automated drafting and design production tools, based on numeric and algorithmic programs. They help engineers manipulate their designs, simulate and check out their circuits, spot errors, and produce a finished plan that is acceptable to another machine or to a human being.

However, traditional CAD/CAE tools do not create designs that did not first originate in the head of some designer. They have little understanding of their task, and consequently, they do very little to help designers with the conceptual design job. Refinement of a design is done by the designer, not by the CAD/CAE system. When a circuit simulator produces unexpected results, engineers must rely on their own resources to understand why.

Similarly, although the formal math of circuit theory is a powerful tool, it is much too detailed and complicated to give engineers an intuitive idea of how circuits work. As such, it is more suited to circuit analysis than design. In designing circuits, engineers tend to use intuitive understanding, heuristic knowledge, and informal reasoning rather than mathematical analyses. Only after the conceptualization of ideas for a circuit design does the process graduate to the stages of analysis and circuit simulation.

WHAT AI CAN DO

Although still in its infancy, work in the application of AI technology to VLSI design is in progress at major semiconductor producers, such as Fairchild IBM, and AT&T Bell Laboratories, as well as at academic institutions. Progress is slow but steady, especially in the area of design synthesis. Although construction of VLSI design assistants is not around the corner, neither have design synthesis snags been hit which require a major technological breakthrough to build practical systems.

AI-based VLSI work is occurring worldwide in the areas of capturing heuristic VLSI design knowledge and representing design knowledge (which is highly visual) in knowledge bases. Efforts are also under way to build AI programs that can diagnose circuit faults, and search, select, and modify preexisting circuit designs in catalogs to produce a circuit tailored to a user's specifications.

These knowledge-based engineering capabilities do not necessarily require specialized, dedicated AI hardware. A number of vendors of conventional computers have come out with AI environments and languages for engineering workstations. Meanwhile, several AI vendors have integrated AI workstations with conventional software capabilities. These combination systems add up to the ability to include AI capabilities in routinely used CAD/CAE systems.

AI/VLSI SPIN-OFFS

The first practical contributions of AI to VLSI design have been AI spin-offs rather than knowledge-based products for VLSI design. They include the application of AI programming languages, tools, and hardware to VLSI design. For example, Silicart, Inc., a custom chip house in Montreal, Canada, is using Lisp, Prolog, and associated tools to design chips on Lisp machines. Another example is Tektronix, which has developed circuit-diagnostic programs, using the Smalltalk language, on an engineering workstation specialized for AI.

Several advantages accrue from using AI languages for VLSI design. Many of these relate to the complexity and large number of elements that VLSI programs handle. AI languages are particularly good at solving problems that involve representations of complex structures. This makes them suitable for manipulating the complex structures of VLSI problems. They are also much more modular and interactive than conventional languages, which makes it easier to debug, incrementally refine, add to, and manage large, complex VLSI programs.

Rule-based programming further simplifies large VLSI problems by allowing designers to specify knowledge applicable to different aspects of VLSI design in

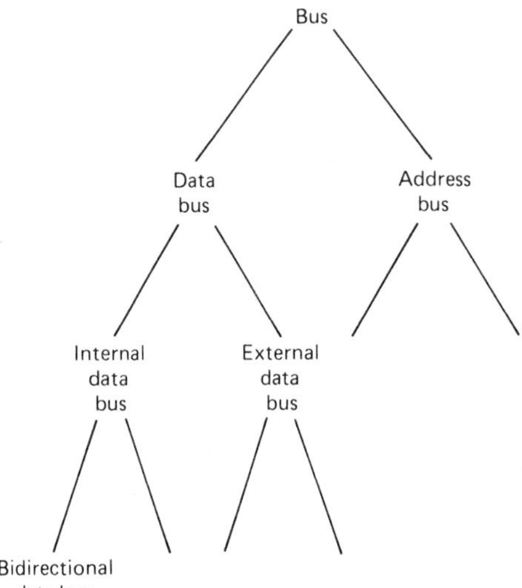

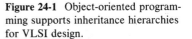

Figure 24-1 Object-oriented programming supports inheritance hierarchies for VLSI design.

the form of modular rules. The rules and the rule interpreter then manage and apply themselves, when applicable, without requiring programmers to explicitly specify all program control.

The Prolog language had some additional advantages for AI-based VLSI design. Prolog's backtracking mechanism (process of guessing at a solution path and backing up to a previous branch point to try another solution if the guess is wrong) provides an easy and automatic way to test the effectiveness of certain substructures in some parts of a VLSI design. It also provides an easy way to explore the consequences of a small number of choices, without programmers having to write the search, choice, and backup-and-try-elsewhere routines for exploration purposes.

Object-oriented programming provides still more modularity by letting the designer encapsulate procedures with local components and data structures (objects) of a design. Since these procedures are hidden from other components and structures, programmers need not worry about adversely affecting the other components and structures when modifying a procedure. This minimizes code changes.

The organization of components and structures into inheritance heirarchies in object-oriented programming also provides benefits for VLSI designers. Normally, the most generic components are at the top of a hierarchy and the more specific components are at the bottom (Figure 24-1). Procedures and attributes of components lower in the hierarchy are inherited from their parents. These hierarchies can also show, at a glance, how components higher in hierarchy are related to those below (Figure 24-2). As each lower-level circuit is created, it knows instantly how it is related to others already created. The inherited

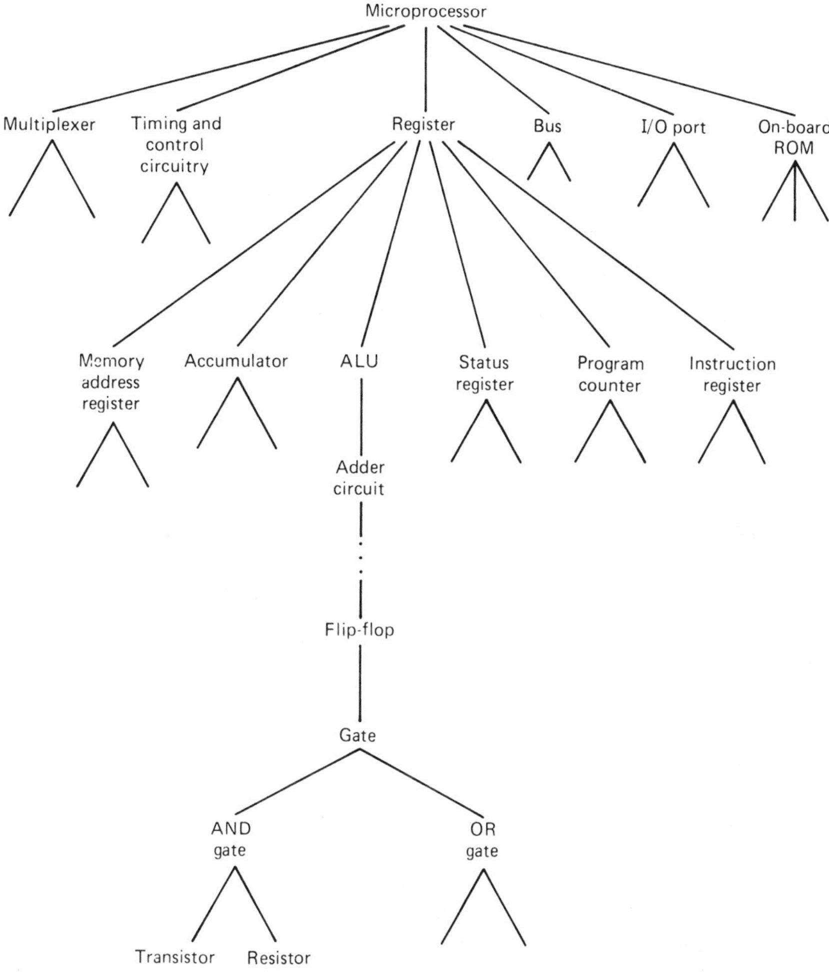

Figure 24-2 Object-oriented programming supports relationship hierarchies for VLSI design.

procedures, along with the encapsulation of procedures with objects, facilitates rapid prototyping of VLSI programs.

Another AI spin-off that is very important to VLSI is advanced human-machine interfaces. Highly visual and easy-to-manipulate interfaces were never the primary objective of AI, but they are one of the features of AI environments that were developed to facilitate complex AI program design. Beyond the application of traditional AI tools and techniques to VLSI design is the idea of an intelligent assistant. By definition, this design assistant would accept a functional specification of behavior (what the circuit should do) and semiautomatically generate an organic specification (design of how the circuit should do its job).

However, designers can intervene in the process and give advice in a form like: "If you ever see a situation like this, then do that." This kind of system is actually a full-fleged, rule-based knowledge-based system.

A DESIGN ASSISTANT

One knowledge-based system for VLSI design, called the Design Automation Assistant (DAA), has been developed at Carnegie-Mellon University, with knowledge engineering work performed at AT&T Bell Labs. Written in OPS5, the DAA is a rule-based, forward-chaining design consultant for designing microprocessors. It contains about 400 rules which examine the algorithmic description of the behavior a designer wants from a microprocessor. From the algorithmic description, the DAA proposes a functional description, indicating how the designer should construct pieces of a microprocessor architecture.

Although complex, the microprocessor domain was chosen for the knowledge system, because there are many well-tested configurations for various subsystems in microprocessors. The DAA rules recognize these configurations and their parts, and have the knowledge to understand whether they make sense under the current conditions. The rules also contain knowledge about how to implement various design features.

Input to DAA has the form of a behavioral description in ISPS (Instruction Set Processor Specification), an algorithmic language commonly used in the design automation community to describe computer and some chip architectures. The ISPS description generates a data-flow representation of chip design called the *value trace* (directed acyclic graph). The nodes of the value trace graph, called *operators*, represent operations to be performed. The arcs, called *values*, represent the data flow from one operator to another.

The value trace is used jointly by the DAA knowledge system and a conventional design automation program for microprocessor design decisions. The two programs cooperate. They use the value trace as their basis for analyzing, optimizing, and making decisions about the control and data parts of the chip design.

The conventional program, which in some ways acts like an optimizing compiler, can perform such tasks as eliminating duplicated operators and control steps and eliminating redundant hardware. DAA can change the order of control operations specified in the ISPS description, change the amount of parallelism, and map operations to functional level hardware modules (such as an adder or register) (Thomas et al., 1983). To manipulate the value trace, and thus the processor design, DAA uses heuristic rules. The finalized value trace can then be converted into a schematic.

A single value trace can produce different schematics that represent different hardware implementations. DAA uses its VLSI design knowledge to decide which implementation to synthesize. In one design decision, for example, the DAA

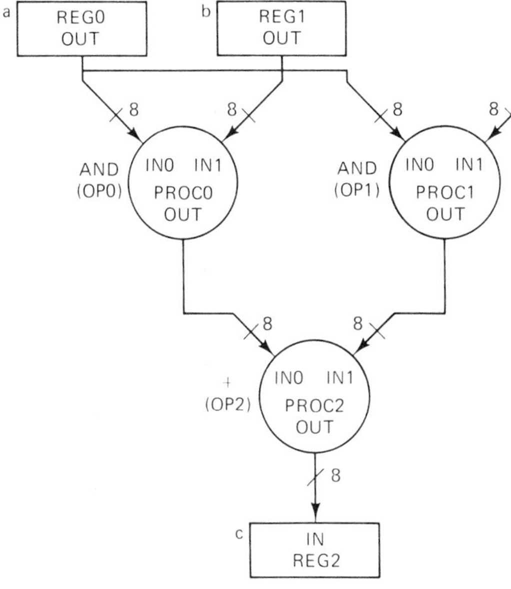

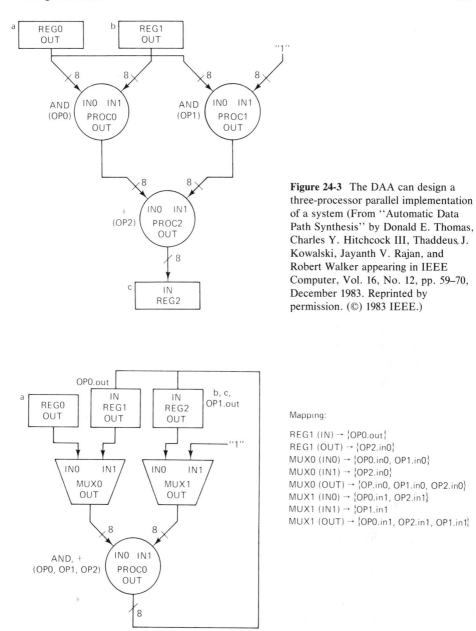

Figure 24-3 The DAA can design a three-processor parallel implementation of a system (From "Automatic Data Path Synthesis" by Donald E. Thomas, Charles Y. Hitchcock III, Thaddeus J. Kowalski, Jayanth V. Rajan, and Robert Walker appearing in IEEE Computer, Vol. 16, No. 12, pp. 59–70, December 1983. Reprinted by permission. (©) 1983 IEEE.)

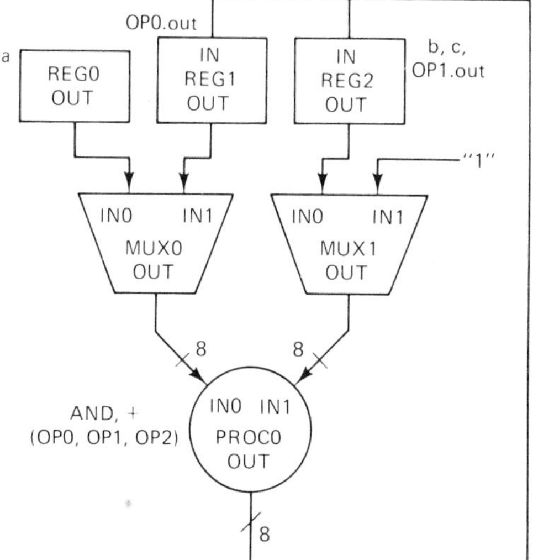

Mapping:

REG1 (IN) → {OP0.out}
REG1 (OUT) → {OP2.in0}
MUX0 (IN0) → {OP0.in0, OP1.in0}
MUX0 (IN1) → {OP2.in0}
MUX0 (OUT) → {OP.in0, OP1.in0, OP2.in0}
MUX1 (IN0) → {OP0.in1, OP2.in1}
MUX1 (IN1) → {OP1.in1
MUX1 (OUT) → {OP0.in1, OP2.in1, OP1.in1}

Figure 24-4 Using multiplexers, the DAA can design a maximally serial, single processor implementation of a system that originally used three processors (From "Automatic Data Path Synthesis" by Donald E. Thomas, Charles Y. Hitchcock III, Thaddeus J. Kowalski, Jayanth V. Rajan, and Robert Walker appearing in IEEE Computer, Vol. 16, No. 12, pp. 59–70, December 1983. Reprinted by permission. (©) 1983 IEEE.)

```
RULE: Add-Multiplexer
IF: Most currennt active context is to create a link
    AND the link should go from a source port to a destination port
    AND the module of the source port is not a multiplexer
    AND there is a link from another module to the same destination
        port
    AND this other module is not a multiplexer
-->
    THEN: Create a multiplexer module
    AND connect the multiplexer to the destination port
    AND connect the source port and destination port link to the
        multiplexer
    AND move the other link from the destination port to the
        multiplexer
```

Figure 24-5 English translation of a DAA rule about multiplexers (From "Automatic Data Path Synthesis" by Donald E. Thomas, Charles Y. Hitchcock III, Thaddeus J. Kowalski, Jayanth V. Rajan, and Robert Walker appearing in IEEE Computer, Vol. 16, No. 12, pp. 59–70, December 1983. Reprinted by permission. (©) 1983 IEEE.)

made some cost-speed trade-offs by adding multiplexers and eliminating parallelism in an architecture. In so doing, it reduced to one the three processors that originally handled certain groups of operations.

Figure 24-3 represents these groups of operations—OP0, OP1, and OP2—as they can be implemented in hardware, using three processors—PROC0, PROC1, and PROC2. This three-processor, parallel implementation results in high performance but requires much hardware. Another implementation, which satisfies the same specifications, makes do with a single processor (Figure 24-4). Which implementation is preferable is one type of design decision that DAA makes. In so doing, it serializes the operations, allocates the operations to various control steps, and maps them through multiplexers to different registers. DAA rules also specify the connection of links, and supply multiplexers where necessary.

The DAA has two rules that know about multiplexers. One, whose English translation is shown in Figure 24-5, creates a multiplexer to multiplex connections if a multiplexer does not already exist. The other rule indicates how to make a connection through a multiplexer that is already in place.

In prototype form, the DAA has been used to produce a design for the Mostek 6502 microprocessor (Figure 24-6). In an even more impressive design project, the DAA produced its own architectural design for the IBM System 370 computer, on a single chip. The DAA-designed System 370 contains 8-, 24-, and 64-bit buses; 32-, 64-, and 68-bit ALUs; six memory arrays; and a large number of registers. Compared with IBM's own implementation of the 370 computer on a chip, the DAA-designed chip has an extra arithmetic-logic unit for floating-point operations, less bus serialization, and a cache memory instead of certain registers. IBM designers who developed the IBM single-chip implementation compared the

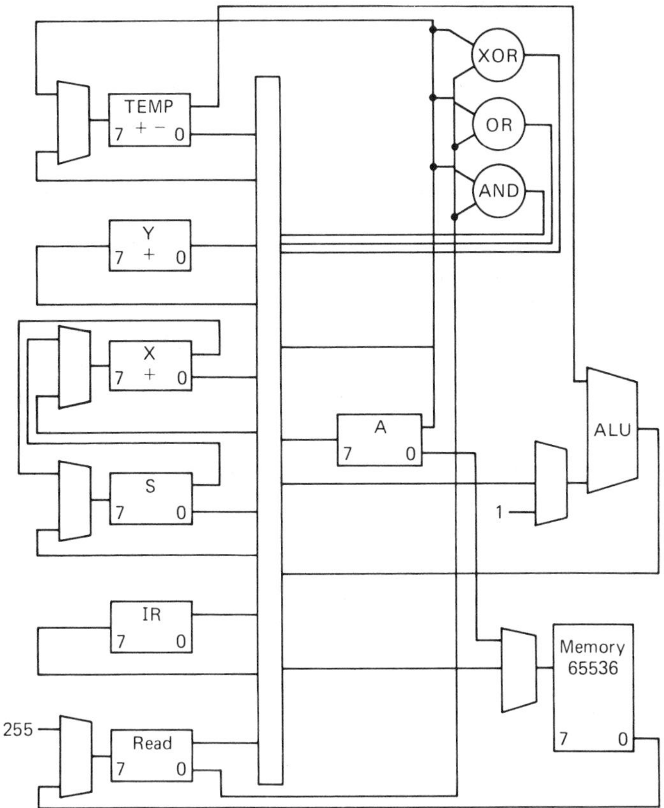

Figure 24-6 MCS6502 eight-bit data path designed by DAA (From "Automatic Data Path Synthesis" by Donald E. Thomas, Charles Y. Hitchcock III, Thaddeus J. Kowalski, Jayanth V. Rajan, and Robert Walker appearing in IEEE Computer, Vol. 16, No. 12, pp. 59–70, December 1983. Reprinted by permission (©) 1983 IEEE.)

two architectures and proclaimed the design of the DAA-produced System 370 to be "the quality of IBM's better designers" (Kowalski and Thomas, 1984).

Both CMU and Bell Labs researchers are separately working to interface the DAA to other tools used in producing VLSI parts.

ACQUIRING VLSI DESIGN KNOWLEDGE

Most companies involved in developing knowledge-based systems for VLSI design agree that the knowledge acquisition process is more problematic than for most traditional manufacturing and business AI systems. The problem stems from the visual orientation of the VLSI design task. It is, unfortunately, difficult to verbalize spatial knowledge and difficult for a rule to capture a visual scene.

For example, in one unsuccessful attempt at acquiring knowledge for the DAA, the design experts were shown block representations of a system, indicating ports, timing, and so on, and asked about modifications to be made to satisfy goals. But VLSI designers prefer a schematic diagram to a block representation because the schematic visually shows design experts information that otherwise requires a well-labeled block representation together with verbal notes.

A technique involving a computer-aided-design system also failed. In this technique, VLSI design experts were shown a design on a CAD screen. The design experts had to enter commands to the system, and the design automatically changed in response to their commands. The knowledge engineer observing was supposed to record all the changes that the experts made and transform them into rules. This technique backfired because the experts became too involved with inputting the proper commands to make the computer respond as desired.

The initial interview sessions with VLSI design experts, for construction of the DAA, produced war stories, jokes, and stories about how they had solved various difficult problems, but minimal knowledge of how they performed VLSI design. Yet these experts were experienced, had been successful in their designs, and were able to teach the subject of VLSI design to others. Furthermore, as long as they were presented with new problems in a specific design, they could explain how to solve them. But they had difficulty enumerating the possible problems that could be encountered.

Knowledge for the DAA prototype was finally gathered with the aid of a simple VLSI knowledge acquisition technique designed by Donald Thomas (CMU) and Thaddeus Kowalski (AT&T Bell Labs). Design experts were given a microprocessor schematic, covered with small pieces of removable cardboard. The purpose of the cardboard was to focus the expert's attention only on the piece of the design that might need modification, and to indicate to the knowledge engineer the piece of the design being focused on. The designers studied the schematic. It was then covered and the experts asked to make changes in the design to accommodate factors such as greater speed, less area, or better power utilization. The proposed changes were added to the knowledge system, a new schematic was generated, and the process was repeated.

It took about a week for the knowledge- and design-engineers to become adept at communicating information about specific areas of design. At that point, better results were obtained by asking explicit questions, and the cardboard was dispensed with.

TOP-DOWN VLSI DESIGN

The acquisition of VLSI design knowledge is one of many puzzle pieces that needs to be popped into place to construct knowledge-based VLSI design programs. The number of possible designs is huge. The goals and constraints on the design often conflict and continuously evolve. As good as heuristics may be,

AI solutions to very large, complex problems are inefficient, and possibly intractable, unless the size and complexity are reduced by first decomposing the problem into smaller, manageable parts—a kind of divide-and-conquer approach.

How to decompose the VLSI problem is still an open question and the subject of active research. A VLSI design problem starts with a specification and outputs a description of a chip architecture. The path from specification to output is not generally a single step, except for algorithmic problems.

Silicon compilers, for example, which are the closest thing to a commercial system for automated chip design, pass from specification to chip design. They do for chips what programming language compilers do for programming languages. A borderline case between AI and conventional systems, silicon compilers use prewritten procedures (involving registers, arithmetic and logical operations, and other chip design and layout tasks) out of a software library. They compile these procedures into microcode instructions for a chip mask. But although they automate some of the VLSI design process, silicon compilers are not considered by most of the AI community to be AI because they perform straightforward, algorithmic procedures that must first exist in a human expert's head.

Creative VLSI design is not algorithmic and is too complex to automate directly. What must be done, instead, is to decompose the abstract specifications into increasingly less complex specifications until one is reached that can be managed. The techniques involved in decomposing VLSI specifications are similar to those used in standard "top-down" software engineering practices.

For example, to design a microprocessor, a designer might decompose the microprocessor into its component parts: arithmetic-logic unit, memory unit, central processing unit, and I/O ports. Each of these parts might be further decomposed (for example, into registers and memory cells) and described, and decomposed again until manageable subcircuits and primitive concrete components are reached. Clearly, the decomposed parts must be able to interact and be reintegrated.

A different way to subdivide the VLSI design problem is according to different abstract views of the same entities on the chip being designed. One view might describe activity in the chip in terms of components with terminals or ports that are connected in a certain way. Another view might describe objects, possibly mathematically, according to behavior. This corresponds to the logic level of design and is useful in deciding if the chip will have the desired functionality. Still another view might be more physical and have timing information involved.

The views are further refined into still smaller subproblems which, by nature, interact. Interactions between the subproblems are represented by constraints, and the designer must attend to these constraints to avoid trouble with the solution of other subproblems. Constraints are of various types; some may be described by mathematical behavior, others, by characterizations such as performance goals and quality goals.

The specifications at various steps of refinement can be described in various functional programming languages that can accommodate specifications as abstract as architecture and as concrete as circuits and arithmetic-logic units. If the behavior of a circuit is described in a functional programming language, the structure of the circuit is also implicit. Therefore, as far as AI programs are concerned, the VLSI design goal is to be able to describe circuit specifications in a circuit design programming language so that they can be compiled for input into a knowledge-based program. The knowledge program will contain knowledge of circuits, components, and constraints. Using this knowledge, it will transform the behavioral specifications into a parts list of primitive concrete components, an activity list, structural descriptions describing connections and subcomponent relationships, and ultimately, layout.

VLSI DESIGN CATALOGS

It goes without saying that much work remains before knowledge-based systems that allow specifications as input and design descriptions as output become a commercial reality. Meanwhile, VLSI designers would find their work greatly shortened if they could use AI capabilities to build on existing work.

To reduce the constant reinvention of the VLSI wheel, Fairchild is developing a smart catalog of VLSI designs. The catalog allows designers to reuse already invented designs, although they might need some modification for reuse.

The difference between retrieving VLSI designs from a catalog and retrieving data from a database is the method of describing what to retrieve. Database users retrieve data based on a name of a field or a key word. VLSI designers must be able to retrieve designs based on descriptions of a function that they need. Their description may not quite correspond to what is in the catalog. Therefore, a VLSI catalog needs intelligent retrieval capabilities that can infer what designers want from their descriptions and match their descriptions as closely as possible to what exists in the catalog.

The catalog returns a representation of a design that contains the design's structure and function. The structure indicates how the circuit design is connected. The function indicates what the design does, its various behaviors, the justification for different design decisions pertaining to this particular design, and the purpose of individual components included in the design.

Typically, when designers retrieve a design, it is almost, but not quite, what they want. It may be simpler to modify the design to make it fit their context exactly than to reinvent the design, especially when the design is as complex as those in VLSI circuits. The magnitude of productivity increases through retrieving, reusing, and modifying existing designs can be seen by reverting to a classic city layout analogy. It may be possible to design and lay out New York City in only a month if the city planners are allowed to reuse existing parks and buildings, but modify them, for example, by facing them differently or changing the entrances and exits to fit the streets. With the intent of further increasing VLSI designers' productivity, Rutgers University has programs under development to automate the incremental modification of design procedures after they have been retrieved from a design catalog.

One such program, appropriately called Redesign, compares a circuit function and the designer's desired function for the circuit. The real and desired functions might have slight differences, such as a parallel instead of a serial output. Several Redesign rules may know how to convert parallel to serial output, for example, through a shift register or through a counter and multiplexer. Various knowledge system rules might also exist not only to eliminate differences in circuits, but also to select which alternatives are best to eliminate the differences based on whether the designers are trying to optimize speed, area, or something else.

The Rutgers work is still experimental. However, one successful project involved an electronic circuit that contained all the circuitry for a 24-line display for a computer. The modification program redesigned the digital circuitry to produce a bigger display.

VERIFICATION

At Fairchild, such an incrementally modified design would be returned to the catalog for future use. But Fairchild goes further. Software engineers there have AI tools under development that could first be used to prove, theoretically, that the newly designed or modified circuit is correct. This is a difficult problem since proving such correctness for any reasonably-sized program has generally been intractable for human beings.

The Fairchild correctness-proving method essentially involves theorem proving. The designer specifies the structure, function, and behavior of the design. These are described in terms of algebraic equations. At the same time, the correctness prover, based on its own observations, infers the structure, function, and behavior of the design. It also constructs a series of equations to model its inferences about the design. The verification problem then boils down to proving these expressions equivalent by reducing them to the same canonic form.

The design is hierarchically structured, and the equations model structure, function, and behavior at each level of the hierarchy. Consequently, there are a large number of equations. Fairly straightforward procedures exist to massage these equations to prove whether or not they are equivalent. However, simplifications, transformations, and solutions of algebraic equations are not feasible, if they can be done at all, with conventional computing languages. Such proofs yield, instead, to symbolic processing.

Fairchild uses a special-purpose theorem prover program written in Prolog to prove the equations equivalent. The program is special purpose in that it not only manipulates expressions and equations, but also contains knowledge of the types of mathematics and transformations that work in proving circuits correct.

SMALLTALK HAS FEW WORDS AND MANY PICTURES

As knowledge-based circuit engineering systems stand right now, they can perform some design, but not necessarily optimally, and they can provide some assistance to designers. Commercial development of expert engineering systems has been slowed not only by the size and complexity of the engineering problems targeted for AI solution, but by their visual and spatial orientation, which makes them difficult to describe to people or computers and difficult for human experts to systematize even to themselves.

Still, progress is ongoing, using various techniques and languages. For Tektronix, for example, Smalltalk is the method of choice for graphically oriented circuit problems.

Smalltalk is an object-oriented programming language developed at Xerox. Aside from its modularity and data/procedure encapsulation advantages, Smalltalk is especially adaptable for engineering applications because it is unusually supportive of graphics. In fact, it is one of the few languages that make it easier to put up a graphical representation than a textural one, because Smalltalk treats text as graphics.

Tektronix is using Smalltalk's visual capabilities in a prototype instrument-diagnostic knowledge-based system, to troubleshoot circuit boards in Tektronix equipment. Designed by Tektronix software engineers James Alexander and Michael Freiling, the FG502 Troubleshooting Assistant Prototype (FG502-Tasp) provides technicians with advice and assistance in repairing a malfunctioning Tektronix FG502 function generator. Also under development is a knowledge system for fixing the 2213 oscilloscope. These systems are part of a larger system called Detektr (Development Environment for Tektronix Troubleshooters). Detektr is a knowledge system-building tool to help technicians and instrument designers rapidly construct troubleshooting assistant knowledge systems focused on the repair of a single instrument.

Troubleshooting problems at Tektronix are similar to those in other fields. It is a burden to retain a large body of expertise to service instruments after they are no longer sold. The turnover rate for experienced troubleshooters is very high. Experienced technicians are difficult to find. As they acquire experience, technicians tend to move up the ladder into careers in such areas as sales, engineering, marketing, and sales support. This is unfortunate for a company's service organization because the major economic payoff for a service group results from a productivity increase in the lower-level technicians.

Tektronix is not alone in claiming that the life cycle of a technician at a company is only two to five years. Visually oriented knowledge systems, in the fields of engineering, instrumentation, testing and measurement—are a way to preserve their expertise.

THE CIRCUIT-BOARD EXPERT

The troubleshooting assistant's first troubleshooting tasks involve the active devices on a major block of the Tektronix function generator. It is not designed to handle passive devices such as resisters because the probability of passive-device failure is relatively small, and therefore a small economic payoff is gained by a large amount of effort.

The philosophy and goals underlying the Tektronix knowledge-based troubleshooting systems are a productivity increase and economic payoff through a general system that can fix most of the instruments returned to the shop, rather than any possible failure of an instrument. Unusual problems are passed on to more experienced, higher-level technicians for personal attention.

Smalltalk became the troubleshooting assistant's language of choice as a result of one summer of discussions with technicians in the Tektronix service organization. By their own admission, what the technicians view as the most helpful adjunct to their work is the availability of a variety of methods and representations used to think about devices that they are troubleshooting—schematic, physical embodiment, pictures, and descriptions—contained in one place. In addition, they want automatic mediation between schematic, circuit board map, parts description, and troubleshooting information and advice.

Troubleshooting is normally done with troubleshooting manuals, which require constant mediation between different representations of a single device. Worse, in the schematic, circuit-board-map representation, numbered parts, descriptive parts information, and problem discussions are scattered throughout the manual. In addition, descriptive and problem information may be located either in the manual or on a computer and written either in the English language or in programming code. Neither English nor programming code is an efficient means of communicating circuit information.

Hence the Detektr development environment and applications were designed with a user interface that supports user communications primarily via graphics. A typical system screen provides cross-referencing between the schematic, block representation of the corresponding circuit board and the parts description (Figure 24-7). A technician unfamiliar with the device being tested can determine the location of the component on the circuit board by pointing to the corresponding schematic symbol. This will cause the circuit-board component to be highlighted and a parts listing and description to be displayed. Similarly, pointing to a circuit-board component or choice of a part from the parts list causes highlighting of the part on the schematic or other diagrams.

The Smalltalk graphics environment, and communications through graphics and pointing, also enable the troubleshooting assistant to provide more effective direction to the technician. As shown in Figure 24-7, when the technician is asked to measure a voltage (or other) value at N19 (Node 19), its location is visually identified by a probe icon in both the schematic and the circuit-board map. At the

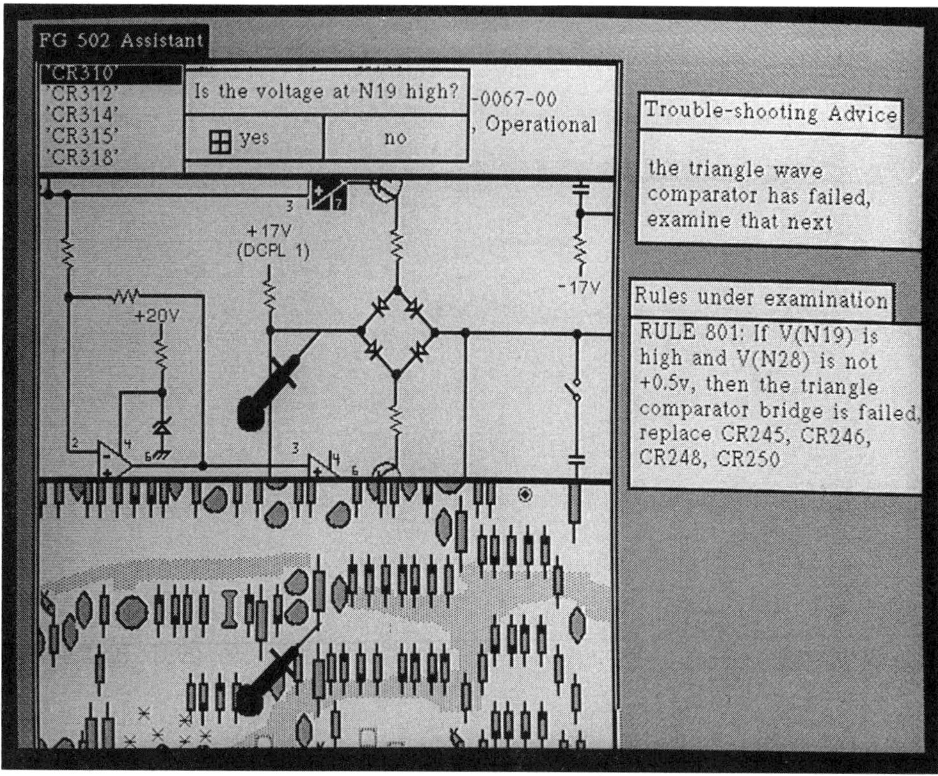

Figure 24-7 Panes in a repair window of the expert troubleshooting system (Tektronix Inc.)

same time, the rule under examination, shown in another window, explains its rationale for its own actions or requests.

Technicians can examine key locations on an instrument to check out measurements. Using a mouse, they can point to key points of a circuit and ask to see, displayed on the screen, the expected waveform on a simulated oscilloscope.

Sooner or later, use of the English language is necessary to diagnose a failure or display advice. However, even during the question, diagnosis, and advice phases, the expert system communicates as much as possible graphically. For example, as the knowledge system chains through its troubleshooting rules, technicians can track troubleshooting progress without needing to read the rules, because the system highlights different test points. Even the troubleshooting advice is partially given graphically, in that technicians need not translate references such as Transistor-350, IC-604, or Diode-245 into circuit board locations, because they are highlighted automatically.

When the diagnosis is complete and accepted by the troubleshooter as

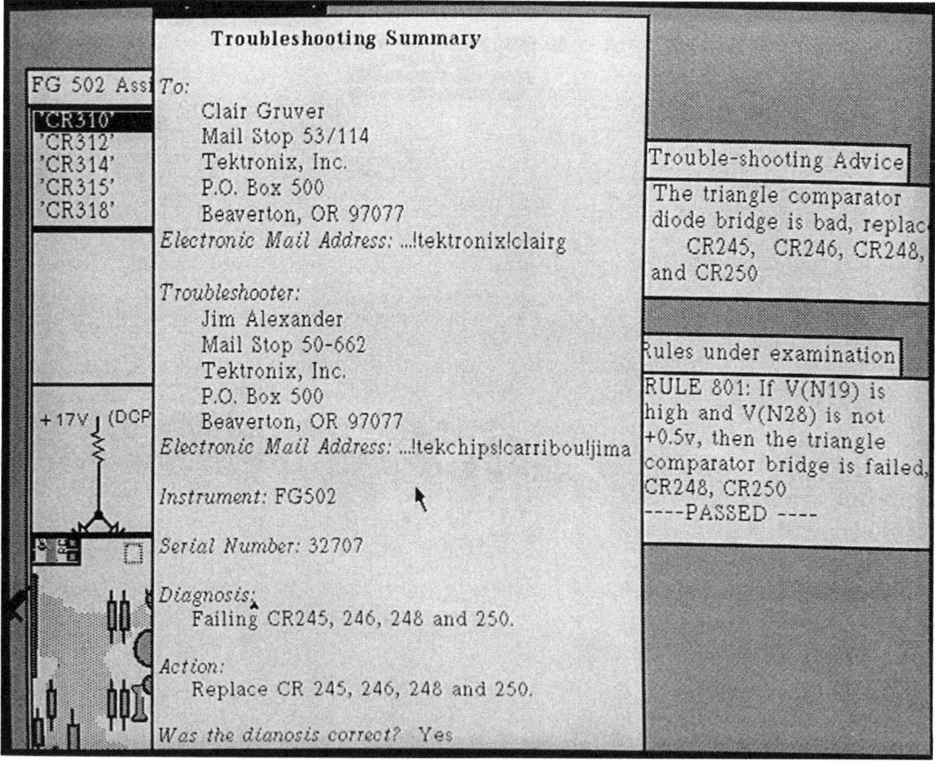

Figure 24-8 Expert system generated repair report (Tektronix Inc.)

accurate, the expert system automatically generates the repair report (Figure 24-8). Automated report generation turned out to be a favorite service of technicians. The ability of supervisors to get the reports so that they can take timely action is equally valuable in terms of customer satisfaction.

SMALLTALK KNOWLEDGE SYSTEM TOOLS

The knowledge-based troubleshooting assistant has two major parts: the diagram manager and the knowledge base manager. The diagram manager knows how to draw and display components and different representations of an instrument and waveforms. It also knows how to manage the relationships between components in different windows and how to highlight parts of circuits. The knowledge base contains knowledge, in the form of rules. The rules diagnose component failures in the instrument. They also communicate with the graphics representation of the component and highlight items in question.

Some code necessary for the operation of the diagram manager and the knowledge base manager was constructed by Tektronix for its applications and would also have to be constructed by other users for their purposes. Much knowledge system construction, however, is facilitated not only because a Smalltalk environment contains program development and debugging tools, but because tools and code that are part of the Smalltalk environment are inherited by the knowledge system under construction.

Inheritance occurs because Smalltalk is an object-oriented language. It allows programmers to create classes of objects and specific objects, in addition to procedures to manipulate the objects. Components, pictures, instrument representations, and windows are typical circuit-board troubleshooting assistant classes of objects. Transistor-350 is a specific object. Draw, highlight, and store locations are procedures.

Smalltalk objects are arranged in a hierarchy of classes. Classes lower in the hierarchy inherit procedures and attributes from those higher in the hierarchy. Circuit-board components are located low down in the class hierarchy. Each component knows its name and location in a picture or diagram. It inherits from the Smalltalk environment code, higher in the hierarchy, the ability to draw, display, and highlight itself. However, programmers can, if they wish, customize this code for a specific object. Also inherited from the Smalltalk environment are a variety of primitives for storing locations of all the parts of a picture, pointing to parts, checking to see what is being pointed at, and sending messages to objects to update themselves.

Code for cross-referencing components in different representations, such as schematics and block diagrams, is programmer defined rather than being inherited from the Smalltalk environment. So are program components such as the rule processor. Once defined, however, this code never need be rewritten, because it is inherited by future troubleshooting programs built in the Smalltalk environment. Moreover, the programmer-defined program components can be composed partially of predefined inherited code and partially of programmer-defined code. Any inherited code may be modified and customized. This inheritance scheme allows programmers to accomplish a great deal with minimal work.

BUILDING A KNOWLEDGE SYSTEM

To build a circuit-board diagnostic knowledge system, a programmer begins by identifying the objects in the system and arranging them into some kind of hierarchical structure. One object high in the hierarchy is the rule processor, whose procedures will be inherited by objects all the way down the hierarchy. Further down the hierarchy are rule objects and graphics objects. Although their subobjects are located in different classes, they interact together.

Graphics objects include pictures and circuit-board maps. Rule objects include individual rules. In fact, each rule in the system is a single object, essentially of the IF-THEN form. The Smalltalk object can receive and send messages. They execute their encapsulated procedures when they receive a message to do so.

For example, when pointed at, a part in the parts list might send a message to both the schematic and the circuit-board picture to "highlight" the corresponding part. A rule object might receive a message to test its condition part and see if it is true. Other operations that can be performed on a rule include initialize it, create it, and value (test and return the value).

The inference mechanism in this Smalltalk system works similarly to a Lisp or OPS5 forward-chaining system, such as DEC's XCON. It tests the condition part of a rule to see if it matches information contained in a working memory. If it matches, the inference mechanism executes the operation indicated in the THEN part of the rule. This may add new information to working memory. This pattern-matching procedure continues until there are no more rules that can be fired or until the system is explicitly stopped. At that point, a solution is assumed to be found.

The form of Detektr's rules, which take five arguments, is as follows:

```
RULE (NUMBER; IF; THEN; QUESTION; POINT)
```

NUMBER is simply the rule number. IF is the pattern to test against working memory to see if the condition is true or false. THEN indicates an operation to perform. QUESTION is an English string that can be used as a question to generate a value if it is not in the rule base, for example, by asking the user. (A nil question is written if no question is appropriate at some point.) POINT indicates a set of nodes to point at as the system asks a question or makes a statement. A right-hand window of Figure 24-8 shows an English translation of the Smalltalk version of a rule.

Like other rule-based expert systems, a rule processor consists of a pattern matcher, an action executer, an indexer, and a control mechanism. The pattern matcher tests the condition parts of a rule to see if it is true. The action executer is the code that executes the action part of the rule. The indexer provides an efficient way to access rules. The control mechanism controls the order in which the rules are processed.

Detektr's pattern matcher uses Smalltalk's prewritten comparison methods and dictionary that provide keys and associated retrieval values. The IF clause of a rule is compared to the facts collected during a consultation and stored in the dictionary to see if they match.

In the control mechanism, the programmer writes an algorithm that describes the way the system selects the next rules to test and execute. Detektr's designers built their rule processor control mechanism by dividing the rules into blocks. Within each block, the processor begins with the first rule and examines the rules sequentially. This sequential examination is efficient as long as the number of rules per block is kept small.

To enter new rules in the knowledge base, programmers decide which block of a circuit they are interested in. Smalltalk windows can be opened, via pointing, that display rules that concentrate on each one of those blocks. Rules are then simply added or modified and saved to become part of the system.

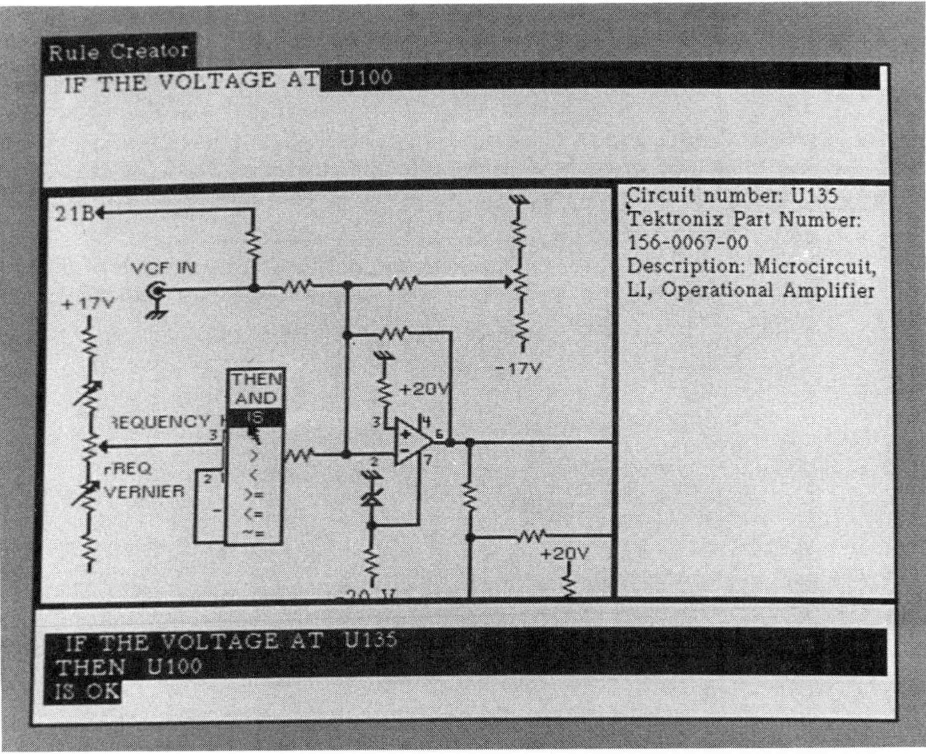

Figure 24-9 Menu system for creating rules (Tektronix Inc.)

To expedite the knowledge acquisition process and make it easier to add rules to an existing expert system, Tektronix is evolving a structured English interface language for users to add rules. Called GLIB (General Language for Instrument Behavior), the language provides a choice of vocabulary for expressing specifications, components, and observations about the behavior of general analog devices.

One way to use this structured language for rule acquisition is via a menu system. The menu displays alternative choices for each word in the rule as it is being selected (Figure 24-9). For example, users might build a rule (which always begins with IF THE) by first being given a choice of VOLTAGE and CURRENT. If, as in Figure 24-9, voltage is selected, the next choice to be made is whether the voltage is of a single point (with respect to ground) or between two points. Therefore, the user choice, after "IF THE VOLTAGE" has been generated, is AT or BETWEEN. Next, the user may reference the node in the schematic by either pointing to it or typing in the name. In this way, the user would choose and generate an entire rule correctly.

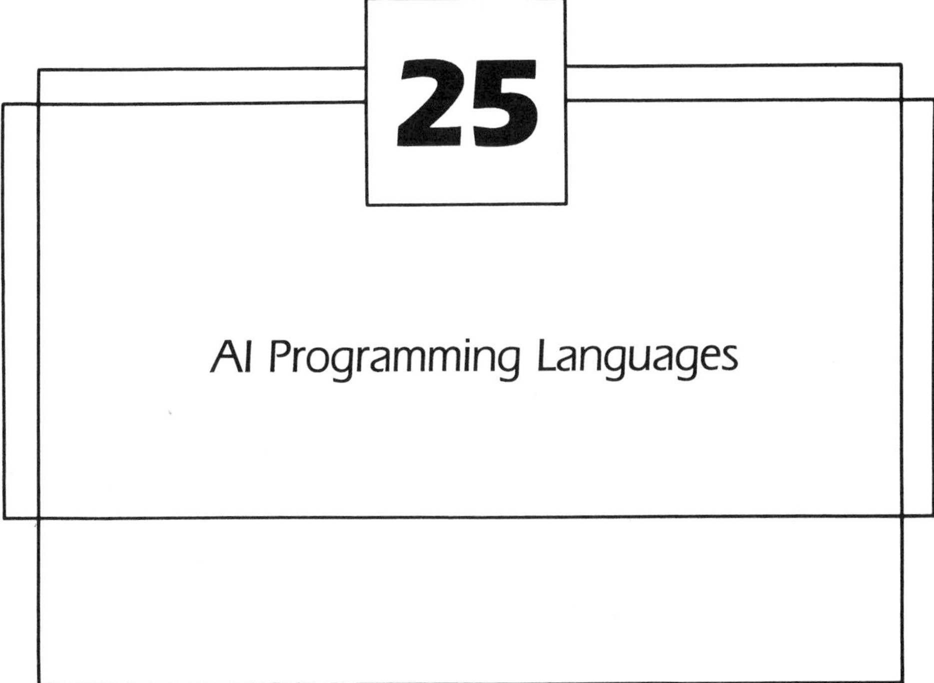

25 AI Programming Languages

AI programs have hardly had a chance to show what they can do. Yet Lisp, the chief AI language until now, already has a rival—Prolog—for the affections of AI programmers.

The original Lisp language was developed in the late 1950s by John McCarthy at MIT. To the uninitiated viewing Lisp for the first time, the most outstanding Lisp feature is the large number of parentheses—sometimes nested 12 to 20 deep—surrounding its instructions.

AI programmers are casual about the parentheses which help keep the language syntax simple, clear to the computer, and can be checked and managed by a computer program. However, AI programmers see Lisp not just as a language, but as an environment. Unlike other language systems, this environment contains both the language and a large number of development tools built over many years and totally integrated with the language.

In contrast to Lisp, the Prolog language is a relative newcomer with few tools. Yet Prolog has already been chosen by the Japanese as the language for their fifth-generation computer project.

Although the languages differ in several respects, anything that can be written in one language can be written in the other. What is more, facilities not available in either Lisp or Prolog can be built upon them.

Both Lisp and Prolog are symbolic manipulation languages, and both can handle a form of mathematics known as predicate calculus logic. Predicate calculus is a logic that provides a way to describe objects and relationships in the world so that it is possible to check formally to see if they are valid. This logic can be used to validly infer the new information from the original.

Despite their similarities, Lisp and Prolog each have different orientations. In particular, Lisp programs are collections of independent procedures called functions. This procedure or functional orientation makes Lisp more akin to conventional programming languages than Prolog. For its part, Prolog is based on logic with certain built-in theorem-proving mechanisms.

Since Lisp, and its tools and environments, are built and tested, it will certainly be the AI language of choice for some time to come. Still, Prolog has enormous potential because of its unique benefits. It is easily readable (if the programs are not too large), and it provides relational database and query capabilities. A programmer can directly express natural-language grammars in Prolog. In addition, to some degree Prolog lends itself to parallel processing—performing several tasks simultaneously. Since AI programs have a tendency to consume a great deal of machine processing power, parallel processing capabilities could, in the future, be necessary to run large AI programs.

BACKTRACKING: CONTROL BY LOOKING FOR DEAD ENDS

Alas, Prolog has some grave drawbacks. Chief among these is the fact that Prolog is limited to a single control mechanism, called *backtracking*. A program's control mechanism provides the means to select what program instructions to execute next. The conventional IF-THEN-ELSE and DO-WHILE statements are control structures, as are XCON's strategies for selecting particular rules to execute next (Chapter 17).

With backtracking as the control mechanism, if a rule that a program selects does not lead to a solution, the program retraces its steps to some decision point and selects another rule. Ultimately, after enough wrong paths are tried, the program control backtracks to select the rules that lead to a solution.

Unfortunately, unlike programs written in Lisp, the problem-solving mechanisms in Prolog generate goals and subgoals to strive for, but have no easy way to determine the best rules to select or the most likely paths to pursue to reach those goals and subgoals. Thus there is no easy way to automatically control a search and zero in a goal. Consequently, a large search can result in an exponentially large computation.

There is a way around the control problem. David Warren, developer of the DEC-10 Prolog compiler, suggests that Prolog program users can alleviate the backtracking problem if they order their goals to minimize searches. To order the goals properly, the designer must simply write queries so that the goals with the least number of solutions appear before those with more solutions. For example, to query "Who in a large company are salespeople, earn greater than $10,000, and work in a small branch in London?" first find the salespeople in London and then determine their salaries. In other words, write the query to read: "Who in a large company are salespeople who work in a small branch in London and earn greater than $10,000?" The Prolog compiler will read and execute the query goals from left to right.

HISTORY MAY REPEAT ITSELF

Even if the Prolog backtracking problem can be solved, many AI programmers are wary of Prolog. There simply have been too many logic-based languages, with great promise, that have failed. One such language, Planner, invented by Carl Hewitt of MIT in the late 1960s, created as great a stir then in the AI community as Prolog did subsequently. Although Planner even had some capabilities that Prolog lacks (it could reason forward and backward, whereas Prolog can only reason backward), it had to be abandoned as the inherent limitations of a language based only on logic were discovered.

As a result of previous logic language problems, but also because Prolog provides some major benefits, most of the AI community has adopted a wait-and-see attitude. Although preferring the greater versatility of Lisp, most AI experts feel that over the next several years Lisp will change to incorporate many Prolog features. Consequently, the future of the two major AI languages is still undecided, but they may evolve in the direction of hybridization.

LISP

Four key points differentiate Lisp from traditional programming languages. First, the basic programming units in Lisp are known as *S-expressions* (for "symbolic expressions"). An S-expression may be an *atomic symbol* such as H, 4, PLUS, or EYECOLOR. Or it may be a *list* of atomic symbols (or other S-expressions, thus making this definition recursive).

The atomic symbols or lists are grouped together in parentheses, such as (PLUS 4 3), (ON TYPEWRITER DESK), (EYECOLOR HAZEL), and (#PUMP 32004465). In fact, the name "Lisp" means "list processing language." This fact suggests that a main feature of Lisp is its ability to manipulate lists. The first two lists above can be evaluated directly (where "evaluation" means "perform the function indicated by the first atom in the list"). The last two lists (which describe eye color and a pump number) might represent knowledge in a frame-based expert system.

The second key point about Lisp is that Lisp uses what is called *prefix notation* to express functions. In prefix notation, operators, such as PLUS, are written first, followed by operands (such as the numbers to be added) from left to right. An example of prefix notation is (PLUS 4 3). In contrast, algebra uses *infix notation*, such as 4 plus 3 where the operator is located between the operands.

The third point is that expressions in Lisp are independent functions that state an action or purpose. Because Lisp programs are composed of these independent functions, and each function contains independent separate S-expressions, many sets of parentheses are required to clarify Lisp programs for computers.

The various Lisp functions can be mathematical, such as (PLUS 4 3). Special functions, called *predicates*, are also allowed. A predicate evaluates to

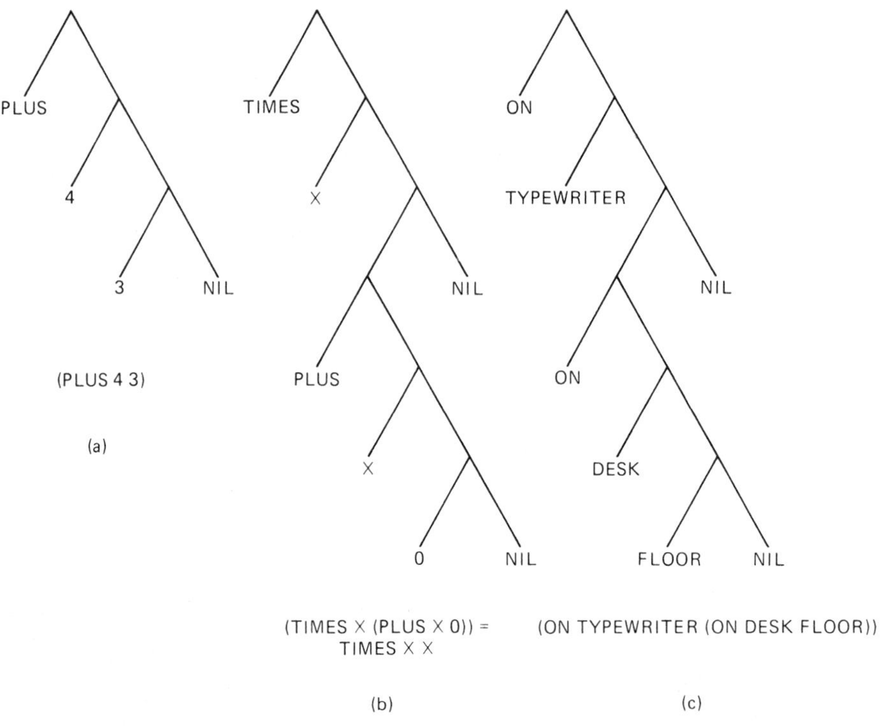

Figure 25-1 Lisp's primary data structure is a binary tree, which can be evaluated.

true or false (false is called NIL in Lisp). Examples of predicate functions are (equal disk disk_drive) or (on typewriter desk). Some Lisp functions construct lists; others take lists apart. Also, Lisp programmers may define their own functions, which may be nested and frequently are recursive.

Lisp functions are evaluated independently as soon as a function is entered. This fact makes Lisp a highly interactive language which gives fast answers—necessary features for the exploratory programming and rapid prototyping capabilities needed to develop AI programs.

The fourth key point about Lisp is that Lisp's primary data structure is a binary tree, with nodes and leaves. This binary tree represents all Lisp lists. In addition to building, extending, and concatenating binary trees, it is possible to dissect and interrogate a tree using only two operators. One operator, CAR, gives the left subtree. The other operator, CDR, gives the right subtree. For example in Figure 25-1a, CAR of the tree that represents (PLUS 4 3) is PLUS. CDR is (4 3). NIL indicates the end of a list or branch of the tree. Combinations of CAR and CDR such as (CAR(CDR)), shortened to CADR, pick out the left side of the right subtree, in this case, 4.

Clearly, even complex forms of expressions such as those shown in Figure

25-1 are easily evaluated with conventional programming techniques. Consider, however, symbolic expressions, such as those shown in Figure 25-1b and c. These types of symbolic expressions, used in conjunction with a small number of Lisp operators, and the Lisp features mentioned above, allow the writing of very compact Lisp programs to perform evaluation and processing which is impractical in conventional languages.

TREE SURGERY

Lisp evaluates the S-expression (TIMES X (PLUS X 0)), shown by the tree in Figure 25-1b by simplifying it to "TIMES XX." Although this is only a very simple example, Lisp can manipulate and simplify highly complex mathematical expressions.

Lisp also handles large complex structures, with branches that represent logic (such as AND, OR, NOT, EXCLUSIVE OR). These are used in logic circuit design and analysis. For these tasks, Lisp programs, which are composed of functions that recursively call each other, traverse the tree. These functions use the CAR and CDR functions to pick symbols off the tree. Then they determine if the picked-off symbols are atomic symbols or particular logic functions. Based on the findings, the functions recursively call the appropriate function and pass it arguments for evaluation.

To determine and make inferences about relationships between objects in an office, a Lisp program can traverse the tree in Figure 25-1c. Such a program uses the CAR function to pick off the predicate function ON. During the evaluation process, the function recursively calls the function ON, and passes the CDR of the tree branch [which in this case is (DESK FLOOR)] as an argument. Thus the Lisp program knows that the typewriter is on the desk, which is on the floor.

It is important to note that the list that represents data has the same form as a list that represents a program. Since there is no differentiation between program data, it is possible to pass an entire program as data to another program. This, in turn, makes it possible to write Lisp programs to construct structures, which are themselves programs, and then execute them.

Because of the difference in the way that Lisp versus conventional programming languages execute a program, this capability is more than just theoretical. It is possible to write a program (program 1) to write another program (program 2) in most programming languages. Unfortunately, program 1 cannot execute program 2 because to do so, the programming language compiler would have had to allocate memory for program 2, compile it, and link it to certain computer library routines before it began to execute program 1. Clearly, this is impossible because at that time program 2 did not exist.

In contrast to conventional languages, Lisp dynamically allocates memory and links the program to the library routines. The compilation step, in advance, is not necessary. As program 1 runs and creates program 2, Lisp dynamically allocates the necessary memory for newly created program 2, dynamically links it to the library routines, and therefore, it is able to run.

MANY VERSIONS OF LISP

A number of different (nonstandard) versions of Lisp exist. The major versions include MacLisp, developed at MIT, and Interlisp, developed at Bolt Beranek and Newman but associated with Xerox Corp. In general, MacLisp is noted for its efficiency and programmer facilities, while Interlisp places more emphasis on its user interfaces and automatic performing of user tasks.

Out of these original versions of Lisp came Zetalisp (an extension of MacLisp, also called Lisp Machine Lisp), and Common Lisp [a new Lisp version standardized and supported by the Lisp machine companies, the universities and research organizations most involved in AI, the major computer manufacturers and AI software vendors, and the Defense Advanced Research Projects Agency (DARPA)]. Common Lisp is more like Zetalisp than Interlisp. Besides the language syntax and functions, several Zetalisp-like development environment facilities, such as windowing, graphics, and object-oriented programming, are being standardized for Common Lisp.

A host of other Lisp dialects also exist. These include Franz Lisp, which runs under Unix; Portable Standard Lisp (PSL), defined by the University of Utah; Cambridge Lisp, developed at Bath University and Cambridge Computer Laboratory; T-Lisp, from Yale; Scheme—an MIT List which is implemented in both software and in silicon, and several Lisp versions for 8-bit and 16-bit microprocessors and personal computers.

PROLOG

As mentioned earlier, the four major advantages of Prolog are its readability, and relational database, natural-language interface, and parallel processing capabilities.

Like logic statements, it is easy to read Prolog statements, declaratively, as English statements about what is true in the world. For example, statements such as

```
physician (Roslyn).
volunteer (Carol).
worksin (Roslyn, New_York).
earns (Roslyn 70,000).
?- staff(X), worksin(X, New_York),
earns (X, salary), salary >30,000.
```

are typical Prolog declarative statements. The first three statements can form part of a Prolog relational database. They state (or declare) that Roslyn is a physician,

Carol is a volunteer, Roslyn works in New York, and Roslyn earns $70,000. The last statement is a query that asks: "Who are the staff in New York who earn more than $30,000?" The "X" indicates the missing information that the query is trying to find. Logic statements such as these make it easy to implement a database and query language in Prolog.

The Prolog statements above can also be read procedurally, as an algorithm, to solve a problem. For example, implicit in the Prolog query is a procedure that directs the computer to pick a hospital staffer, find out whether he or she works in New York, check the salary, and determine if that salary is greater than $30,000.

Unlike conventional databases, which store only conventional data, Prolog databases may also contain rules. The combination of rules and data in a database often eliminates the need to write query programs. For example, the rule

```
earns (X, 0) :-volunteer (X).
```

which says "X (an arbitrary person) earns 0 (or $0.00) if X is a volunteer," may be added to the database statements above. (The :- symbol indicates an IF-THEN rule.) The advantage of such a rule, incorporated in the database, is that the query

```
?- earns (X, 0).
```

meaning who earns $0.00, returns the answer, "Carol," without a programmer, or even a sophisticated end user, having to write a program to determine the answer.

Another advantage of Prolog is its suitability for writing natural-language front ends for databases. The reason is that the Prolog syntax allows the rules of a natural-language grammar to be expressed directly as Prolog statements. A Prolog processor automatically parses the English sentence and applies the appropriate rules in order to represent the meaning of the sentence. In any other language, Lisp included, it is necessary to build a special-purpose system, including data structures to represent the rules of the language, parser, and analyzer to do the same natural-language task that Prolog does automatically.

Prolog runs on Symbolics', Xerox's, and TI's Lisp Machines and on a variety of mainframes, minicomputers, workstations, and PCs.

PARALLEL PROCESSING

Prolog may be suitable for programming very high performance parallel machines. It may be more difficult to adapt conventional programming languages and Lisp, designed for sequential von Neumann machines, to parallel architectures. Parallelism associated with conventional and Lisp languages and von Neumann machines simply means that the computer can perform some operations that are part of a single instruction in parallel. For example, if an instruction directs the computer to add two numbers, then the parts of that instruction are performed in parallel such as data type (checking to see that only similar data types, such as integers or real numbers, are added) and overflow checks (to see that the data fit in the registers).

However, conventional languages and machines cannot execute different instructions in the program in parallel. For example, if instruction-1 said to add 10 to 12, instruction-2 said to subtract 43 from 59, and instruction-3 said to multiply the results, the conventional machine would execute these instructions sequentially. It could not execute instructions 1 and 2 simultaneously and coordinate and feed the results into instruction-3 except under certain conditions and also with special compiler enhancements.

How much Prolog is oriented toward parallel processing is controversial. "The reason that Prolog lends itself to parallel processing is not because of what is in the language, but what is not in it," says David Warren. For example, unlike Prolog, conventional languages have assignment statements. With assignment statements, a program assigns a value and stores it in memory. If two processes simultaneously execute, access, and change the same memory, side effects and conflicts between the two processes can occur. Since Prolog has no assignment statements, these problems do not arise.

But some experts doubt Prolog's parallelism claim. Carl Hewitt, for example, professor of electrical engineering and computer science at MIT and creator of the earlier logic-based language, Planner, points out how backtracking is incompatible with parallelism. With a backtracking approach (and backtracking is Prolog's only control mechanism), a program tries a second alternative only after a first already explored alternative has failed—a technique mutually exclusive with parallelism. So although Prolog programs can perform, for example, operations on two sides of an AND and OR function in parallel, their parallelism capabilities are still very limited.

With the aim of achieving parallel processing capabilities, several companies and universities are investigating parallel processing languages built on Lisp. One of these is Actors, under development at MIT. Actors integrates functional and object-oriented programming. Its functional element is called an *actor*. An actor in many ways resembles a function, but it has added capabilities similar to those found in object-oriented programming. For example, like objects in object-oriented programs, an actor can receive messages. In response to the message, an actor can take three kinds of actions. It can change its local state to become another actor. It can create more actors. Or it can send more messages.

The advantage to organizing a language as a message-passing system is the ability it provides to send, receive, and react to messages in parallel and thus perform multiple tasks concurrently. The actors language is further adapted toward parallel processing because it has no assignment command. The problem with assignment commands is that they create dependencies that are difficult to cope with during parallel operations. Actors substitutes a "become" command for an assignment command. With the "become" statement, it is able to perform the needed operations normally performed with assignment statements but without the dependency disadvantages.

HIGH-LEVEL AI LANGUAGES

Notwithstanding all the brouhaha about Lisp, and more recently Prolog, most AI programming is not done directly in Lisp anyway (and it is too early to tell about Prolog).

Lisp and Prolog are both the equivalent of assembly languages for AI programming. Just as Fortran, Cobol, and Pascal operate on top of and compile to assembly languages, so higher-level rule-based and frame-based languages operate on top of Lisp, compile into Lisp, and use Lisp features.

Some of these high-level AI languages are developed by companies or university groups for their internal use. They reflect the way that these companies and groups think about knowledge, reasoning, and problem-solving strategies. Other languages are extensions of Lisp that incorporate specialized terminology and procedures for a particular application domain, such as VLSI. In addition, the various AI application development tools each have their own programming language for knowledge engineering.

Like any high-level language compared to assembler, these AI languages handle low-level details so that programmers can concentrate on the program to be solved. For expert systems, low-level details handled include the method of representing knowledge in machine-readable form, the building of pattern matchers that are used to infer information and draw conclusions, and the implementation of control mechanisms that guide the sequence of problem-solving steps.

One of the most widely used high-level AI languages is a rule-based forward-chaining language known as OPS5. Developed at Carnegie-Mellon University by Charles Forgy, it is the language used to program expert systems such as DEC's XCON and XSEL and Hazeltine's Opgen.

OPS5 programs look like a set of IF-THEN rules called *productions*. These rules are stored in a section of memory called *production memory*. They operate on database type of expressions (similar to Pascal record structures) stored in a section of memory called *working memory*.

The OPS5 problem-solving technique is an iterative match-rules-and-perform-action cycle (known as the recognize-act cycle). When a program executes, an OPS5 interpreter evaluates the rules to see which have IF or conditional parts that match expressions currently in working memory. If any match, the interpreter performs the action indicated in the THEN part of that rule. If more than one rule is satisfied by finding a match, the interpreter selects one according to a series of OPS5 conflict resolution policies and executes the action (THEN) part of the rule. If no rules have conditional parts that match information in working memory, the interpreter halts.

Much of the time, execution of a rule's action part changes working memory by adding, deleting, or modifying one or more expressions there. The interpreter then reevaluates the rules by reiterating the recognize-act cycle. This process is iterated until the program halts either because the interpreter encounters a rule that explicitly directs the program to halt or because none of the conditional parts of the rule are true. Presumably, when the program halts, the problem is solved.

OPS5 (and other rule-based language) programs differ from Lisp and conventional programs in two respects. One difference is that conventional programs indicate the state of the problem being executed by assigning values to variables. With OPS5 programs, the expressions that are put in working memory indicate the current state of the problem.

The second difference between conventional or Lisp programs and OPS5 rule-based programs is the way the program handles flow of control. In conventional programs, flow of control is based on sequential execution of statements or control constructs in the language that direct which statements should be executed next. Control constructs include IF-THEN-ELSE (conditional branching), DO-WHILE (loops), and subroutine and function calls. In contrast, OPS5 program control flow is based on a search for rules which have patterns that match patterns in working memory. The interpreter executes those rules, changes working memory, and repeats the cycle to find a rule that matches the new information in working memory.

WORKING MEMORY

Typically, information in working memory looks like a list of objects and the attributes and values that describe them. For example, the following working memory expression indicates that monkey 1 is a brown monkey, measuring 3 feet in height, located at coordinates 5–7, on a ladder.

```
(monkey
  ↑name     monkey 1
  ↑color    brown
  ↑height   3
  ↑at       3–5
  ↑on       ladder)
```

The object described here is a monkey. Its attributes are name, color, height, at, and on. The corresponding values are monkey1, brown, 3, 5–7, and ladder.

Attributes and values need not be physical descriptions of the object being described. Predicates also indicate relationships between objects, such as "↑on ladder," which indicates "monkey on ladder." Nor does the information being described need to involve a physical object. For example, the following working memory expression describes a fact with attributes of factname, indexname, and cumulative direction having corresponding values of closing status, Dow Jones Index, and down.

```
(fact
   ↑factname          closingstatus
   ↑indexname         dow-jones-index
   ↑cumul-direction   down)
```

Attributes are indicated by the symbol ↑, which precedes them. The order in which the attribute/value pairs appear does not matter; nor do spaces, tabs, and new lines. OPS5 format is free. Each OPS5 working memory expression is enclosed in parentheses.

OPS5 RULES

An OPS5 rule consists of an open parenthesis, the symbol "p", a name for the rule, the conditional part of the rule (left hand side), the symbol →, the action part of the rule (right hand side), and a close parenthesis. For example, in the Ana stock report generation system's rule 002 in Figure 25-2, "create-message-mixed-up" is the name of the rule. (Rules 000 through 009 in this chapter are excerpted from the Ana stock report generation system, created by Karen Kukich at Carnegie Mellon University/Bell Communications Research. The Ana system collects data from the Dow Jones News Service database, determines which data represent significant events in the day's stock market data, and generates natural-language messages about these events. The rules have been simplified for clarity.) The conditional part of the rule is everything between the rule name and the symbol →; the action part is everything after the →.

The conditional part of a rule consists of one or more *patterns*. Any of the parenthesized expressions in the rule such as (goal ↑ status active ↑ operation create-messages) is a pattern.

Patterns can also contain variables. Variables are indicated by their enclosure within angle brackets, as in <x>. A variable in a pattern may match anything. However, repetitions of the same variable in a rule must match the same value everywhere. For example, the following rule can only describe a cube (Forgy, 1981).

```
(block   ↑length <x>   ↑width <x>   ↑height <x>)
```

The action part of a rule contains various types of actions to perform. These include actions to change working memory, perform input and output, add new rules, call user-written subroutines, and stop firing rules. For example, "make" directs the OPS5 system to create and add the new information, which follows the symbol "make," to working memory. "Remove" deletes information from working memory. "Modify" changes one or more values in working memory.

```
                         **RULE 002**
(p create-message-mixed-up        RULE 002
  (goal                           ; If there is a goal            1
   ↑status active                 ; which is active
   ↑operation create-messages)    ; to create messages
  (fact                           ; And there is a fact           2
  ↑factname closingstatus         ; which is the closing status
  ↑indexname dji                  ; of the Dow Jones Index
  ↑cumul-direction up)            ; had a cummulative direction of up
  (fact                           ; And there is a fact           3
  ↑factname advancedeclines       ; about advances and declines
  ↑indexname nyse                 ; on the New York Stock Exchange
  ↑advances <x> ↑declines > <x>)  ; that says the declines exceeded
                                    the advances


-->
   (make message                  ; Then create a message
    ↑topic genmkt                 ; whose topic is general market
                                    status
    ↑subtopic mix                 ; whose subtopic is mixed
    ↑subjectclass mkt             ; concerning the market
    ↑time close))                 ; at closing time
```

Figure 25-2 A typical OPS5 rule contains an open parenthesis, the symbol "p", a name for the rule, a conditional part (LHS), the symbol →, an action part (RHS), and a close parenthesis. (Karen Kukich)

Other actions include "openfile," "closefile," and "default," which manipulate files; "write," which outputs information; and "halt," which halts the interpreter.

During program execution, the OPS5 interpreter compares each pattern in the conditional part of a rule with the patterns in working memory to determine if the pattern matches any of them. If all the patterns in the rule's conditional part are satisfied (by finding a match), the action part of the rule is executed (Forgy, 1981).

REASONING

An OPS5 program starts its recognize-act cycle when one or more database-type records, of the kind found in working memory, are explicitly placed into working memory. This causes some rule's conditional part to become satisfied. Therefore, that rule's action part is executed by the interpreter. This, in turn, causes either more patterns to be added or existing ones to be deleted or modified. Consequently, other rules are satisfied and can be executed.

The rules in OPS5 programs are unsequenced and unstructured. Therefore, unlike conventional languages with sequencing, loops, branches, and subroutines, they offer no direct clues to their order of execution; in fact, any rule can fire at any time. The order in which the rules were entered also has no bearing on when they will be executed.

To select which rules to execute, the OPS5 interpreter evaluates all the rules on every cycle. However, it does not evaluate them sequentially. Instead, it must cleverly narrow the rule search space because programs might consist of 2000 rules and contain 500 objects in the database when the program starts. If, on every cycle, the interpreter tried to sequentially match all of working memory against all the rules in such a large program, the search for the appropriate rule to execute would be too inefficient to be practical.

WHO'S IN CONTROL?

OPS5 uses two major methods to narrow the search and otherwise improve efficiency. It builds an index into the rules so that the interpreter can easily find rules relevant to the current information in working memory. It also remembers information about partially satisfied rules so that on each evaluation of the rules, not everything has to be recomputed.

The index structure is based on the order in which live experts, whose knowledge is encoded in the program rules, execute different processes. Experts typically perform certain tasks that they consider appropriate for certain situations or contexts. When knowledge engineers encode the expert's knowledge in an OPS5 program, they give that context a name, usually called a *context name* or *goal name*. They then make that context or goal name an attribute and value of all the rules that they want to fire in that situation. Therefore, all the rules that apply to each problem-solving task share the same context name.

For example, all the XCON rules that apply to the task of assigning a power supply might share the attribute and value (↑ context assign-power-supply . . .). In the rule in Figure 25-2, the attribute (goal ↑ operation create-messages) shares the attribute name "operation" and value "create-messages" with all other rules that pertain to the creation of messages. Some other goal names in the Ana stock report generation system are "express-messages" and "select-predicate."

When the programmer enters the rules, the interpreter builds a large discrimination network (type of index structure) based on the condition parts of all the rules, including on the context or goal names. At execution time, it runs the data in working memory through this discrimination network to determine which rules could apply to these data.

Early in this determination-of-relevancy process, the context names or goal names of working memory expressions and rules are compared to see if a match exists. Only those rules for which a match between context names exists are actually considered for evaluation during the recognize-act cycle while that particular context (problem-solving step) is being processed.

The number of rules with the same context name are comparatively small in number. By definition, they are all pertinent to the same specific situation or problem-solving task. None of the other rules in the program are given that same context name. Therefore, only a small number of relevant rules are actually considered during the match-rules-and-perform-action cycle for any particular situation.

The programmer does not have to be aware of OPS5's indexing structure. In fact, from the programmer's point of view, the entire OPS5 language consists of only IF-THEN rules and the database-type expressions in working memory. This makes it very easy for a programmer to add rules. The programmer merely needs to specify for each rule the conditions under which it is appropriate to execute. It is the interpreter that decides in what sequence to execute the rules.

CONFLICT RESOLUTION

The interpreter uses several techniques to decide which rules to execute. The first line technique is to select the rules that are applicable to a particular context.

The rules that are applicable to the context under consideration are evaluated to see if their conditional parts match the patterns in working memory. The aim of this match process is to find one rule, all of whose patterns can be matched, and then perform the actions specified by that rule.

However, it is possible that more than one rule will have totally satisfied conditional parts. This competing set of rules is called a *conflict set*. Only one rule from this conflict set will be executed. The interpreter follows several criteria in order to select which rule in the conflict set to execute. The most important of these are time stamps and specificity.

The time stamp criterion requires all data in working memory to have associated time stamps that indicate when the data were created or last modified. Given a choice, OPS5 selects the rule that matches data that were most recently added to working memory rather than data which have been there for the longest time. The rationale is that the most recently used data are likely to be the most relevant.

For example, rule 001, in Figure 25-3, is a top-level rule from the Ana stock report generation system that sets three high-level goals for generating a daily stock report. The order in which the goals are stated is reversed from the order in which the stock report generation system will attend to them, because the OPS5 recency principle dictates that the most recently added working memory element will be attended to first.

A consequence of this strategy is that OPS5 systems are unlikely to be distracted from the task that they are currently processing. Furthermore, the time stamp strategy, in combination with the context name matching strategy, provides OPS5 programs with some humanlike features. In particular, once OPS5 begins processing a task, it does all it can on that task, and the various aspects of that task, before proceeding to another.

```
                     **RULE 001**

(p generate-report                                    ; RULE 001
    (goal  ↑status active  ↑operation generate-report)
    . . .

-->
    . . .
    (remove 1)
    (make goal  ↑status pending express-messages)
    (make goal  ↑status pending organize-messages)
    (make goal  ↑status active  create-messages))
```

Figure 25-3 OPS5 rule 001 sets three high-level goals for generating a daily stock market report. (Karen Kukuch)

SPECIFICITY

The second conflict resolution criterion, specificity, specifies that given a choice of two totally satisfied rules, OPS5 selects the rule with very specific conditions as opposed to rules with more general conditions. The rationale here is that knowledge that is highly specific is more likely to be the most appropriate because it is specialized for the task at hand (Forgy, 1981).

The very specific rules are written so that they are the rules with the greatest number of data items, in their conditional parts, to match. Choosing the most specific rule therefore results in the OPS5 interpreter choosing the longest rule from the conflict set. This choice is analogous to a cabinetmaker who chooses a large set of every standard-sized drill bit instead of a set of only the six most common size bits. (Similarly, a human being would probably choose the full gauntlet of different-length musical notes to write a symphony instead of only semi- and demisemiquavers.)

How conflict resolution through specificity operates is illustrated by the resolution of the competition between rules 007, 008, and 009 in Figure 25-4. These are three rules used to make a syntactic choice to express a stock report message. The message consists of phrases commonly associated with patterns and actions in a stock market report. The phrases that indicate the day's events, such as "TURNED IN A MIXED SHOWING," "FINISHED THE DAY WITH A SLIGHT LOSS," and "IN MIXED TRADING," have been generated by prior program rules. However, the phrases can be combined and expressed in several ways. For example, the mixed-market message might be expressed in a sentential (simple sentence) form as in "STOCKS TURNED IN A MIXED SHOWING," or as a prepositional phrase, as in THE MARKET CLOSED OUT THE DAY WITH A SLIGHT LOSS "IN MIXED TRADING."

The choice is made using both syntactic and pragmatic constraints. Syntactic constraints include grammatical correctness of expression, availability of certain phrasal forms (such as prepositional phrases) in memory, and satisfaction

```
(p syntactic-form-sentence-004                              ; RULE 007
    (goal  ↑status active  ↑operation select-syntax)          ; 1
    (sentence-requirement  ↑status nil)                       ; 2

-->

    (remove 1)
    (make syntactic-form    ↑form sentence)
    (modify 2  ↑status satisfied))


(p syntactic-form-prepositional-002                         ; RULE 008
    (goal  ↑status active  ↑operation select-syntax)           ; 1
    (sentence-requirement  ↑status satisfied                   ; 2
    (phraselex  ↑phrasetype pred  ↑focus in  prepp <> nil)     ; 3

-->

    (remove 1)
    (make syntactic-form  ↑form prepositional))


( syntactic-form-period-001                                ; RULE 009
    (goal   ↑status active  ↑operation select-syntax)         ;1
    (sentence-requirement  ↑status satisfied)

-->

    (make punctuation  ↑form period)
    (modify 2  ↑status nil))
```

Figure 25-4 Conflict resolution (Karen Kukich)

of a sentence-requirement. (The sentence-requirement dictates that every compound-complex sentence contains at least one complete sentence.) Pragmatic constraints limit the number of messages to be included in one sentence and require the varying of sentence lengths.

The syntactic choices shown in Figure 25-4 are either a sentential or a prepositional phrasal form for the message. Rule 007 selects the sentential form. Rule 008 selects a prepositional phrase. Rule 009 ends the sentence and prepares to begin the next.

Rules 007 and 008 are satisfied depending on whether a complete sentence has not yet been formed (sentence-requirement ↑ status nil), or a complete sentence has been formed and a prepositional phrase is also available in working memory (↑ prepp<>nil). However, rules 008 and 009 are competing rules because both are satisfied if the active operation is select-syntax and a complete sentence has already been formed. For example, both are satisfied after expres-

```
(p goal-changer                          ; RULE 000
        (goal  ↑status pending)
        - (goal  ↑status active)

-->
        (modify 1  ↑status active))
```

Figure 25-5 OPS5 rule for changing a goal (Karen Kukich)

sion of the message, THE MARKET CLOSED OUT THE DAY WITH A SLIGHT LOSS.

The competition, which determines what to do next, can be resolved because rule 008 contains an extra set of data items that indicates the existence of a phrasal lexical element of type predicate, currently in focus (under consideration), which is a prepositional phrase. The OPS5 specificity principle dictates the selection of rule 008 over 009 on the grounds that if an appropriate prepositional phrase exists in working memory, it must have been generated to provide better (more specific) information than a more general sentence that ends without including it. Therefore, the sentence generated would include the prepositional phrase, IN MIXED TRADING. However, if a prepositional phrase was not available to satisfy rule 008, then rule 008 fails and is not included in the conflict set. The less specific rule 009, which has fewer constraints, is still satisfied and is the rule selected. The selection of rule 009 indicates that the expert program cannot think of any other syntactic form for this current message, given the fact that the sentence requirement has been satisfied. Therefore, it adds a period to the sentence and modifies the sentence-requirement status to nil (''modify 2'' indicates ''modify the second condition element''). Once the sentence is ended by adding a period, the program is ready to begin a new sentence. Since a new sentence does not yet have its sentence-requirement satisfied, rule 007 can fire. The cycle then repeats with new phrases created by other rules expressed as messages in simple sentences or with prepositional phrases, subordinate sentences, and so on.

When there are no more messages left to express, either the program is finished or it goes on to processing another goal. OPS5 rules are written so that only goals whose status is active may be attended to. A goal whose status is ''pending'' can be changed only by the demon rule 000 shown in Figure 25-5.

The goal change is accomplished by the demon rule through the specificity principle. At some processing point, everything in working memory will have been attended to, modified, or deleted. Nothing will be left to match the rules that are applicable to a particular goal except the most nonspecific rule of all, the demon rule, which does nothing more than state the status of the goal. At that time, the demon rule is selected and it causes the next goal status to be modified from pending to active.

These and other techniques make the OPS5 interpreter responsible for flow of control in a program and leave the programmer to just write rules. However, programmers do have some control over the program control.

For example, OPS5 allows programmers to create an assertion that specifies a particular type of task that is necessary to perform at some point. In some respects, this is similar to calling a particular function or procedure in traditional programming.

Actually, OPS5 programmers lack control only in the sense that they can leave traditional sequencing of instructions to the interpreter—a convenient feature for incrementally adding rules. However, they can, if they wish, control the program based on how they write the rules. For example, in Figure 25-3 the order of the goals dictates the order in which subtasks will be carried out.

WHY RULE-BASED LANGUAGES?

Any programming language, such as Pascal, Lisp, and OPS5, gives programmers the ability to execute conditional statements. What OPS5 (and other rule-based languages) provides, in contrast to procedural languages (including Lisp), is the ability to easily use more complex conditionals, to use more of them, and to use them more frequently.

For example, DEC's XCON contains more than 5500 rules or conditionals. It is difficult, if not impossible, for human beings to keep track of this many IF-THEN statements in a conventional program and debug it. Modification of such a program is generally a nasty, massive procedure that requires a rewrite, redebug, and retest.

The OPS5 paradigm is appropriate to use for programs with such a large number and complexity of conditionals. OPS5 programmers do not need to keep track of them nor to specify program flow of control. Instead, the rules are added to the OPS5 program in an unstructured and unsequenced manner. The interpreter keeps track of these rules and decides the proper sequence to execute them.

There are some other cases where the OPS5 paradigm is appropriate. One is when the programmer needs to modify the program often, or just to explore a particular program design. The lack of structure and sequencing of the rules, and the offloading of control to the OPS5 interpreter, facilitates program modification and exploratory programming.

Another case, appropriate for OPS5 techniques, occurs when the flow of control of a program is very complex. This means that control jumps around very frequently or, more important, it moves around in ways that programmers cannot perceive when they begin writing the program. This situation is common to many AI programs.

Still, while the OPS5 strategies make it easy for programmers to add rules and rely on their firing at the right time, the programmers must write these rules so that the interpreter always selects the right one. This rule-writing task requires programmers to identify the interacting pieces of knowledge and set them up so that when they compete, at conflict resolution time the one that fires naturally is the appropriate one.

Unfortunately, it is not always easy to identify all the interactions between the individual pieces of knowledge and to encode them so that the conflict resolution strategy selects the intended rule. Frequently, the only way to ensure that the right rule fires at the right time is through trial and error. And since identification of the interacting knowledge is a human rather than a programming procedure, knowledge engineering is still held by many to be an art rather than a science, and is expected to remain that way for some time.

BLOCK-STRUCTURED AI LANGUAGES

Expert systems typically pose large, diverse problems, of which some parts are conveniently solved by rule-based procedures, but other parts may be more efficiently solved by conventional programming techniques. Seeking to integrate the two solution methods in one paradigm, Charles Forgy, the inventor of OPS5, has extended that rule-based language to also include structured programming concepts characteristic of Pascal, C, Ada, and others (Forgy, 1983).

Called OPS83, the hybrid language version permits expressions and subroutine calls in the conditional parts of rules. It includes ordinary functions and procedures. It supports rules, but the action (THEN) parts of rules have the same syntax and semantics as the body of a procedure. This syntax includes structured programming constructs such as the BEGIN-END blocks, IF-THEN-ELSE branches, and FOR loops.

Further similarities to conventional languages such as Pascal and Ada are the data typing facility, which allows programmers to define and use their own data types instead of needing to spend time simulating data types not found in the language. Subroutines called from within rules can manipulate these programmer-defined types. To change one of these programmer-defined types, the programmer need only redefine the type and rewrite the functions that manipulate values of that type. The rules, however, require no changes. Finally, working memory elements in OPS83 are almost identical to records in structured languages.

These features provide a number of advantages to systems developers. Clearly, it is easier for programmers familiar with a language like Pascal to learn the Pascal-like OPS83. In addition, the procedural sublanguage incorporated in OPS83 results in programs that are smaller and execute at higher speed, with fewer rule firings. The functions and procedural constructs in the language make it easier to implement algorithms with a smaller program. Because programmers can call functions and subroutines from rules, OPS83 programs can be more modular and therefore easier to maintain.

```
type location =
    record
        x:integer;
        y:integer
    end;

type locvec = array[1..2] of integer;

type imagset =
    record
        len:integer;
        vals:array[1..64] of record rpart:real; ipart:real end
    end;
```

Figure 25-6 Pascal type declarations (Charles Forgy)

```
type location = record
  (
    x:integer;
    y:integer;
  );

type locvec = array(2:integer);

type imagset = record
  (
    len:integer;
    vals:array(64:record(rpart:real; ipart:real));
  );
```

Figure 25-7 OPS83 type declarations (Charles Forgy)

```
function fib(N:integer):integer;
    var K, FK, PREV, T:integer;
    begin
    FK := 1;
    PREV := 0;
    for K := 2 to N do
        begin
        T := FK + PREV;
        PREV := FK;
        FK := T
        end;
    fib := FK
    end;
```

Figure 25-8 Pascal subroutine to generate Fibonacci numbers (Charles Forgy)

```
function fib(&N:integer):integer
  {
    local &K:integer, &FK:integer,
          &PREV:integer, &T:integer
    &FK = 1;
    &PREV = 0;
    for &K = (2 to &N)
      {
        &T = &FK + &PREV;
        &PREV = &FK;
        &FK = &T;
      };
    return (&FK);
  };
```

Figure 25-9 OPS83 subroutine to generate Fibonacci numbers (Charles Forgy)

OPS83 IS LIKE PASCAL

Like Pascal, OPS83 is an infix language. It uses the symbol ";" to delimit statements rather than using parentheses. A word beginning with the character "&", such as in "&X", signals a variable.

Type declarations in Pascal and OPS83 are similar. For example, the Pascal declarations in Figure 25-6 correspond to the OPS83 declarations in Figure 25-7.

Subroutines are also similar. The subroutine to generate Fibonacci numbers in Figure 25-8 corresponds to the OPS83 subroutine in Figure 25-9. However, OPS83 subroutines are more restricted than those in Pascal. For example, unlike Pascal, one subroutine declaration may not be declared inside the body of another subroutine.

Declarations for OPS5 working memory elements are relatively simple. However, the OPS83 working memory element declaration methods allow the declaration of much more complex structures. For example, OPS83 elements can contain records of records, records of arrays, arrays of records, and so on, nested arbitrarily deeply.

OPS83 rules execute the same recognize-act cycle as OPS5. However, the condition and action parts of rules can contain Pascal-like expressions and subroutines.

26

AI Computer Hardware: The Software Environments

Most AI software for developing AI systems is implemented on specialized hardware which represents the state of the art in workstation/computer system design. Optimized for symbolic rather than numeric processing, these workstation/computers have certain common design goals and features not generally found in standard computers. For example, they are designed to efficiently run programs written in Lisp, the most popular AI language. Hence they are known as Lisp computers. Also, since AI programs are large and complex, Lisp-oriented computers are designed for efficient program development as well as efficient program execution.

Program development efficiency features include high-resolution, bit-mapped, physically large graphics displays with overlapping windows, mice, large memories, networking capabilities, and interactive, integrated AI programming tools. AI programmers need the special considerations provided by these program development features not only because AI programs are large and complex, but also because the programs are, a priori, ill-specified and ill-understood. A bonus of incorporating all the aforementioned software (and hardware) features into one workstation/computer is that AI environments are unsurpassed as software development environments for any large, complex programs—AI or otherwise.

As for program execution efficiency, one important feature in AI computers is a pipelined architecture that supports parallel processing. Although not as sophisticated as the parallel processing architectures being sought for fifth-generation computers, this design allows certain operations within one instruction to be executed in parallel with each other—speeding the execution of many program instructions. Another speed feature used in some Lisp machines is a microcode compiler available to the user. It compiles Lisp program source code directly to system microinstructions (microcode). Machine microcode is "lower level" and easier for computers to execute than assembly code or machine code.

It is important to note that it is impossible to separate AI hardware from software. Lisp computers are put together mostly with standard off-the-shelf components. What makes them special is their architecture, which is optimized to execute their software. Aside from architecture, the most distinguishing characteristic of Lisp computers is their software environment, which is the reason that Lisp computers are used to develop AI systems even when standard computers are able to do the job. Often, this software environment is intimately tied to Lisp computer hardware. Therefore, any discussion of AI computers must include as much software as hardware information.

OF MICE AND WINDOWS

AI developers generally view large amounts of information in many windows on their screens at one time (Figure 26-1). Consequently, very high resolution graphics and larger-than-usual screens are needed, as well as mice to get around the maze of windows.

Whether windows and mice are really needed in conventional computers is controversial. For AI development, however, there is no question that windows and mice increase productivity.

Windows allow AI developers to build a general framework for their system and then create and view different knowledge-representation structures, coded procedures, and parts of the framework simultaneously, in different windows. In addition, programmers do not build AI systems sequentially; instead, they switch back and forth between various parts of the system as they gain feedback about what their system knows and does. Windows reduce the waiting times for new displays to be generated when programmers switch between tasks because the displays are preserved in separate windows.

These windows may be widely separated and there may be many of them. So a mouse is handy because it allows users to sweep a pointer across the screen between commands located in different windows far faster than they could with a cursor key on the keyboard.

VERY LARGE PERSONAL COMPUTERS

Lisp computers are dedicated personal computers. To most people, who think of a personal computer as a machine that resembles an IBM PC or the Apple Macintosh, applying the term "personal computer" to the large Lisp computers is disequilibrating. IBM PCs and Macintoshes are personal "microcomputers," little things compared with Lisp computers, which are really dedicated, personal

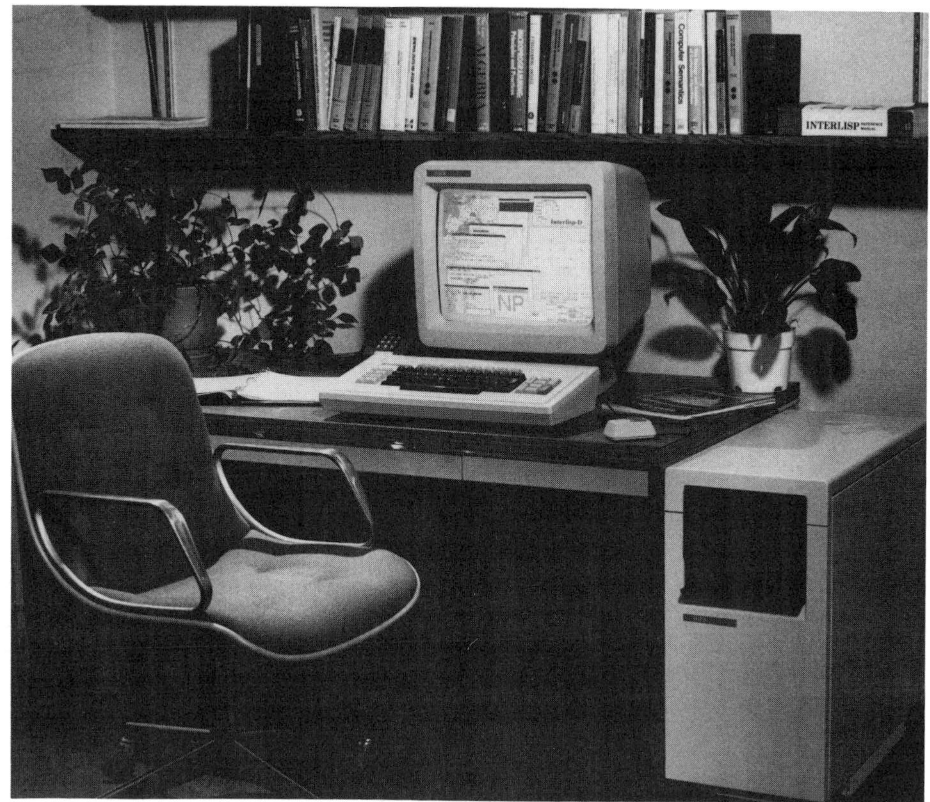

Figure 26-1 Specalized Lisp machines feature a graphical application development environment (Xerox Corp.)

minicomputers, often with more capacity than the mainframes originally used for AI development. However, Lisp machine sizes are decreasing (Figure 26-2).

In the early AI days, before Lisp computers came along, AI work was done on time-shared mainframe computers, primarily DEC System 10s and 20s. These were million-dollar machines with less memory that could be dedicated to one user or program than that of the current Lisp computers. Unfortunately, this time-sharing hardware limited the development of large, complex AI programs.

Intuitively, it may seem that if time-sharing systems such as DEC 10s and 20s have relatively large physical memories to support many users, they must also support very large programs. But, the machine's total memory makes little difference to an individual user or program. The architecture of the machine is designed so that there is a maximum address space that can be conveniently assigned to any one user or program.

A time-sharing machine is delivered with a certain set of memory-mapping registers that can address a certain amount of virtual address space. Normally,

Figure 26-2 Lisp machines are growing smaller (Symbolics, Inc.)

each user gets a set of memory-mapping registers and an associated assigned memory space. In the case of the DEC System 10, the memory-mapping registers and each machine instruction, has 18 bits to specify the address of a memory location. Unfortunately, the amount of memory that can be addressed by 18 bits was just too small for early AI designers to develop most modern AI programs.

Even if money was no object and it was acceptable to assign a $1 million machine to one user, the multiple mapping registers would make it awkward for a programmer to use multiple users' address spaces. Programs can easily refer to anything within their own address space. However, to refer to other addresses would burden the user with the need not only to allocate memory, but to coordinate which set of mapping registers was allocated to various functions in a program. And the point of Lisp is to remove these types of burdens from users and leave them free to concentrate on AI programs.

There are tricks to get around this memory problem. However, most of those tricks result in extra overhead to emulate in software what Lisp computers do in hardware. The extra overhead decreases performance—and unhappily, performance is another sore point for AI processing. AI programs often require huge amounts of computation to solve a problem. Consequently, AI program performance on most machines shared with other users was not considered acceptable, especially during development.

If the lack of a dedicated, high-performance machine was not bad enough, program development problems were exacerbated because time-sharing interfaces are not only unfriendly, they are often downright hostile.

THE AGE OF THE LISP COMPUTER

The methods and tricks to get around both the memory and flexibility limitations became so complicated that in the late 1970s, researchers went off and invented Lisp computers. The earliest Lisp computers were designed at two research labs: one at Massachusetts Institute of Technology and the other at Xerox Corp.'s Palo Alto Research Laboratories.

In August 1980, Xerox announced its first Lisp computer, which it had kept hidden from the peering eyes of competing manufacturers. That prompted two sets of researchers at MIT to license the MIT-developed Lisp computer and form two more companies: Symbolics, Inc. and Lisp Machine, Inc. (LMI). By September 1981, both these companies had also announced their machines. The Lisp computers from Symbolics and LMI, and the Explorer, the 1985-announced Lisp computer from Texas Instruments (TI), are descendents of the MIT Lisp Machine.*

SIZE

All the Lisp computers provide large address spaces and are quite powerful. Typically, they provide the processing power of a supermini computer, and as they increasingly take advantage of new silicon technologies, they will provide still greater processing power.

MULTIPURPOSE

By definition, Lisp computers are optimized to execute symbolic processing languages such as Lisp. However, they also handle numeric processing such as calculations. In addition, their environments make excellent programming tools for developing all sorts of software.

NETWORKING

The Lisp computers all support extensive networking interfaces. Networking capabilities and file sharing are actually a productivity enhancement for any complex program development by groups of software engineers, not only AI designers.

Traditionally, AI development centers have included many machines and lots of different users who share files, confer together, and are likely to use different machines at any time. Therefore, AI centers usually keep one machine as

* These four companies became three when in the second quarter of 1987 LMI filed for protection under chapter 11 of the federal bankruptcy laws.

a file server. All files are stored here. Users can switch to their hearts' delight among machines in different buildings. They simply load their files into their current machine via the network.

PROGRAMMING LANGUAGES

As the name implies, all the Lisp computers run the Lisp programming language. However, several varieties of Lisp exist, most an outgrowth of two original Lisp dialects. One is Interlisp, developed at Xerox and Bolt Beranek and Newman. The other is Maclisp, which came out of MIT. These dialects differ primarily in that Interlisp emphasizes its user interface, whereas performance has always been the foremost consideration in Maclisp.

The Xerox Lisp computers run Interlisp-D, an Interlisp implementation with an environment whose philosophy is DWIM (Do What I Mean). For Interlisp to DWIM, it tries to make sense out of whatever the programmer does.

With its eye toward implementing DWIMming, Interlisp provides an editor that edits the actual data structure (syntax tree) that represents a program, rather than editing files. Since the form of a data structure emphasizes meaning, a data structure-based editor reduces editing errors. This internal representation also makes it easy to write programs that can modify other programs.

Meaning is inherent in the data structure because the Lisp data structure, by definition, is always a well-formed program. Programmers can make changes to the data structure provided that their changes still net them a well-formed program. For example, they can switch two arms (consequences) of a conditional (THEN and ELSE clauses) because the Interlisp system knows that these arms are well-formed expressions and can be exchanged (Figure 26-3). Similarly, programmers can move parentheses around in certain well-formed ways.

The emphasis on editing the program structure gives programmers some productivity leverage because the Interlisp system understands what they are editing. In exchange, they sometimes give up some performance because of the overhead required to diagnose and fix problems and perform many user interface tasks.

The data structure approach also restricts programmers' freedom to create, insert, and experiment with malformed program structures during program development. This freer capability is allowed by the Zetalisp (also called Lisp Machine Lisp) environment, which more conventionally edits programs as text files rather than data structures.

The Symbolics, LMI, and TI computers all run versions of Zetalisp. A derivative and superset of Maclisp, Zetalisp's philosophy is to provide a powerful, high-performance set of tools for the programmer. While also providing a programming environment unexcelled in the conventional computing world, Zetalisp emphasizes the broader range of language facilities, more conventional programming notions, greater programmer responsibility, and minimal structure.

```
Lisp:    (IF (LISTP A) THEN (CONS B A)
                      ELSE (LIST B A))
```

Meaning: If the datum A is a list, then CONS B on the front;
Else make a 2 element list whose first element is B and whose second element is A.
(CONS inserts a new element in the front of a list.)

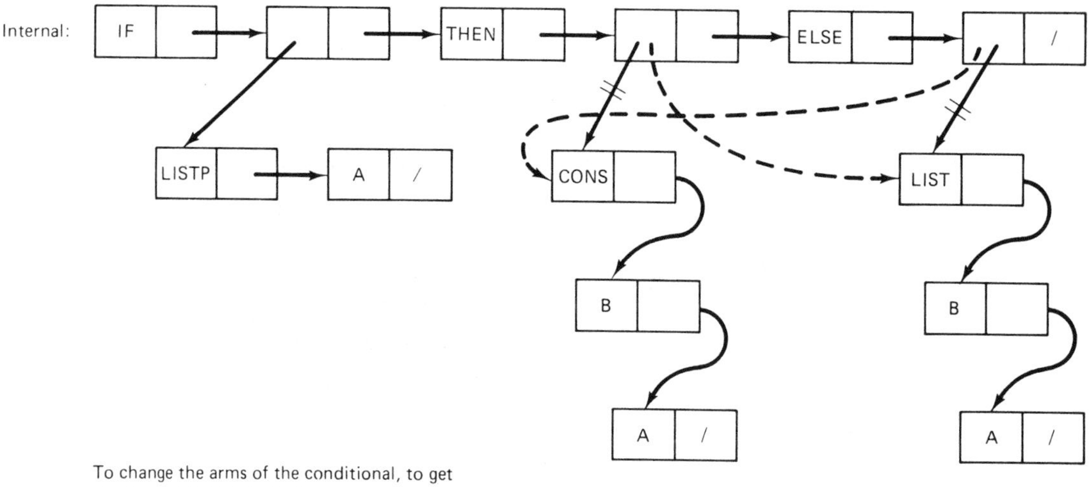

To change the arms of the conditional, to get

```
(IF (LISTP A) THEN (LIST B A)
              ELSE (CONS B A))
```

Just replace the solid links with the dashed ones. Nothing else changes.

Note: By convention: /means NIL.
Pointer to atoms are shown by writing the atom name in the pointer cell.
Links to other cells are shown by a line with an arrow.
Physical layout is not significant.

Figure 26-3 Interlisp programmers edit the data structure that represents a program rather than editing a file. (Beau Sheil)

The editing of files instead of data structures and the emphasis on minimal versus a deep level of structure and programmer restrictions are the fundamental differences between Interlisp and Zetalisp. Each approach has characteristic strengths and weaknesses. Yet the differences in the philosophy of the two approaches have fairly evenly split the Lisp community.

Differences notwithstanding, the Symbolics, LMI, and TI computers sell Interlisp compatibility packages so that Zetalisp users can debug and run Interlisp programs. In addition, all the companies' Lisp computers run Common Lisp, a dialect of Maclisp developed, standardized, and supported by most organizations involved in AI, including universities, research institutions, and the major computer manufacturers and AI software vendors, as well as the Lisp machine companies and the Defense Advanced Research Projects Agency (DARPA).

The Lisp computers can handle non-Lisp languages as well. Symbolics, for example, has integrated Fortran-77, Pascal, Ada, C, OPS5, and Prolog into its

Lisp environment. The high-level languages integrated with Lisp produce Lisp code when they are compiled. Integrating these languages into the Symbolics Lisp environment allows the integrated high-level language automatic access to the extensive array of software development tools.

OBJECT-ORIENTED PROGRAMMING

All the Lisp computers extend Lisp with some form of object-oriented programming. This is a type of programming that bundles objects with procedures and attributes about the object (Chapter 7).

Objects, in object-oriented programming, correspond to traditional program data. When programmers define an object, they also define operations (behaviors) it can perform. These operations, called *methods* in object-oriented programming, correspond to conventional programming procedures.

Unlike in conventional programs, however, an object rather than a procedure is the main focus of attention. Objects receive messages, and depending on what message they receive, they react by executing a specified method.

The objects can be arranged in a hierarchy where the most generic (abstract) objects are at the highest levels of the hierarchy and the most specific ones at the bottom. For example, an expert system that assists in the installation of computers might have a hierarchy of objects in it to define the different kinds of computers that exist. A generic computer with its descriptions and methods would be at the top level. Lisp computers and general-purpose computers, each with their descriptors, would be instances of the object "computer." Getting more specific, the Symbolics 3600, the Xerox 1186, and the TI Explorer, with their descriptors would be instances of Lisp computers. A specific Symbolics computer in a certain location would be the most specific instance of all.

Lower-level objects can inherit methods from higher-level objects. Or they can elect to override the higher-level methods with methods unique to them. For example, as soon as a Symbolics Lisp computer is turned on, it knows it should run Lisp because it is an instance of a Lisp computer which contains methods instructing it about the Lisp language. However, it contains its unique methods about Zetalisp and about program execution based on its own hardware architecture.

The Xerox Lisp computers support CommonLoops, an extension of Common Lisp that provides object-oriented programming for both Common Lisp and Interlisp. Symbolics and TI offer Flavors as their object-oriented programming system. A *flavor* is essentially an object. Like objects, it can exist as part of a hierarchy, it can have specific instances, and it is encapsulated with methods that operate on an instance of a flavor. Both Flavors' flavors and CommonLoops' objects differ from objects in early object-oriented programming languages, such as Smalltalk, in their ability to inherit characteristics from multiple parent flavors that are hierarchically unrelated. For example, a flavor that represents a Lisp

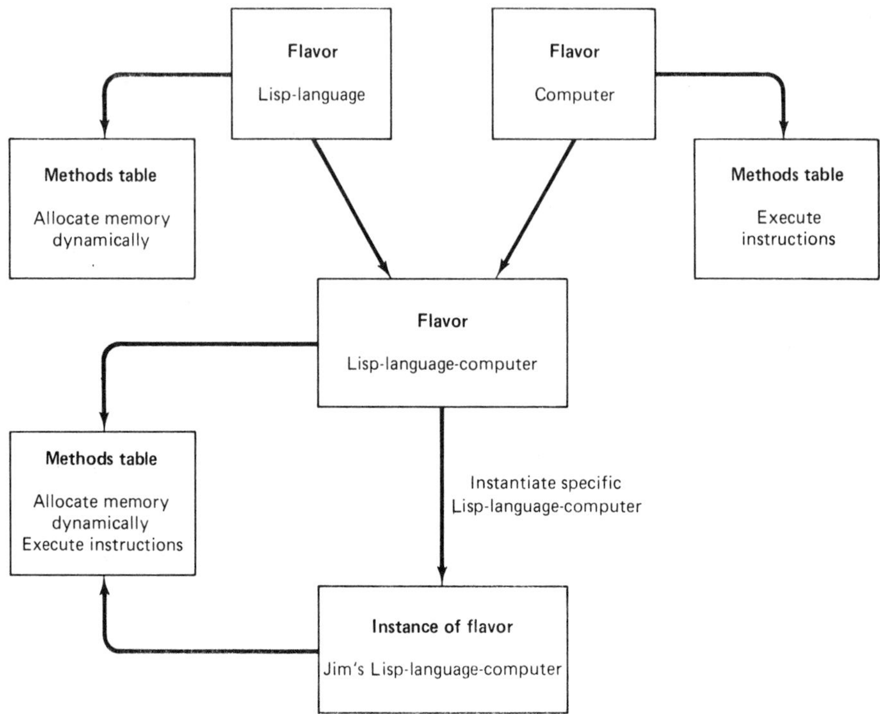

Figure 26-4 Inheritance of characteristics from multiple hierarchically unrelated parents in Flavors.

computer derives its instance variables (characteristics) and methods from parent flavors that represent a "computer" and "the Lisp programming language" (Figure 26-4).

Object-oriented programming promotes modularity and reusability of program code. The modularity is the result of defining modular procedures and encapsulating them with an associated object or flavor. Consequently, if it is necessary to change an object, procedure, or data structure, widespread program modification is not required. Moreover, there is little danger of inadvertently affecting an unrelated object or its associated procedures or data structures. The reusability of program code is the result of inheriting, instead of rewriting, procedures.

These object-oriented programming methods shield users from program implementation problems and permit large, complex programs to be developed easily.

WINDOWS

Lisp computer windows differ from traditional computer window systems in their flexibility and control, which, in turn, stems from differences in their underlying technology. In other words, a Lisp window is more than just a geometrical shape that resembles a window. Each window has specific behaviors, or associated procedures, that define how the window is to react under various circumstances. A simple key or mouse command causes the window to react as defined. The many behaviors possible are relatively easy to write and manage. The reason for the ease of management and control is the object-oriented programming technology that underlies Lisp computer windows.

In Lisp computers, a window is an object or a flavor. Its defined behaviors might instruct it to use a reverse video mode, change size, redraw itself, accept new characters, or move in front of another window.

New and complex window behaviors are relatively easily defined because many attributes and procedures can be inherited instead of needing to be rewritten with subsequent program retesting and debugging.

In contrast to the Lisp computer windows, the windows on general-purpose systems are just virtual screens. The user can shift characters into and out of the window. But there are no behavior characteristics associated with the windows.

Specific programs procedures may be written to allow users to realize, move, or perform other window operations on general-purpose computers. However, new procedures and data descriptions (such as a new type of window) are written afresh. Then the entire program must be tested for any new bugs caused by interactions between the old and new code. This conventionally oriented technique makes window control and management a more difficult task and thus makes it less likely that many window control operations will be written.

SUPPORTING SOFTWARE DEVELOPMENT

By far, the most interesting feature of Lisp computers is their user interface, which supports exploratory programming and rapid prototyping. This interface is actually a complete environment whose characteristics and resulting benefits are a composite of all the individual Lisp language features, Lisp computer features and tools (some of which have been discussed previously) and the fact that they are integrated.

The Lisp computer environment plays maid and manager to its users. Tools in the environment know the syntax and stylistic rules of the Lisp variant being used. Exercising their managerial skills, they reinforce users by blinking when parentheses don't match, positioning themselves over suspicious parenthesis errors, and indenting program lines.

Lisp tools keep track of every change users make to records, files, variables, macros, or data structures during an editing session. When the users are done, the tools root out any changes to code and recompile it. And if a user wishes to examine an earlier program version, the tools reconstruct the original environment.

The Lisp environments contain numerous tools for program editing, debugging, incremental compiling, dynamic linking, and program management, together with the standard workstation tools for file management and electronic mail. However, it is not the tools per se that are noteworthy. To some extent, similar tools are available on mainframes, minicomputers, and professional workstations, especially under the Unix operating system.

In these other programming environments, the tools are separate and independent. Consequently, to use the tool system, the programmer must enter one tool, operate on a file, save the file, exit the tool, enter another tool, and repeat the cycle. As a result, these unintegrated tools-oriented environments consume an extensive amount of time in file interactions and entering and exiting of the various tools. This time-consuming nuisance irks even personal computer users of less complex integrated programs, who claim that the enter/exit cycle decreases their productivity.

SPEEDING SOFTWARE DEVELOPMENT

Lisp computers eliminate the enter/exit requirements, in addition to a host of other software development problems, because the program development tools are fully integrated. This high degree of integration allows software developers to switch between tools and program-support functions while they are still in the editor.

To allow this switch, the command set of the editor is extended to include commands that allow access to all the tools and management functions. As a result, programmers can login to the editor, edit a program for a while, compile a modified segment, and execute the program, all without ever leaving the editor.

If an error is encountered, a single key or mouse stroke from the editor allows programmers to access a window-oriented debugger and obtain a trace of their program. After discovering the error, they use the editor to repair the program, and with another single keystroke reenter the run-time environment and continue execution from the point where the error occurred—also all without leaving the editor. As all these processes happen, the original program listing as well as information about the state of the program, the compilation, trace, modifications, and program execution remain on the screen, in different windows so that the programmer can compare, contrast, and find relationships.

From a hardware point of view, this kind of integration requires, among other things, a large address space such as Lisp machines support. In conventional computers where hardware is a scarcer resource and memory is limited, use of hardware and memory must be optimized. One way to do that is to break down the software support tools into small chunks and allow only one at a time to be present in memory.

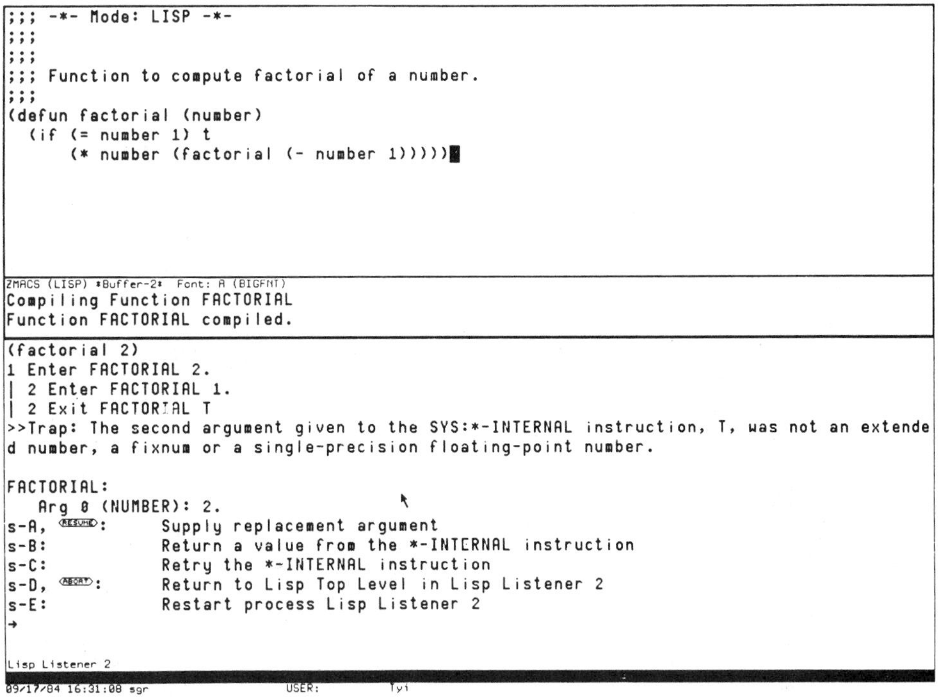

```
;;; -*- Mode: LISP -*-
;;;
;;;
;;; Function to compute factorial of a number.
;;;
(defun factorial (number)
  (if (= number 1) t
      (* number (factorial (- number 1)))))
```

```
ZMACS (LISP) *Buffer-2* Font: A (BIGFNT)
Compiling Function FACTORIAL
Function FACTORIAL compiled.
```

```
(factorial 2)
1 Enter FACTORIAL 2.
| 2 Enter FACTORIAL 1.
| 2 Exit FACTORIAL T
>>Trap: The second argument given to the SYS:*-INTERNAL instruction, T, was not an extende
d number, a fixnum or a single-precision floating-point number.

FACTORIAL:
   Arg 0 (NUMBER): 2.
s-A, RESUME:     Supply replacement argument
s-B:             Return a value from the *-INTERNAL instruction
s-C:             Retry the *-INTERNAL instruction
s-D, ABORT:      Return to Lisp Top Level in Lisp Listener 2
s-E:             Restart process Lisp Listener 2
→

Lisp Listener 2
09/17/84 16:31:08 sgr            USER:          Tyi
```

Figure 26-5 The Symbolics Zmacs editor (Symbolics Inc.)

A PROGRAM DEVELOPMENT EXAMPLE

An example of how the Lisp machines' integration of various program development tools and processes works is shown in Figure 26-5 (produced on a Symbolics 3600 machine) (Spoerl, 1984). If the factorial program shown in the top window portion of the figure was created (complete with bugs) using the Symbolic Zmacs editor, software developers could call the compiler simply by typing "control-shift-C." The compiler would then compile the program function indicated by the cursor position at the time. The typeout area in the middle of the screen would then display the function or procedure and the steps of the compilation as they complete.

As shown in the bottom window, execution of this program would reveal an error condition because the system expects a number 1, instead of a T, for True. Another keystroke switches the programmer to the window debugger (as opposed to a line-oriented debugger, which also exists) to investigate the error further.

The window-oriented debugger divides the screen into several subwindows or panes (Figure 26-6). In the top pane, a system feature called the Inspector displays the disassembled machine code with an arrow pointing to the instruction that caused the error.

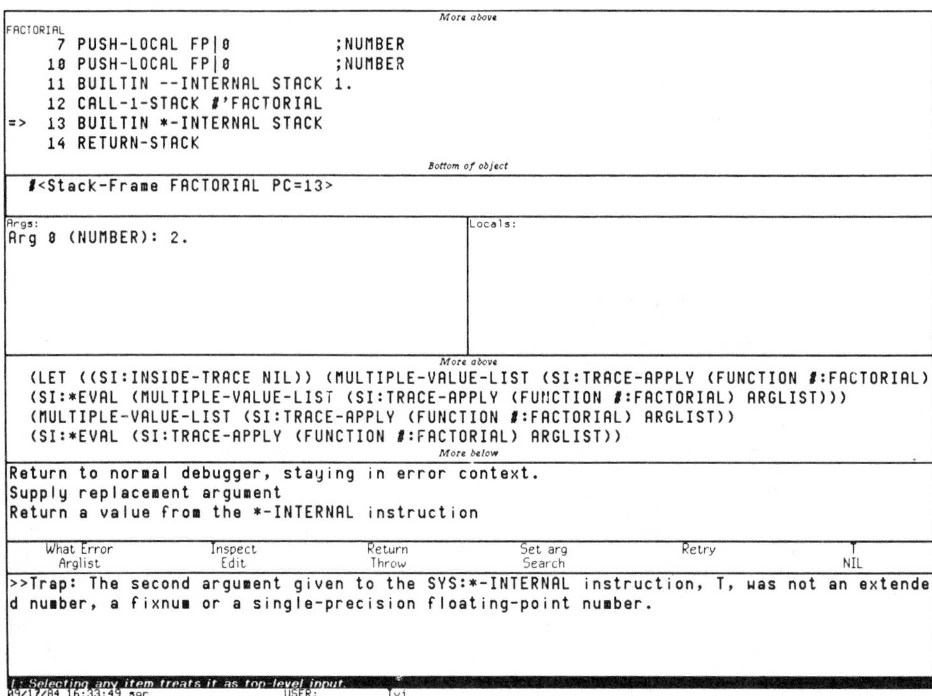
More above
FACTORIAL
7 PUSH-LOCAL FP|0 ;NUMBER
10 PUSH-LOCAL FP|0 ;NUMBER
11 BUILTIN --INTERNAL STACK 1.
12 CALL-1-STACK #'FACTORIAL
=> 13 BUILTIN *-INTERNAL STACK
14 RETURN-STACK
Bottom of object
#<Stack-Frame FACTORIAL PC=13>
Args:
Arg 0 (NUMBER): 2.
Locals:
More above
(LET ((SI:INSIDE-TRACE NIL)) (MULTIPLE-VALUE-LIST (SI:TRACE-APPLY (FUNCTION #:FACTORIAL)
(SI:*EVAL (MULTIPLE-VALUE-LIST (SI:TRACE-APPLY (FUNCTION #:FACTORIAL) ARGLIST)))
(MULTIPLE-VALUE-LIST (SI:TRACE-APPLY (FUNCTION #:FACTORIAL) ARGLIST))
(SI:*EVAL (SI:TRACE-APPLY (FUNCTION #:FACTORIAL) ARGLIST))
More below
Return to normal debugger, staying in error context.
Supply replacement argument
Return a value from the *-INTERNAL instruction
What Error
Arglist
Inspect
Edit
Return
Throw
Set arg
Search
Retry
T
NIL
>>Trap: The second argument given to the SYS:*-INTERNAL instruction, T, was not an extended number, a fixnum or a single-precision floating-point number.
I: Selecting any item treats it as top-level input.
09/17/84 16:33:49 sgr USER: Tyi

Figure 26-6 The Symbolics window-oriented debugger (Symbolics Inc.)

These integrated software development features apply not only to programs written in Lisp, but also to programs written in high-level languages, such as Fortran, Pascal, or Prolog, that are integrated with the Lisp environment. Debugging of these non-Lisp programs is done at the source code level for the particular language in question. If the program were written in one of these high-level languages, that program's source code would be shown (on the screen and in the figure) with the arrow pointing to the line where the error was detected. This allows a Fortran, Pascal, or Prolog programmer to take advantage of the Lisp software environment without knowing Lisp.

The second pane in Figure 26-6 displays a history of the system calls before and after the call that invoked the error handler. A third pane contains the debugger's command menus. Users may choose any of the commands by pointing with the mouse. The menu includes commands to return an arbitrary value from any stack frame, to restart any function call within a stack, and to recover from the error and proceed if possible. A single keystroke calls up an editor window for correcting the source file containing the function in error.

DYNAMIC LINKING AND LOADING

Traditional tool environments would now require the programmer to exit the debugger or editor and then first recompile, next relink, and then reload the program, or at least the segment just modified. Lisp environments, however, allow compilation to proceed without exiting the editor. In addition, memory management, binding of variables, linking, and loading are performed dynamically at run time.

The dynamic linking and loading has two benefits. First, it allows programmers to defer constraints on their programs as long as possible so that they can be more sure of their program specifications and design. Second, after compilation the program is ready to be executed without further ado. In contrast, the long delays for recompiles, relinks, and reloads that occur in traditional tools-oriented program development environments slow down the program development process and are a nuisance.

GARBAGE COLLECTION

If the Lisp environment is to take over the chore of dynamically allocating memory for a large program, it will soon allocate itself out of memory, unless it has a means to reclaim memory when it is no longer needed. The memory no longer needed is generally sitting out somewhere in the computer, unused, unreferenced, and inaccessible by any parts of the program in use. It is therefore referred to as *garbage*. Computerized reclamation of this garbage, called *garbage collection*, is done by a garbage collection program.

During execution time, this garbage collection program must check all the structures in memory to identify which memory is still in use and which is available for reuse and may therefore be returned to a *free space* for future allocation. This is a time-consuming, memory-expensive process.

Lisp systems used to wait until free memory was totally exhausted but more storage space was needed. At that time, the Lisp system would temporarily suspend its computations, identify and collect all garbage, and return unused memory locations to the free space list. It then resumed its computations, accumulated more garbage until it was out of memory, and paused for another garbage collection session.

With the advent of Lisp computers with their very large address space, the pauses (about four or five minutes for a large address space) became too long to be acceptable for interactive computing and new garbage collection algorithms had to be developed. Among the new techniques are garbage collection algorithms that appear to operate concurrently with other Lisp machine processes. In reality, the new Lisp garbage collectors operate by collecting memory garbage incrementally and continuously, whenever free processing time allows it. Different

Lisp machines and concurrent garbage collectors use different algorithms. They may aim for efficiency through microcode or through hardware support. They are similar, however, in that they solve the pause problem by doing their job gradually, instead of in one fell swoop which often manages to occur at a critical time.

A RAPID PROTOTYPING EXAMPLE

AI programs are complex and often not well understood. For this reason, the integrated AI tools, graphical environments, debugging and program management features, and object-oriented programming capabilities, resident on Lisp computers, support software development. In addition, the Lisp language and AI program architectures and techniques are designed to allow exploration of programming strategies for ill-specified problems. These methods and architectures are applicable to development and rapid prototyping of any complex programs, not just knowledge systems.

For example, because Lisp data elements can be treated as a single generic data type, variables can reference any type of object. This makes it easy to build on, or use, previously designed routines. Also, because Lisp programs view other programs as data, it is possible to generate, evaluate, and easily analyze a Lisp expression or program transformation on the fly.

Lisp's dynamic compilation, linking, and memory allocation, which allow programmers to defer many programming decisions until run-time and, therefore, to easily change the behavior of a module, have already been discussed. Other Lisp advantages are the extremely modular AI program architectures that allow programs to be developed and prototyped incrementally. Not only are knowledge-based programs' knowledge base, inference mechanism, and control mechanism independent, but the rules, frames, and other knowledge chunks are modular, unsequenced, and relatively independent.

Texas Instruments (TI) recognized and took advantage of AI tools, environments, and languages when it developed its natural language system, NaturalLink, and its decision-tree software, Arborist. NaturalLink was prototyped in a Lisp environment but subsequently translated into the C programming language. Arborist also was prototyped in a Lisp environment, but the Lisp version was migrated to run on TI's Professional PC and Business Pro computers and IBM's PCs, XTs, ATs, and compatibles.

Arborist differs from other decision-tree software in that it allows users to directly evaluate and modify the decision-tree display, instead of interacting with tabular data from which graphical decision-tree displays are regenerated (Figure 26-7). David Franke, the primary architect of Arborist, chose to develop the Arborist program in Lisp because editing a tree was a new capability for conventional programs and had ill-defined software functionality. He needed an approach that would let him draw upon tools and interactively build and refine a succession of prototypes based on feedback from the previous ones.

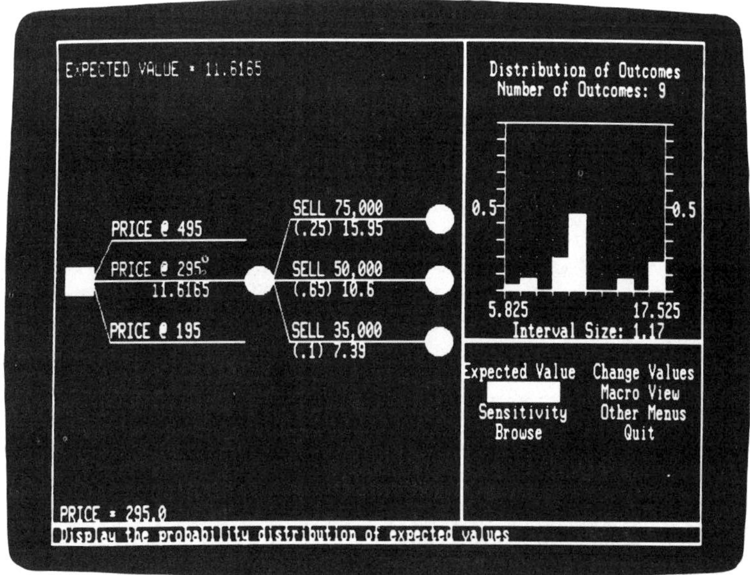

Figure 26-7 Users interact directly with this decision-tree software instead of with tabular data from which a decision tree is generated. (Texas Instruments)

Libraries of already-developed graphics routines and the Lisp-environment tools were of particular importance in helping Franke bootstrap his software into a functional state. It took Franke, then an inexperienced Lisp machine user, only four months to develop a working prototype consisting of the graphics interface, internal representation of the tree, and algorithms to manipulate it.

In migrating the program to the PC, the internal and computational implementations were easy. The I/O portion of the program caused the biggest problems; PC-based Lisps do not support the kinds of graphics supported by Lisp machines. Such problems will be at least partly alleviated when windowing and graphics capabilities are standardized for Common Lisp.

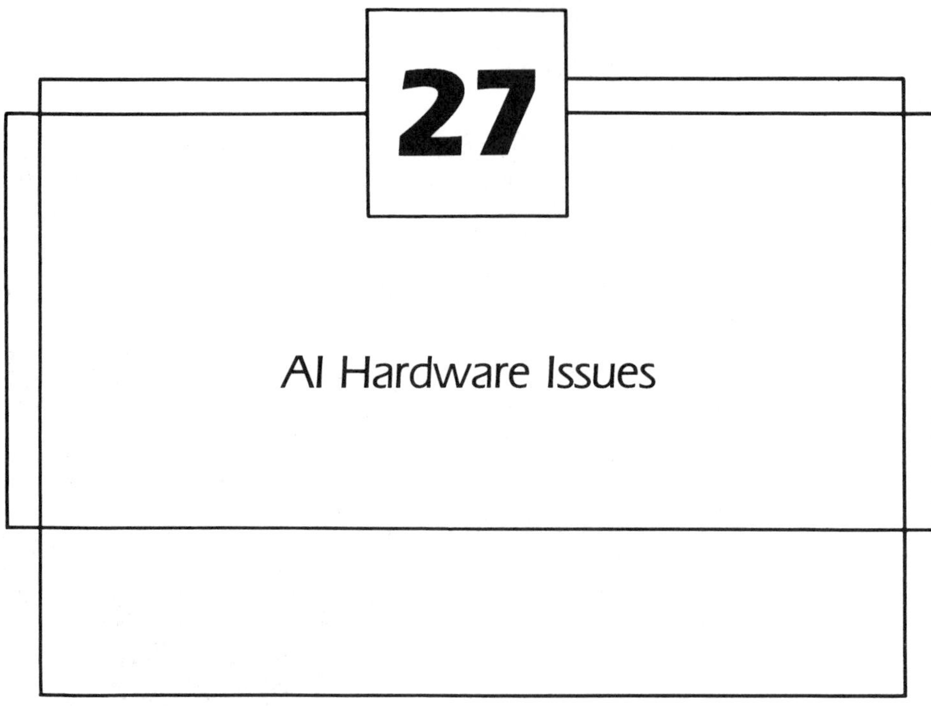

27

AI Hardware Issues

The commercialization of AI has resulted in a change in the market targeted by Lisp computer vendors and necessitated a corresponding series of changes in market approach and computer emphasis. The changes primarily involve decreasing the cost of AI computers and integrating AI hardware and software into conventional computing environments.

THE CHANGING LISP COMPUTER MARKET

The changes occurred almost overnight. Just a short time ago, most Lisp computers were sold to academic institutions and advanced research groups at some companies. At that time, the goals of the AI computer companies were to produce the fastest, most powerful Lisp computers with the best development environments.

The growing market has now shifted to commercial establishments. The commercial market has a different set of requirements and interests than research groups. Commercialization of AI is likely to require the purchase of many AI computers instead of just a few. Consequently, cost becomes a greater factor. Also, in commercial environments, the ability to use the installed bases of hardware and software, and to enhance existing hardware and software with AI capabilities, must be considerations. Moreover, since commercial establishments are more likely to buy several of, instead of a couple of Lisp computers, cost is now destined to play a more prominent role.

In response to need, five classes of hardware have emerged that support AI development and that run fielded production systems: specialized Lisp machines, plug-in board-level computers, conventional minicomputers and mainframes, engineering type workstations, and personal computers. The dividing lines between these classifications are often blurry, and the trend is toward integrating different types of hardware. However, manufacturers of all these types of hardware are taking steps to ensure that their computers satisfy commercial AI requirements.

REDUCING COSTS

The major Lisp machine manufacturers are Symbolics, Texas Instruments (TI), Xerox and Lisp Machine Inc. (LMI).* All of these companies are modifying their Lisp machines to decrease AI hardware costs or support run-time (delivery) machines. Run-time machines are characterized by features such as low cost, ease-of-use by non-programmers, and maintenance support. They usually run the same software as the development machines, but they lack certain features and extra memory needed for serious development work (because they are intended as delivery systems).

Xerox, for example, has a low-cost Lisp development and Lisp delivery machine: the 1185 and 1186. These machines are microcoded and configured to execute Lisp instructions and programs. However, they get economy of scale by using the same hardware (processor, circuitry, etc.) as for the Xerox 6805 office products machine.

LMI's scheme was to design multiuser versions of its Lisp machine series, thus cutting the per user cost. This multiuser feature does not contradict the definition of Lisp machines as single-user machines or Lisp as a single-user language. The machines are multiuser only in the sense that multiple Lisp processors and peripheral components are contained in one main cabinet and an expansion cabinet. The Lisp machine users still have their own personal and dedicated Lisp processors.

Symbolics first cost-savings solution was a delivery version of its Lisp machine. It uses VLSI semi-custom, gate array technology, and CMOS for low power consumption, to reduce the price of the Lisp machine and to reduce the original three-board Lisp processor to one-board. Subsequently, Symbolics implemented its entire Lisp processor on a single CMOS chip. The chip is designed to be integrated into a single board-level Lisp machine that can plug into other manufacturers' computers.

TI has two strategies for making Lisp machines more cost-effective, both based on a TI Lisp-processor board designed around TI's CMOS 1.2 micron Lisp microprocessor chip. The first strategy, exemplified by its Explorer II, delivers a greater performance than its earlier Explorers but at a similar price. The second

* LMI filed for protection under chapter 11 in 1987. However, certain Lisp Machine features that it pioneered became the model on which other Lisp machine vendors are building. These features will be discussed in this chapter.

would be a less expensive Lisp processor board that could be packaged to make a high-performance system-level Lisp machine at a lower price or else tailored to plug into another machine.

INTEGRATING AI AND EXISTING SYSTEMS

Second only to the problem of cost is the need for integration with standard (non-AI) systems. The three most common methods of integrating AI with standard systems are via networking, with a coprocessor card, and by running AI and traditional programs on a single processor.

All the Lisp machines can integrate different types of hardware via networking. Generally, they support networking via Ethernet, the Department of Defense's Transport Control Protocol/Internet Protocol (TCP/IP), IBM's Systems Network Architecture (SNA), and possibly a proprietary protocol such as Digital Equipment Corp.'s Decnet. They also either support, or will shortly support, the Manufacturing Automation Protocol (MAP) and the Technical and Office Protocol (TOP).

All the Lisp machine companies also support coprocessor cards to integrate AI with existing programs. The Lisp and coprocessor card environments generally run in different windows. For example, the Xerox 1185 and 1186 Lisp processors run an 80186-based coprocessor card, allowing the execution of MS-DOS compatible software in a window on the screen. The Lisp and MS-DOS processors can communicate with each other and exchange data. LMI designed its Lisp machines to run Unix and a real-time operating system on separate cards that communicate with the Lisp processor. Symbolics has an Intel 80386-based coprocessor card that allows its Lisp machine users to run MS-DOS and Unix System V.3 software. And TI has a 68020-based coprocessor card running TI's version of Unix System V in its Explorer LX.

To focus on just one example showing the usefulness of coprocessor card integration, the Explorer LX's integrated symbolic and numeric processors are suited to process control and other applications requiring knowledge-based analysis of data. Data acquisition equipment can transmit information to the 68020 processor, while a knowledge system acts as a "watchdog" to identify problems and recommend corrective action.

Such an integrated application is possible because the Explorer LX's Unix coprocessor card provides a multitasking environment for up to sixteen users or devices. They can all communicate with the Lisp processor via shared physical memory or remote procedure calls. The shared memory provides shared data access between Lisp and Unix applications without moving the data from one processor to another. This feature allows knowledge-based applications to watch the execution of, or modify the memory of, Unix applications.

INTEGRATING AI ON CONVENTIONAL MACHINES

Integrating AI and traditional programs on a single processor is possible because the traditional computer manufacturers have been adding AI capabilities to their general-purpose machines. For example, Hewlett-Packard, IBM, Digital Equipment Corp., Tektronix, Sun Microsystems, and Apollo Computer have made AI a major focus. These companies all offer general-purpose workstations. The microprocessors central to these workstations are becoming increasingly more powerful and able to support AI. Clock rates are going up. On-chip caches and memory management units are speeding memory access time.

Garbage collection (cleaning out old data) is still a problem because the architecture of the standard microprocessors does not support data tagging. However, symbolic coprocessor accelerators that offload a significant portion of garbage collection from the CPU are future possibilities.

Meanwhile, available bits in the Intel's 80386 and Motorola's 68030 on-chip paging unit's page descriptors can provide some interim help. Application developers can use these bits to classify and tag pages on a page-by-page basis, which can facilitate garbage collection. The idea is to classify the pages according to the length of their lifetimes. This speeds garbage collection because it narrows the areas to look for garbage. For example, during an incremental garbage run, the garbage collector can scan the tags in the page-descriptor table to look for the most likely areas of memory that have become garbage. Other areas, with allocated pages classified, for example, as static (lives forever) need never to be scanned at all.

MISLEADING BENCHMARKS AND STATISTICS

In general, the best architectures for executing Lisp are those supported by the Lisp machines. This fact is often masked because the newer workstations have been built using the latest silicon technologies, while Lisp machines are just switching over to these chip technologies. Performance differentiation between Lisp machines and traditional computers is further masked by benchmarks that ignore most input/output processing, which is clearly necessary for real-world applications, and graphics processing that is often necessary for AI applications. Moreover, the benchmarks are brief enough not to run into the high-overhead, time-consuming process of garbage collection.

Direct comparisons between Lisp machines and traditional computers can also be misleading in the areas of price and characteristics of the AI environment. For example, unlike traditional computers, Lisp machines are normally bundled with very large amounts of main memory (two to the tens of megabytes) and mass storage capacity (hundreds of megabytes to several gigabytes). When these are added to smaller-scale workstations, the price differences begin to fade.

Lisp machines also support more debugging and program-management tools (bundled with the machine) than general-purpose computers with added AI capabilities. Furthermore, they support a more fully integrated environment. Among other things, Lisp machines integrate the Lisp language with the operating system. Conventional computers generally do not. Consequently, if the operating system does not support windowing and the users step outside Lisp, they lose their windows.

Most important, Lisp machine computing environments are easily modifiable, while conventional computing environments are less, or not at all, modifiable. The ability to easily modify the user's computer environment stems from the object-oriented programming capability that all Lisp machines offer but is lacking in most general-purpose computers. Because windows and other graphical features are programmed with object-oriented techniques, users can easily tailor the computing environment to fit their needs. This capability is a desirable feature in AI program development where customized environments and user interfaces are often an aid to program development and can later become an integral part of the finished program.

THE TRADITIONAL COMPUTER'S SIDE OF THE STORY

The advantages to AI on traditional computers also are several. They are familiar. They tend to cost less (although they may not when sufficient memory, disk storage, and the Lisp language and development environment is added). Traditional computers already exist in an organization's standard computing environment. Integration with existing programs, databases, programming languages, and hardware is simpler. Users can continue to run their routine programs and also gain the benefits of value-added AI capabilities. Management is less likely to feel that it is going out on a limb by making an investment in a strange machine that it has never seen before and that may turn out to be a white elephant.

Many of the conventional computers are capable of performing substantial AI jobs. Many of them integrate the Lisp editor, compiler, program development tools, and computer windows, as Lisp machines do. This integration allows users to develop, compile, and debug a program without leaving the editor.

The conventional computers do not generally support object-oriented programming, and they lack many of the graphical and windowing capabilities of Lisp machines. However, many of these differences may be resolved as Common Lisp standardization specifies these capabilities that will then be supported on standard computers.

DIFFERENT LISP MACHINES

Lisp machines all have similarities in language and environments. However, the various machines exhibit differences in features and emphasis. Some Lisp machines emphasize low cost; others look for speed. Different Lisp machines are oriented differently toward software development. In addition, they use different architectures and techniques to help accomplish similar goals, such as low cost or high speed.

ENVIRONMENT AND PERFORMANCE

Xerox machines, for example, have always been more known in the AI community for their programming environment rather than their execution efficiency. The firm offers a number of machines that target all ends of the AI market.

All the Xerox machines run Interlisp, which is based on Xerox's DWIM (Do What I Mean), or try to make some sense out of what was said, philosophy. However, there may be no free lunch. Although the DWIM techniques increase development efficiency and reduce programmer errors, some users claim the programmer pays in execution efficiency.

Still, improvements keep occurring. The machines' expanded memories and floating point processors speed up execution both in general and for certain specialized computing procedures. The expanded memory makes the AI programs and tools run faster because it reduces the amount of swapping necessary between the main memory and the disk. Previously, there was not enough main memory to store large parts of a program at one time. So part of the program was kept on disk, and when it was needed it was swapped into memory, while a program segment not needed at that time was swapped out to the disk. Although swapping provides a greater amount of (virtual) memory to a program than is actually available for execution at any one time, the large number of disk accesses require a good deal of overhead and slow down performance. With the additional memory, along with the addition of a floating point processor, the Lisp computer normally known for symbolic processing can now also perform computational tasks at a speed that approaches some array processors.

A second factor that differentiates Xerox Lisp computers from others is the large effort put into the compact encoding of data structures and the machine's instruction set. For example, the kernel of the 1108's microstore is only 4K 48-bit words—small enough to be useful in small, relatively inexpensive configurations.

Xerox feels this is an important consideration when it comes to choosing Lisp computers to run, rather than develop, applications at a user site. Many user companies are willing to capitalize a development engineer with $50,000 to $100,000 of machinery. However, a computer company that expects the same pricing structure to apply to users who run applications runs the risk of pricing itself out of the end-user market.

As expected, there are advantages and disadvantages to the Xerox Interlisp machines. On the plus side, in addition to the advantages just mentioned, Xerox machines have a very mature environment with a lot of available software. The main disadvantage is that much of the software is Interlisp-based and Xerox is the only company supporting Interlisp. However, the Xerox machines also run

Common Lisp and Prolog. Common Lisp capabilities facilitate software compatibility with other vendor's Lisp machines and conventional computers that also run the emerging Lisp standard. Both the Xerox Common Lisp and Prolog implementations can use the Interlisp environment and program development tools, as well as the CommonLoops version of object-oriented programming.

LONG WORDS

Although no slouches where programming environments are concerned, LMI, Symbolics, and TI chose to emphasize execution efficiency. The three companies' Lisp machines run Zetalisp and also support Common Lisp. Because they are all descendents of the MIT Lisp machine, they are similar. But they have some differences.

Symbolics' focus for example, has been on improving the MIT machine's architecture. In its commercial machines, Symbolics opted for a hardware-supported tagged architecture to achieve performance. A *tag* is a set of bits that identifies attributes of data, such as data type (integer, binary integer, decimal integer, floating-point number, character string, address, or compiled object code, source code, or a special Lisp object). The tags are transparent to high-level language application programs; they are set by the compiler and used by the machine to determine operations to be performed and to help ensure data integrity and reliability. These tag bits that identify data types stand in contrast to the classical von Neumann architectural techniques, where program instructions define data type information.

There are several advantages to self-identifying (tagged) data. For one, they allow machines to have generic instructions. That is, even though addition of binary integers is performed differently from addition of floating-point numbers, a machine need have only one type of addition instruction. Which type of addition is to be performed (integer, floating point) is determined by examining the tag bits of the instruction operands.

In addition, tagged data support data type checking at run time, instead of just at compile time. At run time, the machine might refuse to add an address to a binary number. Run-time data type checking is important to avoiding invalid operations in Lisp programs because Lisp is an untyped language that executes dynamically. Lisp functions can operate on many different data types, and its dynamic execution capabilities do not permit data type checking during compilation.

Data can be tagged in software (microcode is common with many Lisp machines) or hardware. Symbolics' rationale for hardware tags stems from its observations showing that if the data are tagged in software, a program may require as many words in memory that identify the data types as there are words of data. This is inefficient, since much computer time is spent reading and checking these tags. And Lisp programs, which are large, computationally in-

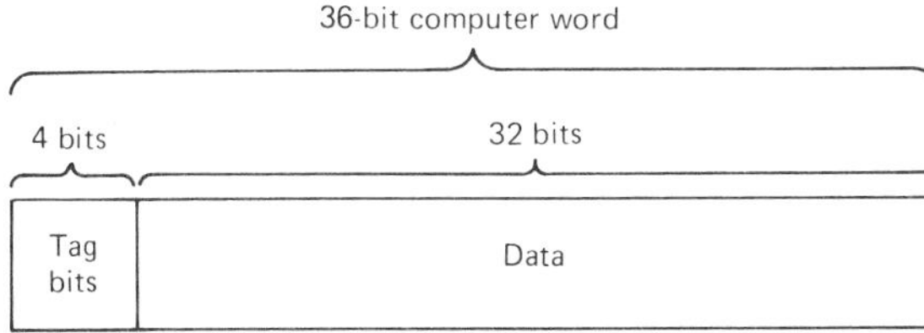

Figure 27-1 Long words with hardware-supported memory tag bits

tensive, and provide run-time data type checking and garbage collection whenever necessary, need speed.

Symbolics machines use words that are 36 bits long, four of which are memory tag bits to detect data types (Figure 27-1). Some newer Lisp machines have 40-bit words, including an 8-bit tag. Either way, execution speed is gained because the data type checking is performed in parallel with the execution of the instruction.

One of Symbolics' goals is to gain enough execution speed to execute one macroinstruction per clock cycle for a particular machine. Toward this end, it applies a combination of techniques. For one, it overlaps its instruction fetch cycle (that part of a machine cycle where the hardware fetches instructions for execution) with current execution (a technique common on high-performance machines). Second, it executes, in parallel, several operations that are part of a single macroinstruction, such as data type checking, overflow checking, and execution of the actual instruction. Third, its generic instructions and tag fields make it possible for one macroinstruction to perform the work of several instructions on conventional machines.

It is important to note, however, that what is considered "parallel" on a Symbolics Computer is not the concept of parallel computing advocated and being researched in several countries as part of their fifth-generation computing efforts. The main difference is that Symbolics can execute only operations that are part of one instruction in parallel. The goal for fifth-generation computers is to be able to partition a program, execute different parts in parallel, and coordinate the different parts. The Symbolics machine runs an enhanced version of Zetalisp, known as Symbolics-Lisp. It runs Common Lisp and has an Interlisp compatibility package. It also runs Fortran 77, Pascal, Ada, C, Prolog, and OPS5.

SPEED THROUGH MICROCODE

LMI retained much of the MIT Lisp machine's architecture in its computers. However, LMI focused on speeding up the basic processor and gaining performance through its microcode compiler, which compiles a certain amount of the programmer-written Lisp source code directly into hardware system microcode.

Microcode is a low-level code that specifies the internal control signals for the operation of basic functional elements in a microprocessor, such as registers.

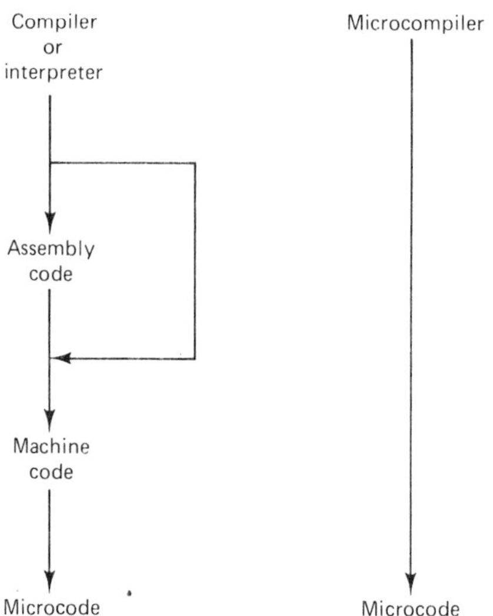

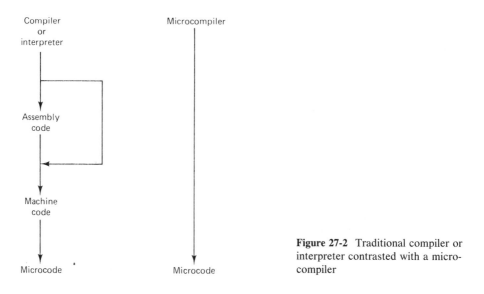

Figure 27-2 Traditional compiler or interpreter contrasted with a microcompiler

Normally, program source code is compiled to assembly code, which is assembled to machine language. More uncommonly, source code is compiled directly to machine code.

Normally, each machine code instruction is made up of a series of microinstructions in control memory (as opposed to macroinstructions, which reside in main memory). Essentially a register transfer language, these microinstructions generate the micro-operations to perform register transfers.

Microinstructions are conceptually similar to macroinstructions in that they deal with memory and register transfers. They differ in that microinstructions are concerned with the control details and hardware resources of a system. Therefore, microprogramming requires a familiarity with, and knowledge of, the hardware organization of components and how they react to each microinstruction. Consequently, microprogramming, if it is done at all, is done by highly technical people. Even so, it is an extremely difficult, time-intensive task. Nonetheless, microprogramming is desirable because it can provide significant speed, improvements, and efficiency.

LMI's contribution to microprogramming and resulting speed was to provide a microcompiler that compiles source code not to the usual machine language, but directly to microcode (Figure 27-2). With this microcompiler, programmers can encode their programs in a high-level language and need not deal with the constraints imposed on them at the low-level hardware of the machine. Yet they have access to the highly efficient microprogram.

LMI's microcompiler is implemented in 64K by 64-bit virtual microprogram memory. Only 16K of physical microcode memory is provided, but microcode in 64K of address space can be used because it is demand paged into 16K of physical RAM. Of this microcode space, 12K is reserved for basic system operations. The remainder is available for users to construct additional, customized instruction sets, or to eliminate execution bottlenecks by microcoding frequently called functions. The advantage of providing the microcode in RAM is the flexibility to alter any of the system code and thus avoid obsoleting the hardware too quickly. Programmers write their changes in high-level source code and depend on the microcompiler to produce the corresponding microcode.

In contrast, microcoded computers typically provide microcode written in ROM. Therefore, the machine's software blueprint is pretty fixed upon delivery. Updating the microcode requires burning a new ROM. Clearly, this is a more expensive, less flexible technique.

UNIQUE TOOLKITS

Like the LMI machines, the architecture of TI's Explorer is similar to the original MIT machine. But TI has put a lot of work into the software, making it more friendly and building tools on top of Lisp. The Explorer, for example, follows users through use of the different tools and offers suggestion menus depending on what the users are doing. The machine also contains several (nontraditional) AI tools including a toolkit to build a natural language interface to applications or databases, relational-database capabilities from Lisp, and a tree editor. The Explorer is based on the Nu Bus (Figure 27-3). Its software includes all the standard Lisp, object-oriented, and integrated AI development, windowing, and menu tools. In addition, it takes advantage of some newer hardware technologies.

For example, the Explorer uses *surface mount* technology for its processor and memory boards. Surface mount technology is a technology for getting more chips, and therefore more functionality, into a given number of square inches on the board. This high chip density enables the Explorer to pack much more functionality on fewer cards and therefore provide almost as much functionality in seven slots (for a single-user, single-processor machine) as was possible previously with other, larger machines.

Beyond the standard AI system software and program development tools, the Explorer differs from other Lisp computers in that it contains a number of productivity toolkits. Some of these implement conventional capabilities on top of the Lisp computer environment, thus eliminating the need for AI developers to build or simulate them. Programmers can use these toolkits to enhance their own productivity, and they can also incorporate toolkit components in their programs, thus passing along many of the toolkit benefits to an application environment.

A Graphics Toolkit, for example, makes it easy to edit and modify graphics interactively in the development environment or to incorporate interactive graphics capabilities in applications. Another toolkit, a Relational Table Manager provides relational database capabilities that can be accessed from within the Lisp environment.

Relational database capabilities have been needed in the past for AI problems that involve handling a large database. For those situations, knowledge-

Figure 27-3 Texas Instruments' Lisp machine, the Explorer (Texas Instruments)

system developers frequently simulate a database capability in a more extensive knowledge base. However, many expert systems' data are representable as standard relational data. Reverting to conventional technology for these data provides an economical method to represent it. The data can then be accessed and manipulated with normal relational commands (select, retrieve, insert, delete) and standard functions (project, join, sort, union, difference, and intersect).

A natural-language facility presents users with a set of windows, each containing menus, that in turn contain words or phrases in English or some other natural language. As with NaturalLink, TI's natural language interface to databases (Chapter 13), users construct sentences by selecting the appropriate words or phrases in individual, active windows, with a mouse. The words and phrases are strung together to form a complete sentence. As the sentence is constructed, the natural language software examines the context of the sentence created so far and decides which windows of items to activate next. As long as users choose an item from the window menu, they can be sure that the line of code they are generating will always be correct.

The Explorer's toolkit provides tools to help build lexicons, grammars, and screen descriptions necessary to tailor a natural language interface to an application. Programmers can extend their AI environment by adding a natural language interface to their own tools, applications, or standard databases. This interface can be passed on to the end user.

Another Explorer toolkit contains knowledge engineering tools which help programmers build their own AI solutions or expert system tools. It includes Prolog development toolkits and a graph representation language called Grasper. The Prolog toolkit contains a Prolog interpreter, a training tool, a knowledge system development tool, and a window-based interface. The Grasper language provides primitives (functions) that allow software developers to describe knowledge base relationships as a directed graph (semantic network), and to create, modify, and otherwise manipulate the objects and relationships described. Nodes in the directed graph represent objects, and edges represent relationships between objects. Grasper differs from other graph manipulation tools in that it also provides object-oriented programming capabilities—an aid in describing, manipulating, and modifying the graph or program developed.

A variety of applications are naturally adapted to directed graphs, and therefore to Grasper representations. In natural-language processing, for example, Grasper represents a grammar as a directed graph; the subject of the sentence is an edge-type (labeled arc) and the values for features of the subject are nodes. In engineering applications, a Grasper graph can represent an OR circuit as seen by a hydraulic, mechanical, and electrical engineer, in terms of parts and types of parts, all of which can be manipulated through Grasper. In business systems, a tool such as Grasper facilitates development of knowledge systems involving manipulation of corporate structures, which are easily represented in a network structure.

For real-world knowledge systems, including areas such as process control, environmental crisis management, and organizational management, perhaps Grasper's integration with other Explorer toolkits is among its biggest attractions. In one integrated application, Grasper was used for analysis in chemical spill systems. Routes of chemical flow, storage areas, drains, and manholes were diagrammed using Grasper. A database was created with nodes, edges, and spaces (collections or views of objects) to chart a large chemical holding area as part of a spill detection and isolation system. Nodes were given values according to what they represented at the actual site and the type of chemicals stored. Pipe routes were defined as labeled edges connecting the nodes. Information about types of chemicals and their flammability and toxicity was input to the database and integrated with the Grasper representation network. Grasper functions were then used to operate on the network and thereby show and analyze real and potential problems in environmental crisis management.

Despite the differences between the MIT Lisp machine descendants (TI's, Symbolics', and LMI's), Scott Fahlman, senior research computer scientist at Carnegie-Mellon University, says "These machines have a strong resemblance to each other. Choosing one boils down to price/performance and which company you are most comfortable dealing with.''

LISP CHIPS AND BOARDS

Smaller power supplies and disk drives are two reasons that Lisp machines are becoming smaller and cheaper. Another major reason is an increase in the number of functions that are implemented in VLSI. TI, for example, under contract to the Defense Advanced Research Projects Agency, designed and built a VLSI-based Lisp CPU. This 553,000 transistor, 1.2 micron CMOS device reduced 60 percent of the original Explorer's two-board Lisp processor into a single chip. TI feels that this chip will enable a Lisp computer to be ''shoebox'' size and will open up the area of embedded symbolic processing just as the microprocessor opened up the world of calculators and personal computers.

The TI Lisp chip is designed into what TI calls a ''Compact Lisp Machine.'' The Compact Lisp Machine is built for very high performance and has militarized specifications. The Lisp chip is also designed into a board-level Lisp processor that can be packaged for use as a standalone Lisp machine (as in the Explorer II) or it can serve as a board-level computer that plugs into non-Lisp machines—TI's and possibly other manufacturers' as well.

Xerox, too, has a single-chip VLSI processor designed to execute the Common Lisp programming language and the CommonLoops object-oriented programming techniques. The chip features a 40-bit tagged architecture. It has a very small instruction set. However, it is not a RISC chip because it supports some complex instructions to execute Lisp functions in addition to simple instructions that execute in one machine cycle. Only the simple instructions are characteristic of RISC machines.

Plans are to implement the chip on boards for use as a standalone Lisp machine or a coprocessor board in Xerox's or other vendors' standard computers. Like the TI Lisp chip, the Xerox VLSI Lisp processor is suitable for packaging in embedded systems, such as intelligent instrument controllers and online-diagnostic equipment.

Symbolics has also mounted an intensive VLSI effort, and it resulted in a VLSI implementation of the company's entire Lisp processor on a single CMOS chip. Size, price, and even performance, however, were only part of the design goals. In a world where users increasingly are demanding application portability across multiple vendors' hardware and application integration with existing data, connectivity and multivendor integration were major factors driving the chip's development.

To achieve these goals, the chip was designed with a new Lisp-machine architecture. This architecture is optimized for VLSI and designed to allow the

Lisp chip to be embedded on a board which, in turn, can be embedded in different manufacturers' conventional computers.

EMBEDDING LISP BOARDS IN CONVENTIONAL COMPUTERS

Because the architectures and memory-handling methods of Lisp processors and conventional computers are so different, the integration of Lisp and conventional computers inside a single chassis is a non-trivial engineering task. This, in itself, creates practicality problems, but with microprogramming being the available means for integrating the Lisp and conventional systems, Symbolics' Lisp-chip architects felt that they would not be able to cost-effectively embed the Lisp machine into different computers unless their design satisfied three basic goals.

For one, all Lisp processing had to be contained on a single-board computer so the Lisp processing could be isolated from the conventional-computer bus. This was necessary because the Lisp processor has a 40-bit word size that includes an 8-bit tag field, while target conventional computers typically have a 32-bit word and bus size with no tag field. Sharing the same bus for memory accesses would require machinations such as reformatting of 40-bit words, extra fetches to accommodate the long words, extra programming, and wasted bits. This would result in bus bottlenecks and decreased throughput.

The second goal stems from the first. Containing all Lisp processing on a single board requires that 100 percent of the Lisp processor fit into a single chip. This is necessary to leave enough room on the board for memory, input/output, bus interfaces, and other chips and circuitry that make up a Lisp computer.

The third goal in making integration practical was to provide a programming language, instead of microcode, for performing the Lisp-system integration tasks. Microcode is used in traditional Lisp machines to define the Lisp machine's instructions; the integrated, graphical environment; and other features that characterize a Lisp machine. The microcode is fast, and since it is implemented in RAM or PROM, it is modifiable. However, programming with microcode is very difficult. There are few tools and debugging aids. Consequently, if the Lisp chip could just provide system integrators with an assembly language (which on a Lisp machine is a Lisp subset) or a high-level language (full Lisp), it could make the task of integrating the Lisp and conventional computers practical to perform.

This problem has been solved for standard microprocessors. They facilitate systems integration by defining an assembly language. The assembly language is based on a microcoded instruction set that is burned into the chip.

Unfortunately, the microcoded instruction sets used on Lisp machines are generally too large to be burned into a single-chip Lisp microprocessor and still leave room for all the other Lisp processor functions. So one of the first things that the Symbolics Lisp chip architects did was to prune the instruction set down to a size that could be burned into the chip.

Little or no penalty was paid for this pruning because equivalent ways were available to perform the same functions. For example, the microcoded instructions dealing with functions such as graphics and floating-point computation were removed, but graphics and floating-point operations were then offloaded to special purpose graphics and floating-point processors. Other instructions that were identified as rarely used (using statistical code-analysis techniques) were removed, but emulated in a microcode routine at the Lisp level. Execution-speed losses for these instructions were compensated by other optimizations. Also, there was no overall performance loss because one of the design goals was to come up with an instruction set that would execute as fast as the system-level Lisp machines execute microcode, if not faster.

The one penalty that Symbolics anticipates for the macrocode-based (rather than microcoded) Lisp machine is loss of the flexibility to microcode the machine to perform specialized tasks. However, with the AI market expanding primarily into commercial establishments, this loss may not be noticed much. Certainly, microprocessor vendors do not usually sell microcodable microprocessors.

As for the remainder of the chip architecture, it was designed with the goals of occupying minimal space, achieving maximum performance, and having on-chip the kinds of components expected on standard microprocessors (Figure 27-4). Like the Intel 80386 and the Motorola 68030, the Lisp chip architects placed the virtual memory management unit on the chip to speed up physical-to-virtual memory mapping. An instruction cache, also on the chip, maintains a high instruction execution rate. A four-way interleaved memory interface on the chip allows a standard MOS memory to supply the processor with instructions or data four times faster than the nominal cycle time of the memory allows. Thus, a memory with a 400 nanosecond access rate could effectively be accessed as if it were a 100 nanosecond memory.

Other on-chip components include a stack cache, hardware support for garbage collections, on-chip error checking and correction, and on-chip message dispatching to facilitate implemention of object-based software like Flavors. This is not to mention on-chip support for Lisp function calls and returns, which is a major source of performance optimization.

LONGER WORDS

Even though Symbolics' original 36-bit word Lisp machines had a 4-bit tag, eight bits have been needed for some time. Therefore, the new Lisp chip was designed with a 40-bit word: 32 bits for data and addresses, and 8 bits for a tag field.

The longer tag field has two major benefits. For one, it simplifies programming because it reduces the complexity necessary to obtain the effect of eight tag bits from a 4-bit field. More specifically, the effect of eight tag bits was achieved by assigning different meanings to the four hardware-supported tag bits depending on the program execution mode. The second benefit of the expanded tag field is a

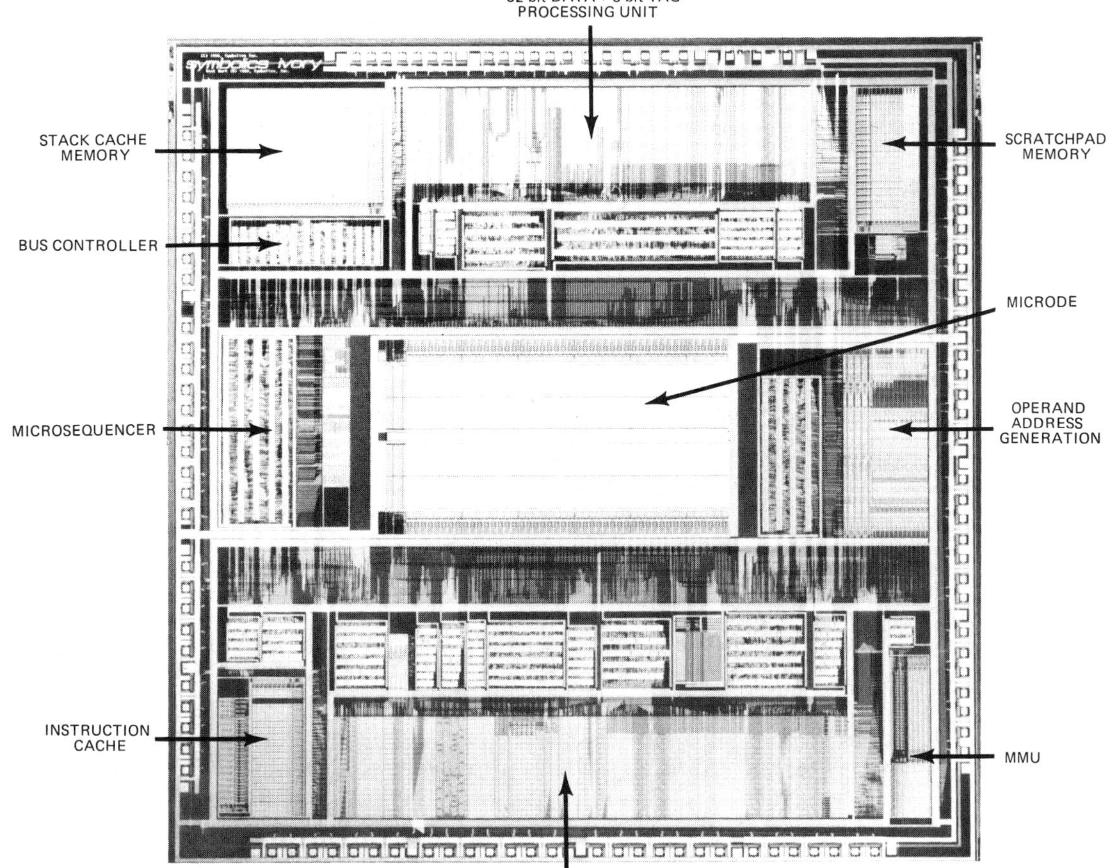

Figure 27-4 Symbolics' Lisp chip.

sixteen times greater address space over that of the 3600 series Lisp machines, even though the address space for the 3600's 36-bit word and the new chip's 40-bit word are nominally the same. They have not really been the same, though, because programmers have been borrowing four bits from the 3600's 32-bit address space to use as extra tags. This left the 3600 with only a 28-bit address field.

Compatibility between the 40-bit word Lisp chip and an industry-standard 32-bit bus is not a problem because the entire Lisp machine, including the Lisp microprocessor, memory, and interface chips, sits on its own board. The Lisp-processor board performs all the Lisp processing, accessing only its own memory on the board. Therefore, there is no need to send 40-bit words across a 32-bit bus. The Lisp and conventional-computer boards normally communicate across the bus just to exchange data. For maximum throughput, just before the data goes out onto the 32-bit bus, the interface software shears off the tag bits and ships out a 32-bit word. Similarly, when data or messages are received, the interface software pops on the tag bits.

AI ON MINICOMPUTERS

The third class of machines for AI are the traditional minicomputers and mainframes—some of which are coming out with single processor versions. These machines include the DEC VAX and Micro VAX, IBM 370s and 4300s, and Data General, Prime, Sperry, NCR, and AT&T minicomputers. Several of these machines run Common Lisp under their native operating system of Unix. Some run a nonstandard version of Lisp.

Most of the conventional computer manufacturers have pretty closely imitated the Lisp machine's integrated AI development environments as far as allowing users to edit, compile, link, debug, and execute their programs from within the editor. Most have also supplied a fair number of AI program development tools.

Besides Lisp, DEC VAXs run OPS5 and Prolog, support Interlisp, and are compatible with Gold Hill Computer's Golden Common Lisp for PCs. The DEC and Data General computers run AI application development tools such as Carnegie Group Inc.'s Knowledge Craft and Language Craft, Teknowledge's S.l, Inference Corp.'s ART, and IntelliCorp's KEE. KEE is a particularly graphic tool, but IntelliCorp is implementing a nongraphical version of KEE that allows it to run on time-sharing systems that don't have extensive graphics capabilities. The IBM machines run an IBM knowledge-system development tool called Expert System Environment/VM (ESE/VM) and Aion Corp.'s Aion Development System (ADS).

"The tools (that DEC supports) were chosen not because of technology, but because the tool companies were willing to implement them in Common Lisp," says Arnold Kraft, former manager of solutions marketing for the intelligent systems technologies group at DEC. As with computer-aided-design and computer-aided-engineering tools, most of the computer companies will offer all the tools and let the market decide.

Meanwhile, several AI tool vendors are translating their tools into C. This will facilitate implementation on a greater number of conventional machines, and also speed up performance there. The underlying language, however, will not be visible to users. They will see only the same tool features as in a Lisp environment.

Lisp applications running on standard minicomputer environments have the advantage of lower cost and easy access to existing databases, programs, and programming languages. Lisp programs implemented on standard computers with conventional architectures can be integrated with conventional programs and programming languages to supply value-added AI features to conventional software.

The integration is possible because libraries of traditional programs are callable from the Lisp editor on conventional general-purpose computers. For example, Lisp on VAX computers is integrated into DEC's VMS operating system and can call the VAX library of programs or VMS utilities.

Disadvantages of Lisp on minicomputers include environments that are less graphic, less friendly, and less modifiable than those on Lisp machines, and also have slower performance. The lack of graphics, however, is not always an obstacle. Run-time systems may not need graphics capabilities. In any case, many graphics differences between Lisp machines and minicomputers may disappear once graphics capabilities are specified by Common Lisp.

A more major problem with AI on time-shared machines is other users. Neither the hardware nor the instruction sets on these machines were designed for Lisp. As a result, Lisp on a time-shared system is instantly visible to other users because it degrades their performance.

Delco Products, a division of General Motors, got around the time-sharing, resource conflict problem by doing their knowledge system development on the night shift, as needed, so they had dedicated use of the company's VAXs. "Choosing a computer with sufficient computing resources for an application and tuning it well in terms of mix of jobs, their priorities, memory allocation, and disk access is an important consideration," says Stephen Dourson, project engineer, knowledge systems, at Delco Products. "If the computer is too small for the AI program, it not only upsets other folks using the system, but the AI project also may drag out and cause skepticism."

However, when it comes to delivery systems, there are other considerations. For example, users with knowledge systems that are attached to MRP and other manufacturing systems, and that heavily access data from these systems, frequently prefer to make the two systems coresident on one minicomputer and view the resulting systems as one large system. Coresidency makes application integration and database access easier. It also reduces file, disk, and integrity maintenance problems. Some applications may even be better served by a large time-sharing computer's I/O and data transfer rates.

In these kinds of cases, users may have to depend on minicomputer vendors improving Lisp speed through hardware and compiler optimizations. An alternative is to develop AI systems using programming languages or tools that do not impact performance so much as Lisp. Examples are the OPS5 language and tools that have been translated into C.

AI ON ENGINEERING WORKSTATIONS

The fourth class of machines used for AI work is the traditional engineering-type workstations, based on the Motorola 68000, National 32032, and Intel 80X86 families, or a proprietary Risc (Reduced Instruction Set Computer) chip and generally running some version of Unix. These machines include Apollo, Sun, Tektronix, and Hewlett-Packard workstations, and the IBM Risc machine.

Unlike minicomputers, workstations are dedicated machines with friendly, graphic interfaces. Workstations have advantages of lower cost and easy compatibility with existing programs. Apollo and Sun Microsystems computer users, for example, can access Unix functions and call other routines written in C, Pascal, or Fortran from within Lisp. Consequently, users can work with their everyday systems, call Lisp to run value-added AI functions, and switch back to their original systems. Development of the value-added AI functions is not a problem because a good Common Lisp implementation, especially on a graphically oriented machine, provides an entry to most large-scale AI application development tools.

The Hewlett-Packard 300 series workstations are an example of the next level of integration of symbolic and numeric computing. The workstations tightly integrate an AI development environment, Common Lisp, Prolog, and object-oriented programming with HP-UX (HP's implementation of Unix System V) running C, Pascal, and Fortran. In this case, integrated means that the AI system provides the same tightly integrated development capabilities for C, Pascal, Fortran, and Unix as it does for Lisp and Prolog. As a result, programmers can incrementally and interactively develop, edit, compile, test, and execute C, Pascal, Fortran, Lisp, and Prolog routines from a single editor. Just as the editor knows Lisp syntax and matches parentheses in Lisp, it knows C, Pascal, and Fortran syntax and checks programming constructs. Just as it performs error checking for Lisp, the editor will catch compile errors in C, Pascal, and Fortran (Figure 27-5). Without leaving the editor, programmers can fix the errors and execute the traditional program. Then, because the non-Lisp object-code files are linked to the Lisp system, developers can interactively evaluate their C, Pascal, and Fortran functions, immediately see the results, determine the function's behavior, and reedit them.

What this means to programmers is that Lisp programmers do not have to learn Unix to develop Unix-based programs or subroutines. At the same time, Unix programmers, who are newcomers to Lisp environments, can develop Lisp and Prolog as well as conventional language programs using familiar Unix tools.

Unlike Lisp machines, however, engineering workstations are not microcoded for Lisp execution. In the past, this meant that they could not match Lisp machines for performance.

This has not turned out to be the case. Increasingly powerful processors are available for workstations. Floating-point processors are being added. Microprocessor clock speeds are going up. And very efficient Common Lisp compilers have been written. Consequently, these workstations are turning out to be very competitive.

There are some differences, however. To get maximum speed on these workstations, it is necessary to program carefully and make sure the declarations

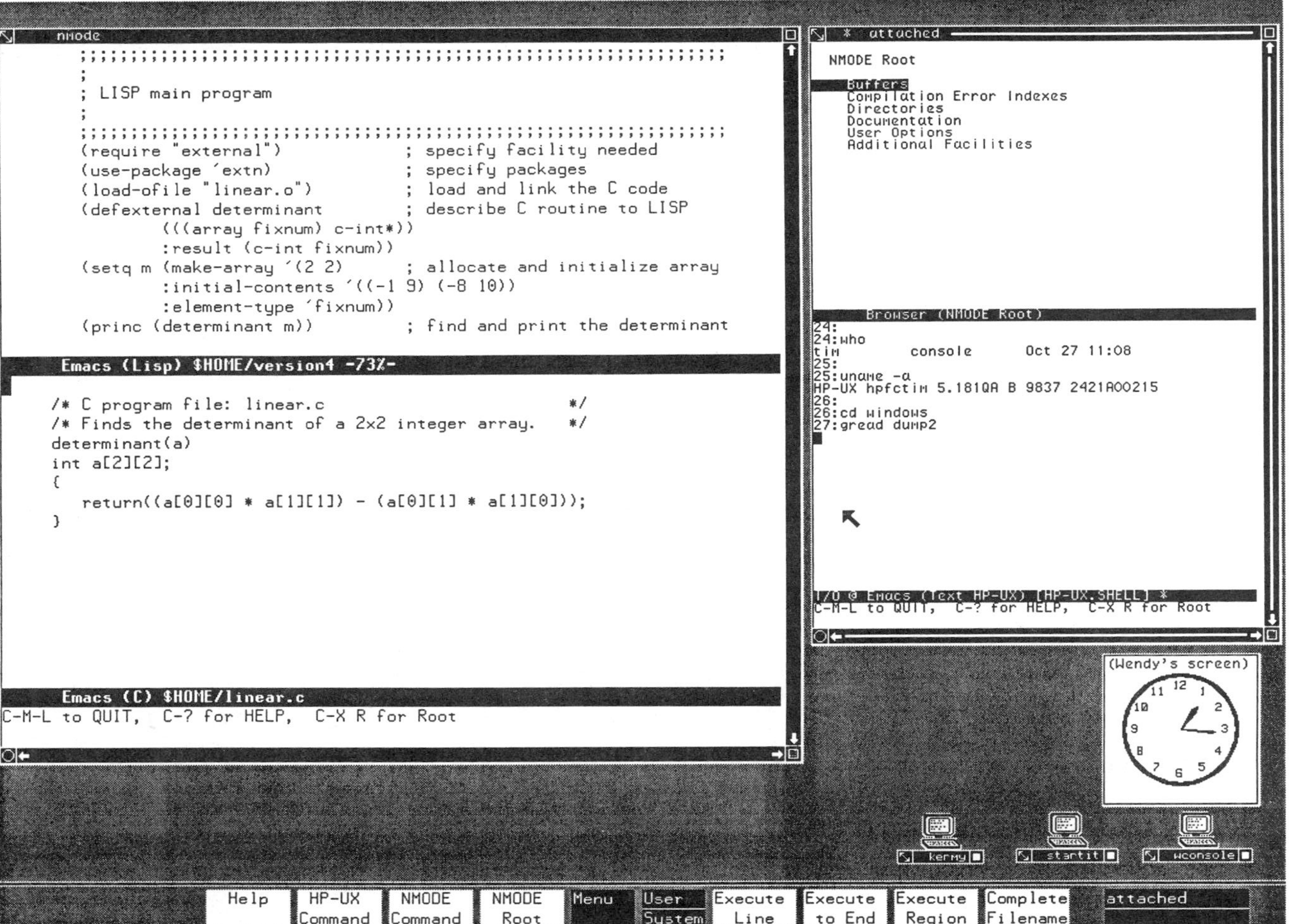

Figure 27-5 In this traditional HP window-oriented Unix workstation, the editor provides a unified programming environment that allows simultaneous development in Lisp, Prolog, and conventional languages; integrated mail and text; and a series of browsers that integrates the various user and programmer tools.

are correct. Data type checking, which helps ensure program correctness, slows down speed. Casually built programs are more likely to run, at speed, on Lisp machines that have hardware support for run-time checking. But programmers can increase performance by sacrificing run-time checking for pieces of code they are sure are correct.

Another problem with workstations occurs when programs get large enough to require garbage collection. This is a high-overhead process. Lisp machines provide hardware support to speed up garbage collection. Garbage collection is a slower operation on numeric processing computers because it is performed in software.

Semiconductor companies are looking at the possibility of building garbage collection chips. Unfortunately, they admit it is very difficult to carry out their ideas without a tagged architecture. A tagged architecture, which is a feature of Lisp machines, is necessary to recognize a pointer (address). Other methods of identifying large amounts of unreferenced areas of memory have so far proved impractical because of performance.

ENGINEERING WORKSTATIONS SPECIALIZED FOR AI

The Tektronix AI workstations run Common Lisp, Prolog, Unix, C, and Franz Lisp, in addition to Smalltalk.

Tektronix's approach to developing its AI workstations was to first choose a general-purpose processor, then make its other design decisions to specialize the machine, in all other ways, in favor of AI capabilities rather than general-purpose work (Figure 27-6). Tektronix had several reasons for designing its AI workstations in this way. In particular, Tektronix is a firm with a large market in the engineering and instrumentation fields. Many of its AI computer design decisions were geared to providing AI capabilities on a machine both optimized for AI and also oriented toward engineering applications.

The 68010 processor is often found in engineering environments, and that is one reason for Tektronix's CPU choice. There is another reason, however. In keeping with its targeted engineering market goals, Tektronix designed its AI workstations to be adapted to running not only Lisp, but also the Smalltalk programming language. Smalltalk is an object-oriented programming language that the firm feels is extremely adapted for engineering applications. The workstations' orientation toward Smalltalk decreases the need for a Lisp processor with an instruction set similar to Lisp's—a characteristic of specialized Lisp machines.

Smalltalk is particularly adaptable for engineering applications because it is unusually supportive of graphics. In its early life, Smalltalk's primary commercial use was its support of graphical interfaces on computers. It also found a role in a newspaper typesetting application, because the application required a good deal of graphical layout work.

Figure 27-6 The Tektronix 4404 AI workstation. (Tektronix, Inc.)

Similarly, development of AI applications in engineering and electronic circuit domains requires a great deal of graphics capabilities. Engineers often tend to think visually, in terms of logic circuits, schematics, and layouts, rather than in terms of the language or even labeled pictures found in many manuals (Chapter 25).

To adapt its workstations for AI, wherever there were trade-offs to consider, Tektronix made optimization decisions in favor of AI functionality. For example, the AI computers were given extra RAM to avoid swapping, since AI programs are memory intensive. In addition, the machine contains a specialized rather than a general-purpose backplane.

The problem with a general-purpose backplane is that it is not optimized for anything because it is not known, a priori, what the system will contain. System performance can therefore degrade, depending on what is plugged into the backplane. AI programs are so computationally intensive that they may not be able to afford this performance degradation. A design decision in favor of a specialized backplane avoids this degradation because the system is not bound to the performance of the least common denominator module that is plugged in.

Further AI benefits are achieved because the central processor handles computing, the display commands, and the display. In contrast, many general-purpose computers offload as many display operations as possible. This improves performance but requires another interface to the general-purpose display engine. Two interfaces make changing the display more difficult and inefficient because changes must be made and coordinated in two places. This prevents AI developers from easily modifying the display and developing their own user interfaces—an important capability for AI applications. To speed performance, however, the AI workstations' display memories are dedicated.

AI ON RISC MACHINES

With a lot of memory and a good compiler, Risc architecture-based machines may, in the long run, surpass Lisp machines. Risc machines are characterized by a simpler instruction set where the goal is to have each instruction execute in one machine cycle. Such a speed may not be possible for general instructions because the computer cannot decode them fast enough.

Risc machines are not new. They were common in the early days of computers, but they evolved into more complex machines with more general instruction sets to make the compiler simpler. Only relatively recently has optimizing compiler technology advanced to the point where fast Risc machines are feasible.

If the microcycle time of a Risc machine compares to the microcycle time of the Symbolics machine, the speeds may also compare. However, Risc machines running Lisp have the same disadvantages as workstations in that they cannot simultaneously achieve run-time checking and maximum speed. And, as with workstations, even if performance barriers are surmounted, memory and mass-storage costs can close the price gap between Lisp machines and Risc machines.

AI ON PCS

The fifth class of computers for running AI tools and applications is PCs. Opinions about the value of PCs for AI applications are divided. The problem is that most serious AI programs require substantial memory. The first generation of PCs, with a maximum of 640K of memory, were mostly limited to Lisp systems suitable for learning Lisp, as entry vehicles into the AI field, and to certain small applications. That did not stop people at companies like Beckman Instruments and Campbell Soup from fielding useful PC-based AI applications on IBM and TI PCs, to provide advice about the use of ultra centrifuges, and to diagnose malfunctions in sterilizers.

The second generation of PCs can address 16 Mbytes of memory and supports virtual memory capabilities. This will remove a big barrier which determines where big and small applications can execute.

Meanwhile, some first generation PCs have incorporated extra features to support AI. TI's Business Pro, for example, is expandable to 15 Mbytes of main

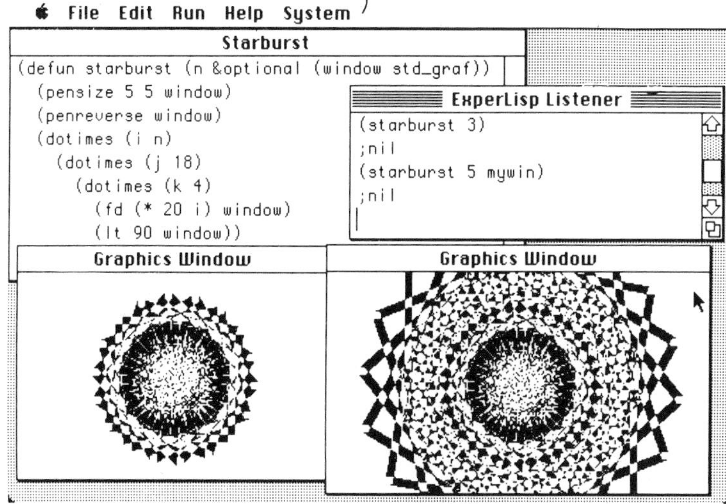

Figure 27-7 A subset of the Symbolics Lisp environment runs on the Apple Computer Macintosh. (ExperTelligence, Inc.)

memory and supports high resolution graphics. It runs Prolog, Common Lisp, Scheme Lisp, and several AI application development tools including TI's Personal Consultant (discussed in Chapter 10). To further increase performance, efforts are being directed toward the development of Lisp processor boards that plug into the Business Pro and are optimized to execute Lisp.

Apple Computer's Macintosh, with its windows, pop up and pull down menus, mouse, high resolution bit-mapper graphics, and memory expandable up to 1.5 Gbytes in the Macintosh II, has many AI-machine features. Recognizing this, ExperTelligence Inc. implemented the Common Lisp and OPS5 languages and a subset of the Symbolics Lisp environment on the Macintosh.

The OPS5 offered is the full language, licensed from Carnegie-Mellon University. It includes the Rete algorithm (developed by Charles Forgy) to speed up execution of large rule bases. Calls from OPS5 into Lisp are allowed.

The Common Lisp implementation, called ExperLisp, uses a 68000-based metacompiler, written in Lisp, that allows programmers to incrementally compile any individual function. To optimize speed, ExperTelligence coded about 400 Lisp primitives in hand-crafted assembly language, rather than in Lisp.

The Macintosh Lisp environment contains traditional, integrated, AI development, debugging, and management tools. Tools include the Lisp Listener, which supports an immediate-execute mode (rather than compiling first) and records a user session and integrated facilities that allow users to edit, compile, test, debug, and execute without leaving the editor (Figure 27-7).

Unfortunately, the limited memory on PCs normally limits the Lisp tools and environment the PCs can use. The problem is that Lisp requires the full language and environment to be loaded for any operation; and Common Lisp contains a lot of language and environment. Recognizing this problem, ExperLisp has another tool that allows programmers to load only the Lisp code that an application requires. Use of such a tool is one way of making AI more feasible for PCs.

The Macintosh-based ExperLisp also provides object-oriented programming capabilities. As in Lisp machines, the object-oriented programming is not only for use in applications, but application developers can use it to tailor the environment.

The alternative is to switch to a conventional language to tailor the environment, which is what most Lisp systems on traditional machines require. It's much easier, however, to use object-oriented techniques. For example, ExperLisp has an object-oriented interface to all 700 Macintosh toolbox commands. The interface allows application developers to treat any Macintosh class as an object, and the toolbox contains more than 60 of these classes dealing with the hardware, ROM, user-interface, and operating system. To customize the software environment or interface to the outside world via machine ports, it is only necessary to send messages to the objects telling them what to do. The messages can be commands in the Macintosh toolbox. If they are, many of the procedures to perform certain actions are pre-written and ready for use.

The ExperLisp language and environment are compatible with the Common Lisp and AI environment on Symbolics' Lisp machines. They were developed on a Symbolics machine along with a cross compiler that produces code for the Macintosh. Consequently, programs developed on Symbolics' machines can execute on the Macintosh. Conversely, with an ExperTelligence utility package, programmers can develop code on the Macintosh and deliver it to a Symbolics machine for execution.

The IBM PC computer line has also gotten an AI boost, particularly from Gold Hill Computer's (and A.I. Architect's Inc.'s) HummingBoard. The HummingBoard is a 16 MHz Intel 80386-based co-processor board that plugs into the PC, XT, or AT. It contains directly addressable on-board memory, which is expandable to 24 Mbyte, an on-board cache memory of 12 Mbyte, and special hardware to perform type checking.

The full Common Lisp runs on the HummingBoard. So does a Gold Hill AI application development tool called "GoldWorks." GoldWorks' knowledge representation and reasoning methods include assertions, rules, frames, forward and backward chaining, object-oriented programming, hypothetical worlds (viewpoints), and a C language interface. It organizes frames into a hierarchy that supports a multiple inheritance mechanism, and it allows users to browse through a graphical representation of this hierarchy.

It goes without saying that the 32-bit processor, memory, special hardware, extensive tool facilities, and full Common Lisp can support fairly demanding AI applications. Of course, a PC does not have all the capabilities of a Lisp machine, and so GoldWorks is limited in speed, display, and ways it can inherit attributes. This has not stopped Coopers & Lybrand from developing an insurance underwriting expert system on a personal computer using GoldWorks. However, the HummingBoard/PC system raises a new question: "When a PC acquires a 32-bit processor, multimegabytes of memory, demand paging, and so on, is it still a PC?" Or, at some point, does it turn into a workstation?

FIFTH-GENERATION COMPUTERS

Lisp machine architectures differ from traditional computer architectures in several ways. Differences include tagged architectures and some parallelism (pipelined architectures). For example, as discussed in Chaper 26, Symbolics' machines support their tagged architectures with hardware that executes certain operations in parallel.

But both U.S. and Japanese researchers are striving for a different type of parallelism than is available from Symbolics, or almost anywhere else for that matter. Parallel execution is currently limited because today's generation of Lisp machines is based on the sequentially oriented von Neumann machine. Despite the parallel execution of different operations in each Symbolics machine's instruction, as far as the programmer is concerned, the machine performs instructions serially. Each instruction manipulates only one set of data or numbers at a time. During this time, much of the logic of the machine goes unused while the CPU awaits the next instruction.

For the next generation, computer designers around the globe want to build machines that execute instructions in different parts of a program in parallel. Parallel computer architectures would allow multiple instructions to manipulate sets of data at the same time, in a general-purpose manner (as opposed to array processors specialized to perform pre-thought-out algorithms and mathematically well-defined operations).

AI researchers are interested in computers with these types of parallel architectures because the current von Neumann machines used for computing are slow, inadequate vehicles for large-scale artificial intelligence system development. Large-scale AI systems often have a large space of possible solutions to search in order to arrive at a goal—the desired or correct solution. This large search space is very time consuming to get through and frequently makes the problem in question intractable.

One way around the problem is to use constraints or heuristics to narrow down the search space so that there are fewer solutions to search. An alternative is to perform the search on a computer with multiple processors that are designed and coordinated so that portions of the search space can be assigned to the different processors. That way the different processors can perform their own searches in parallel with one another and therefore can search a larger space more rapidly.

Many AI developers hope to capitalize on these machines. However, although several machines are under development, and a few have even begun to emerge from laboratories, a number of problems must be solved before fifth-generation machines become practical.

For one, existing programming languages are not suitable for use on computers with parallel architectures because these languages are, by their nature, sequential. This is why new types of programming languages geared to parallel architectures are being developed. The message-passing language, Actors, described in Chapter 25, is an example.

Another concern for parallel computer architectures is the overhead needed for communications between the processors. As the number of connected processors increases, so does the cost of the communications necessary to coordinate the operations performed on the various processors. At some point, the cost of communications will become prohibitive and the performance will either degrade because of excessive communications and coordination overhead or simply no longer be worth the cost.

The last problem of parallel computer architectures is to define what classes of problems are suitable for parallel computer architecture solutions and how to pose these problems to the machine. This is an important point because researchers have noted that if a problem is chosen that is not inherently parallel, the parallel processing machines tend to be slower than conventional ones.

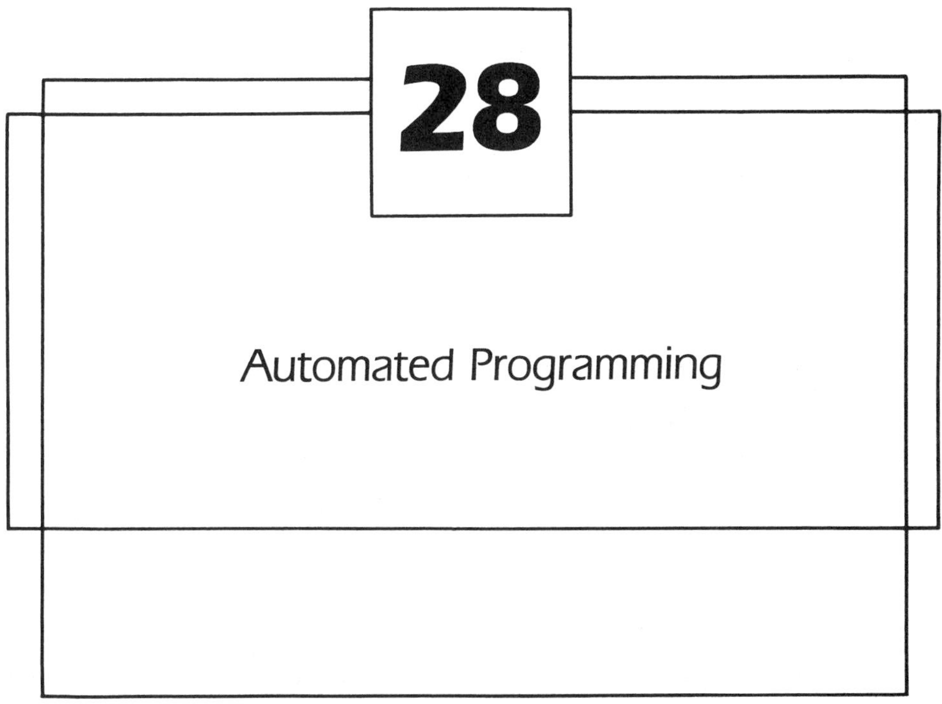

28 Automated Programming

Having reached out to automate every other industry, software is turning inward and using AI principles to provide similar services for itself. It is high time, too, because almost 50 percent of the U.S. work force is employed by information-processing companies. Yet despite the software intensiveness of these companies, most software is painstakingly ground out by hand.

To be sure, over the years the software industry has gotten better at producing software. Programmers have developed tools that help specify, design, code, and verify the software. They have improved human–computer interfaces so as to provide programmers with instant feedback, facilitate their understanding of their program structure, and allow better communication with contractors who specify the program requirements.

But these tools, interfaces, and communications have resulted in only incremental software engineering improvements. Nothing has appeared to give a 10- to 70-fold increase in productivity as happened when assembly languages, which took over from machine languages, were first hailed as the end-all programming productivity tool, and again later when higher-level languages were invented to supplant assembler.

CODE WHILE YOU WAIT

Software professionals believe that a dramatic increase in programming productivity can be brought about by automated programming techniques. In the past there have been a number of claims for automated programming systems. Useful as these systems are, most of them, unfortunately, handle only very simple and narrow domains, such as database retrieval or update. To write programs, they initiate calls to precanned modules or expand existing macros in response to users' commands. Then they string the modules and macros together to build a program.

To automate programs for more complicated domains requires artificial intelligence, and particularly knowledge-based, capabilities. The knowledge base must contain expertise about how programmers use knowledge of both the program's application domain and the program-writing domain to write programs, in addition to knowledge about what makes a good programmer. Clearly, methods must be available to represent this kind of knowledge to a computer. The knowledge system inference mechanism would provide the means to synthesize the program's programming and domain knowledge and the user's specifications to produce complex programs that are executable. To be maximally useful, the automated programming system must be able to accept incomplete programming specifications from users, and then use the system's domain knowledge to fill in missing details.

Creating such an automated AI-based programming system is not an easy task. Therefore, the researchers deemed it best to get started early to identify and work with issues and problems to be surmounted. It is a good thing they started early, because the first problem that cropped up began at the beginning of the program development cycle, when users attempted to describe their requirements. For example, attempts at Information Sciences Institute (ISI) to build program generators that generate formal satellite communications and text processing programs from natural-language specifications revealed that many of the natural-language constructs that people use to express program specifications are not expressible in a formal language. So the ISI group developed GIST, a high-level formal language, whose constructs modeled that of the natural-language descriptions. Unfortunately, like all formal languages, GIST removed all the informal mechanisms, such as overviews, summaries, diagrams, and examples, that make natural-language specifications easy to read and understand.

ISI's solution to this additional problem was to build a natural-language paraphraser that translated formal GIST into a natural-language paraphrase of what the computer understood to be the user's specifications. This expression of specifications in an alternative, easy-to-comprehend form resulted in the discovery of several bugs in the specification. So the natural-language paraphraser, a by-product of the quest for an automatic program generator, was turned into a debugging tool for the program generator.

The goal at ISI is eventually to convert the GIST specification into an efficient program. The question is: To what degree is it possible to automate design decisions?

ISI answers that for complex programs, some strategic decisions concerning, for example, choice of data structure (array, linked list, or bit table), algorithm, or control structure can be automated through heuristic methods. However, programmers must remain in the loop to make the high-level design

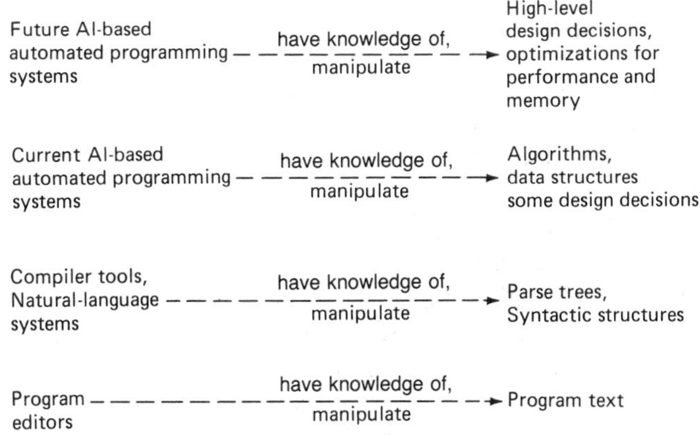

Figure 28-1 The steps toward automated programming

decisions. The reason is the lack of sufficient knowledge about the program design process and how local optimization can be combined to form global optimizations to automate the process. However, once programmers specify their decisions about what optimizations to apply, the program generator can automatically carry them out (Figure 28-1).

Future ISI steps call for techniques that allow the computer itself to make some of the design decisions. One technique is to have the computer look at all the possibilities and analyze the execution time and storage required. Such an analysis must be guided by heuristics. No other method is feasible because the search space of possible programs that can be written is too large.

NEAR-TERM SOLUTIONS

If the software industry waits to develop automated programming tools until all the programming knowledge and representation methods are understood, it will have a long wait. AI-based approaches to software development, however, can provide a number of near-term productivity gains.

As a first step, Lisp, Lisp machines, and the Lisp development environment can be used to create programs that write simple programs. Lisp and the Lisp machine tools are more dynamic and flexible than conventional languages and allow for exploratory programming and easy modification.

These characteristics enabled Schlumberger Ltd. to develop ϕ_0 (phi-naught), an Interlisp-based program-writing program. ϕ_0 uses graphical inputs showing quantitative relationships concerning oil-well logging data to build moderately complex Fortran programs that analyze the oil-well logging data. However, it builds these programs by using a good deal of clever programming rather than pure AI because the program domain is still sufficiently simple.

Crystal, a knowledge-based software development and management system under development at Carnegie Group Inc., is another near-term automated programming solution. Crystal's ultimate goal is an automated software generation program which will apply software development knowledge in a knowledge base to users' specifications which the program can capture. Its shorter term milestones are integrated knowledge-based programs that perform software-project management, configuration management, decision support, and change management.

Crystal's various knowledge bases contain descriptions of software modules and functions, and knowledge of software development activities and module functions. It uses this knowledge to perform a variety of software development activities. For example, it determines the available resources, constraints on the resources, and schedules and monitors software project activities. It scans the knowledge bases to determine if already-constructed modules fit some of a user's specifications and, if so, how the modules should be configured. It consults with software professionals about the design, construction, and testing of code. It also records error reports and proposed error correction changes, determines the effect of the proposed change on existing code, creates new descriptions of, and documentation for, the changed module, and communicates all this maintenance activity to the appropriate people.

The next step toward automating programming is to use AI technology to develop programs under programmers' guidance. Because this task involves so much ill-understood knowledge both of programming and AI, many researchers took an evolutionary approach to the problem, starting small, paralleling the maturation and understanding of software development ideas in industry and AI advances, and incrementally working up to commercial systems.

THE PROGRAMMER'S APPRENTICE

MIT had incremental automation in mind when it began its research into an automated programming tool which it dubbed the Programmer's Apprentice. Even the name "apprentice" suggests that the Programmer's Apprentice is designed to model the apprentice-type relationship and interaction between junior and senior programmers. Like a junior programmer, the Programmer's Apprentice begins its career with fairly modest programming capabilities. It gets smarter during its apprenticeship, until it eventually becomes a master at its tasks. And while the Apprentice is improving its skills, it performs helpful, practical tasks, even to the extent of offloading from the senior programmer the more mundane programming tasks that involve mostly drudgery.

Design decisions remain the province of programmers. However, after they have conceived of and worked out the design, programmers can instruct the Programmer's Apprentice to implement and code the program for them.

The instructions that the programmer issues to the Apprentice are typically only a few lines in length, and they resemble a high-level, generic description of the functionality of features of a desired program. A five-line set of instructions

```
s-X Implement the program as a Sequential_Search.


LOCATE: PROCEDURE(V) RETURNS (...);
  DCL V ...,
      DATA ...,
  DATA = #{the input ARG of the Enumerator};
  DO WHILE '1'B;
    IF #{the Empty_Test of the Enumerator}(DATA)
      THEN RETURN (#{the Failure_(Value});
    IF #{the Test}(DATA)
      THEN RETURN (#{the Success_Value});
    DATA = #{the Step of the Enumerator}(DATA);
  END;
END;
```

Figure 28-2 The Programmer's Apprentice (Richard G. Waters)

might request the Apprentice to write a program that uses a particular data structure, a certain kind of loop, and a specific type of test condition. Acting as a productivity enhancer, the Apprentice then interprets the instructions, checks them for completeness and consistency, fills in the details, and grinds out the code in whatever language is being used. If, during instruction interpretation time, information needed for the program is not yet known, the Apprentice codes a sketchy program, containing ellipses or curly brackets that signify missing information. Programmers can fill in the missing information manually or by issuing further commands.

For example, suppose that a programmer wishes to write a program, called LOCATE, which sequentially searches a vector of integers (the program's sole parameter) for a positive integer (Waters, 1984). If a positive integer is found, the program is to return its index; otherwise, it returns zero. One programmer-input line instructing the Apprentice to write the program LOCATE, with one parameter (Define a program LOCATE with a parameter v), produces the following top-level sketchy PL/1 code:

```
LOCATE: PROCEDURE (V) RETURNS (...);
    DCL V ...;
END;
```

```
s-; Document the program LOCATE.
s-X Display the Failure_Value.


/* The program LOCATE is a Sequential_Search.
    The Enumerator is a Vector_Enumeration which
      enumerates each element "V(I)" in the vector "V".
    The Test is a Positive_Test which determines whether
      the item "V(I)" is greater than zero.
    The Failure_Value is "MIN(0,LBOUND(V,1)-1)".
    The Success_Value is "I".                          */

LOCATE: PROCEDURE(V) RETURNS (FIXED);
  DCL V(*) FIXED,
      I FIXED,
      LIMIT FIXED;
  I = LBOUND(V,1);
  LIMIT = HBOUND(V,1);
  DO WHILE '1'B;
    IF I>LIMIT THEN RETURN (MIN(0,LBOUND(V,1)-1));
    IF V(I)>0 THEN RETURN (I);
```

Figure 28-3 The Programmer's Apprentice (Richard G. Waters)

The next programmer's line might instruct the Apprentice to implement a sequential search procedure. In response, the Apprentice produces a more detailed pseudocode procedure (Figure 28-2). The information between the curly brackets, such as {the input Arg of the Enumerator}, the ellipsis (. . .), and the place held for (DATA), indicate still missing information and may even specify the information that belongs there. The Arg is the initial thing being searched for. The Enumerator enumerates some aggregate data structure whose elements are to be searched. The Test is the condition the program tests to find out if it has found what it was looking for and therefore is done. The Success_Value and Failure_Value specify what to return depending on whether or not a positive integer is found.

As the Apprentice works, the programmer specifies increasingly detailed and precise implementation instructions. For example, a line of input may specify Vector-Enumeration rather than just enumeration, or may instruct the Apprentice to implement the Failure_Value as zero and the Test as a Positive_Test. The Apprentice contains knowledge of search, vector enumeration, and other programming algorithms, and the handling of data type information. It responds to each programmer instruction by gradually filling in the missing information signified by the ellipses. In addition, the Apprentice can create documentation for the program (Figure 28-3). The documentation describes the program in terms of its underlying algorithms.

WHAT MAKES IT TICK?

The process of generating code from programmers' instructions expands the few lines of high-level instructions approximately six- to nine-fold. Because it can perform low-level tasks, such as choosing and implementing a certain loop or data structure, but not the higher-level design chores, the Apprentice enhances programmer productivity less than would a fully automated programming system but far more than traditional software development tools.

Key to the Programmer's Apprentice software skills is its knowledge-based editor. To act on the programmer's specifications, this intelligent editor contains knowledge of different kinds of data structures, loops, and test conditions, what they are, how to implement them, and how to get data into a data or control structure. Since programs are essentially constructed of input and output segments connected by data and control flows, the Apprentice also knows about input/output behavior and properties and parts of, and interrelationships between, data objects. In addition, to generate code that implements the programmer's instructions, the Apprentice understands the generic, conceptual vocabulary of programming design. This abstract programming vocabulary is independent of any particular programming language. However, the Apprentice has a separate, smaller body of knowledge about the specifics of coding data and control structures in various programming languages, such as Ada, Lisp, and PL/1.

To maintain and use all these kinds of knowledge, the Apprentice has a hybrid architecture. It incorporates several kinds of reasoning mechanisms and knowledge bases which cooperate to accomplish a task. Other Apprentice knowledge is intrinsic to the Apprentice's design and is not contained in any knowledge base.

Knowledge bases in the Programmer's Apprentice contain frames, rules, some formal logic, and algorithms. They work together to integrate different stages of the software development cycle. For example, formal logic and theorem-proving techniques are particularly precise methods for expressing and handling programming instructions (and, in the future, high-level specifications) so that they are understood by the computer. (Natural language is too ambiguous for the purpose.) Graph theoretic algorithms are suitable for analyzing data flow and control flow throughout the structure and text of a program. Reasoning about, verifying properties of, and checking data structures, like sets, arrays, and lists, have proved especially susceptible to special purpose automated algebraic reasoning such as the decision procedures of Boolean algebra.

COMMERCIALIZATION AT LAST

The goal of all the automated-programming research is to make knowledge-based automated-programming systems available off-the-shelf. Refine (from Reasoning Systems Inc.) is the first such commercial automated programming system. Based primarily on work performed at Kestrel Institute, it draws on knowledge bases containing programming knowledge and domain-specific knowledge to design and code programs in a variety of application domains. Refine differs from most earlier systems in that it does not take a pseudocode approach. Instead, it takes as its input a specification about the functioning and behavior of a system, compiles it, refines it, and outputs executable code.

During this programming process, Refine makes a knowledge-based choice among algorithms, data structures, and some optimization decisions that could implement a specification in order to select the best ones. As a result, programmers can specify what to do, but they need not tell Refine how to do it. For example, it is not necessary to instruct Refine to perform a "sequential search" to find an element in a "list." It is enough to ask if an element is a member of a set. Refine then uses its knowledge to choose a data structure and it synthesizes the search itself. It may, in fact, decide that the data is more efficiently represented as a tree, in which case a sequential search is probably the wrong thing to do. However, programmers can override Refine's decisions.

To enter specifications, programmers use a formal specification-language that has a domain-specific vocabulary (added by users). This language differs from previous specification languages in that it is integrated with the rest of the programming process and, therefore, does not require programmers to code the executable program in a different, third-generation language (such as Fortran, Pascal, etc.). Refine programmers need use only Refine's specification language for program development.

Although the specification language is formal, it has an English-like syntax. To a large degree, however, at the highest level the language syntax also resembles logic and set theory statements. This makes the Refine language more difficult to learn than languages like Fortran or C. More important, Refine is difficult to learn because the essence of a specification language for an automated programming system is to express functionality in an abstract way, independent of a particular implementation, and to do it essentially for all time, independent of applications as yet unforseen. In contrast, the essence of languages like Fortran and Pascal is to code in a way that is tailored to a specific application. That is one reason why it is so difficult for programmers to reuse, and even maintain, Fortran code.

The abstract nature of Refine's specification language limits the number of people who can learn it easily and use it well. But there are mixed opinions as to whether this will limit its acceptance. Lockheed (a user) doesn't have a problem. Others see acceptance problems for such a tool as depending on whether a company's goal is to prop up mediocre programmers or to amplify excellent programmers.

Nevertheless, it would appear that Refine is not currently a panacea for all software development. It is a new programming paradigm. It requires an investment in learning and time to add domain-specific knowledge. This must be balanced against Refine's ability "to deliver significant productivity gains," says Winston Royce, head of Lockheed's software technology center. For example, as an experiment Lockheed encoded its 306-line Fortran program to implement part of the classic traveling salesman problem (which determines the shortest route to cover the maximum number of cities) in only 26 lines of Refine. Since, in Lockheed's experience, it takes about the same amount of time to produce one line of Fortran as one line of Refine, this represents a productivity gain of 306:26. Other experiments show an expansion factor, between 5 and 10.

Another productivity goal resulting from executable specifications is the ability to validate and maintain specifications, rather than the underlying code. In other words, there is substantial leverage in being able to modify the specifications and have the changes automatically ripple down throughout the program. Decisions are more easily monitored, and policy enforcement and design review more easily achieved. Finally, because Refine is a system for creating programs, it can be used to extend itself (since it is a program). This allows users to customize the automatic programming system with domain-specific language constructs and concepts, which, as will be seen, increase productivity.

Lockheed, Data General (MIS support), General Telephone & Electronics, Advanced Decision Systems (ADS), and MCC number among Refine's users. They are using Refine to develop applications in the areas of Communications, Command, and Control; radar systems, equipment configuration, scheduling, robot planning, and data communication protocols.

Considering the amount of programmer-specific and domain knowledge that must be encoded, in addition to programming tools, Refine is a very memory-intensive system. It runs on Symbolics Lisp machines, but Sun Microsystems workstations and Data General minicomputer implementations will be available next.

The first Refine implementation was designed to generate code in Lisp. The next implementations will generate Ada and C code. But the kind of third-generation language code that Refine generates doesn't matter to Lockheed. Lockheed is using Refine to develop military communications software for embedded systems. When the two-year project is completed, Lockheed says it will take the code that it generates in Refine and compile it directly to the machine language for the target system. It hasn't yet decided how. However, compiling for a target machine is a typical thing that aerospace companies do and, according to Royce, is one of the easier problems to solve.

HOW IS IT USED?

Refine contains a knowledge base, a very-high-level specification language, a rule-based compiler, a language that includes procedural constructs so that programmers may hand-optimize time-critical functions, and the ability for users to extend any of these components. The rules that make up the compiler are program transformation rules, designed to support stepwise refinement. They transform abstract program specifications to a target implementation by successively applying refinement rules that each embody a design decision.

The Refine knowledge base is object-centered. Programs, as well as elements in the application domain, are stored as objects in the knowledge base. Associated with the objects is a large set of attributes that represents characteristics of the objects and also supports software management functions. This object-centered structure makes it very easy for programmers, system tools, and other programs to identify objects, query and manipulate them. For example, program-design rules can apply themselves when applicable because they can easily search the knowledge base for objects that are appropriate for them to manipulate. As a result, it is not necessary for programmers to express how to transform a program component from one state to another. The rules contain the knowledge of how to do this.

A communications system illustrates how Refine works. To use Refine to develop a program, Reasoning Systems recommends beginning by defining the objects in the application domain. Examples of communications-program domain objects are the communications system, transmitters, receivers, channels, encoders, decoders, messages, data compression techniques, data encryption protocols, and noise immunization methods. Domain-independent objects that are also defined include the specification, the program, project schedules, documentation, and testing suites. Programmers would also define attributes for the objects. For example, for the object class of data encoders, they would define attributes such as purpose, input data type, and input data length.

In the first actual program design step, Refine users state the informal functional and real-time behavioral requirements for the system, such as:*

- The system will transmit and receive English text messages at 4800 baud (system bandwidth).
- The content of the messages is proprietary business information to be protected from unauthorized reception.
- The system will transmit and receive over a 9600 baud (channel bandwidth) conditioned telephone line.
- The probability of error in received English characters will be no greater than 0.00001.

* Communications example: courtesy Reasoning Systems.

The requirements are then written in the Refine language syntax. For example, suppose the Refine environment has been customized to include communications-oriented syntaxes, and the system under development is named COMM-SYSTEM-1. These requirements can then be entered into the Refine knowledge base by reading and compiling the following DefObject (''define object'') statement:

```
(DefObject COMM-SYSTEM-1
  the-comm-system
      with-message-type                English-text
      with-system-bandwidth            4800 baud
      with-probability-of-error        0.00001
      with-channel-bandwidth           9600 baud
      with-channel-characteristics     conditioned-telephone-line
      with-security-level              proprietary)
```

Next, system developers would represent the relationships among the knowledge-base objects and facts about the objects. These can be written as assertions. An example is the following condition on correctness of a protocol: a transmitter protocol is correct only if

- all the encoders and decoders employed are correct
- the output data type of each encoder/decoder matches the input data type of its successor encoder (if the message receives further processing before going into the channel)
- the output data type of the final encoder matches the channel
- noise immunization does not precede encryption

This correctness condition on protocol design can be represented in Refine using the following assertion:

```
(Correct p) ⇒   (Empty (incorrect-coders p))
              ∧ (Empty (non-linking-coders p))
              ∧ (Coder-to-channel-match p)
              ∧ (Empty (noise-before-secrecy p))
```

where, for example,

```
(incorrect-coders p)
    = {c : c ∈ (encoding-sequence p) ∧¬ (Correct-coder c)}
```

and

```
(Coder-to-channel-match p)
    = ( (output-data-type (last (encoding-sequence p)))
      = (data-type-of (channel-of p)) )
```

Besides expressing design constraints, assertions can test arbitrary conditions on the design knowledge base. During compilation, consistency enforcement tools use these assertions to guarantee that the resulting implementation meets the constraints expressed in the assertions, and to form a basis for software management tasks such as project management and version control.

The next step after formalizing the requirements is to refine the requirements into a detailed design. The design is refined using IF-THEN type of transformation, or refinement, rules. The first set of refinements transforms the generic system into components that implement it. For example, Refine might transform a generic communications system into a more specific one that has a receiver, channel, transmitter, and also some information, such as input and output data-types, about each of these objects.

The refinements applied via the domain-specific transformation rules are the same as those that an applications engineer applies when designing a system. Normally, this domain knowledge is entered into the rule-base (forming so-called "knowledge packs") when Refine is customized for an application area. Refine uses these knowledge packs to help convert requirements into specifications, thus relieving software designers of much of the task. For example, drawing on the prewritten knowledge packs, Refine can infer, from a communications-software designer's "probability of error" requirement, the need to add a noise encoder to the system. Another refinement rule will then refine the generic noise encoder into a particular Hamming encoder if messages are to be transmitted in packets of fixed length.

The following rule is an example of a transformation rule. It says "if the messages are English text, then add compression encoding to the protocol."

```
TRANS = 'the-transmitter @@                    ;IF the knowledge base has a transmitter
          with-compression-encoder @enc        ;with a data compression encoder named
                                               "enc"
          with-input-data-type @i-d-t'         ;and input data type named "i-d-t"
∧ (undefp enc)                                 ;and the encoder hasn't yet been given a
                                               value
∧ (embedded-in TRANS) = 'the-comm- system      ;and the transmitter has been embedded
                        @@ with-message-       in a communications system that has
                        type English-text'     English text as the message type,
→
(compression-encoder TRANS) =                  ;THEN create a compression encoder
  'the-compression-encoder @ (newsymbol
  'compressor)                                 ;with the name compressor
    with-optimality 0.9                        ; with a value of optimality preset to 0.9
    with-compression-factor 1.3                ; and a data compression factor preset to
                                               1.3
    with-input-data-type @(copyexpr i-d-t)     ;and the same input data type as the
                                               compressor
    with-output-data-type (seq integer)'       ;and the output data type as a sequence
                                               of integers.
```

[*Note:* In Refine, patterns are enclosed in single quotes, the symbol @ indicates a variable in the pattern, the double symbol @@ indicates a wild card variable (a variable whose value doesn't matter).]

This transformation rule refines the transmitter's knowledge-based structure by creating (for the transmitter) a compression encoder object with specified values. Such transformations are performed for all the system's components.

A second set of transformations transforms each of the components into other components that implement them. For example, the transmitter might be further refined to one that performs noise encoding, encryption, and data compression in a certain order. These transformation steps are repeated, producing other components with increasingly detailed attributes, until the program has obtained all the components it needs to meet the specified system requirements, and each of the components can be transformed into functional specifications for that component.

These functional specifications are written in Refine. To produce executable code, the Refine compiler applies a final set of program transformations to transform the specifications into the executable target language.

WHERETO FROM HERE

AI researchers have gone a long way toward automating all stages of the software life cycle. However, significant work remains to be done.

Major automated-programming concerns include user acceptance, the time required to build domain-specific knowledge bases, and efficiency. Refine, for example, met early resistance because it ran only on Lisp machines and produced Lisp code. With the Sun and Data General implementations, and the upcoming Ada and C target languages, that problem is being solved. Another factor limiting acceptance is the initial time required to customize a system with domain-specific knowledge. Adding such knowledge can be like trying to capture a corporation's knowledge of applications and programming.

A greater user acceptance problem stems from the fact that automated programming systems are still preliminary products. Moreover, they entail a new way of thinking about programming. There is a chicken and egg story here. The widespread transfer of this new programming technology may not occur until automated programming becomes accepted enough to teach it in the schools.

By far, however, the biggest automated-programming problem that remains to be solved across the entire field of automated programming is efficiency, meaning how to optimize performance and memory. Simply put, users of automated programming systems can generate correct code faster than they could manually. The code will be easier to maintain. But neither the execution speed nor the memory utilization is as good as it is for programs written by hand.

There are several reasons. First, how to represent the tradeoffs between performance and memory in the design of a program is poorly understood. Second, systems that accept specifications and practice stepwise refinement, rather than requiring programmers to make the implementation decisions, find it very difficult to estimate the efficiency of a target implementation from an early refinement. As a result, an optimal implementation at early levels of refinement may refine down into a slow implementation that occupies lots of space at the target code level. Third, a way to represent the tradeoffs between global and local optimization has yet to be resolved. An implementation may make sense in a local module, but it may make less sense in view of other things going on in a system. Consequently, an automated programming system must know when to sacrifice some local efficiency for overall efficiency.

The notion of a software tool that accepts a programmer's specifications as input, and outputs verified code, is equivalent to automating all of computer science. This is a difficult task because programming is a very complicated activity. However, the programming domain is a potentially fruitful one that will bring great rewards in return for any leverage that can be developed.

29

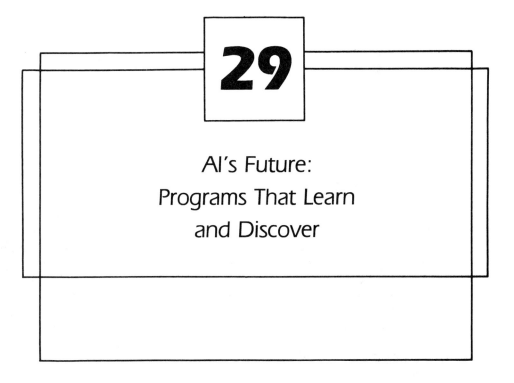

AI's Future: Programs That Learn and Discover

Once the theme that launched a thousand science fiction stories, artificial intelligence is now as real as other previously mythical and fictional themes such as airplanes and submarines. However, AI's economic potential and widespread benefits will remain limited until AI programs become intelligent enough to learn, to some degree, without the intervention of knowledge engineers and programmers.

A LEARNING EXPERIENCE

That no one knows how humans learn (only how to help people learn better) has not stopped people from teaching computers to learn. Many companies are supporting research in computer learning because they think expert systems would be more useful if they could learn. Expert systems are currently limited because they must be hand-crafted by AI experts who are a scant resource. In addition, the process of extracting expert system knowledge from an application expert is an arduous, labor-intensive and long-term process. Finally, expert systems are limited to the narrow domain of their knowledge bases. No matter how much experience they gain, they can never improve their performance unless a human adds new information to their knowledge base.

Therein lies the motivation for building expert systems that learn. For example, GTE needs to ensure automatic reliability and coordination of its increasingly distributed, complicated, heterogeneous, and remotely located telecommunications network. Difficult to ensure with people only for such a complex network, the utility hopes to use AI-based telecommunications software that learns from the experiences of its network nodes how to manage itself. Oil companies want to use expert systems to investigate solutions to oil-field analysis problems by searching for analogies between new and old situations. Atari would like to make its fantasy games more exciting with the help of artificially intelligent "agents" that learn the players' idiosyncrasies and synthesize game responses accordingly.

Fairchild would like to improve its wafer production with the help of AI consultant systems that incorporate not only several forms of learning, but natural language, communications, multiple expert systems and knowledge bases, tools, and simulation systems. Still under development, the consultant system will receive sensory data about Fairchild's factory, interpret them intelligently, and advise and consult with users in natural language, graphics, or speech.

Fairchild plans consultant systems for two domains: the design of complex integrated systems and the manufacture of VLSI products. For these domains, the consultant will use its various kinds of AI software to draw on experiences and learn by analogy in order to perform tasks such as critiquing or improving a design. Moreover, it will be able to learn by deriving information from first principles, and generate rules that incorporate the learned information.

HOW COMPUTERS LEARN

Learning can take many forms, such as learning from examples; learning by experience, precedents, and analogy; and learning from fundamental principles. For each form of learning, computer programs and human beings appear to learn some things similarly. For example, in some learning methods, common in law, mathematics, and business, both computers and human beings study an illustrative example of an object or problem. Then they try to figure out how it differs from an incorrect example. Alternatively, they try to discover relationships between the illustrative and other examples.

Once they know the differences and the relationships, both computers and people may generalize that knowledge so they can apply it appropriately in the future. Or they may simply make a note for future reference of the differences or relationships between correct and incorrect examples.

Patrick Winston (head of the AI laboratory at MIT) has developed several learn-by-example and learn-by-precedent computer programs that have influenced the direction of computer-learning goals in several companies. One program, which guides learning-by-example, presents to the computer an example of a correct arch and several examples of what the computer is told are not arches (Figure 29-1). It is important, however, that the differences between the correct and incorrect arches are small—what Winston calls "near-misses." Winston bases his learning programs on the theory that, like people, computers learn mostly in small steps. According to Winston, "If there is too much to learn, there is too much room for confusion and error." Therefore, he chooses each arch example to teach one idea about an arch.

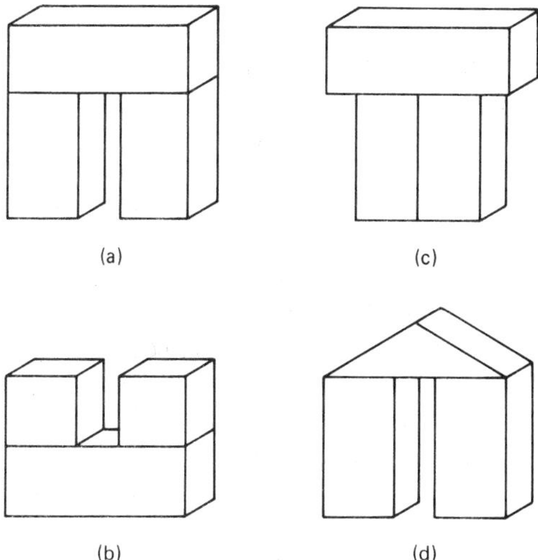

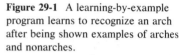

Figure 29-1 A learning-by-example program learns to recognize an arch after being shown examples of arches and nonarches.

For example, the correct example (a) shows that an arch is two vertical bricks and a horizontal brick. The near-misses restrict what can be an arch. The first near-miss (b) teaches that to be an arch, the vertical bricks may not touch. The second near-miss (c) teaches that the vertical bricks must support the horizontal brick. In contrast, the last example (d) identifies an arch whose top is a wedge instead of a brick. This last example makes the definition of an arch more flexible.

To teach the computer to understand arches, Winston's learning program first converts the line drawings of all the arches into semantic-network knowledge representations that describe the arches. Then the program tries to match the correct example of an arch with the corresponding parts of either the near-misses or the more general arch example. It cannot match the examples exactly. So as the program discovers differences that determine what can or cannot be an arch, it modifies the semantic-network representation that correctly describes an arch. The modifications are equivalent to new rules learned about the details and variations of arches.

If there is more than one difference between examples, then to learn from the example it is necessary to rank those differences from most to least important. This ranking of differences is the reason it is so easy for a child to understand a tower, says Marvin Minsky, professor of electrical engineering at MIT. Although characteristics such as stability and strength are important, "the first priority is height, else there is no tower" (Minsky, 1982, pp. 12–14).

PROGRAMS THAT USE WHAT THEY HAVE LEARNED

One goal of learning programs is to eliminate the painful knowledge-acquisition and manual rule-creation process and automate the generation of knowledge-based systems. Systems that can observe, learn, and create new programs based on their learning are the dream of business and industrial organizations that must cope with incessantly changing requirements and environments. Still another goal motivating the development of learning programs is the desire to learn more about how it is possible for human beings to learn. Learning programs make it possible to test educational theories because the computer can be used as a learning-laboratory test environment.

Nobel prize-winning laureate Herbert Simon at CMU, who was one of the people present at the 1956 Dartmouth conference when the field of AI was first defined, is developing learning programs to improve educational techniques. The learning programs, called "adaptive production systems," are systems that learn, write new rules based on what they have learned, and add them to the program. Some of Simon's programs have learned general procedures for solving algebraic equations or for factoring quadratic equations by examining worked out examples of these types of problems.

The learning methods that the programs use date back to the means–end analysis techniques of 1958. The programs compare their expressions with the form of a solution of an algebraic equation. First, they note the differences. Then they apply various operators to eliminate these differences.

As a program discovers actions that take it closer to the goal expression in the example, it notes the conditions that motivated that action. Equipped with this information, the program generalizes the information, builds a rule whose condition part contains the characteristics of this motivating condition, and whose action part, or consequent, is the corresponding action taken.

Hence the adaptive production system can learn from solved mathematics problems and build a program to solve general problems of that type in the future. There are two major difficulties in building such adaptive production systems. One is the task of creating a powerful set of rules that are capable of making new rules. The other difficulty is to get the program to recognize the cues that tell it that the creation of a rule that performs a certain action is appropriate for a particular set of circumstances.

HUMAN-LEARNING LABORATORIES

There has not always been a lot of success in teaching many students the types of mathematics that Simon's programs successfully learned, despite the teaching methods tried. Now, however, the computer provides a controlled laboratory to test out the types and order of examples that are best to present to students, and what types of specific difficulties in learning are likely to be encountered.

In a series of experiments to examine ways to improve classroom teaching, Simon presented the same mathematics examples that formed the teaching basis for his computer programs to six classes in the People's Republic of China. Each class numbered about forty 12- to 13-year-old students.

Using Simon's learning-by-example techniques, rather than a teacher's exposition, the students learned to factor quadratic equations in about twenty minutes. And, based on their ability to do the problems, about 90 percent of them learned. In contrast, in the normal curriculum, two days of the year are allocated to this topic.

But these results are by no means conclusive. As with any set of experiments involving humans, it is very difficult to control, or even know, all the variables involved. Many questions remain to be answered. For example, are two days actually needed, even under normal circumstances, to teach the subject? Also, Simon's experiments were a change from the normal mode of teaching, and experiments have shown that any change from the norm tends to improve human performance.

DISCOVERY AND CREATIVITY

How people learn—both children and adults—has been the subject of ongoing study since the days of Socrates. A much more elusive subject is creativity, and the mental processes involved in great scientific discoveries. Psychologists and educators have studied human creativity and discovery in laboratory situations. They have devised tests for creative thinking and compared test responses of examinees with those of people in the arts and science whose creativity is an accepted fact.

None of this explains, however, how discovery actually comes about or how to teach and increase human creativity. Some precepts underlying discovery have been observed. In particular, although theoretical knowledge is certainly a help, creative discoveries are not necessarily the results of logical inference or deduction. Instead, in the sciences, a good deal of discovery is data driven rather than deduced from theories.

For example, the laws governing electricity and astronomy are not intuitive or immediately logical. They came about when scientists such as Ohm, Kirchoff, and Kepler observed and studied large amounts of data and from those data induced (generalized) Ohm's, Kirchoff's, and Kepler's laws. Only years afterwards did these laws acquire any theoretical base.

Numerous other examples of such data-driven discoveries exist in science. They include Mendel's law of inheritance, Black's law of equilibrium temperatures of mixtures of substances, Mendeleev's formulation of the periodic table of the elements, Gay-Lussac's law for gaseous reactions, and Avogadro's determination of atomic weight.

The human information-processing techniques involved in these discoveries are unknown. Certain features and procedures, however, that have been observed in laboratory studies and in the writings of several prominent scientists are thought to play a large role in the discovery process.

For example, anyone who has ever studied a group of data knows that there are certain patterns that are common in natural data and certain relationships between data that often surface for many types of data. Knowledge of these patterns and relationships is a helpful starting point for induction. In addition, there are a few types of manipulation techniques that make sense to apply to the data in order to investigate the patterns and relationships.

How large a role these procedures play in human discovery, and how much more can be learned about the mental processes involved, remains to be seen. One thing is certain, though: modern computers and computer simulation and AI techniques provide a controlled laboratory for testing some of these hypotheses.

BACON

A CMU program named Bacon, when provided with observed and experimental data, tries to find out if there are any empirical laws hidden in the data. About half a dozen heuristics guide Bacon's induction process by massaging the data in various ways, looking for certain correlations in the data, and trying certain functions that might express any relationships found.

Although certain relationships and manipulation techniques are standard, Bacon is not dependent only on a fixed menu of actions and goals. It builds up new ones recursively or by combining the parts of known relationships and techniques in various ways.

Using heuristic techniques, Bacon has already reinvented a number of our major scientific laws, including Kepler's third law, Ohm's law, the ideal gas laws, and Black's law. One of the more interesting ideas that has come out of Bacon's attempts to discover scientific theories, and possibly key to the process of human induction, is Bacon's ability to invent new concepts along the way. The invented concepts typically involve introducing some new property of the bodies or substances under investigation that will explain the relationship between them and simplify the statement of a law about them.

For example, when Bacon is given certain data about objects that are accelerating, it introduces the notion of mass. It does not go so far as to call it that. But it understands it intuitively, gives it its own name, and then can use the concept or property of mass to help explain acceleration.

What is interesting about this intermediate concept definition is the way it parallels human discovery of some major scientific concepts and theories. Black's law describing the equilibrium temperature of a mixture of two substances is a case in point.*

It was well known in the mid-1700s that if equal volumes of water at different temperatures were mixed, the resulting temperature would be the average of the two. Confusion occurred when the two substances mixed were different. Clearly, the resulting temperature would be some sort of a weighted average. But what type and how much the weighted average had to do with weights or masses was unknown. The idea that a heavy substance such as mercury had less influence on

*This section is based on Bradshaw and others (1983).

the final temperature of a mixture of substance than an equal volume of water, which is so much lighter, was counterintuitive.

In 1760, Joseph Black finally sorted out all the data and formulated the law of equilibrium temperature of a mixture of substances. His successful technique was first to attribute a property, which he called specific heat, to a unit mass of a particular substance, and then use the specific heat to calculate the substance's heat capacity. The substance's heat capacity provided the missing weighting factor needed to determine the final temperature of a mixture that involved that substance.

Not until more than 100 years later did any theoretical basis for Black's law begin to appear. Despite the theoretical lack, Black was the first person to make the inductive leap from the data to the law of temperature equilibrium. The key to his success, just as it has often been the key to Bacon's success, was the idea of defining a new, intermediate concept of specific heat (Bradshaw et al., 1983).

BUT IS IT INTELLIGENCE?

Many people consider the name "artificial intelligence" to be misleading, claiming that AI programs are quite deterministic, and that they all boil down to bits, bytes, and algorithms merely implemented differently from conventional applications. Even within the AI community, many AI experts consider the current generation of AI programs "primitive programs from which some people are getting a lot of mileage." However, as the state of AI programs evolves from these primitive programs to the thinking and learning programs that are closer to human intelligence, the name "artificial intelligence" may become far more meaningful.

This AI evolution, however, will require fundamental conceptual advances in understanding intelligence, understanding meaning, knowledge of how to represent knowledge, how people remember, and how people learn and create. Advancing through this state of AI raises some interesting questions, such as the meaning of meaning, and some paradoxes about why the more difficult knowledge for humans to handle is the easiest for computers and vice versa.

Human beings, for example, develop feelings and attitudes, then simple reasoning skills, and finally, computational skills. But this order of human development is opposite from the order of computer program development. What this means is not certain.

One possibility, Minsky suggests, is that the logical and linguistic parts of the adult mind are far more competent (perhaps better organized) than are the parts of the mind that deal with attitudes, viewpoints, and feelings. This (better organization) may provide an illusion of simplicity (concerning computation processing) (Minsky, 1982).

We may never be able to prove directly how the brain actually organizes and represents knowledge, or what activities take place in the brain when human beings learn. But one thing is certain. If the AI research into computer programs that learn is successful, and researchers discover more about how humans solve problems and acquire new information, that new knowledge gained will provide greater insight into designing better and more complex AI programs. In keeping with the history of AI, today's reasoning programs will no longer be AI; it will be something else, very clever, but not AI.

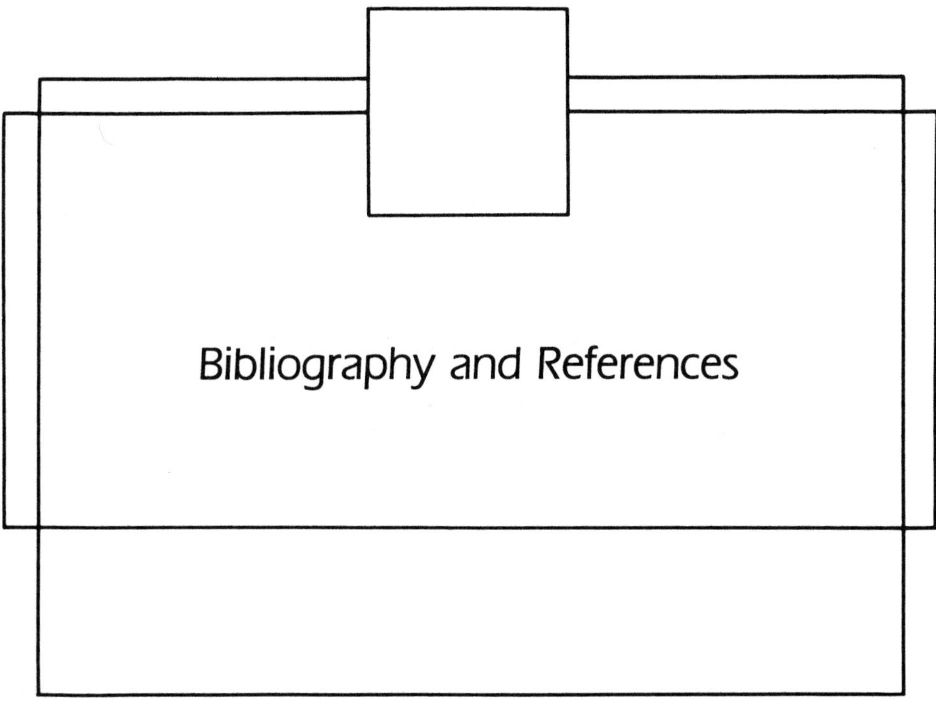

Bibliography and References

SECTION 1: INTRODUCTION TO ARTIFICIAL INTELLIGENCE (CHAPTERS 1 AND 2)

Austin, Howard, "Market Trends in Artificial Intelligence," in *Artificial Intelligence Applications for Business*, Walter Reitman, ed. (Norwood, N.J.: Ablex Publishing Corp., 1984).

Beckman, Frank S., *Mathematical Foundations of Programming* (Menlo Park, Calif.: Addison-Wesley Publishing Co., 1981). (Advanced reading.)

Davis, Randall, "Expert Systems: Where Are We? And Where Do We Go from Here?" *AI Magazine*, Vol. 3, No. 2, Spring 1982, pp. 3–22.

Feigenbaum, Edward A., and Pamela McCorduck, *The Fifth Generation: Artificial Intelligence and Japan's Computer Challenge to the World* (Reading, Mass.: Addison-Wesley Publishing Company, 1983). (General reading about the Japanese challenge to computer technology.)

Freiling, Mike, et al. "Starting a Knowledge Engineering Project: A Step-by-Step Approach," *AI Magazine*, Vol. 6, No. 3, Fall 1985, pp. 150–64.

Harmon, Paul, and David King, *Expert Systems: Artificial Intelligence in Business* (New York: John Wiley & Sons, Inc., 1985). (General reading.)

Hayes-Roth, Frederick, "Knowledge-Based Expert Systems," *Computer*, Vol. 17, No. 10, Oct. 1984, pp. 263–73. (An overview to the technological and commercial state of the art of expert systems.)

Kaplan, S. Jerrold, "The Industrialization of Artificial Intelligence: From By-Line to Bottom Line," *AI Magazine*, Vol. 5, No. 2, Summer 1984, pp. 51–57.

O'Connor, Dennis E., "Using Expert Systems to Manage Change And Complexity in Manufacturing," Digital Equipment Corp., April 1983.

Peters, Thomas J., and Robert H. Waterman, Jr., *In Search of Excellence* (New York: Harper & Row, 1982).

Polit, Stephen, "Rl and Beyond: AI Technology Transfer at DEC," *AI Magazine*, Vol. 5, No. 4, Winter 1985, pp. 76–78.

Taylor, Edward C., "Developing a Knowledge Engineering Capability in the TRW Defense Systems Group," *AI Magazine*, Vol. 6, No. 2, Summer 1985, pp. 58–63.

Turing, Alan M., "Can a Machine Think?" *The World of Mathematics,* Vol. 4, J. R. Newman, ed. (New York: Simon and Schuster, 1954, pp. 2099–2123).

Waterman, Donald A., *A Guide to Expert Systems* (Reading, Mass.: Addison-Wesley Publishing Company, 1986). (General reading.)

Wegner, Peter, "Capital-Intensive Software Technology: Part 3: Knowledge Engineering," *Computer*, Vol. 1, No. 3, July 1984, pp. 33–37. (In the 1990s, software technology will increasingly emphasize knowledge reusability—by both people and computers.)

Wiig, Karl W., "AI: Management's Newest Tool," *Management Review*, August 1986, pp. 24–41.

Winston, Patrick Henry, *Artificial Intelligence*, 2d ed. (Reading, Mass.: Addison-Wesley Publishing Co., 1984). (General reading, but somewhat advanced.)

Winston, Patrick H., and Karen A. Prendergast, eds., *The AI Business* (Cambridge, Mass.: MIT Press, 1984).

SECTION 2: EXPERT/KNOWLEDGE-BASED SYSTEMS (CHAPTERS 3–8)

Barr, Avron, and Edward A. Feigenbaum, eds., *The Handbook of Artificial Intelligence*, Vol. 1 and 2; and Cohen, Paul R., and Edward A. Feigenbaum, eds., Vol. 3 (Los Altos, Calif.: William Kaufmann, Inc., 1981, 1982).

Cox, Brad J., "Object-Oriented Programming: A Power Tool for Software Craftsmen," *Unix Review*, Feb./March 1984.

de Kleer, Johan, "An Assumption-Based TMS (Truth Maintenance System)," *Artificial Intelligence*, Vol. 28, No. 1, 1986. (Advanced reading.)

de Kleer, Johan, et al., "Explicit Control of Reasoning," in *Artificial Intelligence: An MIT Perspective*, Vol. 1, Patrick Henry Winston and Richard Henry Brown, eds. (Cambridge, Mass.: MIT Press, 1979). (Advanced reading.)

Doyle, Jon, "A Glimpse of Truth Maintenance," in *Artificial Intelligence: An MIT Perspective*, Vol. 1, Patrick Henry Winston and Richard Henry Brown, eds. (Cambridge, Mass.: MIT Press, 1979). (Advanced reading.)

"Evaluating Knowledge Engineering Applications," Knowledge Engineering, Teknowledge Inc., Palo Alto, Calif.

Fahlman, Scott E., "Representing and Using Real-World Knowledge," in *Artificial Intelligence: An MIT Perspective*, Patrick Henry Winston and Richard Henry Brown, eds. (Cambridge, Mass.: MIT Press, 1979). (Advanced reading.)

Fikes, Richard, and Tom Kehler, "The Role of Frame-Based Representation in Reasoning," *Communications of the ACM*, Vol. 28, No. 9, Sept. 1985, pp. 904–20.

Genesereth, Michael R., and Matthew L. Ginsberg, "Logic Programming," *Communications of the ACM*, Vol. 28, No. 9, Sept. 1985, pp. 933–41. (Advanced reading.)

Hayes-Roth, Frederick, "Rule-Based Systems," *Communications of the ACM*, Vol. 28, No. 9, Sept. 1985, p. 921–32.

Hayes-Roth, Frederick, Donald A. Waterman, and Douglas B. Lenat, eds., *Building Expert Systems* (Reading, Mass.: Addison-Wesley Publishing Co., 1983).

Hollan, James D., et al., "Steamer: An Interactive Inspectable Simulation-Based Training System," *AI Magazine*, Vol. 5, No. 2, Summer 1984, pp. 15–27.

Kellogg, Charles, "From Data Management to Knowledge Management," *Computer*, Vol. 19, No. 1, Jan. 1986, pp. 75–84.

Kowalski, R., *Logic for Problem Solving* (New York: North-Holland, 1979).

Lecot, Koenraad, and D. Stott Parker, "Control Over Inexact Reasoning," *AI Expert*, Premier 1986, pp. 32–43. (Advanced reading.)

Lenat, Doug, Mayank Prakash, and Mary Shepherd, "CYC: Using Common Sense Knowledge to Overcome Brittleness and Knowledge Acquisition Bottlenecks," *AI Magazine*, Vol. 6, No. 4, Winter 1986, pp. 65–85. (Brittleness and system breakdown are major limitations of large software systems. MCC is addressing the problem.)

Minsky, Marvin, "A Framework for Representing Knowledge," in *The Psychology of Computer Vision*, Patrick Henry Winston, ed. (New York: McGraw-Hill Book Company, 1975).

Mittal, Sanjay, and Clive L. Dym, "Knowledge Acquisition from Multiple Experts," *AI Magazine*, Vol. 6, No. 2, Summer 1985, pp. 32–36.

Nii, Penny H. "Blackboard Systems: The Blackboard Model of Problem Solving and the Evolution of Blackboard Architectures: Part 1," *AI Magazine*, Vol. 7, No. 2, Summer 1986, pp. 38–53, Part 2, *AI Magazine*, Vol. 7, No. 3, Conference 1986, pp. 82–106. (Advanced subject, but readable and informative articles.)

Preau, David S., "Selection of an Appropriate Domain for an Expert System," *AI Magazine*, Vol. 6, No. 2, Summer 1985, pp. 26–30.

Schor, Marshall, I., "Declarative Knowledge Programming Better Than Procedural?" *IEEE Expert*, Vol. 1, No. 1, Spring 1986, pp. 36–43. (Article addresses declarative and procedural knowledge, and the YES/MVS knowledge system that monitors MVS systems.)

Stefik, Mark, and Daniel G. Bobrow, "Object-Oriented Programming: Themes and Variations," *AI Magazine*, Vol. 6, No. 4, Winter 1986, pp. 40–62.

Stevens, Albert, et al., "The Use of a Sophisticated Graphics Interface in Computer-Assisted Instruction," *IEEE CG&A*, March/April 1983.

Zadeh, Lotfi A., "Making Computers Think Like People," *IEEE Spectrum*, Vol. 21, No. 8, August 1984, pp. 26–32. (Article on fuzzy logic.)

Zadeh, Lotfi A., "Test-Score Semantics as a Basis for a Computational Approach to the Representation of Meaning," *Proceedings of the Tenth Annual Conference of the Association for Literary and Linguistic Computing, 1983*. (Advanced reading on fuzzy logic.)

Zadeh, Lotfi A., "Syllogistic Reasoning in Fuzzy Logic and Its Application to Reasoning with Dispositions,'' *Proceedings of the International Symposium on Multiple Valued Logic*, Winnipeg, Canada, 1984. (Advanced reading.)

SECTION 3: AI APPLICATION DEVELOPMENT TOOLS (CHAPTERS 9 & 10)

''A Characterization of Expert System Development Tools for Manufacturing Applications,'' *Final Technical Report*, prepared by the Knowledge Based Systems Laboratory, Dept. of Industrial Engineering, Texas A&M University, College Station, Texas, June 19, 1986.

Clayton, Bruce D., ''ART: Programming Tutorial, Volumes One, Two, and Three,'' Inference Corp., 1986.

Finkel, Ben, ''Tapping into the Knowledge Power of Expert Systems,'' *Computer Design*, March 15, 1986, pp. 95–98. (Article on using RuleMaker to develop expert systems.)

Hayes-Roth, Frederick, Donald A. Waterman, and Douglas B. Lenat, eds., *Building Expert Systems* (Reading, Mass.: Addison-Wesley Publishing Company, 1983).

Holsapple, Clyde W., and Andrew B. Whinston, *Manager's Guide to Expert Systems Using Guru* (Homewood, Ill.: Dow Jones-Irwin, 1986).

Kunz, John, Thomas P. Kehler, and Michael D. Williams, ''Applications Development Using a Hybrid AI Development System,'' *AI Magazine*, Vol. 5, No. 3, Fall 1984, pp. 41–54.

Morris, Paul H., and Robert A. Nado, ''Representing Actions with an Assumption-Based Truth Maintenance System,'' *Proceedings of AAAI 1986*, Vol. 1, pp. 13–17. (Concerning KEE primarily; advanced reading.)

Nardi, Bonnie, and Anne Paulson, ''Multiple Worlds with Truth Maintenance in AI Applications,'' *Proceedings of the Seventh European Conference on Artificial Intelligence*, Vol. 1, July 1986. (Oriented toward KEE.)

Stefik, Mark, et al., ''Knowledge Programming in Loops: Report on an Experimental Course,'' *AI Magazine*, Vol. 4, No. 3, Fall 1983, pp. 3–12.

SECTION 4: UNDERSTANDING LANGUAGE (CHAPTERS 11–14)

Gevarter, W. B., ''An Overview of Computer-Based Natural Language Processing,'' U.S. Department of Commerce, NBSIR 83-2687, April 1983.

Harris, Larry R., ''Natural Language Simplifies Computer Access,'' *Systems & Software*, Jan. 1984, pp. 206–12.

Harris, Larry R., ''Experience with Intellect: Artificial Intelligence Technology Transfer,'' *AI Magazine*, Vol. 5, No. 2, Summer 1984, pp. 43–50.

Kaarsberg, Tina, ''Artificial Intelligence: Software Sophistry,'' *Yale Scientific* (Spring 1981), pp. 25–29. (Article about script-based natural-language systems.)

Johnson, Tim, *Natural Language Computing: The Commercial Applications* (London, England: Ovum Ltd., 1985). (Comprehensive survey.)

''Natural Language Toolkit,'' *Technical Report*, Texas Instruments, 1983.

''Natural Language Technology,'' *Technical Report*, Texas Instruments, 1983.

Rich, Elaine, ''Natural-Language Interfaces,'' *Computer*, Vol. 17, No. 9, Sept. 1984, pp. 39–47.

Nelson, Ruth, ''The First Literate Computers,'' *Psychology Today*, Ziff-Davis Publishing Co., March 1978.

O'Connor, Patrick J., ''Tutoring the Computers,'' *Yale Alumni Magazine and Journal*, Dec. 1981, pp. 10–13. (Article about script-based natural-language systems.)

Schank, Roger, and Robert Abelson, *Scripts, Plans, Goals, and Understanding* (Hillsdale, N.J.: Lawrence Erlbaum Associates Publishers, 1977).

Schank, Roger C., with Peter G. Childers, *The Cognitive Computer* (Reading, Mass.: Addison-Wesley Publishing Co., 1984).

von Limbach, Geoffrey, and Michael B. Taylor, ''Expert System Rules Read Natural Language,'' *Systems & Software*, August 1984, pp. 119–25. (Article about ''Clout.'')

Winograd, Terry, *Language as a Cognitive Process*, Vol. 1 (Reading, Mass.: Addison-Wesley Publishing Co., 1983).

SECTION 5: AI IN INDUSTRY (CHAPTERS 15–18)

Bonissone, Piero P., and Harold E. Johnson, Jr., ''Expert System for Diesel Electric Locomotive Repair,'' *IJCAI Proceeding*, 1983; also *Journal on Forth Application and Research*, Vol. 1.

Bourne, David A., and Mark S. Fox, ''Autonomous Manufacturing: Automating the Job-Shop,'' *Computer*, Vol. 17, No. 9, Sept. 1984, pp. 76–86.

Cynar, Larry, ''Expert Systems Solve Network Problems and Share the Information,'' *Data Communications*, May 1986, pp. 187–92. (Also see Section 7 for AI readings about networks.)

Fox, Mark S., ''The Intelligent Management System: An Overview,'' *Technical Report*, Robotics Institute, Carnegie-Mellon University, August 1981.

Fox, Mark S., et al., ''ISIS: A Constraint-Directed Reasoning Approach to Job Shop Scheduling,'' *Proceedings of the IEEE and NBS Conference on Trends & Applications*, May 1983, pp. 76–81.

Fox, Mark S., et al., ''Techniques for Sensor-Based Diagnosis,'' *Proceedings of IJCAI*, pp. 158–63, 1983.

Fox, Mark S., and Stephen F. Smith, ''ISIS: A Knowledge-Based System for Factory Scheduling,'' *Expert Systems*, Vol. 1, No. 1, 1984.

Frail, Robert P., and Roy S. Freedman, ''Opgen Revisited: Some Methodological Observations on the Delivery of Expert Systems,'' *Proceedings of the Expert Systems in Government Symposium*, IEEE Computer Society, Oct. 1986, pp. 310–17.

Frail, Robert P., and Roy S. Freedman, ''Increasing Support Labor Productivity: Artificial Intelligence Applied to Process Planning,'' *Proceedings of the Conference on Simulation and Training Technology for Increased Military Effectiveness*, Society for Applied Learning Technology, July 1984, pp. 52–56.

Freedman, Roy S., and William Sylvester, ''The Evolution of an Expert System for Process Planning,'' *Proceeding of the Expert Systems in Government Symposium*, IEEE Computer Society, Oct. 1986, pp. 328–34.

Freedman, Roy S., and Robert P. Frail, ''Opgen: The Evolution of an Expert System for Process Planning,'' *AI Magazine*, Vol. 7, No. 4, Winter 1986.

Freedman, Roy S., ''Knowledge-Based Courseware Authoring,'' *Training Technology Journal*, Vol. 1, No. 4, Summer Quarter 1984, pp. 4–9. (Article about AI in education and training.)

Freedman, Roy S., and Jeffrey P. Rosenking, ''Designing Computer-Based Training Systems: Obie-1-Knobe,'' *IEEE Expert*, Vol. 1, No. 2, Summer 1986, pp. 31–38. (Article about use of AI in education and training.)

Kahn, Gary, and John McDermott, ''The Mud System,'' *IEEE Expert*, Vol. 1, No. 1, Spring 1986, pp. 23–32. (Mud is an expert system that provides diagnostic and treatment recommendations to engineers responsible for maintaining desired properties of oil-well drilling fluids.)

Kahn, Gary S., ''From Application Shell to Knowledge Acquisition System,'' Proceedings of IJCAI '87, August 1987. (The concepts underlying troubleshooting tasks and tools to build expert troubleshooting systems.)

Kahn, Gary S. et al., ''TEST: A Model-Driven Application Shell,'' Proceedings of AAAI-87, July 1987. (Strategies used by an expert system tool geared to building diagnostic applications.)

Kak, A. C., et al., ''A Knowledge-Based Robotic Assembly Cell,'' *IEEE Expert*, Vol. 1, No. 1, Spring 1986, pp. 63–83.

Knickerbocker, Carl, ''Integrating AI and Unix Applications,'' *Systems & Software*, Nov. 1984, pp. 139–44. (Article about Picon, real-time systems, and communications between Unix and Lisp systems.)

''Machine Tool Technology,'' *American Machinist*, Vol. 124, No. 10, Oct. 1980, pp. 105–28.

McDermott, John, ''R1: A Rule-Based Configurer of Computer Systems,'' *Artificial Intelligence*, Vol. 1, No. 19, 1982.

McDermott, John, ''R1: The Formative Years,'' *AI Magazine*, Vol. 2, No. 2, Summer 1981, pp. 21–29.

McDermott, John, and Judith Bachant, ''R1 Revisited: Four Years in the Trenches,'' *AI Magazine*, Vol. 5, No. 3, Fall 1984, pp. 21–32.

O'Connor, Dennis E., ''Using Expert Systems to Manage Change and Complexity in Manufacturing,'' Digital Equipment Corp., April 1983.

Pepper, Jeff, and Gary S. Kahn, ''Repair Strategies in a Diagnostic Expert System,'' Proceedings of IJCAI '87, August 1987. (Overview of the troubleshooting task and strategies used by an expert system tool geared to building troubleshooting applications.)

Pepper, Jeff, and Dennis R. Mullins, ''Artificial Intelligence Applied to Audio Systems Diagnosis,'' Proceedings of the International Congress on Transportational Electronics, Dearborn, MI, Oct. 1986. (Overview of the audio diagnosis task and using an expert system tool geared to diagnostic applications to build an audio-systems diagnosis system at Ford Motor Co.)

Reddy, Y. V. Ramana, Mark S. Fox, and Nizwer Husain, ''The Knowledge-Based Simulation System,'' *IEEE Software*, Vol. 3, No. 2, March 1986. (To answer what-if questions, KBS uses AI techniques to model complex organizations, recognize cause-and-effect relations, and generate scenarios automatically.)

Reddy, Y. V., et al., "INET: A Knowledge Based Simulation Model of a Corporate Distribution System," *Proceedings: IEEE and NBS Trends & Applications Conference*, pp. 109–18. (Advanced reading.)

Schor, Marshall I., "Declarative Knowledge Programming Better Than Procedural?" *IEEE Expert*, Vol. 1, No. 1, Spring 1986, pp. 36–43. (Article addresses declarative and procedural knowledge, as well as the YES/MVS knowledge system that monitors MVS systems.)

Seligman, Len, et al., "TEST: An Architecture for Trouble-shooting Systems," Proceedings of AI-87, April 1987. (Article about the characteristics of diagnostics task and an expert system tool for building diagnostic applications.)

Stolfo, Salvatore J., and Greg T. Vesonder, "ACE: An Expert System Supporting Analysis and Management Decision Making," *Technical Report*, Computer Science Department, Columbia University, Oct. 1982. (Oriented toward telecommunications.)

van de Brug, Arnold, Judith Bachant, and John McDermott, "The Taming of R1," *IEEE Expert*, Vol. 1, No. 3, Fall 1986, pp. 33–39.

Winston, Patrick H., and Karen A. Prendergast, eds., *The AI Business* (Cambridge, Mass.: MIT Press, 1984).

Wright, M. Lattimer, et al., "An Expert System for Real-Time Control," *IEEE Software*, Vol. 3, No. 2, March 1986, pp. 16–24. (Article oriented toward microcomputer-based solutions, that combine the best of conventional and expert-system controllers, for use in embedded military applications.)

SECTION 6: AI IN BUSINESS AND FINANCE (CHAPTERS 19–21)

Bic, Lubomir, and Jonathan P. Gilbert, "Learning from AI: New Trends in Database Technology," *Computer*, Vol. 19, No. 3, March 1986, pp. 44–55.

Cohen, P., and M. D. Lieberman, "A Report On Folio: An Expert Assistant for Portfolio Managers," *Proceedings of IJCAI*, 1983, pp. 212–14.

Feinstein, J. L., and F. Siems, "Edass: An Expert System at the U.S. Environmental Protection Agency for Avoiding Disclosure of Confidential Business Information," *Expert Systems*, Vol. 2, No. 2, 1985.

Friedenberg, Robert A., and Ralph L. Hensler, "Strategy and Business Planning for Artificial Intelligence Companies: A Guide for Entrepreneurs," *AI Magazine*, Vol. 7, No. 3, pp. 111–18. (Article is geared to investors.)

Hart, Peter, Amos Barzilay, and Richard O. Duda, "Qualitative Reasoning for Financial Assessments: A Prospectus," *AI Magazine*, Vol. 7, No. 1, Spring 1986, pp. 62–68.

Holsapple, Clyde W., and Andrew B. Whinston, *Manager's Guide to Expert Systems Using Guru* (Homewood, Ill.: Dow Jones-Irwin, 1986).

Kellogg, Charles, "Intelligent Assistant for Knowledge and Information Resource Management," *Proceedings of Eighth International Joint Conference on Artificial Intelligence*, 1983, pp. 170–73.

Koflowitz, Lewis, "Finding Premium Use for Machines," *The American Banker* (The Daily Financial Services Newspaper), June 3, 1985.

New York Times, Oct. 19, 1986, sec. 3, p. 1 (Feature by David Sanger, "Computers are kicking up a furor as they transform the way the financial world bets its money.").

Reitman, Walter, ed., *Artificial Intelligence Applications for Business* (Norwood, N.J.: Ablex Publishing Corp., 1984).

Rieger, Chuck, "From Office Automation to Personal Automation: An AI Perspective," *Technical Report TR-1085*, Scion Corp./University of Maryland, August 1981.

Ruoff, Karen, "Codes: A Database Design Expert System Prototype," *Proceedings of the IEEE Computer Society Conference on Artificial Intelligence Applications*, December 1984.

Shpilberg, David, "One Giant Step for Insurers," *Best's Review: Property/Casualty Insurance Edition*, Vol. 87, No. 1, May 1986.

Shpilberg, David, "A Promising New Frontier," *Best's Review: Property/Casualty Insurance Edition*, Vol. 86, No. 1, May 1985.

Shpilberg, David, Lynford E. Graham, and Harry Schatz, "ExperTAX: An Expert System for Corporate Tax Planning," *Expert Systems*, Vol. 3, No. 3, July 1986.

Wiederhold, Gio., "Knowledge and Database Management," *IEEE Software*, Vol. 1, No. 1, Jan. 1984, pp. 63–73. (Advanced reading.)

Zadeh, Lotfi A., "Making Computers Think Like People," *IEEE Spectrum*, Vol. 21, No. 8, August 1984, pp. 26–32. (Article on fuzzy logic.)

Zadeh, Lotfi A., "Test-Score Semantics as a Basis for a Computational Approach to the Representation of Meaning," *Proceedings of the Tenth Annual Conference of the Association for Literary and Linguistic Computing*, 1983. (Advanced reading on fuzzy logic.)

Zadeh, Lotfi A., "Syllogistic Reasoning in Fuzzy Logic and its Application to Reasoning with Dispositions," *Proceedings of the International Symposium on Multiple Valued Logic*, Winnipeg, Canada, 1984. (Advanced reading on fuzzy logic.)

Zarri, G. P., "Expert Systems and Information Retrieval: An Experiment in the Domain of Biographical Data Management," *International Journal of Man-Machine Studies*, Vol. 20, 1984.

Zarri, G. P., "Inference Techniques for Intelligent Information Retrieval," *Proceedings of the Law and Technology Conference*, Houston, Texas, 1984.

SECTION 7: AI IN SCIENCE, MEDICINE, AND ENGINEERING (CHAPTERS 22–24)

Aikens, Janice S., et al., and Robert J. Fallat, "Puff: An Expert System for Interpretation of Pulmonary Function Data," *Computers and Biomedical Research*, Vol. 16, 1983, pp. 199–208.

Alexander, James H., and Michael J. Freiling, "Smalltalk-80 Aids Troubleshooting System Development," *Systems & Software*, April 1985, pp. 111–18.

Clancey, B. C., and E. H. Shortliffe, eds., *Readings in Medical Artificial Intelligence: The First Decade* (Reading, Mass.: Addison-Wesley Publishing Company, 1984).

Cynar, Larry, "Expert Systems Solve Network Problems and Share the Information," *Data Communications*, May 1986, pp. 187–92.

"Expert Systems in Engineering," special issue of *Computer*, Vol. 19, No. 7, July 1986. (Includes articles on expert systems for VLSI design, mechanical design, strategic defense, power systems, capacity planning for computers systems, fault isolation in electronic equipment, fault diagnosis in space station life support and satellite subsystems, and factory cell simulation in aerospace manufacturing.)

Fallat, Robert J., and Michael G. Snow, "Micropuff—Will it Make Pulmonary Function Test Interpretations a Breeze?" *Education Perspectives*, Vol. II, No. 3, May/June 1984, pp. 14–20.

Goyal, Dr. Shri K., et al., "Compass: An Expert System for Telephone Switch Maintenance," *Expert Systems*, Vol. 2, No. 3, pp. 112–26. (A comprehensive case study of this system.)

Kim, Jin, and John McDermott, "Computer Aids for IC Design," *IEEE Software*, Vol. 3, No. 2, March 1986, pp. 38–47.

Kowalski, Thaddeus J., and Donald E. Thomas, "The VLSI Design Automation Assistant: And IBM System/370 Design," *IEEE Design and Test*, Vol. 1, No. 1, Feb. 1984, pp. 60–69. (Advanced reading.)

Kulikowski, Casimir A., "Expert Medical Consultation Systems," *Journal of Medical Systems*, Vol. 7, No. 3, 1983, pp. 229–34.

McDonald, Clement J., *Action-Oriented Decisions in Ambulatory Medicine* (Chicago, Ill.: Year Book Medical Publishers, Inc., 1981), pp. 1–14.

McDonald, Clement J., "Protocol-Based Computer Reminders: The Quality of Care and the Non-Perfectability of Man," *New England Journal of Medicine*, Vol. 295, Dec. 9, 1976, pp. 1351–55.

McDonald, Clement J., et al., "Data Base Management, Feedback Control, and the Regenstrief Medical Record," *Journal of Medical Systems*, Vol. 7, No. 2, 1983, pp. 111–25.

McDonald, Clement J., et al., "Reminders to Physicians from an Introspective Computer Medical Record: A Two-Year Randomized Trial," *Annals of Internal Medicine*, Vol. 100, 1984, pp. 130–38.

McDonald, Clement J., et al., "A Computer-Based Record and Clinical Monitoring System for Ambulatory Care," *AJPH*, Vol. 67, No. 3, March 1977, pp. 240–45.

McDonald, Clem, et al., "The Regenstrief Clinical Laboratory System," *IEEE Proceedings of the Seventh Annual Symposium on Computer Applications in Medical Care*, 1983, pp. 254–57.

McDonald, Clement J., et al., "CARE: A Real World Medical Knowledge Base," *Proceedings of CompCon*, Spring 1984, pp. 187–91.

Nestler, Eric, "Symbolic Processor Aids Design of Complex Chips," *Computer Design*, Jan. 1985, pp. 147–53.

Pryor, T. A., R. M. Gardner, P. D. Clayton, and H. R. Warner, "The HELP System," *Journal of Medical Systems*, Vol. 7, No. 2, 1983, pp. 87–102.

Purves, William K., "A Biologist Looks at Cognitive AI," *AI Magazine*, Vol. 6, No. 2, Summer 1985, pp. 38–43. (This is a general subject, seen from a biologist's viewpoint.)

Goldberg, Adele, and David Robson, *Smalltalk-80: The Language and Its Implementation* (Reading, Mass.: Addison-Wesley Publishing Company, 1983).

Stach, Jerrold F., "Expert Systems Find a New Place in Data Networks," *Data Communications*, Nov. 1985, pp. 245–61.

Subrahmanyam, P. A., "Synapse: An Expert System for VLSI Design," *Computer*, Vol. 19, No. 7, July 1986, pp. 78–89.

Thomas, Donald E., et al., "Automatic Data Path Synthesis," *Computer*, Vol. 16, No. 12, Dec. 1983, pp. 59–70. (Advanced reading.)

Togai, Masaki, and Hiroyuki Watanabe, "Expert System on a Chip: An Engine for Real-Time Approximate Reasoning," *IEEE Expert*, Vol. 1, No. 3, Fall 1986, pp. 55–62. (Advanced reading.)

Warner, Homer R., et al., "HELP-A Program for Medical Decision-Making," *Computers and Biomedical Research*, 1972, pp. 65–74.

Wong, Carla M., et al, "Application of Artificial Intelligence to Tripple Quadrupole Mass Spectrometry (TQMS)," *IEEE Transactions on Nuclear Science*, Vol. NS-31, No. 1, pp. 804–10.

SECTION 8: ADVANCED TECHNICAL DETAILS PROGRAMMING LANGUAGES (CHAPTER 25)

Bernat, Andrew P., "Multitasking for Common Lisp," *AI Expert*, Premier 1986, pp. 68–79. (Advanced reading.)

Brownston, Lee, et al., *Programming Expert Systems in OPS5: An Introduction to Rule-Based Programming* (Reading, Mass.: Addison-Wesley Publishing Company, 1985).

Forgy, Charles L., "OPS5 Users Manual," *Technical Report*, Department of Computer Science, Carnegie-Mellon University, Pittsburgh, Pa., July 1981.

Forgy, Charles L., "Overview of OPS83," *Technical Report*, Department of Computer Science, Carnegie-Mellon University, August 1983.

Forgy, Charles L., *The OPS83 User's Manual* (Pittsburgh, Pa.: Production Systems Technologies, Inc., 1985).

Goldberg, Adele, and David Robson, *Smalltalk-80: The Language and Its Implementation* (Reading, Mass.: Addison-Wesley Publishing Company, 1983).

Hawkinson, Lowell, "High-Level Languages Based on Lisp Aid Expert System Design," *Computer Technology Review*, Winter 1983, pp. 13–21.

Hewett, Carl, "Concurrency in Intelligent Systems," *AI Expert*, Premier 1986, pp. 44–50. (Article examines concurrency in logic and message-passing languages.)

Kolokouris, Angelos, "Prolog: Programming in Logic," *Systems & Software*, Jan. 1984, pp. 224–30.

Kukich, Karen, "Design of a Knowledge-Based Report Generator," *Proceedings of the 21st Annual Meeting of the Association for Computational Linguistics, MIT*, Cambridge, Mass., June 1983.

Neiman, Dan, and John Martin, "Rule-Based Programming in OPS83," *AI Expert*, Premier 1986, pp. 54–65.

Spoerl, James, "AI Environment Speeds Software Development," *Systems & Software*, August 1984, pp. 111–18.

Steele, Guy L., *Common Lisp: The Language* (Maynard, Mass.: Digital Press, 1985).

Touretzky, David S., *Lisp: A Gentle Introduction to Symbolic Computation* (New York: Harper & Row, 1984).

Winston, Patrick Henry, and Berthold Klaus Paul Horn, *Lisp*, 2d ed. (Reading, Mass.: Addison-Wesley Publishing Co., 1984).

AI COMPUTER HARDWARE (CHAPTERS 26 AND 27)

"3600 Technical Summary," *Symbolics*, Feb. 1983.

Corley, Charles J., and Joyce A. Statz, "Lisp Workstation Brings AI Power to a User's Desk," *Computer Design*, Jan. 1985, pp. 155–62.

Paseman, William G., "Data Flow Concepts Speed Simulation in CAE Systems," *Computer Design*, Jan. 1985, pp. 131–40.

Schink, Steve, "Workstation Unites AI, Number Crunching," *Mini-Micro Systems*, February 1987.

Sheil, Beau, "Power Tools for Programmers," *Datamation*, Feb. 1983, pp. 131–44.

Simons, G. L., "Toward Fifth-Generation Computers," Manchester, England, NCC Publications, 1983.

Spoerl, James, "AI Environment Speeds Software Development," *Systems & Software*, August 1984, pp. 111–18.

"Symbolics Technical Summary," *Symbolics*, Oct. 1985.

AUTOMATED PROGRAMMING (CHAPTER 28)

Barstow, David, "A Perspective on Automatic Programming," *AI Magazine*, Vol. 5, No. 1, Spring 1984, pp. 5–27.

Barstow, David, et al., *Interactive Programming Environments* (New York: McGraw-Hill Book Company, 1984).

Rich, Charles, and Howard Shrobe, "Initial Report on the Programmer's Apprentice," *IEEE Transactions on Software Engineering*, Vol. 4, No. 6, Nov. 1978. (Advanced reading.)

Rich, Charles, and Howard Schrobe, "Design of a Programmer's Apprentice," in *Artificial Intelligence: An MIT Perspective*, Vol. 1, Patrick Henry Winston and Richard Henry Brown, eds. (Cambridge, Mass.: MIT Press, 1979). (Advanced reading.)

Rockmore, Joseph A., "Knowledge-based Software Turns Specifications into Efficient Programs," *Electronic Design*, July 25, 1985, pp. 105–12.

Waters, Richard C., "KBEmacs: Where's the AI?," *AI Magazine*, Vol. 7, No. 1, Spring 1986, pp. 47–56.

Waters, Richard C., "The Programmer's Apprentice: Knowledge-Based Program Editor," *Professional Program Session Record No. 16 on State-of-the-Art Interactive Software Tools*, IEEE Mini/Micro Northeast-84 (Boston, May 1984), pp. 1–9 (also printed in the *Conference Record of IEEE Mini/Micro Northeast-84*). (Advanced reading.)

Waters, Richard C., "The Programmer's Apprentice: Knowledge-Based Programming Editing," *IEEE Transactions on Software Engineering*, Vol. 8, No. 1, Jan. 1982, pp. 1–12. (Advanced reading.)

AI'S FUTURE: PROGRAMS THAT LEARN AND DISCOVER (CHAPTER 29)

Bradshaw, Gary F., Patrick W. Langley, and Herbert A. Simon, "Studying Scientific Discovery by Computer Simulation," *Science*, Vol. 222, No. 4627 (2 Dec. 1983), pp. 971–75.

Elkind, David, *Interpretive Essays on Jean Piaget: Children and Adolescents* (New York: Oxford University Press, 1970).

Gagne, Robert M., "The Learning Requirements for Enquiry," *Journal of Research in Science Teaching*, Vol. 1, 1963, pp. 144–53.

Lenat, Douglas B., "Computer Software for Intelligent Systems," *Scientific American*, Vol. 251, No. 3, Sept. 1984, pp. 204–13.

Michalski, Ryszard S., Jaime G. Carbonell, and Tom M. Mitchell, eds., *Machine Learning: An Artificial Intelligence Approach* (Palo Alto, Calif.: Tioga Press, 1983).

Minsky, Marvin, "The Society Theory of Thinking," in *Artificial Intelligence: An MIT Perspective*, Vol. 1, Patrick Henry Winston and Richard Henry Brown, eds. (Cambridge, Mass.: MIT Press, 1979).

Minsky, Marvin, "K-Lines: A Theory of Memory," (unpublished AI Memo No. 516, June 1979), Massachusetts Institute of Technology, Artificial Intelligence Laboratory.

Minsky, Marvin, "Learning Meaning," (unpublished draft of essay, July 12, 1982), Massachusetts Institute of Technology, Artificial Intelligence Laboratory.

Newell, A., and Herbert A. Simon, *Human Problem Solving* (Englewood Cliffs, N.J.: Prentice-Hall, Inc., 1972).

Piaget, Jean, "Development and Learning," *Journal of Research in Science Teaching*, Vol. 2 (1964), pp. 176–86.

Winston, Patrick H., "Learning by Creating and Justifying Transfer Frames," in *Artificial Intelligence: An MIT Perspective*, Vol. 1, Patrick Henry Winston and Richard Henry Brown, eds. (Cambridge, Mass.: MIT Press, 1979).

Winston, Patrick Henry, *Artificial Intelligence*, 2d ed., Chapters 11 and 12 (Reading, Mass.: Addison-Wesley Publishing Co., 1984). (Basic reading in programs that learn.)

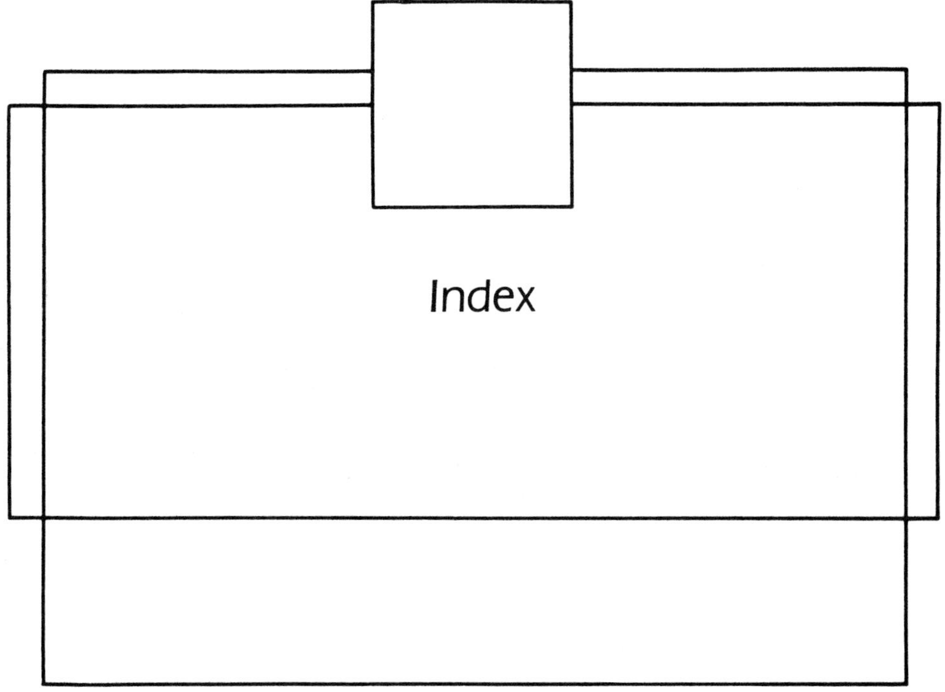

Index

A

B

C

E

F

G

H

L

M

N

O

P

T

U

V

W

X

Y

Z

Announcing. . . .

The Annual Prentice Hall Professional/Technical/Reference Catalog: Books For Computer Scientists, Computer/Electrical Engineers and Electronic Technicians

- Prentice Hall, the leading publisher of Professional/Technical/Reference books in the world, is pleased to make its vast selection of titles in computer science, computer/electrical engineering and electronic technology more accessible to all professionals in these fields through the publication of this new catalog!
- If your business or research depends on timely, state-of-the-art information, The Annual Prentice Hall Professional/Technical/Reference Catalog: Books For Computer Scientists, Computer/Electrical Engineers and Electronic Technicians was designed especially for you! Titles appearing in this catalog will be grouped according to interest areas. Each entry will include: title, author, author affiliations, title description, table of contents, title code, page count and copyright year.
- In addition, this catalog will also include advertisements of new products and services from other companies in key high tech areas.

SPECIAL OFFER!

- Order your copy of The Annual Prentice Hall Professional/Technical/Reference Catalog: Books For Computer Scientists, Computer/Electrical Engineers and Electronic Technicians for only $2.00 and receive $5.00 off the purchase of your first book from this catalog. In addition, this catalog entitles you to special discounts on Prentice Hall titles in computer science, computer/electrical engineering and electronic technology.

Please send me ________________ copies of The Annual Prentice Hall Professional/Technical/Reference Catalog (title code: 62280–3)

SAVE!

If payment accompanies order, plus your state's sales tax where applicable, Prentice Hall pays postage and handling charges. Same return privilege refund guaranteed. Please do not mail cash.

☐ PAYMENT ENCLOSED—shipping and handling to be paid by publisher (please include your state's tax where applicable).
☐ BILL ME for The Annual Prentice Hall Professional/Technical/Reference Catalog (with small charge for shipping and handling).

Mail your order to: Prentice Hall, Book Distribution Center,
Route 59 at Brook Hill Drive,
West Nyack, N.Y. 10994

Name ____

Address ____

City ______________________ State ____________ Zip ____________

I prefer to charge my ☐ Visa ☐ MasterCard

Card Number ______________________ Expiration Date ____________

Signature ____

Offer not valid outside the United States.

Dept. 1

D-PPTR-CS(9)